Lecture Notes in Artificial Intelligence   2381

Subseries of Lecture Notes in Computer Science
Edited by J. G. Carbonell and J. Siekmann

Lecture Notes in Computer Science
Edited by G. Goos, J. Hartmanis, and J. van Leeuwen

T0241846

Springer

Berlin
Heidelberg
New York
Barcelona
Hong Kong
London
Milan
Paris
Tokyo

Uwe Egly   Christian G. Fermüller (Eds.)

Automated Reasoning with Analytic Tableaux and Related Methods

International Conference, TABLEAUX 2002
Copenhagen, Denmark, July 30 – August 1, 2002
Proceedings

 Springer

Series Editors

Jaime G. Carbonell, Carnegie Mellon University, Pittsburgh, PA, USA
Jörg Siekmann, University of Saarland, Saarbrücken, Germany

Volume Editors

Uwe Egly
Technische Univesität Wien, Abteilung Wisssenbasierte Systeme 184/3
Favoritenstr. 9-11, 1040 Vienna, Austria
E-mail: uwe@kr.tuwien.ac.at

Chritian G. Fermüller
Technische Universität Wien, Institut für Computersprachen
AG Theoretische Informatik und Logik 185.2
Favoritenstr. 9-11, 1040 Vienna, Austria
E-mail: chrisf@logic.at

Cataloging-in-Publication Data applied for

Die Deutsche Bibliothek - CIP-Einheitsaufnahme

Automated reasoning with analytic tableaux and related methods : international conference ; tableaux 2002, Copenhagen, Denmark, July 30 - August 1, 2002 ; proceedings / Uwe Egly ; Christian G. Fermüller (ed.). - Berlin ; Heidelberg ; New York ;
Barcelona ; Hong Kong ; London ; Milan ; Paris ; Tokyo : Springer, 2002   (Lecture
notes in computer science ; Vol. 2381 : Lecture notes in   artificial intelligence)
    ISBN 3-540-43929-3

CR Subject Classification (1998): I.2.3, F.4.1, I.2, D.1.6, D,2,4

ISSN 0302-9743
ISBN 3-540-43929-3 Springer-Verlag Berlin Heidelberg New York

Springer-Verlag Berlin Heidelberg New York
a member of BertelsmannSpringer Science+Business Media GmbH

http://www.springer.de

© Springer-Verlag Berlin Heidelberg 2002
Printed in Germany

Typesetting: Camera-ready by author, data conversion by PTP-Berlin, Stefan Sossna e.K.
Printed on acid-free paper   SPIN: 10870473   06/3142   5 4 3 2 1 0

Foreword

This volume contains the research papers presented at the International Conference on Automated Reasoning with Analytic Tableaux and Related Methods (TABLEAUX 2002) held on July 30 – August 1, 2002 in Copenhagen, Denmark, in the context of the third Federated Logic Conference (FLoC 2002). This conference was the continuation of international meetings on the same topic held in Lautenbach (1992), Marseille (1993), Abingdon (1994), St. Goar (1995), Terrasini (1996), Pont-à-Mousson (1997), Oisterwijk (1998), Saratoga Springs (1999), and St Andrews (2000). In 2001 TABLEAUX was part of IJCAR 2001 in Siena. The frame of FLoC 2002 guaranteed once again close contact to the larger Theorem Proving and Logic in Computer Science community. This was in particular witnessed by the talk by Matthias Baaz, jointly invited by CADE-18 and TABLEAUX 2002.

Tableaux and related methods have been found to be a convenient formalism for automating deduction in various non-standard logics as well as in classical logic. This is nicely illustrated by the wide scope of logics that are covered by the papers collected in this volume: among them are linear logic, temporal logics, various modal logics, including hybrid logic and multi-modal logics, fuzzy logics like Gödel- and Łukasiewicz logics, various intermediate logics, quantified boolean logic, and, of course, classical first-order logic in various formats. Some papers mainly address foundational issues, others aim at efficient proof search and applications that include logic programming, reasoning about knowledge and belief, planning, nonmonotonic reasoning, efficient handling of equality, combining theories, and deciding word problems in certain algebraic theories.

Acknowledgements. We would like to thank the members of the program committee, the additional referees, and the members of the TABLEAUX steering committee (all named on the following pages). In particular, we thank Reiner Hähnle – among other duties: conference chair of CADE-18, president of the TABLEAUX steering committee, and member of the FLoC steering committee, the TABLEAUX program committee, and the FLoC organizing committee – who assisted us in many ways. We would also like to thank Gernot Salzer for installing and helping to maintain the software for our web-based reviewing procedure.

May 2002

Uwe Egly
Christian G. Fermüller

Previous Tableaux Workshops/Conferences

1992	Lautenbach, Germany	1993	Marseille, France
1994	Abingdon, England	1995	St. Goar, Germany
1996	Terrasini, Italy	1997	Pont-à-Mousson, France
1998	Oisterwijk, The Netherlands	1999	Saratoga Springs, USA
2000	St Andrews, UK	2001	part of IJACR, Siena, Italy

Invited Speakers

Matthias Baaz	TU Wien, Austria (invited jointly with CADE-18)
Dale Miller	Penn State University, USA

Program and Conference Co-chairs

Uwe Egly	Vienna University of Technology, Austria
Christian Fermüller	Vienna University of Technology, Austria

Program Committee

Peter Baumgartner	University of Koblenz and Landau, Germany
Bernhard Beckert	University of Karlsruhe, Germany
Marcello D'Agostino	University of Ferrara, Italy
Roy Dyckhoff	St Andrews University, UK
Uwe Egly	Vienna University of Technology, Austria
Christian Fermüller	Vienna University of Technology, Austria
Melvin Fitting	City University of New York, USA
Didier Galmiche	LORIA Nancy, France
Rajeev Goré	Australian National University
Jean Goubault-Larrecq	ENS Cachan, France
Reiner Hähnle	Chalmers University of Technology, Sweden
Ian Horrocks	University Manchester, UK
Christoph Kreitz	Cornell University, USA
Reinhold Letz	Munich University of Technology, Germany
Fabio Massacci	University of Trento, Italy
Neil Murray	University at Albany, SU of New York, USA
Nicola Olivetti	University of Turin, Italy

Steering Committee

Elected members

Reiner Hähnle (President)
Peter H. Schmitt (Vice President)
Marcello D'Agostino
Melvin Fitting
Ulrich Furbach
Didier Galmiche

Ex officio members:

Uwe Egly
Christian Fermüller
Rajeev Goré
Fabio Massacci

Additional Referees

Wolfgang Ahrendt
Matthias Baaz
Matteo Baldoni
Piero Bonatti
Serena Cerrito
Koen Claessen
Jürgen Dix
Ulrich Furbach
Laura Giordano
Dominique Larchey-Wendling
Georg Moser
Axel Polleres
Andrew Rowley
Niklas Sörensson
Frieder Stolzenburg
Sergio Tessaris
Helmut Veith
Andrei Voronkov
Kewen Wang

Alessandro Artale
Philippe Balbiani
Dave Barker-Plummer
Mirjana Borisavljevic
Marta Cialdea Mayer
Ingo Dahn
Martin Fränzle
Martin Giese
Bernhard Gramlich
Daniel Mery
Massimo Narizzano
Riccardo Rosati
Renate Schmidt
Colin Stirling
Armando Tacchella
Hans Tompits
Jan von Plato
Arild Waaler
Stefan Woltran

Sponsors

Kurt Gödel Society
Vienna University of Technoloy

Table of Contents

Invited Papers

Research Papers

System Descriptions Papers

Proof Analysis by Resolution
(Abstract)*

Matthias Baaz

Institut für Algebra und Diskrete Mathematik
Technische Universität Wien, Austria

Proof analysis of existing proofs is one of the main sources of scientific progress in mathematics: new concepts can be obtained, e.g., by denoting explicit definitions in proof parts and axiomatizing them as new mathematical objects in their own right. (The development of the concept of integral is a well known example.) All forms of proof analysis are intended to make implicit information of a proof explicit, i.e., visible. Logical proof analysis is mainly concerned with the implicit constructive content of more or less formalized proofs. The following are major examples for logical proof analysis:

- Formal proofs of $(\forall x)(\exists y)P(x, y)$ in computational contexts can be unwinded to proofs of $(\forall x)P(x, \pi(x))$ for suitable programs π.
- Herbrand disjunctions can be extracted from proofs of prenex formulas. Such disjunctions always exist in the case of first-order logic by Herbrand's famous theorem, but can be extracted from many proofs in other systems as well. (C.f. Luckhardt's analysis of the proof of Roth's theorem.) Suitable Herbrand disjunctions can be used to improve bounds or to reduce parametrical dependencies.
- Interpolants can be constructed from proofs of $A \rightarrow B$.[1] Interpolation is the main tool to make implicit definitions explicit via Beth's theorem.[2]

In this talk we concentrate on automatizable logical proof analysis in first-order logic by means of incooperating resolution.

---

* Talk invited jointly by *CADE-18* and *TABLEAUX 2002*. The corresponding paper (extended abstract) appears in the proceedings for *CADE-18*.

[1] An *interpolant* for $A \rightarrow B$ is a formula I such that $A \rightarrow I$ and $I \rightarrow B$ are provable, and I contains only predicate and function symbols common to A and B.

[2] P is *defined implicitly* by $\Sigma(P)$ iff $\Sigma(P) \cup \Sigma(P') \vdash (\forall x)(P(x) \leftrightarrow P'(x))$. P is *defined explicitly* by $\Sigma(P)$ iff $\Sigma(P) \vdash (\forall x)(P(x) \leftrightarrow L(x))$ for some L not containing P.

U. Egly and C.G. Fermüller (Eds.): TABLEAUX 2002, LNAI 2381, p. 1, 2002.

Using Linear Logic to Reason about Sequent Systems*

Dale Miller[1] and Elaine Pimentel[2]

[1] Computer Science and Engineering Department, 220 Pond Lab,
Pennsylvania State University, University Park, PA 16802-6106   USA
dale@cse.psu.edu
[2] Departamento de Matemática,
Universidade Federal de Minas Gerais, Belo Horizonte, M.G.   Brasil
elaine@mat.ufmg.br

Abstract. Linear logic can be used as a meta-logic for the specification of some sequent calculus proof systems. We explore in this paper properties of such linear logic specifications. We show that derivability of one proof system from another has a simple decision procedure that is implemented simply via bounded logic programming search. We also provide conditions to ensure that an encoded proof system has the cut-elimination property and show that this can be decided again by simple, bounded proof search algorithms.

1   Introduction

Various logical frameworks based on intuitionistic logic have been proposed [FM88,Pau89,HHP93] and used for specifying natural deduction proof systems. Given the intimate connection between natural deduction and λ-calculus, applications requiring object-level binding and substitutions have also been successfully implemented in these logical frameworks [Mil00].

In [Mil96], Miller proposed moving from intuitionistic logic to the more expressive setting of linear logic to capture the more general setting of sequent calculus proof system. This use of linear logic has been future explored in [Ric98, Pim01,MP]. In this paper we consider the structure of proofs in the Forum presentation of linear logic in order to show how various aspects of the meta-theory of linear logic can be used to conclude properties of the sequent calculus being specified. In particular, we describe a decision procedure for determining if one encoded proof system is derivable from another and we present conditions and their decision procedure that imply that an encoded proof system satisfies cut-elimination.

After providing an overview of Forum in Section 2 and the encoding into Forum of object-level sequents and inference rules in Section 3, we prove in

---

* Miller has been supported in part by NSF grants CCR-9912387, CCR-9803971, INT-9815645, and INT-9815731. Both authors wish to thank L'Institut de Mathématiques de Luminy, University Aix-Marseille 2 for the support to attend the Logic and Interaction Weeks in February 2002, during which much of this paper was written.

U. Egly and C.G. Fermüller (Eds.): TABLEAUX 2002, LNAI 2381, pp. 2–23, 2002.

Section 4 that deduction between encodings of inference rules is captured by shallow Forum proofs. A decision procedure for determining if the encoding of one proof system is derivable from another proof system then follows by doing bounded depth proof search. Of course, we wish to know if an object-level proof system admits a cut-elimination theorem. Section 5 contains the basic background for this problem and Section 6 contains the main object-level cut-elimination theorem. Section 7 contains a specification and discussion of Girard's Logic of Unity. Finally, we conclude in Section 8.

2   The Forum Presentation of Linear Logic

The Forum presentation of linear logic [Mil96] relies on the connectives $\perp$, $\invamp$, $?$, $\top$, $\&$, $\multimap$, $\Rightarrow$, and $\forall$: this set of connectives is complete for linear logic, in the sense that all other linear logic connectives can be defined from these. Proof search using this collection of connectives can be restricted so that simple goal-directed proof search (using the technical device of multiple-conclusion uniform proofs [Mil93]) is complete. Thus, Forum makes it possible to claim that all of linear logic can be seen as an abstract logic programming language [MNPS91]. Forum has been used to specify a number of computation systems, ranging from object-oriented languages [DM95], imperative programming features [Mil96,Chi95], and a RISC processor [Chi95]. In this paper, we use Forum as a specification language for sequent calculus proof systems. For this purpose, we work often within a weaker fragment of Forum, called *Flat Forum*.

2.1   Flat Forum

A formula of Forum is a *flat goal* if it does not contain occurrences of $\multimap$ and $\Rightarrow$, and all occurrences of the modal $?$ have atomic scope. A formula of the form

$$\forall \bar{y}(G_1 \hookrightarrow \cdots \hookrightarrow G_m \hookrightarrow A_1 \invamp \cdots \invamp A_n), \quad (m, n \geq 0)$$

is called a *flat clause* if $G_1, \ldots, G_m$ are flat goals, $A_1, \ldots, A_n$ are atomic formulas, and occurrences of the symbol $\hookrightarrow$ are either occurrences of $\multimap$ or $\Rightarrow$. The formula $A_1 \invamp \cdots \invamp A_n$ is the *head* of such a clause, while for each $i = 1, \ldots, m$, the formula G_i is a *body* of this clause. If $n = 0$, then we write the head as simply $\perp$ and say that the head is *empty*. A flat clause is essentially a clause of the LinLog system [And92] except that heads of flat clauses may be empty.

A flat Forum formula is logically equivalent to a formula in *uncurried* form, namely, a formula of the form

$$\forall \bar{y}(B \multimap A_1 \invamp \cdots \invamp A_n)$$

where $n \geq 0$, $\bar{y}$ is the list of variables free in the head $A_1 \invamp \cdots \invamp A_n$, all free variables of B are also free in the head, and B may have occurrences of $\exists$, $\otimes$, 1, and $!$, but not in the scope of $\invamp$, $?$, $\&$, $\forall$, $\multimap$, and $\Rightarrow$ (using the terminology

$$\frac{}{\Psi; \Delta \longrightarrow \mathcal{A}, \top, \Gamma; \Upsilon} \top R \qquad \frac{\Psi; \Delta \longrightarrow \mathcal{A}, B, \Gamma; \Upsilon \quad \Psi; \Delta \longrightarrow \mathcal{A}, C, \Gamma; \Upsilon}{\Psi; \Delta \longrightarrow \mathcal{A}, B \,\&\, C, \Gamma; \Upsilon} \,\&\, R$$

$$\frac{\Psi; \Delta \longrightarrow \mathcal{A}, \Gamma; \Upsilon}{\Psi; \Delta \longrightarrow \mathcal{A}, \bot, \Gamma; \Upsilon} \bot R \qquad \frac{\Psi; \Delta \longrightarrow \mathcal{A}, B, C, \Gamma; \Upsilon}{\Psi; \Delta \longrightarrow \mathcal{A}, B \,\otimes\, C, \Gamma; \Upsilon} \,\otimes\, R$$

$$\frac{\Psi; B, \Delta \longrightarrow \mathcal{A}, C, \Gamma; \Upsilon}{\Psi; \Delta \longrightarrow \mathcal{A}, B \multimap C, \Gamma; \Upsilon} \multimap R \qquad \frac{B, \Psi; \Delta \longrightarrow \mathcal{A}, C, \Gamma; \Upsilon}{\Psi; \Delta \longrightarrow \mathcal{A}, B \Rightarrow C, \Gamma; \Upsilon} \Rightarrow R$$

$$\frac{\Psi; \Delta \longrightarrow \mathcal{A}, B[y/x], \Gamma; \Upsilon}{\Psi; \Delta \longrightarrow \mathcal{A}, \forall_\tau x.B, \Gamma; \Upsilon} \forall R \qquad \frac{\Psi; \Delta \longrightarrow \mathcal{A}, \Gamma; B, \Upsilon}{\Psi; \Delta \longrightarrow \mathcal{A}, ?\, B, \Gamma; \Upsilon} \,?\, R$$

$$\frac{B, \Psi; \Delta \xrightarrow{B} \mathcal{A}; \Upsilon}{B, \Psi; \Delta \longrightarrow \mathcal{A}; \Upsilon} decide! \qquad \frac{\Psi; \Delta \longrightarrow \mathcal{A}, B; B, \Upsilon}{\Psi; \Delta \longrightarrow \mathcal{A}; B, \Upsilon} decide?$$

$$\frac{\Psi; \Delta \xrightarrow{B} \mathcal{A}; \Upsilon}{\Psi; B, \Delta \longrightarrow \mathcal{A}; \Upsilon} decide \qquad \frac{}{\Psi; \cdot \xrightarrow{A} A; \Upsilon} initial \qquad \frac{}{\Psi; \cdot \xrightarrow{A} \cdot; A, \Upsilon} initial?$$

$$\frac{}{\Psi; \cdot \xrightarrow{\bot} \cdot; \Upsilon} \bot L \qquad \frac{\Psi; \Delta \xrightarrow{B_i} \mathcal{A}; \Upsilon}{\Psi; \Delta \xrightarrow{B_1 \,\&\, B_2} \mathcal{A}; \Upsilon} \,\&\, L_i \qquad \frac{\Psi; B \longrightarrow \cdot; \Upsilon}{\Psi; \cdot \xrightarrow{?\, B} \cdot; \Upsilon} \,?\, L$$

$$\frac{\Psi; \Delta_1 \xrightarrow{B} \mathcal{A}_1; \Upsilon \quad \Psi; \Delta_2 \xrightarrow{C} \mathcal{A}_2; \Upsilon}{\Psi; \Delta_1, \Delta_2 \xrightarrow{B \,\otimes\, C} \mathcal{A}_1, \mathcal{A}_2; \Upsilon} \,\otimes\, L \qquad \frac{\Psi; \Delta \xrightarrow{B[t/x]} \mathcal{A}; \Upsilon}{\Psi; \Delta \xrightarrow{\forall_\tau x.B} \mathcal{A}; \Upsilon} \forall L$$

$$\frac{\Psi; \Delta_1 \longrightarrow \mathcal{A}_1, B; \Upsilon \quad \Psi; \Delta_2 \xrightarrow{C} \mathcal{A}_2; \Upsilon}{\Psi; \Delta_1, \Delta_2 \xrightarrow{B \multimap C} \mathcal{A}_1, \mathcal{A}_2; \Upsilon} \multimap L \qquad \frac{\Psi; \cdot \longrightarrow B; \Upsilon \quad \Psi; \Delta \xrightarrow{C} \mathcal{A}; \Upsilon}{\Psi; \Delta \xrightarrow{B \Rightarrow C} \mathcal{A}; \Upsilon} \Rightarrow L$$

Fig. 1. The Forum proof system. The rule $\forall R$ has the proviso that y is not free in the lower sequent. In $\&\, L_i$, $i = 1$ or $i = 2$.

of [And92], no synchronous connective is in the scope of an asynchronous connective.) Although uncurried clauses are not Forum clauses, they can easily be rewritten to curried clauses using the following logical equivalences:

$$(B \otimes C) \multimap H \equiv B \multimap C \multimap H \qquad (\exists x.B \ x) \multimap H \equiv \forall x.(B(x) \multimap H)$$

$$(B \oplus C) \multimap H \equiv (B \multimap H) \,\&\, (C \multimap H) \qquad (!\, B) \multimap H \equiv B \Rightarrow H \qquad 1 \multimap H \equiv H.$$

(In the equivalence involving $\exists$, x is not free in H.)

As in Church's Simple Theory of Types [Chu40], both terms and formulas are built using a simply typed λ-calculus. We assume the usual rules of α, β, and η-conversion and we identify terms and formulas up to α-conversion. A term is λ-normal if it contains no β and no η redexes. All terms are λ-convertible to a term in λ-normal form, and such a term is unique up to α-conversion. The substitution notation $B[t/x]$ denotes the λ-normal form of the β-redex $(\lambda x.B)t$. Following [Chu40], we shall also assume that formulas of Forum have type o.

There are two kinds of sequents in Forum, namely, $\Psi; \Delta \longrightarrow \Gamma; \Upsilon$ and $\Psi; \Delta \xrightarrow{B} \Gamma; \Upsilon$. The outermost contexts, labeled here as Ψ and Υ, are the left and right classical contexts: these contexts are sets of formulas. The innermost contexts, labeled here as Δ and Γ, are the left and right linear contexts: these contexts are multisets of formulas. In the second sequent, the formula B over the sequent arrow is also formula and multiset Γ contains only atomic formulas. (Notice that the position of classical and linear contexts is different from that used in sequents within the LU proof system of Girard [Gir93].) The sequent system for Forum is given in Figure 1. The following is a consequence of the soundness and completeness result for Forum [Mil96].

Theorem 1. *Let Ψ be a set of flat clauses, Γ and Δ be multisets of flat goals, and Υ be a set of atomic formulas. Then the sequent $\Psi; \Delta \longrightarrow \Gamma; \Upsilon$ has a proof if and only if $!\Psi, \Delta \vdash \Gamma, ?\Upsilon$ has a proof in linear logic.*

The following lemma holds in general for Forum proofs, but it is particularly relevant here since the scope of ? will always be atomic.

Lemma 1. *If a sequent has a Forum proof, it has a proof in which there are no occurrences of decide? applied to an atomic formula.*

Proof   Permute all occurrences of decide? involving an atomic formula up in a proof until they reach an instance of the initial rule, in which the combination of initial and decide? can be rewritten to an occurrence of initial?.   ∎

Furthermore, a Forum proof of a sequent of the form $\Psi; \Delta \longrightarrow \Gamma; \Upsilon$, where Ψ, Δ, Γ and Υ are as in Theorem 1, is such that there are no occurrences of $\multimap$R, $\Rightarrow$R, and decide? inference rules and the left-hand linear context of all sequents in the proof is a subset of Δ.

3   Representing Sequents and Inference Rules

This section summarizes material found in [MP,Pim01]: see also [Mil96,Ric98] for related material.

Since we now wish to represent one logic and proof system within another, we need to distinguish between the meta-logic, namely, linear logic as presented by Forum, and the various object-logics for which we wish to specify sequent proof systems. Formulas of the object-level will be identified with meta-level terms of type *bool*. Object-level logical connectives will be introduced as needed and as constructors of this type.

A two-sided sequent $\Delta \longrightarrow \Gamma$ is generally restricted so that Δ and Γ are either lists, multisets, or sets of formulas. Sets are used if all three structural rules (exchange, weakening, contraction) are implicit; multisets are used if exchange is implicit; and lists are used if no structural rule is implicit. Since our goal here is to encode object-level sequents into meta-level sequents as directly as possible, and since contexts in Forum are either multisets or sets, we will not be able to represent sequents that make use of lists. It is unlikely, for example, that non-commutative object-logics can be encoded into our linear logic meta theory along the lines we describe below.

3.1 Three Schemes for Encoding Sequents

Consider the well-known, two-sided sequent proof systems for classical, intuitionistic, and linear logic. A convenient distinction between these logics can be described, in part, by where the structural rules of thinning and contraction can be applied. In classical logic, these structural rules are allowed on both sides of the sequent arrow; in intuitionistic logic, no structural rules are allowed on the right of the sequent arrow; and in linear logic, they are not allowed on either sides of the arrow. Thus a classical sequent is a pairing of two sets; a linear logic sequent is a pairing of two multisets; and an intuitionistic sequent is the pairing of a set (for the left-hand side) and a multiset (for the right-hand side). This discussion suggests the following representation of sequents in these three systems. Let $\lfloor \cdot \rfloor$ and $\lceil \cdot \rceil$ be two meta-level predicates, both of type $bool \to o$. These predicates are used to identify which object-level formulas appear on which side of the sequent arrow, and the ? modal is used to mark the formulas to which weakening and contraction can be applied.

We will identify three schemes for encoding sequents. The *linear scheme* encodes the (object-level) sequent $B_1, \ldots, B_n \longrightarrow C_1, \ldots, C_m$ $(n, m \geq 0)$ by the meta-level formula $\lfloor B_1 \rfloor \, \invamp \cdots \invamp \, \lfloor B_n \rfloor \, \invamp \, \lceil C_1 \rceil \, \invamp \cdots \invamp \, \lceil C_m \rceil$ or by the Forum sequent

$$\cdot; \cdot \longrightarrow \lfloor B_1 \rfloor, \ldots, \lfloor B_n \rfloor, \lceil C_1 \rceil, \ldots, \lceil C_m \rceil; \cdot.$$

The *intuitionistic scheme* encodes $B_1, \ldots, B_n \longrightarrow C_1, \ldots, C_m$, where $n, m \geq 0$, with the meta-level formula $?\lfloor B_1 \rfloor \, \invamp \cdots \invamp \, ?\lfloor B_n \rfloor \, \invamp \, \lceil C_1 \rceil \, \invamp \cdots \invamp \, \lceil C_m \rceil$ or by the Forum sequent

$$\cdot; \cdot \longrightarrow \lceil C_1 \rceil, \ldots, \lceil C_m \rceil; \lfloor B_1 \rfloor, \ldots, \lfloor B_n \rfloor.$$

Often intuitionistic sequents are additionally restricted to having one formula on the right. Finally, the *classical scheme* encodes the sequent $B_1, \ldots, B_n \longrightarrow C_1, \ldots, C_m$ $(n, m \geq 0)$ as the meta-level formula

$$?\lfloor B_1 \rfloor \, \invamp \cdots \invamp ?\lfloor B_n \rfloor \, \invamp ?\lceil C_1 \rceil \, \invamp \cdots \invamp ?\lceil C_m \rceil$$

or by the Forum sequent

$$\cdot; \cdot \longrightarrow \cdot; \lfloor B_1 \rfloor, \ldots, \lfloor B_n \rfloor, \lceil C_1 \rceil, \ldots, \lceil C_m \rceil.$$

3.2 Encoding Additive and Multiplicative Inference Rules

We first illustrate how to encode object-level inference rules using the linear scheme.

Consider the specification of the logical inference rules for object-level conjunction, represented here as the infix constant $\wedge$ of type $bool \to bool \to bool$. Consider the additive inference rules for this connective.

$$\frac{\Delta, A \longrightarrow \Gamma}{\Delta, A \wedge B \longrightarrow \Gamma} \wedge L_1 \qquad \frac{\Delta, B \longrightarrow \Gamma}{\Delta, A \wedge B \longrightarrow \Gamma} \wedge L_2 \qquad \frac{\Delta \longrightarrow \Gamma, A \quad \Delta \longrightarrow \Gamma, B}{\Delta \longrightarrow \Gamma, A \wedge B} \wedge R$$

These three inference rules can be specified in Forum using the clauses

$$(\wedge L_1) \quad \lfloor A \wedge B \rfloor \circ\!\!- \lfloor A \rfloor. \qquad (\wedge R) \quad \lceil A \wedge B \rceil \circ\!\!- \lceil A \rceil \,\&\, \lceil B \rceil.$$
$$(\wedge L_2) \quad \lfloor A \wedge B \rfloor \circ\!\!- \lfloor B \rfloor.$$

We shall assume that a formula displayed in this manner actually denote the formula you get when you add the modal ! to the universal closure of the formula displayed. We use the convention that capital letters will generally serve as variables.

Notice that the two clauses for left introduction can be written in the uncurried for as

$$\lfloor A \wedge B \rfloor \circ\!\!- \lfloor A \rfloor \oplus \lfloor B \rfloor.$$

Thus, these additive rules make use of two (dual) meta-level additive connectives: & and $\oplus$. Similarly, the following two clauses encode the multiplicative version of conjunction introduction rules:

$$(\wedge L) \quad \lfloor A \wedge B \rfloor \circ\!\!- \lfloor A \rfloor \,\mathbin{\rotatebox[origin=c]{180}{\&}}\, \lfloor B \rfloor. \qquad (\wedge R) \quad \lceil A \wedge B \rceil \circ\!\!- \lceil A \rceil \circ\!\!- \lceil B \rceil.$$

The equivalent, uncurried form of the right introduction is

$$\lceil A \wedge B \rceil \circ\!\!- \lceil A \rceil \otimes \lceil B \rceil.$$

Thus, these multiplicative rules make use of two (dual) meta-level multiplicative connectives: $\otimes$ and $\mathbin{\rotatebox[origin=c]{180}{\&}}$.

When using either the classical or intuitionistic (hybrid) encoding of an object-level sequent, inference rules can place occurrences of the ? modality where needed with the body of clauses. For example, the additive version of the $(\wedge R)$ rule for a classical sequent is encoded as

$$\lceil A \wedge B \rceil \circ\!\!- ?\lceil A \rceil \,\&\, ?\lceil B \rceil.$$

For additional examples, see Section 3.5.

3.3 Encoding Quantifier Introduction Rules

Using the quantification of higher-order types that is available in Forum, it is a simple matter to encode the inference rules for object-level quantifiers. For example, if we use the linear scheme for representing sequents, then the left and right introduction rules for object-level universal quantifier can be written as

$$(\forall L) \quad \lfloor \forall B \rfloor \circ\!\!- \lfloor Bx \rfloor. \qquad (\forall R) \quad \lceil \forall B \rceil \circ\!\!- \forall x \lceil Bx \rceil.$$

Here, the symbol $\forall$ is used for both meta-level and object-level quantification: at the object-level $\forall$ has the type $(i \rightarrow bool) \rightarrow bool$. Thus the variable B above has the type $i \rightarrow bool$. Consider the Forum sequent $\Psi; \cdot \longrightarrow \lceil \forall B \rceil, \Theta; \cdot$ where Ψ contains the above two clauses. Using *decide*! with the clause for $(\forall R)$ would cause the search for a proof of the above sequent to be reduced to the search for a proof of the sequent $\Psi; \cdot \longrightarrow \lceil By \rceil, \Theta; \cdot$ where y is new. Here, the meta-level eigen-variable y also serves the role of an object-level eigen-variable. Dually, consider the Forum sequent $\Psi; \cdot \longrightarrow \lfloor \forall B \rfloor, \Theta; \cdot$. Using the *decide!* with the clause for $(\forall L)$ would cause proof search to reduce this sequent to the sequent $\Psi; \cdot \longrightarrow \lfloor Bt \rfloor, \Theta; \cdot$ where t is a term of type i. If we restrict appropriately the use of the type i, then terms of type i can be identified with object-level terms.

Notice that the clause for $(\forall L)$ is logically equivalent to the formula

$$\lfloor \forall B \rfloor \circ\!\!- \exists x \lfloor Bx \rfloor.$$

Thus, these quantifier rules make use of two (dual) meta-level quantifiers.

3.4   The Initial and Cut Rules

Up to this point, all the Forum clauses used to specify an inference figure have been such that the head of the clause has been an atom. Clauses specifying the cut and initial rules will have rather different structure. In particular, the initial rule which asserts that the sequent $B \longrightarrow B$ is provable, can be represented simply by the following *initial clause*:

$$(\textit{Initial}) \qquad \lfloor B \rfloor \,\bindnasrepma\, \lceil B \rceil.$$

Notice that this clause has a head with two atoms and no body.

There appear to be several possible ways to encode the cut rule. As a proof rule, cut is given as

$$\frac{\Delta_1 \longrightarrow \Gamma_1, B \qquad \Delta_2, B \longrightarrow \Gamma_2}{\Delta_1, \Delta_2 \longrightarrow \Gamma_1, \Gamma_2} \; Cut$$

Depending on how structural rules are used in this encoding, this cut rule can be specified as one of the following clauses:

(Cut)	$\forall B(\lceil B \rceil \multimap \lfloor B \rfloor \multimap \bot)$	(Cut_1)	$\forall B(?\lceil B \rceil \multimap \lfloor B \rfloor \multimap \bot)$
(Cut_2)	$\forall B(\lceil B \rceil \multimap ?\lfloor B \rfloor \multimap \bot)$	(Cut_3)	$\forall B(?\lceil B \rceil \multimap ?\lfloor B \rfloor \multimap \bot)$

Dual to the initial rule, these clauses have an empty head and two bodies. Other variations on the cut rule also seem possible: namely, one or both of the $\multimap$ can be replaced with $\Rightarrow$. The four displayed possibilities for the cut rule, however, entail these other variations, for example:

$$?\lceil B \rceil \multimap \lfloor B \rfloor \multimap \bot \;\; \vdash \;\; ?\lceil B \rceil \Rightarrow \lfloor B \rfloor \multimap \bot \,.$$

As a result, we shall not consider these variations any further here.

Notice that the *Initial* and *Cut* clauses together proves that $\lfloor \cdot \rfloor$ and $\lceil \cdot \rceil$ are duals of each other: that is, $\forall B(\lfloor B \rfloor \multimap \lceil B \rceil)$ and $\forall B(\lceil B \rceil \multimap \lfloor B \rfloor)$ are proved from these two formulas.

3.5   Example Forum Specifications

Consider a presentation of intuitionistic logic using the logical connective $\supset$, $\cap$, $\cup$, $\forall_i$, $\exists_i$, f_i, and t_i. The usual LJ proof system of Gentzen [Gen69] can be encoded as follows: rules for intuitionistic logic LJ and a cut rule (taken from [MP]).

$(\supset L)$	$\lfloor A \supset B \rfloor \circ\!\!- \lceil A \rceil \circ\!\!- ?\lfloor B \rfloor.$	$(\supset R)$	$\lceil A \supset B \rceil \circ\!\!- ?\lfloor A \rfloor \,\bindnasrepma\, \lceil B \rceil.$
$(\cap L_1)$	$\lfloor A \cap B \rfloor \circ\!\!- ?\lfloor A \rfloor.$	$(\cap R)$	$\lceil A \cap B \rceil \circ\!\!- \lceil A \rceil \,\&\, \lceil B \rceil.$
$(\cap L_2)$	$\lfloor A \cap B \rfloor \circ\!\!- ?\lfloor B \rfloor.$	$(\cup R_1)$	$\lceil A \cup B \rceil \circ\!\!- \lceil A \rceil.$
$(\cup L)$	$\lfloor A \cup B \rfloor \circ\!\!- ?\lfloor A \rfloor \,\&\, ?\lfloor B \rfloor.$	$(\cup R_2)$	$\lceil A \cup B \rceil \circ\!\!- \lceil B \rceil.$
$(\forall_i L)$	$\lfloor \forall_i B \rfloor \circ\!\!- ?\lfloor Bx \rfloor.$	$(\forall_i R)$	$\lceil \forall_i B \rceil \circ\!\!- \forall x \lceil Bx \rceil.$
$(\exists_i L)$	$\lfloor \exists_i B \rfloor \circ\!\!- \forall x\, ?\lfloor Bx \rfloor.$	$(\exists_i R)$	$\lceil \exists_i B \rceil \circ\!\!- \lceil Bx \rceil.$
$(f_i L)$	$\lfloor f_i \rfloor \circ\!\!- \top.$	$(t_i R)$	$\lceil t_i \rceil \circ\!\!- \top.$
(Cut)	$\bot \circ\!\!- ?\lfloor B \rfloor \circ\!\!- \lceil B \rceil.$	$(Initial)$	$\lfloor B \rfloor \,\bindnasrepma\, \lceil B \rceil.$

Theorems that state that one's encoding of a proof system matches the original proof system are often called adequacy theorems. The following such theorem is easily proved by induction of the structure of proofs.

Adequacy Theorem The sequent $B_1, \ldots, B_n \longrightarrow B_0$ has an LJ-proof [Gen69] if and only if the sequent $LJ; \cdot \longrightarrow \lceil B_0 \rceil; \lfloor B_1 \rfloor, \ldots, \lfloor B_n \rfloor$ has a Forum proof. The sequent $B_1, \ldots, B_n \longrightarrow$ has an LJ-proof if and only if $LJ; \cdot \longrightarrow \cdot; \lfloor B_1 \rfloor, \ldots, \lfloor B_n \rfloor$ has a Forum proof $(n \geq 0)$.

A number of other proof systems have been specified in Forum using this particular style of encoding. For example, Gentzen's LK and LJ [Gen69], linear logic, LKQ and LKT [DJS95], an optimization of LJ [LSS93,Dyc92], and Girard's LU [Gir93].

3.6   Advantages of Such Encodings

The encoding of an object-level proof system as Forum clauses has certain advantages over encoding them as inference figures. For example, the Forum specifications do not deal with context explicitly and instead they focus on the formulas that are directly involved in the inference rule. The distinction between making the inference rule additive or multiplicative is achieved in inference rule figures by explicitly presenting contexts and either splitting or copying them. The Forum clause representation achieves the same distinction using meta-level additive or multiplicative connectives. Object-level quantifiers can be handled directly using the meta-level quantification. Similarly, the structural rules of contraction and thinning can be captured together using the ? modal.

Since the encoding of proof systems is natural and direct, we might hope to be able to use the rich meta-theory of linear logic to help in drawing conclusions about object-level proof systems. An example of this kind of meta-level reason is given in [Mil96] where it is shown how a sequent calculus presentation of intuitionistic logic can be transformed into a natural deduction presentation by simple linear logic equivalences.

Since the encodings of object-level encodings result in logic programs (in the sense of Forum) and since there is significant knowledge and tools available to provide automatic and interactive tools to compute with those logic programs, encodings such as those described here can be important for the automation of various proof systems. In this paper, we explore automation of questions such as: Does one object-level sequent follow from the encoding of a proof system? Does one proof system's encoding entail another proof system's encoding? Can cut elimination be proved for the encoded logic? The last question has also been discussed by Avron and Lev [AL01] but their setting is limited the specification of propositional logics based on classical and additive maintenance of context.

There are, of course, some disadvantages to using linear logic as a meta-theory, the principle one being that it will not be possible to capture proof systems requiring non-commutativity. As we shall see, however, significant and interesting proof systems can be encoded into linear logic and for these systems, broad avenues of meta-level reasoning and automation should be available.

4   Entailments between Introduction Rules

We now address the problem of how easy it is to prove that the encoding of some inference rules imply the encoding of some other inference rules. For this purpose, we need to make definitions that restrict flat Forum formulas further so that they encode object-level inference rules. We shall assume that we have fixed a set $\mathcal{Q}$ of unary meta-level predicates all of type $bool \to o$. Object-level logical constants will also be assumed to be fixed. These constants will have types of order 0, 1, or 2 and all will build terms of type $bool$. Examples of object-level constants at various orders are: order 0, true and false; order 1, conjunction and implication; and order 2, universal and existential quantifiers. We shall also assume that object-level quantification is first-order and over one domain, denoted at the meta-level by i.

Definition 1. *An* introduction clause *is a closed flat formula of the form*

$$\forall x_1 \ldots \forall x_n [q(\diamond(x_1, \ldots, x_n)) \leftharpoondown B_1 \leftharpoondown B_2 \leftharpoondown \ldots \leftharpoondown B_m],$$

where $n, m \geq 0$, $\diamond$ is an object-level connective of arity n $(n \geq 0)$, and q is a meta-level predicate. Furthermore, an atom occurring in a body of this clause is either of the form $p(x_i)$ or $p(x_i(y))$ where p is a meta-level predicate and $1 \leq i \leq n$. In the first case, x_i has a type of order 0 while in the second case x_i has a type of order 1 and y is a variable quantified (universally or existentially) in a body of this clause (in particular, y is not in $\{x_1, \ldots, x_n\}$).

Notice that all the encodings of inference rules we have presented so far are examples of *introduction clauses*: the predicates $\lfloor \cdot \rfloor$ and $\lceil \cdot \rceil$ are examples of meta-level predicates. Encodings of inference rules are also allowed to have other predicates defined for, say, side conditions, as long as they can be described using such clauses.

Definition 2. *A* premise atom *is an atomic formula of the form $q(t)$, where q is a meta-level predicate and t is a term of type bool with a variable as its head symbol. A* conclusion atom *is an atomic formula of the form $q(\diamond(x_1, \ldots, x_n))$, where q is a meta-level predicate, $\diamond$ is an object-level connective of arity n, and $x_1, \ldots, x_n$ is a list of variables.*

Definition 3. *Let Π be a Forum proof of the sequent $\Psi; \Delta \longrightarrow \Gamma; \Upsilon$, where Ψ is a set of flat clauses that are either initial, one of the cut clauses, an introduction clause, or a flat goal, Δ and Γ are multisets of flat goals, and Υ is a set of atoms. The* depth *of a Forum proof Π is defined as the maximum number of occurrences of the rules decide or decide! on a branch of Π.*

Notice that if Π is a proof of a sequent of the form $\Psi; \Delta \longrightarrow \Gamma; \Upsilon$, following the restrictions of the definition above, then all sequents in Π are such that the left classical context is equal to Ψ, the right classical context is always a set of atoms, and the two linear contexts are always multisets of flat goals.

It is also a simple matter to see that it is possible to search through all Forum proofs of such sequents which are bounded in depth. The Forum proof system is designed so that the only essential choices that need to be made are those involved with the decide, decide!, and decide? inference rules.

The following lemma can be used to build a decision procedure for certain kinds of inferences between introduction clauses.

Lemma 2. *Let Ψ be a set containing introduction clauses and possibly the initial clause. Let C be an introduction clause. If the sequent $\Psi; \cdot \longrightarrow C; \cdot$ has a proof, it has a proof of depth 3 or less.*

Proof   We first argue that a sequent of the form

$$\Psi, \Delta_1; \Delta_2 \longrightarrow \mathcal{A}_1; \mathcal{A}_2, \qquad (*)$$

where Δ_1 is a set and Δ_2 is a multiset of flat goals over premise atoms and $\mathcal{A}_1$ is a multiset and $\mathcal{A}_2$ is a multiset of premise atoms, is provable if and only if it is provable with a proof of depth 2 or less. This sequent can only be proved using decide or decide!. Let B be the formula that is selected in one of these decide rules. If B is the initial clause, then this proof must have depth 1. Clearly, B is not an introduction clause from Ψ since eventually an instance of the head of that clause must be in either $\mathcal{A}_1$ or in $\mathcal{A}_2$, which is impossible since the instance of a conclusion atom cannot be a premise atom. Thus, B must be from either Δ_1 or Δ_2. A simple argument by structural induction of flat goals shows that in either of these cases, the depth of a proof is limited by 2. In particular, consider the case when B is $? A$, for some premise atom A. Then Δ_2 and $\mathcal{A}_1$ must be empty and the proof has the shape

$$
\frac{\dfrac{\rule{4cm}{0.4pt}}{\Psi, \Delta_1; \cdot \xrightarrow{A} \cdot; \mathcal{A}_2} \; initial?}{\dfrac{\Psi, \Delta_1; A \longrightarrow \cdot; \mathcal{A}_2}{\Psi, \Delta_1; \cdot \xrightarrow{? A} \cdot; \mathcal{A}_2} \; ? L} \; decide
$$

Observe that the only rule that can be applied to the middle sequent is decide, since the left linear context is not empty. Also, note that since A is atomic, it must be in $\mathcal{A}_2$ and the last rule on the above proof has to be initial?. The depth in this case is exactly 2. The other cases of depending on the structure of B are similar and simpler.

Now consider a provable sequent of the form

$$\Psi, \Delta_1; \Delta_2 \longrightarrow A; \cdot, \qquad (**)$$

where Δ_1 is a set and Δ_2 is a multiset of flat goals over premise atoms and A is a conclusion atom. This sequent can be proved only using decide! with an introduction clause from Ψ since the atoms in Δ_1 and Δ_2 are premise atoms. The result of completing the backchaining leaves possibly several sequents that need to be proved, but all of these are of form $(*)$ above. Thus, sequents of the form $(**)$ can be proved in height 3 or less.

Finally, a sequent of the form $\Psi; \cdot \longrightarrow C; \cdot$ has a proof if and only if the right-rules for Forum reduce it to sequents of the form $(**)$ above. Thus, such a sequent is provable if and only if it has a proof of depth 3 or less. ∎

Lemma 2 shows that deciding whether or not one inference rule is derivable from other inference rules is rather simple: if such a derivation is possible, a very shallow proof witnesses that fact.

5   Canonical and Coherent Proof Systems

In the inference systems we shall consider, the set of meta-level predicates $\mathcal{Q}$ is exactly the set $\{\lfloor \cdot \rfloor, \lceil \cdot \rceil\}$. In Section 7, we consider the *LU* proof system of Girard [Gir93] and there we will use additional meta-level predicates.

Definition 4. *Fix $\mathcal{Q}$ to be the set $\{\lfloor \cdot \rfloor, \lceil \cdot \rceil\}$. A canonical proof system is a set $\mathcal{P}$ of flat Forum clauses such that (i) the initial clause is a member of $\mathcal{P}$, (ii) exactly one cut clause is a member of $\mathcal{P}$, and (iii) all other clauses in $\mathcal{P}$ are introduction clauses with the additional restriction that, for every pair of atoms of the form $\lfloor T \rfloor$ and $\lceil S \rceil$ in a body, the head variable of T differs from head variable of S. A formula that statisfies condition (iii) is also called a* canonical *clause.*

Definition 5. *Consider a canonical proof system $\mathcal{P}$ and an object-level connective, say, $\diamond$ of arity $n \geq 0$. Consider all the (uncurried) formulas in $\mathcal{P}$ that specify a left-introduction rule for $\diamond$. These would be of the form*

$$\forall \bar{x}(\lfloor \diamond(x_1, \ldots, x_i) \rfloor \circ\!\!- L_1) \quad \cdots \quad \forall \bar{x}(\lfloor \diamond(x_1, \ldots, x_i) \rfloor \circ\!\!- L_p) \quad (p \geq 0)$$

Similarly, consider all the (uncurried) formulas in $\mathcal{P}$ that specify a right-introduction rule for $\diamond$. These would be of the form

$$\forall \bar{x}(\lceil \diamond(x_1, \ldots, x_i) \rceil \circ\!\!- R_1) \quad \cdots \quad \forall \bar{x}(\lceil \diamond(x_1, \ldots, x_i) \rceil \circ\!\!- R_q) \qquad (q \geq 0)$$

All of these $p + q$ displayed formulas can be replaced by the following two clauses

$$\forall \bar{x}(\lfloor \diamond(x_1, \ldots, x_i) \rfloor \circ\!\!- L_1 \oplus \cdots \oplus L_p) \ \text{and} \ \ \forall \bar{x}(\lceil \diamond(x_1, \ldots, x_i) \rceil \circ\!\!- R_1 \oplus \cdots \oplus R_q)$$

(An empty $\oplus$ is written as the linear logic additive false 0.) We shall say that these last two formulas represent the introduction rules for $\diamond$ in their defini-tion form. While these formulas are not generally formulas of Forum, they are equivalent to the $p + q$ Forum formulas.

Definition 6. *Consider a canonical proof system $\mathcal{P}$ and an object-level connec-tive, say, $\diamond$ of arity $n \geq 0$. Let the formulas*

$$\forall \bar{x}(\lfloor \diamond(x_1, \ldots, x_n) \rfloor \circ\!\!- B_l) \quad \text{and} \quad \forall \bar{x}(\lceil \diamond(x_1, \ldots, x_n) \rceil \circ\!\!- B_r)$$

be the definition form for the left and right introduction rules. Let C be the cut clause that appears in $\mathcal{P}$. The object-level connective $\diamond$ has dual *left and right introduction rules if $!\, C \vdash \forall \bar{x}(B_l \multimap B_r \multimap \bot)$ in linear logic.*

Definition 7. *A canonical system is called* coherent *if the left and right intro-duction rules for each object-level connective are duals.*

Example 1. Consider the specification of *LJ* in Section 3.5. The introduction rules for $\cap$, for example, in definition form are the two formulas

$$\forall A \forall B(\lfloor A \cap B \rfloor \circ\!\!- ?\lfloor A \rfloor \oplus ?\lfloor B \rfloor) \quad \text{and} \quad \forall A \forall B(\lceil A \cap B \rceil \circ\!\!- \lceil A \rceil \,\&\, \lceil B \rceil).$$

The definition form for the introduction rules for the other logical connectives can be computed easily. In the end, to determine that the *LJ* specification is coherent, the following must be proved:

$$
\begin{array}{ll}
(\supset) & !\, Cut_2 \vdash \forall A \forall B [(?\lfloor A \rfloor \oplus ?\lceil B \rceil) \multimap (\lceil A \rceil \,\&\, \lceil B \rceil) \multimap \bot] \\
(\cap) & !\, Cut_2 \vdash \forall A \forall B [(\lceil A \rceil \otimes ?\lfloor B \rfloor) \multimap (?\lfloor A \rfloor \,\bindnasrepma\, \lceil B \rceil) \multimap \bot] \\
(\cup) & !\, Cut_2 \vdash \forall A \forall B [(?\lfloor A \rfloor \,\&\, ?\lfloor B \rfloor) \multimap (\lceil A \rceil \oplus \lceil B \rceil) \multimap \bot] \\
(\forall_i) & !\, Cut_2 \vdash \forall B [\exists x (?\lfloor Bx \rfloor) \multimap \forall x \lceil Bx \rceil \multimap \bot] \\
(\exists_i) & !\, Cut_2 \vdash \forall B [\forall x (?\lfloor Bx \rfloor) \multimap \exists x \lceil Bx \rceil \multimap \bot] \\
(t_i) & !\, Cut_2 \vdash 0 \multimap \top \multimap \bot \\
(f_i) & !\, Cut_2 \vdash \top \multimap 0 \multimap \bot
\end{array}
$$

All of these sequents have simple Forum proofs.

Definition 8. *A Forum proof is said to* encode *an object-level cut-free proof if no occurrence of the decide! inference rule is used on a cut clause.*

Definition 9. *The* degree *$d(B)$ of an object-level formula B is the number of occurrences of object-level logical connectives in B. Thus, $d(A) = 0$ if and only if A is atomic. Logical constants of arity 0 have degree 1. If a cut-clause is used in a decide! rule in a Forum proof, then the* degree *of that occurrence of decide! is the degree of the object-level formula used to instantiate that occurrence of the cut clause. The degree of a Forum proof Π, written as $d(\Pi)$, is the multiset of the degree of all occurrences of decide! in the proof. Thus, a Forum proof Π encodes a cut-free object-level proof if and only if $d(\Pi)$ is the empty multiset.*

We now show that, for coherent systems, it is possible to exchange a Forum proof by another one with a smaller degree: here we use the multiset well-ordering [DM79] induced by the ordering on non-negative integers.

Lemma 3. *Let $\mathcal{P}$ be a coherent system, Ψ be a set, Δ be a multiset of flat goals which contain no occurrences of object-level logical constants, and Γ be a multiset and Υ be a set of atomic formulas. If there is a Forum proof Π of the sequent $\mathcal{P}, \Psi; \Delta \longrightarrow \Gamma; \Upsilon$ such that $d(\Pi)$ contains a positive integer, then there is a proof of the same sequent with smaller multiset order.*

Proof   We shall first assume that the cut clause in $\mathcal{P}$ is the clause without the ? modal. Let Π be a Forum proof for $\mathcal{P}, \Psi; \Delta \longrightarrow \Gamma; \Upsilon$ such that $d(\Pi)$ contains a positive integer. There is thus a subproof of Π of the form

$$
\frac{
\frac{\Pi_1}{\mathcal{P}, \Psi; \Delta_1 \longrightarrow \lfloor D \rfloor, \Gamma_1; \Upsilon'} \quad \frac{\Pi_2}{\mathcal{P}, \Psi; \Delta_2 \longrightarrow \lceil D \rceil, \Gamma_2; \Upsilon'}
}{
\frac{\mathcal{P}, \Psi; \Delta_1, \Delta_2 \xrightarrow{\lceil D \rceil - \circ \lfloor D \rfloor - \circ \perp} \Gamma_1, \Gamma_2; \Upsilon'}{
\frac{\mathcal{P}, \Psi; \Delta_1, \Delta_2 \xrightarrow{\forall B(\lceil B \rceil - \circ \lfloor B \rfloor - \circ \perp)} \Gamma_1, \Gamma_2; \Upsilon'}{\mathcal{P}, \Psi; \Delta_1, \Delta_2 \longrightarrow \Gamma_1, \Gamma_2; \Upsilon'}}
}
$$

where $D = \diamond(D_1, \dots, D_n)$ for some object-level connective $\diamond$, $n \geq 0$, and $\Upsilon \subseteq \Upsilon'$.

We may assume that the occurrences of $\lfloor D \rfloor$ in Π_1 and of $\lceil D \rceil$ in Π_2 are *principal formulas* in their respective proofs: that is, these proofs end with a decide or decide! rule and these atoms are the ones rewritten by the backchaining step. If this is not the case, the decide or decide! rule together with the cut clause can be permuted upward in the Forum proof.

We can distinguish three cases. In one case, Π_1 ends in a decide of an initial clause: thus Γ_1 is $\lceil D \rceil$, Δ_1 is empty, the displayed proof fragment above can be replaced by Π_2, and the degree of the resulting proof decreases. In another case, Π_2 ends in a decide of an initial clause, Γ_2 is $\lfloor D \rfloor$, Δ_2 is empty, the displayed proof fragment above can be replaced by Π_1, and the degree of the resulting proof decreases. The only other case is that Π_1 and Π_2 end in a decide or decide! rule selecting some formula from $\mathcal{P}$, Ψ, and Δ_1 or Δ_2, respectively. Since D must contain an object level logical constant and since the formulas in Ψ, Δ_1, and Δ_2 do not contain such constants, the only possible selections are of formulas from $\mathcal{P}$. Thus, there are clauses

$$\forall \bar{x}. \lfloor \diamond(x_1, \dots, x_i) \rfloor \circ\!- B_l \quad \text{and} \quad \forall \bar{x}. \lceil \diamond(x_1, \dots, x_i) \rceil \circ\!- B_r$$

in $\mathcal{P}$ such that Π_1 and Π_2 are the following two proofs:

$$
\frac{\Pi_1'}{\mathcal{P}, \Psi; \Delta_1 \longrightarrow \theta B_l, \Gamma_1; \Upsilon'}{\mathcal{P}, \Psi; \Delta_1 \longrightarrow \lfloor D \rfloor, \Gamma_1; \Upsilon'} \qquad \frac{\Pi_2'}{\mathcal{P}, \Psi; \Delta_2 \longrightarrow \theta B_r, \Gamma_2; \Upsilon'}{\mathcal{P}, \Psi; \Delta_2 \longrightarrow \lceil D \rceil, \Gamma_2; \Upsilon'}
$$

where θ is the appropriate substitution for the variables in $\bar{x}$. (Here we have assumed that the clauses in $\mathcal{P}$ are written in the logically equivalent uncurried form). Finally, since $\mathcal{P}$ is a coherent system, we know that $Cut; \theta B_l, \theta B_r \longrightarrow \perp; \cdot$ is provable.

Using the soundness and completeness theorem for Forum (Theorem 1) the three sequents

$$!\mathcal{P}, !\Psi, \Delta_1 \vdash \theta B_l, \Gamma_1, ?\Upsilon' \qquad !\mathcal{P}, !\Psi, \Delta_2 \vdash \theta B_r, \Gamma_2, ?\Upsilon' \quad !Cut, \theta B_l, \theta B_r \vdash \perp$$

are provable in linear logic. Using cut twice, we can then conclude that

$$!\mathcal{P}, !\Psi, \Delta_1, \Delta_2 \vdash \Gamma_1, \Gamma_2 ?\Upsilon'$$

is provable in linear logic (remember that $Cut \in \mathcal{P}$) and by cut-elimination in linear logic and Theorem 1, we have that

$$\mathcal{P}, \Psi; \Delta_1, \Delta_2 \longrightarrow \Gamma_1, \Gamma_2; \Upsilon'$$

has a Forum proof. The process of translating to and from linear logic and using cut-elimination in linear logic will not change the degree of the Forum proof except to replace the one selected occurrence with possibly several smaller uses of decide! with Cut in the proof of $!Cut, \theta B_l, \theta B_r \vdash \perp$. As a result, the degree of the overall proof has reduced.

If the cut clause in $\mathcal{P}$ has the modal ?, the result follows with a slightly different proof. ∎

As an immediate corollary of this lemma, if the sequent $\mathcal{P}, \Psi; \Delta \longrightarrow \Gamma; \Upsilon$ (assuming the restrictions of this lemma) has a proof with a degree containing a positive integer, that sequent has a proof with a degree that contains at most zeros. That is, this lemma shows how to reduce object-level cuts to only object-level atomic cuts. The following result shows that, in fact, these cuts can be removed.

Lemma 4. *Let C be a canonical clause that encodes an introduction rule and let $\mathcal{P}$ be a coherent system. If $!\mathcal{P} \vdash C$ in linear logic then there is an object-level cut-free Forum proof of $\mathcal{P}; \cdot \longrightarrow C; \cdot$.*

Proof   Given that $!\mathcal{P} \vdash C$ in linear logic, there is a Forum proof of the sequent $\mathcal{P}; \cdot \longrightarrow C; \cdot$. Applying right introduction rules to this sequent forces the sequent $\mathcal{P}, \Psi; \Delta \longrightarrow A; \cdot$, where Ψ is a set and Δ is a multiset of premise atoms and A is a conclusion atom, to have a Forum proof Π. Given that all clauses in Ψ are flat clauses, a simple induction show that every sequent occurring in Π is of the form $\mathcal{P}, \Psi; \Delta' \xrightarrow{\{B\}} \Gamma; \Upsilon$ where $\Delta' \subseteq \Delta$, Γ is a multiset of flat goals, Υ is a set of atomic formulas and $\{B\}$ indicates that a flat clause labeling the arrow might be present.

Using Lemma 3, we can conclude that Π contains only atomic object level cuts. We now argue that these cuts can be removed. If Π is not object-level cut-free, there is a subproof of Π of the form

$$\cfrac{\cfrac{\begin{matrix}\Pi_1 \\ \mathcal{P}, \Psi; \Delta_1 \longrightarrow \lfloor D \rfloor, \Gamma_1; \Upsilon'\end{matrix} \quad \begin{matrix}\Pi_2 \\ \mathcal{P}, \Psi; \Delta_2 \longrightarrow \lceil D \rceil, \Gamma_2; \Upsilon'\end{matrix}}{\mathcal{P}, \Psi; \Delta_1, \Delta_2 \xrightarrow{\forall B(\lceil B \rceil -\circ \lfloor B \rfloor -\circ \perp)} \Gamma_1, \Gamma_2; \Upsilon'}}{\mathcal{P}, \Psi; \Delta_1, \Delta_2 \longrightarrow \Gamma_1, \Gamma_2; \Upsilon'} \; decide!$$

where Π_1 and Π_2 are object-level cut-free Forum proofs, $\Upsilon \subseteq \Upsilon'$, and D is an object-level atomic formula.

We can distinguish three possibilities for the last inference rules of Π_1 and Π_2. If Π_1 ends a decide! with the initial clause then Δ_1 is empty and Γ_1 is the multiset set containing just $\lceil D \rceil$. In that case, the entire displayed proof can be replaced by Π_2, which removes one decide! on a cut-clause. Similarly, if Π_2 ends a decide! with the initial clause, then the displayed proof can be replaced by Π_1. Finally, the last inference rules of Π_1 and Π_2 could be (meta-level) left-introduction rules: in Π_1 a formula could be selected from Ψ or Δ_1 for backchaining and in Π_2 a formula could be selected from Ψ or Δ_2 for backchaining. In these cases, the formula $\lfloor D \rfloor$ would be a subformula of a formula in Ψ or Δ_1 and $\lceil D \rceil$ would be a subformula of a formula in Ψ or Δ_2. Then both $\lfloor D \rfloor$ and $\lceil D \rceil$ occur in bodies of the clause C, something that is explicitly ruled out by the definition of canonical proof systems (Definition 4).

For the case where another cut rule is present in $\mathcal{P}$, the analysis is the same except that either one or both of $\lfloor D \rfloor$ and $\lceil D \rceil$ could be in the right classical context and references to the Forum rule initial might need to be initial?. ∎

This result is important since it provides a way of controlling the use of cut clauses during proof search. In general, it is desirable to control meta-level proof search when clauses with empty head are available. Using the decide inference rule with such clauses can produce redundant steps in a proof, in a possibly endless process. The same behavior can be observed at the object-level with the use of a cut rule.

Next, we describe a decision procedure for determining if a proof system is derivable from another.

Theorem 2. *Let $\mathcal{P}$ be a coherent proof system. Let Ψ be a set of canonical clauses together with a cut clause and the initial clause and let P be the formula $!\,C_1 \& \ldots \& !\,C_m$ where $\Psi = \{C_1, \ldots, C_m\}$. If there is a proof in Forum of $\mathcal{P}; \cdot \longrightarrow P; \cdot$ then it has a proof of depth less than or equal to 3.*

Proof   Clearly, $\mathcal{P}; \cdot \longrightarrow P; \cdot$ is provable with depth less than or equal to 3 if and only if for all $C \in \Psi$, the Forum sequent $\mathcal{P}; \cdot \longrightarrow C; \cdot$ is provable with depth less than or equal to 3. Thus, we only need to prove this depth restriction for $\mathcal{P}; \cdot \longrightarrow C; \cdot$ for $C \in \Psi$.

The case where C is the initial clause is trivial since $C \in \mathcal{P}$. In the case that C is a cut rule, the proof of $\mathcal{P}; \cdot \longrightarrow C; \cdot$ must look like

$$\frac{\begin{array}{c}\Pi\\ \mathcal{P}; \lfloor B \rfloor, \lceil B \rceil \longrightarrow \cdot; \cdot\end{array}}{\mathcal{P}; \cdot \longrightarrow \forall B. \lfloor B \rfloor \multimap \lceil B \rceil \multimap \bot; \cdot}$$

where B is an eigen-variable of the proof. Using Lemma 3, we may assume that the rest of this proof contains only object-level atomic cuts. Furthermore, the last inference rule of Π must be decide! using a cut rule. Thus, Π must be of the form

$$\cfrac{\cfrac{\quad}{\mathcal{P}; \cdot \overset{\lfloor B \rfloor}{\longrightarrow} \lfloor D \rfloor; \cdot} \; initial}{\mathcal{P}; \lfloor B \rfloor \longrightarrow \lfloor D \rfloor; \cdot} \; decide \qquad \cfrac{\cfrac{\quad}{\mathcal{P}; \cdot \overset{\lceil B \rceil}{\longrightarrow} \lceil D \rceil; \cdot} \; initial}{\mathcal{P}; \lceil B \rceil \longrightarrow \lceil D \rceil; \cdot} \; decide$$

$$\cfrac{}{\mathcal{P}; \lfloor B \rfloor, \lceil B \rceil \overset{\forall B(\lceil B \rceil \multimap \lfloor B \rfloor \multimap \bot)}{\longrightarrow} \cdot; \cdot}$$

where D is some object-level atomic formula, which must be B. In this case, the depth is 2. If another cut rule with occurrences of ? is present in $\mathcal{P}$, the depth is 3.

The remaining case is where C encodes an introduction rule. Then it follows from Lemma 3 that the cut rule of $\mathcal{P}$ is not used. Lemmas 2 then provides us with our conclusion: if the cut rule is removed from $\mathcal{P}$, we are left with only the initial rule and introduction clauses. ∎

Notice that if the encoded proof system $\mathcal{P}$ entails the encoded system Ψ (as describe in the above theorem), then a simple consequence of cut-elimination at the meta-level is that whenever $\mathcal{P}$ proves a object-level sequent, the proof system Ψ also proves that same sequent.

6   Cut-Elimination for Coherent Systems

The cut-elimination theorem for a particular logic can often be divided into two parts. The first part shows that a cut involving a non-atomic formula can be replaced by possibly multiple cuts involving subformulas of the original cut formula. This part of the proof works because left and right introduction rules for each logical connective are duals (formalized here in Definition 6). The second part of the proof argues how cuts with atomic formulas can be removed. Cut-elimination for coherent object-level proof systems is proved similarly: Lemma 3 shows that non-atomic cuts can be removed and the following theorem proves that object-level atomic cuts can also be removed.

Theorem 3. *Let $\mathcal{P}$ be a coherent system and B be an object-level formula. If $!\mathcal{P} \vdash B$ is provable (that is, if there is an object-level proof of B using the proof system encoded as $\mathcal{P}$), then there is an object-level cut-free proof of the Forum sequent $\mathcal{P}; \cdot \longrightarrow \lceil B \rceil; \cdot$.*

Proof   Since $\lceil B \rceil$ is an atomic meta-level formula and $\mathcal{P}$ contains only flat formulas, the left linear context is empty for all sequents in the proof Π of $\mathcal{P}; \cdot \longrightarrow \lceil B \rceil; \cdot$. Also, any formula that occurs in the right classical context of any sequent in Π is atomic.

Assume that Π is not free of object-level cuts. That is, there is a subproof of Π of the form

$$\cfrac{\cfrac{\Pi_1}{\mathcal{P}; \cdot \longrightarrow \lfloor D \rfloor, \Gamma_1; \Upsilon} \qquad \cfrac{\Pi_2}{\mathcal{P}; \cdot \longrightarrow \lceil D \rceil, \Gamma_2; \Upsilon}}{\cfrac{\mathcal{P}; \cdot \overset{\forall B(\lfloor B \rfloor \multimap \lceil B \rceil \multimap \bot)}{\longrightarrow} \Gamma_1, \Gamma_2; \Upsilon}{\mathcal{P}; \cdot \longrightarrow \Gamma_1, \Gamma_2; \Upsilon} \; decide!}$$

such that Π_1 and Π_2 are object-level cut-free, Γ_1 and Γ_2 are multisets of atomic formulas, and D is an object-level formula. As before, we may also assume that $\lfloor D \rfloor$ is a principal formula in Π_1. By Lemma 3, we may assume that D is actually an object-level atomic formula. Thus the last rule of Π_1 must be decide! over the *Initial* rule, since Π_1 is cut-free and the heads of all the other clauses in $\mathcal{P}$ (except *Initial*) have an object-level connective. Hence, Γ_1 is $\lceil D \rceil$ and the subproof displayed above can be replaced by Π_2, which is cut-free by hypothesis. Thus, we have eliminated one instance of the use of the object-level cut rule. This procedure shows that it is possible to eliminate all the top-most cuts. Continuing in this manner, we can finally arrive at a object-level cut-free proof of $\mathcal{P}; \cdot \longrightarrow \lceil B \rceil; \cdot$. ∎

To determine that a proof system satisfies cut-elimination, we can check if its encoding as flat clauses is coherent, since this guarantees cut-elimination for the encoded proof system (Theorem 3). Thus, the complete automation of proof of cut-elimination for coherent systems is given by the following result:

Theorem 4. *Determining whether or not a canonical proof system is coherent is decidable. In particular, determining if a cut clause proves the duality of the definitions of introduction rules for a given connective can be done by bounding proof search to a depth of $v + 2$ where v is the maximum number of meta-level atomic subformulas in the bodies of the introduction clauses.*

Proof   Assume that we have a given coherent proof system $\mathcal{P}$. For every object-level logical constant $\diamond$, let the introduction rules be given in definition format as

$$\forall \bar{x}(\lfloor \diamond(x_1, \ldots, x_i) \rfloor \circ\!\!-\ B_l) \quad \text{and} \quad \forall \bar{x}(\lceil \diamond(x_1, \ldots, x_i) \rceil \circ\!\!-\ B_r)$$

By coherence, $Cut \vdash \forall \bar{x}(B_l \multimap B_r \multimap \bot)$ in linear logic. Let C be the curried form of $\forall \bar{x}(B_l \multimap B_r \multimap \bot)$ and consider the Forum sequent $Cut; \cdot \longrightarrow C; \cdot$. Various right rules will decompose this sequent to a set of sequents of the form $Cut, \Psi; \Delta \longrightarrow \cdot; \cdot$ where Ψ is a set and Δ is a multiset of flat goals that do not contain any occurrences of object-level logical constants. Thus, we need to describe a decision procedure for the Forum provability of such sequents.

Let Π be a proof for the sequent $Cut, \Psi; \Delta \longrightarrow \cdot; \cdot$ above mentioned. Unless $\Delta = \bot$ or $\bot \in \Psi$ and $\Delta = \emptyset$ (in which cases the proof is trivial), Π is not cut-free. We claim that every cut formula is a subformula of some formula in Ψ or Δ. In fact, no formula is added to the left-hand side of sequents in Π and the formulas on the right-hand side of sequents are introduced by decide! on the cut rule. Then Π has the form:

$$
\cfrac{
\cfrac{
\cfrac{\cfrac{\Pi_1}{Cut, \Psi; \Delta_1' \longrightarrow \lceil B \rceil, \Gamma_1; \Upsilon} \ \ldots}{\vdots}{Cut, \Psi; \Delta_1 \longrightarrow \lceil B \rceil; \cdot} \qquad
\cfrac{\cfrac{\Pi_2}{Cut, \Psi; \Delta_2' \longrightarrow \lfloor B \rfloor, \Gamma_2; \Upsilon} \ \ldots}{\vdots}{Cut, \Psi; \Delta_2 \longrightarrow \lfloor B \rfloor; \cdot}
}{Cut, \Psi; \Delta \xrightarrow{\forall B(\lfloor B \rfloor \multimap \lceil B \rceil \multimap \bot)} \bot; \cdot} \ \forall L, \multimap L
}{Cut, \Psi; \Delta \longrightarrow \bot; \cdot} \ \ decide!
$$

where Π_1 and Π_2 are cut-free, $\Delta_i' \subseteq \Delta_i$ and Γ_1 and Γ_2 are multisets of atoms, introduced after various applications of decide! on the cut rule. Let $\Gamma_1' = \Gamma_1 \cup \lceil B \rceil$. Since Π_1 is cut-free, its last rule has to be decide! selecting one formula from Ψ (and in this case Δ_1' is empty) or decide selecting one formula from Δ_1' (Δ_1' is a singleton). That is, the last inference rule of Π_1 is of the form:

$$\frac{Cut, \Psi; \cdot \xrightarrow{D} \Gamma_1'; \Upsilon}{Cut, \Psi; \Delta_1' \longrightarrow \Gamma_1'; \Upsilon}$$

Hence every formula in Γ_1' is a subformula of D, a formula in Ψ or in Δ_1'. Moreover, all the formulas in Γ_1' must follow from the formula D and hence the number of formulas in Γ_1' cannot exceed the number of the atomic subformulas of D.

Note that the total number of formulas in Γ_1' is exactly the number of cuts applied in this path of the proof Π. Hence, for every branch of the proof, the number of decide! on cut rules is less than or equal to the maximum number of atomic subformulas of formulas in Ψ and Δ and this is less or equal to v. Since the number of decide or decide! in a branch of Π over a formula in Ψ or Δ is at most 2 (? has atomic scope), the maximum depth is $v + 2$.

A similar result holds if the cut rule in the proof system is one with the ? modal. ∎

For example, it is possible to prove coherence for LJ by bounding proof search at depth 4 during the check for duality.

7   LU

In [Gir93], Girard introduced the sequent system LU (logic of unity) in which classical, intuitionistic, and linear logics appear as fragments. In this logic, all three of these logics keep their own characteristics but they can also communicate via formulas containing connectives mixing these logics. The key to allowing these logics to share one proof system lies in using *polarities*. In terms of the encoding we have presented here, polarities allow the meta-level atom $\lfloor B \rfloor$ be replaced by $?\lfloor B \rfloor$ if B is positive and the meta-level atom $\lceil B \rceil$ be replaced by $?\lceil B \rceil$ if B is negative. This possibility of replacement is in contrast to the examples of classical and intuitionistic sequent proof systems presented earlier where $\lfloor \cdot \rfloor$ and $\lceil \cdot \rceil$ atoms are either all preceded by the ? modal or all are not so prefixed. The neutral polarity is also available and corresponds to the case where this replacement with a ? modal is not allowed. Many of the LU inference rules for classical and intuitionistic connectives are specified in Figure 2. The definition of the predicates $pos(\cdot)$, $neg(\cdot)$, and $neu(\cdot)$ can be directly obtained from the various polarity tables given in [Gir93].

As noted before, LU is not canonical since the side conditions in its rules require meta-level predicates other than simply $\lfloor \cdot \rfloor$ and $\lceil \cdot \rceil$. For a future work, we intend to generalize the notion of canonical clauses in order to handle more general systems like LU. Still, it is possible to introduce the notions of coherence

Identity and structure

$\lfloor B \rfloor \mathbin{⅋} \lceil B \rceil.$

$\qquad \bot \;\circ\!\!- \lfloor B \rfloor \;\circ\!\!- \lceil B \rceil.$

$\qquad \lceil N \rceil \;\circ\!\!- \;?\lceil N \rceil \;\Leftarrow neg(N).$

$\qquad \lfloor P \rfloor \;\circ\!\!- \;?\lfloor P \rfloor \;\Leftarrow pos(P).$

Conjunction

$\lceil u \wedge v \rceil \;\Leftarrow\; \lceil u \rceil \;\Leftarrow\; \lceil v \rceil \qquad\qquad \Leftarrow pos(u) \oplus pos(v).$

$\lceil u \wedge v \rceil \;\circ\!\!-\; \lceil u \rceil \;\&\; \lceil v \rceil \qquad\qquad \Leftarrow notpos(u) \;\&\; notpos(v).$

$\lfloor u \wedge v \rfloor \;\circ\!\!-\; ?\lfloor u \rfloor \mathbin{⅋} ?\lfloor v \rfloor \qquad\quad \Leftarrow pos(u) \oplus pos(v).$

$\lfloor u \wedge v \rfloor \;\circ\!\!-\; \lfloor u \rfloor \oplus \lfloor v \rfloor \qquad\qquad \Leftarrow notpos(u) \;\&\; notpos(v).$

Intuitionistic implication

$\lceil u \supset v \rceil \;\circ\!\!-\; ?\lfloor u \rfloor \mathbin{⅋} \lceil v \rceil.$

$\lfloor u \supset v \rfloor \;\Leftarrow\; \lceil u \rceil \;\circ\!\!-\; \lfloor v \rfloor.$

Quantifiers

$\lceil \forall_c u \rceil \;\circ\!\!-\; \forall x \, ?\lceil ux \rceil.$

$\lfloor \forall_c u \rfloor \;\Leftarrow\; \lfloor ux \rfloor.$

$\lceil \exists_c u \rceil \;\Leftarrow\; \lceil ux \rceil.$

$\lfloor \exists_c u \rfloor \;\circ\!\!-\; \forall x \, ?\lfloor ux \rfloor.$

Disjunction

$\lceil u \vee v \rceil \;\circ\!\!-\; !\lceil u \rceil \oplus !\lceil v \rceil \qquad\qquad \Leftarrow notneg(u) \;\&\; notneg(v).$

$\lceil u \vee v \rceil \;\circ\!\!-\; ?\lceil u \rceil \mathbin{⅋} ?\lceil v \rceil \qquad\qquad \Leftarrow (pos(u) \;\&\; neg(v)) \oplus (neg(u) \;\&\; notneu(v)).$

$\lceil u \vee v \rceil \;\circ\!\!-\; \lceil u \rceil \mathbin{⅋} ?!\lceil v \rceil \qquad\qquad \Leftarrow neg(u) \;\&\; neu(v).$

$\lceil u \vee v \rceil \;\circ\!\!-\; ?!\lceil u \rceil \mathbin{⅋} \lceil v \rceil \qquad\qquad \Leftarrow neu(u) \;\&\; neg(v).$

$\lfloor u \vee v \rfloor \;\circ\!\!-\; ?\lfloor u \rfloor \;\&\; ?\lfloor v \rfloor \qquad\qquad \Leftarrow notneg(u) \;\&\; notneg(v).$

$\lfloor u \vee v \rfloor \;\Leftarrow\; \lfloor u \rfloor \;\Leftarrow\; \lfloor v \rfloor \qquad\qquad \Leftarrow (pos(u) \;\&\; neg(v)) \oplus (neg(u) \;\&\; notneu(v)).$

$\lfloor u \vee v \rfloor \;\circ\!\!-\; \lfloor u \rfloor \;\Leftarrow\; ?\lfloor v \rfloor \qquad\qquad \Leftarrow neg(u) \;\&\; neu(v).$

$\lfloor u \vee v \rfloor \;\Leftarrow\; ?\lfloor u \rfloor \;\circ\!\!-\; \lfloor v \rfloor \qquad\qquad \Leftarrow neu(u) \;\&\; neg(v).$

Classical implication

$\lceil u \Rightarrow v \rceil \;\circ\!\!-\; ?\lfloor u \rfloor \mathbin{⅋} ?\lceil v \rceil \qquad\qquad \Leftarrow (neg(u) \;\&\; neg(v)) \oplus (pos(u) \;\&\; notneu(v)).$

$\lceil u \Rightarrow v \rceil \;\circ\!\!-\; \lceil v \rceil \oplus \lfloor u \rfloor \qquad\qquad \Leftarrow neg(u) \;\&\; pos(v).$

$\lfloor u \Rightarrow v \rfloor \;\circ\!\!-\; \lceil u \rceil \;\&\; \lfloor v \rfloor \qquad\qquad \Leftarrow neg(u) \;\&\; pos(v).$

$\lfloor u \Rightarrow v \rfloor \;\Leftarrow\; \lceil u \rceil \;\Leftarrow\; \lfloor v \rfloor \qquad\qquad \Leftarrow (neg(u) \;\&\; neg(v)) \oplus (pos(u) \;\&\; notneu(v)).$

Fig. 2. *LU* rules

and duality in *LU* using extra clauses: these clauses play the role of the *Cut* rule on determining the dual predicates for polarity.

Since in *LU* formulas have only one polarity, it is reasonable to consider the clauses:

$$notpos(u) \;\multimap\; (neu(u) \oplus neg(u)).$$
$$notneg(u) \;\multimap\; (neu(u) \oplus pos(u)).$$
$$notneu(u) \;\multimap\; (neg(u) \oplus pos(u)).$$
$$pos(u) \;\multimap\; neg(u) \multimap 0.$$
$$pos(u) \;\multimap\; neu(u) \multimap 0.$$
$$neg(u) \;\multimap\; neu(u) \multimap 0.$$

The first three clauses define the predicates $notpos(\cdot)$, $notneg(\cdot)$ and $notneu(\cdot)$ while the last three indicate that $pos(\cdot)$, $neg(\cdot)$ and $neu(\cdot)$ are dual predicates. Let $\mathcal{L}$ be the set of clauses above. It is straightforward to prove the following for LU: for every connective $\diamond$ of LU, if the left and right introduction clauses for $\diamond$ in their definition form are:

$$\forall \bar{x}(\lfloor \diamond(x_1, \ldots, x_i)\rfloor \circ\!\!-\ B_l) \quad \text{and} \quad \forall \bar{x}(\lceil \diamond(x_1, \ldots, x_i)\rceil \circ\!\!-\ B_r)$$

then

$$!\,\mathcal{L}, !\,Cut, !\,Pos, !\,Neg \vdash \forall \bar{x}(B_l \multimap B_r \multimap \bot) \qquad (\ast\ast\ast)$$

in linear logic. Here, Neg is the third and Pos the fourth clause in Figure 2. This suggests that such an entailment might be used as a natural generalization of coherence to this setting.

Example 2. Consider the definition form for the left and right introduction rules for the conjunction:

$$\lceil u \wedge v \rceil \circ\!\!-\ !(\lceil u \rceil \,\&\, \lceil v \rceil \,\&\, (pos(u) \oplus pos(v))) \oplus ((\lceil u \rceil \,\&\, \lceil v \rceil) \otimes !(notpos(u) \,\&\, notpos(v))).$$

$$\lfloor u \wedge v \rfloor \circ\!\!-\ (?\lfloor u \rfloor \,\invamp\, ?\lfloor v \rfloor \otimes !(pos(u) \oplus pos(v))) \oplus \lfloor u \rfloor \oplus \lfloor v \rfloor \otimes !(notpos(u) \,\&\, notpos(v)).$$

Due to the $\oplus$ operator that occurs on B_r and B_l, the proof of the sequent $(\ast\ast\ast)$ will have four sub-proofs, two of them inferring the same polarity for each object-level formula involved and the other two with incompatible polarities for at least one formula. If the polarities are the same, the proof follows mostly as the usual duality check described in Section 5 (some extra steps may be necessary due to the compact way in which the set of rules of LU was written). On the other hand, if dual polarities appear the proof follows easily and the only rules applied are the last rules listed in $\mathcal{L}$.

The intuitive way we motivated a notion of coherence for LU suggests that it may be possible to extend the definitions and results obtained in earlier sections to more elaborate proofs systems containing certain kinds of side conditions.

8   Conclusion and Future Work

We have argued here that the use of linear logic as a meta-logic for the specification of sequent calculi allows us to use some of the meta-theory of linear logic to draw conclusions about the object-level proof systems. For example, the notion of duality within coherent proof systems is basically the notion of de Morgan duals in linear logic. The proof of Lemma 3, used to prove object-level cut-elimination, makes a critical use of meta-level cut-elimination. We also showed that for coherent proof systems, the question of whether or not one proof system's encoding entails another proof system's encoding is decidable.

An implementation of Forum can also provide a vehicle for the implementation of a number of object-level proof systems. To experiment with the decision procedures described in this paper, the authors used a simple and direct implementation of the Forum proof system within λProlog [NM88]: this implementation could then be used to do proof search restricted to bounded depth.

There are certainly numerous directions for future work related to what has been presented here. For example, most sequent calculi remain complete when restricting to atomically closed initial sequents. Checking the completeness of such a restriction should certainly be handled using techniques such as those for proving that coherent proofs systems satisfy cut-elimination. Also, there have been various proposals for non-commutative variants of classical linear logic [AR99,GS01,Ret97]: it would be interesting to see if these can be used to capture non-commutative object-level logics in a manner done here.

Finally, while we addressed the question of whether or not an inference rule is derivable from other inference rules, the more interesting and useful question is whether or not an inference rule is *admissible* in another proof system. For this, induction is generally required. It seems natural to consider adding to linear logic forms of induction along the lines found in [MM00,Pim01].

References

[AL01]   Arnon Avron and Iddo Lev. Canonical propositional gentzen-type systems. In R. Goré, A. Leitsch, and T. Nipkow, editors, *IJCAR 2001*, volume 2083 of *LNAI*, pages 529–544. Springer-Verlag, 2001.

[And92]   Jean-Marc Andreoli. Logic programming with focusing proofs in linear logic. *Journal of Logic and Computation*, 2(3):297–347, 1992.

[AR99]   V. Michele Abrusci and Paul Ruet. Non-commutative logic I: The multiplicative fragment. *Annals of Pure and Applied Logic*, 101(1):29–64, 1999.

[Chi95]   Jawahar Chirimar. *Proof Theoretic Approach to Specification Languages*. PhD thesis, University of Pennsylvania, February 1995.

[Chu40]   Alonzo Church. A formulation of the simple theory of types. *Journal of Symbolic Logic*, 5:56–68, 1940.

[DJS95]   Vincent Danos, Jean-Baptiste Joinet, and Harold Schellinx. LKQ and LKT: sequent calculi for second order logic based upon dual linear decompositions of classical implication. In Girard, Lafont, and Regnier, editors, *Workshop on Linear Logic*, pages 211–224. London Mathematical Society Lecture Notes 222, Cambridge University Press, 1995.

[DM79]   Nachum Dershowitz and Zohar Manna. Proving termination with multiset orderings. *Communications of the ACM*, 22(8):465–476, 1979.

[DM95]   Giorgio Delzanno and Maurizio Martelli. Objects in Forum. In *Proceedings of the International Logic Programming Symposium*, 1995.

[Dyc92]   Roy Dyckhoff. Contraction-free sequent calculi for intuitionistic logic. *Journal of Symbolic Logic*, 57(3):795–807, September 1992.

[FM88]   Amy Felty and Dale Miller. Specifying theorem provers in a higher-order logic programming language. In *Ninth International Conference on Automated Deduction*, pages 61–80, Argonne, IL, May 1988. Springer-Verlag.

[Gen69]   Gerhard Gentzen. Investigations into logical deductions. In M. E. Szabo, editor, *The Collected Papers of Gerhard Gentzen*, pages 68–131. North-Holland Publishing Co., Amsterdam, 1969.

[Gir93]   Jean-Yves Girard. On the unity of logic. *Annals of Pure and Applied Logic*, 59:201–217, 1993.

[GS01]   Alessio Guglielmi and Lutz Straßburger. Non-commutativity and MELL in the calculus of structures. In L. Fribourg, editor, *CSL 2001*, volume 2142 of *LNCS*, pages 54–68, 2001.

[HHP93]   Robert Harper, Furio Honsell, and Gordon Plotkin. A framework for defining logics. *Journal of the ACM*, 40(1):143–184, 1993.

[LSS93]   Patrick Lincoln, Andre Scedrov, and Natarajan Shankar. Linearizing intuitionistic implication. In *Annals of Pure and Applied Logic*, pages 151–177, 1993.

[Mil93]   Dale Miller. The π-calculus as a theory in linear logic: Preliminary results. In E. Lamma and P. Mello, editors, *Proceedings of the 1992 Workshop on Extensions to Logic Programming*, number 660 in LNCS, pages 242–265. Springer-Verlag, 1993.

[Mil96]   Dale Miller. Forum: A multiple-conclusion specification language. *Theoretical Computer Science*, 165(1):201–232, September 1996.

[Mil00]   Dale Miller. Abstract syntax for variable binders: An overview. In John Lloyd and et. al., editors, *Computational Logic - CL 2000*, number 1861 in LNAI, pages 239–253. Springer, 2000.

[MM00]   Raymond McDowell and Dale Miller. Cut-elimination for a logic with definitions and induction. *Theoretical Computer Science*, 232:91–119, 2000.

[MNPS91]   Dale Miller, Gopalan Nadathur, Frank Pfenning, and Andre Scedrov. Uniform proofs as a foundation for logic programming. *Annals of Pure and Applied Logic*, 51:125–157, 1991.

[MP]   Dale Miller and Elaine Pimentel. Linear logic as a framework for specifying sequent calculus. To appear in the Proceedings of Logic Colloquium 1999.

[NM88]   Gopalan Nadathur and Dale Miller. An Overview of λProlog. In *Fifth International Logic Programming Conference*, pages 810–827, Seattle, August 1988. MIT Press.

[Pau89]   Lawrence C. Paulson. The foundation of a generic theorem prover. *Journal of Automated Reasoning*, 5:363–397, September 1989.

[Pim01]   Elaine Gouvêa Pimentel. *Lógica linear e a especificação de sistemas computacionais*. PhD thesis, Universidade Federal de Minas Gerais, Belo Horizonte, M.G., Brasil, December 2001. (written in English).

[Ret97]   Christian Retoré. Pomset logic: a non-commutative extension of classical linear logic. In *Proceedings of TLCA*, volume 1210, pages 300–318, 1997.

[Ric98]   Giorgia Ricci. *On the expressive powers of a Logic Programming presentation of Linear Logic (FORUM)*. PhD thesis, Department of Mathematics, Siena University, December 1998.

A Schütte-Tait Style Cut-Elimination Proof for First-Order Gödel Logic

Matthias Baaz and Agata Ciabattoni*

Technische Universität Wien, A-1040 Vienna, Austria
{agata,baaz}@logic.at

Abstract. We present a Schütte-Tait style cut-elimination proof for the hypersequent calculus **HIF** for first-order Gödel logic. This proof allows to bound the depth of the resulting cut-free derivation by $4_{\rho(d)}^{|d|}$, where $|d|$ is the depth of the original derivation and $\rho(d)$ the maximal complexity of cut-formulas in it. We compare this Schütte-Tait style cut-elimination proof to a Gentzen style proof.

1 Introduction

The most important cut-elimination methods in first-order proof theory are the *Gentzen style* procedure [10] (and its variants in the context of natural deduction calculi) and the *Schütte-Tait style* procedure [13,14]. The latter has been originally introduced to deal with infinitary calculi. From a procedural point of view, these methods differ by their *cut selection rule*: the Gentzen style method selects a highest cut, while the Schütte-Tait style method a largest one (w.r.t. the number of connectives and quantifiers). Consequently, e.g., Gentzen style procedures, generally, will not terminate on calculi with ω rules.

In this paper we formulate cut-elimination proofs, according to both methods, for the hypersequent calculus **HIF** for first-order Gödel logic $\mathbf{G}_\infty$. This logic, also known as intuitionistic fuzzy logic [16], can be axiomatized extending intuitionistic logic *IL* by the linearity axiom $(A \supset B) \vee (B \supset A)$ and the shifting law of universal quantifier $\forall x(A(x) \vee B) \supset \forall x A(x) \vee B$, where x does not occur free in B. **HIF** has been defined in [8] by incorporating Gentzen's original calculus **LJ** for *IL* as a sub-calculus and adding to it an additional layer of information by allowing **LJ**-sequents to live in the context of finite multisets of sequents (called *hypersequents*). This opens the possibility to define new rules that, "exchanging information" between different sequents, allow to prove both the linearity axiom and the shifting law of universal quantifier.

The Schütte-Tait style cut-elimination proof introduced in this paper establishes non-elementary primitive recursive bounds for the length of the cut-free proofs in **HIF** in terms of the length and the maximal complexity of cut-formulas in the original proof. Consequently, corresponding bounds apply to the length of Herbrand disjunctions (mid-hypersequents) as well as the length of derivations in the chaining calculus described in [5] for the prenex fragment of $\mathbf{G}_\infty$.

---

* Research supported by EC Marie Curie fellowship HPMF–CT–1999–00301

U. Egly and C.G. Fermüller (Eds.): TABLEAUX 2002, LNAI 2381, pp. 24–37, 2002.
© Springer-Verlag Berlin Heidelberg 2002

Finally, this paper allows to compare both the Gentzen and the Schütte-Tait style procedures in the more general context of the hypersequent notation.

2   Syntax and Semantic of First-Order Gödel Logic

Propositional finite-valued Gödel logics have been introduced by Gödel in 1933 [11] to show that intuitionistic logic does not have a characteristic finite matrix. Dummett [9] later generalized these to an infinite set of truth-values, and showed that the set of its tautologies – **LC** – is axiomatized extending intuitionistic logic by the linearity axiom $(A \supset B) \vee (B \supset A)$.

The language of Gödel logics is identical to that of classical logic (or intuitionistic logic, for that matter). More precisely, we use the binary *connectives* $\wedge, \vee$, and $\supset$ and the *truth constant* $\perp$. $\neg A$ is defined as $A \supset \perp$. *Object variables* are denoted by $x, y, \ldots$; the usual existential and universal *quantifiers*, $\forall$ and $\exists$, refer to these variables. *Bound* and *free* occurrences of variables are defined as usual. Moreover, for every $n \geq 0$, there is an infinite supply of n-ary *predicate symbols* and *function symbols*. Constants are considered as 0-ary function symbols. *Terms* and *formulas* are inductively defined in the usual way. Propositional variables are identified with predicate symbols of arity 0.

In this work we consider the first-order Gödel logic $\mathbf{G}_\infty$ defined over the real unit interval $[0, 1]$ [1], also known as *intuitionistic fuzzy logic* [16].

An *interpretation* $\mathcal{I}$ in $\mathbf{G}_\infty$ consists of a non-empty *domain* D and a *valuation function* $v_{\mathcal{I}}$ that maps constants and object variables to elements of D and n-ary function symbols to functions from D^n into D. $v_{\mathcal{I}}$ extends in the usual way to function mapping all terms of the language to an element of the domain. Moreover, $v_{\mathcal{I}}$ maps every n-ary predicate symbol P to a function from D^n into $[0, 1]$. The truth-value of an atomic formula $A \equiv P(t_1, \ldots, t_n)$ is thus defined as

$$v_{\mathcal{I}}(A) = v_{\mathcal{I}}(P)(v_{\mathcal{I}}(t_1), \ldots, v_{\mathcal{I}}(t_n)).$$

For the truth constant $\perp$ we have $v_{\mathcal{I}}(\perp) = 0$.

The semantics of propositional connectives is given by

$$v_{\mathcal{I}}(A \supset B) = \begin{cases} 1 & \text{if } v_{\mathcal{I}}(A) \leq v_{\mathcal{I}}(B) \\ v_{\mathcal{I}}(B) & \text{otherwise,} \end{cases}$$

$$v_{\mathcal{I}}(A \wedge B) = \min(v_{\mathcal{I}}(A), v_{\mathcal{I}}(B)) \qquad v_{\mathcal{I}}(A \vee B) = \max(v_{\mathcal{I}}(A), v_{\mathcal{I}}(B)).$$

To assist a concise formulation of the semantics of quantifiers we define the *distribution* of a formula A and a free variable x with respect to an interpretation $\mathcal{I}$ as $\text{Distr}_{\mathcal{I}}(A(x)) = \{ \text{val}_{\mathcal{I}'}(A(x)) \mid \mathcal{I}' \sim_x \mathcal{I} \}$, where $\mathcal{I}' \sim_x \mathcal{I}$ means that $\mathcal{I}'$ is exactly as $\mathcal{I}$ with the possible exception of the domain element assigned to x. The semantics of quantifiers is given by the infimum and supremum of the corresponding distribution:

$$v_{\mathcal{I}}((\forall x)A(x)) = \inf \text{Distr}_{\mathcal{I}}(A(x)) \quad v_{\mathcal{I}}((\exists x)A(x)) = \sup \text{Distr}_{\mathcal{I}}(A(x)).$$

---

[1] Different topologies on the set of truth values induce different first-order Gödel logics.

A formula A is a *tautology* iff for all $v_\mathcal{I}$, $v_\mathcal{I}(A) = 1$. Moreover A is a *logical consequence* of a set of formulas Γ (in symbols $\Gamma \models_{\mathbf{G}_\infty} A$) iff, for all $v_\mathcal{I}$, $\min\{v_\mathcal{I}(\gamma) \mid \gamma \in \Gamma\} \leq v_\mathcal{I}(A)$.

A Hilbert style calculus for $\mathbf{G}_\infty$ is obtained by extending **LC** with the shifting law of universal quantifier $\forall x(A(x) \lor B) \supset \forall x A(x) \lor B$, where x does not occur free in B, see, e.g., [12].

3 Hypersequent Calculi for $\mathbf{G}_\infty$

In [8] an analytic calculus for $\mathbf{G}_\infty$ has been introduced. This calculus —called **HIF**[2]— uses hypersequents, a natural generalization of Gentzen sequents, see [3]. **HIF** is based on Avron's hypersequent calculus **GLC** for **LC** [2].

The most significant feature of **HIF** is its close relation to Gentzen's sequent calculus **LJ** for intuitionistic logic [10]. Indeed, **HIF** contains **LJ** as a sub-calculus and simply adds it an additional layer of information by allowing **LJ**-sequents to live in the context of finite multisets of sequents, as well as suitable (external) structural rules to manipulate sequents with respect to their contexts. In particular, the crucial rule of the calculus **HIF**, added to **LJ**, is the so called communication rule (*com*). It is this rule which increases the expressive power of **HIF** compared to **LJ**.

Recall that a *sequent* is an expression of the form $\Gamma \Rightarrow A$, where Γ is a multiset of formulas and A may be empty.

Definition 1. *A* hypersequent *is a multiset*

$$\Gamma_1 \Rightarrow A_1 \mid \ldots \mid \Gamma_n \Rightarrow A_n$$

where for every $i = 1, \ldots, n$, $\Gamma_i \Rightarrow A_i$ *is a sequent, called* component *of the hypersequent.*

The interpretation of the symbol " $\mid$ " is disjunctive.

In **HIF** the rules for connectives and quantifiers, as well as the internal structural rules, are those of **LJ**. The only difference is the presence of a context G representing a (possibly empty) hypersequent. The structural rules are divided into *internal* and *external rules*. The former deal with formulas within components. These are weakening and contraction. The external rules manipulate whole components within a hypersequent. These are external weakening (EW), contraction (EC), as well as the (*com*) rule. More precisely, **HIF** consists of

Axioms and Cut Rule

$$A \Rightarrow A \ \ (id) \qquad \bot \Rightarrow \ \ (\bot) \qquad \frac{G \mid \Gamma \Rightarrow A \quad G \mid A, \Gamma \Rightarrow C}{G \mid \Gamma \Rightarrow C} \ (cut)$$

---

[2] **HIF** stands for Hypersequent calculus for Intuitionistic Fuzzy logic.

Internal Structural Rules

$$\frac{G \mid \Gamma \Rightarrow C}{G \mid \Gamma, A \Rightarrow C} \ (w, l) \qquad \frac{G \mid \Gamma \Rightarrow}{G \mid \Gamma \Rightarrow A} \ (w, r) \qquad \frac{G \mid \Gamma, A, A \Rightarrow C}{G \mid \Gamma, A \Rightarrow C} \ (c, l)$$

External Structural Rules

$$\frac{G}{G \mid \Gamma \Rightarrow A} \ (EW) \qquad\qquad \frac{G \mid \Gamma \Rightarrow A \mid \Gamma \Rightarrow A}{G \mid \Gamma \Rightarrow A} \ (EC)$$

$$\frac{G \mid \Gamma_1, \Gamma_2 \Rightarrow A \quad G \mid \Gamma_1, \Gamma_2 \Rightarrow B}{G \mid \Gamma_1 \Rightarrow A \mid \Gamma_2 \Rightarrow B} \ (com)$$

Logical Rules

$$\frac{G \mid \Gamma, A \Rightarrow B}{G \mid \Gamma \Rightarrow A \supset B} \ (\supset, r) \qquad\qquad \frac{G \mid \Gamma \Rightarrow A \quad G \mid B, \Gamma \Rightarrow C}{G \mid \Gamma, A \supset B \Rightarrow C} \ (\supset, l)$$

$$\frac{G \mid \Gamma \Rightarrow A \quad G \mid \Gamma \Rightarrow B}{G \mid \Gamma \Rightarrow A \wedge B} \ (\wedge, r) \qquad\qquad \frac{G \mid \Gamma, A_i \Rightarrow C}{G \mid \Gamma, A_1 \wedge A_2 \Rightarrow C} \ (\wedge_i, l)_{i=1,2}$$

$$\frac{G \mid \Gamma \Rightarrow A_i}{G \mid \Gamma \Rightarrow A_1 \vee A_2} \ (\vee_i, r)_{i=1,2} \qquad\qquad \frac{G \mid \Gamma, A \Rightarrow C \quad G \mid \Gamma, B \Rightarrow C}{G \mid \Gamma, A \vee B \Rightarrow C} \ (\vee, l)$$

$$\frac{G \mid A(t), \Gamma \Rightarrow C}{G \mid (\forall x)A(x), \Gamma \Rightarrow C} \ (\forall, l) \qquad\qquad \frac{G \mid \Gamma \Rightarrow A(a)}{G \mid \Gamma \Rightarrow (\forall x)A(x)} \ (\forall, r)$$

$$\frac{G \mid A(a), \Gamma \Rightarrow C}{G \mid (\exists x)A(x), \Gamma \Rightarrow C} \ (\exists, l) \qquad\qquad \frac{G \mid \Gamma \Rightarrow A(t)}{G \mid \Gamma \Rightarrow (\exists x)A(x)} \ (\exists, r)$$

where $(\forall, r)$ and $(\exists, l)$ must obey the eigenvariable condition: the free variable a must not occur in the lower *hypersequent*.

Definition 2. *In the above rules, Γ and C are called* internal contexts *while G, external context. For each rule, the components not in the external context are called* active components. *In the conclusion of each logical rule, the formula in the active component that does not belong to the internal context is called* principal formula.

Remark 1. By the presence of (c, l) and (w, l) (resp. (EW) and (EC)), one can derive equivalent versions of the above rules with *multiplicative* internal (resp. external) contexts (see, e.g., [17] for this terminology).

In fact, **HIF** has been originally defined in [8] using a different version of the communication rule, namely

$$\frac{G \mid \Pi_1, \Gamma_1 \Rightarrow A \quad G \mid \Pi_2, \Gamma_2 \Rightarrow B}{G \mid \Pi_1, \Pi_2 \Rightarrow A \mid \Gamma_1, \Gamma_2 \Rightarrow B} \ (com')$$

However, using (w, l) and (c, l), (com) and (com') are interderivable (see [3]).

Definition 3. *The* complexity $|A|$ *of a formula A is inductively defined as follows:*

- $|A| = 0$ *if A is atomic*
- $|A \wedge B| = |A \vee B| = |A \supset B| = \max(|A|, |B|) + 1$
- $|\forall x A(x)| = |\exists x A(x)| = |A| + 1$

The right (left) rank *of a cut is the number of consecutive hypersequents containing the cut formula, counting upward from the right (left) upper sequent of the cut.*

For the cut-elimination proof in the next section, following Tait [14], we shall consider an equivalent version of **HIF** without explicit (internal and external) contraction rules. In this calculus, we call it **HIF**^set, hypersequents are considered as *sets* of components, each one of them is a sequent $\Gamma \Rightarrow A$, where Γ is a *set* of formulas. Henceforth, we denote with $\{S_1\} \cup \ldots \cup \{S_n\}$ a hypersequent in **HIF**^set whose components are $S_1, \ldots, S_n$. Rules, are then changed accordingly. Moreover, we only consider atomic axioms, that is of the form

$$A \Rightarrow A \quad \text{and} \quad \bot \Rightarrow \quad \text{where } A \text{ is an atomic formula}$$

Lemma 1. *In* **HIF**^set *non atomic axioms can be derived from atomic axioms.*

A derivation d in **HIF** (or **HIF**^set) is considered, as usual, as an upward rooted tree of hypersequents generated from subtrees by applying the inference rules. This allows for the following definitions:

Definition 4. *The* length $|d|$ *of d is the maximal number of inference rules (but weakenings) + 1 occurring on any branch of d.*

Remark 2. A different way to avoid counting the number of applications of (internal and external) weakening rules while counting the length of a derivation, is to internalize these rules into axioms. This is done by considering axioms of the form $G \mid \Gamma, A \Rightarrow A$. Then $|d|$ can be simply defined as the maximal number of hypersequents occurring on any branch of d. However, in this case one has to use the multiplicative version of (com), namely (com'), that affects both Lemma 2.2 (see Remark 3) and Definition 7 below.

Definition 5. *Let d_i, with $i < k$, be the direct subderivations of d. The* cut-rank $\rho(d)$ *of d is defined by induction as:*

- $\rho(d) = 0$ *if d is cut-free*
- $\rho(d) = \max_{i<k} \rho(d_i)$ *if the last inference of d is not a cut;*
- $\rho(d) = \max(|A| + 1, \max_{i<k} \rho(d_i))$, *where A is the cut formula, otherwise.*

Henceforth we write $d \vdash' H$ (resp. $d \vdash H$) if d is a derivation in **HIF** (resp. **HIF**^set) of H.

Definition 6. *We say that a sequent is* n-reduced *if every formula in the antecedent occurs at most n times. A hypersequent is said to be* n-m-reduced *if it is n-reduced and every component in it occurs at most m times.*

Note that a derivation in **HIF**^{set} only contains 1-1-reduced hypersequents.

Let d be a derivation in **HIF**^{set}. Henceforth we will indicate with $w(d)$ (resp. $W(d)$) the maximal number of applications of internal weakening (resp. external weakening) occurring on any branch of d.

Lemma 2. *Let H be a 1-1-reduced hypersequent.*

1. *If $d \vdash' H$, one can find a proof $d' \vdash H$ such that $|d'| \leq |d|$.*
2. *If $d' \vdash H$ one can find a proof $d \vdash' H$ such that $|d| \leq 2|d'| + w(d')$.*

Proof. 1. Straightforward.

2. We show that d does not contain more than two applications of (c, l) and/or (EC) after each inference step in d' (but weakenings). The proof proceeds by induction on $|d'|$. The claim is trivial if H is an axiom. Suppose that the last rule applied in d' is $(\supset, l)$ and d' ends as follows

$$\frac{\vdots\, d'_1 \qquad\qquad \vdots\, d'_2}{G \,\cup\, \{\Gamma, A \supset B \Rightarrow C\}} \;{\scriptstyle(\supset, l)}$$
$$G \,\cup\, \{\Gamma \Rightarrow A\} \quad G \,\cup\, \{\Gamma, B \Rightarrow C\}$$

By induction hypothesis one can find two proofs d''_1 and d''_2 in **HIF** with the required properties of the 1-1-reduced hypersequents $(G \mid \Gamma \Rightarrow A)^{\#}$ and $(G \mid \Gamma, B \Rightarrow C)^{\#}$. Applying to them the $(\supset, l)$ rule one obtains the hypersequent $G^{\#} \,\cup\, \Gamma^{\#}, A \supset B \Rightarrow C$ that can have at most two equal formulas (if $A \supset B \in \Gamma^{\#}$) and two equal components (if the component $\Gamma^{\#}, A \supset B \Rightarrow C$ is in $G^{\#}$). With at most one application of (c, l) and of (EC), one obtains a 1-1-reduced contraction of $G \mid \Gamma, A \supset B \Rightarrow C$. The cases involving the remaining logical rules as well as the cut rule are analogous.

Suppose the last rule applied in d' is (com) and d' ends as follows

$$\frac{\vdots\, d'_1 \qquad\qquad \vdots\, d'_2}{G \,\cup\, \{\Gamma \Rightarrow A\} \,\cup\, \{\Sigma \Rightarrow B\}} \;{\scriptstyle(com)}$$
$$G \,\cup\, \{\Gamma, \Sigma \Rightarrow A\} \quad G \,\cup\, \{\Gamma, \Sigma \Rightarrow B\}$$

By induction hypothesis one can find two proofs d''_1 and d''_2 in **HIF** with the required properties of the 1-1-reduced hypersequents $(G \mid \Gamma, \Sigma \Rightarrow A)^{\#}$ and $(G \mid \Gamma, \Sigma \Rightarrow B)^{\#}$. Applying the (com) rule to them one obtains the hypersequent $G^{\#} \mid \Gamma^{\#} \Rightarrow A \mid \Sigma^{\#} \Rightarrow B$ in which there can be at most two pairwise equal components (if both the components $\Gamma^{\#} \Rightarrow A$ and $\Sigma^{\#} \Rightarrow B$ are in $G^{\#}$). Applying (EC) at most twice, one obtains a 1-1-reduced contraction of $G \mid \Gamma \Rightarrow A \mid \Sigma \Rightarrow B$.

If the last rule applied in d' is (EW) then the corresponding proof in **HIF** does not contain any additional application of (EC) or (c, l). While in the case of internal weakening one can need an additional application of (EC).

Remark 3. Using multiplicative rules in defining **HIF** and **HIF**^{set}, the bound on $|d|$ in Lemma 2.2 does not hold anymore.

3.1   A Schütte-Tait Style Cut-Elimination Proof

Let $d(s)$ and $H(s)$ denote the result of substituting the term s for all free occurrences of x in the proof $d(x)$ and in the hypersequent $H(x)$, respectively.

Lemma 3 (Substitution). *If $d(x) \vdash H(x)$, then $d(s) \vdash H(s)$, with $|d(s)| = |d(x)|$ and $\rho(d(s)) = \rho(d(x))$, where s only contains variables that do not occur in $d(x)$.*

We introduce the notion of *decorated* formulas in a derivation d of $\mathbf{HIF^{set}}$. This notion is intended to trace the cut-formula through d.

Definition 7. *Let $d \vdash H$ and A be a formula in H that is not the cut-formula of any cut in d. The* decoration *of A (in d) is inductively defined as follows: we denote by A^* a decorated occurrence of A. Given a hypersequent H' in d with some (not necessarily all) decorated A. Let R be the rule introducing H'. We distinguish some cases according to R.*

1. *R is a logical rule, e.g.,*

$$\frac{G \cup \{\Gamma' \Rightarrow C'\}}{G \cup \{\Gamma \Rightarrow C\}}$$

   a) *A is principal in R. Suppose $A^* \in \Gamma$. In the active component, $A^* \in \Gamma'$ if and only if A is a side formula of the inference. Moreover, the decoration in the not-active components of the premise of R is as in the conclusion. That is, for each such a component $\{\Sigma \Rightarrow B\} \in G$, $A^* \in \Sigma$ if and only if $A^* \in \Sigma$ of the corresponding component belonging to the conclusion of R.*
      Suppose C is A^*. The decoration of the not-active components of the premise of R is as in the conclusion.
   b) *A is not principal in R. If $A^* \in \Gamma$ (resp. C) then $A^* \in \Gamma'$ (resp. C') in the active component. Moreover, the decoration of the not-active components of the premise of R is as in the conclusion.*
   If R is a two premises rule, the definition is analogous.
2. *R is (EW). The decoration of the components in the premise of R is as in the conclusion.*
3. *R is (w,l) or (w,r). Analogous to case 1.*
4. *R is (com).*

$$\frac{G \cup \{\Gamma, \Sigma \Rightarrow C\} \quad G \cup \{\Gamma, \Sigma \Rightarrow C'\}}{G \cup \{\Gamma \Rightarrow C\} \cup \{\Sigma \Rightarrow C'\}}$$

Suppose $A^* \in \Gamma$. If $A \notin \Sigma$ (or $A^* \in \Sigma$), then $A^* \in \Gamma, \Sigma$ of both the active components in the premises of R. If A occurs in Σ, then $A^* \in \Gamma, \Sigma$ of only one active component in the premises of R. Suppose $A^* \notin \Gamma$. If $A \notin \Gamma$ and $A^* \in \Sigma$, then $A^* \in \Gamma, \Sigma$ of both the active components in the premises of R. If $A \in \Gamma$ and $A^* \in \Sigma$, then $A^* \in \Gamma, \Sigma$ of only one active component in the premises of R. The decoration in the not-active components in the premises of R is as in the conclusion.

If C (and/or C') is A^*, then so is in the active component $\{\Gamma, \Sigma \Rightarrow C\}$ (and/or $\{\Gamma, \Sigma \Rightarrow C'\}$). The decoration in the not-active components of the premises of R is as in the conclusion.

5. R is (cut). Analogous to case 1(b).

Remark 4. Due to the (com) rule, the decoration of A (in d) is not unique.

Lemma 4 (Inversion).

(i)   If $d \vdash G \ \cup \ \{\Gamma, A \vee B \Rightarrow C\}$ then one can find $d_1 \vdash G \ \cup \ \{\Gamma, A \Rightarrow C\}$ and $d_2 \vdash G \ \cup \ \{\Gamma, B \Rightarrow C\}$

(ii) If $d \vdash G \ \cup \ \{\Gamma, A \wedge B \Rightarrow C\}$ then one can find $d_1 \vdash G \ \cup \ \{\Gamma, A, B \Rightarrow C\}$

(iii) If $d \vdash G \ \cup \ \{\Gamma \Rightarrow A \wedge B\}$ then one can find $d_1 \vdash G \ \cup \ \{\Gamma \Rightarrow A\}$ and $d_2 \vdash G \ \cup \ \{\Gamma \Rightarrow B\}$

(iv) If $d \vdash G \ \cup \ \{\Gamma \Rightarrow A \supset B\}$ then one can find $d_1 \vdash G \ \cup \ \{\Gamma, A \Rightarrow B\}$

(v)   If $d \vdash G \ \cup \ \{\Gamma, \exists x A(x) \Rightarrow C\}$ then one can find $d_1 \vdash G \ \cup \ \{\Gamma, A(a) \Rightarrow C\}$

(vi) If $d \vdash G \ \cup \ \{\Gamma \Rightarrow \forall x A(x)\}$ then one can find $d_1 \vdash G \ \cup \ \{\Gamma \Rightarrow A(a)\}$

such that $\rho(d_i) \leq \rho(d)$ and $|d_i| \leq |d|$, for $i = 1, 2$.

Proof. (i) Let us consider the decoration of $A \vee B$ in d starting from $G \cup \{\Gamma, (A \vee B)^* \Rightarrow C\}$. To obtain the required derivation $d_1 \vdash G \ \cup \ \{\Gamma, A \Rightarrow C\}$ (resp. $d_2 \vdash G \ \cup \ \{\Gamma, B \Rightarrow C\}$), we delete all the right (resp. left) subderivations above any application of $(\vee, l)$ in which the decorated formula $(A \vee B)^*$ is principal and we replace every component $\psi, (A \vee B)^* \Rightarrow D$ in the derivation with $\psi, A \Rightarrow D$ (resp. $\psi, B \Rightarrow D$). (Recall that all axioms are atomic). Clearly $|d_i| \leq |d|$ and $\rho(d_i) \leq \rho(d)$, for $i = 1, 2$.

The remaining cases are analogous.

Remark 5. $(\supset, l)$, $(\forall, l)$ and $(\exists, r)$ are not invertible. Concerning $(\vee, r)$, one has $G \ \cup \ \{\Gamma \Rightarrow A \vee B\}$ can be inverted to $G \ \cup \ \{\Gamma \Rightarrow A\} \ \cup \ \{\Gamma \Rightarrow B\}$ (slightly changing the above bounds). The Schütte-Tait style cut-elimination procedure presuppose that at least one of the two premises of the cut rule is invertible. As we shall see, we will use (i), (iii), (iv), (v) and (vi). Of course we could choose (ii) instead of (iii) or the inversion of $(\vee, r)$ instead of (i). However, the latter choice will transform **LJ**-derivations into derivations containing hypersequents with more than one component.

In the following we write $d, H \ \vdash \ G$ if d is a proof in **HIF**$^\mathrm{set}$ of G from the assumption H. Moreover, $H[^B /_A]$ will indicate the hypersequent H in which we uniformly replace A by B.

Lemma 5. *Let $d \vdash G \ \cup \ \{\Gamma, A^* \Rightarrow B\}$, where A^* is an atomic formula decorated in d that is not the cut formula of any cut in d. One can find a proof $d', \{\Sigma \Rightarrow A\} \vdash G \ \cup \ \{\Gamma, \Sigma \Rightarrow B\}$ such that $|d'| \leq |d|$ and $\rho(d') = \rho(d)$.*

Proof. We replace A^* everywhere in d with Σ. The decorated formula originates

1. in an axiom. Then the axiom is transformed into $\Sigma \Rightarrow A$,
2. by an internal weakening. The weakening on A^* is replaced by stepwise weakenings of formulas B, where $B \in \Sigma$. Note that this does not affect the length of the resulting proof,
3. by an external weakening. The weakening in the component C is replaced by a weakening on $C[^\Sigma/_{A^*}]$.

The resulting proof d' is correct as it can be shown by induction on $|d'| + w(d') + W(d')$.

Lemma 6 (Reduction). *Let $d_0 \vdash G \cup \{\Gamma \Rightarrow A\}$ and $d_1 \vdash G \cup \{\Gamma, A \Rightarrow C\}$ both with cut-rank $\rho(d_i) \leq |A|$. Then we can find a derivation $d \vdash G \cup \{\Gamma \Rightarrow C\}$ with $\rho(d) \leq |A|$ and $|d| \leq 2(|d_0| + |d_1|)$.*

Proof. If A is $\perp$ the proof is trivial. Suppose A atomic ($\neq \perp$). The claim follows by Lemma 5 and subsequent concatenation with the proof d_0. Suppose A not atomic.

– $A = B \supset D$. Let us consider the decoration of A in d_1 starting from $G \cup \{\Gamma, (B \supset D)^* \Rightarrow C\}$. We first replace in d_1 all the components $\{\Psi, (B \supset D)^* \Rightarrow C'\}$ by $\{\Psi, \Gamma \Rightarrow C'\}$. Note that this does not result in a correct proof anymore. We have then to consider the following "correction steps" according to the cases in which the decorated formula originates:
   (i) as principal formula of a logical inference,
   (ii) by an internal weakening,
   (iii) by an external weakening.
   (i) We replace every original inference step of the kind

$$
\frac{G' \cup \{\Psi \Rightarrow B\} \quad G' \cup \{\Psi, D \Rightarrow C'\}}{G' \cup \{\Psi, (B \supset D)^* \Rightarrow C'\}} \; {\scriptstyle(\supset,\mathrm{l})}
$$

by (let $G'' = G' \cup G$)

$$
\frac{(G'' \cup \{\Psi, \Gamma \Rightarrow B\})[^\Gamma/_{A^*}] \quad \dfrac{\vdots \, d_0'}{G'' \cup \{\Gamma, \Psi, B \Rightarrow D\}}}{\dfrac{G'' \cup \{\Psi, \Gamma \Rightarrow D\} \qquad\qquad (G'' \cup \{\Psi, \Gamma, D \Rightarrow C'\})[^\Gamma/_{A^*}]}{G'' \cup \{\Psi, \Gamma \Rightarrow C'\}}}
$$

(adding some internal and external weakenings) where $d_0' \vdash G \cup \{\Gamma, B \Rightarrow D\}$ is obtained by the Inversion Lemma.

(ii) The weakening on $(B \supset D)^*$ is replaced by stepwise weakenings of formulas X, where $X \in \Gamma$. Note that this does not affect the length of the resulting proof.

(iii) The weakening on the component C is replaced by a weakening on $C[^\Gamma/_{(B \supset D)^*}]$.

The replacement of components containing decorated formulas $B \supset D$ does not change the length of the proof tree wich remains $\leq |d_1|$ and the cut-rank, which remains $\leq \rho(A)$. This holds also for the correction steps (ii) and (iii), since only weakenings are added. Correction step (i) uses d_0' (with suitable weakenings) as subproof deriving the missing premise of the cut rules replacing $(\supset, l)$ inferences of $(B \supset D)^*$. Therefore $|d| \leq |d_0'| + |d_1| + 2 \leq |d_0| + |d_1| + 2 \leq 2(|d_0| + |d_1|)$.

- Cases $A = B \wedge D$ and $A = \forall x A(x)$ are treated analogously.
- $A = \exists x A(x)$. Let us consider the decoration of A in d_0 starting from $G \cup \{\Gamma \Rightarrow (\exists x A(x))^*\}$. We first replace in d_0 all the components $\{\Psi \Rightarrow (\exists x A(x))^*\}$ by $\{\Psi \Rightarrow C\}$. As in the previous case, this does not result in a correct proof anymore. Correction steps (ii) and (iii) are as above. While if $\exists x A(x)$ originates as principal formula of a logical inference, we replace every original inference step of the kind

$$\frac{\vdots}{G' \cup \{\Psi \Rightarrow A(t)\}} \quad (\exists, l)$$
$$\overline{G' \cup \{\Psi \Rightarrow (\exists x A(x))^*\}}$$

by

$$\frac{G \cup (G' \cup \{\Psi, \Gamma \Rightarrow A(t)\})[{}^C/_{(\exists x A(x))^*}] \qquad G \cup G' \cup \{\Gamma, \Psi, A(t) \Rightarrow C\} \;\; {}^{\vdots\, d_1'(t)}}{G' \cup G \cup \{\Psi, \Gamma \Rightarrow C\}} \;\; (\text{cut})$$

(adding some external weakenings) where $d_1'(t) \vdash G \cup \{\Gamma, A(t) \Rightarrow C\}$ is obtained by the Inversion Lemma (and Substitution Lemma).

Correction step (i) uses $d_1'(t)$ (with suitable weakenings) as subproof deriving the missing premise of the cut rules replacing $(\exists, r)$ inferences of $(\exists x A(x))^*$. Therefore $|d| \leq |d_0| + |d_1'(t)| + 1 \leq |d_0| + |d_1| + 1 \leq 2(|d_0| + |d_1|)$.

- Case $A = B \vee D$ is treated analogously.

Theorem 1 (Cut-elimination). *If $d \vdash H$ and $\rho(d) > 0$, then we can find a derivation $d' \vdash H$ with $\rho(d') < \rho(d)$ and $|d'| \leq 4^{|d|}$.*

Proof. Proceeds by induction on $|d|$. We may assume that the last inference of d is a cut

$$\frac{G \cup \{\Gamma \Rightarrow A\} \;\; {}^{\vdots\, d_0} \qquad G \cup \{\Gamma, A \Rightarrow C\} \;\; {}^{\vdots\, d_1}}{G \cup \{\Gamma \Rightarrow C\}}$$

(eventually with subsequent weakenings) with $\rho(d) = |A| + 1$. For otherwise the result follows by the induction hypothesis (making use of the fact that our rules all have finitely many premises).

By the induction hypothesis we have $d_0' \vdash G \cup \{\Gamma \Rightarrow A\}$ and $d_1' \vdash G \cup \{\Gamma, A \Rightarrow C\}$ both with cut rank $\rho(d_i') \leq |A|$ and $|d_i'| \leq 4^{|d_i|}$, with $i = 1, 2$. The Reduction Lemma gives a derivation d' with $\rho(d') \leq |A| < \rho(d)$ and $|d'| \leq 2(|d_0'| + |d_1'|) \leq 2(4^{|d_0|} + 4^{|d_1|}) \leq 4^{\max(d_0, d_1) + 1} = 4^{|d|}$.

Let $4_0^n = n, 4_{k+1}^n = 4^{4_k^n}$.

Corollary 1. *If $d \vdash H$, one can find a cut-free proof $d' \vdash H$ with $|d'| \leq 4_{\rho(d)}^{|d|}$.*

Corollary 2. *If $d' \vdash H$, one can find a cut-free derivation d of H in **HIF** such that $|d| \leq 2 \cdot 4_{\rho(d')}^{|d'|} + w(d'')$, where d'' is the corresponding cut-free derivation in **HIF**^{set}.*

Proof. Immediately follows by Corollary 1 together with Lemma 2.

Note that $w(d'')$ can be easily bounded, e.g., by the total number of occurrences of formulas in d''.

Remark 6. Substitution, Inversion and Reduction Lemma, as well as Lemma 5 transform proofs in **HIF**^{set} without applications of (com) and only containing singleton hypersequent, into proofs with the same properties. Therefore the above Schütte-Tait style cut-elimination proof, with the given bound, also holds for **LJ** in the set theoretic notation.

3.2   A Gentzen Style Cut-Elimination Proof

In this section we describe, for comparison, a Gentzen style cut-elimination proof for **HIF**.

Recall that the cut-elimination method of Gentzen proceeds by eliminating the uppermost cut by a double induction on the complexity c of the cut formula and on the sum r of its left and right ranks. In fact, in **LJ**, by the presence of the internal contraction rule one has to consider a derivable generalization of the cut rule, namely, the multi-cut rule

$$\frac{\Gamma \Rightarrow A \quad \Gamma', A^n \Rightarrow B}{\Gamma, \Gamma' \Rightarrow B} \; (mcut)$$

where A^n stands for $A, \ldots, A$ (n times), see, e.g., [15].

Due to the presence of (EC), in hypersequent calculi (and, in particular, in **HIF**) one cannot directly apply Gentzen's argument to show that $(*)$ if $G \mid \Gamma \Rightarrow A$ and $G \mid \Gamma, A^n \Rightarrow B$ are cut-free provable in **HIF**, so is $G \mid \Gamma \Rightarrow B$. A simple way to overcome this problem, is to modify Gentzen's original *Hauptsatz* allowing to reduce certain cuts *in parallel*. E.g., in [2], Avron has used the following induction hypothesis:

$(**)$ If both the hypersequents $G := G' \mid \Gamma_1 \Rightarrow A \mid \ldots \mid \Gamma_n \Rightarrow A$ and $H := H' \mid \Sigma_1, A^{n_1} \Rightarrow B_1 \mid \ldots \mid \Sigma_k, A^{n_k} \Rightarrow B_k$ are cut-free provable in **GLC**, then so is $H' \mid G' \mid \Gamma, \Sigma_1 \Rightarrow B_1 \mid \ldots \mid \Gamma, \Sigma_k \Rightarrow B_k$ where $\Gamma = \Gamma_1, \ldots, \Gamma_n$. It is not hard to see that this formulation is, in fact, equivalent to $(*)$. As we shall see, Avron's induction hypothesis also works for **HIF**.

In analogy with Lemma 2.10 of [15], one can show

Lemma 7. *Let $d(a)$ be a proof in **HIF** of a hypersequent S containing the variable a. If throughout the proof, we replace a by a term t, containing only variables that do not occur in $d(a)$, we then obtain a proof $d(t)$ ending with the hypersequent S' obtained by replacing a by t in S.*

Theorem 2 (Cut-elimination). *If a hypersequent H is derivable in* **HIF** *then it is derivable in* **HIF** *without using the cut rule.*

Proof. We show $(**)$ by induction on the pair (c, r). In addition to Avron's proof in [2], we have to consider the cases involving quantifiers. More precisely, let γ and δ be the proofs of G and H, respectively. We consider the following cases:

1. both γ and δ end in some rules for quantifiers such that the principal formula of both rules is just the cut formula;
2. either γ or δ ends in a rule for quantifiers whose principal formula is not the cut formula.

1. Suppose that both γ and δ end in a rule for $\forall$ and the principal formulas of both rules is the cut formula. For instance, δ is

$$\begin{array}{c} \vdots\, \delta_1 \\ \hline H' \mid \Sigma_1, A(a), (\forall x A(x))^{n_1-1} \Rightarrow B_1 \mid \ldots \mid \Sigma_k, (\forall x A(x))^{n_k} \Rightarrow B_k \\ \hline H' \mid \Sigma_1, (\forall x A(x))^{n_1} \Rightarrow B_1 \mid \ldots \mid \Sigma_k, (\forall x A(x))^{n_k} \Rightarrow B_k \end{array} (\forall, l)$$

and γ is

$$\begin{array}{c} \vdots\, \gamma_1 \\ \hline G' \mid \Gamma_1 \Rightarrow A(a) \mid \ldots \mid \Gamma_n \Rightarrow \forall x A(x) \\ \hline G' \mid \Gamma_1 \Rightarrow \forall x A(x) \mid \ldots \mid \Gamma_n \Rightarrow \forall x A(x) \end{array} (\forall, r)$$

Applying the induction hypothesis to both γ and δ_1 one gets a proof δ' of $H' \mid G' \mid \Sigma_1, \Gamma, A(a) \Rightarrow B_1 \mid \ldots \mid \Sigma_k, \Gamma \Rightarrow B_k$, where $\Gamma = \Gamma_1, \ldots, \Gamma_n$, while applying the induction hypothesis to γ_1 and δ one gets a proof γ' of $H' \mid G' \mid \Gamma_1 \Rightarrow A(a) \mid \Sigma_1, \Gamma_2, \ldots, \Gamma_n \Rightarrow B_1 \mid \ldots \mid \Sigma_k, \Gamma_2, \ldots, \Gamma_n \Rightarrow B_k$. We now apply again the induction hypothesis, based on the reduced complexity of the cut formula, to γ' and δ'. The desired result is obtained by several applications of $(c, l), (w, l)$ and (EC).

2. Suppose that δ ends as follows

$$\begin{array}{c} \vdots\, \delta_1 \\ \hline G' \mid \Gamma_1, A(a) \Rightarrow C \mid \ldots \mid \Gamma_n \Rightarrow C \\ \hline G' \mid \Gamma_1, \exists x A(x) \Rightarrow C \mid \ldots \mid \Gamma_n \Rightarrow C \end{array} (\exists, l)$$

Applying the induction hypothesis to the proof γ of the hypersequent $H' \mid \Sigma_1, C^{n_1} \Rightarrow B_1 \mid \ldots \mid \Sigma_k, C^{n_k} \Rightarrow B_k$ and to δ_1 one gets a proof γ' of (a) $H' \mid G' \mid \Sigma_1, \Gamma, A(a) \Rightarrow B_1 \mid \ldots \mid \Sigma_k, \Gamma, A(a) \Rightarrow B_k$, where $\Gamma = \Gamma_1, \ldots, \Gamma_n$. Due to the eigenvariable condition, one cannot directly apply the $(\exists, l)$ rule to (a) in order to obtain the desired result, namely,

$$H' \mid G' \mid \Sigma_1, \Gamma, \exists x A(x) \Rightarrow B_1 \mid \ldots \mid \Sigma_k, \Gamma, \exists x A(x) \Rightarrow B_k.$$

However, the above hypersequent can be obtained from γ' by several applications of $(\exists, l)$, (com') (i.e. (com) + (w, l)) and (EC). The proof of it proceeds by induction on k. Base case: $k = 1$, the claim follows applying the $(\exists, l)$ rule (and Lemma 7). Let $k > 1$. From γ', using only $(\exists, l)$, (com) and (EC), one can derive $H' \mid G' \mid \Sigma_1, \Gamma, \exists x A(x) \Rightarrow B_1 \mid H$, where H stands for $\Sigma_2, \Gamma, A(a) \Rightarrow B_2 \mid \ldots \mid \Sigma_k, \Gamma, A(a) \Rightarrow B_k$. Indeed, by Lemma 7 one can find a proof $\gamma'[b]$ of (b) $H' \mid G' \mid \Sigma_1, \Gamma, A(b) \Rightarrow B_1 \mid \ldots \mid \Sigma_k, \Gamma, A(b) \Rightarrow B_k$, where b is a new variable not occurring in γ'. The derivation of $H' \mid G' \mid \Sigma_1, \Gamma, \exists x A(x) \Rightarrow B_1 \mid H$ is then as follows (we omit contexts that are not involved in the derivation)

$$
\cfrac{
\cfrac{
\cfrac{(a) \qquad\qquad (b)}{\Sigma_1, \Gamma, A(b) \Rightarrow B_1 \mid \Sigma_3, \Gamma, A(b) \Rightarrow B_3 \mid \cdots \mid \Sigma_k, \Gamma, A(b) \Rightarrow B_k \mid H}{}^{(\star)} \quad (a)
}{
\cfrac{\vdots \qquad\qquad \vdots}{\Sigma_1, \Gamma, A(b) \Rightarrow B_1 \mid H}{}^{(\star)}
}{}^{(\star)}
}{\Sigma_1, \Gamma, \exists x A(x) \Rightarrow B_1 \mid H}{}^{(\exists, l)}
$$

where $(\star)$ stands for (com') and (EC).

Remark 7. In [8] the proof of the cut-elimination theorem in Gentzen style has been formulated without using the "extended multi-cut rule" $(\ast\ast)$. However, as pointed out by Avron, in hypersequent calculi Gentzen's argument works only (as in the case of **LJ** or **LK** without the multi-cut rule) if a suitable notion of decoration is formulated (see, e.g., the "history technique" in [1]).

3.3 Final Remarks

Schütte-Tait style cut-elimination methods make use of the partial (at least one side) invertibility of all logical rules: one side of the cut is reduced immediately. It is easy to see that these methods generally lead to smaller cut-free proofs than the ones obtained with Gentzen style procedures, especially if we admit deletion of subproofs ending with hypersequents containing axioms, e.g.,

$$
\cfrac{
\cfrac{\vdots\, d_1}{
\cfrac{G \mid \Pi \Rightarrow A \supset B}{G \mid B, A, \Pi \Rightarrow A \supset B}{}^{(w,l)}
}
\qquad
\cfrac{
\cfrac{
\cfrac{A \Rightarrow A \quad B \Rightarrow B}{G \mid A \supset B, A \Rightarrow B}{}^{(\supset,l)(EW)}
\qquad
\cfrac{A \Rightarrow A \quad B \Rightarrow B}{G \mid A \supset B, A \Rightarrow B}{}^{(\supset,l)(EW)}
}{G \mid A \supset B, A \Rightarrow B \wedge B}{}^{(\wedge,r)}
}{G \mid A \supset B, B, A, \Pi \Rightarrow B \wedge B}{}^{(w,l)'s}
}{G \mid B, A, \Pi \Rightarrow B \wedge B}{}^{(cut)}
$$

Indeed, here the Inversion Lemma yields $G \mid B, A, \Pi \Rightarrow B$ and the subproof d_1 is deleted, while a Gentzen style procedure inevitably shifts the cut inside d_1. (See [7] for a comparison on the complexity of Gentzen and Schütte-Tait style procedures in classical first-order logic).

On the other hand, Schütte-Tait style procedures are more arbitrary than Gentzen style procedures (see, e.g., Remark 4), which use the exact properties of the calculus under consideration. In addition, Gentzen style procedures are local and they work even in the case of deductions from arbitrary atomic assumptions closed under cut.

Finally, note that both Gentzen and Schütte-Tait style procedures transform intuitionistic proofs into intuitionistic proofs (within **HIF**): new applications of the (com) rule are not introduced in eliminating cuts. Therefore cut-free derivations even for propositional formulas might lead to long cut-free proofs (recall that the validity problem in intuitionistic logic is P-space complete while the same problem in **LC** is in co-NP). This is not the case, when eliminating cuts from derivations in the sequent-of-relations calculus for **LC** defined in [4] (see also [6]). In this latter calculus, all the rules are invertible. However, it cannot be modified in a simple way in order to include quantifiers.

References

1. A. Avron: A constructive analysis of RM. *J. Symbolic Logic*, 52: 939–951, 1987.
2. A. Avron: Hypersequents, logical consequence and intermediate logics for concurrency. *Annals of Mathematics and Artificial Intelligence*, 4: 225–248, 1991.
3. A. Avron: The Method of Hypersequents in the Proof Theory of Propositional Nonclassical Logics. In W. Hodges, M. Hyland, C. Steinhorn and J. Truss editors, *Logic: from Foundations to Applications, European Logic Colloquium* Oxford Science Publications. Clarendon Press. Oxford. 1–32. 1996.
4. M. Baaz, A. Ciabattoni, C. Fermüller: Cut-Elimination in a Sequents-of-Relations Calculus for Gödel Logic. In *International Symposium on Multiple Valued Logic (ISMVL'2001)*, 181–186. IEEE. 2001.
5. M. Baaz, A. Ciabattoni, C. Fermüller: Herbrand's Theorem for Prenex Gödel Logic and its Consequences for Theorem Proving. In *Proceedings of Logic for Programming and Automated Reasoning (LPAR'2001)*, LNAI 2250, 201–216. 2001.
6. M. Baaz, A. Ciabattoni, C. Fermüller: Sequent of Relations Calculi: a Framework for Analytic Deduction in Many-Valued Logics. In M. Fitting and E. Orlowska editors, *Theory and applications of Multiple-Valued Logics*. To appear.
7. M. Baaz, A. Leitsch: Comparing the complexity of cut-elimination methods. In *Proceedings of Proof Theory in Computer Science*, LNCS 2183, 49–67. 2001.
8. M. Baaz, R. Zach: Hypersequents and the proof theory of intuitionistic fuzzy logic. In *Proceedings of Computer Science Logic (CSL'2000)*, LNCS 1862, 187–201. 2000.
9. M. Dummett: A Propositional Logic with Denumerable Matrix. *J. of Symbolic Logic*, 24: 96–107. 1959.
10. G. Gentzen: Untersuchungen über das logische Schliessen I, II. *Mathematische Zeitschrift*, 39: 176–210, 405–431. 1934.
11. K. Gödel: Zum Intuitionistischen Aussagenkalkul. *Ergebnisse eines mathematischen Kolloquiums*, 4: 34–38. 1933.
12. P. Hájek: *Metamathematics of Fuzzy Logic*. Kluwer. 1998.
13. K. Schütte: *Beweistheorie*. Springer Verlag. 1960.
14. W.W. Tait: Normal derivability in classical logic. In *The Sintax and Semantics of infinitary Languages*, LNM 72, 204–236. 1968.
15. G. Takeuti: *Proof Theory*. North-Holland. 1987.
16. G. Takeuti, T. Titani: Intuitionistic fuzzy logic and intuitionistic fuzzy set theory. *J. of Symbolic Logic*, 49: 851–866. 1984.
17. A.S. Troelstra and H. Schwichtenberg: Basic Proof Theory. Cambridge University Press. 1996

Tableaux for Quantified Hybrid Logic*

Patrick Blackburn[1] and Maarten Marx[2]

[1] INRIA, Lorraine, Nancy, France. `patrick@aplog.org`
[2] ILLC, University of Amsterdam, The Netherlands. `marx@science.uva.nl`

Abstract. We present a (sound and complete) tableau calculus for Quantified Hybrid Logic (*QHL*). *QHL* is an extension of orthodox quantified modal logic: as well as the usual $\Box$ and $\Diamond$ modalities it contains names for (and variables over) states, operators $@_s$ for asserting that a formula holds at a named state, and a binder $\downarrow$ that binds a variable to the current state. The first-order component contains equality and rigid and non-rigid designators. As far as we are aware, ours is the first tableau system for *QHL*.

Completeness is established via a variant of the standard translation to first-order logic. More concretely, a valid *QHL*-sentence is translated into a valid first-order sentence in the correspondence language. As it is valid, there exists a first-order tableau proof for it. This tableau proof is then converted into a *QHL* tableau proof for the original sentence. In this way we recycle a well-known result (completeness of first-order logic) instead of a well-known proof.

The tableau calculus is highly flexible. We only present it for the constant domain semantics, but slight changes render it complete for varying, expanding or contracting domains. Moreover, completeness with respect to specific frame classes can be obtained simply by adding extra rules or axioms (this can be done for every first-order definable class of frames which is closed under and reflects generated subframes).

1   Introduction

Hybrid logic is an extension of modal logic in which it is possible to name states and to assert that a formula is true at a named state. Hybrid logic uses three fundamental tools to do this: nominals, satisfaction operators, and the $\downarrow$-binder. Nominals are special propositional symbols that are true at precisely one state in any model: nominals 'name' the unique state they are true at. A satisfaction operator has the form $@_s$ where s is a nominal. A formula of the form $@_s\phi$ asserts that ϕ is true at the state named by the nominal s. Finally, a formula of the form $\downarrow s.\phi$ binds all occurrences of the nominal s in ϕ to the current state of evaluation — that is, it makes s a name for the current state. (Actually, so that we don't have to worry about accidental binding in the course of tableau proofs, we shall distinguish between ordinary nominals, which cannot be bound, and 'state variables' which are essentially bindable nominals.)

* This research was supported by the Netherlands Organization for Scientific Research (NWO, grants# 612.000.106 and 612.062.001). This work was carried out as part of the INRIA funded partnership between LIT (Language and Inference Technology, ILLC, University of Amsterdam) and LED (Langue et Dialogue, LORIA, Nancy).

U. Egly and C.G. Fermüller (Eds.): TABLEAUX 2002, LNAI 2381, pp. 38–52, 2002.

Hybrid logic has a lengthy history (see the web page `www.hylo.net` for further information), and over the years it has become clear that adding the hybrid apparatus of nominals (and state variables), satisfaction operators, and $\downarrow$ to modal logic often results in systems with better logical properties than the original. But most previous work on hybrid logic has examined the effects of hybridizing *propositional* modal logics. What about *quantified* (first-order) hybrid logic?

In fact, strong evidence already exists that quantified hybrid logic (QHL) is also better behaved logically than orthodox quantified modal logic. In [2], the only recent paper devoted to the topic, it is shown that a very general interpolation theorem holds in QHL (as is well known interpolation almost never holds in orthodox quantified modal logic [3]). The purpose of the present paper is to show that QHL is well behaved in another respect: just as in the propositional case, it is possible to define simple and intuitive tableau systems. We shall present a tableau system for QHL which handles equality, and rigid and non-rigid designators.

Our method for proving completeness is very simple and inspired by Jerry Seligman's paper [10]. Instead of redoing a proof we use existing results. Correspondence theory and its notion of a standard translation $ST(\cdot)$ places the model theory of (propositional and first-order) modal logic firmly into first-order logic [12,13]. Our plan is the following. We prove completeness for our tableaux calculus by taking a proof P for $ST\phi$ in a proven complete first-order calculus, and transform P into a proof P' for ϕ in our calculus. The tableaux system we use is by Fitting, in particular the one presented in [4]. This strategy works in hybrid logic because it has an equivalent expression for every subformula which might occur in a first-order proof of a translated formula.

Outline of paper. The paper starts with a definition of first-order hybrid logic. Then we present the tableau system in three natural parts. The forth section is devoted to completeness issues. Again we split them up into three natural parts. This section ends with a very general completeness result. Finally we draw conclusions.

2   Quantified Hybrid Logic

We first define the syntax of QHL. We have a set NOM of nominals, a set SVAR of state variables, a set FVAR of first-order variables, a set CON of first-order constants, a set IC of unary function symbols, and predicates of any arity (note that predicates of nullary arity are simply propositional variables). The *terms* of the language are the constants from CON, the first-order variables from FVAR and the terms generated by the rule

$$\text{if } q \in \mathsf{IC} \text{ and } s \in \mathsf{NOM} \cup \mathsf{SVAR}, \text{ then } @_s q \text{ is a term.}$$

(For readers familiar with propositional hybrid logic, this notation may come as a surprise: we are combining a satisfaction operator with a term to make a new term. But as the semantics defined below will show, overloading the @ notation in this way is quite natural: $@_s q$ will be the value of the non-rigid term q at the world named by s.)

The *atomic formulas* are all symbols in NOM and SVAR together with the usual first-order atomic formulas generated from the predicate symbols and equality using the terms. *Complex formulas* are generated from these according to the rules

$$\neg\phi \mid \phi \wedge \psi \mid \phi \vee \psi \mid \phi \rightarrow \psi \mid \exists x\phi \mid \forall x\phi \mid \Diamond\phi \mid \Box\phi \mid @_n\phi \mid \downarrow w.\phi.$$

Here $x \in \mathsf{FVAR}$, $w \in \mathsf{SVAR}$ and $n \in \mathsf{NOM} \cup \mathsf{SVAR}$.

These formulas are interpreted in first-order modal models with constant domains. A QHL model is a structure $(W, R, D, I_{nom}, I_w)_{w \in W}$ such that

- (W, R) is a modal frame;
- I_{nom} is a function assigning members of W to nominals;
- for every $w \in W$, (D, I_w) is an ordinary first-order model such that
  - $I_w(c) = I_{w'}(c)$, for all $w, w' \in W$ and constants c;
  - $I_w(q) \in D$, for q a unary function symbol;
  - $I_w(P) \subseteq {}^k D$, for P a k-ary predicate symbol.

To interpret formulas with free variables we use special two-sorted assignments. A QHL *assignment* is a function g from SVAR $\cup$ FVAR to $W \cup D$ which sends state variables to members of W and first-order variables to elements of D. Given a model and an assignment g, the interpretation of terms t, denoted by $\bar{t}$, is defined as

$$
\begin{array}{lll}
\bar{x} & = g(x) & \text{for } x \text{ a variable} \\
\bar{c} & = I_w(c) & \text{for } c \text{ a constant and some } w \in W \\
\overline{@_n q} & = \begin{cases} I_{I_{nom}(n)}(q) & \text{if } n \text{ a nominal} \\ I_{g(n)}(q) & \text{if } n \text{ a state variable.} \end{cases} & \text{for } q \text{ a unary function symbol}
\end{array}
$$

Formulas are now interpreted as usual. With g_d^x we denote the assignment which is just like g except that $g(x) = d$. $\mathfrak{M}, g, s \Vdash \phi$ means that ϕ holds in model $\mathfrak{M}$ at state s under the assignment g. The inductive definition is

$$
\begin{array}{lll}
\mathfrak{M}, g, s \Vdash P(t_1, \ldots, t_n) & \Longleftrightarrow & \langle \bar{t}_1, \ldots, \bar{t}_n \rangle \in I_s(P) \\
\mathfrak{M}, g, s \Vdash t_i = t_j & \Longleftrightarrow & \bar{t}_i = \bar{t}_j \\
\mathfrak{M}, g, s \Vdash n & \Longleftrightarrow & I_{nom}(n) = s, \text{ for } n \text{ a nominal} \\
\mathfrak{M}, g, s \Vdash w & \Longleftrightarrow & g(w) = s, \text{ for } w \text{ a state variable} \\
\mathfrak{M}, g, s \Vdash \neg\phi & \Longleftrightarrow & \mathfrak{M}, g, s, \not\Vdash \phi \\
\mathfrak{M}, g, s \Vdash \phi \wedge \psi & \Longleftrightarrow & \mathfrak{M}, g, s \Vdash \phi \text{ and } \mathfrak{M}, g, s \Vdash \psi \\
\mathfrak{M}, g, s \Vdash \phi \vee \psi & \Longleftrightarrow & \mathfrak{M}, g, s \Vdash \phi \text{ or } \mathfrak{M}, g, s \Vdash \psi \\
\mathfrak{M}, g, s \Vdash \phi \rightarrow \psi & \Longleftrightarrow & \mathfrak{M}, g, s \Vdash \phi \text{ implies } \mathfrak{M}, g, s \Vdash \psi \\
\mathfrak{M}, g, s \Vdash \exists x \phi & \Longleftrightarrow & \mathfrak{M}, g_d^x, s \Vdash \phi, \text{ for some } d \in D \\
\mathfrak{M}, g, s \Vdash \forall x \phi & \Longleftrightarrow & \mathfrak{M}, g_d^x, s \Vdash \phi, \text{ for all } d \in D \\
\mathfrak{M}, g, s \Vdash \Diamond\phi & \Longleftrightarrow & \mathfrak{M}, g, t \Vdash \phi \text{ for some } t \in W \text{ such that } Rst \\
\mathfrak{M}, g, s \Vdash \Box\phi & \Longleftrightarrow & \mathfrak{M}, g, t \Vdash \phi \text{ for all } t \in W \text{ such that } Rst \\
\mathfrak{M}, g, s \Vdash @_n \phi & \Longleftrightarrow & \mathfrak{M}, g, I_{nom}(n) \Vdash \phi \text{ for } n \text{ a nominal} \\
\mathfrak{M}, g, s \Vdash @_w \phi & \Longleftrightarrow & \mathfrak{M}, g, g(w) \Vdash \phi \text{ for } w \text{ a state variable} \\
\mathfrak{M}, g, s \Vdash {\downarrow}w.\phi & \Longleftrightarrow & \mathfrak{M}, g_s^w, s \Vdash \phi.
\end{array}
$$

3   The Tableau Calculus

The tableau system can be divided into three natural pieces: **(A)** the propositional rules, the $\Diamond$ and $\Box$ rules and the rules for @; **(B)** the rule for $\downarrow$; **(C)** the rules for (first-order) quantification and equality. The blocks of rules taken separately form a complete calculus for the appropriate reducts. In particular:

1. **A** is complete for the propositional modal language expanded with nominals and @. (We name this system $\mathcal{HL}(@)$; in the literature it is often called the *basic hybrid language*.)
2. **A** $\cup$ **B** is complete for $\mathcal{HL}(@, \downarrow)$, the expansion of $\mathcal{HL}(@)$ with state variables and the $\downarrow$ binder;
3. **A** $\cup$ **B** $\cup$ **C** is complete for QHL.

Some terminology. As usual, a tableau branch is *closed* if it contains ϕ and $\neg\phi$, where ϕ is a formula. A tableau is closed if each branch is closed. A branch is *atomically closed* if it closes on an atom and its negation. A *(tableau) proof* of a hybrid sentence ϕ is a closed tableau beginning with $\neg@_s\phi$, where s is a nominal not occurring in ϕ.

3.1 Tableau for $\mathcal{HL}(@)$

A key feature of our tableau is that all modal formulas occurring in a proof are grounded to a named world by their label. (This same feature also occurs in labelled tableau for propositional modal logic [8,7].)

Grounding to a named state is implemented in our system by ensuring that all formulas occurring in proofs are of the form $@_s\phi$ or $\neg@_s\phi$ for s a nominal. Thus the propositional rules become

```
Conjunctive rules
  @_s(φ ∧ ψ)      ¬@_s(φ ∨ ψ)      ¬@_s(φ → ψ)
  ─────────       ──────────       ──────────
    @_s φ           ¬@_s φ            @_s φ
    @_s ψ           ¬@_s ψ           ¬@_s ψ

Disjunctive rules
  @_s(φ ∨ ψ)           ¬@_s(φ ∧ ψ)            @_s(φ → ψ)
  ───────────────     ────────────────      ────────────────
  @_s φ | @_s ψ       ¬@_s φ | ¬@_s ψ       ¬@_s φ | @_s ψ

Negation rules
  ¬@_s ¬φ            @_s ¬φ
  ───────           ───────
   @_s φ             ¬@_s φ
```

To these we add rules for diamond and box. In the diamond rules, t is a nominal which does not occur on the branch.

```
Diamond rules
     @_s ◇φ             ¬@_s □φ
    ────────           ────────
     @_s ◇t             @_s ◇t
     @_t φ             ¬@_t φ

Box rules
  @_s □φ,  @_s ◇t     ¬@_s ◇φ,  @_s ◇t
  ──────────────     ────────────────
      @_t φ               ¬@_t φ
```

Finally the rules for @. There are two rewrite rules to delete nestings of @. Next, as $@_s t$ really means that s and t are equal, there are rules to handle equality. These three rules are direct analogues of the reflexivity and replacement rules in Fitting's first-order tableau system [4]. As we will use them often, we gave them separate names.

@ rules

$$\frac{@_s@_t\phi}{@_t\phi} \quad \frac{\neg@_s@_t\phi \;\; [s \text{ on the branch}]}{\neg@_t\phi} \quad \frac{}{@_s s} \text{[Ref]} \quad \frac{@_s t \;\; @_s\varphi}{@_t\varphi} \text{[Nom]} \quad \frac{@_s t \;\; @_r\Diamond s}{@_r\Diamond t} \text{[Bridge]}$$

The following rules can be derived: $\dfrac{@_s t}{@_t s}$ [Sym] $\dfrac{@_s t \;\; @_t r}{@_s r}$ [Trans] $\dfrac{@_s t \;\; @_t\varphi}{@_s\varphi}$ [Nom^{-1}]

Example. Below we give a tableau proof for $(\Diamond p \wedge \Diamond\neg p) \to (\Box(q \to n) \to \Diamond\neg q)$. Here n is a nominal and p, q are propositional variables. The formula expresses that if a state has two successors, then if it has at most one q successor, it has at least one $\neg q$ successor. Note that this is not expressible in ordinary modal logic. In ordinary modal logic we cannot put an upper bound on the number of successors.

1. $\neg@_s(\Diamond p \wedge \Diamond\neg p \to (\Box(q \to n) \to \Diamond\neg q))$
2. $@_s(\Diamond p \wedge \Diamond\neg p)$
3. $\neg@_s(\Box(q \to n) \to \Diamond\neg q)$
4. $@_s\Diamond p$
5. $@_s\Diamond\neg p$
6. $@_s\Box(q \to n)$
7. $\neg@_s\Diamond\neg q$
8. $@_s\Diamond t$
9. $@_t p$
10. $@_s\Diamond r$
11. $@_r\neg p$
12. $@_t(q \to n)$

13.1 $\neg@_t q$	14. $@_t n$
13.2 $\neg@_t\neg q$	15. $@_r(q \to n)$
13.3 $@_t q$	

	16.1 $\neg@_r q$	17. $@_r n$
	16.2 $\neg@_r\neg q$	18. $@_n r$
	16.3 $@_r q$	19. $@_t r$
		20. $@_r p$
		21. $\neg@_r p$

In this, 2 and 3 are from 1 by a conjunctive rule; 4,5,6,7 are from 2 and 3 by conjunctive rules; 8,9,10,11 are from 4 and 5 by diamond rules; 12 is from 6 and 8 by box; 13.1 and 14 are from 12 by a disjunctive rule; 13.2 is from 7 and 8 by box; 13.3 is from 13.2 by a negation rule. The branch closes on 13.3 and 13.1.

15 is from 6 and 10 by box; 16.1 and 17 are from 15 by a disjunctive rule; 16.2 is from 10 and 7 by box; 16.3 is from 16.2 by a negation rule. The branch closes on 16.1 and 16.3.

18 is from 17 by the derived Sym rule; 19 is from 18 and 14 by the derived Trans rule; 20 is from 19 and 9 by the Nom rule; 21 is from 11 by a negation rule. The final branch closes on 20 and 21.

3.2 Tableau for $\mathcal{HL}(\downarrow, @)$

To obtain a complete tableau system for the expansion of $\mathcal{HL}(@)$ with variables over states and the binder $\downarrow$, we only need to add the following two rewrite rules to the rules for $\mathcal{HL}(@)$:

Downarrow rules	
$@_s\downarrow w.\phi$	$\neg@_s\downarrow w.\phi$
$@_s\phi[s/w]$	$\neg@_s\phi[s/w]$

Here $[s/w]$ means substitute s for all free occurrences of w in ϕ. Because s is always a nominal, whence cannot be quantified over, we do not have to worry about accidental bindings. As an example the reader can try to prove the validities $\downarrow w.\Diamond w \to (p \to \Diamond p)$ and $\downarrow w.\Box\Diamond w \to (\Diamond\Box p \to p)$.

3.3 Tableau for QHL

A complete tableau system for quantified hybrid logic consists of the $\mathcal{HL}(\downarrow, @)$ system, plus the (adjusted) rules for the quantifiers and equality from Fitting's system (see [4]) for first-order logic with equality, plus two rules relating equalities across worlds. In the existential rules, c is a parameter which is new to the branch. As parameters are never quantified over, the substitution $[c/x]$ is free for the formula $\phi(x)$. In the universal rules, t is any grounded term on the branch (thus either a first-order constant, a parameter or a grounded definite description). A grounded definite description is a term $@_n q$ for n a nominal and q a non-rigid designator from IC.

Existential rules	
$@_s\exists x\phi(x)$	$\neg@_s\forall x\phi(x)$
$@_s\phi(c)$	$\neg@_s\phi(c)$

Universal rules	
$@_s\forall x\phi(x)$	$\neg@_s\exists x\phi(x)$
$@_s\phi(t)$	$\neg@_s\phi(t)$

Besides Fitting's [4] Reflexivity (Ref) and Replacement (RR) rules, there are three extra rules for equality. The first (called DD) states that if n and m denote the same state, then $@_n q$ and $@_m q$ denote the same individual. The second and third (both called @=) embody that equality is a rigid predicate: if two terms are the same in one world, they are the same in every world. Because these two rules peel the leading $@_n$ from equalities, reflexivity and replacement can be kept in the old format. In the Replacement rule, $\phi[u]$ denotes $\phi(t)$ with some of the occurrences of t replaced by u.

QHL Equality rules				
$\dfrac{}{t=t}$[Ref]	$\dfrac{t=u,\ \ \phi(t)}{\phi[u]}$[RR],	$\dfrac{@_n m}{@_n q = @_m q}$[DD]	$\dfrac{@_n(t_i = t_j)}{t_i = t_j}$[@=]	$\dfrac{\neg@_n(t_i = t_j)}{\neg(t_i = t_j)}$[@=]

Example. The most interesting examples deal with equality and rigid and non-rigid designators. Consider the sentence *Caroline is Miss America*. When formalising this let c be a rigid designator denoting Caroline and q a non-rigid designator denoting Miss America. Then $\downarrow x.(c = @_x q)$ means *Caroline is the present Miss America*. It is true in a state w if $I_w(c) = I_w(q)$. This formula has the following relation with the $\square$ operator:

(1) $\not\models (\downarrow w.c = @_w q) \rightarrow \square \downarrow w.c = @_w q$

(2) $\models (\downarrow w.c = @_w q) \rightarrow \downarrow w.\square c = @_w q.$

A falsifying model for the sentence in (1) is given by two worlds n and m, with Rnm, and a domain $\{a, b\}$ with the interpretation $I_n(c) = I_m(c) = I_n(q) = a$ and $I_m(q) = b$. Then (1) fails at world n. When downarrow has wide scope in the consequent, the formula becomes true. Here is the tableau proof:

1. $\neg @_n((\downarrow w.c = @_w q) \rightarrow \downarrow w.\square (c = @_w q))$
2. $@_n \downarrow w.c = @_w q$
3. $\neg @_n \downarrow w.\square (c = @_w q)$
4. $@_n(c = @_n q)$
5. $\neg @_n \square (c = @_n q)$
6. $@_n \lozenge m$
7. $\neg @_m(c = @_n q)$
8. $c = @_n q$
9. $\neg (c = @_n q).$

In this, 2 and 3 are from 1 by a conjunctive rule; 4 and 5 are from 2 and 3 by a downarrow rule, respectively; 6 and 7 are from 5 by a diamond rule; 8 and 9 are from 4 and 7 by an @= rule, respectively.

4   Soundness and Completeness

The argument to establish soundness follows the familiar pattern: show that satisfiability is preserved by each tableau rule application. This is easy to check and left to the reader. Completeness will be established using the standard translation and a complete first-order inference system. We use the system that is closest to the one presented here: the tableau calculus for first-order logic with equality from Fitting [4] with the reflexivity and replacement rules (restricted to atoms). The main line of the argument is the following. We need to establish that every valid QHL sentence has a QHL tableau proof. The standard translation preserves validity, thus a QHL sentence ϕ is valid if and only if the first-order sentence $\mathsf{ST}\phi$ is valid. For valid $\mathsf{ST}\phi$, there exists a closed first-order tableau proof T starting with $\neg \mathsf{ST}\phi$. Our task is to transform this closed first-order proof T starting with $\neg \mathsf{ST}\phi$ into a closed QHL tableau proof T' starting with $\neg \phi$.

Most of the work concerns the modalities and the @ operator, because with these the standard translation creates the largest change in syntactic structure. For this reason we present the completeness proof for the simplest logic $\mathcal{HL}(@)$ separately. After that, the rest will be easy.

Before we can continue we have to settle two things. We change Fitting's first-order tableau rules a little bit in order to better cope with translations of modal formulas. Besides that we have to use a modified translation. We start with the former.

In order to save on inductive proofs and definitions, we assume from now on that the QHL language contains as primitive logical operators only $\neg, \wedge, \Box, @_s, \downarrow w.$ and $\forall v$. Clearly this is without loss of generality because the other operators can be defined in terms of these.

4.1   Tableau Rules for Relativized Quantifiers

The translation of a box modality yields a relativized universal formula of the form $\forall x(A(x) \to C(x))$, with $A(x)$ an atom. For these relativized universals, a more efficient tableau rule exists than the combination of universal and $\to$ rule together. In fact it is nothing but Modes Ponens. For t a closed term,

Modes Ponens (MP)
$\dfrac{A(t),\ \forall x(A(x) \to \phi(x))}{\phi(t)} \qquad \dfrac{A(t),\ \neg \exists x(A(x) \wedge \phi(x))}{\neg \phi(t)}$

We change Fitting's calculus such that on universals relativized by an atom the normal universal rules cannot be applied, but MP can. This is easily seen to be complete (cf., also [11]). We can make a further reduction in complexity in the case the antecedent is an equality. Then the statement just expresses a substitution. We also add the following rules to Fitting's calculus and make the proviso that universal and existential rules are never applied to quantified sentences relativized by an equality.

Substitution Rules
$\dfrac{\forall x(x = t \to \phi(x))}{\phi(t)} \quad \dfrac{\exists x(x = t \wedge \phi(x))}{\phi(t)} \quad \dfrac{\neg \forall x(x = t \to \phi(x))}{\neg \phi(t)} \quad \dfrac{\neg \exists x(x = t \wedge \phi(x))}{\neg \phi(t)}$

4.2   Translation Using Predicate Abstraction

Unfortunately, the standard translation does not square well with the intention to change one proof into another because it does not preserve syntactic structure. Because we want to transform a proof for the translation of ϕ into a proof for ϕ, we need to translate backwards as well. It is crucial that applying the backwards translation to the translation of ϕ yields ϕ again. This is simply not obtainable by the standard translation or obvious variants.

An example might explain why not. We can read $@_s(p \wedge q)$ as saying that state s has the property $p \wedge q$. As we want to translate proposition letters to one place predicates, in first-order logic we can only say then that s has property p and s has property q. This is of course logically equivalent, but syntactically different. We would like to have machinery which can turn formulas into predicates, so that we can speak about the property "p and q". The lambda calculus provides precisely this: $\langle \lambda x.(Px \wedge Qx) \rangle$ denotes the property of being P and Q. The formula $\langle \lambda x.(Px \wedge Qx) \rangle(s)$ serves then as an excellent proxy for $@_s(p \wedge q)$.

We work in first-order logic with predicate abstraction restricted to variables ranging over individuals. Thus we only add a piece of syntactic sugar. The expressive power of the language remains the same, it is just first-order logic. For a thorough introduction to real predicate abstraction in modal logic we refer to [6].

Suppose ϕ is a first-order formula and x a first-order variable. Then $\langle \lambda x.\phi \rangle$ is a predicate abstract. Its free variable occurrences are the free variable occurrences of ϕ except for x. Predicate abstracts behave as unary predicate symbols; new atomic formulas from predicate abstracts $\langle \lambda x.\phi \rangle$ can be made by the rule

$$\text{if } t \text{ is a term, then } \langle \lambda x.\phi \rangle(t) \text{ is a formula.}$$

Examples are $\langle \lambda x.Px \rangle(t)$ and $\langle \lambda x.Px \wedge Qx \rangle(s)$. The new formulas get their meaning by performing β-*reduction:*

$$\text{the } \beta\text{-reduction of } \langle \lambda x.\phi \rangle(t) \text{ is } \phi[t/x].$$

The meaning of $\langle \lambda x.\phi \rangle(t)$ is simply the meaning of $\phi[t/x]$. This shows that the expressive power remains the same. Our convention is that in λ expressions, the . takes wide scope, thus $\langle \lambda x.\phi \wedge \psi \rangle = \langle \lambda x.(\phi \wedge \psi) \rangle$.

In order to handle predicate abstracts in tableau proofs, we need only add two very simple rules to Fitting's system. The rules just implement β-reduction. Here they are

Abstract rules	
$\langle \lambda x.\phi \rangle(t)$	$\neg \langle \lambda x.\phi \rangle(t)$
$\phi[t/x]$	$\neg\phi[t/x]$

Fitting's tableau system with the two abstract rules added is a complete inference system for the expansion of first-order logic with λ abstraction with variables ranging over individuals [5].

We are ready to define the new standard translation AT for the propositional hybrid language, together with its inverse AT^-. In a certain sense, this translation can be traced back to the paper [9] in which McCarthy and Hayes introduce the situation calculus. $AT_y(\phi)$ and $AT_y^-(\phi)$ are defined in the same way but with x and y interchanged, e.g., $AT_y(p) := Py$ and $AT_y(\Box\phi) := \langle \lambda y.\forall x(Ryx \to AT_x(\phi)) \rangle(y)$.

$$
\begin{aligned}
AT_x(p) &:= Px \\
AT_x(n) &:= x = n \\
AT_x(\neg\phi) &:= \langle \lambda x.\neg AT_x(\phi) \rangle(x) \\
AT_x(\phi \wedge \psi) &:= \langle \lambda x.AT_x(\phi) \wedge AT_x(\psi) \rangle(x) \\
AT_x(\Box\phi) &:= \langle \lambda x.\forall y(Rxy \to AT_y(\phi)) \rangle(x) \\
AT_x(@_n\phi) &:= \langle \lambda x.\forall x(x = n \to AT_x(\phi)) \rangle(x)
\end{aligned}
$$

$$
\begin{aligned}
AT_x^-(Px) &:= p \\
AT_x^-(x = n) &:= n \\
AT_x^-(\langle \lambda x.\neg\phi \rangle(x)) &:= \neg AT_x^-(\phi) \\
AT_x^-(\langle \lambda x.\phi \wedge \psi \rangle(x)) &:= AT_x^-(\phi) \wedge AT_x^-(\psi) \\
AT_x^-(\langle \lambda x.\forall y(Rxy \to \phi) \rangle(x)) &:= \Box AT_y^-(\phi) \\
AT_x^-(\langle \lambda x.\forall x(x = n \to \phi) \rangle(x)) &:= @_n AT_x^-(\phi)
\end{aligned}
$$

The following properties of AT and AT^- hold, for every $\mathcal{HL}(@)$ formula ϕ,

(3) $AT_x(\phi)$ is always a formula of the form $\langle \lambda x.\psi \rangle(x)$ or Px or $x = n$.

(4) $AT_x^-(AT_x(\phi)) = \phi$, and similarly when x is replaced by y.

(5) ϕ is $\mathcal{HL}(@)$ valid iff $AT_x(\phi)$ is first-order valid.

(3) follows from the definition. (4) is proved by induction on the complexity of the $\mathcal{HL}(@)$ formula. (5) is immediate by performing β-reduction and the well-known result on the standard translation.

4.3   Completeness for $\mathcal{HL}(@)$

Theorem 1. *The $\mathcal{HL}(@)$ tableau calculus is complete.*

We now specify an algorithm for turning a closed Fitting tableau for the formula $AT_x(\phi)[c/x]$ (where c is a parameter) into a closed $\mathcal{HL}(@)$ tableau for $@_c\phi$. Some terminology will be useful. A literal is a grounded formula of the form

$$P(t) \mid t = u \mid Rtu \mid \langle \lambda x.\phi \rangle(t) \mid \langle \lambda y.\phi \rangle(t), \text{ or its negation.}$$

Define the following translation $(\cdot)^*$ from positive literals to $\mathcal{HL}(@)$ sentences

$$\begin{aligned}
P(t)^* &:= @_t p \\
(t = u)^* &:= @_t u \\
(Rtu)^* &:= @_t \Diamond u \\
(\langle \lambda x.\phi \rangle(t))^* &:= @_t AT_x^-(\langle \lambda x.\phi \rangle(x)) \\
(\langle \lambda y.\phi \rangle(t))^* &:= @_t AT_y^-(\langle \lambda y.\phi \rangle(y)).
\end{aligned}$$

For negative literals $(\neg\phi)$, we set $(\neg\phi)^* = \neg\phi^*$.

We recapitulate: AT translates a hybrid formula into a first-order formula and AT^- translates them backwards. The translation $(\cdot)^*$ translates literals occurring in a first-order tableau proof into hybrid formulas. Note that these literals may contain parameters introduced in the proof. The crucial connection between the forward and backward translations is that they preserve syntactic structure: for ϕ a hybrid formula and t a nominal or parameter,

(6) $(AT_x(\phi)[t/x])^* = @_t\phi$ and $(\neg AT_x(\phi)[t/x])^* = \neg@_t\phi$.

Property (6) follows immediately from the definition of $(\cdot)^*$ and (4).

We are ready to specify the algorithm. Let T be a closed Fitting tableau for the formula $AT_x(\phi)[c/x]$. Without loss of generality we may assume that T is atomically closed. Let T' simply be T with all literals replaced by their $(\cdot)^*$ translation and all other formulas removed.

Claim T' is $\mathcal{HL}(@)$ tableau proof for ϕ.

We first observe that T' starts with $\neg@_c\phi$. This is because T starts with the literal $\neg AT_x(\phi)[c/x]$ whose $*$ translation is $\neg@_c\phi$ by (6).

Table 1. Corresponding replacement proofs

First-order proof	Corresponding $\mathcal{HL}(@)$ proof
$\dfrac{t = u, P(t)}{P(u)}$ [RR]	$\dfrac{@_t u, @_t p}{@_u p}$ [Nom]
$\dfrac{t = u, v = t}{v = u}$ [RR]	$\dfrac{@_t u, @_v t}{@_v u}$ [Nom$^-$1]
$\dfrac{t = u, vRt}{vRu}$ [RR]	$\dfrac{@_t u, @_v \Diamond t}{@_v \Diamond u}$ [Bridge].

Secondly, every branch in T' closes. This is because T branches close on literals, which we all move over to T', keeping the negation signs in place. We now show that T' is a correct $\mathcal{HL}(@)$ tableau, i.e. that every formula l^* in T' is derived from $\neg @_c \phi$ by a finite number of $\mathcal{HL}(@)$ rule applications. We prove by induction on the structure of the literals that for all literals l, l' in T, for all literals l_1, l_2 produced from l, l' by applying rules, the literals l_1^*, l_2^* can be obtained from l^*, l'^* by applying a (derived) rule in T'.

There is only one zero premise rule. Ref can introduce literals $t = t$ in T, which can be matched by the hybrid Ref rule producing $(t = t)^* = @_t t$.

On literals which are not λ-formulas we can only perform Replacement, which we handle later. Every literal in T which is a λ-formula has the form $\langle \lambda z. AT_z(\psi) \rangle(t)$, for z either x or y, and ψ an $\mathcal{HL}(@)$ formula. Its $(\cdot)^*$ translation is $@_t \psi$ by (6). This gives us with the cases presented in Table 2. This table is read as follows. On the left are first-order proofs with annotations indicating which rule is applied on what to obtain the result. On the right are the $\mathcal{HL}(@)$ proofs which derive the $(\cdot)^*$ translated results from the $(\cdot)^*$ translated premises, again annotated.

We assumed Replacement only works on positive literals. The possible instantiations of literals in which t is replaced are

$$t = v, v = t, vRt, tRv, P(t) \text{ and } \langle \lambda z.\phi \rangle(t).$$

In Table 1 the application of the replacement rule is given on the left while the corresponding $\mathcal{HL}(@)$ proof on the $(\cdot)^*$ images of the formulas is on the right. As the cases for $P(t)$, $t = v$, tRv and $\langle \lambda z.\phi \rangle(t)$ are all by applications of Nom, we only show the case for $P(t)$.

We considered all possible applications of all rules on all possible literals. Thus T' is a $\mathcal{HL}(@)$ tableau.

4.4   Completeness for $\mathcal{HL}(\downarrow, @)$

Theorem 2. *The tableau system for $\mathcal{HL}(\downarrow, @)$ is complete.*

Table 2. Corresponding proof rules

Case	FO tableau		$\mathcal{HL}(@)$ tableau	
$\neg$, pos	(1) $\langle \lambda x.\neg AT_x(\phi)\rangle(t)$		(1) $@_t \neg\phi$	
	(2) $\neg AT_x(\phi)[t/x]$	(1), λ	(2) $\neg@_t\phi$	(1), Neg
$\neg$ neg	(1) $\neg\langle \lambda x.\neg AT_x(\phi)\rangle(t)$		(1) $\neg@_t\neg\phi$	
	(2) $\neg\neg AT_x(\phi)[t/x]$	(1), $\neg\lambda$		
	(3) $AT_x(\phi)[t/x]$	(2), $\neg\neg$	(2) $@_t\phi$	(1), Neg
$\wedge$ pos	(1) $\langle \lambda x.AT_x(\phi) \wedge AT_x(\psi)\rangle(t)$		(1) $@_t(\phi \wedge \psi)$	
	(2) $AT_x(\phi)[t/x] \wedge AT_x(\psi)[t/x]$	(1), λ		
	(3) $AT_x(\phi)[t/x]$	(2), Con	(2) $@_t\phi$	(1), Con
	(4) $AT_x(\psi)[t/x]$	(2), Con	(3) $@_t\psi$	(1), Con
$\wedge$ neg	(1) $\neg\langle \lambda x.AT_x(\phi) \wedge AT_x(\psi)\rangle(t)$		(1) $\neg@_t(\phi \wedge \psi)$	
	(2) $\neg[AT_x(\phi)[t/x] \wedge AT_x(\psi)[t/x]]$	(1), $\neg\lambda$		
	(3) $\neg AT_x(\phi)[t/x] \mid \neg AT_x(\psi)[t/x]$	(2), Dis	(2) $\neg@_t\phi \mid \neg@_t\psi$, (1), Dis	
@ pos	(1) $\langle \lambda x.\forall x(x = n \rightarrow AT_x(\phi))\rangle(t)$		(1) $@_t @_n\phi$	
	(2) $\forall x(x = n \rightarrow AT_x(\phi))$	(1), λ		
	(3) $AT_x(\phi)[n/x]$	(2), Sub	(2) $@_n\phi$	(1), @
@ neg	(1) $\neg\langle \lambda x.\forall x(x = n \rightarrow AT_x(\phi))\rangle(t)$		(1) $\neg@_t @_n\phi$	
	(2) $\neg\forall x(x = n \rightarrow AT_x(\phi))$	(1), $\neg\lambda$		
	(3) $\neg AT_x(\phi)[n/x]$	(2), Sub	(2) $\neg@_n\phi$	(1), @
$\square$ pos	(1) $\langle \lambda x.\forall y(Rxy \rightarrow AT_y(\phi))\rangle(t)$		(1) $@_t\square\phi$	
	(2) Rtn		(2) $@_t n$	
	(3) $\forall y(Rty \rightarrow AT_y(\phi))$	(1), λ		
	(4) $AT_y(\phi)[n/y]$	(2), (3) MP	(3) $@_n\phi$	(1),(2), $\square$
$\square$ neg	(1) $\neg\langle \lambda x.\forall y(Rxy \rightarrow AT_y(\phi))\rangle(t)$		(1) $\neg@_t\square\phi$	
	(2) $\neg(\forall y(Rty \rightarrow AT_y(\phi)))$	(1), $\neg\lambda$		
	(3) Rtc	(2), Exi	(2) $@_t\Diamond c$	(1), $\Diamond$
	(4) $\neg AT_y(\phi)[c/y]$	(2), Exi	(3) $\neg@_c\phi$	(1), $\Diamond$

With all the groundwork done, the proof is very easy. We have to extend the translation to incorporate the variables and downarrow formulas. We assume that x and y are new variables. The translation and its inverse for the state variables and downarrow is simply

$$AT_x(w) := x = w$$
$$AT_x^-(x = w) := w$$
$$AT_x(\downarrow w.\phi) := \langle \lambda x.\forall w(w = x \rightarrow AT_x(\phi))\rangle(x)$$
$$AT_x^-(\langle \lambda x.\forall w(w = x \rightarrow \phi)\rangle(x)) := \downarrow w.AT_x^-(\phi).$$

In a straightforward way, the properties (3)–(6) still hold. Then the completeness proof amounts to showing that Fitting's rules applied to translations of downarrow formulas can be transformed to applications of the downarrow rules. On these translations only substitutions can be applied. This case is similar to the @ case, so we do not spell it out.

4.5 Completeness for QHL

Theorem 3. *The tableau system for QHL is complete.*

Again the proof is simple after we made the needed straightforward adjustments. The translation and its inverse for the full QHL language is obtained by adding the following rules to the ones already existing:

$$
\begin{aligned}
AT_x(P(t_1,\ldots,t_k)) &:= P'(x,t_1,\ldots,t_k) \\
AT_x(t_i = t_j) &:= \langle \lambda x.t_i = t_j \rangle(x) \\
AT_x(\forall v\phi) &:= \langle \lambda x.\forall v\, AT_x(\phi) \rangle(x)
\end{aligned}
$$

$$
\begin{aligned}
AT_x^-(P'(x,t_1,\ldots,t_k)) &:= P(t_1,\ldots,t_k) \\
AT_x^-(\langle \lambda x.t_i = t_j \rangle(x)) &:= t_i = t_j \\
AT_x^-(\langle \lambda x.\forall v\phi \rangle(x)) &:= \forall v\, AT_x^-(\phi)
\end{aligned}
$$

The translation $(\cdot)^*$ is extended for the new literals as follows:

$$
\begin{aligned}
P'(s,t_1,\ldots,t_k)^* &:= @_s P(t_1,\ldots,t_n) \\
(t_i = t_j)^* &:= t_i = t_j.
\end{aligned}
$$

We don't translate the QHL terms $@_s q$ but just pretend they are first-order terms $q(s)$. Again, properties (3)–(6) still hold. (The first-order tableau calculus has to respect the two sorts of course. For example, $\forall x P'(s,x)$ does not yield the not correctly typed $P'(s,s)$ by universal instantiation.) The atomic hybrid formula $t_i = t_j$ is translated as $\langle \lambda x.t_i = t_j \rangle(x)$. This is done to have a syntactic analogue of $@_s(t_i = t_j)$. In a first-order proof, β-reduction can be applied to $\langle \lambda x.t_i = t_j \rangle(s)$ or its negation, yielding $t_i = t_j$ and $\neg t_i = t_j$, respectively. This proof step corresponds to an application of one of the $@ =$ rules on the $(\cdot)^*$ translations in a QHL tableau.

It is immediate that the quantifier rules can be mimicked in QHL tableaux (provided they respect the sorts).

For the application of replacement, there are now terms $@_n q$ for q a non-rigid designator and n a nominal. The replacement rule in a first-order proof can then with the premise $n = m$ replace $@_n q$ by $@_m q$ in any atom. But $n = m$ back-translates to $@_n m$ and from that the QHL equality rule DD yields $@_n q = @_m q$. Now replacement in QHL with this premise on the translated atom yields the translated result.

Thus all first-order rules have a corresponding QHL analogue and we are done.

4.6 Completeness for Specific Frame Classes

We only considered the (quantified) hybrid logic of the class of all frames. Here we establish completeness for every elementary first-order definable class of frames which is closed under and reflects generated subframes. A class of frames is closed under generated subframes if all generated subframes of its members are in the class. A class reflects generated subframes if whenever $\mathcal{F}$ is in the class and $\mathcal{F}$ is a generated subframe of $\mathcal{F}'$, then also $\mathcal{F}'$ is in the class. Note that this implies that the class is closed under disjoint unions. Closure under and reflection of generated subframes is a requirement which reflects the local evaluation of modal formulas.[1]

We recall from [1], that every such elementary class of frames is definable by a first-order sentence $\forall y \gamma(y)$, in which $\gamma(y)$ is equivalent to a pure hybrid $\mathcal{HL}(@, \downarrow)$ sentence γ' (i.e., without propositional variables nor nominals). As AT preserves meaning we may without loss of generality assume that $\gamma(y) = AT_y(\gamma')$.

Let such a class K be defined by $\forall y \gamma(y)$. Then a QHL sentence ϕ is valid on K iff $\forall y \gamma(y) \to AT_x(\phi)[c/x]$ for c a new parameter is first-order valid. In that case, there is a first-order tableau proof starting with

1. $\forall y \gamma(y)$
2. $\neg AT_x(\phi)[c/x]$.

Whence the proof will develop almost as for $AT_x(\phi)[c/x]$ except that for any state parameter or nominal s, $\gamma(s)$ may be introduced on the branch. This insight leads to the following rule to be added to the QHL tableau system:

$$\frac{}{@_s \gamma'} \quad \text{for } s \text{ on the branch.}$$

Now every time a $\gamma(s)$ is added to the branch in the first-order proof, we apply the new rule on s in the QHL proof. Because of the assumption on the form of γ, translating $\gamma(s)$ by $(\cdot)^*$ yields $@_s \gamma'$. Thus we have shown

Theorem 4. *Let γ a pure nominal free hybrid sentence which axiomatises the class of frames K. Then adding the above rule to the QHL tableau calculus yields completeness for the quantified hybrid logic of the class of frames K.*

---

[1] **Added in proof.** Balder ten Cate together with the first author of the present paper (from now on referred to as BC) have proposed a proof system for $\mathcal{HL}(@)$ which is complete for frame classes defined by formulas of the form $\forall \bar{x} \exists \bar{y} \phi(\bar{x}, \bar{y})$, in which ϕ is an $\mathcal{HL}(@)$ formula starting with $@_{x_1}$ and the quantifiers bind all nominals $\bar{x}$ and $\bar{y}$ occurring in ϕ. A natural example is $\forall x_1 x_2 x_3 \exists y @_{x_1}(@_{x_1} \Diamond x_2 \wedge @_{x_1} \Diamond x_3 \to @_{x_2} \Diamond y \wedge @_{x_3} \Diamond y)$ defining the class of confluent frames.

BC claim that adding the rule (*) below to the $\mathcal{HL}(@)$ tableaux calculus given here is complete for the class of frames defined by $\forall \bar{x} \exists \bar{y} \phi(\bar{x}, \bar{y})$. This result is most easily proved using the developed theory of translations, as follows: Assume a $\mathcal{HL}(@)$ formula ψ is valid on the class of frames defined by $\forall \bar{x} \exists \bar{y} \phi(\bar{x}, \bar{y})$. Then $\forall \bar{x} \exists \bar{y} AT_{x_1}(\phi(\bar{x}, \bar{y})) \to AT_x(\psi)[c/x]$ for c a new parameter is FO valid. Thus there is a first-order tableau proof of it starting with $\forall \bar{x} \exists \bar{y} AT_{x_1}(\phi(\bar{x}, \bar{y}))$, $\neg AT_x(\psi)[c/x]$. Our goal is to turn this tableau into an $\mathcal{HL}(@)$ tableau as before. The only new thing we have to mimic is an application of universal instantiation followed by existential elimination to $\forall \bar{x} \exists \bar{y} AT_{x_1}(\phi(\bar{x}, \bar{y}))$. This is exactly what rule (*) of BC is doing.

$$(*) \frac{}{\overline{\phi(\bar{s}, \bar{t})}} \quad \text{for } \bar{s} \text{ nominals on the branch and all } \bar{t} \text{ nominals new to the branch.}$$

Analogous to the proof in this subsection, completeness now follows.

5   Conclusions

The positive effects of hybridization in propositional logic extend well to the first-order case. In fact, one could argue that the need for hybridization is felt much stronger in first-order modal logic. The field is plagued with failures of desirable properties, and consequently more difficult and obscure than its propositional counterpart. Here we have presented an extremely general completeness theorem (Theorem 4) covering virtually all modally interesting elementary frame classes. In a companion paper we have shown that the calculus can be used to construct interpolants. Interpolation is one of the properties which fail in many quantified modal logics. This theorem also extends to all frame classes from Theorem 4. These very general results indicate that the additions to the syntax are natural and extremely useful.

The paper contained two important ideas. First and foremost is the proof method for showing completeness. An almost standard translation was used in a non-trivial way to transfer a first-order result into the modal setting. In the hybrid language, this was particularly easy, as it contains such first-order proof-elements as parameters. In orthodox modal logic, too many completeness proofs are repeated with only tiny changes. Maybe hybridization is needed to change modal logic into a field in which standard results are recycled instead of proofs. It's worth the price.

The second idea is our treatment of definite descriptions like *Miss America*. In QHL it is not possible to write intensional terms as in Montague's IL. The hidden variables in intensional terms cause many technical problems and make IL mathematically complicated. The use of @ to ground non-rigid designators to states is a simple remedy.

References

1. C. Areces, P. Blackburn, and M. Marx. Hybrid logics: Characterization, interpolation and complexity. *Journal of Symbolic Logic*, 66(3):977–1010, 2001.
2. C. Areces, P. Blackburn, and M. Marx. Repairing the interpolation lemma in quantified modal logic. Report PP-2001-19, ILLC. To appear in Annals of Pure and Applied Logic.
3. K. Fine. Failures of the interpolation lemma in quantified modal logic. *Journal of Symbolic Logic*, 44(2):201–206, 1979.
4. M. Fitting. *First Order Logic and Automated Theorem Proving (second edition)*. Springer Verlag, 1996.
5. M. Fitting. *Types, Tableaus, and Gödel's God*. Unpublished Draft, 1999.
6. M. Fitting and R. Mendelsohn. *First–Order Modal Logic*. Kluwer, 1998.
7. D. Gabbay. *Labelled Deductive Systems*. Oxford University Press, 1996.
8. R. Goré. Tableau methods for modal and temporal logics. In M D'Agostino, et al editors, *Handbook of Tableau Methods*, pages 297–396. Kluwer Academic Publishers, 1999.
9. John McCarthy and Patrick J. Hayes. Some philosophical problems from the standpoint of artificial intelligence. In B. Meltzer and D. Michie, editors, *Machine Intelligence 4*, pages 463–502. Edinburgh University Press, 1969.
10. J. Seligman. Internalization: The case of hybrid logic. *Journal of Logic and Computation*, 11(5):671–689, 2001.
11. R. Smullyan. *First Order Logic*. Springer–Verlag, 1968.
12. J. van Benthem. *Modal Logic and Classical Logic*. Bibliopolis, Naples, 1983.
13. J. van Benthem. Correspondence theory. In D.M. Gabbay and F. Guenther, editors, *Handbook of Philosophical Logic*, volume 2, pages 167–248. Reidel, Dordrecht, 1984.

Tableau-Based Automated Deduction for Duration Calculus

Nathalie Chetcuti-Sperandio

Institut de Recherche en Informatique de Toulouse
118 route de Narbonne, 31062 Toulouse CEDEX 04, France
chetcuti@irit.fr

Abstract. Duration Calculus is a temporal logic introduced to specify real-time systems. It is a very expressive but undecidable logic. In this paper we turn our attention to a decidable fragment for which we develop a tableau-based decision method taking into account some semantic restrictions.

1 Introduction

Within the framework of reactive system modelling, temporal logics were developed during the eighties. Qualitative constraints between events such as

The system will stop after someone presses the emergency-stop button

can be expressed through these logics whereas quantitative constraints such as

If someone presses the emergency-stop button then the system will stop within five seconds

cannot. The need to express such information led to the development of so-called real-time logics (usually extensions of existing temporal logics) from the second half of the eighties onwards. Among these logics lies Duration Calculus (DC) [ZHR91]. This calculus is able to express formally important real-time problems like the specification of the behaviour of schedulers [YZ94]; it has also been used, *e.g.*, to specify the requirements of the classical gas burner [RRH93], to give a semantics to communicating processes sharing a processor and to specify their scheduler [ZHRR92], to specify controllers automatically synthesized from these specifications [Frä96], *etc.* This formalism is based on Interval Temporal Logic [HMM83] with an additional notion of *duration* in a state, *i.e.* the duration for which a system stays in a particular state.

First the states of a system are modelled as boolean combinations of basic states. These *state expressions* are interpreted as boolean functions on temporal points. Fig. 1 represents the interpretation of some state expression. Next durations, such as the length of a temporal interval, the duration for which the system stays in a given state in the course of a temporal interval (illustrated by the hatched zone of Fig. 2), *etc.*, can be expressed by *terms*. Finally the proper *formulae* of the language enable one to model temporal properties, especially durationwise properties. These formulae are interpreted on intervals. For example formula $\phi_1; \phi_2$ is true on interval $[d, f]$ if there is a point t within $[d, f]$ such that ϕ_1 is true on subinterval $[d, t]$ and ϕ_2 is true on subinterval $[t, f]$

U. Egly and C.G. Fermüller (Eds.): TABLEAUX 2002, LNAI 2381, pp. 53–69, 2002.
© Springer-Verlag Berlin Heidelberg 2002

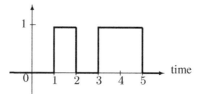

Fig. 1. Interpretation of a state expression.

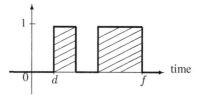

Fig. 2. Time spent in a given state in the course of interval $[d, f]$.

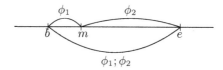

Fig. 3. Intuitive meaning of operator *chop*.

(see Fig 3). The obvious corollary of the expressiveness of DC is its great complexity. To develop automated proof procedures in order to exploit this logic, considering syntactical or semantic restrictions of DC becomes then interesting.

If time is dense (modelled, *e.g.*, by the set of real numbers), two decidable fragments of propositional DC were identified: the propositional fragment of DC without nearly any quantitative information (this logic losing thus a great part of its real-time specificity) [ZHS93], and the propositional fragment of DC in which quantitative information and negation of formulae are restricted [Frä97]. On the other hand the decidable fragments of propositional DC can be enlarged with semantic restrictions [Frä97,SVHP98]. For example, one of the restrictions consists in imposing a bounded number of state changes within finite time on systems.

The automation of reasoning in DC concerns several problems:

- satisfiability: is there a model which satisfies a given formula [CSFdC00] ?
- validity: is a given formula satisfied in all models [SS94] ?
- model-checking: is a given formula satisfied in a given model [Frä02] ?

It should be noted that according to the considered syntactical restrictions the problems of satisfiability and of validity are not necessarily equivalent.

This paper deals with the satisfiability problem of formulae from the first isolated decidable fragment [ZHS93], for restricted models. This fragment corresponds to propositional DC without nearly any quantitative information: one can only specify that a temporal interval is a point or a proper interval. Moreover state changes of systems modelled by this language can occur solely at integer temporal points, time being represented by the set of real numbers (Fig. 1 presents a permissible behaviour and Fig. 4 a forbidden one). This restriction is fully justified for systems which can change states only at regular intervals. It is the case in particular of clock-driven systems.

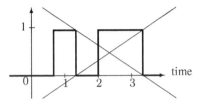

Fig. 4. A forbidden interpretation of a state expression in time-wise discrete models.

We chose to tackle this problem, *viz.* determining the satisfiability of formulae from the chosen fragment and for the chosen semantics, by means of a tableau method. It consists in trying to build a model of a formula ; in case of failure, the formula under consideration is unsatisfiable.

Usually a tableau is a tree, the nodes of which are labelled by formulae. A step-by-step procedure applies extension rules to a tree initially possessing an only node, called *root*, to which the formula to be satisfied is attached. An extension rule is represented as a pattern of tree: $\dfrac{S_1}{S_2|\ldots|S_j}$ where S_1, S_2 and S_3 are conjunctions (expressed in the form of sets) of formulae and where branching expresses disjunction. The intended meaning of an extension rule is as follows: if a leaf n of a tree T contains a set of formulae matching S_1 then the rule applies to n and adds j sons to n, each son containing the corresponding instantiation of $S_1, \ldots$ or S_k. When no more extension rule applies to the current tree this one is called a *tableau* of the initial formula. If a leaf of the tableau possesses some consistency properties, it is *open*. From an open tableau (that is to say, having an open leaf) a model of the initial formula can be built, this formula being thus satisfiable. If the tableau has no open leaf, the initial formula is unsatisfiable.

Owing to the adopted semantics $\neg(\phi_1; \phi_2)$-like formulae can be processed. Such a formula is satisfied over an interval $[d, f]$ if *for all points t* of $[d, f]$ either $\neg\phi_1$ is satisfied over interval $[d, t]$, or $\neg\phi_2$ is satisfied over interval $[t, f]$ (see Fig. 5). Given that time is modelled by the set of real numbers there is an infinite uncountable number of points in interval $[d, f]$ (if it is proper). But thanks to the chosen models we showed that actually it was sufficient to process the formula for a finite number of points, judiciously selected. To determine the maximal number of points to retain it is necessary to fix a limit to the length of the interval over which the initial formula may be satisfied.

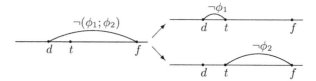

Fig. 5. Satisfaction of $\neg(\phi_1; \phi_2)$ for a point of interval $[d, f]$.

The proposed procedure is

- sound: a tableau built from a satisfiable formula is open because of the property of satisfiability preservation by extension rules,
- and complete: an open tableau has an open branch, the elements of which are satisfiable, among others the initial formula from which the tableau has been built.

Furthermore this procedure terminates: on the one hand every branch of a tableau is finite, thanks notably to the priority given to the application of the rule stopping the building of a branch, on the other hand a tableau has only a finite number of branches. This paper is organised as follows: we introduce the fragment of DC under consideration in the next section. Then in section 3 we set out the tableau method we developed. We end with the soundness, completeness and termination of the presented method in section 4, before concluding.

2 Time-Wise Discrete Duration Calculus

2.1 Syntax

The syntactical restrictions occur at the levels of terms and formulae: on the one hand the language has no more terms, on the other hand the only quantitative constraint expressible by formulae deals with the length of intervals – nil or strictly positive.

State Expressions. State expressions are built from state variables (the basic states of a system) and classical boolean operators: $\sigma ::= s \mid \neg\sigma \mid \sigma \wedge \sigma$ where s is a state variable.

Formulae. Formulae are defined in the following way: $\phi ::= \top \mid \lceil\rceil \mid \lceil\sigma\rceil \mid \neg\phi \mid \phi \wedge \phi \mid \phi; \phi$ where σ is a state expression.

2.2 Semantics

The temporal domain is modelled by the set of the positive real numbers $\mathbb{R}^+$. $\mathbb{I}$ will denote the set of closed intervals. An interpretation $\mathcal{I}$ associates with each state variable, a boolean function over temporal points: $\mathbb{R}^+ \longrightarrow \{0, 1\}$. It is extended into a function associating with each state expression, a boolean function over temporal points. State variables, hence state expressions, are finitely varied, *i.e.* they may have only a finite number of discontinuities on a bounded interval, state expressions being thus Riemann-integrable on all bounded interval.

A formula is interpreted as a boolean function over intervals: $\mathbb{I} \longrightarrow \{false, true\}$. The semantics of a formula w.r.t. a model $(\mathcal{I}, [b, e])$, where $[b, e]$ is an interval, is defined by induction in the following way:

- $(\mathcal{I}, [b, e]) \models \top$
- $(\mathcal{I}, [b, e]) \models \lceil \rceil$ iff $b = e$, this formula specifies that the length of the interval of interpretation is nil, that is to say this one is a point,
- if σ is a state expression then $(\mathcal{I}, [b, e]) \models \lceil \sigma \rceil$ iff $\int_b^e \mathcal{I}(\sigma)(t)dt = e - b$ and $b < e$: the state expression σ is equal to 1 almost everywhere in the current interval, this one being a proper interval,
- if ϕ is a formula then $(\mathcal{I}, [b, e]) \models \neg\phi$ iff $(\mathcal{I}, [b, e]) \not\models \neg\phi$,
- if ϕ_1 and ϕ_2 are formulae then $(\mathcal{I}, [b, e]) \models \phi_1 \wedge \phi_2$ iff $(\mathcal{I}, [b, e]) \models \phi_1$ and $(\mathcal{I}, [b, e]) \models \phi_2$,
- if ϕ_1 and ϕ_2 are formulae then $(\mathcal{I}, [b, e]) \models \phi_1; \phi_2$ iff $\exists t \in [b, e]$ such that $(\mathcal{I}, [b, t]) \models \phi_1$ and $(\mathcal{I}, [t, e]) \models \phi_2$.

We present here the semantic restrictions we shall consider throughout this paper.
First an interpretation $\mathcal{I}$ is *time-wise discrete* [Frä97] if for all state variable s,
$$\forall k \in \mathbb{N}, \ \forall \delta, \delta' \in (0, 1), \ \mathcal{I}(s)(k + \delta) = \mathcal{I}(s)(k + \delta')$$
In such an interpretation discontinuity points of state expressions are integers. By extension we shall call *time-wise discrete model* a model the interpretation of which is time-wise discrete.

Next we define k-satisfiability on models the intervals of which have a restricted length: it is to be equal to k.

Definition 1 (k-satisfiability). *Let k belong to $\mathbb{N}^*$. A model $(\mathcal{I}, [d, f])$ k-satisfies formula ϕ, denoted by $(\mathcal{I}, [d, f]) \models_k \phi$, if $f - d = k$ and $(\mathcal{I}, [d, f]) \models \phi$.*

2.3   Properties of Time-Wise Discrete Models

Considering time-wise discrete interpretations implies several properties. In particular, owing to lemma 2 to satisfy a $\neg(\phi_1; \phi_2)$-like formula it suffices to satisfy a finite number of formulae.

Lemma 1. *Let t_1 and t_2 be real numbers such that $t_1 < t_2$ and such that there is $n \in \mathbb{N}$ such that $n < t_1 < n + 1$ and $n < t_2 < n + 1$. For all formula ϕ, for all time-wise discrete interpretation $\mathcal{I}$ and for all real number r different from t_1 and from t_2*

1. *if $r < t_1$ then $(\mathcal{I}, [r, t_1]) \models \phi$ iff $(\mathcal{I}, [r, t_2]) \models \phi$,*

2. *if $r > t_2$ then $(\mathcal{I}, [t_1, r]) \models \phi$ iff $(\mathcal{I}, [t_2, r]) \models \phi$,*

3. *if $t_1 < r < t_2$ then $(\mathcal{I}, [t_1, r]) \models \phi$ iff $(\mathcal{I}, [r, t_2]) \models \phi$.*

This lemma is illustrated by Fig. 6.

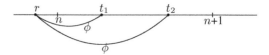

(a) Illustration of point 1.

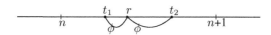

(b) Illustration of point 2.

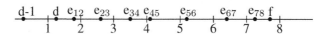

(c) Illustration of point 3.

Fig. 6. Illustration of lemma 1.

Lemma 2. *Let $[d, f]$ be an interval. For all integer i within $(d - 1, f)$, let $e_{i(i+1)}$ be a number within $(d, f) \cap (i, i+1)$. Let S be the set $\{d, f\} \cup (\mathbb{N} \cap [d, f]) \cup \{e_{i(i+1)} : i \in \mathbb{N} \cap (d - 1, f)\}$, ϕ_1 and ϕ_2 be formulae and $\mathcal{I}$ be a time-wise discrete interpretation. If $\forall t \in S$, $(\mathcal{I}, [d, t]) \models \phi_1$ or $(\mathcal{I}, [t, f]) \models \phi_2$ then $\forall \theta \in [d, f]$, $(\mathcal{I}, [d, \theta]) \models \phi_1$ or $(\mathcal{I}, [\theta, f]) \models \phi_2$.*

Example 1. To satisfy a $\neg(\phi_1; \phi_2)$-like formula over interval $[d, f] = [1.25, 7.7]$, it suffices to consider the following points: numbers 1.25 and 7.7, all the integers within interval $[1.25, 7.7]$ and for all integer e within interval $(0.25, 7.7)$ a number within interval $[1.25, 7.7] \cap (e, e + 1)$.

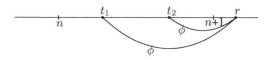

$$S = \{1.25, e_{12}, 2, e_{23}, 3, e_{34}, 4, e_{45}, 5, e_{56}, 6, e_{67}, 7, e_{78}, 7.7\}$$

3   Tableau Method

The specificities of a tableau-based method concern on the one hand the formulae labelling the nodes, on the other hand the extension rules. In the current case nodes contain labelled formulae $[d, f] : \phi$, labelled state expressions $(d, f) : \sigma$ and (qualitative or quantitative) constraints on variables. Intuitively $[d, f] : \phi$ (resp. $(d, f) : \sigma$) is "satisfied" if there are an interpretation $\mathcal{I}$ such that $(\mathcal{I}, [d, f]) \models \phi$ (resp. $\forall t \in [d, f), \mathcal{I}(\sigma)(t) = 1$).

We show here how to build a tableau for a given formula, then, if this tableau is open, how to associate a model of the original formula with it. Finally we present some tableau properties used in the proofs of soundness and completeness.

Let $\mathcal{P} = \{p_0, \ldots, p_{k+1}\}$, $\mathcal{M} = \{m_{01}, \ldots, m_{k(k+1)}\}$ and $\mathcal{S} = \mathcal{P} \cup \mathcal{M}$. The elements of $\mathcal{P}$ and $\mathcal{M}$ will be handled like variables. $\mathcal{P}$ will be interpreted as the set of the integers within $[0, k+1]$ and every element $m_{i(i+1)}$ of $\mathcal{M}$ will be interpreted as a non-integer real number within $(i, i+1)$. We shall denote by π_j ($j \in \mathbb{N}$) any element of $\mathcal{P}$.

3.1 Extension Rules

There are four types of extension rules: a stop rule which detects inconsistencies (Tab. 1), rules applying to formulae and generating formulae or constraints (Tab. 2a, 2b and 2c), rules applying to formulae and producing state expressions (Tab. 3) and rules applying to state expressions (Tab. 4).

We comment on some of these rules below.

Stop Rule. The information represented by formulae are partly translated by constraints. From them the stop rule (Tab. 1) detects potential inconsistencies. If so, this rule stops the building of the current branch.

Table 1. Stop Rule

inconsistent set of constraints
STOP

Formula Rules. In Tab. 2a, 2b and 2c are presented rules applying to formulae and generating formulae or constraints. Rules POINT, DOUBLE NEGATION FOR, AND FOR, NOT AND FOR and CHOP mimic the semantics of the considered formulae in a very natural way. The other rules call for some comments which we detail hereafter.

Rule VERUM. As $\top$ is always satisfiable it is sufficient (but necessary) to make sure that the considered interval is an actual interval, hence the constraint generated by rule VERUM.

Rule FALSUM. $\neg\top$ can never be satisfied: rule FALSUM generates an inconsistent set of constraints so that the stop rule may detect the inconsistency of the current branch.

Rule NOT POINT. Formula $\neg\lceil\rceil$ is satisfied over interval $[d, f]$ if the constraint $f - d \neq 0$ is satisfied, *i.e.* if the constraint $d < f$ or the constraint $f < d$ is satisfied. On the other hand $[d, f]$ being an interval the constraint $d \leq f$ must be satisfied. Consequently only the constraint $d < f$ may be satisfied, which is expressed by rule NOT POINT.

Table 2a. Formula rules

VERUM	FALSUM
$\dfrac{[d,f]:\top}{d\leq f}$	$\dfrac{[d,f]:\neg\top}{d\leq f, f<d}$

POINT	NOT POINT
$\dfrac{[d,f]:\lceil\rceil}{d=f}$	$\dfrac{[d,f]:\neg\lceil\rceil}{d<f}$

AND FOR	NOT AND FOR
$\dfrac{[d,f]:\phi_1\wedge\phi_2}{[d,f]:\phi_1,[d,f]:\phi_2}$	$\dfrac{[d,f]:\neg(\phi_1\wedge\phi_2)}{[d,f]:\neg\phi_1\|[d,f]:\neg\phi_2}$

DOUBLE NEGATION FOR	CHOP
$\dfrac{[d,f]:\neg\neg\phi}{[d,f]:\phi}$	$\dfrac{[d,f]:\phi_1;\phi_2}{[d,t]:\phi_1,[t,f]:\phi_2}$ t new

Table 2b. Formula rules: rules NOT CHOP 1 and NOT CHOP 2

NOT CHOP 1

$$[d,f]:\neg(\phi_1;\phi_2)$$

$[d,f]:\neg(\phi_1;\phi_2)$ $t<d$	$[d,f]:\neg(\phi_1;\phi_2)$ $f<t$	$[d,f]:\neg(\phi_1;\phi_2)$ $[d,t]:\neg\phi_1$ $d\leq t\leq f$	$[d,f]:\neg(\phi_1;\phi_2)$ $[t,f]:\neg\phi_2$ $d\leq t\leq f$

$$t\in\mathcal{S}\cup\{d,f\}$$
apply once only for a given t and a given labelled formula

NOT CHOP 2

$$[d,f]:\neg(\phi_1;\phi_2)$$

$[d,f]:\neg(\phi_1;\phi_2)$ $d=f$	$[d,f]:\neg(\phi_1;\phi_2)$ $0<f-d<1$ $[d,t]:\neg\phi_1$ $d<t<f$	$[d,f]:\neg(\phi_1;\phi_2)$ $0<f-d<1$ $[t,f]:\neg\phi_2$ $d<t<f$	$[d,f]:\neg(\phi_1;\phi_2)$ $f-d\geq 1$

$$t\text{ new}$$
apply once only to a given labelled formula

Rules NOT CHOP 1, NOT CHOP 2 *and* NOT CHOP 3. The goal of rules NOT CHOP 1, NOT CHOP 2 and NOT CHOP 3 is to implement lemma 2.

Let $\neg(\phi_1;\phi_2)$ be the formula to be satisfied over interval $[d,f]$. For all element t of some set of points (detailed hereafter), either $\neg\phi_1$ is satisfied over $[d,t]$, or $\neg\phi_2$ is satisfied over $[t,f]$.

The set S of the points to be considered (example 1) consists of

Table 2c. Formula rules: rule NOT CHOP 3

NOT CHOP 3
$$[d, f] : \neg(\phi_1; \phi_2) \text{ (beginnning \dots)}$$

$[d, f] : \neg(\phi_1; \phi_2)$	$[d, f] : \neg(\phi_1; \phi_2)$	$[d, f] : \neg(\phi_1; \phi_2)$
$p \leq d$	$0 < p - d < 1$	$0 < p - d < 1$
	$f - p \geq 1$	$f - p \geq 1$
	$d < t < p$	$d < t < p$
	$[d, t] : \neg\phi_1$	$[t, f] : \neg\phi_2$

t new

$p \in \mathcal{P}$

apply once only for a given p and a given labelled formula

$$[d, f] : \neg(\phi_1; \phi_2) \text{ (\dots continuation \dots)}$$

$[d, f] : \neg(\phi_1; \phi_2)$	$[d, f] : \neg(\phi_1; \phi_2)$	$[d, f] : \neg(\phi_1; \phi_2)$	$[d, f] : \neg(\phi_1; \phi_2)$
$0 < p - d < 1$	$0 < p - d < 1$	$0 < p - d < 1$	$0 < p - d < 1$
$0 < f - p < 1$	$0 < f - p < 1$	$0 < f - p < 1$	$0 < f - p < 1$
$d < t_1 < p$	$d < t_1 < p$	$d < t_1 < p$	$d < t_1 < p$
$p < t_2 < f$	$p < t_2 < f$	$p < t_2 < f$	$p < t_2 < f$
$[d, t_1] : \neg\phi_1$	$[d, t_1] : \neg\phi_1$	$[t_1, f] : \neg\phi_2$	$[t_1, f] : \neg\phi_2$
$[d, t_2] : \neg\phi_1$	$[t_2, f] : \neg\phi_2$	$[d, t_2] : \neg\phi_1$	$[t_2, f] : \neg\phi_2$

t_1, t_2 new

$$[d, f] : \neg(\phi_1; \phi_2) \text{ (\dots ending of rule NOT CHOP 3)}$$

$[d, f] : \neg(\phi_1; \phi_2)$	$[d, f] : \neg(\phi_1; \phi_2)$	$[d, f] : \neg(\phi_1; \phi_2)$	$[d, f] : \neg(\phi_1; \phi_2)$
$p - d \geq 1$	$p - d \geq 1$	$p - d \geq 1$	$f \leq p$
$f - p \geq 1$	$0 < f - p < 1$	$0 < f - p < 1$	
	$p < t < f$	$p < t < f$	
	$[d, t] : \neg\phi_1$	$[t, f] : \neg\phi_2$	

t new

- d and f,
- any integer between d and f,
- for all integer p between $d - 1$ and f, any number strictly between p and $p + 1$ and strictly between d and f.

Rule NOT CHOP 2 handles the special case where the length of interval $[d, f]$ is strictly less than 1. When S consists only of d and f, for $\neg(\phi_1; \phi_2)$ to be satisfied over interval $[d, f]$, it is enough either for $\neg\phi_1$ to be satisfied over $[d, t]$, or for $\neg\phi_2$ to be satisfied over $[t, f]$, where t is a point strictly between d and f.

In the most general case, rules NOT CHOP 1 and NOT CHOP 3 apply. Rule NOT CHOP 1 undertakes the following points:

- d and f,
- any integer between d and f,
- for all integer p such that p and $p + 1$ are between d and f, any number strictly between p and $p + 1$.

In Example 1, it concerns the set $\{1, 25; 2; e_{23}; 3; e_{34}; 4; e_{45}; 5; e_{56}; 6; e_{67}; 7; 7, 7\}$. Rule NOT CHOP 3 generates the missing two points, namely e_{12} and e_{78}.

In outline, there are four cases depending on whether d and f are integers. When an interval bound is not an integer, rule NOT CHOP 3 generates a point between the considered bound and its lower or upper whole part ; Fig. 7 presents the three configurations (with respect to $p \in \mathcal{P}$) in which rule NOT CHOP 3 generates new points.

Formula $\rightarrow$ State Expression Rules. The rules presented in Tab. 3 apply to formulae and produce state expressions (indirectly as for rule NOT INTEGRAL).

Table 3. Formula $\rightarrow$ state expression rules

INTEGRAL $[d, f] : \lceil \sigma \rceil$				NOT INTEGRAL $[d, f] : \neg \lceil \sigma \rceil$	
$(d^-, f^+) : \sigma$ $d < f$ $d^- < d < d^+$ $d^+ - d^- = 1$ $f^- < f < f^+$ $f^+ - f^- = 1$	$(d^-, f^+) : \sigma$ $d < f$ $d^- < d < d^+$ $d^+ - d^- = 1$ $f^- = f = f^+$	$(d^-, f^+) : \sigma$ $d < f$ $d^- = d = d^+$ $f^- < f < f^+$ $f^+ - f^- = 1$	$(d^-, f^+) : \sigma$ $d < f$ $d^- = d = d^+$ $f^- = f = f^+$	$[t_1, t_2] : \lceil \neg \sigma \rceil$ $d \le t_1 < t_2 \le f$ t_1 and t_2 new	$f - d = 0$

Rule INTEGRAL. Rule INTEGRAL develops formula $\lceil \sigma \rceil$. This one is satisfied over a proper interval $[d, f]$ if σ is 1 nearly everywhere over $[d, f]$. Furthermore, as we consider time-wise discrete models, σ will be 1 necessarily nearly everywhere over $[d^-, f^+]$, where d^- is the lower whole part of d and f^+ is the upper whole part of f. Rule INTEGRAL expresses in particular the various potential constraints between a bound and its whole parts (lower and upper) depending on whether that one is an integer.

Rule NOT INTEGRAL. Formula $\neg \lceil \sigma \rceil$ is satisfied over interval $[d, f]$ if σ is not equal to 1 nearly everywhere over $[d, f]$ or if $[d, f]$ is a temporal point. Therefore either the length of interval $[d, f]$ is nil, or there is a proper subinterval $[t_1, t_2]$ of $[d, f]$ such that σ is equal to 0 (*i.e* $\neg \sigma$ is equal to 1) nearly everywhere.

State Expression Rules. The rules applying to state expressions are presented in Tab. 4. We shall consider that state expressions are labelled by *integer*-bound intervals. This hypothesis shall be proved in lemma 4.

The meaning of rules DOUBLE NEGATION EXP and AND EXP being easily understandable, we shall not explain them.

Rules NOT AND EXP 1 *and* NOT AND EXP 2. Let $\neg(\sigma_1 \wedge \sigma_2)$ be a state expression to be "satisfied" over interval $[d, f)$ (where d and f are integers), *i.e.* we search for a time-wise discrete interpretation $\mathcal{I}$ such that $\forall t \in [d, f), \mathcal{I}(\neg \sigma_1)(t) = 1$ or $\mathcal{I}(\neg \sigma_2)(t) = 1$. Since

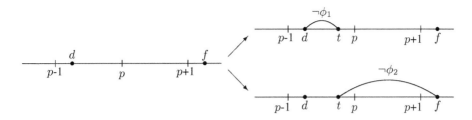

(a) Case where $0 < p - d < 1$ and $f - p \geq 1$.

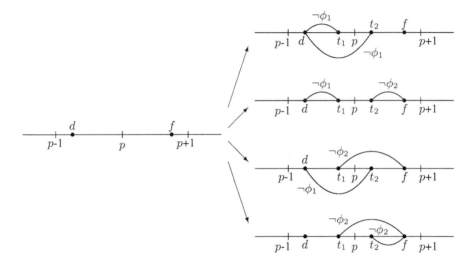

(b) Case where $0 < p - d < 1$ and $0 < f - p < 1$.

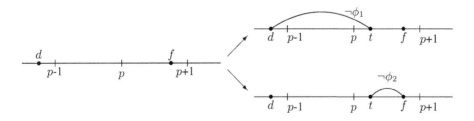

(c) Case where $p - d \geq 1$ and $0 < f - p < 1$.

Fig. 7. Illustration of rule NOT CHOP 3 for $p \in \mathcal{P}$.

the sought interpretation is time-wise discrete, it is piecewise constant, more precisely it is constant over any unit-long interval bounded by integers.

Rules NOT AND EXP 1 and NOT AND EXP 2 take advantage of this property. First rule NOT

Table 4. State expression rules

DOUBLE NEGATION EXP

$$\frac{(d, f) : \neg\neg\sigma}{(d, f) : \sigma}$$

AND EXP

$$\frac{(d, f) : \sigma_1 \wedge \sigma_2}{(d, f) : \sigma_1, (d, f) : \sigma_2}$$

NOT AND EXP 1

$$(d, f) : \neg(\sigma_1 \wedge \sigma_2)$$

$(d, f) : \neg(\sigma_1 \wedge \sigma_2)$ $p \leq d$	$(d, f) : \neg(\sigma_1 \wedge \sigma_2)$ $f \leq p$	$(d, p) : \neg(\sigma_1 \wedge \sigma_2)$ $(p, f) : \neg(\sigma_1 \wedge \sigma_2)$ $d < p < f$

$$p \in \mathcal{P}$$
apply once only for a given p
and a given labelled state expression

NOT AND EXP 2

$$(d, f) : \neg(\sigma_1 \wedge \sigma_2)$$

$f - d > 1$ $(d, f) : \neg(\sigma_1 \wedge \sigma_2)$	$f - d = 1$ $(d, f) : \neg\sigma_1$	$f - d = 1$ $(d, f) : \neg\sigma_2$	$d = f$

do not apply if $f - d > 1$ is deducible from the constraints of the father node

INTERVAL DISJUNCTION: s is a state variable

$$(d_1, f_1) : s, (d_2, f_2) : \neg s$$

$(d_1, f_1) : s, (d_2, f_2) : \neg s$ $f_1 \leq d_2$	$(d_1, f_1) : s, (d_2, f_2) : \neg s$ $f_2 \leq d_1$

do not apply if $f_1 \leq d_2$ or $f_2 \leq d_1$ is deducible from the constraints of the father node

---

AND EXP 1 divides interval $[d, f)$ into unit-long integer-bounded subintervals (Fig. 8). Secondly rule NOT AND EXP 2 splits state expression $\neg(\sigma_1 \wedge \sigma_2)$ over any unit-long integer-bounded interval into either $\neg\sigma_1$, or $\neg\sigma_2$ (Fig. 9).

Rule INTERVAL DISJUNCTION. Rule INTERVAL DISJUNCTION avoids the situation where a state variable and its negation would both be equal to 1 over overlapping intervals (Fig. 10).

3.2   Tableau Computation

We set out here how to compute the tableau of a formula, then if it proves to be open how to build a model of the starting formula.

Definition 2 (Tableau). *Let ϕ be a formula, k belong to $\mathbb{N}^*$ and $(T_0, T_1, \ldots, T_i)$ be a series of trees such that*

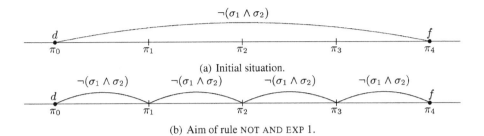

(a) Initial situation.

(b) Aim of rule NOT AND EXP 1.

Fig. 8. Illustration of rule NOT AND EXP I.

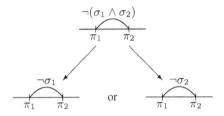

Fig. 9. Result of the application of rule NOT AND EXP 2.

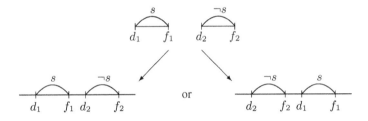

Fig. 10. Result of the application of rule INTERVAL DISJUNCTION.

- T_0 is a single node containing $p_1 - p_0 = 1, \ldots, p_{k+1} - p_k = 1$, $p_0 < m_{01} < p_1$, $\ldots, p_k < m_{k(k+1)} < p_{k+1}$, where p_i and $m_{i(i+1)}$ are variables, and $[b_1, b_2] : \phi$, $p_0 \leq b_1 \leq b_2 \leq p_{k+1}$, $b_2 - b_1 = k$ where b_1 and b_2 are variables.
- $\forall j < i, T_{j+1}$ is obtained by applying an extension rule to T_j.

If no extension rule is applicable to T_i, it is called a k-tableau of formula ϕ.

Strategy. In order to ensure the termination of the tableau computation, it is essential to define a stategy to apply extension rules: the application of the stop rule has priority.

Now we specify the vocabulary we shall use and explain how to associate a model with an open node.
A *whole variable* either belongs to $\mathcal{P}$, or is a t^- or t^+-like variable. We shall call *whole constraint* a constraint comprising only whole variables. Intuitively whole variables will be valued by integers and t^- (resp. t^+) is the inferior (resp. superior) whole part of t.

Let $\mathcal{B}$ be a tableau branch. We shall denote $\mathcal{C}(\mathcal{B})$ the set of constraints appearing in branch $\mathcal{B}$. Likewise if n is a node, $\mathcal{C}(n)$ will represent the set of constraints belonging to n. Lastly if c is a constraint, $\mathcal{C}(\mathcal{B}) \vdash c$ (resp. $\mathcal{C}(n) \vdash c$) means that constraint c is deducible from the set of constraints $\mathcal{C}(\mathcal{B})$ (resp. $\mathcal{C}(n)$).

An *open node* is such that the set of whole constraints has a whole solution within $[0, k]$, extensible to the whole set of constraints. Accordingly the set of constraints of an open node is consistent.

Definition 3 (Model associated with an open node). *Let n be an open node. The model $(V, \mathcal{I})$ associated with n is such that*

- V *is a valuation of the variables appearing in the constraints of n such that*
  - *the set of constraints is satisfied,*
  - $V(p_0) = 0$,
  - *whole variables are valued by a natural number,*
- *and $\mathcal{I}$ is an interpretation of the state variables of n such that for all state variable s, for all variable t, if there are variables t_1 and t_2 such that $V(t_1) \leq t < V(t_2)$ and $(t_1, t_2) : s$ belongs to node n then $\mathcal{I}(s)(t) = 1$, else $\mathcal{I}(s)(t) = 0$.*

3.3   Properties of k-Tableaux

There is no difficulty about the proofs of the auxiliary lemmas presented in this subsection, hence they will be omitted.

If a labelled formula $[d, f] : \phi$ or a labelled state expression $(d, f) : \sigma$ appears in an open branch $\mathcal{B}$, the model $(V, \mathcal{I})$ associated with the terminal node of $\mathcal{B}$ must be such that $[V(d), V(f)]$ is an actual interval, that is to say $V(d) \leq V(f)$:

Lemma 3. *Let ϕ be a formula (resp. σ be a state expression) and d and f be two variables. If $[d, f] : \phi$ (resp. $(d, f) : \sigma$) belongs to an open branch $\mathcal{B}$ then $\mathcal{C}(\mathcal{B}) \vdash d \leq f$.*

The following lemma will ensure that the model associated with an open terminal node is time-wise discrete.

Lemma 4. *Let $(d, f) : \sigma$ be a labelled state expression appearing in a tableau. d and f are whole variables.*

Corollary 1. *The interpretation built from an open terminal node is time-wise discrete.*

4   Soundness and Completeness

First the tableau method presented in this paper is sound, *i.e.* the k-tableau of a formula k-satisfiable by a time-wise discrete model is open. This method is also complete: if the k-tableau of a formula is open then this one is k-satisfiable by a time-wise discrete model. Finally the decision procedure terminates.

The reader interested in the full proofs of soundness, completeness and termination can find them in [CS01].

4.1 Soundness

The following lemma states that for all rule if all the elements of the father node are satisfiable then all the elements of one of the sons are satisfiable.

Lemma 5 (Satisfiability preservation). *Let n be the (open) father node of a rule. Let V be a valuation and let $\mathcal{I}$ be a time-wise discrete interpretation such that*

- *if $[d, f] : \phi \in n$ then $V(d) \leq V(f)$ and $(\mathcal{I}, [V(d), V(f)]) \models \phi$,*
- *if c is a constraint belonging to n then V satisfies c (whole variables being valued by integers),*
- *if $(d, f) : \sigma \in n$ then $V(d) \leq V(f)$ and for all variable t such that $V(d) \leq t < V(f)$, $\mathcal{I}(\sigma)(t) = 1$.*

There is a son n' of n such that there is a valuation V' such that

- *if $[d, f] : \phi \in n'$ then $V'(d) \leq V'(f)$ and $(\mathcal{I}, [V'(d), V'(f)]) \models \phi$,*
- *if c is a constraint belonging to n' then V' satisfies c (whole variables being valued by integers),*
- *if $(d, f) : \sigma \in n'$ then $V'(d) \leq V'(f)$ and for all variable t such that $V'(d) \leq t < V'(f)$, $\mathcal{I}(\sigma)(t) = 1$.*

The soundness of our method can be deduced from the previous lemma:

Corollary 2 (Soundness). *Let ϕ be a formula and k be a natural number. If ϕ is k-satisfiable by a time-wise discrete model then ϕ has an open k-tableau.*

Proof. If ϕ is k-satisfiable in a time-wise discrete model then there are a time-wise discrete interpretation $\mathcal{I}$ and an interval $[d, f]$ such that $[d, f] \subseteq [0, k + 1]$, $f - d = k$ and $(\mathcal{I}, [d, f]) \models \phi$. The (open) root of a tableau for ϕ contains $[b_1, b_2] : \phi$, $p_0 \leq b_1 \leq b_2 \leq p_{k+1}$, $b_2 - b_1 = k$, $p_1 - p_0 = 1, \ldots, p_{k+1} - p_k = 1$, $p_0 < m_{01} < p_1, \ldots,$ $p_k < m_{k(k+1)} < p_{k+1}$, where b_1, b_2, p_i and $m_{i(i+1)}$ are variables. Let V be a valuation such that $V(b_1) = d$, $V(b_2) = f$, $\forall i \in \{0, \ldots, k\}$, $V(p_i) = i$ and $\forall i \in \{0, \ldots, k - 1\}$, $i < V(m_{i(i+1)}) < i + 1$. Then V satisfies all the constraints of the root (whole variables being valued by integers) and $(\mathcal{I}, [V(b_1), V(b_2)]) \models \phi$. Owing to lemma 5, there is a branch of the tableau such that this property is preserved for any node ; such a branch is open and can be built recursively: the root of the branch is the root of the tree, then for all non terminal node of the branch, one has just to choose a son node satisfying the property stated above (such a node exists thanks to lemma 5). $\square$

4.2 Completeness

The proof of the completeness of our method is particularly long and intricate. Moreover it calls for two lemmas (stated hereafter) themselves quite technical. That is the reason why we shall not give the complete proofs.

To prove the completeness of our method we show that each labelled formula of an open branch $\mathcal{B}$ is satisfiable (theorem 1). With this in view we first have to prove that each labelled state expression of $\mathcal{B}$ is, in a way, "satisfiable" (lemma 7). When the labelled state expression under consideration is $(d, f) : \neg(\sigma_1 \wedge \sigma_2)$-like, interval $[d, f]$ can be partitioned into unit intervals where either $\neg\sigma_1$, or $\neg\sigma_2$ will be valued to 1. This property is the subject of the following lemma.

Lemma 6. *Let* $(d, f) : \neg(\sigma_1 \wedge \sigma_2)$ *belong to an open branch* $\mathcal{B}$ *and let* $M = (\mathtt{V}, \mathcal{I})$ *be the model associated with the terminal node of* $\mathcal{B}$. *There are* $\pi_0, \ldots, \pi_n \in \mathcal{P}$ *such that*

(i) $\mathtt{V}(\pi_0) = \mathtt{V}(d)$

(ii) $\mathtt{V}(\pi_n) = \mathtt{V}(f)$

(iii) $\pi_{j+1} - \pi_j = 1 \in \mathcal{B}$ ($j \in \{0, \ldots, n-1\}$)

(iv) $(\pi_j, \pi_{j+1}) : \neg\sigma_1 \in \mathcal{B}$ *or* $(\pi_j, \pi_{j+1}) : \neg\sigma_2 \in \mathcal{B}$ ($j \in \{0, \ldots, n-1\}$).

Lemma 7. *Let* ϕ *be a formula, the* k-*tableau of which is open and let* $\mathcal{B}$ *be an open branch of that tableau ;* $M = (\mathtt{V}, \mathcal{I})$ *is the model associated with the terminal node* n *of* $\mathcal{B}$. *For all variables* d *and* f, *for all state expression* σ, *if* $(d, f) : \sigma \in \mathcal{B}$ *then for all variable* t *such that* $\mathtt{V}(d) \le t < \mathtt{V}(f)$, $\mathcal{I}(\sigma)(t) = 1$.

Theorem 1 (Completeness). *Let* ϕ *be a formula and* k *be a natural number. If* ϕ *has an open* k-*tableau then* ϕ *is* k-*satisfiable by a time-wise discrete model.*

Proof. Let ϕ be a formula for which an open k-tableau exists and let $\mathcal{B}$ be an open branch of that tableau ; $M = (\mathtt{V}, \mathcal{I})$ is the model associated with the terminal node n of $\mathcal{B}$. According to corollary 1, $\mathcal{I}$ is a time-wise discrete interpretation. Next note that, according to definition 3, $\mathtt{V}(p_0) = 0$. So it is sufficient to show that for all labelled formula $[d, f] : \psi$ of $\mathcal{B}$, ψ is satisfied by $(\mathcal{I}, [\mathtt{V}(d), \mathtt{V}(f)])$. Then it will follow that $(\mathcal{I}, [0, k]) \models \phi$ (resp. $(\mathcal{I}, [\mathtt{V}(b_1), \mathtt{V}(b_2)]) \models \phi$ and $\mathtt{V}(b_2) - \mathtt{V}(b_1) \le k$).

4.3   Termination

The termination of our method follows from the fact that the extension rules have the "subelement property" after a finite number of applications.

The critical point of the proof deals with $(d, f) : \neg(\sigma_1 \wedge \sigma_2)$-like labelled state expressions: rule NOT AND EXP I may loop. Applications of this rule build a partition of interval $[d, f]$ into unit intervals. For each step the set E of the endpoints of the intervals of the partition under construction is ordered strictly. Moreover for all labelled state expression $(d', f') : \neg(\sigma_1 \wedge \sigma_2)$ appearing in the current branch, d' and f' belong to E and are consecutive, with respect to the elements of E. Applying rule NOT AND EXP I twice on the same element of E yields an inconsistency. In that case the application of the stop rule, which has priority, freezes the construction of the current branch.

By proving that in any saturated branch there is a node to which no extension rule may apply, neither to labelled formulae, nor to labelled state expressions, we show that any branch of a tableau is finite. In addition each extension rule generates a finite number of son nodes, so a tableau has a finite number of branches. We obtain hence the termination of our method (Th. 2).

The lemmas necessary for this proof being especially technical, we shall omit them.

Theorem 2 (Termination). *The building of a* k-*tableau for a formula from the fragment under consideration terminates.*

5   Conclusion

In this paper we defined a sound and complete decision method for a fragment of DC. It is thus possible to determine the satisfiability of a formula over a bounded-long interval. We consider now implementating this method in order to apply it to real cases and to measure its practical efficiency. We also need to study the complexity of the proposed method to measure its theoretical efficiency.

Moreover, carrying on with our study initiated in [CSFdC00] we attempt to define decision procedures for more expressive fragments of DC. Finally we consider doing a similar work for other real-time logics for which the model-checking problem has been privileged.

References

[CS01]   Nathalie Chetcuti-Sperandio. *Déduction automatique en calcul des durées basée sur la méthode des tableaux*. PhD thesis, Université Toulouse 3, December 2001.

[CSFdC00]   N. Chetcuti-Sperandio and L. Fariñas del Cerro. A Mixed Decision Method for Duration Calculus. *Journal of Logic and Computation*, 10(6):877–895, 2000.

[Frä96]   M. Fränzle. Synthesizing Controllers from Duration Calculus. In *FTRTFT'96*, volume 1135 of *LNCS*, pages 168–187, 1996.

[Frä97]   M. Fränzle. *Controller Design from Temporal Logic: Undecidability Need Not Matter*. PhD thesis, Christian-Albrechts-Universität, Kiel, Germany, 1997.

[Frä02]   M. Fränzle. Model-Checking Dense-Time Duration Calculus. *Formal Aspects of Computing*, 2002. To appear.

[HMM83]   J. Halpern, Z. Manna, and B. Moszkowski. A Hardware Semantics Based on Temporal Intervals. In *ICALP'83*, volume 154 of *LNCS*, pages 278–291, 1983.

[RRH93]   A. P. Ravn, H. Rischel, and K. M. Hansen. Specifying and Verifying Requirements of Real-Time Systems. *IEEE Transactions on Software Engineering*, 19(1):41–55, 1993.

[SS94]   J. U. Skakkebæk and P. Sestoft. Checking Validity of Duration Calculus Formulas. Technical Report ID/DTH JUS 3/1, Technical University of Denmark, 1994.

[SVHP98]   M. Satpathy, D. Van Hung, and P. K. Pandya. Some Decidability Results for Duration Calculus under Synchronous Interpretation. In *FTRTFT'98*, volume 1486 of *LNCS*, pages 186–197, 1998.

[YZ94]   Z. Yuhua and C. Zhou. A Formal Proof of the Deadline Driven Scheduler. In *FTRTFT'94*, volume 863 of *LNCS*, pages 756–775, 1994.

[ZHR91]   C. Zhou, C. A. R. Hoare, and A. P. Ravn. A calculus of durations. *information processing letters*, 40(5):269–276, 1991.

[ZHRR92]   C. Zhou, M. R. Hansen, A. P. Ravn, and H. Rischel. Duration Specifications for Shared Processors. In *FTRTFT'92*, volume 571 of *LNCS*, pages 21–32, 1992.

[ZHS93]   C. Zhou, M. R. Hansen, and P. Sestoft. Decidability and Undecidability Results for Duration Calculus. In *STACS '93*, volume 665 of *LNCS*, pages 58–68, 1993.

Linear Time Logic, Conditioned Models, and Planning with Incomplete Knowledge

Marta Cialdea Mayer and Carla Limongelli

Università di Roma Tre, Dipartimento di Informatica e Automazione

Abstract. The "planning as satisfiability" paradigm, which reduces solving a planning problem P to the search of a model of a logical description of P, relies on the assumption that the agent has complete knowledge and control over the world. This work faces the problem of planning in the presence of incomplete information and/or exogenous events, still keeping inside the "planning as satisfiability" paradigm, in the context of linear time logic.

We give a logical characterization of a "conditioned model", which represents a plan solving a given problem together with a set of "conditions" that guarantee its executability. During execution, conditions have to be checked by means of sensing actions. When a condition turns out to be false, a different "conditioned plan" must be considered. A whole conditional plan is represented by a set of conditioned models. The interest of splitting a conditional plan into significant sub-parts is due to the heavy computational complexity of conditional planning.

The paper presents an extension of the standard tableau calculus for linear time logic, allowing one to extract from a single open branch a conditioned model of the initial set of formulae, i.e. a partial description of a model and a set of conditions U guaranteeing its "executability". As can be expected, if U is required to be minimal, the analysis of a single branch is not sufficient. We show how a global view on the whole tableau can be used to prune U from redundant conditions. In any case, if the calculus is to be used with the aim of producing the whole conditional plan off-line, a complete tableau must be built. On the other hand, a single conditioned model can be used when planning and execution (with sensing actions) are intermingled. In that case, the requirement for minimality can reasonably be relaxed.

1 Introduction

The specification of a planning problem P consists of an initial state, a goal to be achieved and a set of actions that the agent can execute. A (linear) plan solving P is a sequence of actions that, when executed, lead from the initial state to a goal state. Most approaches to planning work under the assumption that the agent has complete knowledge of the world, its actions have deterministic effects and the world changes are caused only by the agent's actions. Conditional planning faces problems where such assumptions are dropped. The approach followed by most of the recent work on this area consists in extending partial-order planning

U. Egly and C.G. Fermüller (Eds.): TABLEAUX 2002, LNAI 2381, pp. 70–84, 2002.

algorithms to find "conditional plans" (see, for instance, [9,11]). Some logical approaches to conditional planning have also been proposed: either based on deduction [4,8,13], or on model checking [3,10].

An effective logical approach to (non-conditional) planning is based on the "planning as satisfiability" paradigm, where planning is reduced to a satisfiability problem, either in classical propositional logic [6,7] or linear time logic (LTL) [1, 2]: a planning problem can be described by a set Σ of formulae, in such a way that any model of Σ describes a plan solving the problem and vice-versa.

For instance, let us consider the problem where the agent has to enter a room, passing through a door, that is initially closed. Following the methodology proposed in [1,2], the problem can be described in LTL by means of the following set of formulae:

$$\Sigma = \{\ \Box(do\_pass \rightarrow open),$$
$$\Box(do\_open \rightarrow \neg open),$$
$$\Box(\bigcirc in \equiv (in \wedge \neg do\_pass) \vee (\neg in \wedge do\_pass)),$$
$$\Box(\bigcirc open \equiv open \vee do\_open),$$
$$\neg in \wedge \neg open,$$
$$\Diamond in\ \}$$

The first two formulae represent the preconditions for the executability of the actions do_pass and do_open, respectively. The third and fourth formulae are the reformulation in LTL of Reiter's "successor state axioms" [12]. The fifth formula represents the agent's knowledge about the initial state, and the last one represents the goal. Any model of Σ represents a plan solving the problem. For instance, the model where do_open is true at state 0, do_pass is true at state 1 and in is true at state 2. The plan extracted from such a model is the sequence of actions $\langle do\_open, do\_pass \rangle$.

However planning by satisfiability relies on the assumption that the agent has complete knowledge and control over the world. Let us consider, for instance, the same problem as before, but where the agent does not know whether the door is initially open or closed. The problem is represented in LTL by the set Σ_0, obtained from Σ by replacing the initial state formula $\neg in \wedge \neg open$ with $\neg in$. Since there is no information about the state of the door in the initial situation, no model of Σ_0 represents a correct plan.

Incomplete knowledge about the initial state is not the only source of uncertainty. When the world is not under the agent's complete control, the state of the world at a given time point cannot be predicted simply on the base of what holds before and the agent's actions. For example, let us assume that the agent can open the door but the effect of the action is guaranteed for the next state only, for instance because other agents may pass by and open or close the door; the agent must enter the room and exit again. The problem is represented by the set Σ_1 obtained from Σ_0 by relaxing the successor state axiom for $open$ and modifying the goal formula:

$$\Sigma_1 = \{ \, \Box(do\_pass \to open),$$
$$\Box(do\_open \to \neg open),$$
$$\Box(\bigcirc in \equiv (in \land \neg do\_pass) \lor (\neg in \land do\_pass)),$$
$$\Box(do\_open \to \bigcirc open),$$
$$\neg in,$$
$$\Diamond(in \land \Diamond \neg in) \, \}$$

In such cases, conditional planning solves the problems by means of *conditional plans*. For instance, a conditional plan solving the problem represented by Σ_1 is:

IF the door is open
THEN pass; afterwards, IF the door is open
      THEN pass
      ELSE open the door and pass
  ELSE open the door and pass;
    afterwards, IF the door is open
      THEN pass
      ELSE open the door and pass

The execution of a conditional plan requires sensing: during execution, at each IF/THEN/ELSE branching, the agent checks the state of the world and follows the respective branch. A conditional plan can be represented by a tree: each node N represents a property that must be checked at execution time, the left subtree of N is the conditional plan that must be executed if N turns out to be true, the right subtree is the plan to be executed when N is false.

A conditional plan P can be seen as a set of "*conditioned plans*", each corresponding to a branch in the tree representing P. For instance, the conditional plan above can be split into the following set of "complementary" conditioned plans:

 1) IF the door is open THEN pass;
   afterwards, IF the door is open THEN pass
 2) IF the door is open THEN pass;
   afterwards, IF the door is closed THEN open the door and pass
 3) IF the door is closed THEN open the door and pass;
   afterwards, IF the door is open THEN pass
 4) IF the door is closed THEN open the door and pass;
   afterwards, IF the door is closed THEN open the door and pass.

Each conditioned plan can in turn be described by means of a linear plan (a sequence of actions) together with a set of conditions guaranteeing the executability of the plan. For instance, the third plan above can be represented by the pair:

$\langle \, \langle$ do_open, do_pass, do_pass $\rangle$,
 $\{$ the door is closed at state 0, the door is open at state 2 $\} \, \rangle$

The interest of splitting a conditional plan into significant sub-parts is due to the heavy computational complexity of conditional planning [13]. Instead of producing the whole conditional plan off-line, and then executing it, we can consider the possibility that planning and execution (with sensing actions) are intermingled. In that case, a single conditioned plan can be generated at first. During its execution, its conditions are checked by means of sensing actions. When a condition turns out to be false, a different (complementary) conditioned plan is generated and considered. Conditional planning can be reduced to the search for a set of complementary conditioned plans.

In this work we give a logical characterization of a "conditioned model" of a set Σ of LTL-formulae (describing a planning problem) (Section 2). A conditioned model, which represents a conditioned plan, is a pair $\langle S, U \rangle$, where S is a partial description of a temporal model of Σ and U a set of conditions that guarantee the "executability" of S.

In Section 3 we describe a tableau calculus that allows us to extract a conditioned model $\langle S, U \rangle$ of Σ from a single open branch of a tableau for Σ. As can be expected, if U is required to be minimal, the analysis of a single branch is not sufficient. We show (Section 4) how a global view on the whole tableau can be used to prune U from redundant conditions. In any case, if the calculus is to be used with the aim of producing the whole conditional plan off-line, a complete tableau must be built. Section 5 concludes this work.

2   Conditioned Models

We consider the language of linear time logic over a set of propositional letters $\mathbb{P}$ built by means of the connectives $\neg$, $\wedge$, $\vee$ and the future time $\square$ (always), $\Diamond$ (eventually), $\bigcirc$ (next). Implication and double implication are defined symbols. For convenience, we restrict the language to formulae in negation normal form, and consider negation over non atomic formulae as a defined symbol too:

$$\neg(A \vee B) \equiv_{def} \neg A \wedge \neg B \qquad \neg(A \wedge B) \equiv_{def} \neg A \vee \neg B \qquad \neg \neg A \equiv_{def} A$$
$$\neg \square A \equiv_{def} \Diamond \neg A \qquad \neg \Diamond A \equiv_{def} \square \neg A \qquad \neg \bigcirc A \equiv_{def} \bigcirc \neg A$$

For our aims, a non standard way of describing the semantics of LTL is more convenient. It makes use of *labelled formulae*, i.e. expressions of the form $n : A$ where $n \in \mathbb{N}$ and A is an LTL-formula. If ℓ is a literal, then $n : \ell$ is a labelled literal. A set S of labelled literals is consistent if it does not contain both $n : p$ and $n : \neg p$ for any $n \in \mathbb{N}$ and $p \in \mathbb{P}$. It is complete if for all $n \in \mathbb{N}$ and all $p \in \mathbb{P}$, either $n : p \in S$ or $n : \neg p \in S$.

A temporal interpretation $\mathcal{M}$ is a consistent and complete set of labelled literals. If $\mathcal{M}$ is an interpretation of $\mathbb{P}$, $n \in \mathbb{N}$ and A is a formula, the relation $\mathcal{M} \models n : A$ corresponds to the usual satisfiability relation $\mathcal{M}_n \models A$ (the n-th state of $\mathcal{M}$ satisfies A) and is recursively defined as follows:

1. $\mathcal{M} \models n : \ell$ iff $n : \ell \in \mathcal{M}$, when ℓ is a literal;
2. $\mathcal{M} \models n : A \wedge B$ iff $\mathcal{M} \models n : A$ and $\mathcal{M} \models n : B$;
3. $\mathcal{M} \models n : A \vee B$ iff either $\mathcal{M} \models n : A$ or $\mathcal{M} \models n : B$;
4. $\mathcal{M} \models n : \bigcirc A$ iff $\mathcal{M} \models n + 1 : A$;

5. $\mathcal{M} \models n : \Box A$ iff for all $k \geq n$, $\mathcal{M} \models k : A$;
6. $\mathcal{M} \models n : \Diamond A$ iff for some $k \geq n$, $\mathcal{M} \models k : A$.

An LTL-formula A is true in $\mathcal{M}$ (and $\mathcal{M}$ is a model of A) iff $\mathcal{M} \models 0 : A$. If Σ is a set of formulae, $\mathcal{M} \models \Sigma$ iff $\mathcal{M} \models A$ for all $A \in \Sigma$. From now on, a set Σ of LTL-formulae is considered equivalent to $\{0 : A \mid A \in \Sigma\}$.

The rest of this section introduces the notion of conditioned model and its main desirable properties.

Definition 1. *If S is a set of labelled formulae, the* history of S up to n, $h(S, n)$, *is*

$$\{k : \ell \mid k : \ell \in S, \ \ell \text{ is a literal, and } k \leq n\}$$

Let S_0 be a set of formulae representing a planning problem, according to the method proposed in [2] (but for the fact that incomplete information is allowed). In particular, we assume that the agent's tasks and goals are represented by formulae of the form $\Diamond G$, where G is classical (the approach can easily be extended to nested goals, assuming only that G does not contain any occurrence of the $\Box$ operator). If $\mathcal{M}$ is a model of S_0, we are interested in extracting a set of conditions ensuring the executability of the plan represented by $\mathcal{M}$, to solve the problem represented by S_0. In other words, we want to "explain" the executability of $\mathcal{M}$. In general, however, it is not the whole model $\mathcal{M}$ that has to be explained, but only a finite fragment of the model, up to the achievement of the goals. The following definitions formalize this concept.

Definition 2. *Let S_0 be a set of labelled formulae, $\mathcal{M}$ a model of S_0, $S \subseteq \mathcal{M}$ and $U \subseteq S$. Then U is a (sufficient) set of conditions* explaining S in the context of S_0 *(briefly, U explains S in S_0) iff*

for all $n : \ell \in S - U$: $S_0, h(U, n - 1) \models n : \ell$.

The condition above amounts to saying that, for all $n : \ell \in S - U$ and for every model $\mathcal{M}'$ of S_0, if $\mathcal{M}'$ is also a model of the subset $h(U, n - 1)$ of the history of U up to $n - 1$, then $\mathcal{M}' \models n : \ell$, too. In informal terms, $h(U, n)$ "explains", in the context of S_0, all that happens, according to S, up to the n-th state. If S implies that the goals are achieved before the n-th step, then $h(U, n - 1)$ actually guarantees the achievement of the goals.

Definition 3. *Let S_0 be a set of labelled formulae representing a planning problem. A* conditioned model *of S_0 is a pair $\langle S, U \rangle$, where $S \subseteq \mathcal{M}$ for some model $\mathcal{M}$ of S_0, U explains S in S_0 and S satisfies the goals in S_0, i.e. for all $0 : \Diamond G \in S_0$, $S \models n : G$ for some n.*

A conditioned plan solving the problem encoded by Σ can be extracted from the set U of conditions of a conditioned model of Σ, by dropping negative literals representing actions and splitting the rest of U into the set of atoms representing actions and the fluents (conditions guaranteeing the executability of the plan).

For instance, let us consider the set Σ_1 of Section 1, and the following subset S of one of its models:

$$S = \{\, 0 : open, \; 0 : do\_pass, \; 0 : \neg do\_open, \; 0 : \neg in,$$
$$1 : \neg open, \; 1 : \neg do\_pass, \; 1 : do\_open, \; 1 : in,$$
$$2 : open, \; 2 : do\_pass, \; 2 : \neg do\_open, \; 2 : in,$$
$$3 : open, \; 3 : \neg do\_pass, \; 3 : \neg do\_open, \; 3 : \neg in\}$$

S implies that all the goals are achieved at the third state. The set:

$$U = \{\, 0 : open, \; 0 : do\_pass, \; 0 : \neg do\_open$$
$$1 : \neg open, \; 1 : \neg do\_pass, \; 1 : do\_open,$$
$$2 : do\_pass, \; 2 : \neg do\_open,$$
$$3 : open, \; 3 : \neg do\_pass, \; 3 : \neg do\_open\}$$

is a set explaining S in Σ_1. In fact:

$$S - U = \{0 : \neg in, \; 1 : in, \; 2 : open, \; 2 : in, \; 3 : \neg in\}$$
$$h(U, -1) = \varnothing$$
$$h(U, 0) = \{0 : open, \; 0 : do\_pass, \; 0 : \neg do\_open\}$$
$$h(U, 1) = h(U, 0) \cup \{1 : \neg open, \; 1 : \neg do\_pass, \; 1 : do\_open\}$$
$$h(U, 2) = h(U, 1) \cup \{do\_pass, \; 2 : \neg do\_open\}$$

and

$$\Sigma_1 \models 0 : \neg in \qquad\qquad \Sigma_1, \; h(U, 1) \models 2 : in$$
$$\Sigma_1, \; h(U, 0) \models 1 : in \qquad\qquad \Sigma_1, \; h(U, 2) \models 3 : \neg in$$
$$\Sigma_1, \; h(U, 1) \models 2 : open$$

Omitting the negative "action" literals, U can be read as saying:

IF $0 : open$, $0 : do\_pass$, $1 : \neg open$, $1 : do\_open$, and $2 : do\_pass$,
THEN the goal is achieved.

The conditioned plan that is extracted from U is then:

$\langle 0 : do\_pass, \; 1 : do\_open, \; 2 : do\_pass \rangle$ if $\{0 : open, \; 1 : \neg open\}$

Obviously, if $U = S$, then $\langle S, U \rangle$ is trivially a conditioned model of Σ. So, we are interested in finding "non trivial" sets of conditions. This issue is addressed in Section 4.

3   Conditional Tableaux

This section introduces a tableau system that, given a set Σ of satisfiable LTL-formulae, allows one to compute a conditioned model of Σ. The calculus is mainly a labelled version of the standard tableau system for LTL [16]. Moreover, to each labelled formula is associated a set of "conditions" C, in such a way that, when a non empty set C is associated to $n : \ell$, then $n : \ell$ is included in the set of conditions to be computed.

Tableau nodes are *conditioned labelled formulae* (cl-formulae), i.e. expressions of the form $n : A$ *if* C, where $n : A$ is a labelled formula and C is a set of labelled formulae (parentheses will sometimes enclose cl-formulae to enhance readability).

A cl-formula $n : A$ *if* $\emptyset$ is abbreviated by $n : A$. If Σ is a set of LTL-formulae, the initial tableau for Σ is the one-branch tableau whose nodes are $0 : A$ for all $A \in \Sigma$.

The next definition introduces some useful notions.

Definition 4.

1. If K is a tableau branch, then

$$forms(K) = \{n : A \mid (n : A \text{ if } C) \in K \text{ for some } C\}$$

2. The notion of history is generalized to sets K of cl-formulae as follows:

$$h(K, n) = \{k : \ell \mid k : \ell \in forms(K), \ \ell \text{ is a literal, and } k \leq n\}$$

$$\frac{n : A \wedge B \text{ if } C}{\begin{array}{l} n : A \text{ if } C \\ n : B \text{ if } C \end{array}} \ (\alpha)$$

$$\frac{n : A \vee B \text{ if } C}{n : A \text{ if } C \cup \{n : \neg B\} \qquad n : B \text{ if } C \cup \{n : \neg A\}} \ (\beta)$$

$$\frac{n : \Box A \text{ if } C}{\begin{array}{l} n : A \text{ if } C \\ n : \bigcirc\Box A \text{ if } C \end{array}} \ (\nu)$$

$$\frac{n : \Diamond A \text{ if } C}{n : A \text{ if } \{n : A\} \cup C \qquad n : \bigcirc\Diamond A \text{ if } \{n : \neg A\} \cup C} \ (\pi)$$

$$\begin{array}{l} \vdots \ (K) \\ \dfrac{n : \bigcirc A \text{ if } C}{n+1 : A \text{ if } C'} \ (\bigcirc) \qquad \text{where } C' = \emptyset \text{ if } h(K, n) \models C, \\ \qquad\qquad\qquad\qquad \text{ otherwise } C' = C. \end{array}$$

Fig. 1. The conditional tableaux expansion rules

Tableaux are expanded by means of the rules displayed in Figure 1. In the $\bigcirc$-rule, K is the branch being expanded. Note that the call to a theorem prover for LTL required by such a rule can be expected to face a quite simple problem, since $h(K, n)$ is a set of cl-literals.

Next we define when a branch is complete and when it is closed, what is the set $U(K)$ extracted from a branch, and the temporal interpretation represented by a branch.

Definition 5. *Let K be a tableau branch.*

1. *K is completely expanded at n (or n-complete) iff every non-literal formula labelled with $k \leq n$ in K has been expanded.*
2. *K is looping if there are m, p with $p > 0$ such that K is completely expanded at $m + p$ and*

$$\{A \mid m : \bigcirc A \in forms(K)\} = \{A \mid m + p : \bigcirc A \in forms(K)\}$$

   Then K is said to be "periodic" with starting index $m + 1$ and period p.
3. *K is complete if it is either looping or n-complete for all n.*
4. *K contains an unsatisfied eventuality if $n : \Diamond A \in forms(K)$ and:*
   a) *either K is p-complete for all p or periodic with starting index $m \geq n$, and $k : A \notin forms(K)$ for all $k \geq n$;*
   b) *or K is periodic with starting index $m < n$ and period p, and $k : A \notin forms(K)$ for all k such that $m \leq k \leq m + p$.*
5. *K is closed if one of the following conditions holds:*
   a) *$forms(K)$ contains a formula $n : A$ and its negation $n : \neg A$.*
   b) *K is complete and it contains some unsatisfied eventuality.*
6. *$lits(K) = \{n : \ell \mid \ell$ is a literal and $n : \ell \in forms(K)\}$*
7. *$U(K) = \{n : \ell \mid \ell$ is a literal, $n : \ell \notin K$ and $(n : \ell$ if $C) \in K$ for some $C \neq \emptyset\}$*
8. *$unfold(K)$ is the model (rather, the set of models) represented by K:*

$$unfold(K) = \begin{cases} lits(K) & \text{if } K \text{ is not a looping branch} \\ lits(K) \cup \{k + p + i : \ell \mid k + i : \ell \in lits(K), i \in \mathbb{N}\} \\ \quad \text{if } K \text{ is periodic with starting index } k \\ \quad \text{and period } p \end{cases}$$

9. *A tableau is complete iff all its branches are complete. It is closed iff all its branches are closed.*

If K is a complete and open branch in a tableau for K_0, then $unfold(K)$ represents a model of K_0 (see Theorem 1 below) and $U(K)$ is the set of conditions explaining $lits(K)$ in the context of K_0 (Theorem 2). As an example, consider the following set of sentences, representing a simplified planning problem:

$$\Sigma = \{ \neg in, \ do\_pass \rightarrow open, \ \bigcirc in \equiv do\_pass, \ \Diamond in \}$$

A branch in a tableau for such a set of sentences shown in Figure 2, where the order in which the nodes are expanded is displayed on the right. The cl-literals in the branch are

$$\{0 : \neg in, \ 0 : open \text{ if } \{0 : do\_pass\}, \ 0 : do\_pass \text{ if } \{0 : \bigcirc in\}, \\ 1 : in, \ 1 : in \text{ if } \{1 : in\}\}$$

and $U(K) = \{0 : open, \ 0 : do\_pass\}$.

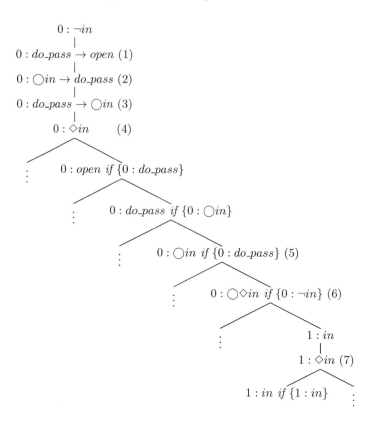

Fig. 2. A branch in a tableau for $\{\neg in, do\_pass \rightarrow open, \bigcirc in \equiv do\_pass, \Diamond in\}$

3.1   Properties of the Calculus

The semantics of cl-formulae just ignores the "conditional" part:

$$\mathcal{M} \models (n : A \text{ if } C) \quad \text{iff} \quad \mathcal{M} \models n : A$$

The other basic semantical notions are extended to cl-formulae in the obvious way.

It can easily be recognized that, if the C-parts of the tableau nodes are ignored, the calculus is a labelled version of the standard tableau calculus for LTL [16]: the time point at which a given formula is assumed to hold is identified by its numerical label, instead of its "context", i.e. the whole set of formulae labelling a tableau node. From this equivalence it follows that:

Theorem 1. *If $\mathcal{M} \models \Sigma$ then there is a branch K in any tableau for Σ such that $\mathcal{M} \models K$, hence in particular $lits(K) \subseteq \mathcal{M}$. Vice-versa, every complete and open branch K in a tableau for Σ represents a model of Σ: i.e. for all $\mathcal{M}$, if $unfold(K) \subseteq \mathcal{M}$, then $\mathcal{M} \models \Sigma$.*

As a consequence, the calculus is sound and complete in the standard sense. The main concern of this work consists however in showing that $U(K)$ is a set of conditions explaining $lits(K)$ in the context of the initial tableau. The next theorem states in fact that $U(K)$ is large enough.

Theorem 2. *Let K be a complete and open branch in a tableau for K_0. Then $\langle lits(K), U(K) \rangle$ is a conditioned model of K_0.*

Proof. By Theorem 1, $unfold(K) \models K_0$, therefore $lits(K)$ is a subset of a model of K_0. The fact that, for all labelled literal $n : \ell \in K - U(K)$:

$$K_0, h(U(K), n - 1) \models n : \ell$$

is proved by showing that, if $n : A$ *if* C is a node in a branch K of a tableau initialized with K_0, then

$$K_0, h(U(K), n - 1), C \models n : A$$

The latter assertion can easily be proved by induction on tableaux.

Finally, let $0 : \Diamond G$ be a goal in K_0. Since K does not contain any unsatisfied eventuality, $n : G \in forms(K)$ for some $n \geq 0$, and, since K is complete and G is classical, $lits(K) \models n : G$. Therefore $lits(K)$ satisfies all the goals in K_0.

Assuming that the $\bigcirc$-rule is never applied to a formula $n : \bigcirc A$ before another rule is applied to any formula labelled by n, it can be shown that if $(n : \ell$ *if* $C) \in K$, where K is a tableau branch, and $h(U(K), n - 1) \models C$, then $n : \ell \notin U(K)$. However, if K is any complete and open branch in a tableau initialized with K_0, then $U(K)$ is not necessarily a minimal set of conditions explaining $lits(K)$ in the context of K_0, i.e. a minimal subset X of $lits(K)$ such that for all $n : \ell \in lits(K) - X$, $K_0, h(X, n - 1) \models n : \ell$. It may even happen that some $n : \ell$ belongs to $U(K)$, for some complete and open branch K in a tableau initialized with K_0, even if $K_0 \models n : \ell$. Consider for instance $K_0 = \{0 : A \lor B, 0 : A \to p, 0 : B \to p\}$. Clearly, $K_0 \models 0 : p$, although $0 : p$ occurs "conditioned" in any branch in a tableau for K_0. Figure 3 shows a branch in a tableau for K_0.

4   Minimality

Let S_0 be a set of labelled formulae, and $\langle S, U \rangle$ a conditioned model of S_0. Then U is a minimal set of conditions explaining S in the context of S_0 iff no proper subset of U explains S in S_0.

Consider for instance the set Σ of Section 3 (page 77) and the corresponding set of labelled formulae:

$$S_0 = \{\, 0 : \neg in,\ 0 : do\_pass \to open,\ 0 : \bigcirc in \equiv do\_pass,\ 0 : \Diamond in \,\}$$

Let S be the following subset of a model of S_0:

$$S = \{0 : \neg in,\ 0 : open,\ 0 : do\_pass,\ 1 : in\}$$

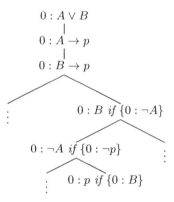

Fig. 3. A branch in a conditional tableau for $\{A \vee B,\ A \rightarrow p,\ B \rightarrow p\}$

A minimal set X such that for all $n : \ell \in S - X$: $S_0, h(X, n - 1) \models n : \ell$ is $X = \{0 : do\_pass,\ 0 : open\}$ (X represents the conditioned plan "IF $0 : open$ THEN $0 : do\_pass$"). In fact $S - X = \{0 : \neg in,\ 1 : in\}$ and

$$S_0 \models 0 : \neg in$$
$$S_0,\ 0 : do\_pass,\ 0 : open \models 1 : in$$

And no subset of X explains S in S_0. In fact, $S_0 \not\models 0 : open$ and $S_0 \not\models 0 : do\_pass$, so that both $0 : open$ and $0 : do\_pass$ must be in X.

Note that the notion of "minimal explanation" adopted here is different from the corresponding notion used in abductive reasoning. In that context, X would not be considered "minimal", since $S_0,\ 0 : do\_pass \models 0 : open$.

The following result shows that minimality of a set U of conditions is equivalent to a property that can be checked "locally", i.e. without considering all the proper subsets of U.

Lemma 1. *If $\langle S, U \rangle$ is a conditioned model of S_0, then U is minimal if and only if for all $n : \ell \in U$: $S_0, h(U, n - 1) \not\models n : \ell$.*

Proof. In fact, let us assume that U is not minimal, i.e. for some $n : \ell \in U$ $X = U - \{n : \ell\}$ explains S in S_0. Since $n : \ell \notin X$, $S_0, h(X, n - 1) \models n : \ell$. Therefore also $S_0, h(U, n - 1) \models n : \ell$ (since $X \subset U$).

Vice versa: let us assume that for some $n : \ell \in U$, $S_0, h(U, n - 1) \models n : \ell$. Consider $X = U - \{n : \ell\}$ and any $k : \ell' \in S - X$. If $k = n$ and $\ell' = \ell$, then $S_0, h(X, k - 1) \models k : \ell'$ by hypothesis. Otherwise, $k : \ell' \in S - U$, therefore $S_0, h(U, k - 1) \models k : \ell'$. Since $S_0, h(U, k - 1) \models n : \ell$, then also $S_0, h(U, k - 1) - \{n : \ell\} \models k : \ell'$, i.e. $S_0, h(X, k - 1) \models k : \ell'$. Therefore U is not minimal.

By Theorem 1, minimality of $U(K)$ can be obtained if the following "simplification rule" is added to the calculus:

$$\begin{array}{c} \vdots \ (K) \\ \hline n : \ell \ if \ C \\ \hline n : \ell \end{array} \qquad \begin{array}{l} \text{if } K_0, h(K, n-1) \models n : \ell, \\ \text{where } K_0 \text{ is the initial tableau} \end{array}$$

However, the recursive call to the theorem prover required by this rule would be quite expensive.

Here we present an alternative method, consisting in filtering $U(K)$ with information obtained by a global view on the tableau. Intuitively, in order to check whether $K_0, h(K, n-1) \models n : \ell$, the tableau for K_0 that is being built is exploited.

The next definition introduces a subset of $U(K)$ which can be proved to be minimal.

Definition 6. *Let $\mathcal{T}$ be a tableau for K_0 and K a complete and open branch in $\mathcal{T}$. Then*

$$U^*(K) = U(K) - \{n : \ell \mid \text{ for all branches } K_i \text{ in } \mathcal{T}, \ K_i, h(K, n-1) \models n : \ell\}$$

Remark 1. If $n : \ell \in U(K) - U^*(K)$, then $K_0, h(K, n-1) \models n : \ell$. In fact, let us assume (by contraposition) that $K_0, h(K, n-1) \not\models n : \ell$, for some $n : \ell \in U(K)$, and $\mathcal{M}$ is a model of $K_0 \cup h(K, n-1) \cup \{n : \neg\ell\}$. By Theorem 1, there is a branch K_i in $\mathcal{T}$ such that $\mathcal{M} \models K_i$, and consequently $K_i, h(K, n-1) \not\models n : \ell$, i.e. $n : \ell \in U^*(K)$.

We note, first of all, that, in the context of K_0, $h(K, n)$ and $h(U^*(K), n)$ are equivalent:

Lemma 2. *If K is a complete and open branch in a tableau for K_0, then for all $n : \ell \in lits(K)$, $K_0, h(U^*(K), n) \models n : \ell$.*

Proof. By Theorem 2, $lits(K)$ and $U(K)$ are equivalent in the context of K_0, i.e. for all $n : \ell \in lits(K)$, $K_0, h(U(K), n) \models n : \ell$. Therefore, it suffices to show that, in the context of K_0, $U(K)$ and $U^*(K)$ are equivalent, i.e. that for all $n : \ell \in U(K)$, $K_0, h(U^*(K), n) \models n : \ell$. If $n : \ell \in U^*(K)$, trivially $K_0, h(U^*(K), n) \models n : \ell$. Let us assume then that $n : \ell \in U(K)$ and $n : \ell \notin U^*(K)$, i.e. for all branches K_i in $\mathcal{T}$, $K_i, h(K, n-1) \models n : \ell$. We prove that $K_0, h(U^*(K), n) \models n : \ell$ by induction on n.

1. If $n = 0$ and $K_i \models 0 : \ell$ for all branches K_i in $\mathcal{T}$, then $K_0 \models 0 : \ell$ by Remark 1, since $h(K, n-1) = \emptyset$.
2. If $n > 0$, let us assume (inductive hypothesis) that for all $k < n$ and $k : \ell \in U(K)$, $K_0, h(U^*(K), k) \models k : \ell$, i.e. if $k < n$ then $U(K)$ and $U^*(K)$ are equivalent in the context of K_0. Since, by hypothesis, for all branches K_i in $\mathcal{T}$, $K_i, h(K, n-1) \models n : \ell$, by Remark 1 $K_0, h(K, n-1) \models n : \ell$. By Theorem 2, $K_0, h(U(K), n-1) \models n : \ell$; by the inductive hypothesis, $K_0, h(U^*(K), n-1) \models n : \ell$, since $n-1 < n$, and then also $K_0, h(U^*(K), n) \models n : \ell$.

The next theorem establishes that $U^*(K)$ indeed explains $lits(K)$ in K_0, i.e. that $U^*(K)$ is still "large enough".

Theorem 3. *Let $\mathcal{T}$ be a complete tableau for K_0 and K an open branch in $\mathcal{T}$. Then for all $n : \ell \in K - U^*(K)$, $K_0, h(U^*(K), n - 1) \models n : \ell$.*

Proof. Exploiting Lemma 2, it is sufficient to prove that for all $n : \ell \in K - U^*(K)$: $K_0, h(K, n - 1) \models n : \ell$. If $n : \ell \in K - U(K)$, this follows from Theorem 2. If $n : \ell \in U(K) - U^*(K)$, then $K_0, h(K, n - 1) \models n : \ell$ follows from Remark 1.

Finally, we prove that $U^*(K)$ is minimal:

Theorem 4. *Let $\mathcal{T}$ be a tableau for K_0 and K a complete and open branch in $\mathcal{T}$. Then $U^*(K)$ is a minimal set of conditions for $lits(K)$ in K_0, i.e. for all $n : \ell \in U^*(K)$, $K_0, h(U^*(K), n - 1) \not\models n : \ell$.*

Proof. We show that if $K_0, h(U^*(K), n - 1) \models n : \ell$, then $n : \ell \notin U^*(K)$. Let us assume that $K_0, h(U^*(K), n - 1) \models n : \ell$, hence also $(\star)$ $K_0, h(K, n - 1) \models n : \ell$. If $n : \ell \notin U(K)$, then also $n : \ell \notin U^*(K)$. So, it is sufficient to show that if $n : \ell \in U(K)$ then for any branch K_i in the tableau, $K_i, h(K, n - 1) \models n : \ell$. Let us assume, by absurd, that for some branch K_i and some interpretation $\mathcal{M}$, $\mathcal{M} \models K_i \cup h(K, n - 1) \cup \{n : \neg\ell\}$. Since trivially a model of any branch of the tableau is also a model of a sub-branch, $\mathcal{M} \models K_0 \cup h(K, n - 1) \cup \{n : \neg\ell\}$, contradicting $(\star)$.

Computing a minimal set of conditions explaining $lits(K)$ in K_0 is necessarily more expensive than computing a non-necessarily minimal one. A way how this can be achieved is the following: after having built a complete and open branch K and computed $U(K)$, all the other open branches $K_1, ..., K_m$ are considered. For each n such that a literal $n : \ell$ belongs to $U(K)$, $h(K, n - 1)$ is added to K_i, for all $i = 1, ..., m$, and the branches obtained in that way are (possibly) expanded further to obtain complete ones. If $n : \ell$ occurs in all the open branches obtained in this way, then $n : \ell$ is eliminated from $U(K)$. In fact, obviously, $K_i, h(K, n - 1) \models n : \ell$ if and only iff $n : \ell$ occurs in all the open branches in a tableau for $K_i \cup h(K, n - 1)$. This method can be applied in an incremental fashion, considering in turn all the literals labelled by 0, then the literals labelled by 1, and so on. In such a way, the recursive calls to the theorem prover exploit the work already done sofar.

5   Concluding Remarks

In this work we have defined the notion of conditioned model of a set of formulae Σ, that consists of a partial description S of a model of Σ together with a set U of conditions guaranteeing the "executability" of S. Moreover, we propose an extension of the standard tableau calculus for LTL so that a conditioned model of a set Σ of formulae can be extracted from any complete and open branch of a tableau for Σ. As can be expected, the set U of conditions extracted from the analysis of a single branch is not necessarily minimal. In order to prune U from redundant conditions, the whole tableau must be built and each of its open branches possibly expanded further.

When not only a single conditioned plan is looked for, but a whole set of complementary ones, the construction of a single tableau branch is not sufficient in any case. We notice, in this respect, that the theorem prover `ptl` [5] used by the planning system described in [2] (and whose comparison with other existing planning systems has given encouraging results) builds the whole graph representing a tableau, before a single branch is analysed in order to extract a model. Conditional planning can therefore be accomplished by means of a non-substantial modification of the algorithm underlying `ptl`.

As a further remark, we observe that the requirement for minimality can reasonably be relaxed when a single conditioned model is to be used because planning and execution (with sensing actions) are intermingled. On the other hand, some preliminary experiments with a simple prototype, implementing the system described in this work, have always produced a minimal set $U(K)$ explaining $lits(K)$ in the context of the initial set of formulae.

Note, finally, that the same machinery can deal with *conformant planning* [15], i.e. the search for non-conditional plans succeeding no matter which of the allowed states the world is actually in. A conformant plan in fact corresponds to a conditioned plan with empty conditions.

Directions for future work include:

- the definition of a calculus aiming at producing *finite* temporal models of the initial set of formulae, in view of the fact that a plan consists of a finite sequence of actions. The calculus would be simplified in this case by the absence of open looping branches (by Lemma 4.5 in [14], such models can be discarded). Possibly, also the computation of a minimal set of conditions is simplified.
- The study of reasonable rules acting on the C-part of cl-formulae and allowing one to restrict the set of conditions associated with a branch.
- The analysis of the syntactical form of the encoding of planning problems, and its possible relations with minimality.

Acknowledgements. The authors thank the anonymous referees of this work for their precious comments and suggestions.

References

1. S. Cerrito and M. Cialdea Mayer. Using linear temporal logic to model and solve planning problems. In F. Giunghiglia, editor, *Proceedings of the 8th International Conference on Artificial Intelligence: Methodology, Systems, Applications (AIMSA'98)*, pages 141–152. Springer, 1998.
2. M. Cialdea Mayer, A. Orlandini, G. Balestreri, and C. Limongelli. A planner fully based on linear time logic. In S. Chien, S. Kambhampati, and C.A. Knoblock, editors, *Proc. of the 5th Int. Conf. on Artificial Intelligence Planning and Scheduling (AIPS-2000)*, pages 347–354. AAAI Press, 2000.

3. A. Cimatti, M. Roveri, and P. Traverso. Strong planning in non-deterministic domains via model checking. In *Proc. of the International Conference on AI Planning and Scheduling (AIPS'98)*. AAAI Press, 1998.

4. A. Finzi, F. Pirri, and R. Reiter. Open world planning in the Situation Calculus. In *Proceedings of the 7th Conference on Artificial Intelligence (AAAI-00) and of the 12th Conference on Innovative Applications of Artificial Intelligence (IAAI-00)*, pages 754–760. AAAI Press, 2000.

5. G. L. J. M. Janssen. *Logics for Digital Circuit Verification. Theory, Algorithms and Applications*. CIP-DATA Library Technische Universiteit Eindhoven, 1999.

6. H. Kautz and B. Selman. Planning as satisfiability. In B. Neumann, editor, *10th European Conference on Artificial Intelligence (ECAI)*, pages 360–363. Wiley & Sons, 1992.

7. H. Kautz and B. Selman. Pushing the envelope: Planning, propositional logic, and stochastic search. In *Proc. of the 13th National Conference on Artificial Intelligence (AAAI-96)*, pages 1202–1207. AAAI Press / The MIT Press, 1996.

8. H. Levesque. What is planning in the presence of sensing? In *Proc. of the 13th National Conference on Artificial Intelligence, AAAI-96*, pages 1139–1146. AAAI Press, 1996.

9. M. A. Peot and D. E. Smith. Conditional nonlinear planning. In J. Hendler, editor, *Proc. of the First International Conference on Artificial Intelligence Planning Systems*, pages 189–197. Morgan Kaufmann, 1992.

10. M. Pistore and P. Traverso. Planning as model checking for extended goals in non-deterministic domains. In *Proc. IJCAI'01*. AAAI Press, 2001.

11. L. Pryor and G. Collins. Planning for contingencies: a decision-based approach. *Journal of Artificial Intelligence Research*, 4:287–339, 1996.

12. R. Reiter. The frame problem in the situation calculus: A simple solution (sometimes) and a completeness result for goal regression. In V. Lifschitz, editor, *Artificial Intelligence and mathematical theory of computation: Papers in honor of John McCarthy*, pages 359–380. Academic Press, 1991.

13. J. Rintanen. Constructing conditional plans by a theorem-prover. *Journal of Artificial Intellingence Research*, 10, 1999.

14. A. P. Sistla and E. M. Clarke. The complexity of propositional linear temporal logics. *Journal of the ACM*, 32(3):733–749, 1985.

15. D. E. Smith and D. S. Weld. Conformant Graphplan. In *Proc. of the 15th National Conference on Artificial Intelligence (AAAI-98)*, pages 889–896, 1998.

16. P. Wolper. The tableau method for temporal logic: an overview. *Logique et Analyse*, 28:119–152, 1985.

A Simplified Clausal Resolution Procedure for Propositional Linear-Time Temporal Logic*

Anatoli Degtyarev, Michael Fisher, and Boris Konev**

Logic and Computation Group, Department of Computer Science
University of Liverpool, Liverpool L69 7ZF, UK
{A.Degtyarev,M.Fisher,B.Konev}@csc.liv.ac.uk

Abstract. The clausal resolution method for propositional linear-time temporal logics is well known and provides the basis for a number of temporal provers. The method is based on an intuitive clausal form, called SNF, comprising three main clause types and a small number of resolution rules. In this paper, we show how the normal form can be radically simplified and, consequently, how a simplified clausal resolution method can be defined for this important variety of logic.

1 Introduction

As computational systems become more complex, it is increasingly important to be able to *verify* that the system behaves as required. While a computational system can be tested in many ways, it is only through *formal* verification that we have the possibility of establishing the correctness of the system in *all* possible situations. However, complex systems in turn require powerful formal notations, in particular logics such as *temporal logic*. Temporal logics are extensions of classical logic, with operators that deal with time. They have been used in a wide variety of areas within Computer Science and Artificial Intelligence, for example robotics [17], databases [18], hardware verification [10] and agent based systems [16]. In particular, propositional temporal logics have already made significant impact within Computer Science, having been applied to:

- the specification and verification of distributed or concurrent systems [14];
- the synthesis of programs from temporal specifications [15,13];
- the semantics of executable temporal logic [9];
- algorithmic verification via model-checking [10,2]; and
- knowledge representation and reasoning [6,1,20].

In developing such techniques, temporal proof is often required, and we base our work on practical proof techniques on the clausal resolution approach to temporal logic. The clausal resolution method for propositional linear-time temporal logics provides the basis for a number of temporal provers. The method is based on an intuitive clausal form, called SNF, comprising three main clause types and a small number of resolution rules [7]. While the approach has been shown to be competitive [11,12], we here re-address the

---

* Work supported by both EPSRC (grant GR/L87491) and the University of Liverpool (RDF).
** On leave from Steklov Institute of Mathematics at St.Petersburg

U. Egly and C.G. Fermüller (Eds.): TABLEAUX 2002, LNAI 2381, pp. 85–99, 2002.

basic form of the resolution method. In particular, we here show that the normal form can be radically simplified and, following on from this, a simplified resolution method can be defined for this important variety of temporal logic. Thus, the main benefits of the reductions described in this paper are that they produce a temporal normal form that

- provides a cleaner separation between classical and temporal reasoning,
- ensures more streamlined use of simplified temporal resolvents (without the need for further transformation),
- is simpler, involving only one (unconditional) eventuality formula, and
- since there is only one eventuality, then no heuristics/strategy is needed for choosing which temporal formula to apply temporal resolution to.

It turns out that if a given problem contains only one conditional eventuality clause, then the simplified resolution can be applied immediately without any reductions. At the same time we show the necessity to reduce conditional eventuality clauses to unconditional ones if a problem contains more than one eventuality.

We believe that all of these factors, as well as simplifying the method itself, will have significant impact upon practical temporal resolution tools.

The structure of the paper is as follows. In §2, we provide an overview of the propositional temporal logic considered and the normal form used (see [7] for further details). We then proceed to describe and analyse two key reductions:

1. from *conditional* eventuality clauses to *unconditional* eventuality clauses (§4);
2. from *multiple* unconditional eventuality clauses to a *single* unconditional eventuality clause (§7).

These reductions not only radically simplify the normal form and the resolution calculus, but initial results indicate that they can improve the speed of practical resolution systems in certain cases.

The simplified clausal resolution procedure is given in §3 and §5. The case of one eventuality is considered in §6. The results of these sections refine those given in [3]; an extension of the simplified resolution calculus to fragments of first-order temporal logic has been considered in [4,5].

2   Preliminaries

We define the temporal logic we use based on the following symbols:

- atomic propositions $Prop = a, b, c \ldots, p, q, r \ldots$;
- Boolean operators $\neg, \wedge, \Rightarrow, \equiv, \vee$, **true** ('true'), **false** ('false');
- temporal operators   **start** ('at the initial moment of time'), $\square$ ('always in the future'), $\Diamond$ ('at sometime in the future'), $\bigcirc$ ('at the next moment'), $\mathcal{S}$ ('since', a past-time operator).

For the interpretation of the formulas in the logic, we use discrete structures $\mathfrak{M} = \langle S, I \rangle$ where $S = s_0, s_1, s_2, \ldots$ is a linearly ordered infinite sequence of states such that each state, s_i $(0 \le i)$, represents those elements of $Prop$ which are satisfied at the ith moment of time, and I is an interpretation function $Prop \to 2^S$. Below we define a relation '$\models$', which evaluates temporal formulas at an index $i \in \mathbb{N}$ in a model $\mathfrak{M}$ abbreviating with $\mathfrak{M}_I(p)$ a subset of S where p is true (we omit the standard definitions of the Boolean operators).

$$
\begin{array}{lll}
(\mathfrak{M}, i) \models p & \text{iff} & i \in \mathfrak{M}_I(p) \quad [\text{for } p \in Prop] \\
(\mathfrak{M}, i) \models \textbf{start} & \text{iff} & i = 0 \\
(\mathfrak{M}, i) \models \Box B & \text{iff} & \text{for each } j, \text{ if } i \le j \text{ then } (\mathfrak{M}, j) \models B \\
(\mathfrak{M}, i) \models \Diamond B & \text{iff} & \text{there exists } j \text{ such that } i \le j \text{ and } (\mathfrak{M}, j) \models B \\
(\mathfrak{M}, i) \models \bigcirc B & \text{iff} & (\mathfrak{M}, i+1) \models B \\
(\mathfrak{M}, i) \models A \mathcal{S} B & \text{iff} & \text{there exists a } k \in \mathbb{N}, \text{ such that } 0 \le k < i \text{ and } (\mathfrak{M}, k) \models B \\
& & \text{and, for all } j \in \mathbb{N}, \text{ if } k \le j < i \text{ then } (\mathfrak{M}, j) \models A
\end{array}
$$

Definition 1 (Satisfiability). *A formula R is satisfiable if, and only if, there exists a model $\mathfrak{M}$ such that $(\mathfrak{M}, 0) \models R$.*

Definition 2 (Validity). *A formula R is valid if, and only if, it is satisfiable in every possible model, i.e. for each $\mathfrak{M}$, $(\mathfrak{M}, 0) \models R$.*

Clausal temporal resolution, introduced in [8], operates on formulas in Separated Normal Form (SNF):

$$
\Box \bigwedge_i A_i,
$$

where each A_i is known as a *PLTL-clause* and must be one of the following forms with each particular k_a, k_b, l_c, l_d, and l representing a literal.

$$
\begin{array}{ll}
\textbf{start} \Rightarrow \bigvee_c l_c & \text{an } \textit{initial} \text{ PLTL-clause} \\
\bigwedge_a k_a \Rightarrow \bigcirc \bigvee_d l_d & \text{a } \textit{step} \text{ PLTL-clause} \\
\bigwedge_b k_b \Rightarrow \Diamond l & \text{a } \textit{eventuality (sometime)} \text{ PLTL-clause}
\end{array}
$$

(For convenience, the outer '$\Box$' and '$\wedge$' connectives are usually omitted.)
An eventuality PLTL-clause is called *unconditional* if it has the form $\Diamond l$.

   It is known [7] that a PLTL-formula is satisfiable if, and only if, a set of temporal clauses is satisfiable. When a temporal formula is translated into the SNF form (see [7] for full details), we essentially apply a set of the transformation rules based upon the renaming of complex expressions by new propositions and upon the substitution of temporal operators by their fixpoint definitions.

3   Temporal Resolution for the Unconditional Eventuality Case

We extend the notion of a PLTL-clause by allowing arbitrary Boolean combinations of propositions and giving a simplified normal form called *Divided Separated Normal Form (DSNF)*. Further, we consider unconditional eventuality PLTL-clauses only (and give a reduction to this case). We (ambiguously) refer to these new entities as *clauses*.

A *propositional temporal specification*, SP, is a triple consisting of:

1. an universal part, $\mathcal{U}$, given by a set of propositional formulas (clauses);
2. an initial part, $\mathcal{I}$, with the same form as the universal part; and
3. a step part, $\mathcal{S}$, given by a set of propositional step temporal clauses of the form:

$$P \Rightarrow \bigcirc Q \qquad (step \text{ clause}),$$

where P and Q are Boolean combinations of propositional symbols[1].

(To relate these new clauses with the old ones, we note that the initial part corresponds to initial PLTL-clauses, step part corresponds to step clauses, and any clause C from the universal part can be represented by the pair: **start** $\Rightarrow C$, **true** $\Rightarrow \bigcirc C$.)

An *unconditional eventuality temporal problem*, P, whose satisfiability we are interested in, consists of a temporal specification SP with

4. an eventuality part, $\mathcal{E}$, given by a set of unconditional eventuality clauses of the form $\Diamond l$, where l is a literal.

This combination is denoted $\mathsf{P} = \mathsf{SP} \cup \mathcal{E}$.

A literal l from an eventuality clause is called an *eventuality literal*. Step clauses will also be referred to as *step rules*. Without loss of generality, we can assume that there are no two different temporal step clauses with the same left-hand sides.

In what follows we will not distinguish between a finite set of formulas $\mathcal{X}$ and the conjunction $\bigwedge \mathcal{X}$ of formulas in it. To each unconditional eventuality temporal problem, we associate the formula

$$\mathcal{I} \wedge \Box \mathcal{U} \wedge \Box \mathcal{S} \wedge \Box \mathcal{E}.$$

When we talk about particular properties of temporal problems (e.g., satisfiability, validity, logical consequences etc) we mean properties of the associated formula. The similar agreement takes place for specifications.

The inference system we use consists of an (implicit) *merging operation*

$$\frac{P_1 \Rightarrow \bigcirc Q_1, \ldots, P_n \Rightarrow \bigcirc Q_n}{\bigwedge\limits_{j=1}^{n} P_i \Rightarrow \bigcirc \bigwedge\limits_{j=1}^{n} Q_i} \quad,$$

(whose result is a logical consequence of its premises) and the following inference rules[2]. Due to our understanding of the temporal problem, the premises and conclusion of the rules are (implicitly) closed under $\Box$ operator.

Let $A \Rightarrow \bigcirc B$, $A_i \Rightarrow \bigcirc B_i$ be merged step rules, $\mathcal{U}$ be the (current) universal part of the problem.

– *Step resolution rule w.r.t.* $\mathcal{U}$: $\quad \dfrac{A \Rightarrow \bigcirc B}{\neg A} \; (\bigcirc_{res}^{\mathcal{U}})$, where $\mathcal{U} \cup \{B\} \vdash \bot$.

---

[1] We could still restrict ourselves (e.g., for implementation purposes) to formulas in clausal form: $(p_1 \wedge p_2 \wedge \ldots \wedge p_k) \Rightarrow \bigcirc (q_1 \vee q_2 \vee \ldots \vee q_l)$.
[2] Note that, if the premises of the rules are given in clausal form, the result of applying these rules is a clause (or set of clauses for the sometime resolution rule).

- *Sometime resolution rule w.r.t. $\mathcal{U}$*

$$\frac{A_1 \Rightarrow \bigcirc B_1, \quad \ldots, \quad A_n \Rightarrow \bigcirc B_n \quad \Diamond l}{(\bigwedge_{i=1}^{n} \neg A_i)} \ (\Diamond_{res}^{\mathcal{U}}),$$

where $A_i \Rightarrow \bigcirc B_i$ are *merged* step rules such that the *loop* side conditions

$$\mathcal{U} \cup \{B_i, l\} \vdash \perp \quad \text{and} \quad \mathcal{U} \cup \{B_i, \bigwedge_{j=1}^{n} \neg A_j\} \vdash \perp \quad \text{for all} \quad i \in \{1, \ldots, n\}$$

are satisfied. (The side conditions imply validity of $\bigvee A_j \Rightarrow \square \bigcirc \neg l$. Indeed, $\bigvee A_j \Rightarrow \bigvee \bigcirc B_j \equiv \bigcirc \bigvee B_j \Rightarrow \bigcirc \neg l$ and $\bigvee A_j \Rightarrow \bigvee \bigcirc B_j \equiv \bigcirc \bigvee B_j \Rightarrow \bigcirc \bigvee A_j$; the formula $\bigvee A_j$ can be considered as an *invariant formula*.)
- *Sometime termination rule w.r.t. $\mathcal{U}$*
  The contradiction $\perp$ is derived and the derivation is (successfully) terminated if $\mathcal{U} \cup \{l\} \vdash \perp$, where l is an eventuality literal.
- *Initial termination rule w.r.t. $\mathcal{U}$*
  The contradiction $\perp$ is derived and the derivation is (successfully) terminated if $\mathcal{U} \cup \mathcal{I} \vdash \perp$.

Successful termination means that a given problem is unsatisfiable.

Note 1. All clauses generated by our inference rules are universal. Hence, the proof procedure does not change the Initial, Step and Eventuality parts of the temporal problem. As to the Universal part, it is extended step by step until one of termination rules is applied.

Note 2. The *sometime resolution rule* above can be thought of as two separate rules:

- *Induction rule w.r.t. $\mathcal{U}$*

$$\frac{A_1 \Rightarrow \bigcirc B_1, \quad \ldots, \quad A_n \Rightarrow \bigcirc B_n}{(\bigvee_{i=1}^{n} A_i) \Rightarrow \bigcirc \square \neg l} \ (ind^{\mathcal{U}}),$$

(with the same side conditions as the sometime resolution rule above).
- *Pure sometime resolution*[3]

$$\frac{(\bigvee_{i=1}^{n} A_i) \Rightarrow \bigcirc \square \neg l \quad \Diamond l}{\neg (\bigvee_{i=1}^{n} A_i)} \ (\Diamond_{res}).$$

---

[3] We could as well formulate this rule in a more "traditional" form, with $\bigcirc \Diamond l$ as the second premise of the rule. However, note that $\Phi \wedge \square \bigcirc \Diamond l$ is satisfiable if, and only if, $\Phi \wedge \square \Diamond l$ is satisfiable for any temporal formula Φ.

4 Reduction to the Unconditional Eventuality Case

Suppose we are interested in satisfiability of $\Phi \cup \{\Box(P \Rightarrow \Diamond q)\}$, where Φ is a set of propositional temporal formulas. Let us consider two clauses:

$$\Box((P \wedge \neg q) \Rightarrow waitforQ) \tag{1}$$

$$\Box((waitforQ \wedge \bigcirc\neg q) \Rightarrow \bigcirc waitforQ) \tag{2}$$

where $waitforQ$ is a new propositional symbol. The first clause is universal, the second is translated into a step clause $waitforQ \Rightarrow \bigcirc(q \vee waitforQ)$. Let us note that clauses (1) and (2) are logical consequences of a formula $\Box(q \equiv \neg waitforQ)$.

Theorem 1. $\Phi \cup \{\Box(P \Rightarrow \Diamond q)\}$ *is satisfiable if, and only if,* $\Phi \cup \{(1),(2)\} \cup \{\Box\Diamond\neg waitforQ\}$ *is satisfiable.*

Proof. ($\Rightarrow$)   Let $\mathfrak{M}$ be a model of $\Phi \cup \{\Box(P \Rightarrow \Diamond q)\}$. Let us extend this model by a new proposition $waitforQ$ such that, in the extended model, $\mathfrak{M}'$, formulas (1), (2) and $\Box\Diamond\neg waitforQ$ would be true. In order to define the truth value of $waitforQ$, in n-th moment, $n \in \mathbb{N}$, we consider two cases depending on whether $\mathfrak{M} \models \Box\Diamond P$ or $\mathfrak{M} \models \Diamond\Box\neg P$.

 – Assume $\mathfrak{M} \models \Box\Diamond P$. Together with $\Box(P \Rightarrow \Diamond q)$, this implies that $\mathfrak{M} \models \Box\Diamond q$. For every $n \in \mathbb{N}$ let us put

$$(\mathfrak{M}', n) \models \neg waitforQ \;\Leftrightarrow\; (\mathfrak{M}', n) \models q \qquad (\Leftrightarrow (\mathfrak{M}, n) \models q).$$

 – Assume $\mathfrak{M} \models \Diamond\Box\neg P$. There are two possibilities:
   • $\mathfrak{M} \models \Box\neg P$. In this case let us put $(\mathfrak{M}', n) \models \neg waitforQ$ for all $n \in \mathbb{N}$.
   • There exists $m \in \mathbb{N}$ such that $(\mathfrak{M}, m) \models P$ and, for all $n > m$, $(\mathfrak{M}, n) \models \neg P$. These conditions imply, in particular, that there is $k \geq m$ such that $(\mathfrak{M}, k) \models q$ if the formula is satisfiable. Now we define $waitforQ$ in $\mathfrak{M}'$ as follows:

$$\begin{array}{ll}(\mathfrak{M}', n) \models \neg waitforQ \;\Leftrightarrow\; (\mathfrak{M}', n) \models q & \text{if } n < k, \\ (\mathfrak{M}', n) \models \neg waitforQ & \text{if } n \geq k.\end{array}$$

It is easy to see that $\mathfrak{M}'$ is a required model.

($\Leftarrow$)   Let us show that $\Box(P \Rightarrow \Diamond q)$ is a logical consequence of $\Phi \cup \{(1),(2)\} \cup \{\Box\Diamond\neg waitforQ\}$.
Let $\mathfrak{M}'$ be a model of $\Phi \cup \{(1),(2)\} \cup \{\Box\Diamond\neg waitforQ\}$. By contradiction, suppose $\mathfrak{M}' \not\models \Box(P \Rightarrow \Diamond q)$, that is, $\mathfrak{M}' \models \Diamond(P \wedge \Box\neg q)$. Let $m \in \mathbb{N}$ be an index such that $(\mathfrak{M}', m) \models P$ and for all $n \geq m$, $(\mathfrak{M}', n) \models \neg q)$. Then from (1) and (2) we conclude that for all $n \geq m$ $(\mathfrak{M}', n) \models waitforQ)$ holds. However, this conclusion contradicts the formula $\Box\Diamond\neg waitforQ$ which is true in $\mathfrak{M}'$.

Lemma 1. *The growth in size of the problem following the reduction from a conditional to an unconditional eventuality temporal problem is linear in the number of conditional eventualities occurring in the given problem.*

Proof. Follows from the proof of Theorem 1.

Example 1. Consider the following set of formulas containing two eventuality literals:

$$1.\ a \wedge \neg l_1 \wedge \neg l_2$$
$$2.\ \Box(a \Rightarrow \bigcirc(\neg a \wedge (l_1 \vee l_2) \wedge (\neg l_1 \vee \neg l_2)))$$
$$3.\ \Box((\neg a \wedge l_1 \wedge \neg l_2) \Rightarrow \bigcirc(\neg a \wedge l_1 \wedge \neg l_2))$$
$$4.\ \Box((\neg a \wedge \neg l_1 \wedge l_2) \Rightarrow \bigcirc(\neg a \wedge \neg l_1 \wedge l_2))$$
$$5.\ \Box(a \Rightarrow \Diamond l_1)$$
$$6.\ \Box(a \Rightarrow \Diamond l_2)$$

We reduce it to an unconditional eventuality problem as given by Theorem 1.

$$\mathcal{I} = \big\{\, 1.\ a \wedge \neg l_1 \wedge \neg l_2 \,\big\}$$

$$\mathcal{U} = \left\{ \begin{array}{l} 9.\ a \wedge \neg l_1 \Rightarrow wl_1 \\ 10.\ a \wedge \neg l_2 \Rightarrow wl_2 \end{array} \right\} \quad \mathcal{S} = \left\{ \begin{array}{l} 2.\ a \Rightarrow \bigcirc(\neg a \wedge (l_1 \vee l_2) \wedge (\neg l_1 \vee \neg l_2)) \\ 3.\ (\neg a \wedge l_1 \wedge \neg l_2) \Rightarrow \bigcirc(\neg a \wedge l_1 \wedge \neg l_2) \\ 4.\ (\neg a \wedge \neg l_1 \wedge l_2) \Rightarrow \bigcirc(\neg a \wedge \neg l_1 \wedge l_2) \\ 7.\ wl_1 \Rightarrow \bigcirc(l_1 \vee wl_1) \\ 8.\ wl_2 \Rightarrow \bigcirc(l_2 \vee wl_2) \end{array} \right\}$$

$$\mathcal{E} = \left\{ \begin{array}{l} 11.\ \Diamond \neg wl_1 \\ 12.\ \Diamond \neg wl_2 \end{array} \right\}$$

The derivation given below involves the following merged step clauses:

$$13.\ (a \wedge wl_1 \wedge wl_2) \Rightarrow \bigcirc((\neg a \wedge \neg l_1 \wedge l_2 \wedge wl_1) \vee (\neg a \wedge l_1 \wedge \neg l_2 \wedge wl_2))$$
$$14.\ (\neg a \wedge l_1 \wedge \neg l_2 \wedge wl_2) \Rightarrow \bigcirc(\neg a \wedge l_1 \wedge \neg l_2 \wedge wl_2)$$
$$15.\ (\neg a \wedge \neg l_1 \wedge l_2 \wedge wl_1) \Rightarrow \bigcirc(\neg a \wedge \neg l_1 \wedge l_2 \wedge wl_1)$$

(Clause 13 is obtained by merging clauses 2, 7 and 8, clause 14 by merging 3 and 8, and clause 15 by merging 4 and 7.)

Clause 14 gives a loop for resolution with 12, and clause 15 gives a loop for resolution with 11 resulting in two new universal clauses:

$$16.\ a \vee \neg l_1 \vee l_2 \vee \neg wl_2 \qquad [\text{ sometime resolution 14 and 12 }]$$
$$17.\ a \vee l_1 \vee \neg l_2 \vee \neg wl_1 \qquad [\text{ sometime resolution 15 and 11 }]$$

Let $\mathcal{U}_1$ be $\mathcal{U} \cup \{16, 17\}$. Then the step resolution of 13 with respect to $\mathcal{U}_1$ can be applied:

$$18.\ \neg a \vee \neg wl_1 \vee \neg wl_2 \qquad [\text{ step resolution 13 w.r.t } \mathcal{U}_1]$$

Let $\mathcal{U}_2$ be $\mathcal{U}_1 \cup \{18\}$. Because $\mathcal{U}_2 \cup \mathcal{I} \vdash \perp$, the initial termination rule can be applied and the derivation is terminated. It follows that the given set of formulas is unsatisfiable.

5   Completeness of Simplified Resolution

From consideration of the models, it straightforwardly follows that:

Theorem 2 (soundness). *Temporal resolution rules preserve satisfiability.*

To show completeness of the simplified system we adapt the completeness proof of the original system [7] as follows.

Notation. We consider interpretations (or valuations) of a set of propositional symbols (or atoms) $\mathcal{L}$ as Boolean functions over $\mathcal{L}$, that is, functions $I: \mathcal{L} \to \{0, 1\}$. A proposition $p \in \mathcal{L}$ is called *true* in I if, and only if, $I(p) = 1$ and *false* otherwise. This notion of truth and falsehood is extended in the usual way to literals and formulas built over $\mathcal{L}$. If E is an atom, literal, or formula such that E is true in I, then we write $I \models E$, and we write $I \not\models E$ if E is false in I.

Definition 3 (behaviour graph). *Given a specification* $SP = < \mathcal{U}, \mathcal{I}, \mathcal{S} >$ *over a set of propositional symbols* $\mathcal{L}$*, we construct a finite directed graph G as follows. The nodes of G are interpretations of* $\mathcal{L}$*, and an interpretation, I, is a node of G if* $I \models \mathcal{U}$*.*

For each node, I, we construct an edge in G to a node I' if, and only if, the following condition is satisfied:

- *For every step rule* $(P \Rightarrow \bigcirc Q) \in \mathcal{S}$*, if* $I \models P$ *then* $I' \models Q$*.*

A node, I, is designated an initial node of G if $I \models \mathcal{I} \cup \mathcal{U}$*. The* behavior graph H *of* SP *is the maximal subgraph of G given by the set of all nodes reachable from initial nodes.*

It is easy to see the following relation between behavior graphs of two temporal problems when one of them is obtained by extending the universal part of the other.

Lemma 2. *Let* $SP_1 = < \mathcal{U}_1, \mathcal{I}, \mathcal{S} >$ *and* $SP_2 = < \mathcal{U}_2, \mathcal{I}, \mathcal{S} >$ *be two specifications over the same set of propositional symbols such that* $\mathcal{U}_1 \subseteq \mathcal{U}_2$*. Then the behavior graph* H_2 *of* SP_2 *is a subgraph of the behavior graph* H_1 *of* SP_1*.*

Proof. The graph H_2 is the maximal subgraph of H_1 given by the set of all nodes whose interpretations satisfy $\mathcal{U}_2$ and that are reachable from the initial nodes of H_1 whose interpretations also satisfy $\mathcal{U}_2$. □

Definition 4. *Let* I, I' *be nodes of a graph H. We denote the relation "I' is an immediate successor of I" by* $I \to I'$*, and the relation "I' is a successor of I" by* $I \to^+ I'$*.*

Lemma 3 (existence of a model). *Let* $P = SP \cup \mathcal{E}$ *be an unconditional eventuality temporal problem. Let H be the behavior graph of* SP *such that both the set of initial nodes of H is non-empty and the following condition is satisfied:*

$$\forall I \forall l \exists I' (I \to^+ I' \wedge I' \models l), \tag{3}$$

where I, I' *are nodes of H and* $\Diamond l \in \mathcal{E}$*. Then* P *has a model.*

Proof. It follows from the conditions of the lemma that all paths through H are infinite. We can construct a model for P as follows. Let I_0 be an initial node of H and $l_1, \ldots, l_m$ be all eventuality literals of $\mathcal{E}$. Let π be the infinite path $I_0, I_1, \ldots, I_{k_1}, I_{k_1+1}, \ldots, I_{k_2}, \ldots,$ where for all $i \geq 0$ and $j \geq 1$, $I_{k_{mi+j}} \models l_j$. It follows by the construction of the behavior graph that the sequence of interpretations given by π is a model for P.

Indeed, all nontemporal clauses and all step clauses of P are satisfied on this sequence immediately by the definition of the behavior graph of SP. Now, let us take an eventuality clause $\Diamond l_j$ and a node I_ν on π. By construction of π, there is a node $I_{k_{mi+j}}$ such that $I_\nu \to^+ I_{k_{mi+j}}$ and $I_{k_{mi+j}} \models l_j$. It implies that $\Diamond l_j$ is satisfied at the moment ν. □

Note. This lemma remains valid in the case when a temporal problem does not contain eventualities. In this case the (sufficient) condition assumes the form

$$\forall I \exists I'(I \rightarrow^+ I'), \tag{4}$$

which simply says that P has a model if all paths through H are infinite.

Theorem 3 (completeness). *If an unconditional eventuality problem $\mathsf{P} = \mathsf{SP} \cup \mathcal{E}$ is unsatisfiable then the temporal resolution procedure will derive a contradiction when applied to it.*

Proof. The proof proceeds by induction on the number of nodes in the behavior graph H of SP, which is finite. Let $\mathsf{SP} =< \mathcal{U}, \mathcal{I}, \mathcal{S} >$. If H is empty then the set $\mathcal{U} \cup \mathcal{I}$ is unsatisfiable. In this case the derivation is successfully terminated by the initial termination rule.

Now suppose H is not empty. Let I be a node of H which has no successors. In this case there exists a set of step rules $\{P_1 \Rightarrow \bigcirc Q_1, \ldots, P_m \Rightarrow \bigcirc Q_m\}$, $m > 0$, such that for all $1 \leq i \leq m$, $I \models P_i$ but the set $\mathcal{U} \cup \{Q_1, \ldots Q_m\}$ is unsatisfiable. So, we can derive by the step resolution rule a new clause $\neg P_1 \vee \ldots \vee \neg P_m$. Adding this clause to the set $\mathcal{U}$ results in removing the node I because $I \not\models \neg P_1 \vee \ldots \vee \neg P_m$. Let us note that if $m = 0$ the set $\mathcal{U}$ would be unsatisfiable in contradiction to the supposition H is not empty.

Now we consider another possibility when all nodes of H have a successor. Note that in this case $\mathcal{E}$ cannot be empty. Because P is unsatisfiable the following condition (the negation of condition (3) concerning the existence of a model given in lemma 3) holds:

$$\exists I \exists l \forall I'(I \rightarrow^+ I' \Rightarrow I' \not\models l), \tag{5}$$

where I, I' are nodes of H and $l \in \mathcal{E}$.

Let I_0 be a node defined by the first quantifier in condition (5), and l_0 be an eventuality literal defined by the second one.

Let $\mathcal{I}$ be a finite nonempty set of indexes such that $\{I_n \mid n \in \mathcal{I}\}$ is the set of all successors of I_0. (It is possible that $0 \in \mathcal{I}$.) Let $I_{n_1}, \ldots I_{n_k}$ be the set of all immediate successors of I_0.

Let R_0 (R_n) be the set of all step rules of $\mathcal{S}$ whose left-hand sides are satisfied by I_0 (I_n). Let $A_0 \Rightarrow \bigcirc B_0$ ($A_n \Rightarrow \bigcirc B_n$) be the result of applying the merging operation to all clauses in R_0 (R_n) simultaneously.

Consider the following two cases depending on the emptiness of either R_0 or any $R_n, n \in \mathcal{I}$.

1. Let R_0 be empty. It implies, that $\mathcal{U} \vdash \neg l$. Indeed, since $I_{n_1}, \ldots I_{n_k}$ is the set of all immediate successors of I_0, it holds that $I_{n_1}, \ldots I_{n_k}$ are all possible models of $\mathcal{U}$. Because for all $j \in \{n_1, \ldots, n_k\}$ it holds $I_j \not\models l_0$, we can conclude that $\mathcal{U} \vdash \neg l_0$. Now, we can apply the sometime termination rule as this contradicts $\Diamond l_0$.
   The same argument holds if any of the sets $R_n, n \in \mathcal{I}$, is empty.
2. Let R_0 and R_n (for every $n \in \mathcal{I}$) be non empty. Then we have:

a) $\mathcal{U} \cup \{B_0\} \vdash \neg l_0$ and $\mathcal{U} \cup \{B_n\} \vdash \neg l_0$ for all $n \in \mathcal{I}$.

Indeed, by arguments similar to given above at (1) we conclude that $I_{n_1}, \ldots, I_{n_k}$ are all interpretations of $\mathcal{U} \cup \{B_0\}$. Since $I_{n_1} \not\models l_0, \ldots, I_{n_k} \not\models l_0$ it follows that $\mathcal{U} \cup \{B_0\} \vdash \neg l_0$.

The same holds for every node I_n and every conjunction B_n, $n \in \mathcal{I}$.

b) $\mathcal{U} \cup \{B_n\} \vdash \bigvee\limits_{j \in \{0\} \cup \mathcal{I}} A_j$ for all $n \in \{0\} \cup \mathcal{I}$.

Again, consider the case $n = 0$ (for other indexes arguments are similar). Since $I_{n_1}, \ldots, I_{n_k}$ are all possible interpretations of $\mathcal{U} \cup \{B_0\}$ and for every $j \in \{n_1, \ldots, n_k\}$ $I_j \vdash A_j$ holds we can conclude that $\mathcal{U} \cup \{B_0\} \vdash \bigvee\limits_{j \in \{n_1, \ldots, n_k\}} A_j$.

Therefore, the sometime resolution rule

$$\frac{\{A_j \Rightarrow \bigcirc B_j \mid j \in \{0\} \cup \mathcal{I}\} \qquad \Diamond l_0}{(\bigwedge\limits_{j \in \{0\} \cup \mathcal{I}} \neg A_j)} \ (\Diamond^{\mathcal{U}}_{res}).$$

can be applied. Then, the node I_0 will is removed from H (recall that $I_0 \vdash A_0$ by construction of A_0) together with the set of its successors. $\qquad \square$

6   Conditional Single Eventuality

Our simplified resolution technique relies on the translation from conditional eventualities to unconditional ones (Theorem 1). Here we show that, if a temporal problem is given in DSNF with only one conditional eventuality rule of the form[4]

$$P \Rightarrow \Diamond \bigcirc l,$$

then we do not actually need to carry out *any translation*. Instead of the sometime termination rule, we now use

- *Sometime negation rule for single eventuality w.r.t.* $\mathcal{U}$

$$\frac{P \Rightarrow \bigcirc \Diamond l}{\neg P} \ (\Diamond^{\mathcal{U}}_{neg})$$

where $\mathcal{U} \cup \{l\} \vdash \perp$ (or $\mathcal{U} \vdash \neg l$).

The modified sometime resolution rule now takes the following form

- *Sometime resolution rule for single eventuality w.r.t.* $\mathcal{U}$

$$\frac{A_1 \Rightarrow \bigcirc B_1, \quad \ldots, \quad A_n \Rightarrow \bigcirc B_n \quad P \Rightarrow \bigcirc \Diamond l}{(\bigwedge\limits_{i=1}^{n} \neg A_i) \vee \neg P} \ (\Diamond^{\mathcal{U}}_{s-res})$$

with the usual loop side conditions.

---

[4] This is not the exact DSNF form—we here extend it to the conditional eventuality case. Note further the following equivalence $(P \Rightarrow \Diamond l) \equiv (P \Rightarrow (l \vee \Diamond \bigcirc l)) \equiv ((P \wedge \neg l) \Rightarrow \Diamond \bigcirc l)$. If we have more than one eventuality rule sharing the same eventuality literal, e.g., $P_1 \Rightarrow \bigcirc \Diamond l$, $P_2 \Rightarrow \bigcirc \Diamond l$, we replace them with the combined rule $((P_1 \vee P_2) \Rightarrow \bigcirc \Diamond l)$, which is equivalent w.r.t. satisfiability to the given pair of eventuality rules.

Theorem 4. *Temporal resolution rules for the single eventuality case preserve satisfiability.*

Proof. Follows straightforwardly from consideration of the models.   □

Lemma 4 (existence of a model: single eventuality). *Let $P = SP \cup \{P \Rightarrow \bigcirc \Diamond l\}$ be a single eventuality temporal problem. Let H be the behavior graph of SP such that all paths through H are infinite and the following condition is satisfied:*

$$\forall I(I \models P \Rightarrow \exists I'(I \rightarrow^+ I' \wedge I' \models l)), \tag{6}$$

where I, I' are nodes of H. Then P has a model.

Proof. Similar to the proof of Lemma 3.   □

Theorem 5 (completeness: single eventuality). *If a problem $P = SP \cup \{P \Rightarrow \bigcirc \Diamond l\}$ is unsatisfiable, then the temporal resolution procedure will derive a contradiction when applied to it.*

Proof. The proof is obtained by analysing the proof of Theorem 3 given above. It remains the same for the case when H contains nodes with no successor.

If all nodes in H have a successor, because of Lemma 4, the counterpart of the condition (6) now has the following form:

$$\exists I(I \models P \wedge \forall I'(I \rightarrow^+ I' \Rightarrow I' \not\models l)). \tag{7}$$

Let I_0 be a node of H determined by the first quantifier of (7).

If case (1) of the previous proof holds (i.e. $\mathcal{U} \models \neg l$), node I_0 will be deleted from the graph because of the sometime negation rule (recall that $I_0 \models P$).

If case (2) holds, node I_0 will be deleted because of the conclusion of the sometime resolution rule for single eventuality: $(\bigwedge_{i=1}^{n} \neg A_i) \vee \neg P$.   □

Example 2. Let us replace the two eventuality clauses of the example 1 by a single eventuality clause and show that the resulting problem is still unsatisfiable.

1. $a \wedge \neg l_1 \wedge \neg l_2$
2. $\Box(a \Rightarrow \bigcirc(\neg a \wedge (l_1 \vee l_2) \wedge (\neg l_1 \vee \neg l_2)))$
3. $\Box((\neg a \wedge l_1 \wedge \neg l_2) \Rightarrow \bigcirc(\neg a \wedge l_1 \wedge \neg l_2))$
4. $\Box((\neg a \wedge \neg l_1 \wedge l_2) \Rightarrow \bigcirc(\neg a \wedge \neg l_1 \wedge l_2))$
5. $\Box(a \Rightarrow \Diamond\bigcirc(\neg l_1 \wedge \neg l_2))$

The following DSNF corresponds to this problem[5]:

$$\mathcal{I} = \{ 1.\ a \wedge \neg l_1 \wedge \neg l_2 \}$$
$$\mathcal{U} = \{ 6.\ l_{\neg l_1 \wedge \neg l_2} \Rightarrow (\neg l_1 \wedge \neg l_2) \} \quad \mathcal{S} = \left\{ \begin{array}{l} 2.\ a \Rightarrow \bigcirc(\neg a \wedge (l_1 \vee l_2) \wedge (\neg l_1 \vee \neg l_2)) \\ 3.\ (\neg a \wedge l_1 \wedge \neg l_2) \Rightarrow \bigcirc(\neg a \wedge l_1 \wedge \neg l_2) \\ 4.\ (\neg a \wedge \neg l_1 \wedge l_2) \Rightarrow \bigcirc(\neg a \wedge \neg l_1 \wedge l_2) \end{array} \right\}$$
$$\mathcal{E} = \{ 7.\ a \Rightarrow \Diamond\bigcirc l_{\neg l_1 \wedge \neg l_2} \}$$

We see that step clauses $2, 3, 4$, taken together with the universal clause 6, form a loop for the single eventuality temporal resolution with clause 7. The resulting universal clause, $\neg a$, contradicts the initial clause.

---

[5] When introducing a new name for the positive occurrence of the subformula $\neg l_1 \wedge \neg l_2$, we use implication rather than equivalence; this technique goes back to [19].

Example 3 (Example 1 cont.). We show now that if the given DSNF contains more than one eventuality clause, reduction to the unconditional case is necessary. (I.e. the inference system described in this section is not complete for the general case.)

Consider the original set of temporal formulas from Example 1. The step resolution rule cannot be applied to the problem. Clauses 3 and 4 form a loop for eventuality rules 6 and 5 respectively; however, the temporal resolvents (by the rule $\Diamond^{\mathcal{U}}_{s-res}$) are tautologies: $a \lor \neg l_1 \lor l_2 \lor \neg a$ (resp., $a \lor l_1 \lor \neg l_2 \lor \neg a$).

Note 3. Instead of an *eventuality literal* we could introduce a notion of an *eventuality expression* giving eventuality rules the form $P \Rightarrow \Diamond \bigcirc Q$ where P, Q are arbitrary Boolean combinations of propositional symbols. It is not difficult to check that our inference system is adapted to such reformulation straightforwardly—we do not distinguish between eventuality expressions Q_1 and Q_2 if $\mathcal{U} \vdash (Q_1 \equiv Q_2)$, i.e. they are equivalent with respect a given universal part. Let us remind that during the derivation the universal part of a given problem is not narrowed. Alternatively, we could rename these eventuality expressions taking into consideration the equivalence, and introducing the same name for equivalent expressions.

7   Reduction to the Single Eventuality Problem

We reduce now a temporal problem with several unconditional eventualities to a single eventuality temporal problem (first, in the language with past-time operator '$\mathcal{S}$').

Lemma 5. $SP \cup \{\Box \Diamond Q_i\}_{i \in I}$ *is satisfiable if, and only if,* $SP \cup \{l \land \Box(l \Rightarrow \Diamond \bigcirc (\bigwedge_{i \in I} (\neg l \, \mathcal{S} \, Q_i) \land l))\}$ *is satisfiable, where l is a new propositional symbol.*

Proof. Let us reformulate the given problem in a two-sorted temporal language with variables over $\mathbb{N}$ for the temporal sort:

$$SP \cup \{\forall n \exists m (n \leq m \land Q_i(m))\}_{i \in I}$$

(meaning that each $Q_i, i \in I$, is satisfied infinitely often). This problem is equivalent with respect to satisfiability to the following (this can easily be checked by considering possible models):

$$SP \cup \{\forall n \exists m (m > n \land \bigwedge_{i \in I} \exists k_i (n \leq k_i < m \land Q_i(k_i)))\} \tag{8}$$

which states, informally, that for each moment of time, n, there is a moment $m > n$, such that all eventualities $Q_i, i \in I$, are satisfied "after n and before m". We prove that given a model for (8) it is possible to find a model for

$$SP \cup \{l \land \Box(l \Rightarrow \Diamond \bigcirc (\bigwedge_{i \in I} (\neg l \, \mathcal{S} \, Q_i) \land l))\} \tag{9}$$

and vice versa.

First, consider a model $\mathfrak{M}$ for (8). We construct a model $\mathfrak{M}'$ for (9) by extending $\mathfrak{M}$ with a new proposition l and defining its value as follows. Formula (8) states that for each moment of time, n, there exists a future moment, m, when a certain property holds, defining thus a function $m(n)$. Let us construct a sequence of times defined by (8) starting from 0, i.e. $m_0 = 0$, $m_2 = m(0), \ldots, m_{j+1} = m(m_j)$; and let us also define y in $\mathfrak{M}'$ to be **true** at those times and **false** everywhere else. Note that, for all $i \in I$ and $j \geq 0$, there exists a moment $k_i : m_j \leq k_i < m_{j+1}$ such that $Q_i(k_i)$. Therefore, $(\mathfrak{M}, m_{j+1}) \models \bigwedge_{i \in I} (\neg y \, \mathcal{S} \, Q_i)$; hence, $(\mathfrak{M}, m_j) \models \Diamond\bigcirc(\bigwedge_{i \in I} (\neg l \, \mathcal{S} \, Q_i) \wedge l)$, making (9)

true in $\mathfrak{M}'$.

Let $\mathfrak{M}$ be a model for (9); we show that it is also a model for (8). It is enough to show that for infinitely many n's there exists an m such that $(m > n)$ and $\bigwedge_{i \in I} \exists k_i (n \leq k_i < m \wedge Q_i(k_i))$ holds. For $j \geq 1$, let us consider the sequence m_j $(m_j > 0)$ of all moments such that $(\mathfrak{M}, m_j) \models \bigwedge_{i \in I} (\neg l \, \mathcal{S} \, Q_i) \wedge l$ (note that there are infinitely many such moments); let $m_0 = 0$. We can see that for all $j \geq 0$, $n = m_j$, and $m = m_{j+1}$, the formula $\bigwedge_{i \in I} \exists k_i (n \leq k_i < m \wedge Q_i(k_i))$ is true in $\mathfrak{M}$. Indeed, $(\mathfrak{M}, n) \models l$, $(\mathfrak{M}, m) \models l$; by semantics of the operator "since", $(\mathfrak{M}, m) \models \bigwedge_{i \in I} (\neg l \, \mathcal{S} \, Q_i)$ means that $(\mathfrak{M}, m) \models \bigwedge_{i \in I} \exists k_i (n \leq k_i < m \wedge Q_i(k_i))$. $\qquad\square$

Lemma 6. *Formula $\square(A \Rightarrow (B \, \mathcal{S} \, C))$ is satisfiable if, and only if, the temporal specification*

$$(\neg s) \quad \wedge \quad \square(A \Rightarrow s) \quad \wedge \quad \square((C \vee (B \wedge s)) \equiv \bigcirc s)$$

is satisfiable, where s is a new propositional symbol. (The first clause goes into the initial part, the second into the universal part, and the third can be represented by two step clauses).

Proof. Follows straightforwardly from consideration of possible models. $\qquad\square$

Corollary 1. *Any propositional temporal problem with an arbitrary number of eventuality clauses is equivalent, by satisfiability, to a single eventuality propositional temporal problem.*

Lemma 7. *The growth in size of the problem following the reduction from DSNF to a single eventuality temporal problem is linear in the number of eventualities occurring in the DSNF form.*

Proof. Follows from the above transformation. $\qquad\square$

Example 4 (Example 1 cont.). We reduce now the given set of formulas to a single eventuality problem.

$$\mathcal{I} = \left\{ \begin{array}{l} 1.\ a \wedge \neg l_1 \wedge \neg l_2 \\ 18.\ l \\ 19.\ \neg s_1 \\ 20.\ \neg s_2 \end{array} \right\}$$

$$\mathcal{U} = \left\{ \begin{array}{l} 13.\ a \wedge \neg l_1 \Rightarrow w l_1 \\ 14.\ a \wedge \neg l_2 \Rightarrow w l_2 \\ 15.\ Q_1 \Rightarrow s_1 \\ 16.\ Q_2 \Rightarrow s_2 \\ 17.\ l \wedge \neg Q \Rightarrow w Q \end{array} \right\}$$

$$\mathcal{E} = \{21.\ \Diamond \neg w Q\}$$

$$\mathcal{S} = \left\{ \begin{array}{l} 2.\ a \Rightarrow \bigcirc(\neg a \wedge (l_1 \vee l_2) \wedge (\neg l_1 \vee \neg l_2)) \\ 3.\ (\neg a \wedge l_1 \wedge \neg l_2) \Rightarrow \bigcirc(\neg a \wedge l_1 \wedge \neg l_2) \\ 4.\ (\neg a \wedge \neg l_1 \wedge l_2) \Rightarrow \bigcirc(\neg a \wedge \neg l_1 \wedge l_2) \\ 5.\ w l_1 \Rightarrow \bigcirc(l_1 \vee w l_1) \\ 6.\ w l_2 \Rightarrow \bigcirc(l_2 \vee w l_2) \\ 7.\ Q \Rightarrow \bigcirc(Q_1 \wedge Q_2 \wedge l) \\ 8.\ (\neg w l_1 \vee \neg l \wedge s_1) \Rightarrow \bigcirc s_1 \\ 9.\ w l_1 \wedge (l \vee \neg s_1) \Rightarrow \bigcirc \neg s_1 \\ 10.\ (\neg w l_2 \vee \neg l \wedge s_2) \Rightarrow \bigcirc s_2 \\ 11.\ w l_2 \wedge (l \vee \neg s_2) \Rightarrow \bigcirc \neg s_2 \\ 12.\ w Q \Rightarrow \bigcirc(Q \vee w Q) \end{array} \right\}$$

The derivation of a contradiction is rather lengthy for this example; we omit it due to lack of space. We note that it enjoys the following property: Instead of two loops needed for Example 1, one is enough. However, the following example shows that it is not always the case.

Example 5. The following single unconditional eventuality temporal problem

$$\mathcal{I} = \{ 1.\ a \wedge \neg l \}$$
$$\mathcal{U} = \emptyset \qquad \mathcal{S} = \begin{cases} 2.\ a \wedge \neg l \Rightarrow \bigcirc ((a \wedge \neg l) \vee (a \wedge l)) \\ 3.\ a \wedge l \Rightarrow \bigcirc (\neg a \wedge \neg l) \\ 4.\ \neg a \wedge \neg l \Rightarrow \bigcirc (\neg a \wedge \neg l) \end{cases}$$
$$\mathcal{E} = \{ \Diamond l \}$$

requires two applications of the sometime resolution rule.

Indeed, the behavior graph for this problem consists of three vertices, I_0, I_1, I_2 (see Fig. 1). One application of the sometime resolution rule deletes the node I_2; then, the node I_1 can be deleted by the step resolution rule; after that, one more application of the sometime resolution is needed to delete the node I_0.

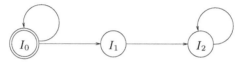

Fig. 1. Behavior graph for the problem. $I_0 = \{a, \neg l\}$; $I_1 = \{a, l\}$; $I_2 = \{\neg a, \neg l\}$.

8   Conclusion

In this paper, we have addressed the problem of simplifying, still further, the clausal resolution approach described in [7]. We have shown how to reduce conditional eventualities, i.e formulas of the form $\Box(P \Rightarrow \Diamond q)$, to unconditional eventualities, i.e. $\Box \Diamond q'$, and how to reduce problems containing multiple formulate of the form $\Diamond r$, to problems containing just one. This not only allows us to simplify the normal form required (from that defined in [7]) to a more streamlined version, but has also allowed us to introduce a set of simplified resolution rules. For example, in [7], the resolvent generated by applying temporal resolution to the formula $A \Rightarrow \bigcirc \Box \neg l$ and $\Diamond l$ will be $(\neg A)\,\mathcal{U}\,l$, while we have here shown that the resolvent can be as simple as $\neg A$.

In addition to providing both a much simpler normal form for temporal formula, and a streamlined resolution process, the reductions described in this paper can, we believe, form the basis of temporal resolution provers with greatly improved efficiency. Thus, our future work in this area mainly involves the incorporation of the techniques described here to develop improved temporal provers.

References

1. A. Artale and E. Franconi. Temporal description logics. In *Handbook of Temporal Reasoning in Artificial Intelligence*. To appear.

2. E. Clarke, O. Grumberg and D. A. Peled. *Model Checking*. MIT Press, 2000.
3. A. Degtyarev and M. Fisher. Propositional temporal resolution revisited. In *Proc. of 7th UK Workshop on Automated Reasoning (ARW)*, London, July 2000.
4. A. Degtyarev and M. Fisher. An Extension of Propositional Temporal Resolution. In *Proc. UK Workshop on Automated Reasoning (ARW)*, York, March 2001.
5. A. Degtyarev and M.Fisher. Towards First-Order Temporal Resolution. In Proc. *KI 2001*, volume 2174 of *LNCS*. Springer Verlag, 2001.
6. R. Fagin, J. Halpern, Y. Moses, and M. Vardi. *Reasoning About Knowledge*. MIT Press, 1996.
7. M. Fisher, C. Dixon, and M. Peim. Clausal temporal resolution. *ACM Transactions on Computation Logic*, 2(1), January 2001.
8. M. Fisher. A resolution method for temporal logic. In *Proc. 12th Int. Joint Conf. on Artificial Intelligence (IJCAI)*. Morgan Kaufman, 1991.
9. M. Fisher. An introduction to executable temporal logics. *Knowledge Engineering Review*, 11:43–56, 1996.
10. G. J. Holzmann. The Model Checker Spin. *IEEE Trans. on Software Engineering*, 23(5):279–295, May 1997. Special Issue on Formal Methods in Software Practice.
11. U. Hustadt and R. Schmidt. Scientific Benchmarking with Temporal Logic Decision Procedures *Proc. Int. Conf. on Principles of Knowledge Representation & Reasoning*, 2002.
12. U. Hustadt and R. Schmidt. Formulae which Highlight Differences between Temporal Logic and Dynamic Logic Provers In *Issues in the Design and Experimental Evaluation of Systems for Modal and Temporal Logics*, Italy, 2001.
13. O. Kupferman and M. Vardi. Synthesis with incomplete informatio. In *Advances in Temporal Logic*. pp.109-128. Kluwer, 2000.
14. Z. Manna and A. Pnueli. *The Temporal Logic of Reactive and Concurrent Systems: Specification*. Springer, 1992.
15. A. Pnueli and R. Rosner. On the synthesis of a reactive module. In *Proc. 16th ACM Symp. Princip. Prog. Lang.*, pp.179–190, 1989.
16. A. S. Rao and M. P. Georgeff. Decision procedures for BDI logics. *Journal of Logic and Computation*, 8(3):293–342, 1998.
17. M. P. Shanahan. *Solving the Frame Problem*. MIT Press, 1997.
18. A. Tansel, editor. *Temporal Databases: theory, design, and implementation.* Benjamin/Cummings, 1993.
19. G. Tseitin. On the complexity of derivations in propositional calculus. In *Studies in Constructive Mathematics and Mathematical Logic*, 1968.
20. F. Wolter and M. Zakharyaschev. Temporalizing description logics. In *Frontiers of Combining Systems II*, pp.379–401. Research Studies Press LTD, England, 2000.

Modal Nonmonotonic Logics Revisited: Efficient Encodings for the Basic Reasoning Tasks*

Thomas Eiter, Volker Klotz, Hans Tompits, and Stefan Woltran

Institut für Informationssysteme 184/3, Technische Universität Wien,
Favoritenstraße 9–11 , A-1040 Vienna, Austria,
{eiter,volker,tompits,stefan}@kr.tuwien.ac.at

Abstract. Modal nonmonotonic logics constitute a well-known family of knowl-edge-representation formalisms capturing ideally rational agents reasoning about their own beliefs. Although these formalisms are extensively studied from a the-oretical point of view, most of these approaches lack generally available solvers thus far. In this paper, we show how variants of Moore's autoepistemic logic can be axiomatised by means of quantified Boolean formulas (QBFs). More specif-ically, we provide polynomial reductions of the basic reasoning tasks associated with these logics into the evaluation problem of QBFs. Since there are now effi-cient QBF-solvers, this reduction technique yields a practically relevant approach to build prototype reasoning systems for these formalisms. We incorporated our encodings within the system QUIP and tested their performance on a class of benchmark problems using different underlying QBF-solvers.

1 Introduction

Modal nonmonotonic logics constitute one of the basic categories of approaches formal-ising certain aspects of human common-sense reasoning. In contrast to other well-known nonmonotonic reasoning frameworks, like, e.g., default logic [35], logic programming with negation as failure [16,34], or circumscription [28], modal nonmonotonic logics employ the language of modal logic to realise nonmonotonicity. More specifically, the aim is to model the behaviour of an ideally rational agent reasoning about its own beliefs, by means of a unary operator L. Informally, $L\phi$ means that the agent believes ϕ. Given a set T of formulas as initial premises, referred to as *theories*, introspection properties generate sets of total beliefs, called *expansions*. Different introspection principles have been proposed in the literature, yielding different classes of modal nonmonotonic logics.

Although modal nonmonotonic logics have been extensively studied from a theoret-ical point of view (for a recent work discussing proof-theoretical issues, cf., e.g., [1]), besides some early attempts about implementational issues [4,2,21,3], most of these ap-proaches lack generally available solvers thus far. This despite the fact that recent years witnessed an increasing amount of successful implementations for various nonmono-tonic formalisms, mostly for the answer-set programming paradigm, as realised, e.g., by the state-of-the-art solvers dlv [14] and smodels [31] implementing the stable model semantics for logic programs, or the default-logic prover DeReS [6].

---

* This work was partially supported by the Austrian Science Fund Project P15068.

U. Egly and C.G. Fermüller (Eds.): TABLEAUX 2002, LNAI 2381, pp. 100–114, 2002.
© Springer-Verlag Berlin Heidelberg 2002

In this paper, we describe a general method to build a prototype reasoning system for modal nonmonotonic logics, based on a reduction approach. The central idea is to translate a given reasoning task into a quantified Boolean formula (QBF) and then applying some sophisticated QBF-solver to evaluate the translated QBF. The existence of efficient QBF-solvers, like, e.g., the systems developed by Cadoli *et al.* [5], Giunchiglia *et al.* [18], Rintanen [37], Letz [25], or Feldmann *et al.* [15], makes this reduction approach practicably applicable.

Concerning the particular reductions, we provide efficient (polynomial-time) translations of reasoning tasks for the following modal nonmonotonic logics: Moore's autoepistemic logic [29], nonmonotonic logic **N** [26] (also called *iterative autoepistemic logic*), reasoning with parsimoniously grounded expansions [13], and Konolige's system of moderately grounded expansions [24].

From a theoretical point of view, the feasibility of the current approach relies on the observation that the evaluation problem of quantified Boolean formulas, QSAT, is PSPACE-complete, so any decision problem in PSPACE can be polynomially reduced to QSAT. In fact, the evaluation problem for QBFs having prenex normal form with $i - 1$ quantifier alternations is complete for the i-th level of the polynomial hierarchy. Since the reasoning tasks considered in this paper belong to the second and third level of the polynomial hierarchy, respectively, efficient translations to QBFs with one or two quantifier alternations must exist.

A similar approach for solving various reasoning tasks belonging to the area of nonmonotonic reasoning has been realised in the system QUIP [11,10,12,7,32]. This prototypical implementation currently handles the computation of the main reasoning tasks for logic-based abduction, default logic, a consistency-based approach to belief revision, and equilibrium logic, a generalisation of the stable model semantics for logic programs. We implemented the translations for modal nonmonotonic logics by incorporating them into the system QUIP.

Reduction methods to QBFs naturally generalise similar approaches for problems in NP; these latter problems can in turn be solved by translating them (in polynomial time) to SAT, the satisfiability problem of classical propositional logic (see e.g., [22] for such an application in Artificial Intelligence). Besides the implementation of different nonmonotonic reasoning tasks as realised by the system QUIP, successful applications based on reductions to QBFs have also been applied to conditional planning [36].

In order to conduct some experimental evaluation of our translations, we tested their implementation in the system QUIP based on a class of benchmark problems using different underlying QBF-solvers. More specifically, we used the solvers ssolve [15], QuBe [18], and semprop [25] on randomly generated problem instances covering a complete easy-hard-easy pattern.

2   Preliminaries

We deal with propositional languages and use the logical symbols $\top$, $\bot$, $\neg$, $\vee$, $\wedge$, and $\rightarrow$ to construct formulas in the standard way. We write $\mathcal{L}_\mathcal{P}$ to denote a language over an alphabet $\mathcal{P}$ of *propositional variables* or *atoms*. Formulas are denoted by Greek lower-case letters (possibly with subscripts).

Given an alphabet $\mathcal{P}$, we define a disjoint alphabet $\mathcal{P}'$ as $\mathcal{P}' = \{p' \mid p \in \mathcal{P}\}$. Accordingly, for a formula $\alpha \in \mathcal{L}_\mathcal{P}$, we define α' as the result of replacing in α each atom p from $\mathcal{P}$ by the corresponding atom p' in $\mathcal{P}'$. This is defined analogously for sets of formulas. Observe that this priming mechanism can be applied in an iterative manner, yielding, e.g., formulas of form α'' whose underlying alphabet $\mathcal{P}''$ is disjoint from both $\mathcal{P}$ and $\mathcal{P}'$.

Quantified Boolean formulas (QBFs) generalise ordinary propositional formulas by the admission of quantifications over propositional variables (QBFs are denoted by Greek upper-case letters). Informally, a QBF of form $\forall p \exists q\, \Phi$ means that for all truth assignments of p there is a truth assignment of q such that Φ is true. For instance, it is easily seen that the QBF $\exists p_1 \exists p_2\, ((p_1 \rightarrow p_2) \wedge \forall p_3 (p_3 \rightarrow p_2))$ evaluates to true.

The precise semantical meaning of QBFs is defined as follows. First, some ancillary notation. An occurrence of a variable v in a QBF Φ is *free* iff it does not appear in the scope of a quantifier $\mathsf{Q}v$ ($\mathsf{Q} \in \{\forall, \exists\}$), otherwise the occurrence of v is *bound*. If Φ contains no free variables, then Φ is *closed*, otherwise Φ is *open*. Furthermore, $\Phi[v_1/\psi_1, \ldots, v_n/\psi_n]$ denotes the result of uniformly substituting the free occurrences of variables v_i in Φ by ψ_i ($1 \leq i \leq n$).

By an *interpretation*, I, we understand a set of variables. Informally, a variable v is true under I iff $v \in I$. In general, the truth value, $\nu_I(\Phi)$, of a QBF Φ under an interpretation I is recursively defined as follows:

1. if $\Phi = \top$, then $\nu_I(\Phi) = 1$;
2. if $\Phi = \bot$, then $\nu_I(\Phi) = 0$;
3. if $\Phi = v$ is an atom, then $\nu_I(\Phi) = 1$ if $v \in I$, and $\nu_I(\Phi) = 0$ otherwise;
4. if $\Phi = \neg\Psi$, then $\nu_I(\Phi) = 1 - \nu_I(\Psi)$;
5. if $\Phi = (\Phi_1 \wedge \Phi_2)$, then $\nu_I(\Phi) = min(\{\nu_I(\Phi_1), \nu_I(\Phi_2)\})$;
6. if $\Phi = (\Phi_1 \vee \Phi_2)$, then $\nu_I(\Phi) = max(\{\nu_I(\Phi_1), \nu_I(\Phi_2)\})$;
7. if $\Phi = (\Phi_1 \rightarrow \Phi_2)$, then $\nu_I(\Phi) = 1$ iff $\nu_I(\Phi_1) \leq \nu_I(\Phi_2)$;
8. if $\Phi = \forall v\, \Psi$, then $\nu_I(\Phi) = \nu_I(\Psi[v/\top] \wedge \Psi[v/\bot])$;
9. if $\Phi = \exists v\, \Psi$, then $\nu_I(\Phi) = \nu_I(\Psi[v/\top] \vee \Psi[v/\bot])$.

We say that Φ is *true under I* iff $\nu_I(\Phi) = 1$, otherwise Φ is *false under I*. If $\nu_I(\Phi) = 1$, then I is a *model* (or *satisfying truth assignment*) of Φ. Likewise, for a set S of formulas, if $\nu_I(\Phi) = 1$ for all $\Phi \in S$, then I is a model of S. If Φ has some model, then Φ is said to be *satisfiable*. If Φ is true under any interpretation, then Φ is *valid*. Observe that a closed QBF is either valid or unsatisfiable, because closed QBFs are either true under each interpretation or false under each interpretation. Hence, for closed QBFs, there is no need to refer to particular interpretations.

In the sequel, we employ the following abbreviation in the context of QBFs: For an indexed set $P = \{p_1, \ldots, p_n\}$ of propositional variables and a quantifier $\mathsf{Q} \in \{\forall, \exists\}$, we let $\mathsf{Q}P\, \Phi$ stand for the formula $\mathsf{Q}p_1\mathsf{Q}p_2 \cdots \mathsf{Q}p_n\, \Phi$.

3   Translations

In this section, we show how several modal nonmonotonic logics can be mapped to QBFs in polynomial time.

The language of each modal nonmonotonic logic contains the unary modal operator L, where $L\phi$ intuitively means that ϕ is believed. By $\mathcal{L}_L$ we denote the language obtained from $\mathcal{L}$ by the adjunction of L. Finite subsets of $\mathcal{L}_L$ are referred to as *autoepistemic theories*, or simply as *theories*, and are identified with the conjuction of their elements.

Formulas of the form $L\phi$ are treated like propositional atoms and are called *modal atoms*.

The following notational convention will be applied: If $S \subseteq \mathcal{L}_L$, then $\neg S = \{\neg\phi \mid \phi \in S\}$. For an autoepistemic theory T, M_T denotes all modal atoms of T, and M_T^0 denotes all modal atoms of T which are not in the scope of another L-operator.

Autoepistemic theories represent an initial set of premises, generating sets of total knowledge, called *expansions*. The specific definition of an expansion depends on the nonmonotonic logic at hand, and incorporates differing notions of *groundedness*.

For all modal nonmonotonic logics introduced in the sequel, we provide reductions of the following reasoning tasks into QBFs:

1. compute all expansions of a given autoepistemic theory;
2. given an autoepistemic theory T and a formula ψ, check whether T possesses some expansion containing ψ ("brave reasoning"); and
3. given an autoepistemic theory T and a formula ψ, check whether ψ is contained in all expansions of T ("skeptical reasoning").

3.1 Autoepistemic Logic

A *stable expansion* [29] of an autoepistemic theory $T \subseteq \mathcal{L}_L$ is a set of formulas $E \subseteq \mathcal{L}_L$ such that

$$E = Cn(T \cup \{L\phi \mid \phi \in E\} \cup \{\neg L\phi \mid \phi \in \mathcal{L}_L \setminus E\}), \tag{1}$$

where $Cn(\cdot)$ is the classical consequence operator with respect to the extended language $\mathcal{L}_L$. A weakening of this concept is that of a *stable set*: $S \subseteq \mathcal{L}_L$ is stable if S satisfies the following three conditions: (i) $S = Cn(S)$, (ii) $\phi \in S$ implies $L\phi \in S$, and (iii) $\phi \notin S$ implies $\neg L\phi \in S$.

Following Niemelä [30], there is a one-to-one correspondence between stable expansions and *full sets*, which are defined as follows: Let $T \subseteq \mathcal{L}_L$ be an autoepistemic theory. Call $\Lambda \subseteq M_T \cup \neg M_T$ T-*full* iff, for all $L\phi \in M_T$, (i) $T \cup \Lambda \models \phi$ iff $L\phi \in \Lambda$, and (ii) $T \cup \Lambda \not\models \phi$ iff $\neg L\phi \in \Lambda$.

Furthermore, the following relation is defined: Given a set $T \subseteq \mathcal{L}_L$ and a modal formula ψ, $T \models_L \psi$ iff $T \cup SB_T(\psi) \models \psi$, where $SB_T(\psi) = \{L\phi \in M_\psi^0 \mid T \cup SB_T(\phi) \models \phi\} \cup \{\neg L\phi \in \neg M_\psi^0 \mid T \cup SB_T(\phi) \not\models \phi\}$.

Proposition 1 ([30]). *Let T be an autoepistemic theory. Then, the function SE_T, defined as*

$$SE_T(\Lambda) = \{\phi \in \mathcal{L}_L \mid T \cup \Lambda \models_L \phi\},$$

gives a bijective mapping from the set of T-full sets to the set of stable expansions of T. Moreover, $SE_T(\Lambda)$ is the unique stable expansion S of T such that

$$\Lambda = (M_T \cup \neg M_T) \cap (\{L\phi \mid \phi \in S\} \cup \{\neg L\phi \mid \phi \notin S\}).$$

Example 1. Let $T = \{Lp \rightarrow p\}$. This theory has two stable expansions, one containing p and Lp, the other containing $\neg Lp$. Concerning the first expansion, the corresponding T-full set is $\Lambda_1 = \{Lp\}$, since $T \cup \{Lp\} \models p$ holds. The second expansion is characterised by the T-full set $\{\neg Lp\}$, since we have that $T \cup \{\neg Lp\} \not\models p$. Observe that $SE_T(\Lambda_2)$ does neither contain p nor $\neg p$.

It has been argued in the literature [24,26] that the first expansion is in some sense counterintuitive, since the assertion of p is based solely on the assumption that p is believed. The following subsections will deal with variations of autoepistemic logic which circumvent this problem.

For an autoepistemic theory T having propositional variables V and for a set M of new modal atoms, the following QBF will be used as a basic module:

$$\mathcal{F}_{ael}[T, M] = \forall V \left(T \rightarrow \bigwedge_{L\phi \in M} (L\phi \rightarrow \phi) \right) \wedge \bigwedge_{L\phi \in M} \left(\neg L\phi \rightarrow \exists V (T \wedge \neg\phi) \right).$$

This QBF reflects the conditions for full sets. In fact, we have the following characterisation:

Proposition 2 ([11]). *An autoepistemic theory $T \subseteq \mathcal{L}_L$ has at least one stable expansion iff $\mathcal{F}_{ael}[T, M_T]$ is satisfiable. Moreover, the satisfying truth assignments of $\mathcal{F}_{ael}[T, M_T]$ are in a one-to-one correspondence to the full sets of T.*

Thus, due to Proposition 1, the satisfying truth assignments of $\mathcal{F}_{ael}[T, M_T]$ are in a one-to-one correspondence to the stable expansions of T.

Example 2. We show the functioning of module $\mathcal{F}_{ael}[\cdot, \cdot]$ by using the theory $T = \{Lp \rightarrow p\}$ from Example 1. In this case, we have $M_T = \{Lp\}$ and $V = \{p\}$. So, $\mathcal{F}_{ael}[T, M_T]$ is given by

$$\forall p \Big((Lp \rightarrow p) \rightarrow (Lp \rightarrow p) \Big) \wedge \Big(\neg Lp \rightarrow \exists p((Lp \rightarrow p) \wedge \neg p) \Big). \tag{2}$$

Since Lp is the single free variable of (2), there are only two interpretations serving as potential models of $\mathcal{F}_{ael}[T, M_T]$, viz. $\emptyset$ and $\{Lp\}$.

Observe that the first conjunct of (2) evaluates trivially to true, since $(Lp \rightarrow p) \rightarrow (Lp \rightarrow p)$ is a tautology. Thus, it remains to analyse the second conjunct. Clearly, $\neg Lp \rightarrow \exists p((Lp \rightarrow p) \wedge \neg p)$ evaluates to true if Lp is set to true. Hence, $\{Lp\}$ is a model of $\mathcal{F}_{ael}[T, M_T]$. On the other hand, setting Lp to false makes $\exists p((Lp \rightarrow p) \wedge \neg p)$ true as well, since $(Lp \rightarrow p) \wedge \neg p$ reduces to $\neg p$ in this case, and there is quite obviously an interpretation which makes $\neg p$ true. Hence, $\emptyset$ is also a model of $\mathcal{F}_{ael}[T, M_T]$. Invoking Proposition 2 yields the expected result that T possesses two stable expansions, one containing Lp, and the other containing $\neg Lp$.

Using Niemelä's relation $\models_L$ as a basis for describing autoepistemic inference tasks, one has to deal with the recursive nature of this relation. However, such recursive definitions are extremely unhandy to be expressed as QBFs. In the following, we give an alternative method to decide containment of a formula in a stable expansion.

Lemma 1. *Let T be an autoepistemic theory, $SE_T(\Lambda)$ a stable expansion of T, and ψ a formula. Then, for any subformula χ of ψ and any $L\phi \in M_T \cap M_\chi^0$, we have that $L\phi \in \Lambda$ iff $L\phi \in SB_{T\cup\Lambda}(\chi)$.*

This lemma gives evidence that any possible element $L\phi \in M_T$ used in the recursive computation of an assertion $T \cup \Lambda \models_L \psi$ has equal polarity in the two sets $SB_{T\cup\Lambda}(\chi)$ and Λ. Like the full-set characterisation of stable models of T, it turns out that the remaining modal atoms of ψ can be utilised analogously to describe membership of formulas in stable models.

Lemma 2. *Let T, $SE_T(\Lambda)$, and ψ be as in Lemma 1. Then, $\psi \in SE_T(\Lambda)$ iff there exists some $\Lambda^+ \subseteq (M_\psi \setminus M_T) \cup \neg(M_\psi \setminus M_T)$ such that $T \cup \Lambda \cup \Lambda^+ \models \psi$, where Λ^+ satisfies the following conditions, for each $L\phi \in M_\psi \setminus M_T$:*

(i) $T \cup \Lambda \cup \Lambda^+ \models \phi$ *iff* $L\phi \in \Lambda^+$; *and*
(ii) $T \cup \Lambda \cup \Lambda^+ \not\models \phi$ *iff* $\neg L\phi \in \Lambda^+$.

We get the following translations into QBFs:

Theorem 1. *Let T be an autoepistemic theory and ψ a formula. Furthermore, let V be the set of propositional atoms occurring in T or ψ, and let $M^+ = M_\psi \setminus M_T$. Define*

$$\mathcal{F}_{ael}^{cred}[T, \psi] = \exists M^+ \Big(\mathcal{F}_{ael}[T, M_T \cup M_\psi] \wedge \forall V(T \rightarrow \psi) \Big); \quad and$$

$$\mathcal{F}_{ael}^{skept}[T, \psi] = \exists M^+ \Big(\mathcal{F}_{ael}[T, M_T \cup M_\psi] \wedge \neg \forall V(T \rightarrow \psi) \Big).$$

Then:

(i) *T has a stable expansion containing ψ iff $\mathcal{F}_{ael}^{cred}[T, \psi]$ is satisfiable. Moreover, the satisfying truth assignments of the free variables M_T in $\mathcal{F}_{ael}^{cred}[T, \psi]$ are in a one-to-one correspondence to the stable expansions of T containing ψ.*
(ii) *ψ is contained in all stable expansions of T iff the QBF $\neg \exists M_T(\mathcal{F}_{ael}^{skept}[T, \psi])$ evaluates to true.*

Intuitively, brave reasoning via $\mathcal{F}_{ael}^{cred}[T, \psi]$ works as follows. The first conjunct in the scope of the quantifier $\exists M^+$ determines the T-full set Λ as well as the set Λ^+ satisfying conditions (i) and (ii) of Lemma 2, and the second conjunct, $\forall V(T \rightarrow \psi)$, checks, with respect to the selected variables from $M_T \cup M_\psi$ corresponding to $\Lambda \cup \Lambda^+$, whether $T \cup \Lambda \cup \Lambda^+ \models \psi$ holds. As for skeptical reasoning, observe that the models of $\mathcal{F}_{ael}^{skept}[T, \psi]$ correspond to those T-full sets *not* containing ψ. Obviously, if no such set exists (i.e., if $\neg \exists M^+ \mathcal{F}_{ael}^{skept}[T, \psi]$ evaluates to true), ψ is a skeptical consequence of T.

3.2   Nonmonotonic Logic N

As illustrated by Example 1, Moore's autoepistemic logic admits stable expansions which are not sufficiently grounded in the premises. To circumvent this problem, several more restrictive groundedness conditions have been proposed. The nonmonotonic logic **N** [26] eliminates unfounded expansions by representing the positive introspection part in the fixed-point condition (1) in terms of a modified consequence operator. More specifically, define the inference relation $\vdash_{\mathbf{N}}$ by adding the *necessitation rule* $\phi/L\phi$ to the postulates of the classical derivability relation $\vdash$. Accordingly, let $Cn_{\mathbf{N}}(T) = \{\phi \mid T \vdash_{\mathbf{N}} \phi\}$. Then, E is an **N**-*expansion* of T iff

$$E = Cn_{\mathbf{N}}(T \cup \{\neg L\phi \mid \phi \in \mathcal{L}_L \setminus E\}). \tag{3}$$

Example 3. Reconsider Example 1, where we argued that the expansion $SE_T(\{Lp\})$ of the theory $T = \{Lp \rightarrow p\}$ is counterintuitive. This expansion is not an **N**-expansion. To see this, since $Lp \notin Cn_{\mathbf{N}}(T)$ and $Lp \notin Cn_{\mathbf{N}}(T \cup \{\neg L\phi \mid \phi \in \mathcal{L}_L \setminus E\})$ for any set E of formulas containing Lp, it follows that no set E containing Lp fulfills Condition 3. It is easy to see that the stable expansion $SE_T(\{\neg Lp\})$ is, however, an **N**-expansion of T.

In order to express **N**-expansions in terms of QBFs, we need a suitable characterisation of the derivability operator $\vdash_{\mathbf{N}}$.

Proposition 3 ([20]). *Let T be an autoepistemic theory, ψ a formula, and $M = M_T^0 \cup M_\psi^0$. Then, $T \vdash_{\mathbf{N}} \psi$ iff there exists no set $K \subseteq M$ such that*

(i) $T \cup K \not\models \psi$; and
(ii) for each $L\phi \in M \setminus K$, $T \cup K \not\models \phi$.

Proposition 3 allows the construction of a QBF representing the relation $T \vdash_{\mathbf{N}} \psi$ in the following way. Let T be an autoepistemic theory, ψ an autoepistemic formula, V the set of propositional variables occurring in T or ψ, and $M \subseteq (M_T^0 \cup M_\psi^0)$. Then, $\Phi_{\mathbf{N}}[T, \psi, M]$ is defined as

$$\neg \exists M' \Big(\exists M \exists V (T \wedge \bigwedge_{L\phi' \in M'} (L\phi' \rightarrow L\phi) \wedge \neg \psi) \wedge$$

$$\bigwedge_{L\phi' \in M'} (\neg L\phi' \rightarrow \exists M \exists V (T \wedge \bigwedge_{L\phi' \in M'} (L\phi' \rightarrow L\phi) \wedge \neg \phi)) \Big).$$

Theorem 2. *For any autoepistemic theory T and any formula ψ, $T \vdash_{\mathbf{N}} \psi$ holds iff $\Phi_{\mathbf{N}}[T, \psi, M_T^0 \cup M_\psi^0]$ is true.*

N-expansions can be characterised by means of full sets as follows:

Proposition 4 ([19]). *Let T be an autoepistemic theory T and let Λ be T-full. Then, $SE_T(\Lambda)$ is an **N**-expansion of T iff*

$$T \cup \{\neg L\phi \mid \neg L\phi \in \Lambda\} \vdash_{\mathbf{N}} \{L\phi \mid L\phi \in \Lambda\}.$$

Obviously, each **N**-expansion of a theory T is also a stable expansion of T, but not vice versa. This is reflected by the following characterisations, in which we add an additional conjunct to rule out those models which correspond to stable expansions but not to **N**-expansions.

Theorem 3. *Let T be an autoepistemic theory and ψ a formula. Furthermore, let* $\Lambda^+ = \bigwedge_{L\phi \in M_T}(L\phi \rightarrow L\phi')$ *and* $\Lambda^- = \bigwedge_{L\phi \in M_T}(\neg L\phi \rightarrow \neg L\phi')$, *and consider the following QBFs:*

$$\mathcal{F}_{ael}[T, M_T] \wedge \Phi_{\mathbf{N}}[T' \wedge \Lambda^-, \Lambda^+, M_{T'}]; \tag{4}$$

$$\mathcal{F}_{ael}^{cred}[T, \psi] \wedge \Phi_{\mathbf{N}}[T' \wedge \Lambda^-, \Lambda^+, M_{T'}]; \tag{5}$$

$$\neg \exists M_T \big(\mathcal{F}_{ael}^{skept}[T, \psi] \wedge \Phi_{\mathbf{N}}[T' \wedge \Lambda^-, \Lambda^+, M_{T'}]\big). \tag{6}$$

Then:

(i) *T has an $\mathbf{N}$-expansion iff (4) is satisfiable. Moreover, the satisfying truth assignments of the free variables M_T in (4) are in a one-to-one correspondence to the $\mathbf{N}$-expansions of T.*

(ii) *T has an $\mathbf{N}$-expansion containing ψ iff (5) is satisfiable. Moreover, the satisfying truth assignments of the free variables M_T in (5) are in a one-to-one correspondence to the $\mathbf{N}$-expansions of T containing ψ.*

(iii) *ψ is contained in all $\mathbf{N}$-expansions of T iff (6) is true.*

Although the notion of an $\mathbf{N}$-expansion overcomes some difficulties arising with stable expansions (cf. Example 3), there are still some unwanted features of nonmonotonic logic $\mathbf{N}$.

As a case in point, consider the theory $T = \{\neg L \neg Lp \rightarrow p\}$. T has two $\mathbf{N}$-expansions: one containing $\neg L \neg Lp$ (and thus p, by propositional inference, and Lp, by the rule of necessitation), the other containing $L \neg Lp$, but neither p nor $\neg p$. Hence, here we have the situation that the objective (i.e., non-modal) part of one $\mathbf{N}$-expansion (namely the one containing neither p nor $\neg p$) is a proper subset of the objective part of the other $\mathbf{N}$-expansion, which, in some sense, is undesirable.

Note that, as shown in [19], all of the reasoning problems discussed so far lie at the second level of the polynomial hierarchy. It is easily verified that the corresponding encodings (1)–(6) yield QBFs possessing one quantifier alternation. Thus, our transformations reflect the inherent complexity of the expressed tasks. Moreover, since the reductions are constructible in polynomial time, they are, in this sense, *efficient*.

We proceed with two approaches which impose a minimality criterion on expansions. These systems were shown to be located at the third level of the polynomial hierarchy [13]. Consequently, our subsequent encodings possess an additional quantifier alternation.

3.3   Parsimoniously Grounded Expansions

Parsimoniously grounded expansions [13] are a natural strengthening of the concept of stable expansions requiring that the objective (i.e., non-modal) part of a stable expansion must be minimal with respect to set inclusion compared to all other stable expansions.

We define the following partial order: Let $S_1, S_2 \subseteq \mathcal{L}_L$ be stable sets. Then, $S_1 \preceq S_2$ iff $S_1 \cap \mathcal{L} \subseteq S_2 \cap \mathcal{L}$. As usual, we write $S_1 \prec S_2$ if $S_1 \preceq S_2$ and $S_2 \not\preceq S_1$.

A stable expansion E_1 of T is *parsimonious* iff there is no stable expansion E_2 of T such that $E_2 \prec E_1$.

Proposition 5 ([13]). *Let E_1, E_2 be stable expansions of T_1 and T_2, respectively. Then, $E_2 \preceq E_1$ iff $F_{T_1}(E_1) \models F_{T_2}(E_2)$, where $F_T(E)$ is the propositional formula resulting from T by substituting all modal atoms $L\phi$ in T by $\top$ if $L\phi \in E$, and by $\bot$ otherwise.*

We define the following modules: Let S, T be autoepistemic theories, and V the propositional atoms occurring in S or T. Furthermore, let $\hat{S}$ be the result of replacing in S (uniformly) all modal atoms $L\phi$ by $L\phi'$, providing $L\phi \in M_S$. Then:

$$\Phi_\prec[S, T] = \forall V(T \rightarrow \hat{S}) \wedge \neg\forall V(\hat{S} \rightarrow T);$$
$$\Phi_{pars}[T] = \neg\exists M_{T'}\Big(\Phi_\prec[T, T] \wedge \mathcal{F}_{ael}[T', M_{T'}]\Big).$$

Theorem 4. *Let T be an autoepistemic theory and ψ a formula. Consider the following QBFs:*

$$\mathcal{F}_{ael}[T, M_T] \wedge \Phi_{pars}[T]; \tag{7}$$
$$\mathcal{F}_{ael}^{cred}[T, \psi] \wedge \Phi_{pars}[T]; \tag{8}$$
$$\neg\exists M_T\big(\mathcal{F}_{ael}^{skept}[T, \psi] \wedge \Phi_{pars}[T]\big). \tag{9}$$

Then:

(i)   *T has a parsimoniously grounded expansion iff (7) is satisfiable. Moreover, the satisfying truth assignments of the free variables M_T in (7) are in a one-to-one correspondence to the parsimoniously grounded expansions of T.*

(ii) *T has a parsimoniously grounded expansion containing ψ iff (8) is satisfiable. Moreover, the satisfying truth assignments of the free variables M_T in (8) are in a one-to-one correspondence to the parsimoniously grounded expansions of T containing ψ.*

(iii) *ψ is contained in all parsimoniously grounded expansions of T iff (9) is true.*

3.4   Moderately Grounded Expansions

Konolige [24] suggested to restrict stable expansions to *moderately grounded expansions*, defined as follows: Let E be a stable expansion of T. Then, E is moderately grounded iff there is no stable set S such that $T \subseteq S$ and $S \prec E$.

The difference between this notion of groundedness and parsimoniously grounded expansions is illustrated by the following example:

Example 4. Consider the autoepistemic theory $T = \{Lp \rightarrow p, p \rightarrow q, Lq\}$. This theory has one parsimoniously grounded expansion, $E = SE_T(\{Lp, Lq\})$. But E is not moderately grounded, since

$$F = \{\phi \mid T \cup \{\neg Lp, Lq\} \models_L \phi\}$$

is a stable set containing T, and the objective part of F is a proper subset of the objective part of E, i.e., $F \prec E$ holds.

We proceed with a characterisation of moderately grounded expansions required for our subsequent QBF encoding.

Proposition 6 ([13]). *A stable expansion E of T is moderately grounded iff there exists no set $\Gamma \subseteq M_T \cup \neg M_T$ such that Γ is T^+-full, where $T^+ = T \cup \{\phi \mid L\phi \in \Gamma\}$, and $SE_{T^+}(\Gamma) \prec E$.*

We define the following QBF module:

$$\Phi_{mod}[T] = \neg \exists M_{T'} \Big(\Phi_{\prec}[S, T] \wedge \mathcal{F}_{ael}[S', M_{S'}] \Big),$$

with $S = T \wedge \bigwedge_{L\phi \in M_T}(L\phi \to \phi)$. Observe that $M_T = M_S$, and thus $M_{T'} = M_{S'}$.

Theorem 5. *Let T be an autoepistemic theory and ψ a formula. Consider the following QBFs:*

$$\mathcal{F}_{ael}[T, M_T] \wedge \Phi_{mod}[T]; \tag{10}$$

$$\mathcal{F}_{ael}^{cred}[T, \psi] \wedge \Phi_{mod}[T]; \tag{11}$$

$$\neg \exists M_T \big(\mathcal{F}_{ael}^{skept}[T, \psi] \wedge \Phi_{mod}[T] \big). \tag{12}$$

Then:

(*i*)   *T has a moderately grounded expansion iff (10) is satisfiable. Moreover, the satisfying truth assignments of the free variables M_T in (10) are in a one-to-one correspondence to the moderately grounded expansions of T.*

(*ii*) *T has a moderately grounded expansion containing ψ iff (11) is satisfiable. Moreover, the satisfying truth assignments of the free variables M_T in (11) are in a one-to-one correspondence to the moderately grounded expansions of T containing ψ.*

(*iii*) *ψ is contained in all moderately grounded expansions of T iff (12) is true.*

4   Implementation

Our methodology for expressing several modal nonmonotonic logics in terms of quantified Boolean formulas is motivated by the availability of several practically efficient QBF-solvers. Among the different tools, there is a propositional theorem prover, `boole`,[1] based on *binary decision diagrams*, a system using a generalised resolution principle [23], several provers implementing an extended Davis-Putnam procedure [5,15,18, 25,37], as well as a distributed algorithm running on a PC-cluster [15]. With the exception of `boole`, these tools do not accept arbitrary QBFs, but require the input formula to be in *prenex conjunctive normal form*. To avoid an exponential increase of formula size, *structure-preserving normal-form translations* [8,9,33] can be used to translate a general QBF into the required normal form. In contrast to the usual normal-form translations based on distributivity laws, structure-preserving normal-form translations introduce

---

[1] The system, together with its source code, can be downloaded from the Web at URL `http://www.cs.cmu.edu/~modelcheck/bdd.html`.

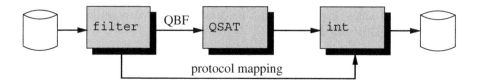

Fig. 1. Architecture to use different QBF-solvers.

new labels for subformula occurrences and are polynomial in the length of the input formula.

The translations discussed in the previous section are implemented as a special module of the reasoning system **QUIP** [11,10,12,7,32], which is a prototype tool for solving several nonmonotonic reasoning tasks based on reductions to QBFs. The general architecture of **QUIP** is depicted in Figure 1. **QUIP** consists of three parts, namely the `filter` program, a QBF-evaluator, and the interpreter `int`. The input filter translates the given problem description (in our case, a modal nonmonotonic theory and a specified reasoning task) into the corresponding quantified Boolean formula, which is then fed into the QBF-evaluator. The current version of **QUIP** provides interfaces to most of the sequential QBF-solvers mentioned above. For the solvers requiring prenex normal form, the QBFs are translated into structure-preserving normal form. The result of the QBF-evaluator is interpreted by `int`. Depending on the capabilities of the employed QBF-evaluator, `int` provides an explanation in terms of the underlying problem instance (e.g., listing all stable expansions of a given autoepistemic theory). This task relies on a protocol mapping of internal variables of the generated QBF into concepts of the problem description which is provided by `filter`.

5   Experimental Results

In this section, we report some experimental results conducted on the implementations of the translations from Section 3. We focus here on the encodings for autoepistemic logic (cf. Proposition 2 and Theorem 1), since these translations represent, in some sense, the core parts for the other formalisms we considered. More specifically, we tested the computational behaviour, in terms of running time, of three different QBF solvers using a class of randomly generated benchmark problems, representing skeptical autoepistemic reasoning. The employed solvers are `ssolve` [15], `QuBe` [18], and `semprop` [25]. These solvers have been chosen because they turned out to be the most efficient ones on some preparatory tests.

The problem instances used here are built up as follows: We consider autoepistemic theories of form

$$T = \{ p_1 \leftrightarrow Lp_1 , \ldots , p_n \leftrightarrow Lp_n , \neg L\phi \rightarrow u \},$$

where ϕ is a randomly generated propositional formula on atoms $p_1, \ldots, p_m$ $(m \geq n)$ not containing u, and the task is to check whether u is contained in all stable expansions

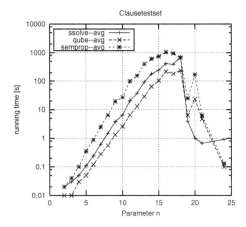

Fig. 2. Running times with varying parameter n and $l = 35$ and $m = 26$ fixed.

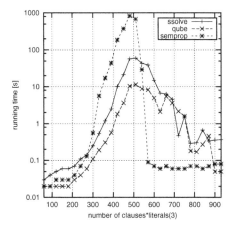

Fig. 3. Running times with varying parameter l and $m = 60$ and $n = 4$ fixed.

of T. This particular class of problems is taken from the Π_2^p-hardness proof of skeptical autoepistemic reasoning, following Gottlob [19]. Thus, in some sense, these problems are responsible for the inherent worst-case complexity of skeptical autoepistemic reasoning.

For the specific tests, we chose ϕ to be in conjunctive normal form built up by l clauses each of which containing three literals. The distribution of the variables p_i in ϕ is in flavour of other benchmark methodologies [17,27] and tries to capture computationally hard instances.

All tests have been performed on Pentium II/450 MHz processors with 128MB RAM running the Linux operating system. The running time is measured in seconds (with an upper time limit set to 1000s) and comprises the sum of both user time and system time.

In the first test set, ϕ is build over $m = 26$ variables and $l = 35$ clauses. We set up 21 sample sets, each containing 50 randomly generated formulas, by varying n from 2 to 24. Figure 2 depicts the observed running times. In the second test set, the number of clauses of ϕ is assumed to be varying, where m was set to 60 and n to 4. Each sample set contains again 50 formulas. Figure 3 shows the results. Note that the y-axes in both graphs are scaled logarithmically.

Observe that the figures indicate quite clearly that the considered test sets cover a complete easy-hard-easy pattern. To wit, in Figure 2, the instances with $n < 15$ are easily evaluated to true, whilst instances with $n > 21$ are easily evaluated to false, and the so-called *phase transition*—containing the most difficult problems—is located in the interval $16 \leq n \leq 21$. A similar phase transition occurs in Figure 3 between 400 and 600.

The most significant result of both tests is that, in general, there is no best solver. Each of the three solvers under consideration outperforms the others on certain instances. While QuBe seems to be most effective on formulas evaluating to true, semprop significantly outperforms the other ones on the instances with $l * 3 \geq 550$ in the second test.

Figure 2 reveals also another interesting behaviour. Here, for both QuBe and semprop, there is a significant peak at $n = 20$, which is not present for ssolve. This peak results from a single instance (out of the 50 tested) which turned out to be hard for QuBe and semprop, but apparently not for ssolve. This, in turn, demonstrates that invoking several solvers in parallel is quite useful in practice.

Clearly, generally speaking, it is a matter of more comprehensive tests in order to obtain a better understanding where the difficulties in solving QBFs of the current kind arise, and thus to be able to provide valuable hints to developers of QBF-solvers.

6   Conclusion

In this paper, we considered the compilation of reasoning tasks into quantified Boolean formulas as an approach to realise prototype reasoning engines for several modal non-monotonic logics. The need for these logics in Artificial Intelligence has been well recognised in the literature. However, in contrast to other nonmonotonic-reasoning formalisms like default logic or logic programming with negation as failure, none of the considered approaches currently possesses publicly available solvers.

The investigated decision problems belong to the second and third level of the polynomial hierarchy, respectively, and are thus, from a computational point of view, "intractable". The translations described here are polynomial-time constructible and their existence is guaranteed by corresponding complexity results.

The employed framework is a natural generalisation of a similar method successfully applied to problems in NP. In general, the use of QBFs for knowledge representation purposes has been advocated in the literature [5,37], and, besides the current framework, reductions of other reasoning tasks to QBFs have been discussed in [36,11].

We reported some experiments using the implementation of our encodings for autoepistemic logic. Due to the absence of available solvers for modal nonmonotonic logics, we focused here on a comparison of different QBF-solvers, constituting core engines for the system QUIP.

Finally, a particular advantage of our modular approach is the straightforward ability to *parallelise* the entire evaluation process. On the one hand, this can be done by using different provers in parallel, and, on the other hand, by using the distributed QBF-solver PQsolve [15].

Future issues include a more thorough experimental evaluation, as well as investigating possible optimisations of the current translations.

References

1. P. Bonatti and N. Olivetti. Sequent Calculi for Propositional Nonmonotonic Logics. *ACM Transactions on Computational Logic*, 2002. To appear.
2. G. Brewka. Tweety - Still Flying: Some Remarks on Abnormal Birds, Applicable Rules and a Default Prover. In *Proc. AAAI-86*, pages 8–12, 1986.
3. G. Brewka. *Nonmonotonic Reasoning: Logical Foundations of Commonsense*. Cambridge University Press, 1991.
4. G. Brewka and K. Wittur. Nichtmonotone Logiken. Universität Bonn, Informatik Berichte 40, 1984.
5. M. Cadoli, A. Giovanardi, and M. Schaerf. An Algorithm to Evaluate Quantified Boolean Formulae. In *Proc. AAAI-98*, pages 262–267, 1998.
6. P. Cholewinski, W. Marek, and M. Truszcyński. Default Reasoning System DeReS. In *Proc. KR-96*, pages 518–528, 1996.
7. J. Delgrande, T. Schaub, H. Tompits, and S. Woltran. On Computing Solutions to Belief Change Scenarios. In *Proc. ECSQARU-01*, pages 510–521, 2001.
8. E. Eder. *Relative Complexities of First-Order Calculi*. Vieweg Verlag, 1992.
9. U. Egly. On Different Structure-preserving Translations to Normal Form. *Journal of Symbolic Computation*, 22:121–142, 1996.
10. U. Egly, T. Eiter, V. Klotz, H. Tompits, and S. Woltran. Computing Stable Models with Quantified Boolean Formulas: Some Experimental Results. In *Proc. AAAI Spring Symposium-01*, pages 53–59, 2001.
11. U. Egly, T. Eiter, H. Tompits, and S. Woltran. Solving Advanced Reasoning Tasks Using Quantified Boolean Formulas. In *Proc. AAAI-00*, pages 417–422, 2000.
12. U. Egly, V. Klotz, H. Tompits, and S. Woltran. A Toolbox for Abduction: Preliminary Report. In *Proc. IJCAR-Workshop on Theory and Applications of Quantified Boolean Formulas*, pages 29–39, 2001.
13. T. Eiter and G. Gottlob. Complexity of Reasoning with Parsimonious and Moderately Grounded Expansions. *Fundamenta Informaticae*, 17(1-2):31–53, 1992.
14. T. Eiter, N. Leone, C. Mateis, G. Pfeifer, and F. Scarcello. A Deductive System for Non-monotonic Reasoning. In *Proc. LPNMR-97*, pages 363–374, 1997.
15. R. Feldmann, B. Monien, and S. Schamberger. A Distributed Algorithm to Evaluate Quantified Boolean Formulas. In *Proc. AAAI-00*, pages 285–290, 2000.
16. M. Gelfond and V. Lifschitz. The Stable Model Semantics for Logic Programming. In *Proc. ICLP-88*, pages 1070–1080, 1988.
17. I. P. Gent and T. Walsh. Beyond NP: The QSAT Phase Transition. In *Proc. AAAI-99*, pages 648–653, 1999.
18. E. Giunchiglia, M. Narizzano, and A. Tacchella. QUBE: A System for Deciding Quantified Boolean Formulas Satisfiability. In *Proc. IJCAR-01*, pages 364–369, 2001.

19. G. Gottlob. Complexity Results for Nonmonotonic Logics. *Journal of Logic and Computation*, 2(3):397–425, 1992.
20. G. Gottlob. Translating Default Logic into Standard Autoepistemic Logic. *Journal of the ACM*, 42(4):711–740, 1995.
21. U. Junker and K. Konolige. Computing the Extensions of Autoepistemic and Default Logic with a TMS. In *Proc. AAAI-90*, pages 278–283, 1990.
22. H. Kautz and B. Selman. Planning as Satisfiability. In *Proc. ECAI-92*, pages 359–363, 1992.
23. H. Kleine-Büning, M. Karpinski, and A. Flögel. Resolution for Quantified Boolean Formulas. *Information and Computation*, 117(1):12–18, 1995.
24. K. Konolige. On the Relation Between Default and Autoepistemic Logic. *Artificial Intelligence*, 35(3):343–382, 1988.
25. R. Letz. Advances in Decision Procedures for Quantified Boolean Formulas. In *Proc. IJCAR-Workshop on Theory and Applications of Quantified Boolean Formulas*, pages 55–64, 2001.
26. W. Marek and M. Truszczyński. Modal Logic for Default Reasoning. *Annals of Mathematics and Artificial Intelligence*, 1:275–302, 1990.
27. F. Massacci. Design and Results of the Tableaux-99 Non-classical (Modal) Systems Comparison. In *Proc. TABLEAUX-99*, pages 14–18, 1999.
28. J. McCarthy. Circumscription - A Form of Nonmonotonic Reasoning. *Artificial Intelligence*, 13:27–39, 1980.
29. R. C. Moore. Semantical Considerations on Nonmonotonic Logic. *Artificial Intelligence*, 25(1):75–94, 1985.
30. I. Niemelä. On the Decidability and Complexity of Autoepistemic Reasoning. *Fundamenta Informaticae*, 17:117–155, 1992.
31. I. Niemelä and P. Simons. Smodels: An Implementation of the Stable Model and Well-Founded Semantics for Normal Logic Programs. In *Proc. LPNMR-97*, pages 420–429, 1997.
32. D. Pearce, H. Tompits, and S. Woltran. Encodings for Equilibrium Logic and Logic Programs with Nested Expressions. In *Proc. EPIA-01*, pages 306–320. Springer, 2001.
33. D. A. Plaisted and S. Greenbaum. A Structure Preserving Clause Form Translation. *Journal of Symbolic Computation*, 2(3):293–304, 1986.
34. T. Przymusinski. Stable Semantics for Disjunctive Programs. *New Generation Computing Journal*, 9:401–424, 1991.
35. R. Reiter. A Logic for Default Reasoning. *Artificial Intelligence*, 13(1–2):81–132, Apr. 1980.
36. J. Rintanen. Constructing Conditional Plans by a Theorem Prover. *Journal of Artificial Intelligence Research*, 10:323–352, 1999.
37. J. Rintanen. Improvements to the Evaluation of Quantified Boolean Formulae. In *Proc. IJCAI-99*, pages 1192–1197, 1999.

Tableau Calculi for the Logics of Finite k-Ary Trees

Mauro Ferrari[1], Camillo Fiorentini[1], and Guido Fiorino[2]

[1] Dipartimento di Scienze dell'Informazione, Università degli Studi di Milano
Via Comelico, 39, 20135 Milano, Italy
[2] CRII, Università dell'Insubria,Via Ravasi 2, 21100 Varese, Italy

Abstract. We present tableau calculi for the logics $\mathbf{D}_k$ $(k \geq 2)$ semantically characterized by the classes of Kripke models built on finite k-ary trees. Our tableau calculi use the signs $\mathbf{T}$ and $\mathbf{F}$, some tableau rules for Intuitionistic Logic and two rules formulated in a hypertableau fashion. We prove the Soundness and Completeness Theorems for our calculi. Finally, we use them to prove the main properties of the logics $\mathbf{D}_k$, in particular their constructivity and their decidability.

1 Introduction

In recent years there has been a growing interest (see [1,3,4,6,7,8,10,11]) in proof-theoretical characterization of *propositional intermediate logics*, that is logics laying between Intuitionistic and Classical Logic. This interest is motivated by the applications of some of these logics. As an example we recall *Dummett-Gödel Logic*, studied for its relationship with multi-valued and fuzzy logics [14]; *Jankov Logic* and *here-and-there Logic*, studied for their application to Logic Programming [15,16].

Apart from the cases of Intuitionistic and Classical Logic, the proof-theoretical characterization of Intermediate Logics given in the literature relies on variations of the standard sequent calculi or tableau calculi. As an example, the tableau calculi for the interpolable Intermediate Logics described in [1,10, 11] use new signs besides the usual signs $\mathbf{T}$ and $\mathbf{F}$ (we remark that the calculi of [10,11] give rise to space-efficient decision procedures). However, this approach seems hard to apply to several families of interesting Intermediate Logics. Another approach relies on hypersequent calculi, a natural generalization of sequent calculi; e.g., in [3] a hypersequent characterization of Dummett-Gödel Logic is presented, while in [7] the authors extend this approach to some families of Intermediate Logics with bounded Kripke models. However, also the approach based on hypersequent calculi or hypertableau calculi (the dualized version of hypersequents presented in [6]) seems to be inadequate to treat some Intermediate Logics and further variations are needed. An example is given in [6], where the notion of path-hypertableau calculus is introduced to treat the intermediate logic of finite-depth Kripke models.

Despite the wide research in this field, we remark that all the intermediate logics studied in the above mentioned papers fail to be *constructive*, where

U. Egly and C.G. Fermüller (Eds.): TABLEAUX 2002, LNAI 2381, pp. 115–129, 2002.

we call *constructive* any intermediate logic **L** satisfying the *disjunction property*: $A \lor B \in \mathbf{L}$ implies $A \in \mathbf{L}$ or $B \in \mathbf{L}$. As it is well-known, there exists a continuum of constructive intermediate logics [5,9], but, as far as we know, no proof-theoretical characterizations of constructive logics are known, apart from those given in [2]. In that paper *generalized tableau calculi* for the constructive logics $\mathbf{D}_k$ ($k \geq 2$) and for the constructive *Kreisel-Putnam Logic* are presented; however, such calculi are far from being genuine tableau calculi and are highly inefficient. Indeed, they are obtained by adding to the intuitionistic tableau calculus a special rule allowing us to introduce, at any point of the derivation, a suitable **T**-signed instance of the schema characterizing the logic.

In this paper we provide tableau calculi for the intermediate constructive logics $\mathbf{D}_k$ ($k \geq 2$) of finite k-ary trees. $\mathbf{D}_k$ is the set of all the formulas valid in every Kripke model built on a finite k-ary tree. These logics have been introduced in [13], where a finite axiomatization of every $\mathbf{D}_k$ is given, and their decidability is proved. Our proof-theoretical characterization is based on a *hybrid* tableau calculus that uses the two usual signs **T** and **F**, some tableau rules for Intuitionistic Logic and two rules formulated in a hypertableau fashion (a structural rule and a purely logical rule). Then we use such calculi to provide a proof of the main properties of the logics $\mathbf{D}_k$, in particular their constructivity and their decidability.

The paper is organized as follows: in Section 2 we introduce the logics $\mathbf{D}_k$ providing both the axiomatization and the semantical characterization in terms of families of Kripke models. In Section 3 we introduce the calculi $\mathbf{TD}_k$ and we prove that they characterize the logics $\mathbf{D}_k$. Finally, in Section 4 we use these calculi to prove the main properties of the logics $\mathbf{D}_k$.

2   Preliminaries

Here we consider the propositional language based on a denumerable set of atomic symbols and the logical constants $\bot, \land, \lor, \rightarrow$. We denote with $p, q, \ldots$, possibly with indexes, the atomic symbols and with $A, B, \ldots$, possibly with indexes, arbitrary formulas. Moreover, as usual in the setting of intermediate logics, $\neg A$ is defined as $A \rightarrow \bot$. **Int** and **Cl** denote respectively the set of intuitionistically and classically valid formulas.

An *intermediate propositional logic* (see, e.g., [5]) is any set L of formulas satisfying the following conditions: (i) L is consistent; (ii) **Int** $\subseteq$ L; (iii) L is closed under modus ponens; (iv) L is closed under propositional substitution (where a *propositional substitution* is any function mapping every propositional variable to a formula). It is well-known that, for any intermediate logic L, L $\subseteq$ **Cl**.

Many intermediate logics can be semantically characterized by families of Kripke models. A *(propositional) Kripke model* (see, e.g., [5]) is a structure $\underline{K} = \langle P, \leq, \Vdash \rangle$, where $\langle P, \leq \rangle$ is a *poset* (partially ordered set), and $\Vdash$ (the *forcing relation*) is a binary relation between elements of P and atomic symbols such that, for every atomic symbol p, $\alpha \Vdash p$ implies $\beta \Vdash p$ for every $\beta \in P$ such that $\alpha \leq \beta$. The forcing relation is extended to arbitrary formulas as follows:

1. $\alpha \not\Vdash \bot$;
2. $\alpha \Vdash B \wedge C$ iff $\alpha \Vdash B$ and $\alpha \Vdash C$;
3. $\alpha \Vdash B \vee C$ iff $\alpha \Vdash B$ or $\alpha \Vdash C$;
4. $\alpha \Vdash B \rightarrow C$ iff, for every $\beta \in P$ such that $\alpha \leq \beta$, $\beta \Vdash B$ implies $\beta \Vdash C$.

We write $\alpha \not\Vdash A$ to mean that $\alpha \Vdash A$ does not hold. We remark that, according to the above interpretation, $\alpha \Vdash \neg A$ iff, for every $\beta \in P$ such that $\alpha \leq \beta$, we have $\beta \not\Vdash A$.

It is easy to check that the forcing relation meets the monotonicity condition:

Proposition 1. *For every formula A, Kripke model $\underline{K} = \langle P, \leq, \Vdash \rangle$ and element α in $\underline{K}$, if $\alpha \Vdash A$ then $\beta \Vdash A$ for every $\beta \in P$ such that $\alpha \leq \beta$.*

Given a Kripke model $\underline{K} = \langle P, \leq, \Vdash \rangle$, we write $\alpha < \beta$ to mean that $\alpha \leq \beta$ and $\alpha \neq \beta$. Given $\alpha \in P$, we call *immediate successor* of α (in $\underline{K}$) any $\beta \in P$ such that $\alpha < \beta$ and, for every $\gamma \in P$, if $\alpha \leq \gamma \leq \beta$ then either $\gamma = \alpha$ or $\gamma = \beta$. We call *final element* of $\underline{K}$ any $\phi \in P$ such that, for every $\alpha \in P$, if $\phi \leq \alpha$ then $\phi = \alpha$. It is easy to check that a *final element* ϕ of $\underline{K}$ behaves like a classical interpretation, that is, for every formula A, either $\phi \Vdash A$ or $\phi \Vdash \neg A$.

A formula A *is valid in a Kripke model* $\underline{K}$ if $\alpha \Vdash A$ for all $\alpha \in P$. If $\mathcal{K}$ is a non empty class of Kripke models, A *is valid in* $\mathcal{K}$ if it is valid in every model of $\mathcal{K}$.

For every $k \geq 2$, let (D_k) be the axiom schema

$$\bigwedge_{i=0}^{k} \left((p_i \rightarrow \bigvee_{j \neq i} p_j) \rightarrow \bigvee_{j \neq i} p_j \right) \rightarrow \bigvee_{i=0}^{k} p_i$$

and let $\mathbf{D}_k$ denote the closure under modus ponens and propositional substitution of the set containing **Int** and all the instances of the axiom schema (D_k). As shown in [13] every $\mathbf{D}_k$ $(k \geq 2)$ is an intermediate logic and the sequence $\{\mathbf{D}_k\}_{k \geq 2}$ has the following properties:

- $\cap_{k \geq 2} \mathbf{D}_k = \mathbf{Int}$;
- For every $k \geq 2$, $\mathbf{D}_k \supset \mathbf{D}_{k+1}$;
- For every $k \geq 2$, $\mathbf{D}_k$ has the *disjunction property*: that is, for every formula of the kind $A \vee B$, if $A \vee B \in \mathbf{D}_k$, then $A \in \mathbf{D}_k$ or $B \in \mathbf{D}_k$;
- Every D_k is decidable.

Now, let $\mathcal{T}_k$ be the the family of all the Kripke models $\underline{K} = \langle P, \leq, \Vdash \rangle$ where:

- $\langle P, \leq \rangle$ is a finite tree;
- Given $\alpha \in P$, α has at most k immediate successors in $\langle P, \leq \rangle$.

In [13] the following result is proved:

Theorem 1. *For every $k \geq 2$, $A \in \mathbf{D}_k$ iff A is valid in $\mathcal{T}_k$.*

Hence the above result shows that every logic $\mathbf{D}_k$ is characterized by the class of finite k-ary trees.

The above quoted properties of the logics $\mathbf{D}_k$ are proved in [13] by means of semantical tools. In particular the decidability of $\mathbf{D}_k$ relies on the decidability of the second order theory describing the validity of formulas in $\mathcal{T}_k$ and the disjunction property follows from a property of the class of models $\mathcal{T}_k$. In the following sections we introduce a tableau calculus for every $\mathbf{TD}_k$ and then we use the properties of such a calculus to deduce the decidability and the disjunction property for $\mathbf{D}_k$.

3   The Sequence of Tableau Calculi $\mathbf{TD}_k$ $(k \geq 2)$

A *signed formula* (*swff* for short) is an expression of the form $\mathbf{T}X$ or $\mathbf{F}X$ where X is any formula. The meaning of the signs $\mathbf{T}$ and $\mathbf{F}$ is as follows: given a Kripke model $\underline{K} = \langle P, \leq, \Vdash \rangle$ and a swff H, $\alpha \in P$ *realizes* H (in symbols $\alpha \triangleright H$) if $H \equiv \mathbf{T}X$ and $\alpha \Vdash X$, or $H \equiv \mathbf{F}X$ and $\alpha \nVdash X$. $\alpha \ntriangleright H$ means that $\alpha \triangleright H$ does not hold. α realizes a set of swff's S ($\alpha \triangleright S$) if α realizes every swff in S. By Proposition 1, if $\alpha \triangleright \mathbf{T}X$ then $\beta \triangleright \mathbf{T}X$ for every $\beta \in P$ such that $\alpha \leq \beta$. On the other hand, if $\alpha \triangleright \mathbf{F}X$, then can exist $\beta \in P$ such that $\alpha \leq \beta$ and $\beta \ntriangleright \mathbf{F}X$.

A *hyperset* is an expression of the form

$$S_1 \mid \ldots \mid S_n$$

where, for all $i = 1, \ldots, n$, S_i is a set of swff's. S_i is called a *component* of the hyperset. We call *simple hyperset* a hyperset containing exactly one component. A *configuration* is an expression of the form

$$\Psi_1 \parallel \ldots \parallel \Psi_m$$

where, for all $i = 1, \ldots, m$, Ψ_i is a hyperset. Ψ_i is called a *component* of the configuration. A *simple configuration* is a configuration where every component is a simple hyperset.

The intended meaning of the symbol $\mid$ is conjunctive while the one of the symbol $\parallel$ is disjunctive. Formally, given a Kripke model $\underline{K} = \langle P, \leq, \Vdash \rangle$, $\underline{K}$ *realizes a hyperset* $S_1 \mid \ldots \mid S_n$ if, for every $i = 1, \ldots, n$, there exists $\alpha_i \in P$ such that $\alpha_i \triangleright S_i$. On the other hand, $\underline{K}$ *realizes a configuration* $\Psi_1 \parallel \ldots \parallel \Psi_m$ if there exists a hyperset Ψ_j, with $j \in \{1, \ldots, m\}$, such that $\underline{K}$ realizes Ψ_j.

The rules of Table 1 are common to all the calculi $\mathbf{TD}_k$ for $k \geq 2$ and are independent of the parameter k. The rule properly characterizing the tableau calculus $\mathbf{TD}_k$ is D_k and it will be introduced in a while. Before that we introduce some notations. First of all, in the rules of the calculus $\mathbf{TD}_k$, we simply denote with $S, H_1, \ldots, H_h$ the set $S \cup \{H_1, \ldots, H_h\}$. The rules apply to configurations but, to simplify the notation, we omit the components of the configuration not involved in the rule. E.g., the schema

$$\frac{S_1 \parallel \ldots \parallel S, \mathbf{T}(A \wedge B) \parallel \ldots \parallel S_n}{S_1 \parallel \ldots \parallel S, \mathbf{T}A, \mathbf{T}B \parallel \ldots \parallel S_n} \mathbf{T}\wedge$$

illustrates an application of the $\mathbf{T}\wedge$-rule. In every rule we distinguish two parts: the *premise*, that is the configuration above the line, and the *conclusion*, that is the configuration below the line. We remark that all the rules of Table 1 but

Table 1. Rules common to all the $\mathbf{TD}_k$

$$\frac{S, \mathbf{T}(A \wedge B)}{S, \mathbf{T}A, \mathbf{T}B} \mathbf{T}\wedge \qquad \frac{S, \mathbf{F}(A \wedge B)}{S, \mathbf{F}A \parallel S, \mathbf{F}B} \mathbf{F}\wedge$$

$$\frac{S, \mathbf{T}(A \vee B)}{S, \mathbf{T}A \parallel S, \mathbf{T}B} \mathbf{T}\vee \qquad \frac{S, \mathbf{F}(A \vee B)}{S, \mathbf{F}A} \mathbf{F}\vee_1 \qquad \frac{S, \mathbf{F}(A \vee B)}{S, \mathbf{F}B} \mathbf{F}\vee_2$$

$$\frac{S, \mathbf{T}A, \mathbf{T}(A \rightarrow B)}{S, \mathbf{T}A, \mathbf{T}B} \mathbf{T}\rightarrow Atom \text{ with } A \text{ an atom}$$

$$\frac{S, \mathbf{T}((A \wedge B) \rightarrow C)}{S, \mathbf{T}(A \rightarrow (B \rightarrow C))} \mathbf{T}\rightarrow\wedge \qquad \frac{S, \mathbf{T}((A \vee B) \rightarrow C)}{S, \mathbf{T}(A \rightarrow C), \mathbf{T}(B \rightarrow C)} \mathbf{T}\rightarrow\vee$$

$$\frac{S, \mathbf{T}((A \rightarrow B) \rightarrow C)}{S, \mathbf{F}(A \rightarrow B), \mathbf{T}((A \rightarrow B) \rightarrow C) \parallel S, \mathbf{T}C} \mathbf{T}\rightarrow\rightarrow$$

$$\frac{S_1 \mid \ldots \mid S_i \mid \ldots \mid S_n}{S_i} \text{Weak}$$

Weak only involve simple configurations (both the premise and the consequence of such rules are simple configurations). On the other hand, Weak has a non simple configuration as premise and a simple configuration as consequence; on the contrary, as we will see, the rule D_k properly characterizing $\mathbf{TD}_k$ has a simple configuration as premise and (in general) a non simple configuration as consequence.

We call *main set of swff's* of a rule the set of swff's that are in evidence in the premise of the rule; when the main set of swff's of a rule contains just a swff we call it the *main swff* of the rule. As an example, $\mathbf{T}(A \wedge B)$ is the main swff of the rule $\mathbf{T}\wedge$ while $\{\mathbf{T}A, \mathbf{T}(A \rightarrow B)\}$ is the main set of swff's of the rule $\mathbf{T} \rightarrow Atom$. The rule Weak is a structural rule; it acts on components of a hyperset and it does not have a main set of swff's.

The rule properly characterizing the calculus $\mathbf{TD}_k$ is D_k that applies to the premise

$$S, \mathbf{F}(A_1 \rightarrow B_1), \ldots, \mathbf{F}(A_n \rightarrow B_n), \mathbf{T}((C_1 \rightarrow D_1) \rightarrow E_1), \ldots, \mathbf{T}((C_m \rightarrow D_m) \rightarrow E_m)$$

Let

$$U = \{\mathbf{F}(A_1 \rightarrow B_1), \ldots, \mathbf{F}(A_n \rightarrow B_n)\}$$
$$V = \{\mathbf{T}((C_1 \rightarrow D_1) \rightarrow E_1), \ldots, \mathbf{T}((C_m \rightarrow D_m) \rightarrow E_m)\}$$

and let $U \cup V$ be the main set of swff's of the rule. Now, let Σ_U be the set containing all the subsets of U different from U itself and the empty set. We remark that the cardinality of Σ_U is $2^n - 2$. We denote with Σ_U^k the set of all the *complete k-sequences* of Σ_U, that is the set of all the sequences $\Phi_1, \ldots, \Phi_h$ of elements of Σ_U such that:

- $h \leq k$;
- $\bigcup_{1 \leq i \leq h} \Phi_i = U$.

We associate with every sequence $\sigma \equiv \Phi_1, \ldots, \Phi_h$ belonging to Σ_U^k the hyperset

$$\mathcal{H}_\sigma \equiv S_c, \Phi_1, \Psi_1 \mid \ldots \mid S_c, \Phi_h, \Psi_h$$

where, $S_c = \{\mathbf{T}A \mid \mathbf{T}A \in S\}$ and, for $i = 1, \ldots, h$

$$\Psi_i = \{\mathbf{T}E \mid \mathbf{T}((C \to D) \to E) \in V \text{ and } \mathbf{F}(C \to D) \notin \Phi_i\}$$
$$\cup \{\mathbf{T}((C \to D) \to E) \mid \mathbf{T}((C \to D) \to E) \in V \text{ and } \mathbf{F}(C \to D) \in \Phi_i\}$$
$$\cup \{\mathbf{T}((C \to D) \to E) \mid \mathbf{T}((C \to D) \to E) \in V \text{ and } \mathbf{F}(C \to D) \notin U\}$$

The rule D_k is

$$\frac{S, \mathbf{F}(A_1 \to B_1), \ldots, \mathbf{F}(A_n \to B_n), \mathbf{T}((C_1 \to D_1) \to E_1), \ldots, \mathbf{T}((C_m \to D_m) \to E_m)}{S_c, \Gamma_1, \Delta_1 \parallel \ldots \parallel S_c, \Gamma_n, \Delta_n \parallel \mathcal{H}_{\sigma_1} \parallel \ldots \parallel \mathcal{H}_{\sigma_r}} D_k$$

where $\sigma_1, \ldots, \sigma_r$ are all the complete k-sequences in Σ_U^k and, for $i = 1, \ldots, n$

$$\Gamma_i = U \setminus \{\mathbf{F}(A_i \to B_i)\} \cup \{\mathbf{T}A_i, \mathbf{F}B_i\}$$
$$\Delta_i = \{\mathbf{T}(B_i \to E) \mid \mathbf{T}((A_i \to B_i) \to E) \in V\}$$
$$\cup \{\mathbf{T}((C \to D) \to E) \in V \mid C \to D \not\equiv A_i \to B_i\}$$

The following is an example of application of D_2 where the components of the consequence occur in different lines

$$\frac{\mathbf{F}(A \to B), \mathbf{F}(C \to D), \mathbf{F}(E \to G), \mathbf{T}((A \to B) \to H)}{\begin{array}{c} \mathbf{T}A, \mathbf{F}B, \mathbf{F}(C \to D), \mathbf{F}(E \to G), \mathbf{T}(B \to H) \parallel \\ \mathbf{F}(A \to B), \mathbf{T}C, \mathbf{F}D, \mathbf{F}(E \to G), \mathbf{T}((A \to B) \to H) \parallel \\ \mathbf{F}(A \to B), \mathbf{F}(C \to D), \mathbf{T}E, \mathbf{F}G, \mathbf{T}((A \to B) \to H) \parallel \\ \mathbf{F}(A \to B), \mathbf{T}((A \to B) \to H) \mid \mathbf{F}(C \to D), \mathbf{F}(E \to G), \mathbf{T}H \parallel \\ \mathbf{F}(C \to D), \mathbf{T}H \mid \mathbf{F}(A \to B), \mathbf{F}(E \to G), \mathbf{T}((A \to B) \to H) \parallel \\ \mathbf{F}(E \to G), \mathbf{T}H \mid \mathbf{F}(A \to B), \mathbf{F}(C \to D), \mathbf{T}((A \to B) \to H) \parallel \\ \mathbf{F}(A \to B), \mathbf{F}(C \to D), \mathbf{T}((A \to B) \to H) \mid \mathbf{F}(A \to B), \mathbf{F}(E \to G), \mathbf{T}((A \to B) \to H) \parallel \\ \mathbf{F}(A \to B), \mathbf{F}(C \to D), \mathbf{T}((A \to B) \to H) \mid \mathbf{F}(C \to D), \mathbf{F}(E \to G), \mathbf{T}H \parallel \\ \mathbf{F}(A \to B), \mathbf{F}(E \to G), \mathbf{T}((A \to B) \to H) \mid \mathbf{F}(C \to D), \mathbf{F}(E \to G), \mathbf{T}H \end{array}} D_2$$

We remark that, if $U = \{\mathbf{F}(A_1 \to B_1)\}$ the corresponding instance of D_k is

$$\frac{S, \mathbf{F}(A_1 \to B_1), \mathbf{T}((C_1 \to D_1) \to E_1), \ldots, \mathbf{T}((C_m \to D_m) \to E_m)}{S_c, \mathbf{T}A_1, \mathbf{F}B_1, \Delta_1} D_k$$

which is a purely intuitionistic rule.

A set S of swff's is *contradictory* if one of the following conditions holds:

1. $\mathbf{T}A \in S$ and $\mathbf{F}A \in S$;
2. $\mathbf{T}\bot \in S$.

A hyperset $S_1 \mid \ldots \mid S_n$ is *contradictory* if at least one of the S_i is contradictory and a configuration $\Psi_1 \parallel \ldots \parallel \Psi_m$ is *contradictory* if all the Ψ_i are contradictory. It is easy to check that:

Proposition 2. *If a configuration is contradictory then it is not realizable in any Kripke model.*

Given the tableau calculus $\mathbf{TD}_k$, a $\mathbf{TD}_k$-*proof table for a configuration* $\mathcal{K}_1$ is a finite sequence of configurations $\mathcal{K}_1, \ldots, \mathcal{K}_n$, where the configuration $\mathcal{K}_{i+1}$ is obtained from $\mathcal{K}_i = \Psi_1 \| \ldots \| \Psi_m$ by applying a rule to a non-contradictory hyperset. A *closed* $\mathbf{TD}_k$-*proof table* is a $\mathbf{TD}_k$-proof table $\mathcal{K}_1, \ldots, \mathcal{K}_n$ where the last configuration is contradictory. Closed $\mathbf{TD}_k$-proof tables are the proofs of our calculus $\mathbf{TD}_k$. A formula A *is provable in* $\mathbf{TD}_k$ if there exists a closed $\mathbf{TD}_k$-proof table for the configuration $\{\mathbf{F}A\}$ (the configuration consisting of the set $\{\mathbf{F}A\}$ only).

Now, our aim is to prove that, for every $k \geq 2$, the calculus $\mathbf{TD}_k$ is sound and complete with respect to the class of Kripke models $\mathcal{T}_k$. As usual the main step of the Soundness Theorem consists in proving that the rules of the calculus preserve realizability.

Lemma 1. *If the premise of a rule of* $\mathbf{TD}_k$ *is realized in a model* $\underline{K} \in \mathcal{T}_k$, *then the consequence of the rule is realized in* $\underline{K}$.

Proof. We only analyze the case of the rule D_k the other cases being trivial. So, let us assume that $\underline{K} = \langle P, \leq, \Vdash \rangle \in \mathcal{T}_k$ and that an element $\alpha \in P$ realizes the set of swff's $\Gamma = S \cup U \cup V$, where S is any set of swff's and

$$U = \{\mathbf{F}(A_1 \to B_1), \ldots, \mathbf{F}(A_n \to B_n)\}$$
$$V = \{\mathbf{T}((C_1 \to D_1) \to E_1), \ldots, \mathbf{T}((C_m \to D_m) \to E_m)\}$$

Now, since $\underline{K}$ is finite, there exists an element β such that $\alpha \leq \beta$, $\beta \rhd U$ and, for every $\gamma > \beta$, $\gamma \not\rhd U$. We have two cases:

Case 1: There exists an $i \in \{1, \ldots, n\}$ such that $\beta \rhd \{\mathbf{T}A_i, \mathbf{F}B_i\}$. This implies that $\beta \rhd \Gamma_i$ where $\Gamma_i = U \setminus \{\mathbf{F}(A_i \to B_i)\} \cup \{\mathbf{T}A_i, \mathbf{F}B_i\}$; moreover, since $\alpha \leq \beta$, $\beta \rhd S_c \cup V$ and, since $\beta \rhd \mathbf{T}((A_i \to B_i) \to E)$ implies $\beta \rhd \mathbf{T}(B_i \to E)$, we get $\beta \rhd S_c, \Gamma_i, \Delta_i$.

Case 2: For every $i \in \{1, \ldots, n\}$, $\beta \not\rhd \{\mathbf{T}A_i, \mathbf{F}B_i\}$. Then, for every $\mathbf{F}(A_i \to B_i) \in U$ there exists $\gamma \in P$ such that $\beta < \gamma$ and $\gamma \rhd \{\mathbf{T}A_i, \mathbf{F}B_i\}$. Let Θ be the set of all $\gamma \in P$ such that $\beta < \gamma$ and $\gamma \rhd \{\mathbf{T}A_i, \mathbf{F}B_i\}$ for some $\mathbf{F}(A_i \to B_i) \in U$. Since $\underline{K} \in \mathcal{T}_k$, β has at most k immediate successors. Let $\delta_1, \ldots, \delta_h$ ($h \leq k$) be the distinct immediate successors of β such that there exists $\gamma \in \Theta$ such that $\delta_i \leq \gamma$. Let, for $i = 1, \ldots, h$

$$\Phi_i = \{\mathbf{F}(A \to B) \in U \mid \delta_i \rhd \mathbf{F}(A \to B)\}$$
$$\Psi_i = \{\mathbf{T}E \mid \mathbf{T}((C \to D) \to E) \in V \text{ and } \mathbf{F}(C \to D) \notin \Phi_i\}$$
$$\cup \{\mathbf{T}((C \to D) \to E) \mid \mathbf{T}((C \to D) \to E) \in V \text{ and } \mathbf{F}(C \to D) \in \Phi_i\}$$
$$\cup \{\mathbf{T}((C \to D) \to E) \mid \mathbf{T}((C \to D) \to E) \in V \text{ and } \mathbf{F}(C \to D) \notin U\}$$

Since $\cup_{i=1}^h \Phi_i = U$, $\sigma = \Phi_1, \ldots, \Phi_h$ is a complete k-sequence of Σ_U^k. Clearly $\delta_i \rhd \Phi_i$; moreover, since $\delta_i \rhd V$ and, for all $\mathbf{F}(C \to D) \notin \Phi_i$, $\delta_i \Vdash C \to D$, it holds that $\delta_i \rhd \Psi_i$. Therefore, $\delta_i \rhd S_c, \Phi_i, \Psi_i$ for all $i \in \{1, \ldots, h\}$ and the hyperset $\mathcal{H}_\sigma$ is realized in $\underline{K}$. Thus, both in Case 1 and in Case 2, β realizes the conclusion of D_k. $\square$

From the above lemma we deduce that, if A is not valid in $\mathcal{T}_k$, then no closed $\mathbf{TD}_k$-proof table for $\{\mathbf{F}A\}$ can exist. Indeed, let $\underline{K} = \langle P, \leq, \Vdash \rangle$ be a model of $\mathcal{T}_k$ such that A is not valid in $\underline{K}$ and let us assume that there exists a closed $\mathbf{TD}_k$-proof table τ for $\{\mathbf{F}A\}$. Since $\underline{K}$ realizes $\{\mathbf{F}A\}$, by the previous lemma, $\underline{K}$ realizes the last configuration of τ against Proposition 2. It follows that A is not provable in $\mathbf{TD}_k$, hence:

Theorem 2 (Soundness). *If A is provable in $\mathbf{TD}_k$, then A is valid in $\mathcal{T}_k$.*

Now, a finite set S of swff's is $\mathbf{TD}_k$-*consistent* if no $\mathbf{TD}_k$-proof table starting from S is closed. To prove the completeness of $\mathbf{TD}_k$ we provide a procedure that, given a finite and $\mathbf{TD}_k$-consistent set S of swff's, allows us to build a Kripke model $\underline{K}_\mathbf{D}(S)$ whose root realizes S. Our technique is similar to the one used in [1], which is an adaptation of Fitting's one described in [12]. The construction consists of two steps. In the first step we construct the sequence $\{S_i\}_{i \in \omega}$ of sets of swff's and the set of swff's $\overline{S}$, called the *node set of S*. $\overline{S}$ will be the root of the model $\underline{K}_\mathbf{D}(S)$ and its forcing relation is determined by the signed atoms belonging to $\overline{S}$. In the second step we construct the *successor sets* $\Delta_1, \ldots, \Delta_h$ of $\overline{S}$. The model $\underline{K}_\mathbf{D}(S)$ will be constructed by iterating the two steps on $\Delta_1, \ldots, \Delta_h$.

Let us consider a finite and $\mathbf{TD}_k$-consistent set S of swff's and let $A_1, \ldots, A_n$ be any listing of swff's of S (without repetitions of swff's). Starting from this listing we construct the sequence $\{S_i\}_{i \in \omega}$ of sets of swff's defined as follows:

- $S_0 = S$;
- Let $S_i = \{H_1, \ldots, H_u\}$; then

$$S_{i+1} = \bigcup_{H_j \in S_i} \mathcal{U}(H_j, i),$$

where, setting $S'_j = \mathcal{U}(H_1, i) \bigcup \cdots \bigcup \mathcal{U}(H_{j-1}, i) \bigcup \{H_j, \ldots, H_u\}$, $\mathcal{U}(H_j, i)$ is defined as follows:

($\mathcal{N}$1) If $H_j \equiv \mathbf{T}(A \wedge B)$, then $\mathcal{U}(H_j, i) = \{\mathbf{T}A, \mathbf{T}B\}$.

($\mathcal{N}$2) If $H_j \equiv \mathbf{F}(A \wedge B)$, then $\mathcal{U}(H_j, i) = \{\mathbf{F}A\}$ if $(S'_j \setminus \{H_j\}) \bigcup \{\mathbf{F}A\}$ is $\mathbf{TD}_k$-consistent and $\mathcal{U}(H_j, i) = \{\mathbf{F}B\}$ otherwise.

($\mathcal{N}$3) If $H_j \equiv \mathbf{T}(A \vee B)$, then $\mathcal{U}(H_j, i) = \{\mathbf{T}A\}$ if $(S'_j \setminus \{H_j\}) \bigcup \{\mathbf{T}A\}$ is $\mathbf{TD}_k$-consistent and $\mathcal{U}(H_j, i) = \{\mathbf{T}B\}$ otherwise.

($\mathcal{N}$4) If $H_j \equiv \mathbf{T}(A \to B)$ with A an atom, then $\mathcal{U}(H_j, i) = \{\mathbf{T}B\}$ if $\mathbf{T}A \in S'_j$, and $\mathcal{U}(H_j, i) = \{H_j\}$ otherwise.

($\mathcal{N}$5) If $H_j \equiv \mathbf{T}((A \wedge B) \to C)$, then $\mathcal{U}(H_j, i) = \{\mathbf{T}(A \to (B \to C))\}$.

($\mathcal{N}$6) If $H_j \equiv \mathbf{T}((A \vee B) \to C)$, then $\mathcal{U}(H_j, i) = \{\mathbf{T}(A \to C), \mathbf{T}(B \to C)\}$.

($\mathcal{N}$7) If $H_j \equiv \mathbf{T}((A \to B) \to C)$ and $\mathbf{F}(A \to B) \notin S'_j$, then $\mathcal{U}(H_j, i) = \{\mathbf{T}C\}$ if $(S'_j \setminus \{H_j\}) \bigcup \{\mathbf{T}C\}$ is $\mathbf{TD}_k$-consistent and $\mathcal{U}(H_j, i) = \{H_j, \mathbf{F}(A \to B)\}$ otherwise. If $\mathbf{F}(A \to B) \in S'_j$ then $\mathcal{U}(H_j, i) = \{H_j\}$.

($\mathcal{N}$8) If H_j is a signed atom or $H_j \equiv \mathbf{F}(A \to B)$ or $H_j \equiv \mathbf{F}(A \vee B)$, then $\mathcal{U}(H_j, i) = \{H_j\}$.

It is easy to check, by induction on $i \geq 0$, that, if S is $\mathbf{TD}_k$-consistent, then every S_i is $\mathbf{TD}_k$-consistent. Moreover, since S is finite, every S_i is finite and there exists an index j such that $S_i = S_j$ for every $i \geq j$. Let u be the first index such that $S_u = S_{u+1}$. We call *node set* of S the set $\overline{S} = S_u$ and we call $\{S_0, \ldots, S_u\}$ the *sequence generating* $\overline{S}$. We remark that different listings $A_1, \ldots, A_n$ of the swff's of S give rise to different sequences $\{S_i\}_{i \in \omega}$ and to different node sets of S.

The *successor* sets of $\overline{S}$ are defined as follows:

($\mathcal{S}1$) If $\overline{S}$ contains at least one swff $H \equiv \mathbf{F}(A \lor B)$, then the only *successor* sets of $\overline{S}$ are $U_1 = (\overline{S} \setminus \{H\}) \cup \{\mathbf{F}A\}$ and $U_2 = (\overline{S} \setminus \{H\}) \cup \{\mathbf{F}B\}$. We call U_1 and U_2 the *successor sets corresponding to the* $\mathbf{F}\lor$-*rule*.

($\mathcal{S}2$) If $\overline{S}$ does not contain swff's of the kind $\mathbf{F}(A \lor B)$ and contains at least one swff of the kind $\mathbf{F}(A \to B)$, then let:

$$U = \{\mathbf{F}(A \to B) \mid \mathbf{F}(A \to B) \in \overline{S}\}$$
$$V = \{\mathbf{T}((C \to D) \to E) \mid \mathbf{T}((C \to D) \to E) \in \overline{S}\}$$
$$S = \overline{S} \setminus (U \cup V)$$

and let

$$S_c, \Gamma_1, \Delta_1 \parallel \cdots \parallel S_c, \Gamma_n, \Delta_n \parallel \mathcal{H}_{\sigma_1} \parallel \cdots \parallel \mathcal{H}_{\sigma_r}$$

be the configuration obtained by applying the rule D_k to the set $S \cup U \cup V$ where the main set of swff's is $U \cup V$. Since, by hypothesis, $\overline{S}$ is $\mathbf{TD}_k$-consistent, at least a component of this configuration is $\mathbf{TD}_k$-consistent, let $\Phi_1 \mid \ldots \mid \Phi_h$ $(1 \leq h \leq k)$ be such a component. By applying the Weak-rule we deduce that all the Φ_i are $\mathbf{TD}_k$-consistent. The only successor sets of $\overline{S}$ are $\Phi_1, \ldots, \Phi_h$. We call $\Phi_1, \ldots, \Phi_h$ the *successor sets corresponding to the* D_k-*rule*.

We remark that if $\overline{S}$ is finite and $\mathbf{TD}_k$-consistent then every successor set of $\overline{S}$ is finite and $\mathbf{TD}_k$-consistent; moreover $\overline{S}$ has k successor sets at most.

Given a finite and $\mathbf{TD}_k$-consistent set S of swff's, we use the construction above to define the structure $\underline{K}_{\mathbf{D}}(S) = \langle P, \leq, \Vdash \rangle$ as follows:

1. $\overline{S} \in P$, where $\overline{S}$ is a *node set* of S;
2. For every $\overline{\Gamma} \in P$ and for every *successor* set Δ of $\overline{\Gamma}$, let $\overline{\Delta}$ be a *node set* of Δ. Then $\overline{\Delta}$ is a member of P and $\overline{\Delta}$ is an *immediate successor* of $\overline{\Gamma}$ in $\underline{K}_{\mathbf{D}}(S)$;
3. $\leq$ is the transitive and reflexive closure of the *immediate successor* relation;
4. For every atom p and for every $\overline{\Gamma} \in P$, $\overline{\Gamma} \Vdash p$ iff $\mathbf{T}p \in \overline{\Gamma}$.

Now, we have to prove that the structure $\underline{K}_{\mathbf{D}}(S)$ defined above is a Kripke model of $\mathcal{T}_k$. In particular we need to prove the finiteness of $\langle P, \leq \rangle$; to this aim we introduce the notion of *degree* and *weight*. Given a formula A, the *degree of* A, denoted by $dg(A)$, is defined as follows:

- if $A \equiv p$, where p is an atom, or $A \equiv \bot$, then $dg(A) = 0$;
- if $A \equiv B \wedge C$ or $A \equiv B \vee C$, then $dg(A) = dg(B) + dg(C) + 1$;
- if $A \equiv p \to B$ where p is an atom, then $dg(A) = dg(B) + 2$;
- if $A \equiv (B \wedge C) \to D$, then $dg(A) = dg(B \to (C \to D)) + 1$;
- if $A \equiv (B \vee C) \to D$, then $dg(A) = dg(B \to D) + dg(C \to D) + 1$;
- if $A \equiv (B \to C) \to D$, then $dg(A) = dg(B \to C) + dg(C \to D) + 1$.

It is easy to prove that $dg(A \to B) > dg(A) + dg(B)$. Given a swff $H \equiv \mathbf{T}A$ or $H \equiv \mathbf{F}A$, the *degree* of H is $dg(H) = dg(A)$. For a finite set of swff's S and a swff $H \in S$, the *weight* $\mathrm{wg}(H, S)$ of H in S is:

$$\mathrm{wg}(H, S) = \begin{cases} 0 & \text{if } H \equiv \mathbf{F}(A \to B) \text{ and } \mathbf{T}((A \to B) \to C) \in S \\ dg(H) & \text{otherwise} \end{cases}$$

The *weight* $\mathrm{wg}(S)$ of a finite set S of swff's is $\mathrm{wg}(S) = \sum_{H \in S} \mathrm{wg}(H, S)$.

Lemma 2. *Let Γ be a finite and $\mathbf{TD}_k$-consistent set of swff's and let $\overline{\Gamma}$ be a node set of Γ.*

(i) *If $\{\Gamma_0, \dots \Gamma_u\}$ is the sequence generating $\overline{\Gamma}$, $\mathrm{wg}(\Gamma_{i+1}) \leq \mathrm{wg}(\Gamma_i)$ for every $i \in \{0, \dots, u-1\}$.*

(ii) *If Δ is a successor set of $\overline{\Gamma}$, $\mathrm{wg}(\Delta) < \mathrm{wg}(\overline{\Gamma})$.*

Proof. The proof of Point (i) is trivial. Indeed, one can see that, if R is any rule of Table 1 different from $\mathbf{T} \to\to$, Φ is the premise of R and Ψ is any component of the consequence of R, it holds that $\mathrm{wg}(\Psi) < \mathrm{wg}(\Phi)$. In the case of the $\mathbf{T} \to\to$-rule, $\mathrm{wg}(S \cup \{\mathbf{T}C\}) < \mathrm{wg}(S \cup \{\mathbf{T}((A \to B) \to C)\})$, while $\mathrm{wg}(S \cup \{\mathbf{T}((A \to B) \to C)\}) = \mathrm{wg}(S \cup \{\mathbf{F}(A \to B), \mathbf{T}((A \to B) \to C)\})$, since $\mathrm{wg}(\mathbf{F}(A \to B), S \cup \{\mathbf{T}((A \to B) \to C)\}) = 0$.

As for Point (ii), if Δ is a successor set corresponding to the rule $\mathbf{F}\vee$ the proof is trivial. Now, let us consider the case where Δ is a successor set of $\overline{\Gamma}$ corresponding to the rule D_k. Then $\overline{\Gamma} = S \cup U \cup V$ where $U = \{H \in \overline{\Gamma} \mid H \equiv \mathbf{F}(A \to B)\}$, $V = \{H \in \overline{\Gamma} \mid H \equiv \mathbf{T}((C \to D) \to E)\}$ and $S = \overline{\Gamma} \setminus (U \cup V)$. Let us suppose that

$$U = \{\mathbf{F}(A_1 \to B_1), \dots, \mathbf{F}(A_n \to B_n)\}$$
$$V = \{\mathbf{T}((C_1 \to D_1) \to E_1), \dots, \mathbf{T}((C_m \to D_m) \to E_m)\}$$

We have two cases, according to the $\mathbf{TD}_k$-consistent hyperset used to build up the successor set Δ.

Case 1: Δ is the only successor set of $\overline{\Gamma}$. In this case $\Delta = S_c \cup \Gamma_i \cup \Delta_i$ where $1 \leq i \leq n$ and

$$\Gamma_i = U \setminus \{\mathbf{F}(A_i \to B_i)\} \cup \{\mathbf{T}A_i, \mathbf{F}B_i\}$$
$$\Delta_i = \{\mathbf{T}(B_i \to E) \mid \mathbf{T}((A_i \to B_i) \to E) \in V\}$$
$$\cup \{\mathbf{T}((C \to D) \to E) \in V \mid C \to D \not\equiv A_i \to B_i\}$$

If $\mathrm{wg}(\mathbf{F}(A_i \to B_i), \overline{\Gamma}) > 0$ then there is no swff of the kind $\mathbf{T}((A_i \to B_i) \to C)$ in V and $\Delta_i \equiv V$. Since $dg(A_i \to B_i) > dg(A_i) + dg(B_i)$, it is easy to check that $\mathrm{wg}(\Delta) < \mathrm{wg}(\overline{\Gamma})$. On the other hand, if $\mathrm{wg}(\mathbf{F}(A_i \to B_i), \overline{\Gamma}) = 0$, then V contains at least a swff of the kind $\mathbf{T}((A_i \to B_i) \to C)$ and we can write the sets $\overline{\Gamma}$ and Δ as follows:

$$\overline{\Gamma} = \Xi \cup \{\mathbf{F}(A_i \to B_i)\} \cup \{\mathbf{T}((A_i \to B_i) \to C_1), \dots, \mathbf{T}((A_i \to B_i) \to C_q)\}$$
$$\Delta = \Xi_c \cup \{\mathbf{T}A_i, \mathbf{F}B_i\} \cup \{\mathbf{T}(B_i \to C_1), \dots, \mathbf{T}(B_i \to C_q)\}$$

where $q \geq 1$ and $\{\mathbf{T}((A_i \to B_i) \to C_1), \dots, \mathbf{T}((A_i \to B_i) \to C_q)\}$ is the set of all the $\mathbf{T}$-signed implicative formulas occurring in $\overline{\Gamma}$ having $A_i \to B_i$ as antecedent. Now, given two sets of swff's Θ and Λ, let us denote with $\mathrm{wg}_\Theta(\Lambda) = \sum_{H \in \Lambda} \mathrm{wg}(H, \Theta)$. It is easy to check that:

$$\mathrm{wg}(\overline{\Gamma}) = \mathrm{wg}_{\overline{\Gamma}}(\Xi) + dg((A_i \to B_i) \to C_1) + \cdots + dg((A_i \to B_i) \to C_q)$$
$$\mathrm{wg}(\Delta) \leq \mathrm{wg}_\Delta(\Xi_c) + dg(A_i) + dg(B_i) + dg(B_i \to C_1) + \cdots + dg(B_i \to C_q)$$

Since $\mathrm{wg}_\Delta(\Xi_c) \leq \mathrm{wg}_{\overline{\Gamma}}(\Xi)$, $dg(A_i) + dg(B_i) + dg(B_i \to C_1) < dg((A_i \to B_i) \to C_1)$ and $dg(B_i \to C_j) < dg((A_i \to B_i) \to C_j)$ for every $j \in \{2, \dots, q\}$, it follows that $\mathrm{wg}(\Delta) < \mathrm{wg}(\overline{\Gamma})$.

Case 2: $\overline{\Gamma}$ has at least two successor sets. In this case, following the definition of D_k, we can write $\Delta = S_c \cup U_1 \cup \overline{V}_1 \cup V_2$, where $U_1 \subset U$ and $U_1 \neq \emptyset$ and

$$\overline{V}_1 = \{\mathbf{T}E \mid \mathbf{T}((C \to D) \to E) \in V \text{ and } \mathbf{F}(C \to D) \notin U_1\}$$
$$V_2 = \{\mathbf{T}((C \to D) \to E) \mid \mathbf{T}((C \to D) \to E) \in V \text{ and } \mathbf{F}(C \to D) \in U_1\}$$

On the other hand, we can write $\overline{\Gamma}$ as $S \cup U_1 \cup U_2 \cup V_1 \cup V_2$ where $U_2 = U \setminus U_1$ and $V_1 = \{\mathbf{T}((C \to D) \to E) \in V \mid \mathbf{F}(C \to D) \notin U_1\}$ (we recall that $U_1 \neq \emptyset$ and $U_2 \neq \emptyset$). We notice that $\mathrm{wg}_\Delta(S_c) \leq \mathrm{wg}_{\overline{\Gamma}}(S)$. Moreover, if $\mathrm{wg}(\mathbf{F}(A \to B), \overline{\Gamma}) = 0$, where $\mathbf{F}(A \to B) \in U_1$, then there exists C such that $\mathbf{T}((A \to B) \to C) \in V_2$, hence $\mathrm{wg}(\mathbf{F}(A \to B), \Delta) = 0$ as well; it follows that $\mathrm{wg}_\Delta(U_1) = \mathrm{wg}_{\overline{\Gamma}}(U_1)$. Finally, if $V_1 \neq \emptyset$, then $\overline{V}_1 \neq \emptyset$ and $\mathrm{wg}_\Delta(\overline{V}_1) < \mathrm{wg}_{\overline{\Gamma}}(V_1)$. To prove that $\mathrm{wg}(\Delta) < \mathrm{wg}(\overline{\Gamma})$ we have to consider two cases.

(i) There exists $\mathbf{F}(A \to B) \in U_2$ such that $\mathrm{wg}(\mathbf{F}(A \to B), \overline{\Gamma}) > 0$. Then $\mathrm{wg}_{\overline{\Gamma}}(U_2) > 0$, therefore $\mathrm{wg}(\Delta) < \mathrm{wg}(\overline{\Gamma})$.

(ii) For all $\mathbf{F}(A \to B) \in U_2$, $\mathrm{wg}(\mathbf{F}(A \to B), \overline{\Gamma}) = 0$. Since $U_2 \neq \emptyset$, there exist $\mathbf{F}(A \to B) \in U_2$ and $\mathbf{T}((A \to B) \to C) \in V_1$, hence $V_1 \neq \emptyset$ and $\mathrm{wg}_\Delta(\overline{V}_1) < \mathrm{wg}_{\overline{\Gamma}}(V_1)$. This implies that $\mathrm{wg}(\Delta) < \mathrm{wg}(\overline{\Gamma})$. $\square$

Now, we have all the elements needed to prove that $\underline{K}_\mathbf{D}(S)$ is a Kripke model of $\mathcal{T}_k$.

Lemma 3. *Let S be a finite and $\mathbf{TD}_k$-consistent set of swff's and let $\underline{K}_\mathbf{D}(S) = \langle P, \leq, \Vdash \rangle$ be the structure defined above. Then $\underline{K}_\mathbf{D}(S)$ is a Kripke model of $\mathcal{T}_k$.*

Proof. By construction of $\underline{K}_{\mathbf{D}}(S)$ it is easy to check that $\langle P, \leq \rangle$ is a poset; moreover, since $\mathbf{T}p \in \overline{\Gamma}$ implies that $\mathbf{T}p$ belongs to every successor set of $\overline{\Gamma}$, the forcing relation $\Vdash$ is well defined. Hence $\underline{K}_{\mathbf{D}}(S)$ is a Kripke model and, always by construction, every element of $\langle P, \leq \rangle$ has k immediate successors at most. To conclude the proof we only have to show that $\langle P, \leq \rangle$ is finite. Let us assume that $\langle P, \leq \rangle$ is not finite; then, since $\langle P, \leq \rangle$ is a finite branching tree, there is an infinite chain $\overline{\Gamma}_0 < \overline{\Gamma}_1 < \ldots$ in $\langle P, \leq \rangle$. Since every $\overline{\Gamma}_i$ is finite and $\mathbf{TD}_k$-consistent, by the above lemma $\mathrm{wg}(\overline{\Gamma}_0) > \mathrm{wg}(\overline{\Gamma}_1) > \ldots$, which leads to a contradiction. Hence $\langle P, \leq \rangle$ is finite and this concludes the proof.   □

Lemma 4. *Let S be a finite and $\mathbf{TD}_k$-consistent set of swff's and let $\underline{K}_{\mathbf{D}}(S) = \langle P, \leq, \Vdash \rangle$ be defined as above. Let $\overline{\Gamma} \in P$ and let $\{\Gamma_0, \ldots, \Gamma_u\}$ be the sequence generating $\overline{\Gamma}$. For every $i \in \{0, \ldots, u\}$ and every $H \in \Gamma_i$, $\overline{\Gamma} \triangleright H$ in $\underline{K}_{\mathbf{D}}(S)$.*

Proof. The proof is by induction on $dg(H)$.
Basis: If $dg(H) = 0$, then $H \equiv \mathcal{S}p$, with p atom, and, by construction of $\underline{K}_{\mathbf{D}}(S)$, if $\mathcal{S}p \in \Gamma_i$ then $\mathcal{S}p \in \Gamma_u = \overline{\Gamma}$. If $\mathcal{S} \equiv \mathbf{T}$ then, by definition of forcing, $\overline{\Gamma} \triangleright \mathbf{T}p$; if $\mathcal{S} \equiv \mathbf{F}$ then, by consistency of $\overline{\Gamma}$, $\mathbf{T}p \notin \overline{\Gamma}$ and hence $\overline{\Gamma} \triangleright \mathbf{F}p$.
Step: Let us suppose that the assertion holds for every H' such that $dg(H') < dg(H)$. The proof goes by cases on the structure of H. We give only few cases. If $H \equiv \mathbf{F}(A \rightarrow B)$ and $H \in \Gamma_i$, then, by construction, $H \in \overline{\Gamma}$. Since $\underline{K}_{\mathbf{D}}(S)$ is finite, there exists $\overline{\Delta} \in P$ such that $\overline{\Delta} \geq \overline{\Gamma}$, $H \in \overline{\Delta}$ and $\{\mathbf{T}A, \mathbf{F}B\}$ is included in a successor set Λ of $\overline{\Delta}$. By induction hypothesis $\overline{\Lambda} \triangleright \{\mathbf{T}A, \mathbf{F}B\}$, thus $\overline{\Gamma} \triangleright \mathbf{F}(A \rightarrow B)$. If $H \equiv \mathbf{T}((A \rightarrow B) \rightarrow C)$ and $H \in \Gamma_i$, then, by construction, either $\mathbf{T}C \in \Gamma_j$ with $j > i$, or $\{\mathbf{T}((A \rightarrow B) \rightarrow C), \mathbf{F}(A \rightarrow B)\} \subseteq \overline{\Gamma}$. In the former case, by induction hypothesis, we immediately get $\overline{\Gamma} \triangleright \mathbf{T}C$ and hence $\overline{\Gamma} \triangleright H$. In the latter case, let $\overline{\Lambda} \in P$ such that $\overline{\Lambda} \geq \overline{\Gamma}$; if $H \in \overline{\Lambda}$, then, by construction, $\mathbf{F}(A \rightarrow B) \in \overline{\Lambda}$, and by induction hypothesis $\overline{\Lambda} \nVdash A \rightarrow B$. If $H \notin \overline{\Lambda}$, then there exist $\overline{\Theta}_1, \overline{\Theta}_2 \in P$ such that $\overline{\Gamma} \leq \overline{\Theta}_1 < \overline{\Theta}_2 \leq \overline{\Lambda}$, $H \in \overline{\Theta}_1$, $\mathbf{F}(A \rightarrow B) \in \overline{\Theta}_1$ and $H \notin \overline{\Theta}_2$, with $\overline{\Theta}_2$ a successor set of $\overline{\Theta}_1$ corresponding to the D_k-rule. If $\mathbf{T}C \in \overline{\Theta}_2$ then, by induction hypothesis, $\overline{\Theta}_2 \triangleright \mathbf{T}C$, hence $\overline{\Lambda} \Vdash C$. On the other hand, if $\mathbf{T}A, \mathbf{T}(B \rightarrow C) \in \overline{\Theta}_2$, then, by induction hypothesis, $\overline{\Theta}_2 \triangleright \mathbf{T}A$ and $\overline{\Theta}_2 \triangleright \mathbf{T}(B \rightarrow C)$, hence $\overline{\Lambda} \Vdash A$ and $\overline{\Lambda} \Vdash B \rightarrow C$. Therefore, if $\overline{\Lambda} \Vdash A \rightarrow B$, then $\overline{\Lambda} \Vdash C$. Thus we have proved that, for every $\overline{\Lambda} \in P$ such that $\overline{\Lambda} \geq \overline{\Gamma}$, if $\overline{\Lambda} \Vdash A \rightarrow B$, then $\overline{\Lambda} \Vdash C$ and this implies $\overline{\Gamma} \Vdash (A \rightarrow B) \rightarrow C$ and $\overline{\Gamma} \triangleright H$.   □

Theorem 3 (Completeness of $\mathbf{TD}_k$). *If A is valid in $\mathcal{T}_k$, then A is provable in $\mathbf{TD}_k$.*

Proof. Suppose that there is no closed $\mathbf{TD}_k$-proof table for $\{\mathbf{F}A\}$, then $\{\mathbf{F}A\}$ is a $\mathbf{TD}_k$-consistent set of swff's. By Lemma 4, $\mathbf{F}A$ is realizable in the model $\underline{K}_{\mathbf{D}}(\{\mathbf{F}A\}) \in \mathcal{T}_k$, hence A is not valid in $\mathcal{T}_k$.   □

4   Properties of D_k

First of all, we remark that in the calculus $\mathbf{TD}_k$ the swff's of the kind $\mathbf{F}(A \vee B)$ are treated by two rules. This implies a non deterministic choice in the construction of a proof table. Of course, we can replace the rules $\mathbf{F}\vee_1$ and $\mathbf{F}\vee_2$ with the deterministic rule

$$\frac{S, \mathbf{F}(A \vee B)}{S, \mathbf{F}A, \mathbf{F}B} \mathbf{F}\vee'$$

The resulting calculus $\mathbf{TD}'_k$ is trivially valid for $\mathbf{D}_k$. As for the completeness, we have to change the construction of the counter model $\underline{K}_\mathbf{D}(S)$ as follows: add the case

($\mathcal{N}9$) If $H_j \equiv \mathbf{F}(A \vee B)$, then $\mathcal{U}(H_j, i) = \{\mathbf{F}A, \mathbf{F}B\}$

to the definition of node set and do not consider case $\mathcal{S}1$ in the definition of successor set (thus, in this case the only successor sets are those corresponding to the $\mathbf{D}_k$-rule).

We have chosen to present the main calculus for $\mathbf{TD}_k$ with the rules $\mathbf{F}\vee_1$ and $\mathbf{F}\vee_2$ since they allow us to get an immediate and syntactical constructivity proof for $\mathbf{D}_k$.

Theorem 4. *For every $k \geq 2$, if $A \vee B$ is provable in $\mathbf{TD}_k$ then either A or B is provable in $\mathbf{TD}_k$.*

Proof. If $A \vee B$ is provable in $\mathbf{TD}_k$ then there exists a closed $\mathbf{TD}_k$-proof table τ for $\mathbf{F}(A \vee B)$. Since the first rule of τ is either $\mathbf{F}\vee_1$ or $\mathbf{F}\vee_2$, τ either contains a closed $\mathbf{TD}_k$-proof table for $\mathbf{F}A$ or a closed $\mathbf{TD}_k$-proof table for $\mathbf{F}B$.   □

Let us consider the rule characterizing the calculus $\mathbf{TD}_k$. Let $\Gamma = S \cup U \cup V$ where $U = \{\mathbf{F}(A_1 \rightarrow B_1), \ldots, \mathbf{F}(A_n \rightarrow B_n)\}$ and $V = \{\mathbf{T}((C_1 \rightarrow D_1) \rightarrow E_1), \ldots, \mathbf{T}((C_m \rightarrow D_m) \rightarrow E_m)\}$. Since any complete k-sequence of Σ_U^k is also a complete $(k+1)$-sequence of Σ_U^{k+1}, any component of the configuration $\mathcal{C}$ obtained by applying $\mathbf{D}_k$ to S is also a component of the configuration $\mathcal{C}'$ obtained by applying the rule $\mathbf{D}_{k+1}$ to S. This immediately implies that if $\{\mathbf{F}A\}$ has a closed $\mathbf{TD}_{k+1}$-proof table then it also has a closed $\mathbf{TD}_k$-proof table, therefore $\mathbf{D}_k \supseteq \mathbf{D}_{k+1}$. Moreover, since (D_{k+1}) is not valid in the class of models $\mathcal{T}_k$, by the Completeness Theorem we get:

Theorem 5. *For every $k \geq 2$, $\mathbf{D}_k \supset \mathbf{D}_{k+1}$.*

We describe a procedure to decide $\mathbf{D}_k$ extracted from the completeness theorem for our tableau calculus. Here, for the sake of simplicity, we consider the tableau calculus $\mathbf{TD}'_k$. Following the construction of the counter model $\underline{K}_\mathbf{D}(S)$, we can define the procedure $\Pi(\Gamma)$ of Table 2 that, taken as input a set Γ of swff's, returns *true* if and only if Γ is $\mathbf{TD}'_k$-consistent. The procedure $Apply(\Gamma)$ called in Π takes as input a set Γ of swff's and returns a configuration $\mathcal{C}_P$ obtained by selecting a main set of swff's P in Γ (if it exists) and applying a rule of $\mathbf{TD}'_k$ to Γ considering P as the main set of swff's. We remark that lines 1-12 implement the cases $\mathcal{N}1-\mathcal{N}8$ of Section 3 and case $\mathcal{N}9$ above of the construction of the node set, while lines 13-15 implement the construction of the successor sets (case $\mathcal{S}2$ of Section 3). From the completeness of the decision procedure we get:

Table 2. The procedures $\Pi(\Gamma)$ and $Apply(\Gamma)$

$\Pi(\Gamma)$

```
 1  if Γ is contradictory
 2     then return false
 3     else  C = Apply(Γ)
 4  if C has Γ as only component
 5     then return true
 6  if C is a simple configuration S₁ ∥ ... ∥ Sₙ
 7     then for i := 1 to n
 8           do if Π(Sᵢ) = true
 9                 then return true
10           return false
11  if C is a non simple configuration Ψ₁ ∥ ... ∥ Ψₙ
12     then
13           for i := 1 to n
14           do  Let  Ψᵢ = S₁ⁱ | ... | Sₕᵢⁱ
15              for j := 1 to hᵢ
16              do if Π(Sᵢ) = false
17                    then  goto 13
18           return true
19           return false
```

$Apply(\Gamma)$

```
 1  if Γ contains at least a swff H of the kind T(A ∧ B) or T(A ∨ B) or F(A ∧ B)
       or T((A ∧ B) → C) or T((A ∨ B) → C)
 2     then  select such an H
 3           return C_{H}
 4  if Γ contains at least a set P of the kind {T(A → B), TA} with A an atom
 5     then  select such a set P
 6           return C_P
 7  if Γ contains at least a swff H of the kind T((A → B) → C) such that F(A →
       B) ∉ Γ
 8     then  select such an H
 9           return C_{H}
10  if Γ contains at least a swff H of the kind F(A ∨ B)
11     then  select such an H
12           return C_{H}
13  if Γ contains at least a swff H of the kind F(A → B)
14     then  select such an H
15           return C_{H}
16  return Γ
```

Theorem 6. *For every $k \geq 2$, $\mathbf{D}_k$ is decidable.*

To conclude the paper, we point out that the rule $\mathbf{D}_k$ is intrinsically inefficient, indeed the number of hypersets in the consequence of the rule is exponential in the number of $\mathbf{F}$-signed implicative formulas occurring in the premise. Despite this, our decision procedure is more efficient than the one based on generalized tableau given in [2], where in the proof one has to introduce a super-exponential number of instances of the axiom shema (D_k).

References

1. A. Avellone, M. Ferrari, and P. Miglioli. Duplication-free tableau calculi and related cut-free sequent calculi for the interpolable propositional intermediate logics. *Logic Journal of the IGPL*, 7(4):447–480, 1999.
2. A. Avellone, P. Miglioli, U. Moscato, and M. Ornaghi. Generalized tableau systems for intermediate propositional logics. In D. Galmiche, editor, *Proceedings of the 6th International Conference on Automated Reasoning with Analytic Tableaux and Related Methods: Tableaux '97*, volume 1227 of *LNAI*, pages 43–61. Springer-Verlag, 1997.
3. A. Avron. Hypersequents, logical consequence and intermediate logics for concurrency. *Annals for Mathematics and Artificial Intelligence*, 4:225–248, 1991.
4. M. Baaz and C. G. Fermüller. Analytic calculi for projective logics. *Lecture Notes in Computer Science*, 1617:36–50, 1999.
5. A. Chagrov and M. Zakharyaschev. *Modal Logic*. Oxford University Press, 1997.
6. A. Ciabattoni and M. Ferrari. Hypertableau and path-hypertableau calculi for some families of intermediate logics. In R. Dyckhoff, editor, *TABLEAUX 2000, Automated Reasoning with Analytic Tableaux and Related Methods*, volume 1947 of *LNAI*, pages 160–174. Springer-Verlag, 2000.
7. A. Ciabattoni and M. Ferrari. Hypersequent calculi for some intermediate logics with bounded Kripke models. *Journal of Logic and Computation*, 11(2):283–294, 2001.
8. R. Dyckhoff. A deterministic terminating sequent calculus for Gödel-Dummett logic. *Logic Journal of the IGPL*, 7(3):319–326, 1999.
9. M. Ferrari and P. Miglioli. Counting the maximal intermediate constructive logics. *Journal of Symbolic Logic*, 58(4):1365–1401, 1993.
10. G. Fiorino. An $O(n \log n)$-SPACE decision procedure for the propositional Dummett Logic. *Journal of Automated Reasoning*, 27(3):297–311, 2001.
11. G. Fiorino. Space-efficient Decision Procedures for Three Interpolable Propositional Intermediate Logics. *Journal of Logic and Computation*, To appear.
12. M.C. Fitting. *Intuitionistic Logic, Model Theory and Forcing*. North-Holland, 1969.
13. D.M. Gabbay and D.H.J. De Jongh. A sequence of decidable finitely axiomatizable intermediate logics with the disjunction property. *Journal of Symbolic Logic*, 39:67–78, 1974.
14. P. Hájek. *Metamathematics of fuzzy logic*. Kluwer, 1998.
15. D. Pearce. A new logical characterization of stable models and answer sets. In J. Dix, L.M. Pereira, and T. Przymusinski, editors, *Non-Monotonic Extensions of Logic Programming*, volume 1216 of *LNAI*, pages 57–70. Springer-Verlag, 1997.
16. D. Pearce. Stable inference as intuitionistic validity. *Journal of Logic Programming*, 38(1):79–91, 1999.

A Model Generation Style Completeness Proof for Constraint Tableaux with Superposition

Martin Giese

Institut für Logik, Komplexität und Deduktionssysteme,
Universität Karlsruhe, Germany
giese@ira.uka.de

Abstract. We present a calculus that integrates equality handling by superposition into a free variable tableau calculus. We prove completeness of this calculus by an adaptation of the *model generation* [2,15] technique commonly used for completeness proofs of resolution calculi. The calculi and the completeness proof are compared to earlier results of Degtyarev and Voronkov [7].

1 Introduction

Efficient equality handling for first order tableaux or related calculi, like matings or the connection method, has been problematic for a long time. It is generally believed that only techniques based on ordered rewriting can sufficiently reduce the search space of equality reasoning to make it tractable. It was also believed that the best approach to the integration of free variable tableaux and equality handling would be to search for *simultaneous rigid E-unifiers* [9] of disequations on the tableau and use these to close branches instead of usual unifiers. So the overall idea was to solve the rigid E-unification problems using ordered rewriting techniques.

Unfortunately, simultaneous rigid E-unification was later shown to be undecidable [6].[1] The outlined plan could thus only be implemented using incomplete procedures for E-unification. Experimenting with such a setting however, it turned out that the *combination* of a first order theorem prover and an incomplete solver for rigid E-unification problems seemed to be complete despite the incompleteness of the unification machinery, though nobody knew exactly why. In 1997, Degtyarev and Voronkov finally showed completeness for such a combination [7,8], and thus for a tableau calculus with integrated superposition-based equality handling.

One might have expected that all problems would be solved after this discovery. A number of publications would follow, providing variations on the theme, like what is known as 'basic ordered paramodulation' in the resolution community, or a version with universal variables (see e.g. [12]), or hyper tableaux [4] with equality. Curiously enough, this has not happened! We surmise that

---

[1] This was only shown in 1996, invalidating a number of attempts at a completeness proof that were based on the opposite assumption.

U. Egly and C.G. Fermüller (Eds.): TABLEAUX 2002, LNAI 2381, pp. 130–144, 2002.
© Springer-Verlag Berlin Heidelberg 2002

the reason for this is the complexity of Degtyarev and Voronkov's completeness proof: It is over ten pages long, and very technical, although the proof of one of the theorems used is not even included in the cited papers.

In this paper we present calculi similar to (a clausal version of) the one presented in [7], though we prefer to integrate the superposition process into the tableau calculus instead of defining a separate calculus for rigid E-unification. We then show the completeness of this calculus using an adaptation of the technique called *model generation*, well known for resolution calculi, see [2,15].In particular, we can use many ideas of Nieuwenhuis and Rubio that worked for them in the setting of resolution with constraint propagation. Apart from being significantly shorter than the proof of Degtyarev and Voronkov, our proof has the advantage of requiring only few additional ingredients not known from resolution. This makes it easy to produce tableau versions of variants known for resolution, like basic ordered paramodulation or hyper resolution resp. hyper tableaux. Some parts of this paper are elaborated in more detail in [11].

In Sect. 2 we review some common notions and notations. Our calculus is described in Sect. 3. The main result, namely completeness, is presented in Sect. 4. A discussion of a certain relative termination property and related issues follows in Sect. 5. We then try to demonstrate the versatility of the model generation technique for tableau completeness proofs in Sect. 6 by applying it to rigid basic ordered paramodulation. Finally, some possible fields for further research are identified in Sect. 7.

2   Preliminaries

We shall assume a fixed signature consisting of function symbols with fixed arity, constant symbols being considered as functions of arity zero, and a single binary predicate symbol '$\doteq$' denoting equality. The equality symbol is handled in a symmetric way, i.e. two formulae $s \doteq t$ and $t \doteq s$ are considered identical. A literal is either an equation $s \doteq t$ or a negated equation $\neg s \doteq t$. A clause is a finite set of literals.

An interpretation is a congruence relation on ground terms. Validity of equations, literals and clauses in a interpretation is defined as usual.[2]

Interpretations will be described by sets of rewrite rules $l \Rightarrow r$. The interpretation induced by a given set R of rewrite rules is the minimal congruence R^* on ground terms, such that lR^*r for all $l \Rightarrow r \in R$.

Furthermore, a fixed total reduction ordering $\succ$ on ground terms will be assumed. This ordering is extended to a total well-founded ordering $\succ_l$ on ground literals as follows: A ground literal is assigned a multiset by $m(s \doteq t) := \{s, t\}$ and $m(\neg s \doteq t) := \{s, s, t, t\}$. Then $l \succ_l l'$ iff $m(l) \gg m(l')$, where $\gg$ is the multiset extension of $\succ$. It is useful to keep the following properties in mind, which are immediate consequences of this definition:

---

[2] This approach is also taken in [15]. Herbrand's Theorem guarantees that for our purposes this is equivalent to defining interpretations with arbitrary carrier sets.

If $s \succ t$ and $s' \succ t'$, then

$$
\begin{array}{lll}
s \doteq t \succ_l s' \doteq t' & \text{iff} & s \succ s' \text{ or } (s = s' \text{ and } t \succ t') \\
s \doteq t \succ_l \neg s' \doteq t' & \text{iff} & s \succ s' \\
\neg s \doteq t \succ_l s' \doteq t' & \text{iff} & s \succeq s' \\
\neg s \doteq t \succ_l \neg s' \doteq t' & \text{iff} & s \succ s' \text{ or } (s = s' \text{ and } t \succ t')
\end{array}
$$

A *position* is a sequence of numbers designating subterms. $s|_p$ is the subterm of s at position p and $s[r]_p$ is the result of replacing the subterm at position p in s by r.

A *constraint* is a first order formula that uses a certain fixed signature and is interpreted over the set of ground terms. There are two predicate symbols with fixed interpretation, namely '$\equiv$' representing (syntactic) equality and $\succ$ for the reduction ordering. We denote conjunction as '$\&$' in constraints. A substitution satisfies a constraint, if the constraint is true under the fixed interpretation when its free variables are assigned values according to the substitution. A constraint is satisfiable, if there is a substitution that satisfies it.

A *constrained literal* is a pair $(\neg)s \doteq t \ll C$ of a literal and a constraint. The intention is that the literal may only be used if the instantiation of the free variables of a tableau satisfies the constraint.

We shall occasionally refer to *rigid* versus *universal* variables. Rigid variables are the free variables introduced by the rule for universal quantifiers of a free variable tableau calculus. They are called rigid because all occurrences of such variables in a tableau have to be instantiated by the same terms. This is very different from the situation in a resolution calculus, where each new clause is implicitly universally quantified and variables in a clause may be instantiated by a different m.g.u. in each resolution step. There are cases where this restriction can be lifted in tableau calculi, i.e. where it is sound to instantiate different occurrences of a free variable differently. If that is the case, one calls the free variable 'universal' for the formula in which it occurs, see [12]. As has been recognized in [5], using universal variables is crucial for efficient equality handling in tableaux. The calculi presented in this paper do *not* use universal variables, but we expect our results to be easily adaptable to calculi that use them.

3   The Calculus

We shall describe a clausal free variable tableau calculus to refute sets of clauses. In such a calculus, there is of course the usual clause extension rule, which expands the tableau by renamings of the literals of one clause. In addition, we want rules to perform superposition between literals on a branch. In principle, e.g. in a ground calculus, the rule should look like this:

$$
\frac{(\neg)s \doteq t \quad l \doteq r}{(\neg)s[r]_p \doteq t}
$$

where p is a position in s, $s|_p = l$, $s \succ t$ and $l \succ r$.

That is, we apply ordered equations on maximal sides of literals.

In a calculus with free variables, the condition $s|_p = l$ becomes a unification problem, and the ordering conditions also depend on the instantiation of free variables. In their calculus,[3] Degtyarev and Voronkov annotate the whole tableau with a constraint to which these unification and ordering conditions are added. They require that constraint to be satisfiable at all times. A consequence of using such a global constraint is that backtracking is required for each superposition application that adds to the global constraint. In order to avoid this, we shall work with *constrained literals* $(\neg)s \doteq t \ll C$, where the constraint C accumulates the unification and ordering conditions of superposition steps needed to derive *this* literal.

Furthermore, Degtyarev and Voronkov delete the literal $(\neg)s \doteq t$ from the branch in a superposition step. Of course, this also can be done only if the procedure backtracks over every superposition step. We choose a non-destructive formulation to avoid backtracking: instead of actually deleting literals, we keep track with each new literal L of a set of literals that *would have been deleted* during the derivation of L in a destructive calculus. These sets, called *histories* can then be used to exclude rule applications, e.g. between L and K if L is in the history of K. We shall write a constrained literal with history as $(\neg)s \doteq t \ll C \cdot h$.

In fact, we go a step further: at each superposition step we delete (or rather simulate deletion of) not only the first premise but both premises, because it turns out that this stronger restriction does not complicate the completeness proof—in a sense, it even becomes more transparent—and it makes it easier to prove the termination property of Sect. 5. Deleting both premises amounts to requiring each literal to be used at most once in the derivation of any other literal. Call the literals introduced on the tableau by the extension rule and not by superposition *ext-literals*. In the history of a literal L, we shall record the ext-literals from which L is derived, and in superposition steps, we shall require these histories to be disjoint.

Formally, we start from an initial empty tableau and expand it by applying certain rules. Tableau nodes are labeled with *constrained literals with histories,* written $L = (\neg)s \doteq t \ll C \cdot h$. The history h is a set of (references to occurrences of) literals on the tableau. Let a set $\mathcal{C}$ of clauses be given. Our calculus has the following three rules:

$$ext \quad \frac{}{L_1 \cdot \{L_1\} \quad | \quad \cdots \quad | \quad L_k \cdot \{L_k\}}$$

where $\{L_1, \ldots, L_k\} = \theta C$, with $C \in \mathcal{C}$
and θ renames each variable in C into a new (free) variable.

$$sup\text{-}p \quad \frac{s \doteq t \ll A \cdot h_1 \qquad l \doteq r \ll B \cdot h_2}{s[r]_p \doteq t \ll s|_p \equiv l \,\&\, s \succ t \,\&\, l \succ r \,\&\, A \,\&\, B \cdot h_1 \cup h_2}$$

where p is a position in s, $s|_p$ is not a variable and $h_1 \cap h_2 = \emptyset$.

---

[3] From now on, we always refer to the 'tableau basic superposition' calculus $\mathcal{TBSE}$ of [7].

$$\neg s \doteq t \ll A \cdot h_1$$
$$l \doteq r \ll B \cdot h_2$$

sup-n $$\overline{\neg s[r]_p \doteq t \ll s|_p \equiv l \ \& \ s \succ t \ \& \ l \succ r \ \& \ A \ \& \ B \cdot h_1 \cup h_2}$$

where p is a position in s, $s|_p$ is not a variable and $h_1 \cap h_2 = \emptyset$.

The superposition rules *sup-p* and *sup-n* are only applied if the constraint of the new literal is satisfiable. The two literals involved as premises in the *sup-p*-rule are required to be distinct,[4] although one might be a renaming of the other.

A ground substitution σ closes a branch $\mathcal{B}$ of a tableau, if there is a constrained negated equation $\neg s \doteq t \ll A \cdot h \in \mathcal{B}$ such that $\sigma s = \sigma t$ (that is syntactic identity) and σ satisfies A. The whole tableau is closed, if there is a single substitution σ that closes all branches simultaneously.

The *sup*-rules implement what is known as *rigid basic superposition*. The term 'rigid' refers to the rigidity of the free variables of our tableau calculus. One talks of superposition when only ordered application of equations is allowed, and *only on the maximal side* of an equation, which in our case is enforced by the constraint $s \succ t$. Finally, the *basic strategy* is a restriction that was first introduced for calculi that work without constraints. In a superposition step of such calculi, a most general unifier μ of $s|_p$ and l is determined, and a literal $\mu(s[r]_p \doteq t)$ is generated. The basicness restriction forbids application of equations on subterms of this literal introduced by the unifier μ. In other words, superposition steps at or below variable positions of $s[r]_p \doteq t$ are excluded. In our constraint based calculus, we get this restriction automatically, because the unifier is encoded in the constraint instead of being actually applied, and because we forbid superpositions at or below variable positions.

Various proof procedures that use this calculus can be designed, differing in their use of backtracking and constraint handling:

- One gets a calculus similar to that of Degtyarev and Voronkov, if one does not keep the constraints together with the literals, but instead gathers them all in one global constraint G that is required to be satisfiable. This introduces a backtracking choice point for each rule application that adds to the global constraint. In addition, branch closure requires backtracking, as usual in free variable tableaux: whenever a negated equation $\neg s \doteq t$ appears on a branch, a backtracking point is introduced and the constraint $s \equiv t$ is added to G. The procedure tries to close the other branches, always keeping G satisfiable, and keeping below a certain instantiation depth limit. If this fails, extension of the branch is continued. If no proof is found within a given depth limit, the whole procedure is restarted with an increased limit (iterative deepening). In contrast to the classic formulation of tableaux, the unifiers generated in superposition applications and branch closures should *not* be applied to the tableau, as this would yield possibilities for new, spurious rule applications on the other branches, weakening the 'basicness' property. Of course, rule

---

[4] We can require this because we have *rigid* variables. With rigid variables, a term can't be unified with one of its proper subterms, so superposition would only be possible at the top position, leading to a trivial equation.

applications on other branches that generate constraints incompatible with the global constraint G need not be considered in this scheme. One can also drop the histories and discard literals used in a *sup*-rule application from the branch instead. Of course, when the procedure backtracks, they have to be reintroduced. The only difference to the calculus of Degtyarev and Voronkov is then that they discard only the first premise in the superposition steps, while we discard both.

- One can avoid the backtracking points introduced by the *sup*-rules by keeping the constraints of literals. These are only added to the global closure constraint G when a branch is closed, and accordingly, backtracking is only needed over branch closures.
- One can use the Incremental Closure technique to avoid backtracking completely, see [10].

Although we prefer the last alternative, our results are equally valid for a backtracking proof procedure.

4   Completeness

The completeness proof follows the usual lines: Assuming that there is no closed tableau for a set of clauses, one constructs an infinite tableau by applying rules exhaustively—in particular, the *ext*-rule has to be applied infinitely often for each clause on each branch. Then one chooses a ground substitution σ for the free variables, such that after applying the substitution to the tableau, every branch contains a sufficient set of ground instances of literals from each of the clauses. From the assumption, it follows that at least one branch $\mathcal{B}$ of the tableau is not closed by σ. From the literals on $\sigma\mathcal{B}$, an interpretation is constructed, which is then shown to be a model for the clause set.

Our proof differs from this standard approach only in the construction of the interpretation and in the proof that the clause set is indeed satisfied by it.

First, we need the following notion:

Definition 1. *Given a set $\mathcal{S}$ of constrained literals with history, a ground substitution σ for all free variables occurring in $\mathcal{S}$, and a set R of ground rewrite rules, the set of* variable-irreducible ground instances of $\mathcal{S}$ under σ with respect to R, *written $irred_R(\sigma, \mathcal{S})$, is the set of all ground literals $(\neg)\sigma l \doteq \sigma r$, where $((\neg)l \doteq r \ll A \cdot h) \in \mathcal{S}$, A is satisfied by σ, and σx is irreducible by R for all variables x occurring in l or r.*

Note that irreducibility is not required for the whole terms σl and σr, but only for the instantiations of variables occurring in them. Also, the instantiation of variables occurring only in the constraint A is allowed to be reducible. We are going to work only on variable-irreducible ground instances of the constrained literals on a branch. The reason for this will become clear later.

We can now define the 'model generation' process, which constructs a ground rewrite system by induction with $\succ_l$ over variable-irreducible ground instances of literals on a branch. The tricky part here is that the rewrite relation that variable-irreducibility refers to is only just being built during the induction.

Definition 2. *Let $\mathcal{S}$ be a set of constrained literals with history and σ a ground substitution for all variables in $\mathcal{S}$. For any ground literal L, we define $\mathrm{Gen}(L) = \{l \Rightarrow r\}$ and say L generates the rule $l \Rightarrow r$, iff*

1. *$L \in irred_{R_L}(\sigma, \mathcal{S})$,*
2. *$L = (l \doteq r)$,*
3. *$R_L^* \not\models L$,*
4. *$l \succ r$, and*
5. *l is irreducible w.r.t. R_L,*

where $R_L := \bigcup_{L \succ_l K} \mathrm{Gen}(K)$ is the set of all previously generated rules. Otherwise, we define $\mathrm{Gen}(L) := \emptyset$. The set of all rules generated by any ground literal is denoted $R_{\mathcal{S},\sigma} := \bigcup_K \mathrm{Gen}(K)$.

Note that only positive equations generate rules. When no confusion is possible about the set $\mathcal{S}$ and the substitution σ, we will just write R instead of $R_{\mathcal{S},\sigma}$. We will need the following two useful lemmas, taken from Nieuwenhuis and Rubio [15]:

Lemma 1. *For any set of constrained literals with history $\mathcal{S}$ and ground substitution σ, the generated set of rules $R = R_{\mathcal{S},\sigma}$ is convergent, i.e. confluent and terminating. The subset R_L is also convergent for any ground literal L.*

Proof. R terminates because $l \succ r$ for all rules $l \Rightarrow r \in R$ (condition 4). To show confluence, by Newman's Lemma, one thus only needs to show local confluence, which follows from the fact that there can be no critical pairs in R. For assume $l \Rightarrow r \in R$ and $l' \Rightarrow r' \in R$ with $l|_p = l'$. Let $l \Rightarrow r$ be generated by a literal K. $l' \Rightarrow r'$ cannot be in R_K, for otherwise condition 5 would have prevented the generation of $l \Rightarrow r$. So $l' \Rightarrow r'$ is generated by a literal K' with $K' \succ_l K$. But then either $l' \succ l$, which is impossible because l' is a subterm of l. Or $l' = l$ and $r' \succ r$, but then l' would be reducible by $l \Rightarrow r$, violating condition 5 for $\mathrm{Gen}(K') = \{l' \Rightarrow r'\}$.

For arbitrary ground literals L, $R_L \subseteq R$, so R_L is also terminating, and R_L cannot contain critical pairs either. Hence, R_L is also convergent. $\qquad\square$

Lemma 2. *For all ground literals L, if $R_L^* \models L$, then $R^* \models L$.*

Proof. Let $R_L^* \models L$.

Case 1: $L = (s \doteq t)$. R contains at least all the rewrite rules of R_L, i.e. $R \supseteq R_L$. Thus, the equation must also hold in R^*.

Case 2: $L = (\neg s \doteq t)$. According to Lemma 1, R_L is convergent, so s and t have distinct normal forms $s' \preceq s$ and $t' \preceq t$ w.r.t. R_L. Now consider rules $l \Rightarrow r \in R \setminus R_L$. By definition of R_L, their generating literals $l \doteq r$ must be larger than L in the literal ordering (they can't be equal because L is a negated equation). By the definition of $\succ_l$, this implies that $l \succ s \succeq s'$ and $l \succ t \succeq t'$. So rules in $R \setminus R_L$ can not further rewrite s' or t', hence these are the normal forms of s and t also w.r.t. R. And as they are distinct, $R^* \models \neg s \doteq t$. $\qquad\square$

Definition 3. *Let S be a set of constrained literals with history and σ a ground substitution for the free variables in S. Two literals $L, K \in S$ are called* variants, *if they are equal up to renaming of free variables, if histories are not regarded.*[5] *They are called* copies *(under σ) if moreover the free variables are assigned the same ground terms under σ. S is called* rich *(under σ), if every literal $L \in S$ has an infinite number of copies with* pairwise disjoint histories *in S.*

For instance, $f(X) \doteq Y \ll X \equiv a \cdot \{L_1, L_2\}$ and $f(U) \doteq V \ll U \equiv a \cdot \{L_1, L_3\}$ are variants. They are also copies under σ if $\sigma X = \sigma U$ and $\sigma Y = \sigma V$.

We can now show the central property of the model R^* constructed in Def. 2, namely that it satisfies all the irreducible instances (w.r.t R) of literals in S under certain conditions.

Lemma 3 (Model Generation). *Let S be a set of constrained literals with history and σ a ground substitution for the free variables in S, such that*

- *S is closed under the application of the sup-p and sup-n rules, and*
- *there is no literal $\neg s \doteq t \ll A \cdot h \in S$ such that $\sigma s = \sigma t$ (syntactically) and σ satisfies A.*
- *S is rich under σ.*

Then $R^* \models L$ for all $L \in \mathit{irred}_R(\sigma, S)$.

Proof. Assume that this were not the case. Then there must be a *minimal* (w.r.t. $\succ_l$) L in $\mathit{irred}_R(\sigma, S)$ with $R^* \not\models L$. We distinguish two cases, according to whether L is an equation or a negated equation:

Case 1: $L = (s \doteq t)$. If $s = t$ syntactically, then clearly $R^* \models L$, so we may assume that $s \succ t$. As $R_L \subseteq R$, we certainly have $L \in \mathit{irred}_{R_L}(\sigma, S)$. Also, due to Lemma 2, we already have $R_L^* \not\models L$. But $\mathrm{Gen}(L) = \emptyset$, because otherwise the rule $s \Rightarrow t$ would be in R, implying $R^* \models L$. As conditions 1 through 4 for L generating a rule are fulfilled, condition 5 must be violated. This means that there is a rule $l \Rightarrow r \in R_L$ that reduces s, so $s|_p = l$ for some position p in s. Now let L be the variable-irreducible (w.r.t. R) instance of a constrained literal $L_0 = (s_0 \doteq t_0 \ll A \cdot h_L) \in S$. Similarly, let $l \Rightarrow r$ be generated by a literal $K = (l \doteq r) \prec_l L$ that is the variable-irreducible (w.r.t. R_K) instance of a constrained literal $K_0 = (l_0 \doteq r_0 \ll B \cdot h_K) \in S$. As S is rich, there are infinitely many copies under σ of L_0 with pairwise disjoint histories. Each of the finitely many elements of h_K can be contained in the history of at most one of these copies, and all the remaining ones have a history disjoint to h_K. So we may assume that L_0 and K_0 are chosen in a way that h_K and h_L are disjoint. Further, it turns out that p must be a non-variable position in s_0, because otherwise, since $s = \sigma s_0$, we would have $p = p'p''$ with $s_0|_{p'} = x$ and $\sigma x|_{p''} = l$, thus σx would be reducible by $l \Rightarrow r \in R$, contradicting the variable-irreducibility of L. From all this, it follows that an application of the *sup-p*-rule between the literals $L_0, K_0 \in S$ is possible:

$$\textit{sup-p} \ \frac{s_0 \doteq t_0 \ll A \cdot h_L \qquad l_0 \doteq r_0 \ll B \cdot h_K}{s_0[r_0]_p \doteq t_0 \ll s_0|_p \equiv l_0 \ \& \ s_0 \succ t_0 \ \& \ l_0 \succ r_0 \ \& \ A \ \& \ B \cdot h_L \cup h_K}$$

---

[5] The variable renaming also applies to the constraints.

As S is required to be closed under rule applications, the resulting literal, call it L_0', must be in S. Now $L' := (s[r]_p \doteq t) = \sigma L_0'$ is a variable-irreducible (w.r.t. R) instance of L_0': indeed, σ obviously satisfies the new constraint. Furthermore, σx is irreducible by R for any variable x occurring in s_0 or t_0. For an x occurring in r_0, σx is known to be irreducible by rules in R_K. But for rules $g \Rightarrow d \in R \setminus R_K$, we have $g \succeq l \succ r \succeq \sigma x$, so g cannot be a subterm of σx. This shows that σx is irreducible by R for all variables x in L_0', so $L' \in \mathit{irred}_R(\sigma, S)$. Moreover, since l and r are in the same R^*-equivalence class, replacing l by r in s does not change the (non-)validity of $s \doteq t$, i.e. $R^* \not\models L'$. And finally, by monotonicity of the rewrite ordering $\succ$, $L \succ_l L'$. This contradicts the assumption that L is the minimal element of $\mathit{irred}_R(\sigma, S)$ which is not valid in R^*.

Case 2: $L = (\neg s \doteq t)$. If $s = t$ syntactically, then the second precondition of this lemma is violated, so we may assume $s \succ t$. Due to Lemma 2, $R_L^* \not\models L$, i.e. $R_L^* \models s \doteq t$. According to Lemma 1, R_L is convergent. Validity of $s \doteq t$ in R_L^* then means that s and t have the same normal form w.r.t. R_L. This normal form must be $\preceq t$, and thus $\prec s$. Therefore, s must be reducible by some rule $l \Rightarrow r \in R_L$ with $s|_p = l$ for some position p. As in case 1, let L be the variable-irreducible (w.r.t. R) instance of a constrained literal $L_0 = (\neg s_0 \doteq t_0 \ll A \cdot h_L) \in S$ and let $l \Rightarrow r$ be generated by a literal $K = (l \doteq r) \prec_l L$ that is the variable-irreducible (w.r.t. R_K) instance of a constrained literal $K_0 = (l_0 \doteq r_0 \ll B \cdot h_K) \in S$. Again as in case 1, p must be a non-variable position in s_0, and we can choose L_0 and K_0 with disjoint histories. It follows that an application of the *sup-n* rule is possible between L_0 and K_0:

$$\text{sup-n} \ \frac{\begin{array}{c} \neg s_0 \doteq t_0 \ll A \cdot h_L \\ l_0 \doteq r_0 \ll B \cdot h_K \end{array}}{\neg s_0[r_0]_p \doteq t_0 \ll s_0|_p \equiv l_0 \ \& \ s_0 \succ t_0 \ \& \ l_0 \succ r_0 \ \& \ A \ \& \ B \cdot h_L \cup h_K}$$

We can now show, in complete analogy with case 1, that $L' := (\neg s[r]_p \doteq t) \in \mathit{irred}_R(\sigma, S)$, $R^* \not\models L'$ and $L \succ_l L'$, contradicting the assumption that L is minimal in $\mathit{irred}_R(\sigma, S)$ with $R^* \not\models L$. $\qquad \square$

We cope with the history restriction here by requiring that S is rich, so we can find enough copies of the required literals that some of them have disjoint histories. Now in the actual completeness proof, we have to extract a rich set of literals from an open branch in such a way that the validity of the irreducible instances of that set will imply the validity of each of the clauses in our clause set.

We now have all the necessary tools to show that our calculus is complete in the sense that there exists a finite closed tableau for any unsatisfiable set of clauses. We are going to show a little more, namely that a closed proof will be found if we simply expand the tableau in a fair way without requiring backtracking. Of course, this property is partly due to the fact that we postpone the instantiation of free variables to a global closure test. If we closed branches one at a time, we would have to backtrack over branch closures, but not—contrary to what is the case in the $\mathcal{TBSE}$ calculus of Degtyarev and Voronkov—over every application of the superposition rules. In order to state the completeness theorem, we need the following definition of a fair proof procedure.

Definition 4. *A proof procedure is a procedure that takes a set of clauses $\mathcal{C}$ and builds a sequence of tableaux $\mathcal{T}_0, \mathcal{T}_1, \mathcal{T}_2, \ldots$ for $\mathcal{C}$ where $\mathcal{T}_0$ is the empty tableau, and each $\mathcal{T}_{i+1}$ results from the application of an ext or sup rule on one of the branches of $\mathcal{T}_i$. A proof procedure finds a proof for $\mathcal{C}$, if one of the $\mathcal{T}_i$ is closed. A proof procedure is* fair, *if in any run, it either finds a proof, or the following holds for the limit $\mathcal{T}$ of the sequence of constructed tableaux:* [6]

- *The ext-rule is applied infinitely often for each clause on every branch of $\mathcal{T}$.*
- *Every possible application of the sup-rules between two literals on a branch of $\mathcal{T}$ has been performed on that branch.*

Theorem 1. *Let $\mathcal{C}$ be an unsatisfiable set of clauses. Then a fair proof procedure for the calculus with histories finds a proof for $\mathcal{C}$.*

Proof. Assume that the procedure does not find a proof. Then it constructs a sequence of tableaux $\mathcal{T}_0, \mathcal{T}_1, \mathcal{T}_2, \ldots$ with a limit $\mathcal{T}$. $\mathcal{T}$ has at least one open branch under any ground substitution for the free variables in $\mathcal{T}$. For assume that under a certain σ all branches are closed. Then there is a literal $\neg s \doteq t$ on every branch with $\sigma s = \sigma t$. Make a new tableau $\mathcal{T}'$ by cutting off every branch below some occurrence of such a literal. Then σ still closes $\mathcal{T}'$ and $\mathcal{T}'$ has only branches of finite length and is finitely branching. Thus, by König's Lemma, $\mathcal{T}'$ must be a finite closed tableau for $\mathcal{C}$. One of the tableaux $\mathcal{T}_i$ must contain $\mathcal{T}'$ as initial sub-tableau, and thus $\mathcal{T}_i$ is closed under σ, contradicting the assumption that the procedure finds no proof.

We now fix the ground substitution σ. Namely, σ should instantiate the free variables introduced by the *ext*-rule in such a way that every branch of $\sigma \mathcal{T}$ contains *infinitely many* occurrences of literals of each ground instance of every clause in $\mathcal{C}$. This is possible because the *ext*-rule is applied infinitely often for each clause on every branch, and using a dovetailing process that lets each of the ground instantiations be used infinitely often.

There must now be a branch $\mathcal{B}$ of $\mathcal{T}$, such that $\mathcal{B}$ is not closed by σ. As there are infinitely many occurrences of literals of each ground instance of every clause on $\mathcal{B}$, and every clause is finite, for every ground instance τC of every clause, there must be at least one literal $L_{\tau C} \in \tau C$, such that there are infinitely many ext-literals $L' \in \mathcal{B}$ with $\sigma L' = L_{\tau C}$.

Collect all these ext-literals $L_{\tau C}$ on $\mathcal{B}$ in a set $\mathcal{I}$. As we are dealing with ext-literals, the histories of literals in $\mathcal{I}$ are disjoint, so $\mathcal{I}$ is rich under σ. Now define $\mathcal{B}^\infty$ to contain all literals of $\mathcal{I}$ as well as all literals on $\mathcal{B}$ derived from literals in $\mathcal{I}$ alone.

As $\mathcal{B}$ is closed under *sup*-rule applications by fairness of the proof procedure, so is $\mathcal{B}^\infty$. Furthermore, $\mathcal{B}^\infty$ is rich, as can be seen by induction on the number n of literals in the history of a given literal L: For $n = 1$, L is an ext-literal, so $L \in \mathcal{I}$. Hence there are infinitely many copies of L with pairwise disjoint histories. For $n > 1$, L must be derived by an application of a *sup*-rule from literals with a history smaller than n. The induction hypothesis guarantees an infinite number of copies with pairwise disjoint histories of these literals in $\mathcal{B}^\infty$.

---

[6] The limit of a sequence of tableaux is defined as the supremum under the initial subtree ordering.

The same rule application is obviously possible between these copies, and as $\mathcal{B}^\infty$ is closed under *sup* applications, one easily sees that there must be infinitely many copies of L.

We apply the model generation of Def. 2 on $\mathcal{B}^\infty$ and σ to obtain a set of rewrite rules $R = R_{\mathcal{B}^\infty,\sigma}$. As $\mathcal{B}^\infty$ and σ satisfy the preconditions of Lemma 3, every variable-irreducible instance of $\mathcal{B}^\infty$ is valid in R^*.

It now remains to show that every clause in $\mathcal{C}$ is valid in R^* to contradict the assumption that $\mathcal{C}$ is unsatisfiable. We do this by showing that all ground instances of clauses in $\mathcal{C}$ are valid. Let τC be a ground instance of $C \in \mathcal{C}$, where τ is a ground substitution for the variables occurring in C. We now define a new substitution τ' such that $\tau'x$ is the normal form w.r.t. R of τx. This makes $\tau'x$ irreducible by R for all variables x of C. Now $\tau'C$ is obtained from τC by replacement of a number of subterms by other subterms equivalent under R^*. Thus $R^* \models \tau C$ iff $R^* \models \tau'C$. By construction of σ and $\mathcal{B}^\infty$, there must be a literal $L \in C$ such that $\theta L \in \mathcal{I} \subset \mathcal{B}^\infty$ for some renaming of variables θ, and such that $\tau'L = \sigma\theta L$. As θL carries no constraint, this makes $\tau'L$ a variable-irreducible instance of θL, so $R^* \models \tau'L$ and accordingly $R^* \models \tau'C$. $\qquad\Box$

5   Termination and Regularity

Our proof of (relative) termination is simpler than the one of Degtyarev and Voronkov because the calculus is more restrictive. Indeed, we can prove termination with the histories alone, without needing arguments about the ordering restrictions expressed in the constraints.

Theorem 2. *Starting from a finite tableau $\mathcal{T}$, only a finite number of sup-rule applications is possible without intervening applications of the ext-rule.*

Proof. As the *sup*-rules do not introduce new branches, it suffices to show this property for each of the finitely many branches of $\mathcal{T}$. The *sup*-rules combine the disjoint history sets of used literals, so the size of the history of the resulting literal is the sum of the sizes of the used literals' histories. In particular, only ext-literals have a history of size one. We show by induction on n that only finitely many literals with a history of at most n literals can be derived. For $n = 1$, this is the case, since we start out with only finitely many ext-literals, and we do not get any new ones. For $n > 1$, a literal must be the result of a *sup*-application between literals of history size less than n. By induction hypothesis, there can be only finitely many of those. Also, there are only finitely many ways to apply a *sup*-rule between two given literals, because the rule applications are determined by the position p at which the terms are overlapped. No history can get larger than the initial number of ext-literals on the branch, so one can only derive a finite number of new literals altogether. $\qquad\Box$

We proved this property to show that our calculus is not inferior to that of Degtyarev and Voronkov in this respect. The flip side of enforcing the termination property using histories is that the calculus is not compatible with the regularity restriction (see e.g. [12]): It is clear from our completeness proof that an arbitrary number of ext-literals with the same instantiation, though with different histories, might be needed.

The situation changes if one discards histories from our calculus. One then loses the termination property, but the calculus becomes compatible with regularity. Indeed, the completeness proof then works without the richness condition, so one literal of every instantiation of every clause on each branch is sufficient. See [11] for a proof simplified in this way.

The question arises whether this happens if one deletes (or uses histories to simulate deletion of) only the first premise of the *sup*-rules, as is done in the calculus of Degtyarev and Voronkov. There is no indication in [7] whether their calculus and completeness proof are compatible with regularity. We have not been able to find a natural restriction of our calculus that enjoys the termination property *and* is compatible with regularity, see [11] for a discussion of the difficulties.

Our restriction to disjoint histories is so strong that it prompts the question whether it is useful in practice. But, of course that question has to be asked of any restriction. Only experimentation can show which restriction is useful to ensure termination in practice. In fact, it is not even clear whether the termination property is of any practical value at all:

- At first sight, the termination property makes it easier to implement a fair proof procedure: One can apply the *sup*-rules exhaustively before resorting to further *ext*-expansions. However, one still needs a fair strategy to choose the next extension clause on a branch. If one can implement an intelligent procedure to do this, one should also be able to choose between extension and superposition. Or, vice versa, if it is sufficient to just put pending *ext*-expansions in a FIFO queue, why should it not be good enough to use the same queue for superposition steps?
- In an efficient tableau prover, particularly in the presence of equality, one needs to take universal variables into account, see [5]. The superposition rules with universal variables correspond essentially to unfailing Knuth-Bendix completion [1], which does not terminate in general. UKBA behaves very well in practice, so it is probably not sensible to artificially introduce additional conditions to enforce termination.
- As noted above, it is not clear whether there is a natural restriction that ensures termination and is compatible with regularity. But regularity is acknowledged to be an important refinement for automated theorem provers.

To summarize, it seems that in an efficient implementation of a tableau calculus with superposition, the termination property is not really important, and maybe cannot even be sensibly maintained at all.

Of course, the termination property can be bestowed on any calculus by a simple trick: One takes an arbitrary fair strategy and codes it into the calculus. As every possible rule application gets scheduled at some point by a fair procedure, and extension with a clause is always possible, it follows that only finitely many *sup*-applications are performed in between.

Admittedly, it is nonsense to code the whole proof procedure into the calculus. But only experimentation can show how far one should go.

6   Tableaux with Basic Ordered Paramodulation

In this section, we shall try to demonstrate how variations of calculi and completeness proofs can be carried over from known results for resolution-based calculi.

There is a more restrictive form of equality handling known in the resolution community as *basic ordered paramodulation* [3]. In comparison to basic superposition, the basicness restriction is strengthened: One forbids paramodulation at or below a position where a previous paramodulation step has taken place. The price to pay is that equations have to be applied on both sides of literals and not only the maximal side as for basic superposition. Still, basic ordered paramodulation seems to be very effective in practice [13].

Using constrained literals, one can easily enforce this stronger basicness restriction by introducing a new free variable in the equality handling rules. The *sup-p* rule becomes:[7]

$$par\text{-}p \quad \frac{s \doteq t \ll A \\ l \doteq r \ll B}{s[X]_p \doteq t \ll X \equiv r \;\&\; s|_p \equiv l \;\&\; l \succ r \;\&\; A \;\&\; B}$$

where p is a position in s, $s|_p$ is not a variable,
and X is a new (free) variable.

Note how the constraint forces X to be instantiated with r, and that the restriction $s \succ t$ is gone.[8] The *par-n*-rule is exactly analogous. This modification is a straightforward adaptation of the formulation of basic ordered paramodulation using constraint inheritance given by Nieuwenhuis and Rubio in [15].

How do we show completeness of our modified calculus? We cite [15]:

> The completeness proof is an easy extension of the previous results by the model generation method. It suffices to modify the rule generation by requiring, when a rule $l \Rightarrow r$ is generated, that both l and r are irreducible by R_C, instead of only l as before, and to adapt the proof of Theorem 5.6 accordingly, which is straightforward.

The Theorem 5.6 referred to is the resolution equivalent of our Lemma 3. They have R_C instead of our R_L because they have to work with ground clauses, where we can use literals. Otherwise, this statement applies exactly to our case.

7   Conclusion and Future Research

We presented a free variable tableau calculus with integrated equality handling using basic superposition rules with constraint propagation. We demonstrated

---

[7] We do not use the disjoint history restriction here in order to make things easier to read. It is no problem to use that restriction with basic ordered paramodulation.

[8] It might seem that introducing a new free variable is not a good idea. But these ones are harmless, as there is no need to search for their instantiation. It is determined by the instantiations of the free variables in r. In a sense, they can be regarded as universal variables restricted by the constraint $X \equiv r$.

how the completeness of such a calculus can be shown using model generation techniques known from resolution calculi with only few additional tableau-specific ingredients. Though completeness of a similar calculus has previously been established in [7], using a different approach, our proof is much shorter, and we have demonstrated that it is easily adapted to related calculi.

We have shown how a termination property can be enforced for such calculi using a disjoint history restriction, and how completeness may be proved in presence of such a restriction. We have also briefly discussed the practical usefulness of the termination property in such calculi.

One area for future research is experimentation with an implementation. In particular, it would be interesting to see what impact various restrictions ensuring the termination property have both on performance of the prover and on implementation complexity.

An obvious extension of our results would be a version that permits predicates other than equality and that does not require problems to be in clausal form. We expect this to be quite easy.

Universal variables are known to be important for efficiency. It is expected that the given calculi and proofs can easily be adapted to incorporate universal variables, but of course this has to be checked in detail. We also plan to investigate how superposition-based equality handling can be incorporated into hyper tableaux [4].

Another important field for research is building in associativity and commutativity or other common equational theories. We expect that this can be done in the same way as for resolution, see e.g. [14].

Finally, it would be (at least theoretically) interesting to find an answer to the question of Sect. 5, namely whether there is a natural restriction that ensures the termination property but is compatible with regularity.

Acknowledgements. I thank Bernhard Beckert, Reiner Hähnle, Peter Schmitt and the anonymous referees for many fruitful discussions and good advice.

References

[1] Leo Bachmair, Nachum Dershowitz, and David A. Plaisted. Completion without failure. In H. Aït-Kaci and M. Nivat, editors, *Resolution of Equations in Algebraic Structures*, volume 2: Rewriting Techniques, pages 1–30. Academic Press, New York, 1989.

[2] Leo Bachmair and Harald Ganzinger. Resolution theorem proving. In Robinson and Voronkov [16], chapter 2, pages 19–99.

[3] Leo Bachmair, Harald Ganzinger, Christopher Lynch, and Wayne Snyder. Basic paramodulation. *Information and Computation*, 121(2):172–192, 1995.

[4] Peter Baumgartner. Hyper Tableaux — The Next Generation. In Harrie de Swart, editor, *Proc. International Conference on Automated Reasoning with Analytic Tableaux and Related Methods, Oosterwijk, The Netherlands*, number 1397 in LNCS, pages 60–76. Springer-Verlag, 1998.

[5] Bernhard Beckert. A completion-based method for mixed universal and rigid E-unification. In Alan Bundy, editor, *Proc. 12th Conference on Automated Deduction CADE, Nancy/France*, LNAI 814, pages 678–692. Springer-Verlag, 1994.

[6] A. Degtyarev and A. Voronkov. The undecidability of simultaneous rigid E-unification. *Theoretical Computer Science*, 166(1-2):291–300, October 1996.

[7] A. Degtyarev and A. Voronkov. What you always wanted to know about rigid E-unification. Technical Report 143, Comp. Science Dept., Uppsala University, 1997.

[8] A. Degtyarev and A. Voronkov. What you always wanted to know about rigid E-unification. *Journal of Automated Reasoning*, 20(1):47–80, 1998.

[9] J. Gallier, S. Raatz, and W. Snyder. Theorem proving using rigid E-unification: Equational matings. In *Proc. IEEE Symp. on Logic in Computer Science*, pages 338–346. IEEE Computer Society Press, 1987.

[10] Martin Giese. Incremental closure of free variable tableaux. In Rajeev Goré, Alexander Leitsch, and Tobias Nipkow, editors, *Proc. Intl. Joint Conf. on Automated Reasoning, Siena, Italy*, LNCS. Springer-Verlag, 2001.

[11] Martin Giese. Model generation style completeness proofs for constraint tableaux with superposition. Technical Report 2001-20, Universität Karlsruhe TH, Germany, 2001. URL: `http://i11www.ira.uka.de/~giese/tr01-20.ps.gz`.

[12] R. Hähnle. Tableaux and related methods. In Robinson and Voronkov [16], chapter 3, pages 100–178.

[13] William McCune. Solution of the Robbins problem. *Journal of Automated Reasoning*, 19(3):263–276, December 1997.

[14] R. Nieuwenhuis and A. Rubio. Paramodulation with built-in AC-theories and symbolic constraints. *Journal of Symbolic Computation*, 23(1):1–21, January 1997.

[15] R. Nieuwenhuis and A. Rubio. Paramodulation-based theorem proving. In Robinson and Voronkov [16], chapter 7, pages 371–443.

[16] Alan Robinson and Andrei Voronkov, editors. *Handbook of Automated Reasoning*. Elsevier Science B.V., 2001.

Implementation and Optimisation of a Tableau Algorithm for the Guarded Fragment

Jan Hladik

Theoretical Computer Science
TU Dresden

Abstract. In this paper, we present SAGA, the implementation of a tableau-based **S**atisfiability **A**lgorithm for the **G**uarded Fragment ($\mathcal{GF}$). Satisfiability for $\mathcal{GF}$ with finite signature is ExpTime-complete and therefore theoretically intractable, but existing tableau-based systems for ExpTime-complete description and modal logics perform well for many realistic knowledge bases. We implemented and evaluated several optimisations used in description logic systems, and our results show that with an efficient combination, SAGA can compete with existing highly optimised systems for description logics and first order logic.

1 Preliminaries

The Guarded Fragment of first order predicate logic ($\mathcal{GF}$) [1] restricts the appearance of quantifiers to formulas of the kind

$$\forall \boldsymbol{x}(G(\boldsymbol{x}, \boldsymbol{y}) \rightarrow \varphi(\boldsymbol{x}, \boldsymbol{y}))$$
$$\text{and} \quad \exists \boldsymbol{x}(G(\boldsymbol{x}, \boldsymbol{y}) \wedge \varphi(\boldsymbol{x}, \boldsymbol{y})) \ ,$$

where $\boldsymbol{x}$ and $\boldsymbol{y}$ are tuples of variables, and $G(\boldsymbol{x}, \boldsymbol{y})$ is an atom, which is called the *guard* of the formula, whereas $\varphi(\boldsymbol{x}, \boldsymbol{y})$ is called the *body*. This fragment has many desirable properties: satisfiability is decidable [1] in 2-ExpTime, which is reduced to ExpTime if the arity of the relations is bounded [12]. It also has the finite model property [1] and a tree model property for a special notion of a tree [12].

$\mathcal{GF}$ can be regarded as a generalisation of modal or description logics to n-ary relations (roles) [1,10]. The more expressive such logics have a comparably high worst-case complexity, e.g. PDL [4] and $\mathcal{SHIQ}$ [23] are ExpTime-complete [29, 22]. However, with optimised tableau algorithms like DLP [28], which decides PDL, and FaCT [19] or RACER [14], which decide $\mathcal{SHIQ}$, satisfiability becomes tractable for various realistic knowledge bases [19,21,15]. This suggests that a tableau algorithm for $\mathcal{GF}$-satisfiability might lead to an implementation that does not consume exponential time in practice.

$\mathcal{GF}$ is also decidable by resolution [9]. To the best of our knowledge, the efficiency of this approach for realistic formulas has not yet been analysed.

U. Egly and C.G. Fermüller (Eds.): TABLEAUX 2002, LNAI 2381, pp. 145–159, 2002.
© Springer-Verlag Berlin Heidelberg 2002

2   A Tableau Algorithm for $\mathcal{GF}$

In [17], a tableau algorithm is presented for the Clique Guarded Fragment ($\mathcal{CGF}$) [11], a generalisation of $\mathcal{GF}$. Its worst-case complexity is 2-NExpTime (NExpTime for signatures with bounded arity), and therefore higher than that of the automata algorithm in [12], but it allows for many of the optimisations known from description logics and therefore promises to lead to an efficient implementation.

Before describing this algorithm, we recall some definitions from [17]. Since our implementation Saga decides satisfiability of $\mathcal{GF}$ and not of $\mathcal{CGF}$, the definitions and the description of the tableau algorithm are restricted to $\mathcal{GF}$ formulas.

Definition 1 (NNF, closure). A formula $\varphi \in \mathcal{GF}$ is in *negation normal form (NNF)* if negation occurs only in front of atoms.

For a $\mathcal{GF}$-sentence φ in NNF, the *closure* $\mathrm{cl}(\varphi)$ is the set of all subformulas of φ. For a set C of constants, $\mathrm{cl}(\varphi, C)$ is the set containing all instantiations of $\mathrm{cl}(\varphi)$ with constants in C.

Table 1. Completion Rules for $\mathcal{GF}$

R∧	if $\varphi \wedge \chi \in \Delta(v)$
	then $\Delta(v) := \Delta(v) \cup \{\varphi, \chi\}$
	unless $\{\varphi, \chi\} \subseteq \Delta(v)$
R∨	if $\varphi \vee \chi \in \Delta(v)$
	then $\Delta(v) := \Delta(v) \cup \{\psi\}$ for a ψ chosen non-deterministically from $\{\varphi, \chi\}$
	unless $\{\varphi, \chi\} \cap \Delta(v) \neq \emptyset$
R≐	if $a \doteq b \in \Delta(v)$
	then for all nodes w that contain a:
	$\quad C(w) := (C(w) \setminus \{a\}) \cup \{b\}$ and $\Delta(w) := \Delta(w)[a \mapsto b]$
	unless $a = b$
R∀	if $\forall \boldsymbol{x}(G(\boldsymbol{x}, \boldsymbol{c}) \to \varphi(\boldsymbol{x}, \boldsymbol{c})) \in \Delta(v)$,
	$\quad$ and there exists a $\boldsymbol{b} \subseteq C(v)$ such that $G(\boldsymbol{b}, \boldsymbol{c}) \in \Delta(v)$
	then $\Delta(v) := \Delta(v) \cup \{\varphi(\boldsymbol{b}, \boldsymbol{c})\}$
	unless $\varphi(\boldsymbol{b}, \boldsymbol{c}) \in \Delta(v)$
R∃	if $\exists \boldsymbol{x}(G(\boldsymbol{x}, \boldsymbol{c}) \wedge \varphi(\boldsymbol{x}, \boldsymbol{c})) \in \Delta(v)$
	then let $\boldsymbol{b}$ be a sequence of new constants with the same length as $\boldsymbol{x}$
	$\quad$ create a son w of v with $C(w) := \boldsymbol{b} \cup \boldsymbol{c}, \Delta(w) := \{G(\boldsymbol{b}, \boldsymbol{c}), \varphi(\boldsymbol{b}, \boldsymbol{c})\}$
	$\quad N(w) := 1 + \max\{N(v) : v \in V \setminus \{w\}\}$
	unless there is a $\boldsymbol{b}, \boldsymbol{c} \subseteq \Delta(v)$ with $\{G(\boldsymbol{b}, \boldsymbol{c}), \varphi(\boldsymbol{b}, \boldsymbol{c})\} \subseteq \Delta(v)$,
	$\quad$ there is a son w of v with $\{G(\boldsymbol{b}, \boldsymbol{c}), \varphi(\boldsymbol{b}, \boldsymbol{c})\} \subseteq \Delta(w)$ for some $\boldsymbol{b}, \boldsymbol{c} \subseteq \Delta(w)$,
	$\quad$ or v is blocked
R↕	if $\varphi(\boldsymbol{c}) \in \Delta(v)$ is an atomic or universally quantified formula,
	$\quad$ and w is a neighbour of v with $\boldsymbol{c} \subseteq C(w)$
	then $\Delta(w) := \Delta(w) \cup \{\varphi(\boldsymbol{c})\}$
	unless $\varphi(\boldsymbol{c}) \in \Delta(w)$

The $\mathcal{GF}$ tableau algorithm operates on a *completion tree*, a vertex labeled tree in which every node stands for a set of constants which appear together in a guard atom.

Definition 2 (Completion Tree, Blocking, Tableau). Let $\varphi \in \mathcal{GF}$ be a sentence in NNF. A *completion tree* $T = (V, E, C, \Delta, N)$ for φ is a vertex labeled tree (V, E) with the function C labeling each node $v \in V$ with a set of constants, Δ labeling each $v \in V$ with a subset of $\mathrm{cl}(\varphi, C(v))$, and N mapping each node to a distinct natural number such that if v is an ancestor of w, then $N(v) < N(w)$.

A node $v \in V$ is called *directly blocked* by a node $u \in V$ if u is not blocked, $N(u) < N(v)$, and there is an injective mapping π from $C(v)$ to $C(u)$ such that for all constants $c \in C(v) \cap C(u)$, $\pi(c) = c$ and for the extension of π to formulas, $\pi(\Delta(v)) = \Delta(u)|_{\pi(C(v))}$, where $\Delta(u)|_{\pi(C(v))}$ denotes the set of all formulas in $\Delta(u)$ containing only constants in $\pi(C(v))$. A node is called *blocked* if it is directly blocked or if its father is blocked.

A completion tree T *contains a clash* if there is a node $v \in V$ such that $\neg(c \doteq c) \in \Delta(v)$ for a constant $c \in C(v)$ or there is an atomic formula φ such that $\{\varphi, \neg\varphi\} \subseteq \Delta(v)$. Otherwise, T is called *clash-free*. A completion tree T is called *complete* if none of the *completion rules* given in Table 1 can be applied to T. A *tableau* is a complete and clash-free completion tree.

For a formula set Φ and constant symbols a, b, we use the notation $\Phi[a \mapsto b]$ to denote the set of formulas in Φ where all occurrences of a are replaced by b.

The blocking condition is *dynamic*, i.e. blockings are not established forever, but they can be canceled later if one of the nodes involved changes (and reappear if the other one changes accordingly).

To decide the satisfiability of a formula φ, a root node n_0 is created with $N(n_0) := 0$, $C(n_0) := \{c\}$ for a random constant c (to prevent empty structures), and $\Delta(n_0) := \{\varphi\}$. Then the completion rules in Table 1 are applied until a tableau is found or a clash occurs. If the rules can be applied in such a way that a tableau is found, "φ is satisfiable" is output, otherwise "φ is unsatisfiable".

Since a satisfiable $\mathcal{GF}$-formula need not have a *finite tree* model, the blocking condition is necessary to ensure termination. It prevents new nodes from being created if there is already another node containing "similar" formulas. If a tableau is found, it can be transformed into a model by *unraveling* the blockings, i.e. replacing a blocked node v with a copy of the node u blocking v. Note that the blocking condition is not equivalent to *subset blocking*, where a node v is blocked by a node u if the label of v is a subset of the label of u: for $\mathcal{GF}$, the image of π need only be a subset of $C(u)$, but restricted to these constants, the labels of u and v have to be equal (modulo π). The proof of correctness, completeness and termination of the algorithm can be found in [17].

3   Implementation

The algorithm described in Section 2 leaves many possibilities for an implementation. To obtain an efficient program, the following issues have to be considered:

Non-determinism. There are two kinds of non-determinism involved in the $\mathcal{GF}$-algorithm: the decision which rule to apply first if several ones are applicable is *don't-care* non-deterministic, i.e. every choice will lead to a correct behaviour of the algorithm, but its efficiency will depend on a good heuristic. The two heuristics implemented in SAGA are described in Section 5.

The decision which disjunct of a disjunction to add to the corresponding node is *don't-know* non-deterministic, i.e. only certain choices will lead to the discovery of a tableau. Therefore, a *branching* and *backtracking* technique is necessary to undo the changes made by the last decision after a clash has occurred. Efficiency will again depend on a good strategy which disjunct to try first.

The data structure *branching point* described in Section 3 is used to enable branching and backtracking: before adding the first disjunct φ to the corresponding node, a new branching point is created that subsequently stores backups of all nodes that are changed as a consequence of adding φ. Three different heuristics for choosing the first disjunct are implemented (cf. Section 5).

Data Structures. The data structure for a node n contains the labels $C(n)$, $\Delta(n)$, and $N(n)$ described in Section 2. Additionally, blockings that were already detected are recorded in the blocking node as well as in the blocked one such that unnecessary testing is avoided.

A branching point b is created by R$\vee$ after choosing a disjunct ψ from a disjunction $\varphi \vee \chi$. It contains a unique *branching identifier (BID)* $I(b)$, a list $C(b)$ of nodes that were created, and a list $M(b)$ of backups of nodes that were modified as a consequence of adding φ, and the other disjunct $O(b) = \chi$ that has to be added to the tree if φ causes a clash.

For a node n, every formula $\varphi \in \Delta(n)$ is labeled with the *dependency set* $D(\varphi, n)$ of branching points it depends on. This enables us to find the right branching point for the backup of a node n if a rule application for φ modifies n, and to use *backjumping* (cf. Section 4).

Functions. Figure 1 shows the function hierarchy: an arrow from f1 to f2 means that f1 invokes f2. The main function construct-tableau(φ) receives a $\mathcal{GF}$ formula as input. It creates a new node n_0 and adds φ to $\Delta(n_0)$. Subsequently, it iteratively calls choose-next-formula(), which uses one of the heuristics described in Section 5 to determine the next formula φ to process and the node n containing φ. The function satisfy(n, φ) applies the corresponding rule by choosing the appropriate function satisfy-and(n, φ), satisfy-all(n, φ) etc. Most of these functions will add new formulas to n, which is performed by add-formula(n, φ). If there are branching points associated with φ, i.e. $D(\varphi, n)$ is not empty, a backup of n is created in the branching point b with $I(b) = \max(D(\varphi, n))$. A possible blocking of n by another node or of another node by n is removed.

For an existential formula $\varphi = \exists x(G(c, x) \wedge \chi(c, x))$, satisfy-ex($n, \varphi$) first invokes blocked($n_i$) for n and its ancestors to check if n is blocked. For this purpose, the function equivalent(n_i, n_j) tries to find a mapping π for two nodes

n_i, n_j from $C(n_i)$ to $C(n_j)$ as described in Definition 2. If such a mapping is found, the function $\texttt{block}(n_i)$ blocks the node n_i and its successors. Otherwise, a new son n_k of n is created with $C(n_k) = C_{\text{old}} \cup C_{\text{new}}$, where $\boldsymbol{d}$ is a vector of new constants for the variables in $\boldsymbol{x}$, C_{old} are the constants in $\boldsymbol{c}$, and C_{new} are the constants in $\boldsymbol{d}$. The guard $G(\boldsymbol{c}, \boldsymbol{d})$ and body $\chi(\boldsymbol{c}, \boldsymbol{d})$ are added to $\Delta(n_k)$, and formulas in $\Delta(n)$ which contain only constants in C_{old} are propagated to $\Delta(n_k)$.

For a disjunction φ, $\texttt{satisfy-or}(n, \varphi)$ invokes $\texttt{choose-alternative}(\varphi)$ to find the first disjunct ψ to add to n. It then calls $\texttt{branch}(n, \psi)$, which creates a new branching point b_{new} and a backup of n in $M(b_{\text{new}})$, and finally adds ψ to n. When a clash occurs, $\texttt{construct-tableau}$ calls $\texttt{backtrack}()$ to return to the last branching point b_i for which there is another alternative, i.e. $O(b_i)$ is not empty: all nodes n created as a consequence of the last branch are removed by $\texttt{delete-node}(n)$, and all nodes modified are replaced with their backups by $\texttt{restore-tree}(\{n_1, \ldots, n_k\})$. Then the remaining alternative from $O(b_i)$ is added to the corresponding node and removed from $O(b_i)$.

R$\updownarrow$ is not implemented as a separate rule, but is applied implicitly whenever a formula is added to a node: when $\texttt{add-formula}$ is invoked for a formula φ and a node n, it calls $\texttt{propagate}(\varphi, \{n_1, \ldots, n_i\})$, which checks if the constants in φ are also contained in the neighbours $n_1, \ldots, n_i$ of n and adds φ to the corresponding nodes.

If a clash occurs and backtracking is impossible, i.e there is no branching point containing another alternative, $\texttt{construct-tableau}$ returns "φ is $\texttt{unsatisfiable}$"; if $\texttt{choose-next-formula}$ finds no more formulas to process, the tree is complete and "φ is $\texttt{satisfiable}$" is returned together with the tableau that was generated.

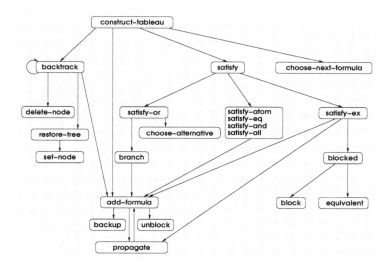

Fig. 1. Function Hierarchy

4   Optimisation

Section 3 describes only a very basic implementation whose performance cannot compete with existing systems for comparably complex logics. To obtain an efficient program, sophisticated optimisation techniques are necessary.

Syntactic Preprocessing. Before SAGA tries to construct a tableau for the input formula φ, it simplifies the syntactic structure of φ to speed up the tableau generation process: obvious tautologies and contradictions are made explicit, a normal form is used which supports their detection by eliminating $\vee$ and $\exists$ and using n-ary conjunctions, and the variables contained in a formula φ are normalised when φ is added to a node. Details can be found in [18] or [19].

Semantic Branching. The naive method to satisfy a disjunction $\varphi \vee \chi$ is to add φ first and, if this causes a clash, add χ afterwards (*Syntactic Branching*). This is rather inefficient because resources have been spent to find out that φ is unsatisfiable in the current tree, but this information is forgotten.

Semantic Branching [7] adds $\neg\varphi \wedge \chi$ to the tree if φ leads to a clash. This makes the information that φ is unsatisfiable explicit and possibly prunes the search space because a tree in which φ is satisfiable is never tested again.

The drawback of semantic branching lies in adding formulas to the tree that are superfluous for a model. If these formulas are complex, they can slow down the tableau generation process because superfluous rule applications take place and superfluous nodes are created. An assessment of the advantages and disadvantages of semantic branching is presented in Section 6.

Backjumping. After a clash, naive backtracking returns to the most recent branching point. Dependency directed backtracking (*backjumping*) [2] instead returns to the most recent branching point *one of the clashing formulas depends on*. Thus, the intermediate BPs, which did not have any influence on the clash, are skipped. The dependency sets described in Section 3 are used to find the right branching point to return to: after a clash between φ and χ in node n, the most recent BP b in $D(\varphi, n) \cup D(\chi, n)$ is determined and the backjump to b is performed.

Boolean Constraint Propagation. Before choosing a disjunct ψ from a disjunction $\varphi \vee \chi$ in a node n and performing a branch for ψ, every disjunct is tested regarding whether it is *closed*, i.e. its negation is already contained in n, or whether it is *open*. If ψ is closed, it is removed from the disjunction (because adding it would lead to an immediate clash), and only the remaining disjuncts are considered for branching (this technique is known as *boolean constraint propagation, BCP* [6]). In particular, if there is only one open disjunct, it is added deterministically to n, and the branch is avoided.

To-do Lists. To efficiently find the next formula to process (i.e. without searching the whole tree constructed so far), a data structure *to-do list* is used. For every kind of formula (atoms, conjunctions, existential restrictions etc.), it contains a list of unblocked nodes which contain un-processed formulas of that kind. These lists are sorted by the node identifiers, which makes it possible to find the "oldest" node containing e.g. an un-processed conjunction in constant time.

5   Heuristics

In this section, the different heuristics implementing the non-deterministic decisions (cf. Section 3) and the different blocking techniques are described.

Branching. The decision which disjunction to choose for the next branch and which one of its disjuncts to test first is crucial for efficiency (cf. Section 6). In SAGA, three different heuristics pursuing different goals are implemented.

MOMS. The heuristic "Maximum Occurrence in disjunctions of Minimum Size" [6] was developed for propositional logic. It considers all clauses (disjunctions) of minimum size and counts the appearances of positive and negative literals (disjuncts). The variable A to branch on is the one with the largest count of A and $\neg A$. If the count for A is larger than the one for $\neg A$, $\neg A$ is tested first and, if this leads to a clash, A is tested afterwards. (MOMS therefore implicitly requires semantic branching.)

The goal is to optimise BCP by increasing the number of closed disjuncts and reaching deterministic expansion as soon as possible. To adapt MOMS for $\mathcal{GF}$, we consider every disjunct appearing in a disjunction of a particular node as a literal and choose the disjunct φ or $\neg\varphi$ for branching in the corresponding way.

One disadvantage of MOMS lies in the fact that it tries the more constrained alternative first, i.e. the alternative that is more likely to fail. This means that it performs nicely for unsatisfiable formulas, but badly for satisfiable ones [18]. Furthermore, it was observed that MOMS interacts adversely with backjumping [19].

iMOMS. Inverted MOMS [18] tries to avoid the disadvantage of being likely to fail with the first alternative by testing φ and $\neg\varphi$ in the opposite order, i.e. it chooses the disjunct which satisfies most of the smallest disjunctions.

Maximise-jump. This heuristic was first used in FaCT [21]. From all disjunctions of a node, it selects the one for which the maximum element in the dependency set is minimal, i.e. the one leading to the furthest backjump. To find the first disjunct to try, FaCT uses a MOMS-style heuristic. In SAGA, the syntactically shortest disjunct is selected because a short formula probably can be tested faster than a long one which is likely to contain existential or universal formulas. Since this approach does not rely on counts of disjuncts like MOMS, we also expect to see the differences in efficiency more clearly.

Choosing the Next Formula. There are two kinds of formulas which are significantly more expensive to process than the remaining ones. Firstly, disjunctions require the creation of a branching point and backups of nodes and, after a clash, all modified nodes have to be restored to their original state. Secondly, for an existential formula in a node n, the blocking test for n has to be performed. Since the blocking condition is defined recursively, each ancestor m_i of n has to be compared with all nodes ℓ_j with $N(\ell_j) < N(m_i)$. For the blocking test itself, all mappings from $C(m_i)$ to $C(\ell_j)$ have to be tested (in the worst case). Therefore, either disjunctions or existential formulas are processed last.

Blocking. The blocking condition for a node n as defined in Section 2 requires $\pi(\Delta(n))$ to be equal to a *restriction* $\Delta(m) \mid_{\pi(C(n))}$ for an ancestor node m. The algorithm also works for an alternate definition of blocking where the same number of constants is required for n and m, i.e. equality of $\Delta(n)$ and $\Delta(m)$ modulo π. This may lead to postponing blocking because the blocking test only succeeds after the creation of some additional nodes, but the test itself becomes significantly more efficient: if the number of constants, atoms, universal formulas etc. is not identical for m and n, it can be aborted immediately without generating a mapping π. In the following, we will refer to the different blocking conditions as *subset-equality blocking* and *equality blocking* respectively.

6   Evaluation of Optimisations and Heuristics

In this section, we present an analysis of the efficiency and the interaction of the heuristics and optimisations described in the previous sections. We used several benchmarks for logics of different expressiveness to see how the heuristics behave for formulas of different complexity: two sets from the "Tableaux 2000 Non-Classical Systems Comparison" (TANCS-2000) [27] benchmark suite and some $\mathcal{GF}$ formulas.

QBF-inv. The "quantified boolean formulas with inverse" benchmark consists of sets of random generated QBF formulas satisfying given parameters, which are translated into the logic $\mathbf{K}^-$ ($\mathbf{K}$ with inverse modality). For this comparison, we used the sets "p-QBF-inv-cnfSSS-K4-Cc-V4-D4" with $c \in \{10, 20, 30, 40, 50\}$, which are the easiest ones, so that even very inefficient combinations of heuristics can still decide some formulas.

PSAT-inv. The random generated "periodic satisfiability with inverse" formulas are translated into the logic $\mathbf{K}^-$ with global axioms. Again, we used the easiest sets "p-psat-inv-cnf-K4-Cc-V4-D4" with $c \in \{20, 30, 40, 50\}$.

GFB. Since the QBF and PSAT formulas contain only unary and binary relations, they do not use the complete expressive power of $\mathcal{GF}$. To see how SAGA performs for "proper" $\mathcal{GF}$ formulas, we generated some (simple) "$\mathcal{GF}$ Benchmark" (GFB) formulas. Each set consists of eight random generated formulas with the same width, depth, and maximum arity of the relations.

The QBF benchmark does not require blocking because termination of the algorithm is ensured by the properties of $\mathbf{K}^-$: each constant exists in at most two nodes, and for every grandson n of a node m the maximum modal depth of a formula in $\Delta(n)$ is strictly shorter than it is in $\Delta(m)$. This property makes it possible to regard the blocking test as another heuristic for this benchmark and thus evaluate its efficiency. For the more expressive logics, this is not possible because blocking must be permanently enabled to ensure termination.

The different blocking conditions *equality* and *subset-equality* (cf. Section 5) can only be compared for GFB because in a tree for QBF or PSAT every node contains exactly two constants and the case of subset-equality blocking for a *proper* subset cannot occur.

To evaluate the heuristics by themselves as well as their interactions, we ran every benchmark with every possible combination of heuristics. The figures in the following sections show how many formulas could be solved with the corresponding combination. On the x-axis, the different branching mechanisms are shown: syntactic branching first, then semantic branching with the different branching heuristics. For every combination of the other optimisations, a separate graph is printed. The different measuring points are connected by lines to improve readability.

The benchmarks were run on the following system: Hardware: Pentium-III (733 MHz), 384 MB RAM, 512 MB swap space; Software: Linux (Kernel 2.2), Allegro Common Lisp 6.0.

QBF. Surprisingly, blocking is the most efficient heuristic. With enabled blocking test, up to 26 formulas can be solved, compared to at most 4 without blocking. Although it is very expensive in the worst case, it is obviously still far more efficient than the expansion of the nodes that could be blocked. This indicates that the simple heuristic of comparing the number of constants, atoms, existential formulas etc. before generating a mapping π (cf. Section 5) is sufficient to achieve an efficient blocking test. The speedup could also be explained by regarding the blocking test as a kind of partial model caching (e.g. [21]), which was observed to be very efficient for the TANCS benchmark [13].

Semantic branching and backjumping also provide a significant speedup. While backjumping leads to a rather constant improvement independent of the other optimisations, the speedup delivered by semantic branching is particularly high for efficient combinations of the other heuristics. iMOMS is slightly worse than maximise-jump, and MOMS is far worse than the other branching heuristics. This is true even if backjumping is disabled, i.e. if selecting maximise-jump effectively means choosing a random disjunct, which shows that the main drawback of MOMS is not the interference with backjumping, but the high probability of failing with the first alternative.

Processing R∃ or R∨ first does not have a significant influence, and syntactic simplification has none at all (it is therefore not recorded in the figures). This is probably caused by the structure of the formulas.

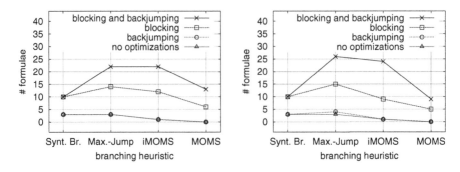

Fig. 2. Heuristics Comparison for QBF with "R∨ Last" (Left) and "R∃ Last" (Right)

PSAT. Semantic branching is by far the most important heuristic, and back-jumping is also very efficient. Regarding the optimal rule sequence, we can observe a significant speedup if R∨ is applied before R∃. An explanation for this behaviour is the blocking test: if it is applied only to propositionally expanded nodes, the probability for blocking is higher.

iMOMS is slightly better than maximise-jump, but the difference is irrelevant for efficient combinations of the other heuristics. The same is true for syntactic simplification: if we have an efficient combination of heuristics, disabling syntactic simplification does not significantly slow down the system. This indicates that, in the presence of semantic branching and backjumping, the efficiency is not affected by minor differences in the branching condition or syntactic redundancy of a formula.

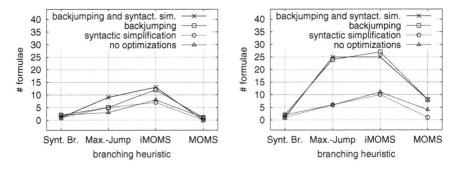

Fig. 3. Heuristics Comparison for PSAT with "R∨ Last" (Left) and "R∃ Last" (Right)

GFB. The results for QBF indicate that blocking, although expensive, results in a speedup. This raises the question if searching for more blocking situations by using subset-equality blocking instead of equality blocking might lead to a further speedup, although the blocking test becomes even more expensive. The measurements show that this is is not the case: subset-equality blocking leads to a higher average time and to fewer solvable formulas. The reason is that in this case, we cannot use the heuristics enabling us to abort the test if a node n is blocked by a node m early if $C(m) > C(n)$, but have to test all subsets of $C(m)$ which have the size of $C(n)$. Syntactic simplification has more influence for GFB than for the other benchmarks, which is probably caused by the simple and random structure of the formulas. The other heuristics behave similarly. (Therefore we do not include a figure.)

Summary. Semantic branching and backjumping deliver a significant speedup for all of our benchmarks. Blocking is useful even when it is not necessary. Among the branching heuristics, maximise-jump and iMOMS perform well, whereas MOMS is slower than choosing a random disjunct. Syntactic simplification does not provide a significant speedup, and the optimal sequence of rule applications differs for the various benchmarks.

7 Comparison with Other Systems

In this section, we examine how well SAGA scales compared to other systems for logics of different complexity, i.e. how fast it can solve formulas from $\mathcal{GF}$ and less expressive logics. We compare our own results with those that were presented in the TANCS-2000 comparison [3] for the QBF-inv/PSAT/PSAT-inv benchmarks.

The comparison systems are DLP [28], a satisfiability tester for PDL [4]; FaCT [20], a tableau algorithm for the description logic $\mathcal{SHIQ}$ [23]; RACE, a TBox and ABox reasoner for the logic $\mathcal{ALCNH}_{R+}$ [16]; and GOST [18], a tableau algorithm for the logic $\mathcal{GF}1^-$ [26], which is a PSPACE-fragment of $\mathcal{GF}$. GOST differs from SAGA in two important aspects: it does not include a blocking test (because it is not necessary to ensure termination for $\mathcal{GF}1^-$), and it uses a simpler backup algorithm: before a branch is performed, the entire tree constructed so far is copied, and during backtracking, the tree is replaced with that copy.

While these systems are tableau algorithms like SAGA and also share most of its optimisations, the last competitor SPASS [30,31] is a resolution-based first-order theorem prover. MSPASS [24] is a SPASS module translating formulas from the syntax of modal or description logics to first order logic so that their satisfiability can be decided with SPASS.

For this comparison, we used a larger set of the QBF and PSAT formulas than in Section 6. The results for DLP, FaCT, MSPASS and RACE were taken from [3] and those for GOST from [18]. The figures in the following sections show, for every system, how many formulas of each set could be solved.

The SAGA benchmarks and the GF benchmark for SPASS were run on the following system: Hardware: Pentium-III (1 GHz), 512 MB RAM, 1 GB swap space; Software: Linux (Kernel 2.2), Allegro Common Lisp 6.0. Timeout: 600sec (QBF), 1000sec (PSAT), 100sec (GFB).

QBF. Figure 4 shows that SAGA is more efficient than GOST and FaCT for most of the sets. While FaCT fails to solve many of the satisfiable formulas from the first sets, (C10/20/30-V4-D4), it performs better for some of the unsatisfiable formulas (C50-V4-D6). It seems that FaCT prunes the search space more efficiently, but needs more time to collect the necessary information.

The comparison with GOST again shows that the blocking test has a positive impact on performance. Furthermore, the more sophisticated backup strategy, though slower for very easy formulas, pays for complex ones: SAGA never aborts because of memory exhaustion, whereas this is often the case for GOST. Obviously, this behaviour is a result of the more space-consuming backup strategy.

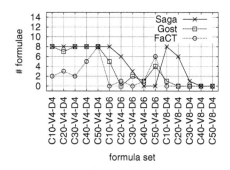

Fig. 4. System Comparison for QBF

PSAT. In order to compare SAGA with as many systems as possible, we ran the the PSAT as well as the PSAT-inv benchmark. Although the results presented in this section were produced on different hardware with different timeouts, the differences between the systems are relatively small. The PSAT formulas with depth 1 were easy for all of the systems. For the harder formulas with depth 2, the differences become visible and it turns out that SAGA is slightly slower than RACE and slightly faster than DLP and MSPASS. For PSAT-inv, SAGA is faster than FaCT and similar to MSPASS. Again, the difference to FaCT is particularly large for satisfiable formulas.

GFB. Figure 6 shows for every set characterised by the width (w) and depth (d) of the formulas and by the maximum arity (r) of the relations how many formulas could be solved. Among the comparison systems, SPASS is the only one that can decide $\mathcal{GF}$ formulas, but, as mentioned before, its characteristics

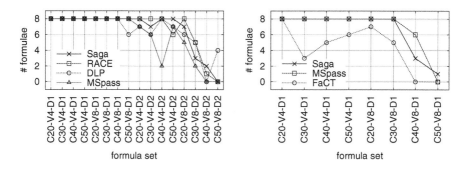

Fig. 5. System Comparison for PSAT (Left) and PSAT-inv (Right)

are quite different from SAGA's. Therefore, it is no surprise that the results are also different: while SAGA handles a large depth (d16) of a formula well, it has problems with relations of a higher arity (r4). SPASS shows the opposite behaviour. The sum of decidable formulas is similar.

Though SAGA works only for a fragment of FO and is not significantly faster than SPASS, the benefit of using a tableau algorithm is having a *decision procedure*, i.e. termination is guaranteed (even if it may consume exponential time).

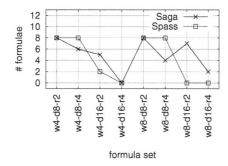

Fig. 6. System Comparison for GFB

8 Conclusion

In this paper, we presented an implementation and empirical analysis of a $\mathcal{GF}$ tableau algorithm. It turned out that, in spite of its worst-case complexity of NEXPTIME (for bounded arity), it performs well for existing benchmark formulas and the $\mathcal{GF}$ formulas we generated. Compared to other systems, SAGA's performance is slightly better than FaCT and similar to DLP, RACE an SPASS

/MSPASS. Sophisticated optimisations, in particular backjumping and semantic branching, are necessary to achieve this result. The blocking test, even when it is not necessary to ensure termination, significantly speeds up the program. However, this depends on the heuristics implemented to abort the test early.

The performance analysis presented in this paper is based on random generated formulas, most of which belong to a small fragment of $\mathcal{GF}$. This enables us to compare SAGA with several existing systems, but it also means that it may not be representative for real-life problems. The behaviour for realistic knowledge bases is subject to further study.

Acknowledgments. The author of this paper is supported by the DFG, Project No. GR 1324/3-3.

References

[1] H. Andréka, J. van Benthem, and I. Németi. Modal languages and bounded fragments of predicate logic. *Journal of Philosophical Logic*, 27(3):217–274, 1998.

[2] A. B. Baker. *Intelligent Backtracking on Constraint Satisfaction Problems: Experimental and Theoretical Results*. PhD thesis, University of Oregon, 1995.

[3] R. Dyckhoff, editor. *Automated Reasoning with Analytic Tableaux and Related Methods, International Conference (TABLEAUX 2000)*, volume 1847 of *Lecture Notes in Artificial Intelligence*. Springer-Verlag, 2000.

[4] M. J. Fischer and R. E. Ladner. Propositional dynamic logic of regular programs. *Journal of Computer and System Science*, 18:194–211, 1979.

[5] E. Franconi, G. De Giacomo, R. M. MacGregor, W. Nutt, and C. A. Welty, editors. *Proceedings of the International Workshop on Description Logics*, Povo - Trento, Italy, 1998. CEUR.

[6] J. W. Freeman. *Improvements to propositional satisfiability search algorithms*. PhD thesis, University of Pennsylvania, 1995.

[7] J. W. Freeman. Hard random 3-SAT problems and the Davis-Putnam procedure. *Artificial Intelligence*, 81:183–198, 1996.

[8] H. Ganzinger, editor. *Proceedings of the 16th International Conference on Automated Deduction (CADE-99)*, volume 1632 of *Lecture Notes in Artificial Intelligence*, Berlin, 1999. Springer-Verlag.

[9] H. Ganzinger and H. de Nivelle. A superposition decision procedure for the guarded fragment with equality. In *14th IEEE Symposium on Logic in Computer Science (LICS)*, Trento, Italy, 1999. IEEE Computer Society Press.

[10] E. Grädel. Guarded fragments of first-order logic: a perspective for new description logics? In Franconi et al. [5]. Extended abstract.

[11] E. Grädel. Decision procedures for guarded logics. In Ganzinger [8].

[12] E. Grädel. On the restraining power of guards. *Journal of Symbolic Logic*, 64:1719–1742, 1999.

[13] V. Haarslev and R. Möller. Consistency testing: The RACE experience. In Dyckhoff [3].

[14] V. Haarslev and R. Möller. Description of the RACER system and ist applications. In D.L. McGuinness, P.F. Patel-Schneider, C. Goble, and R. Möller, editors, *Proceedings of the 2001 International Workshop on Description Logics (DL2001)*, volume 49, Stanford, CA, USA, 2001. CEUR.

[15] V. Haarslev and R. Möller. High performance reasoning with very large knowledge bases: A practical case study. In Bernhard Nebel, editor, *Proceedings of the Seventeenth International Joint Conference on Aritificial Intelligence*. Morgan Kaufman Publishers, San Francisco, USA, 2001.

[16] V. Haarslev, R. Möller, and A.-Y. Turhan. RACE user's guide and reference manual version 1.1. Technical Report FBI-HH-M-289/99, University of Hamburg, CS department, 1999.

[17] C. Hirsch and S. Tobies. A tableau algorithm for the clique guarded fragment. In F. Wolter, H. Wansing, M. de Rijke, and M. Zakharyaschev, editors, *Advances in Modal Logics*, volume 3, Stanford, 2001. CSLI Publications.

[18] J. Hladik. Implementing the n-ary description logic $\mathcal{GF}1^-$. In F. Baader and U. Sattler, editors, *Proceedings of the International Workshop on Description Logics*, Aachen, Germany, 2000. CEUR.

[19] I. Horrocks. *Optimising Tableaux Decision Procedures for Description Logics*. PhD thesis, University of Manchester, 1997.

[20] I. Horrocks. Using an expressive description logic: FaCT or fiction? In A. G. Cohn, L. Schubert, and S. C. Shapiro, editors, *Principles of Knowledge Representation and Reasoning: Proceedings of the Sixth International Conference (KR'98)*. Morgan Kaufmann Publishers, San Francisco, California, 1998.

[21] I. Horrocks and P. F. Patel-Schneider. Optimising description logic subsumption. *Journal of Logic and Computation*, 9(3):267–293, 1999.

[22] I. Horrocks and U. Sattler. A description logic with transitive and inverse roles and role hierarchies. *Journal of Logic and Computation*, 9(3):385–410, 1999.

[23] I. Horrocks, U. Sattler, and S. Tobies. Practical reasoning for expressive description logics. In H. Ganzinger, D. McAllester, and A. Voronkov, editors, *Proceedings of the Sixth International Conference on Logic for Programming and Automated Reasoning (LPAR'99)*, number 1705 in Lecture Notes in Artificial Intelligence, pages 161–180. Springer-Verlag, 1999.

[24] U. Hustadt, R. A. Schmidt, and C. Weidenbach. MSPASS: Subsumption testing with SPASS. In Lambrix et al. [25].

[25] P. Lambrix, A. Borgida, M. Lenzerini, R. Möller, and P. Patel-Schneider, editors. *Proceedings of the International Workshop on Description Logics*, Linköping, Sweden, 1999. CEUR.

[26] C. Lutz, U. Sattler, and S. Tobies. A suggestion for an n-ary description logic. In Lambrix et al. [25].

[27] F. Massacci and F. M. Donini. Design and results of TANCS-2000. In Dyckhoff [3].

[28] P. F. Patel-Schneider. DLP system description. In Franconi et al. [5].

[29] V. R. Pratt. Models of program logics. In *Proceedings of the 20th Annual Symposium on Foundations of Computer Science*, San Juan, Puerto Rico, 1979.

[30] C. Weidenbach. SPASS: Combining superposition, sorts and splitting. In A. Robinson and A. Voronkov, editors, *Handbook of Automated Reasoning*, chapter 27. Elsevier, 1999.

[31] C. Weidenbach, B. Afshordel, U. Brahm, C. Cohrs, T. Engel, E. Keen, C. Theobalt, and D. Topić. System description: SPASS version 1.0.0. In Ganzinger [8].

Lemma and Model Caching in Decision Procedures for Quantified Boolean Formulas

Reinhold Letz

Institut für Informatik
Technische Universität München
D-80290 Munich, Germany
letz@in.tum.de

Abstract. The increasing role of quantified Boolean logic in many applications calls for practically efficient decision procedures. One of the most promising paradigms is the semantic tree format implemented in the style of the DPLL procedure. In this paper, so-called learning techniques like intelligent backtracking and caching of lemmas which proved useful in the pure propositional case are generalised to the quantified Boolean case and the occuring differences are discussed. Due to the strong restriction of the variable selection in semantic tree procedures for quantified Boolean formulas, learning methods are more important than in the propositional case, as we demonstrate. Furthermore, in addition to the caching of lemmas, significant advances can be achieved by techniques based on the caching of models, too. The theoretical effect of these improvements is illustrated by a comparison of the search spaces on pathological examples. We also describe the basic features of the system Semprop, which is an efficient implementation of (some of) the developed techniques, and give the results of an experimental evaluation of the system on a number of practical examples.

1 Introduction

The last years have seen an increasing interest in the language of quantified Boolean formulas (*QBFs*). While in complexity theory the central rôle of this language is obvious from the fact that it represents one of the natural paradigms for characterising the complexity class PSPACE, it has been recognised that QBFs are also suitable in practice, since they offer a concise framework for expressing many problems from planning, abduction, nonmonotonic reasoning, or from intuitionistic, terminological and modal logics. This has motivated the need for efficient decision procedures for QBFs. As a consequence, recently, a number of such procedures have been developed, e.g., QKN [7], Evaluate [2], QSOLVE [4], Decide [9], QuBE [5], or Semprop (the system described in this paper). However, when compared with the procedures available for propositional logic, these procedures are still in their infancy. Furthermore, even for the few procedures available, there is a tendency of *divergence*, in the sense that almost every procedure contains some special adhoc techniques that apply well to some examples, but may not be useful for a generally successful approach.

U. Egly and C.G. Fermüller (Eds.): TABLEAUX 2002, LNAI 2381, pp. 160–175, 2002.
© Springer-Verlag Berlin Heidelberg 2002

In this paper we identify some techniques that are very important if not essential for any powerful and robust QBF procedure. These techniques all subscribe to the so-called *learning* or *look-back* paradigm, i.e., information gathered during the search process is used to prune the remaining search. First, we consider the technique of *dependency-directed backtracking*, which can be seen as one of the simplest learning methods in terms of space and time overhead. We also give experimental evidence that dependency-directed backtracking is of general importance for deciding quantified Boolean formulas.

Another more general paradigm is *caching* of more complex data structures. In its pure form, caching comes in two dual variants, caching of *lemmas* and caching of *models*. We discuss the proof-theoretic background of these methods and the complications arising when moving from propositional to quantified Boolean logic, where the so-called resolvent lemma does no more hold. Unfortunately, the efficient integration of caching methods is much more problematic than using dependency-directed backtracking. First, from a general complexity point of view, since when caching is applied in an uncontrolled manner, the underlying procedure looses the advantage of being a polynomial space procedure. Furthermore, from an implementational point of view, because the integration of lemmas or models is expensive and may significantly decrease the speed of the basic procedure. As a consequence, in propositional logic, caching could not make its way as a standard technique. In the pure propositional case, because of the applicability of powerful *look-ahead* techniques, the use of expensive look-back techniques like caching is often not needed. In this paper we will expound that this situation completely changes when going from propositional to quantified Boolean logic. Since here the applicability of look-ahead techniques is strongly restricted, there exist ridiculously small formulas which are intractable for the currently existing QBF procedures, and these formulas become trivial with caching methods. This suggests that, in contrast to propositional logic, an integration of such methods might be indispensable.

In order to also facilitate the experimental evaluation of the presented learning methods, the methods are currently being implemented in the QBF decision procedure Semprop. We describe the general design decisions for an efficient integration. The key idea by which the mentioned difficulties of integrating lemmas (and models) is avoided is to limit their applicability to certain *path contexts*. With this approach, one may dynamically control the size of the cache by simply adapting the size of the path contexts. We have evaluated the current implementation on a number of practical examples. Although the current implementation does not contain all of the presented methods, the results clearly show that learning is beneficial and that the additional overhead can be kept under control.

The paper is organised as follows. We begin with some preliminaries in the next section. Then, we shortly review the basic paradigms for deciding quantified Boolean formulas with the emphasis on semantic tree procedures. After discussing the main problems of devising an efficient QBF procedure, we present the paradigm of dependency-directed backtracking, as the simplest application of the learning paradigm. Then we turn to the development of more powerful caching methods, first, the case of lemmas, then, the case of models. Subsequently, we consider issues of integrating and implementing the developed methods, and present the results of an experimental evaluation.

2   Preliminaries

We consider quantified Boolean formulas in clausal form, which is sufficient, since there exist efficient translations into this normal form. So a QBF Φ will be of the form $Q_1 x_1 \cdots Q_n x_n S$ where every $Q_i \in \{\exists, \forall\}(1 \le i \le n)$ and where S is a set of propositional *clauses* (i.e, sets of literals) over the variables $x_1, \ldots, x_n$. We also assume that the $x_1, \ldots, x_n$ are pairwise different. $Q_1 x_1 \cdots Q_n x_n$ is called the *prefix* and S the *matrix* of Φ.

For defining the semantics of QBFs, we extend the language with the two Boolean constants $\top$ and $\bot$. A clause in a QBF Φ is *true* if it contains $\top$ or $\neg\bot$; a clause is *false* if it contains neither $\top$, nor $\neg\bot$, nor an *existential* literal, i.e., a literal whose variable is preceded by an $\exists$ in the prefix of Φ; otherwise a clause is called *open*. Furthermore, with $\Phi[l/k]$ we denote the result of substituting l in the matrix of Φ by k. Then the *truth value* of a QBF is defined inductively as follows:

 - A QBF Φ with no variables is *true* if every clause of the matrix of Φ is true.
 - A QBF Φ of the form $\forall x \Phi$ is *true* if both $\Phi[x/\top]$ and $\Phi[x/\bot]$ are true, and a QBF of the form $\exists x \Phi$ is *true* if $\Phi[x/\top]$ or $\Phi[x/\bot]$ is true.

A QBF which is not true is *false*. We will also use the following general notion of a *partial model* or just *model* for short. A *model for* a QBF Φ is any set of literals $M = \{l_1, \ldots, l_n\}$ such that

 - M does not contain $\top$, $\neg\top$, $\bot$ or $\neg\bot$,
 - M is *consistent*, i.e., contains no literal and its complement,
 - the QBF $\Phi[x_1/v_1] \cdots [x_n/v_n]$ is true where, for any $1 \le i \le n$, x_i is the variable of l_i and v_i is $\top$ resp. $\bot$ depending on whether l_i is x_i resp. $\neg x_i$.

3   Semantic Tree Procedures

Before presenting the most natural paradigm for deciding quantified Boolean formulas, we shall shortly mention some other approaches that are occasionally used. One is to transform a QBF into propositional logic, the obvious problem is the exponential blow-up of the formula size. Another is to use resolution on QBFs as described in [7]; here the weaknesses are the same as in propositional logic where resolution turned out to be practically useless (resolution is no PSPACE procedure and difficult to control). In Section 6, however, we will demonstrate that, in order to devise a powerful and robust QBF procedure, a controlled integration of resolution is indispensable.

Certainly, the most natural approach to deciding the truth value of a quantified Boolean formula is by a direct implementation of the semantics. That is, one iteratively splits the problem of deciding a formula of the form $Qx\Phi$ into the two subproblems $\Phi[x/\top]$ and $\Phi[x/\bot]$, as in propositional logic. The resulting proof structure is a *semantic tree*, i.e., a binary tree in which every pair of edges is labeled with a variable and its negation. With the root of the tree we associate the original QBF Φ, and with every node N in the tree with ingoing edge literal x respectively $\neg x$ we associate the QBF $\Psi[x/\top]$ respectively $\Psi[x/\bot]$ where $Qx\Psi$ is the QBF associated with the predecessor node of N. The additional complication of the quantified Boolean case is that we have to distinguish between *existential* and *universal* nodes in the tree depending on whether the literal at the ingoing edge is existentially or universally quantified. When applying a backtracking-driven procedure which constructs a semantic tree in a depth-first manner and considers one branch at a time only, the truth value of a QBF can obviously be checked in linear space.

There are two sources of indeterminism when constructing a semantic tree, (1) on which variable to branch next, and (2) which branch to consider first. In propositional logic, one has total freedom of selection in both respects. Since these choices determine the size of the semantic tree, a lot of effort in SAT research has been devoted to finding clever selection criteria. In the quantified Boolean case, the crucial difference is that the freedom of selection of type (1) is strongly restricted by the prefix order, since existential and universal quantifiers cannot be permuted. So, in general, the next branching variable y of a QBF $Qx\Phi$ has to be of type Q and no other quantifier must precede y in the prefix of the QBF. As we will see, this restriction has severe consequences for the design of efficient QBF procedures.

Example 1. A false quantified Boolean formula:

$$\exists x_1 \forall x_2 \exists x_3 \exists x_4 \big(\underbrace{(\neg x_1 \vee x_2 \vee \neg x_3)}_{c_1} \wedge \underbrace{(x_3 \vee \neg x_4)}_{c_2} \wedge \underbrace{(x_3 \vee x_4)}_{c_3} \wedge \underbrace{(x_1 \vee \neg x_2 \vee \neg x_3)}_{c_4} \big).$$

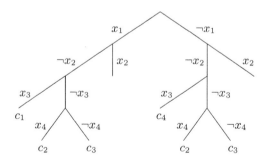

Fig. 1. A semantic tree proof for the falsity of Example 1.

In Figure 1, a semantic tree proof of the falsity of the QBF given in Example 1 is displayed. As a matter of fact, the same partial evaluation technique as in propositional logic may be used to avoid unnecessary splittings: a clausal QBF Φ is true if it contains only true clauses, and Φ is false if it contains a false clause.

In either case, a further splitting on the respective branch can be avoided. In the figure, we have added the false clauses at the respective branches.

In order to achieve a reasonably efficient basic QBF procedure, two other methods from propositional logic are indispensable, which determine the procedure of Davis, (Putnam,) Logemann, and Loveland [3], *DPLL* for short. One is the *unit propagation*, the other the *purity rule*. Both methods are standard in QBF procedures (see [2]).

Unit (propagation) rule. A clause c in a QBF Φ is *unit* if it contains exactly one existential literal with variable, say, x and all the variables of the universal literals in the clause occur to the right of x in the quantifier prefix of Φ. If the QBF Φ associated with a node N in a semantic tree contains a unit clause c with an existential literal x ($\neg x$), then one can split on the variable x. (Immediately afterwards one may label the new node with the subproblem $\Phi[x/\bot]$ ($\Phi[x/\top]$) with the false clause c.)

Purity rule. A literal l occurring in the matrix of a QBF is called *pure* if its complement does not occur in the matrix of the QBF. If the QBF Φ associated with a node N in a semantic tree contains a pure literal x ($\neg x$), then one can split on x and

- when x is existential, ignore the node with the subproblem $\Phi[x/\bot]$ ($\Phi[x/\top]$),
- when x is universal, ignore the node with the subproblem $\Phi[x/\top]$ ($\Phi[x/\bot]$).

Proposition 1. *The unit and the purity rule preserve the correctness of the semantic tree method for QBFs. (For a proof see [2])*

The resulting inference system will be considered as our *basic semantic tree procedure* for QBFs, it is also the common basis of all mentioned systems that are using the semantic tree paradigm.

4   Towards a Powerful QBF Procedure

In the last years, very powerful decision procedures for propositional logic have been developed. Despite the hardness of the problem, those procedures can often decide formulas containing thousands of variables. The question is whether such procedures can be extended to the quantified Boolean case and whether a comparable performance can be achieved. One of the main paradigms used in propositional logic are semantic trees[1]. The techniques applied in propositional semantic tree procedures comprise sophisticated criteria for variable and sign selection, dependency-directed backtracking, the use of lemmas, equivalences (à la Stalmarck) or even symmetries, methods of partitioning the input, etc. Which

---

[1] Another is decision diagrams. It would be interesting to consider extensions of decision diagrams to QBFs, but this is out of the scope of this paper. On the other hand, it is obvious that stochastic methods like GSAT are useless in the quantified Boolean case.

of these techniques should be used in order to obtain a practically efficient QBF procedure? Furthermore, when looking at the few QBF systems that have been developed in the last few years, additional QBF specific methods were developed and implemented like *trivial truth* in [2] or *sampling, inversion of quantifiers*, and *failed literal detection on inner quantifiers* in [9]. For example, the method called "trivial truth" is to abstract the universal variables from a QBF and check whether the resulting formula is true. If so, the original formula must be true, too; if not, nothing is gained, and the runtime overhead of the method is in vain.

In order to avoid the problems of such a divergence, we think that one should first concentrate on the identification and development of some few pruning methods which are beneficial in general. But which methods are of this type? As already mentioned, the chief difference of the quantified Boolean from the propositional case is that the freedom of variable selection is strongly restricted. As a consequence, all the sophisticated methods from propositional logic which aim at avoiding the selection of unfortunate branching variables are often not applicable. In such a situation, we need methods that can remedy the redundancies induced by unfortunate branchings, *after* those branchings have been performed. There are two general approaches of this type. One is *dependency-directed backtracking*, the other is *caching of lemmas and models*.

5   Dependency-Directed Backtracking

When analysing the behaviour of the basic semantic tree procedure for QBFs, as introduced at the end of Section 2, it often occurs that one has to branch on a variable x which afterwards turns out to be irrelevant for the solution of one of its subproblems Φ_1 or Φ_2. This induces an unnecessary search effort.

The natural approach to attacking this problem is *dependency-directed backtracking*, also called *pruning* or *level cut*. Dependency-directed backtracking for QBFs was first published in [5], here we give a more general account. In the QBF case dependency-directed backtracking comes in two very different forms, one for false and one for true subproblems. We start with the description of the method for false subproblems, since this is similar to the propositional case (see, e.g., [8]).

5.1   Dependency-Directed Backtracking for False Subproblems

We will present the method in two versions, one weaker one, but with almost no implementational overhead, and another more expensive method, but with a higher potential of pruning the semantic tree. Evidently, dependency-directed backtracking for false subproblems only applies to existential variables[2].

Dependency-directed backtracking by labeling. Whenever we branch at a node N on an existential variable x producing the subproblems Φ_1 and Φ_2, we label x

---

[2] If two subproblems Φ_1 and Φ_2 result from a universal splitting and Φ could be identified as false, then Φ_2 need not be considered anyway.

as *irrelevant*. When reaching a node in the semantic tree whose associated QBF contains a false clause c, then, for every existential literal in c, we label its variable as *relevant*. If on backtracking we reach the node N, after having identified one of its subproblems, say Φ_1, as false, and if x is labelled as irrelevant, then the subproblem Φ_2 can be considered as false, too, and need not be solved any more.

Dependency-directed backtracking by relevance sets. When reaching a node in the semantic tree whose associated QBF contains a false clause c, then the variables of all existential literals in c are collected in the so-called *relevance set* of the node. If on backtracking we reach a node N with an existential branching variable x after having identified the subproblem at one of its successors, say N_1, as false, then we check whether x is contained in the relevance set R_1 of N_1:

- if not, the subproblem at the other successor N_2 can be considered as false and need not be considered, furthermore, the relevance set of N is set to R_1;
- otherwise, the other successor N_2 has to be processed yielding a relevance set, say, R_2. Then we check whether $x \in R_2$:
  - if not, the relevance set of N is set to R_2;
  - otherwise, i.e., only if $x \in R_1 \cap R_2$, the relevance set of N is set to $R_1 \cup R_2$.

Both methods preserve correctness. Obviously, the runtime overhead of the first method is almost negligible whereas the second method is more time consuming[3]. On the other hand, the second method is strictly more powerful, in the sense that it can achieve a stronger pruning of the search tree. The case where the first method fails is when two variables x and y (with y above x in the tree) are relevant in the subproblem Φ_1 solved first for x, but x and y are both irrelevant in the second subproblem Φ_2 for x. Using the first method the irrelevance of y cannot be identified any more. Both methods are already successfully used in semantic tree procedures for propositional formulas.

5.2   Dependency-Directed Backtracking for True Subproblems

The identification of irrelevant variables for true subproblems has no counterpart in the propositional case, since it affects universal variables only. Also, this problem is harder to handle than the case of false subproblems. In order to comprehend the difficulties, consider the case of a branching on a universal variable producing two subproblems Φ_1 and Φ_2. Assume now, for example, Φ_1 has been identified as true. Under which conditions would we consider the branching on x as irrelevant?

Dependency-directed backtracking by model intersections. As in the false case there are different approaches. The simplest idea is as follows. Certainly, we would consider x as irrelevant if we could re-use the solution tree of the problem Φ_1 as a solution tree for Φ_2, too. This can be expressed in the following more implementation-oriented proposition. For this, we use the following notion. Given a leaf node N of a semantic tree whose formula is true, the set of literals on the branch from the root to N is called *the model at* N.

---
[3] Although it can quite efficiently be implemented using bit vectors.

Proposition 2. *Let T be a semantic tree proof of the truth of a QBF $\Phi[x/\top]$ respectively $\Phi[x/\bot]$. Let further S be the set of open clauses in the matrix of Φ that contain the literal x respectively $\neg x$, and M the set of models at the leaf nodes of T. Then $\Phi[x/\bot]$ respectively $\Phi[x/\top]$ is true if every clause in S contains a literal from $\bigcap M \setminus \{x\}$ respectively $\bigcap M \setminus \{\neg x\}$.*

In order to implement this technique, one simply has to associate with every subproblem identified as true a corresponding *model intersection* set. A closer look at this method shows that it achieves a special version of the technique of trivial truth, mentioned in Section 4. The difference, however, is that here the method is applied on the fly.

Dependency-directed backtracking by model unions. The model intersection method can be made more powerful concerning search pruning by pursuing the following idea. Instead of simply *re-using* the solution tree of a subproblem Φ_1 for its mate Φ_2, one could try to modify it in the following manner. It might be possible to extend the models encountered in the solution of Φ_1 with additional existential literals in such a manner that with those new literals the clauses S in the argumentation above can be made true. This is captured by the following proposition.

Proposition 3. *Let T be a semantic tree proof of the truth of a QBF $\Phi[x/\top]$ respectively $\Phi[x/\bot]$. Let further S be the set of open clauses in the matrix of Φ that contain the literal x respectively $\neg x$, and M the set of models at the leaf nodes of T. Then $\Phi[x/\bot]$ respectively $\Phi[x/\top]$ is true if there exists a set E of existential literals satisfying the following conditions:*

1. every clause in S contains the complement of a literal from E,
2. $E \cap \bigcup M = \emptyset$.

The implementation of this method is similar to the previous one. But the new approach contains indeterminism (finding a set E), whereas the model intersection method is completely deterministic. On the other hand, it can be shown that the model union technique can no more be captured by the trivial truth method mentioned before.

6   Use of Lemmas

In procedures for propositional logic, the use of *lemmas* (also called *nogoods* or *learning*) is indispensible for unsatisfiable formulas which, for no variable selection strategy, have semantic trees of manageable size. In order to comprehend the general idea of lemmas (see also, e.g., [8]), let us consider Example 1 and the proof of its falsity in Figure 1. The tree contains two identical subtrees below the edges labelled with $\neg x_3$. The use of lemmas is the natural approach of avoiding such a duplication. It can be shown that this duplication cannot be avoided by any of the techniques mentioned so far, including dependency-directed backtracking.

In fact, one can construct a class of *very short* false QBF formulas which are intractable for any of the existing QBF procedures based on semantic trees[4].

Example 2. For any $n \geq 1$, let F_n be the QBF of the following form:

$$\exists y_{n+1} \forall x_n \exists y_n \cdots \forall x_1 \exists y_1 S$$

where the matrix S contains the four clauses

$$\neg y_{n+1},\ y_1 \vee y_2,\ \neg y_1 \vee y_2,\ y_1 \vee \neg y_2, \text{ plus the } n-1 \text{ clauses}$$

$$\neg y_j \vee \neg x_j \vee \neg y_{j+1} \vee x_{j+1} \vee y_{j+2}, \text{ for } 1 \leq j \leq n-1.$$

Proposition 4. *The size of any semantic tree proof (including dependency-directed backtracking) of an F_n is exponential in n.*

The existence of intractable formulas for semantic tree procedures is nothing exceptional, but for this formulas the behaviour of semantic tree procedures is so poor that even the system Semprop, which has the best performance on this class, explores a semantic tree with more than 3×10^6 branches for F_{30}, which is a tiny formula of just 33 clauses (as a comparison, for F_{35}, the tree has more than 3×10^7 branches). F_{50} cannot be solved within a day by any of the existing QBF procedures that are based on semantic trees. In contrast, in propositional logic, any decent decision procedure can quickly solve every formula of such a size. The consequence to be drawn from this observation is that lemmas, which are of some use in propositional logic, might really be indispensable in the quantified Boolean case.

6.1   Q-Resolution

As the basis of lemma generation in propositional logic is resolution, its extension to QBFs was introduced in [7] and called *Q-resolution*. Given a QBF Φ with prefix P and matrix S, the $\forall$-*reduct* of a clause c is the clause obtained by removing any universal literal whose variable does not precede in P the variable of an existential literal in c. Furthermore, a clause is *tautological* if it contains $\top$ or $\neg\bot$ or a literal and its negation. Given two non-tautological clauses c_1 and c_2 which contain two complementary existential literals, say, $x \in c_1$ and $\neg x \in c_2$, the *Q-resolvent* of c_1 and c_2 is $(c_1' \setminus \{x\}) \cup (c_2' \setminus \{\neg x\})$ where c_1' and c_2' are the $\forall$-reducts of c_1 and c_2 respectively.

Q-resolution is *sound*, i.e., any resolvent of a true QBF can be added to its matrix without changing its truth value.[5] Recalling the semantic tree given in Figure 1, from the two clauses $c_2 = x_3 \vee \neg x_4$ and $c_3 = x_3 \vee x_4$ the Q-resolvent x_3 can be deduced, which can afterwards be used on the right-hand side to shorten the proof. So, the integration of lemmas, i.e., Q-resolvents in a semantic procedure for QBFs can be beneficial.

---

[4] Whereas those formulae should be trivial for resolution-based systems like [7].

[5] Q-resolution is also *complete*, i.e., from any false QBF Φ the empty clause can be deduced by a sequence of Q-resolution steps. However, for our purposes completeness is of no interest, since we want to use resolution in a limited manner only.

6.2   Semantic Trees with Lemmas

As illustrated with the example discussed above, a natural integration of lemmas into semantic trees could work as follows, let us call this the *standard method*. We associate with every solved false node N_i of the semantic tree a clause $\mathcal{C}(N_i)$, defined inductively as follows.

1. For every false leaf node N, $\mathcal{C}(N)$ is the $\forall$-reduct of the respective clause c at N.
2. If N is a universal false non-leaf node, then we may assume that it has exactly one false successor node N' and set $\mathcal{C}(N) = \mathcal{C}(N')$.
3. If N is an existential false non-leaf node, then it must have two false successor nodes N_1 and N_2. Let w.r.g. x be the literal at the edge leading to N_1 and $\neg x$ the one at the edge to N_2. We may distinguish two cases.
   - Either $\neg x \in \mathcal{C}(N_1)$ and $x \in \mathcal{C}(N_2)$. Then $\mathcal{C}(N)$ is the Q-resolvent of $\mathcal{C}(N_1)$ and $\mathcal{C}(N_2)$.
   - Or, a clause below does not contain the complement of its respective edge literal, say, w.r.g., $\mathcal{C}(N_2)$. [6] This means that x is not needed in the solution of N_2. Then set $\mathcal{C}(N) = \mathcal{C}(N_2)$.

We call the respective semantic tree a *clause-labelled semantic tree*.

6.3   Complications in the QBF Case

There is a crucial difference between propositional and quantified Boolean logic concerning the use of lemmas in semantic trees. In propositional logic, we have the following fundamental result which supports an easy integration of lemmas.

Proposition 5 (Resolvent lemma). *For any clause-labelled semantic tree proof T for the falsity of a QBF without universal variables, i.e., a propositional formula, no clause $\mathcal{C}(N)$ at a node N of T is tautological.*

Unfortunately, the resolvent lemma does no more hold in the general QBF case. The critical situation may be described as follows. In the course of generating a semantic tree, it may happen that an existential variable x is used as a branching literal, although there is some non-selected universal variable y to the left of x in the prefix. This may occur in an application of the unit propagation rule. Now it can occur that two sibling nodes below are labelled with clauses $c_1 = y \vee \neg x \vee \neg z$ and $c_2 = \neg y \vee \vee \neg x \vee \neg z$ with z being an existential variable. Because $\neg x$ blocks the removal of y respectively $\neg y$, the Q-resolvent of both clauses is tautological. Obviously, tautological clauses are not productive for shortening semantic tree proofs.

When faced with this problem, one may simply accept it and use the standard method, with the consequence that in the QBF case fewer productive lemmas are available. As a matter of fact, it does not make sense to restrict the unit rule

---

[6] Note that when using dependency-directed backtracking, at least one of the two clauses must contain the complement of its respective edge literal.

in such a manner that the generation of tautologies is avoided, since the unit rule is one of the driving forces of the procedure. But there is another possibility for avoiding tautologies. Assume, in the mentioned example, that N would be the node above at which the unit rule w.r.t. the existential variable x was applied. Then the respective false leaf successor of N is labelled with a clause c containing x. Now one could try to remedy the tautology generation problem by performing Q-resolution between the clauses c_1 and c and the clauses c_2 and c, thus removing the blocking literal $\neg x$, and afterwards applying Q-resolution to the resulting clauses. Unfortunately, it may not suffice to do this, because other existential literals could be contained and block the $\forall$-reduction. Furthermore, when performing Q-resolution with c, new blocking literals may be imported, leading to some snowball effect. From a practical point of view, any such sophisticated method of tautology avoidance should evaluate the efforts needed to circumvent the generation of a certain tautology with the gain that may be achieved this way, i.e., whether a useful lemma results.

7   Use of Models

As illustrated with the different variants of dependency-directed backtracking, in quantified Boolean logic, most methods have a dual form. The dual form of employing lemmas is the use of models. As a motivation, consider the semantic tree proof shown in Figure 2 of the formula given in Example 3. This proof contains two identical subtrees below the edges labelled with $\neg x_3$. None of the methods developed so far can capture this redundancy.

Example 3. A true QBF $\forall x_1 \exists x_2 \forall x_3 \forall x_4 \exists x_5 (c_1 \wedge c_2 \wedge c_3 \wedge c_4 \wedge c_5)$ where

$$c_1 = x_1 \vee \neg x_3 \vee x_5,$$
$$c_2 = \neg x_1 \vee x_2 \vee x_5,$$
$$c_3 = \neg x_2 \vee x_4 \vee x_5,$$
$$c_4 = x_3 \vee \neg x_4 \vee \neg x_5,$$
$$c_5 = x_2 \vee \neg x_3 \vee \neg x_5.$$

As a natural approach for solving this problem we introduce *model resolution*, which can be viewed as the dual of Q-resolution. Given two models m_1 and m_2 for a QBF Φ containing two complementary universal literals, say, $x \in m_1$ and $\neg x \in m_2$, the *model resolvent* of m_1 and m_2 is the set $(m_1' \setminus \{x\}) \cup (m_2' \setminus \{\neg x\})$ where m_1' is obtained from m_1 by removing any existential literal whose variable does not precede in P the variable of a universal literal in m_1, and analogously for m_2'.

Proposition 6. *If a model resolvent m of two models for a QBF Φ is consistent, then m is a model for Φ.*

How can this method be applied to shorten the proof of Example 3? Consider the situation when the leaf node N_1 at the edge labelled with $\neg x_5$ on the left-hand side is reached. The set of the respective branch literals $m_1 = \{x_1, x_2, \neg x_3, x_4, \neg x_5\}$

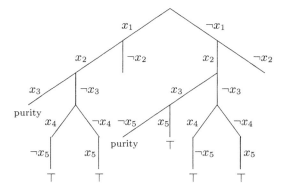

Fig. 2. A semantic tree proof for the truth of Example 3.

is a model for Φ. The essential observation now is that x_1 is redundant in this model, the only clause made true by x is $x_1 \lor \neg x_3 \lor x_5$, but $\neg x_3$ is already in the model. Consequently, it can be *reduced* to $m_1 = \{x_2, \neg x_3, x_4, \neg x_5\}$, which is a model for Φ, too. For the next leaf node N_2 to the right, the same holds for the model $\{x_1, x_2, \neg x_3, \neg x_4, x_5\}$, which can hence be reduced to $m_2 = \{x_2, \neg x_3, \neg x_4, x_5\}$. Now, model resolution can be applied to m_1 and m_2 yielding the model $m = \{x_2, \neg x_3\}$. The model m can then be used to solve the $\neg x_3$-edge on the right-hand side of the tree, since it *subsumes* (is a subset of) the set of literals on the branch. This way the duplication can be avoided. An essential observation of this application of model resolution is that models need to be reduced in order to be beneficial. The problems of integrating model resolution in an efficient manner are the same as for lemmas.

7.1   Use of Models for Exploiting the Independence of Subproblems

Interestingly, there is a technique based on the caching of model information which nicely addresses the problem that standard QBF procedures have with certain formulas containing variable-independent subformulas. One of the simplest formula classes which reveals the weakness of the existing QBF procedures in this respect is the following.

Example 4. $\forall x_1 x_3 \cdots x_{n-1} \exists x_2 x_4 \cdots x_n (c_1 \land \cdots \land c_n)$ where
$c_1 = x_1 \lor x_2$, $c_2 = \neg x_1 \lor \neg x_2$, $c_3 = x_3 \lor x_4$, $c_4 = \neg x_3 \lor \neg x_4$, ..., $c_{n-1} = x_{n-1} \lor x_n$, $c_n = \neg x_{n-1} \lor \neg x_n$.

Such a QBF consists of simple variable-independent subproblems, which could easily be solved separately. However, this simple class is intractable for the standard QBF decision procedures, and there is no obvious general remedy of this weakness. In order to exploit the independence of subproblems, in certain systems, special techniques for partitioning have been integrated (see, for example, [9]). However, one could worsen the problem by introducing connecting variables, which would block the possibility of partitioning the formula.

Such a modified class is shown in the next example.

Example 5. $\forall x_1 x_3 \cdots x_{n-1} x_{n+1} \exists x_2 x_4 \cdots x_n (c_1 \wedge \cdots \wedge c_n)$ where
$c_1 = x_1 \vee x_2 \vee x_3$, $c_2 = \neg x_1 \vee \neg x_2 \vee \neg x_3$, $c_3 = x_3 \vee x_4 \vee x_5$, $c_4 = \neg x_3 \vee \neg x_4 \vee \neg x_5$,
$\ldots$, $c_{n-1} = x_{n-1} \vee x_n \vee x_{n+1}$, $c_n = \neg x_{n-1} \vee \neg x_n \vee \neg x_{n+1}$.

When analysing the behavior of a semantic tree procedure on the previous example, we can make an interesting observation. Given a model m for the formula containing an existential literal, say, $\neg x_i$ and a universal literal x_{i-1} immediately above, then, when switching the signs of both literals, the respectively evaluated QBF's are identical. Consequently, this new partial interpretation m' must be a model of the formula, too. This can be exploited for search pruning, by simply avoiding the search when faced with the partial interpretation m'.

The idea underlying this observation can be generalised to a powerful search pruning mechanism, which is based on the following property of QBF's. Given a QBF Φ with clauses S and a partial interpretation m, with $V(m)$ we denote the set of variables underlying m, i.e. the result of deleting the signs, with $\top(m)$ we denote the set of clauses in S satisfied by m, and with $\mathcal{A}(m)$ we denote the clauses in $S \setminus \top(m)$ which contain complements of literals in m.

Proposition 7 (Sign abstraction). *Given two partial interpretations m and m', if m is a model of Φ, $V(m') \subseteq V(m)$, $\top(m) \subseteq \top(m')$, and $\mathcal{A}(m)$ is empty, then m' is a model of Φ.*

This property can be directly used as a search pruning mechanism, as follows. During the proof process, we cache pairs $\langle m, S \rangle$ where m is a model of Φ and $S = \top(m)$. Then, for every branch m', we check whether $\mathcal{A}(m)$ is empty. If so, we check the other conditions for all pairs in the cache. Interestingly, with this method the mentioned examples can be solved in linear time, even if always the newest few pairs are kept in the cache. That this method is also relevant for practical examples, is demonstrated below.

8   Integration and Implementation of Caching Methods

There have always been attempts to integrate lemmas into propositional semantic tree procedures. However, as experience has shown, it is very difficult to implement lemmas in such a manner that the runtime overhead is not too high. Furthermore, it is hard to find the right trade-off between not to get drowned by the wealth of possible lemmas and keeping such lemmas which are effective in shortening the proof process.

Our approach to overcome these problems is to always generate *conditional lemmas*, i.e. lemmas of the form $m \vdash c$ where c is a clause and m is a certain *path context*, i.e., an initial segment of the literals on the current tree branch. The validity of a lemma is always restricted to m. When on backtracking the lowest literal in m is touched, all lemmas associated with m are automatically deleted. On the one hand, this procedure provides a relatively robust means to control the number of lemmas that are generated, viz., by simply modifying the size of the path context. One the other hand, lemmas will automatically be deleted (see also

[8]). As a general criterion for limiting the number of lemmas, we generate lemmas only at existential branching points where both subtrees are complex. In practice, the size of the context is controlled by the following self-adjusting procedure. We periodically compare the size of the lemma cache with the number of effective uses of lemmas, and adapt the size of the path context accordingly. As our experience with a large number of experiments in propositional and quantified Boolean logic have shown, this procedure can keep the space and time overheads of caching in reasonable bounds and yet achieve a significant reduction of the proof length, so that on average it performs better than methods without caching. This is a crucial difference to the manner learning techniques are currently integrated in the system QuBE. In QuBE no context lemmas (and models) are used, instead the maximal length of a lemma (and model) has to be controlled by the user [6].

The manner how lemmas are represented also deserves some remarks. The lemma associated with a tree node is encoded by using bit vector technology. These bit vectors are destructively modified when moving back from the leaves towards the root of the tree. Whenever we decide to make a lemma available for a future use, this information is converted into the standard data structure used for clauses, viz. a list of pointers to the contained literals, plus some control information. The same bit vector technology can also be used for doing dependency-directed backtracking efficiently. Finally, also the sign abstraction method can be implemented this way, in the current implementation the default cache size for the respective pairs is 10.

In summary, the current implementation of Semprop contains the following of the described features:

- dependency-directed backtracking,
- generation of Q-resolvents according to the standard scheme,
- the sign abstraction method as described in 7.1.

Model caching is currently implemented in the same manner as lemma caching. The system (version semprop240202) is available on the following web page:

http://www.jessen.informatik.tu-muenchen.de/~letz/semprop/

9   Experimental Results

We have tested the current implementation both on randomly generated examples and on structured examples. As randomly generated examples we used the set 3QBF-5CNF of 1000 QBF formulas generated by F. Massacci (download, e.g., from http://frege.mrg.dist.unige.it/star/qube/). The only procedure which can compete with Semprop on these examples is the system QuBE [5]. For both QuBE and Semprop without caching, the median of the solution times per example is less than 100 milliseconds whereas for all other mentioned procedures it is $> 10^4$ seconds on contemporary hardware. So even without caching, Semprop is one of the most powerful QBF procedures around. It is interesting to note that from the mentioned QBF procedures only QuBE and Semprop use forms of dependency-directed backtracking.

Problem		lem	abs	both	Problem		lem	abs	both
adder-2-sat	0.06	0.05	0.01	0.01	lognbwlargea0	0.01	0.02	0.01	0.03
adder-2-uns.	1.86	1.10	1.86	1.18	lognbwlargea1	11.98	3.26	15.51	4.07
blocks3ii.4.3	9.87	4.33	10.15	4.37	lognbwlargeb0	0.02	0.02	0.03	0.03
blocks3ii.5.2	25.19	7.55	27.28	8.26	lognbwlargeb1	63.38	16.98	68.44	17.30
blocks3ii.5.3	> 200	34.88	> 200	37.17	r3*3_15_2.50_0	0.02	0.02	0.02	0.02
blocks3iii.4	50.44	51.22	54.73	55.20	r3*3_15_2.50_1	0.05	0.05	0.02	0.03
blocks3iii.5	2.23	1.78	2.55	1.95	r3*3_15_2.50_2	0.01	0.01	0.01	0.01
chain12v13	0.35	0.37	0.08	0.08	r3*3_15_2.50_3	0.01	0.03	0.02	0.02
chain13v14	0.71	0.75	0.09	0.09	r3*3_15_2.50_4	0.03	0.04	0.03	0.03
chain14v15	1.55	1.58	0.09	0.09	r3*3_15_2.50_5	0.01	0.01	0.01	0.01
chain15v16	3.18	3.27	0.10	0.10	r3*3_15_2.50_6	0.10	0.09	0.10	0.11
chain16v17	6.75	6.91	0.10	0.10	r3*3_15_2.50_7	0.11	0.12	0.10	0.11
chain17v18	14.35	14.58	0.11	0.11	r3*3_15_2.50_8	0.28	0.30	0.20	0.20
chain18v19	30.99	31.42	0.11	0.11	r3*3_15_2.50_9	0.01	0.02	0.02	0.01
chain19v20	65.75	66.63	0.12	0.12	r3*7_15_2.60_0	0.14	0.14	0.14	0.16
chain20v21	143.45	144.08	0.12	0.12	r3*7_15_2.60_1	0.02	0.01	0.02	0.01
chain21v22	> 200	> 200	0.13	0.13	r3*7_15_2.60_2	0.05	0.06	0.05	0.04
chain22v23	> 200	> 200	0.13	0.13	r3*7_15_2.60_3	0.12	0.14	0.13	0.14
chain23v24	> 200	> 200	0.14	0.14	r3*7_15_2.60_4	0.02	0.02	0.04	0.03
impl02	0.01	0.01	0.01	0.01	r3*7_15_2.60_5	0.21	0.22	0.12	0.12
impl04	0.01	0.01	0.01	0.01	r3*7_15_2.60_6	0.07	0.10	0.07	0.06
impl06	0.02	0.02	0.01	0.01	r3*7_15_2.60_7	0.01	0.20	0.14	0.16
impl08	0.05	0.03	0.01	0.01	r3*7_15_2.60_8	0.01	0.01	0.02	0.01
impl10	0.15	0.08	0.01	0.01	r3*7_15_2.60_9	0.01	0.01	0.01	0.01
impl12	0.95	0.43	0.02	0.01	toilet2.1.iv.3	0.01	0.01	0.01	0.01
impl14	5.19	2.16	0.03	0.01	toilet2.1.iv.4	0.01	0.01	0.01	0.01
impl16	19.05	12.43	0.03	0.01	toilet6.1.iv.11	12.24	13.88	13.96	14.86
impl18	163.14	69.68	0.03	0.01	toilet6.1.iv.12	2.23	2.51	2.46	2.62
impl20	> 200	> 200	0.05	0.01	toilet7.1.iv.14	29.45	23.12	32.66	15.06

As structured problems we took the 91 formulas which are also used by QuBE (see http://frege.mrg.dist.unige.it/star/qube/). We compared four variants of Semprop, all using dependency-directed backtracking. In the first column, the results for the system without lemmas and sign abstraction are shown, column 2 shows the results for lemmas without abstraction, column 3 contains results for abstraction without lemmas, and column 4 lemmas and abstraction. Times are given in seconds on a Sun running with about 800 MHz. Problems not listed could not be solved by any of the versions within 200 seconds.

The results clearly show that the full version of the system including lemma caching and sign abstraction is the most successful one, it can solve 58 problems, also the average runtime per problem is smaller. Interestingly, sometimes the different techniques seem to have their special domains where they work very well. For example, the chain class is solved linearly by all systems using sign abstraction, but only exponentially without this method. It is, however, too early to give an explanation of this phenomenon. As a further remark, the currently used standard paradigm for generating lemmas in certain cases produces only tautologies, for example, on the problem toilet6.1.iv.11. Consequently, it seems worthwhile to use a method of tautology avoidance, as mentioned above.

10   Conclusions

In this paper we have investigated the integration of a number of so-called learning techniques in semantic tree-based decision procedures for quantified Boolean formulas. We have considered both the caching of lemmas and models plus a certain abstraction technique based on models. The practical usefulness of these methods could be demonstrated with a significant gain in performance on a number of examples, even for an implementation which does not contain all of the presented methods and hence does not exploit the full power of caching. Consequently, for a full integration of caching, one may expect a further significant improvement in performance.

Acknowledgments. I would like to thank the referees for the instructive comments.

References

1. Bayardo Jr., R.J. and Schrag, R.C. Using CSP look-back techniques to solve real-world SAT instances. In Proceedings AAAI, pages 203-208, 1997.
2. Cadoli, M., Schaerf, M., Giovanardi, A. and Giovanardi, M. An Algorithm to Evaluate Quantified Boolean Formulae and its Evaluation. *Journal of Automated Reasoning* 28(2): 101-142, 2002.
3. Davis, M., Logemann, G. and Loveland, D.W. A Machine Program for Theorem Proving. *Communications of the ACM*, 5(7):394–397, 1962.
4. Feldmann, R., Monien, B. and Schamberger, S. A Distributed Algorithm to Evaluate Quantified Boolean Formulae. In Proceedings of AAAI, pages 285-290, 2000.
5. Giunchiglia, E., Narizzano, M. and Tacchella, A. Backjumping for quantified boolean logic satisfiability. In proceedings of IJCAI, pages 275–281, 2001.
6. Giunchiglia, E., Narizzano, M. and Tacchella, A. Learning for Quantified Boolean Logic Satisfiability In Proceedings AAAI, 2002.
7. Kleine-Büning, H., Karpinsky, M. and Flögel, A. Resolution for Quantified Boolean Formulas, *Information and computation*, 117(1):12-18, 1995.
8. Marques-Silva, J.P. and Sakallah, K.A. GRASP - A New Search Algorithm for Satisfiability. In Proceedings of IEEE/ACM International Conference on Computer-Aided Design, pages 220-227, 1996.
9. Rintanen, J.T. Improvements to the Evaluation of Quantified Boolean Formulae. In Proceedings of IJCAI, pages 1192-1197, 1999.

Integration of Equality Reasoning into the Disconnection Calculus

Reinhold Letz and Gernot Stenz

Institut für Informatik
Technische Universität München
D-80290 Munich, Germany
{letz,stenzg}@in.tum.de

Abstract. Equality handling has always been a traditional weakness of tableau calculi because the typical refinements of those calculi were not compatible with the most successful methods for equality handling. The disconnection tableau calculus represents a new confluent framework well suited for the integration of a large class of different methods for equality handling, as we demonstrate in this paper. We consider both saturation based and goal-oriented methods for equality handling. We also show how specialized equality handling can affect the properties of the calculus at the example of the well-known regularity condition. All the presented approaches of equality handling have been implemented in the theorem prover DCTP and we present the results of an experimental evaluation.

1 Introduction

In the past decade automated theorem proving using tableau style calculi was developed into a number of very successful systems. However, one of the great weaknesses of tableau style theorem proving is that few methods were found for enabling tableau provers to efficiently solve problems containing equality. Approaches like theory unification [Bec98] turned out to be unfeasible in practice; and they additionally presented new completeness and even undecidability problems. A number of variants of Brand's modification method [Bra75] were developed into usable systems [MIL+97] and must be considered as the most successful means of integrating equality reasoning into a tableau framework hitherto. Methods based on ordered equality handling are not compatible with the most successful refinements of tableaux like the connection conditions. In contrast to such refinements the disconnection calculus offers a more robust framework for the integration of various approaches of equality handling. We present some methods based on orderings and some unordered approaches. These approaches extend the calculus [LS01b] which is the basis for the DCTP prover described in [LS01a], where equality was handled in the generic axiomatic way only. In the following, we assume the reader to be familiar with the basic concepts of equational reasoning as summarized in [BG98]. This paper is organized as follows. In the following section, a short introduction to the disconnection calculus will be

U. Egly and C.G. Fermüller (Eds.): TABLEAUX 2002, LNAI 2381, pp. 176–190, 2002.

presented. After briefly reviewing the standard axiomatic approach we show, in Section 4, how the paramodulation rule can be adapted to the calculus. Then, we elucidate that the regularity condition, which is one of the most successful techniques for tableau search pruning, is not compatible with this adaptation. In Section 5 we consider a different, more goal-oriented approach to equality handling based on lazy paramodulation and disagreement sets. Section 6 contains some comments on the implementations of the introduced approaches and the results of the experimental comparisons.

2   The Disconnection Tableau Calculus

The disconnection tableau calculus was first developed in [Bil96]. Essentially, this proof system can be viewed as an integration of Plaisted's *clause linking* method [PL92] into a tableau control structure.

   The original clause linking method works by iteratively producing instances of the input clauses, which are occasionally tested for unsatisfiability by a separate propositional decision procedure. The use of a tableau as a control structure has two advantages. On the one hand, the tableau format restricts the number of clause linking steps that may be performed. On the other hand, the tableau method provides a propositional decision procedure for the produced clause instances, thus making a separate propositional decision procedure superfluous. For the description of the proof method, we use the standard terminology for clausal tableaux. The disconnection tableau calculus consists of a single complex inference rule, the so-called *linking rule*.

> **Linking rule.** Given a tableau branch B containing two literals K and L in tableau clauses c and d, respectively, if there exists a unifier σ for the complement of K and a variable-renamed variant of L, then successively expand the branch with renamings of the two clauses $c\sigma$ and $d\sigma$ as illustrated in Figure 1.

In other terms, we perform a clause linking step and attach the coupled instantiated clauses at the end of the current tableau branch. Afterwards, the respective connection cannot be used any more on the branches expanding B, which explains the naming "disconnection" tableau calculus for the proof method. Additionally, in order to be able to start the tableau construction, one must choose an arbitrary *initial active path* through all the input clauses, from which the initial connections can be selected. This initial active path has to be used as a common initial segment of all proper tableau branches considered later on.

   As branch closure condition we use the same notion as employed in the clause linking method. That is, a branch of a tableau is ∀-*closed* if it contains two literals K and L such that $K\sigma$ is the complement of $L\sigma$ where σ is a substitution mapping all variables in the tableau to a new constant.

   As usual in the development of theorem provers, implementing a simple calculus in its pure form will not result in a competitive system [LS01a]. In order to improve the performance of the system, we have integrated a number of

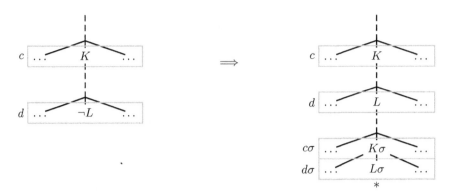

Fig. 1. Illustration of a linking step.

refinements, which preserve completeness and increase the performance of the disconnection tableau calculus tremendously. These refinements include different variations of subsumption, a strong unit theory element and several deletion strategies for redundancy elimination. In addition, we use full tableau pruning similar to the technique of [OS88].

3   Axiomatic Equality Handling

The most generic way of handling equality is by adding a set of axioms to each clause set to be proven that specify the properties of the equality predicate. These axioms contain the basic axioms defining equality as an equivalence relation:

$$x \approx x \quad \text{(Reflexivity)}$$
$$x \approx y \rightarrow y \approx x \quad \text{(Symmetry)}$$
$$x \approx y \wedge y \approx z \rightarrow x \approx z \quad \text{(Transitivity)}$$

In addition to these, a number of *substitution axioms* is required that depend on the signature of the clause set. That is, we require an axiom of the form

$$x \approx y \rightarrow f(\dots, x, \dots) \approx f(\dots, y, \dots)$$

for every argument position of every functor f and axioms of the form

$$x \approx y \wedge P(\dots, x, \dots) \rightarrow P(\dots, y, \dots)$$

for every argument position of every predicate P.

This form of equality handling has two advantages. First, it is easily implemented. That is, actually there is no implementation required on the prover side. There are no additional inference rules and no additional branch closure conditions. The required axiom set can by automatically generated by existing generic tools. The second advantage of axiomatic equality handling is the way that the substitution axioms disconnect the literals to be altered from their clauses.

Unfortunately, axiomatic equality handling also has two major disadvantages, which are the lack of guidance and the immense amount of redundancy introduced into the proof search. Both are caused by the fact that this form of equational reasoning does not exploit orderings and the limitation of any kind of equational inference to top level positions. Access to the inner parts of nested terms can be managed only by successively applying the substitution axioms to generate the altered terms from the inside out.

4   Paramodulation-Based Approaches

Apart from using the equality axioms added to the proof problem, paramodulation is perhaps the most traditional and conservative means of handling equality. It also is the basic inference rule underlying the successful superposition calculus [BG98]. We refer the reader to [Lov78,RW69] for a description of paramodulation in the resolution environment.

The simplest form of paramodulation is unordered paramodulation, where overlapping is allowed in an unrestricted manner with all sides of all equations into all terms. Adaptation of this inference rule to the disconnection calculus leads to the *eq-linking rule* as it was introduced in [Bil96].

> **Eq-linking rule.** Given a tableau branch B containing an equation $s \approx t$ and a literal L in tableau clauses c and d, respectively, if there exists a unifier σ for s and a subterm $L_{|p}$ at position p in L ($L_{|p} \notin VAR(L)$), then successively expand the branch with renamings of the two clauses $c\sigma$ and $d'\sigma$ where $d' = \{s \napprox t\} \cup \{L_{|p}[t]\} \cup (d \setminus \{L\})$, where $L_{|p}[t]$ describes literal L with subterm $L_{|p}$ replaced by t, as illustrated in Figure 2.

Unlike the paramodulation rule of the resolution calculus, eq-linking introduces two independent clauses, the instantiated overlapping equation and the overlapped clause. As these two clauses can be used independently of each other for further inference steps, the equality condition $s \approx t$ has to be added in negated form to the overlapped clause. This way the soundness of inferences involving the overlapped clause can be guaranteed[1], i.e. for every clause c in the tableau there is an input clause c' such that $E \cup c' \models c$, where E is the set of equality axioms for the input clauses. Therefore the soundness of the disconnection calculus with eq-linking as a whole is given. Of course, the eq-linking rule also implies that the length of the tableau clauses can increase. But in order to avoid this lengthening, another means of expressing the connectedness between the equation instance and the overlapped instance would be needed. Yet, there is no straightforward way to do this.

When using paramodulation with resolution calculi, an additional inference rule is required to handle inferences with the reflexivity axiom which is called *reflexivity resolution*. In the disconnection tableau calculus, if the reflexivity axiom is not added to the initial active path, a corresponding rule must be defined:

---

[1] This also guarantees the correctness of tableau pruning [LS01a] in the equality case.

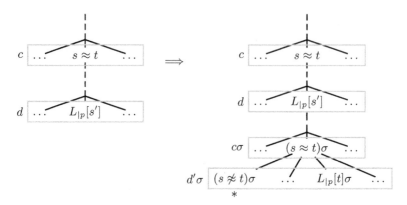

Fig. 2. Tableau paramodulation by the eq-linking rule.

Reflexivity linking. Given a tableau branch B containing an disequation $s \not\approx t$ in clause c, such that there is a most general unifier σ of s and t, then expand the branch with a renaming of $c\sigma$.

The reflexivity property of equality w.r.t. branch closure must be accounted for by either introducing a special closure rule for branches on which a disequation of the form $t \not\approx t$ is placed or by adding the axiom $x \approx x$ to the set of input clauses.

The symmetry property of equality as far as linking steps are concerned is taken care of by the eq-linking-rule. The $\forall$-closure of branches as well as all tests for subsumption and variant deletion must take the symmetry issue into account explicitly.

4.1 Ordered Eq-Linking

The unrestricted unordered form of eq-linking can lead to the generation of a multitude of redundant clauses. The introduction of a term ordering therefore is vital for the success of the method by controlling the symmetry property of equality. As usual, we do this by imposing a reduction ordering on the Herbrand universe of each problem. Overlapping is allowed with the maximal sides of equations only and, in case the overlapped literal is an equality literal, into maximal sides only.[2]

Example 1. Figure 3 depicts a disconnection proof using ordered eq-linking for the clause set marked as "Input clauses". The selected sides of the overlapping equations and the overlapped terms are underlined. In the term ordering of the example $f > g$. All redundant clauses and subgoals have been omitted for brevity. Only the links not involving unit clauses are indicated. When applying link ①, the altered literal $P(g(x))$ is valid only under the assumption $f(x) \approx g(x)$, which

---

[2] In case an equality literal cannot be ordered, both sides are considered maximal.

is expressed by the disequation $f(x) \not\approx g(x)$ added to tableau clause c'. When later c' is used for the ordinary linking step ②, a different equality condition is required in c'' by $f(b) \not\approx g(b)$. This condition is not implied by the path of c'' and therefore the condition has to be proven explicitly. This is done by applying the eq-linking step of link ③. The second clause resulting from that linking step, $\{f(b) \not\approx g(b), g(b) \not\approx g(b), P(g(b)), R(f(b))\}$, is variant-subsumed[3] by c'', but the open subgoal $f(b) \approx g(b)$ already is $\forall$-closed by its path. The remaining open subgoals $P(g(x))$ and $R(f(x))$ are eliminated by tableau pruning (their proofs are identical to the subproof below link application ② anyway).

Note that ordered eq-linking instantiates to unfailing completion with narrowing for unit clauses.

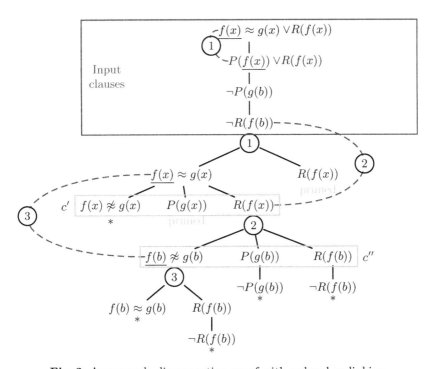

Fig. 3. An example disconnection proof with ordered eq-linking.

4.2 Eq-Linking and Regularity

To give an example for how the integration of a specialized equality handling with additional inference rules can substantially change the properties of a calculus

---

[3] Variant subsumption, as opposed to full clause subsumption, is compatible with the disconnection calculus.

we demonstrate the incompatibility of eq-linking with the *regularity restriction*. A tableau is said to be *regular* if no branch contains any literal more than once. Since in the disconnection tableau calculus all variables are renamed when new clause instances are placed on the tableau, this regularity condition can only be violated by ground literals, so we use the term *ground regularity*.

The introduction of eq-linking significantly alters the behaviour of the calculus. One important surprising consequence of these changes is that the disconnection calculus with eq-linking is incompatible with regularity, i.e. the calculus with said extensions loses its refutation completeness. We show this with the following example.

Let $S = \{\{\neg Q\}, \{Q, P(a), R\}, \{Q, P(a)\}, \{Q, \neg P(b), S\}, \{Q, \neg P(b)\}, \{a \approx b\}\}$. S is equationally unsatisfiable. The tableau in Figure 4 is an open saturated regular disconnection tableau with eq-linking for S which demonstrates the incompleteness.

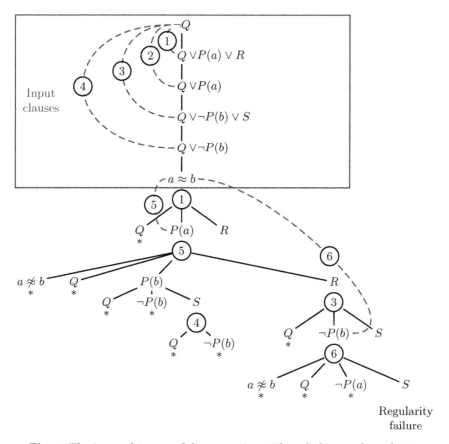

Fig. 4. The incompleteness of disconnection with eq-linking and regularity.

At the subgoal marked with "Regularity failure", links (1), (5), (3) and (6) have been used, leaving only links (2) and (4) available. But the use of either of these links would cause a regularity violation, the former due to the repeated creation of a subgoal $P(a)$, the latter due to $\neg P(b)$.

How does this incompleteness come to be? When showing that ground regularity preserves completeness in the non-equality case, use is made of the concept of variant freeness and of the fact that a ground literal cannot be instantiated any further, i.e. will remain unchanged by any action. Together this means that no instance of a clause containing a ground literal L would occur in a subproof of L. But with eq-linking, this is no longer the case. When solving a ground literal $P(a)$ in a clause C, it is well possible that we apply an equation $a \approx b$ to that literal and create a new eq-instance that is not a variant of C. In the course of creating such an eq-instance, all other literals of C are placed as open subgoals on the tableau once again. And when we take a closer look at the failed proof attempt in Figure 4, we see that the failure is caused by the repeated need to solve a pure subgoal. If in this example the (subsuming) variants without the pure literals had been used for the linkings, no dead-ends in the proof search would have occurred. But the way we selected the links we created redundant subgoals for whose solution the non-redundant clause-variants would have been required, and their use was prevented by the regularity restriction.

The example used to show the incompatibility of ground regularity and eq-linking may seem contrived. Yet, the described phenomenon has been observed in experiments, though the incompleteness was not quite as easily verified.

Nevertheless, it is interesting to observe that the ground regularity restriction is permissible when an axiomatic equality handling is used. So the incompleteness does not arise from the equational nature of a problem, but from the way eq-linking can alter ground literals. With axiomatic equality handling on the other hand, to obtain $P(b)$ with $P(a)$ in a clause C and $a \approx b$ given, an ordinary linking step involving a substitution axiom $\{\neg P(a), a \neq b, P(b)\}$ is performed that does not place potentially redundant literals from C on the tableau again. The use of the substitution axiom takes $P(a)$ out of its clause context and places it in an equational context instead. This particular feature in general can be seen as a disadvantage of axiomatic equational reasoning but, in the case of ground regularity, helps to preserve completeness.

4.3   Rewriting

The huge advances in automated equational reasoning are not due to the use of either paramodulation or orderings by themselves, the most powerful method is the destructive rewriting of terms [KB70,BDP89]. Rewriting can be used both for normalizing the input clause set before the actual proof is begun and as a special way of applying eq-linking, both resulting in a significant reduction of the search space.

However, the application of rewriting to clauses interconnected in a tableau control structure is not trivial. Of course, some rewriting of terms can be easily

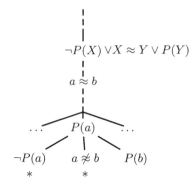

Fig. 5. Altering ground literals with the substitution axiom.

performed in a separate preprocessing phase, before the tableau construction is started.

The rewriting of tableau literals, however, poses problems in theory as well as in implementation. Currently, we use term rewriting in three different ways:

1. Rewriting of the input clauses as part of the formula preprocessing.
2. Normalization of new subgoals w.r.t the current unit equality theory of the problem.
3. Back rewriting of path subgoals with new unit equations.

The preprocessing variant of rewriting is not limited to use in conjunction with any kind of equality handling, however, rewriting proof subgoals is limited to ordered eq-linking. Currently we do not make use of *contextual* rewriting, i.e. the normalization of subgoals w.r.t the equational theory of the current active path.

5   A Variant of Lazy Paramodulation

As an alternative research direction, there have always been attempts to develop methods of equality handling which are compatible with *goal-orientedness*, but at the price of sacrificing compatibility with term orderings. The framework of *lazy paramodulation* developed in the context of E-unification in [GS89] is one particularly suited approach. In eq-linking, there are two different forms of indeterminism which blow up the search space, one is the number of equations that can be applied to a given term position, the other is the number of term positions which have to be considered. While the first form of indeterminism cannot be avoided, in lazy paramodulation, one may completely get rid of the second form of indeterminism by restricting equality inferences to root terms only, as has already been observed in [GS89]. This method of *lazy root paramodulation*, as one may term it, is closely related with Digricoli's RUE [DH86]. These ideas can be integrated into a tableau-based approach as follows. The method is centered around the concept of the disagreement set [4]. We only consider the pure equality case, i.e., where the equality sign is the only predicate symbol, since the extension to the general case is straightforward.

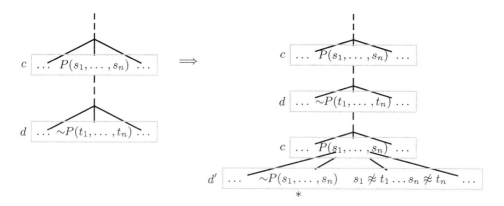

Fig. 6. The disagreement linking rule.

Definition 1 (Disagreement set, substitution). *Given two terms of the form $f(s_1, \ldots, s_n)$ and $f(t_1, \ldots, t_n)$ with identical top function symbol, their disagreement set is the clause $\{s_1 \not\approx t_1, \ldots, s_n \not\approx t_n\}$ and their disagreement substitution is the empty set. The disagreement set of two terms x and t where x is a variable which does not occur in t is the empty set, and their disagreement substitution is the substitution $\sigma = \{x/t\}$. Otherwise the disagreement set of two terms is not defined.*

Using the disagreement set concept, we have additional links between literals of complementary signs and identical predicate symbols, both with unifiable and non-unifiable terms. This leads us to the *disagreement linking rule*:

Definition 2 (Disagreement linking). *Given a tableau branch B containing a disequation K with top terms s and s' and an equation L with top terms t and t' in tableau clauses c and d, respectively, such that s and t have a disagreement set $\mathcal{D}$ and a disagreement substitution σ, then successively expand the branch with renamings of the two clauses $c\sigma$ and $d'\sigma$, where $d' = \mathcal{D} \cup (d \setminus \{L\}) \cup \{s' \not\approx t', s \approx s'\}$. The similar disagreement linking rule for non-equality predicates is illustrated in Figure 6 for an empty substitution σ and literals $P(s_1, \ldots, s_n)$ and $\sim P(t_1, \ldots, t_n)$ of identical predicate symbols but complementary signs.*

---

[4] Note that our use of this term differs from the one used in [DH86], since we uniquely associate exactly one disagreement set with each pair of terms or literals.

To account for the symmetry requirements, equations must be disagreement-linked in both directions and the same necessities apply for $\forall$-closure as for eq-linking. Also the reflexivity axiom $x \approx x$ must be added to the input formula.

Finally, in order to guarantee completeness, we need the following *decomposition rule*:

Definition 3 (Decomposition). *Given a tableau branch B containing a disequation L with top terms s and t in tableau clause d such that s and t have a disagreement set $\mathcal{D}$ and a disagreement substitution σ, then successively expand the branch with renamings of the clause $d'\sigma$, where $d' = \mathcal{D} \cup (d \setminus \{L\})$.*

Further refinements like the viability restriction [DH86] can be applied. Finally, one refinement possible is restricting disagreement linking between equality literals to an arbitrary but fixed (for each instance) side of the equation or disequation. This feature we call *side selection*. In contrast to eq-linking, the side selection restriction does not affect the completeness of disagreement linking and this refinement may lead to an exponential reduction of the search space w.r.t. the original RUE.

Example 2. Let $S = \{\{h(a) \not\approx c\}, \{h(e) \approx d\}, \{h(f) \approx h(b)\}, \{a \approx b\}, \{c \approx d\}, \{e \approx f\}\}$. S is equationally unsatisfiable. Figure 7 depicts a disconnection proof using disagreement linking with side selection for S. The selected sides of equations and disequations are underlined. All redundant clauses and subgoals have been omitted for brevity.

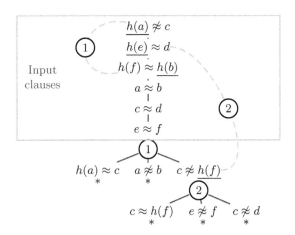

Fig. 7. Example for a disconnection proof with disagreement linking

A further refinement which turns out to be very effective in the context of lazy paramodulation is the so-called *eager variable elimination*.

Eager variable elimination. A clause of the form $x \not\approx t \vee R$, where x does not occur in t can be seen as $x \approx t \Rightarrow R$ and destructively rewritten to $R\{x/t\}$.

The eager variable elimination rule is a special case of reflexivity linking that allows a destructive transformation. It is an equivalence transformation w.r.t. the satisfiability of the clause set for congruent interpretations. Whether this rule preserves completeness, however, is an open problem that was first addressed in [GS89].

The one fundamental disadvantage of disagreement linking is its incompatibility with any sort of orderings. On the other hand it is very restrictive in applying equalities. For example, consider the following satisfiable clause set:

$$\{\{h(f(x)) \not\approx f(x)\}, \{f(x) \approx g(f(y))\}\}$$

The equation $f(x) \approx g(f(y))$ cannot be oriented and therefore will be applied in an entirely unrestricted way, functioning as a term explosion engine. Automatically detecting the satisfiability of this clause set is very difficult, the problem touches the issue of reachability of terms. That problem is undecidable in general and even sub-optimal solutions have a very high complexity [GT01]. Calculi based on superposition and paramodulation, which includes the disconnection tableau calculus with eq-linking do not terminate on this example. However, when using disagreement linking with side selection, there is no possible inference with the h-term and the procedure terminates immediately. This example also shows the way by which the restriction to root positions, which applies to disagreement linking, prunes the search space.

6   Implementation

In [LS01a] we presented the first implementation of the disconnection calculus in the theorem prover DCTP. The DCTP system also took part in the CASC-JC system competition at the IJCAR 2001 conference, however then using only axiomatic equality handling. In order to evaluate the effectiveness of the integrated methods of equality handling, all approaches described in the previous sections have been implemented as part of the prover.

As we explained above, the link concept is very important in the disconnection calculus. So both for eq-linking and disagreement linking we introduced new types of links to be stored separately from non-eq-links. The application of both equality and non-equality is guided by the same weight functions, but there is a fixed alternation scheme between equality and non-equality inferences based on the ratio of equality to non-equality literals in the input[5]. Also, within each category of links, there is a parameterized alternation between using the best links (according to the weight functions) and using the oldest links available.

Rewriting is implemented in three variations. The first is an integral part of the formula preprocessing, along with other techniques such as simplification or tautology elimination. Then, during the proof, open subgoals are normalized by rewriting before they are solved. Finally, eq-linking steps can be applied destructively (deleting the overlapped clause) if the rewrite conditions are fulfilled.

---

[5] More specifically, if ten percent of the input literals are equality literals, then ten percent of the inferences will be equality inferences.

This is currently the way that the rewriting of path literals is done. Currently no indexing techniques are used for rewriting and the only term ordering relation that is currently implemented is a Knuth-Bendix ordering.

It has turned out that ordered eq-linking is far more successful than both unordered eq-linking and disagreement linking. For this reason, most of the development work and experimentation went into ordered eq-linking and rewriting.

The implementation of integration of disagreement linking turned out to be far more complicated than expected. Also, it appears that disagreement linking requires proof search guidance different from that for eq-linking and probably also different search heuristics, which will be the subject of future research. Disagreement linking in the currently implemented form turned out to be least effective of all used approaches for equality handling, but this might to some extent be due to the aforementioned problems.

The following table presents the performance of the different methods for equality handling on the 2894 clause equality problems of the TPTP version 2.4.1.

TPTP	Ordered/Rewr.	Ordered	Unordered	Disagreement	Axiomatic
2894	1080	887	866	522	513

The results of the evaluation of ordered eq-linking clearly indicate the dramatic increase in performance of the prover system, both compared to the version of DCTP without special equality handling and to other state of the art systems. In the following tables, we will present the performance of DCTP with the different equality handling methods and selected other theorem provers for the problems of the CASC-JC system competition held in summer 2001. All computations have been done under the same conditions on the machines of the actual competition.

Prover	Rewrite	Unord.	Disagr.	Axiom.	E-SETHEO	Otter
Attempted	120	120	120	120	120	120
Solved	40	25	18	21	93	31

The above table shows the results for the MIX class of the competition, which was won by E-SETHEO and VampireJC. Allotted time for each problem was 300 seconds. While still being far behind the really successful systems in this category, DCTP with eq-linking performs far better than the competition version[6] and also better than some other well known systems. It also should be noted that DCTP was run on a single strategy only, as opposed to most other systems.

Prover	DCTP/Rewr.	DCTP/Axiom.	GandalfSat	SCOTT	MACE
Attempted	90	90	90	90	90
Solved	50	20	48	41	25

---

[6] The figures have been recomputed after the elimination of a performance-limiting bug.

This table gives the results for the problems of the SAT category (i.e. all problems of this class are satisfiable) of CASC-JC. Billon claimed in [Bil96] that the disconnection approach is particularly suitable for detecting satisfiability. But since most of the problems selected in the SAT class were equality problems, the competition version of DCTP without builtin equality handling had some problems. The new version of DCTP with ordered eq-linking and rewriting in its current state is so successful that it outperforms the competition winner of this class. More importantly, most of the other systems in the SAT class enumerate non-Herbrand models in some way. This is entirely different from what DCTP does and so DCTP can be considered to be complementary to the other methods used in this class and therefore useful as an additional strategy.

7   Conclusion

In this paper we have described different methods of integrating non-axiomatic equality handling into a tableau framework. The disconnection tableau calculus turned out to be well-suited to this task. This allowed for a successful implementation of integrated equality handling in the DCTP prover.

We conclude with a remark concerning the completeness of the presented methods, which were not directly addressed in this paper. The idea for a completeness proof is to extend the model generation arguments used in [LS01b], for example, in the spirit of [Gie02]. However, the concept of what constitutes a model and how such a model is represented significantly changes in the equality case and therefore detailed completeness proofs would be beyond the scope of this paper and will be presented in a future publication.

Acknowledgements. We would like to thank Peter Baumgartner for his unrelenting questions and some fruitful discussions which helped to eliminate a number of errors that could be found in earlier versions of this paper.

References

[BDP89]   L. Bachmair, N. Dershowitz, and D.A. Plaisted. Completion Without Failure. In H. Ait-Kaci and M. Nivat, editors, *Resolution of Equations in Algebraic Structures*, volume 2, pages 1–30. Academic Press, 1989.

[Bec98]   Bernhard Beckert. Rigid *E*-unification. In Wolfgang Bibel and Peter H. Schmitt, editors, *Automated Deduction — A Basis for Applications*, volume I: Foundations, pages 265–289. Kluwer, Dordrecht, 1998.

[BG98]   Leo Bachmair and Harald Ganzinger. Equational reasoning in saturation-based theorem proving. In Wolfgang Bibel and Peter H. Schmidt, editors, *Automated Deduction: A Basis for Applications. Volume I, Foundations: Calculi and Methods*, pages 353–398. Kluwer Academic Publishers, Dordrecht, 1998.

[Bil96]   Jean-Paul Billon.   The disconnection method: a confluent integration
             of unification in the analytic framework. In P. Migliolo, U. Moscato,
             D. Mundici, and M. Ornaghi, editors, *Proceedings of the 5th International
             Workshop on Theorem Proving with analytic Tableaux and Related Meth-
             ods (TABLEAUX)*, volume 1071 of *LNAI*, pages 110–126, Berlin, May15–
             17 1996. Springer.

[Bra75]   Daniel Brand. Proving theorems with the modification method. *SIAM
             Journal on Computing*, 4(4):412–430, 1975.

[DH86]   Vincent J. Digricoli and Malcolm C. Harrison. Equality-based binary res-
             olution. *Journal of the ACM*, 33(2):253–289, April 1986.

[Gie02]   Martin Giese. A model generation style completeness proof for constraint
             tableaux with superposition. In *Proc. International Conference on Auto-
             mated Reasoning with Analytic Tableaux and Related Methods, Copenhagen,
             Denmark*, LNCS. Springer-Verlag, 2002. To appear.

[GS89]   Jean H. Gallier and Wayne Snyder. Complete sets of transformations for
             general *E*-unification. *Theoretical Computer Science*, 67:203–260, 1989.

[GT01]   Thomas Genet and Valérie Viet Tirem Tong. Reachability Analysis of Term
             Rewriting Systems with timbuk. In Andrei Voronkov, editor, *Proceedings of
             the 8th International Conference on Logic for Programming and Automated
             Reasoning (LPAR 2001), Havanna, Cuba*, pages 695–706. Springer, Berlin,
             December 2001.

[KB70]   D.E. Knuth and P.B. Bendix. Simple Word Problems in Universal Algebras.
             In J. Leech, editor, *Computational Algebra*, pages 263–297. Pergamon Press,
             1970.

[Lov78]   Don W. Loveland. *Automated theorem proving: A logical basis*. North
             Holland, New York, 1978.

[LS01a]   Reinhold Letz and Gernot Stenz. DCTP: A Disconnection Calculus Theo-
             rem Prover. In Rajeev Goré, Alexander Leitsch, and Tobias Nipkow, editors,
             *Proceedings of the International Joint Conference on Automated Reasoning
             (IJCAR-2001), Siena, Italy*, volume 2083 of *LNAI*, pages 381–385. Springer,
             Berlin, June 2001.

[LS01b]   Reinhold Letz and Gernot Stenz. Proof and Model Generation with Discon-
             nection Tableaux. In Andrei Voronkov, editor, *Proceedings of the 8th Inter-
             national Conference on Logic for Programming and Automated Reasoning
             (LPAR 2001), Havanna, Cuba*, pages 142–156. Springer, Berlin, December
             2001.

[MIL+97]   Max Moser, Ortrun Ibens, Reinhold Letz, Joachim Steinbach, Christoph
             Goller, Johann Schumann, and Klaus Mayr. SETHEO and E-SETHEO—
             The CADE-13 Systems. *Journal of Automated Reasoning*, 18(2):237–246,
             April 1997.

[OS88]   F. Oppacher and E. Suen. HARP: A tableau-based theorem prover. *Journal
             of Automated Reasoning*, 4:69–100, 1988.

[PL92]   David A. Plaisted and Shie-Jue Lee. Eliminating duplication with the
             hyper-linking strategy. *Journal of Automated Reasoning*, 9(1):25–42, 1992.

[RW69]   G. A. Robinson and L. Wos. Paramodulation and theorem proving in first-
             order theories with equality. *Machine Intelligence*, 4:135–150, 1969.

Analytic Sequent Calculi for Abelian and Łukasiewicz Logics

George Metcalfe[1], Nicola Olivetti[2], and Dov Gabbay[1]

[1] Department of Computer Science, King's College London, Strand, London WC2R
2LS, UK {metcalfe,dg}@dcs.kcl.ac.uk
[2] Department of Computer Science, University of Turin, Corso Svizzera 185, 10149
Turin, Italy olivetti@di.unito.it

Abstract. In this paper we present the first labelled and unlabelled
analytic sequent calculi for abelian logic **A**, the logic of lattice-ordered
abelian groups with characteristic model $\mathbb{Z}$, motivated in [10] as a logic
of *relevance* and in [3] as a logic of *comparison*. We also show that the
so-called *material fragment* of **A** coincides with Łukasiewicz's infinite-
valued logic **Ł**, hence giving us as a significant by-product, labelled and
unlabelled analytic sequent calculi for **Ł**.

1 Introduction

In this paper, we got to $\mathbf{Ł}^+$ without thinking about truth values at all.
Indeed, we had no intention or desire to get to $\mathbf{Ł}^+$; it just happened.
And the usual Łukasiewiczian problems are with us. Mathematically it
is clear - almost *too* clear, one would like to say - but the philosophical
interpretation is not so clear. Accordingly, we should like to try on for size
the idea that $\mathbf{Ł}^+$ is interesting *because* it is a fragment of **A**. Specifically,
it is that fragment of **A** on which one would most naturally hit if guided
by the most familiar accounts of deductive methodology.

Abelian Logic (from A to Z), R. K. Meyer and J. K. Slaney.

Although the infinite-valued Łukasiewicz propositional logic **Ł** possesses a well
developed model theory as the calculus of MV-algebras (see [5] for details), it has
yet to be given a fully satisfying proof theory. Theorem proving approaches in the
literature either fail to be analytic [4,14] or require external calculations such as
solving mixed integer programming problems [7] or determinining Θ-supports of
formulae [12]. A notable exception is the recent work of Aguzzoli and Ciabattoni
[1] where an analytic sequent calculus is provided based on the observation that
a formula valid in **Ł** is also valid in the *finite* Łukasiewicz logic $\mathbf{Ł_n}$ where n is
a function of the number of occurrences of variables in the formula. We take
the view, however, that infinite-valued Łukasiewicz logic both can and should be
viewed as *independent* of the finite-valued logics. Standard presentations of **Ł**,
such as Hilbert-style axiomatisations, Kripke semantics and algebraic semantics,
are generally much simpler than those given for the finite-valued logics and

U. Egly and C.G. Fermüller (Eds.): TABLEAUX 2002, LNAI 2381, pp. 191–205, 2002.

indeed often these logics can be obtained by refining the appropriate system for **Ł**. Moreover **Ł** can be motivated independently as one of the fundamental examples of truth-functional fuzzy logics [8] and also as a theory of subjective probabilities [6] or of Ulam games of twenty questions with lies/errors [5]. Finally, and most relevantly of all to the current endeavour **Ł** can be viewed as a natural fragment of *abelian logic*, the logic of lattice-ordered abelian groups.

Abelian logic, **A**, is motivated by Meyer and Slaney in [10] as a logic of *relevance* and by Casari in [3] as a logic of *comparison*. Many interesting results for abelian logic are presented in these papers, including soundness and completeness theorems for particular Hilbert-style axiomatisations, a proof that the integer group $\mathbb{Z}$ is a characteristic model for **A** (ie ϕ is valid in all lattice-ordered abelian groups iff ϕ is true in $\mathbb{Z}$), and a proof of decidability. Also studied in [10] are *fragments* of **A**, one of which, the *enthymematic* fragment, $\mathbf{A_E}$, turns out to be $\mathbf{Ł^+}$, the positive part of **Ł**. Moreover, as we show here, by taking the *material* fragment, $\mathbf{A_M}$, we obtain **Ł** in full.

Our intention in this paper is to provide cut-free Gentzen-style sequent calculi for abelian logic and hence also for Łukasiewicz logic. We begin with a summary of the literature on abelian logic. Then as a simple first step we give an unlabelled sequent calculus for the *intensional* fragment $\mathbf{A_I}$ (the logic of abelian groups) before moving on to give both labelled and unlabelled calculi for the whole of **A**. We then consider the enthymematic and material fragments, $\mathbf{A_E}$ and $\mathbf{A_M}$ respectively, and show that $\mathbf{A_M} = \mathbf{Ł}$.

2   Abelian Logic

A Hilbert-style axiomatisation of abelian logic is obtained from the positive part of the relevance logic **R** (see [2] for details) by dropping the contraction axiom $(A \to (A \to B)) \to (A \to B)$ and generalising the negation axiom $((A \to f) \to f) \to A$ to $((A \to B) \to B) \to A$, Meyer and Slaney's *axiom of relativity*:

Definition 1 (Abelian Logic, A). $\to, +, \wedge, \vee$ *and* t *are primitive.* **A** *has the following definitions, axioms and rules:*

$D \leftrightarrow \quad A \leftrightarrow B = (A \to B) \wedge (B \to A)$ $\qquad D\neg \quad \neg A = A \to t$

A1 $\quad ((A \vee B) \to C) \leftrightarrow ((A \to C) \wedge (B \to C))$ $\quad$ A6 $\quad A \leftrightarrow (t \to A)$

A2 $\quad ((A + B) \to C) \leftrightarrow (A \to (B \to C))$ $\qquad$ A7 $\quad (A \wedge B) \to A$

A3 $\quad (A \to B) \to ((B \to C) \to (A \to C))$ $\qquad$ A8 $\quad (A \wedge B) \to B$

A4 $\quad ((A \to B) \wedge (A \to C)) \to (A \to (B \wedge C))$ $\quad$ A9 $\quad A \to ((A \to B) \to B)$

A5 $\quad (A \wedge (B \vee C)) \to ((A \wedge B) \vee (A \wedge C))$ $\qquad$ A10 $((A \to B) \to B) \to A$

$$(mp) \ \frac{A \to B, A}{B} \qquad (\wedge I) \ \frac{A, B}{A \wedge B}$$

It turns out (as intended!) that the appropriate models for **A** are lattice-ordered abelian groups:

Definition 2 (Lattice-Ordered Abelian Group (Abelian l-Group)). *An abelian l-group is an algebra $\langle G, +, \vee, \neg, t \rangle$ with binary operations $+$ and $\vee$, a unary operation $\neg$ and a constant t, satisfying the following equations:*

$a1\ t + a = a$	$a5\ a \vee b = b \vee a$
$a2\ a + b = b + a$	$a6\ (a \vee b) \vee c = a \vee (b \vee c)$
$a3\ (a + b) + c = a + (b + c)$	$a7\ a = a \vee a$
$a4\ a + \neg a = t$	$a8\ a + (b \vee c) = (a + b) \vee (a + c)$

In addition, we define: $a \wedge b = \neg(\neg a \vee \neg b)$, $a \rightarrow b = \neg(a + \neg b)$, $a \leftrightarrow b = (a \rightarrow b) \wedge (b \rightarrow a)$ *and* $a \leq b$ *iff* $a \vee b = a$.

Note that $\vee$ and $\wedge$ represent the inf and sup operations respectively. Well known examples of abelian l-groups include the integers $\mathbb{Z} = \langle \mathbb{Z}, +, \vee, -, 0 \rangle$ and the rationals $\mathbb{Q} = \langle \mathbb{Q}, +, \vee, -, 0 \rangle$. Although perfectly respectable *algebraically*, from a *logical* point of view abelian l-groups may seem a little odd. Consider the dual of $+$ for example:

$$\neg a \rightarrow b = \neg(\neg a + \neg b) = (a + \neg a) + (b + \neg b) + \neg(\neg a + \neg b) = (a + b) + (\neg a + \neg b) + \neg(\neg a + \neg b) = a + b$$

That is, fission, intensional *disjunction*, and fusion, intensional *conjunction*, are *exactly the same thing*. In a similar vein we discover that $\neg t = t$, so truth and "canonical" falsity are identified in **A**. Note however that if we take f as a constant with no characteristic axioms or rules whatsoever then we have a falsity that can take *any* value; this will prove useful later on when we look at embedding Łukasiewicz logic in **A**.

   We now develop the formal machinery required to talk about abelian logic.

Definition 3 (Form). *The set of formulae Form is built inductively from the vocabulary* $\{t, +, \vee, \neg, x_1, \ldots, x_n, \ldots\}$ *ie (1) $t \in$ Form, (2) $x_i \in$ Form for all $i \in \mathbb{N}$, (3) if $\phi_1, \phi_2 \in$ Form then $\phi_1 + \phi_2$, $\phi \vee \phi_2$, $\neg\phi_1 \in$ Form.*

Definition 4 (G-valuation). *Given an abelian l-group G a G-valuation is a function $v :$ Form $\rightarrow G$ such that $v(t) = t$, $v(\phi_1 + \phi_2) = v(\phi_1) + v(\phi_2)$, $v(\phi_1 \vee \phi_2) = v(\phi_1) \vee v(\phi_2)$ and $v(\neg\phi_1) = \neg v(\phi_1)$ for all $\phi_1, \phi_2 \in$ Form.*

Definition 5 (Validity). *$\phi \in$ Form is valid in an abelian l-group G iff $v(\phi) \leq t$ for all G-valuations v. ϕ is valid (written $\models \phi$) iff ϕ is valid in all abelian l-groups. A sequent $\phi_1, \ldots, \phi_n \vdash \psi_1, \ldots, \psi_m$ is valid (written $\models \phi_1, \ldots, \phi_n \vdash \psi_1, \ldots, \psi_m$) iff $(\phi_1 + \ldots + \phi_n) \rightarrow (\psi_1 + \ldots + \psi_m)$ is valid where $\varphi_1 + \ldots + \varphi_u = t$ if $u = 0$.*

The nature of validity in **A** is summed up nicely by the following characterisation theorem:

Theorem 1 (Characterisation Theorem for A). *The following are equivalent: (1) ϕ is a theorem of **A**. (2) ϕ is valid in all abelian l-groups. (3) ϕ is valid in $\mathbb{Z}$.*

Proof. See [10]. $\square$

The next proposition shows that we can equally well take our characteristic model to be the rationals.

Proposition 1. $\mathbb{Z} \models \phi$ *iff* $\mathbb{Q} \models \phi$.

Proof. The only-if direction is trivial. For the other direction, suppose we have a valuation v for $\mathbb{Q}$ such that $v(\phi) > 0$. Let $c = gcm\{b : v(p) = a/b, p$ an atomic subformula of $\phi\}$. We take $v'(p) = c.v(p) \in \mathbb{Z}$ for all propositional variables; an easy inductive proof shows that $v'(\psi) = c.v(\psi)$ for all formulae ψ and we are done. $\square$

Using these results we may henceforth identify validity in abelian l-groups with validity in $\mathbb{Z}$ or $\mathbb{Q}$. Consequently we have:

$$\models \phi_1, \ldots, \phi_n \vdash \psi_1, \ldots \psi_m \text{ iff } \phi_1 + \ldots + \phi_n \geq \psi_1 + \ldots + \psi_m \text{ in } \mathbb{Z} \text{ or } \mathbb{Q}$$

3   Proof Theory for A

Thanks to Meyer and Slaney we have for **A** both a *philosophically* motivated Hilbert system presentation and also an elegant *mathematically* motivated semantics. What we seek now is a *proof theory* (ie a Gentzen-style sequent calculus) for **A** that will illuminate connections with other logics, facilitate theorem proving, further philosophical understanding and so on. Also, to look ahead a little, a calculus for **A** will turn out to give us a calculus for Łukasiewicz infinite-valued logic, **L**.

3.1   An Unlabelled Calculus for A

An analytic unlabelled calculus is relatively easy to find for $\mathbf{A_I}$, the *intensional* fragment of abelian logic, that is, the fragment built up from propositional variables $p_1, p_2, \ldots$ and the connectives $+$ and $\rightarrow$, with defined connectives $t = q \rightarrow q$ (for any propositional variable q) and $\neg A = A \rightarrow t$ (note: this is the logic of *abelian groups*). We simply take the procedure used to determine whether or not a linear equation holds in $\mathbb{Z}$; ie for each propositional variable p check that there is the same number of ps on each side of the sequent.

Note 1. In the following $\Gamma, \Delta, \Sigma, \Pi$ etc. are multisets (hence permutation rules are implicit); A, B, C etc. are formulae; Γ, Δ and Γ, A are to be interpreted as $\Gamma \cup \Delta$ and $\Delta \cup \{A\}$ respectively where $\cup$ is multiset union.

Note 2. We say a sequent $Q = \Gamma \vdash \Delta$ succeeds in a sequent calculus SEQ iff a tree can be constructed using the rules of SEQ with Q at its root where every leaf is a rule with no premises (ie an axiom).

Definition 6 (A Sequent Calculus for A_I, AB_i). AB_i *has the following rules:*

$$(id) \qquad A \vdash A \qquad (mingle) \; \frac{\Gamma_1 \vdash \Delta_1 \quad \Gamma_2 \vdash \Delta_2}{\Gamma_1, \Gamma_2 \vdash \Delta_1, \Delta_2}$$

$$(+, l) \; \frac{\Gamma, A, B \vdash \Delta}{\Gamma, A + B \vdash \Delta} \qquad (+, r) \qquad \frac{\Gamma \vdash \Delta, A, B}{\Gamma \vdash \Delta, A + B}$$

$$(\to, l) \; \frac{\Gamma, B \vdash \Delta, A}{\Gamma, A \to B \vdash \Delta} \qquad (\to, r) \qquad \frac{\Gamma, A \vdash \Delta, B}{\Gamma \vdash \Delta, A \to B}$$

Example 1. A proof of $((A \to B) \to B) \to A$ in AB_i:

$$\frac{\dfrac{\dfrac{\dfrac{A \vdash A \quad B \vdash B}{A, B \vdash A, B}}{B \vdash A, A \to B}}{(A \to B) \to B \vdash A}}{\vdash ((A \to B) \to B) \to A}$$

Theorem 2 (Soundness of AB_i). *If $\Gamma \vdash \Delta$ succeeds in AB_i then $\models \Gamma \vdash \Delta$.*

Proof. By induction on the length of a proof in AB_i. We just have to check for each rule that soundness is preserved. For example, for $(\to, r)$ if $\models \Gamma, A \vdash \Delta, B$ then we have $\Sigma_{C \in \Gamma} C + A \geq \Sigma_{D \in \Delta} D + B$ in $\mathbb{Z}$. So $\Sigma_{C \in \Gamma} C \geq \Sigma_{D \in \Delta} D + B - A$ in $\mathbb{Z}$ whence $\models \Gamma \vdash \Delta, A \to B$. Other cases are very similar. □

Proposition 2. *Given multisets of atoms Γ and Δ, if $\models \Gamma \vdash \Delta$ then $\Gamma = \Delta$.*

Proof. Suppose $\models \Gamma \vdash \Delta$ and for some atom q, there are more qs in Δ than in Γ; by taking a suitably large valuation for q in $\mathbb{Z}$ we obtain a contradiction. Similarly if there are more qs in Γ than in Δ we take a suitably large negative valuation for q in $\mathbb{Z}$. □

Proposition 3. *For the rules $(+, l)$, $(+, r)$, $(\to, l)$ and $(\to, r)$, if the conclusion is valid then the premises are valid.*

Proof. For example, for $(\to, l)$ if $\models \Gamma, A \to B \vdash \Delta$ then $\Sigma_{C \in \Gamma} C + B - A \geq \Sigma_{D \in \Delta} D$ in $\mathbb{Z}$. So $\Sigma_{C \in \Gamma} C + B \geq \Sigma_{D \in \Delta} D + A$ in $\mathbb{Z}$ hence $\models \Gamma, B \vdash \Delta, A$. Other cases are very similar. □

Theorem 3 (Completeness of AB_i). *If $\models \Gamma \vdash \Delta$ then $\Gamma \vdash \Delta$ succeeds in AB_i.*

Proof. Given $\models \Gamma \vdash \Delta$ we show that $\Gamma \vdash \Delta$ succeeds in AB_i. Since the rules for $+$ and $\to$ both decrease multiset complexity and by Proposition 3 pass validity from conclusion to premises, they can be applied until we have $\Gamma' \vdash \Delta'$ where Γ' and Δ' are both multisets of atoms and $\models \Gamma' \vdash \Delta'$. But then by Proposition 2 $\Gamma' = \Delta'$ whence $(mingle)$ and (id) can be applied repeatedly to complete the proof. □

We now move on to consider $\mathbf{A}$ in full, built from $\mathbf{A_I}$ with the added connective $\Rightarrow$:

Definition 7 (Positive Implication, $\Rightarrow$). $a \Rightarrow b = t \wedge (a \rightarrow b)$

Proposition 4. *(i)* $a \wedge b = a + (a \Rightarrow b)$ *(ii)* $a \vee b = (b \Rightarrow a) \rightarrow a$

Proof. (i) $a + (a \Rightarrow b) = a + (t \wedge (a \rightarrow b)) = (a + t) \wedge (a + (a \rightarrow b)) = a \wedge b$
(ii) $(b \Rightarrow a) \rightarrow a = \neg((t \wedge (b \rightarrow a)) + \neg a) = \neg((t + \neg a) \wedge ((b \rightarrow a) + \neg a)) = \neg(\neg a \wedge (\neg(b + \neg a) + \neg a)) = \neg(\neg a \wedge (\neg b + (a + \neg a))) = \neg(\neg a \wedge \neg b) = a \vee b$. $\square$

Definition 8 (A Sequent Calculus for Abelian Logic, AB). AB *has the same rules as* AB_i *plus the following:*

$$(emp) \qquad \vdash \qquad\qquad (wk) \quad \frac{\Gamma \vdash \Delta}{\Gamma, A \Rightarrow B \vdash \Delta}$$

$$(\Rightarrow, l) \ \frac{\Gamma, B, B \Rightarrow A \vdash \Delta, A}{\Gamma, A \Rightarrow B \vdash \Delta} \quad (\Rightarrow, r) \ \frac{\Gamma \vdash \Delta \quad \Gamma, A \vdash \Delta, B}{\Gamma \vdash \Delta, A \Rightarrow B}$$

$$(con) \ \frac{\overbrace{\Gamma, \ldots, \Gamma}^{n} \vdash \overbrace{\Delta, \ldots, \Delta}^{n}}{\Gamma \vdash \Delta} \ n > 0$$

Note 3. The following are derived rules of AB:

$$(\wedge, l) \ \frac{\Gamma, A, A \Rightarrow B \vdash \Delta}{\Gamma, A \wedge B \vdash \Delta} \quad (\wedge, r) \ \frac{\Gamma \vdash \Delta, A \quad \Gamma \vdash \Delta, B}{\Gamma \vdash \Delta, A \wedge B}$$

$$(\vee, l) \ \frac{\Gamma, A \vdash \Delta \quad \Gamma, B \vdash \Delta}{\Gamma, A \vee B \vdash \Delta} \quad (\vee, r) \ \frac{\Gamma, B \Rightarrow A \vdash \Delta, A}{\Gamma \vdash \Delta, A \vee B}$$

Our choice of $\Rightarrow$ as a primitive connective is supported here by the observation that although we do not have the subformula property for this calculus, we *almost* do; for the $(\Rightarrow, l)$ rule we have $A \Rightarrow B$ in the conclusion and $B \Rightarrow A$ in the premise. Note however that unlike the rules for the intensional connectives, the left and right rules for $\Rightarrow$, $\vee$ and $\wedge$ are not *symmetrical*.

Example 2. A proof of $(A + (A \Rightarrow B)) \rightarrow B$ in AB:

$$\frac{\dfrac{\dfrac{A \vdash A \quad B \vdash B}{A, B \vdash B, A}}{\dfrac{A, B \Rightarrow A, B \vdash B, A}{\dfrac{A, A \Rightarrow B \vdash B}{\dfrac{A + (A \Rightarrow B) \vdash B}{\vdash (A + (A \Rightarrow B)) \rightarrow B}}}}{}$$

We extend the soundness proof for AB_i to deal with the new rules:

Theorem 4 (Soundness of AB). *If* $\Gamma \vdash \Delta$ *succeeds in* AB *then* $\models \Gamma \vdash \Delta$.

Proof. By induction on the length of a proof in AB. Reasoning in the characteristic model $\mathbb{Z}$, we show that all the new rules preserve soundness.

- $\vdash$ succeeds by (emp). Clearly $\models \vdash$.
- $\Gamma, A \Rightarrow B \vdash \Delta$ follows by (wk) from $\Gamma \vdash \Delta$. If $\models \Gamma \vdash \Delta$, then $\models \Gamma, A \Rightarrow B \vdash \Delta$ since $A \Rightarrow B \geq 0$ in $\mathbb{Z}$.
- $\Gamma \vdash \Delta$ follows by (con) from $\underbrace{\Gamma, \dots, \Gamma}_{n} \vdash \underbrace{\Delta, \dots, \Delta}_{n}$. If $\models \underbrace{\Gamma, \dots, \Gamma}_{n} \vdash \underbrace{\Delta, \dots, \Delta}_{n}$, then dividing by n in $\mathbb{Z}$, $\models \Gamma \vdash \Delta$.
- $\Gamma \vdash \Delta, A \Rightarrow B$ follows by $(\Rightarrow, r)$ from $\Gamma \vdash \Delta$ and $\Gamma, A \vdash \Delta, B$. If $\models \Gamma \vdash \Delta$ and $\models \Gamma, A \vdash \Delta, B$ then given a valuation v, if $v(A) \leq v(B)$ then $v(A \Rightarrow B) = v(B) - v(A)$ and $v(\Gamma) \geq v(\Delta) + v(B) - v(A)$, if $v(A) \geq v(B)$ then $v(A \Rightarrow B) = 0$ and $v(\Gamma) \geq v(\Delta)$. Hence $\models \Gamma \vdash \Delta, A \Rightarrow B$.
- $\Gamma, A \Rightarrow B \vdash \Delta$ follows by $(\Rightarrow, l)$ from $\Gamma, B, B \Rightarrow A \vdash \Delta, A$. If $\models \Gamma, B, B \Rightarrow A \vdash \Delta, A$ then since $v(A \Rightarrow B) = v(B \Rightarrow A) + v(B) - v(A)$ for all valuations v, $\models \Gamma, A \Rightarrow B \vdash \Delta$. $\square$

Our strategy for proving the completeness of AB involves two stages. First we define and prove completeness for a new *labelled* calculus; then we prove the equivalence of the two calculi.

3.2 A Labelled Calculus for A

We introduce labels as a means of representing several unlabelled sequents in one labelled sequent. Unlabelled sequents are obtained from labelled sequents via labelling functions that map each label into the set $\{0, 1\}$, removing *formulae* labelled with a 0 from the sequent and leaving the rest. For example, the sequent $x : p, 1 : q \vdash 1 : p, x : q$ is mapped by a labelling function f to $q \vdash p$ if $f(x) = 0$ and to $p, q \vdash p, q$ if $f(x) = 1$.

Definition 9 (Labels, Labelled Formulae). *A set of labels Lab is generated as follows: (1) $1 \in Lab$, (2) $x_i \in Lab$ for all $i \in \mathbb{N}$, (3) if $x \in Lab$ and $y \in Lab$ then $xy \in Lab$. A labelled formula is of the form $x : A$ where $x \in Lab$ and A is a formula.*

Definition 10 (Labelling Function). *$f : Lab \to \{0, 1\}$ is a labelling function iff: (1) $f(1) = 1$ (2) $f(x_i) \in \{0, 1\}$ for all $i \in \mathbb{N}$ (3) $f(xy) = f(x).f(y)$. f is extended to multisets of formulae by the condition: (4) $f(\Gamma) = \{A \mid x : A \in \Gamma$ and $f(x) = 1\}$.*

Definition 11 (Γ^l, Γ^{ul}). *Given a multiset of unlabelled formulae Γ, $\Gamma^l = \{1 : A \mid A \in \Gamma\}$. Given a multiset of labelled formulae Γ, $\Gamma^{ul} = \{A \mid x : A \in \Gamma\}$.*

Definition 12 (A Labelled Calculus for A). AB_l *has the following rules:*

$(+,l)$ $\qquad \dfrac{\Gamma, x : A, x : B \vdash \Delta}{\Gamma, x : A + B \vdash \Delta}$ $\qquad (+,r)$ $\qquad \dfrac{\Gamma \vdash \Delta, x : A, x : B}{\Gamma \vdash \Delta, x : A + B}$

$(\to,l)$ $\qquad \dfrac{\Gamma, x : B \vdash \Delta, x : A}{\Gamma, x : A \to B \vdash \Delta}$ $\qquad (\to,r)$ $\qquad \dfrac{\Gamma, x : A \vdash \Delta, x : B}{\Gamma \vdash \Delta, x : A \to B}$

$(\Rightarrow,l)$ $\qquad \dfrac{\Gamma, xy : B \vdash \Delta, xy : A}{\Gamma, x : A \Rightarrow B \vdash \Delta}$ $\qquad (\Rightarrow,r)$ $\dfrac{\Gamma, x : A \vdash \Delta, x : B \quad \Gamma \vdash \Delta}{\Gamma \vdash \Delta, x : A \Rightarrow B}$
$\qquad\qquad\qquad y$ a new label

$(succ)$ $\qquad\qquad\qquad \dfrac{\Gamma \vdash \Delta}{\quad}$
$\qquad\qquad$ where Γ and Δ are atomic
$\qquad\qquad$ and there exist labelling
$\qquad\qquad$ functions $f_1, \ldots f_n$ such that
$\qquad\qquad \cup_{i=1}^{n} f_i(\Gamma) = \cup_{i=1}^{n} f_i(\Delta)$

Note 4. The (id), $(mingle)$, (con), (wk) and (emp) rules from the unlabelled calculus are all replaced here by the $(succ)$ rule. Notice in particular that a labelled formula $x : A \Rightarrow B$ can be removed from the left hand side of a sequent by applying $(\Rightarrow, l)$ and setting the new label to 0.

Note 5. A set of linear inequations $S = \{A_1 < B_1, \ldots, A_n < B_n\}$ is inconsistent over $\mathbb{Q}$ iff there exist $\lambda_1, \ldots, \lambda_n \in \mathbb{N}$ with some $\lambda_u > 0$ $(1 \le u \le n)$ such that $\sum_{i=1}^{n} \lambda_i . A_i = \sum_{j=1}^{n} \lambda_j . B_j$. So in particular checking the $(succ)$ rule is equivalent to solving a linear programming problem.

The following example shows that *more than one* labelling function may be required to apply $(succ)$:

Example 3. A proof of $(p \Rightarrow (p \Rightarrow r)) \Rightarrow ((q \Rightarrow (q \Rightarrow r)) \Rightarrow (p \Rightarrow (q \Rightarrow r)))$ in AB_l (note that for convenience we write x instead of $x1$):

$f_1(x) = f_1(y) = 1,\ f_1(z) = f_1(w) = 0,\ f_2(x) = f_2(y) = 0,\ f_2(z) = f_2(w) = 1$
$\cup_{i=1}^{2} f_i(\{xy : r, zw : r, 1 : p, 1 : q\}) = \cup_{j=1}^{2} f_j(1 : r, x : p, xy : p, z : q, zw : q) = \{r, r, p, p, q, q\}$

$$
\cfrac{
\cfrac{
\cfrac{
\cfrac{
\cfrac{xy : r, zw : r, 1 : p, 1 : q \vdash 1 : r, x : p, xy : p, z : q, zw : q}
{xy : r, z : q \Rightarrow r, 1 : p, 1 : q \vdash 1 : r, x : p, xy : p, z : q}}
{xy : r, 1 : q \Rightarrow (q \Rightarrow r), 1 : p, 1 : q \vdash 1 : r, x : p, xy : p}}
{x : p \Rightarrow r, 1 : q \Rightarrow (q \Rightarrow r), 1 : p, 1 : q \vdash 1 : r, x : p}}
{1 : p \Rightarrow (p \Rightarrow r), 1 : q \Rightarrow (q \Rightarrow r), 1 : p, 1 : q \vdash 1 : r}}{}
$$

$$
\cfrac{
\cfrac{
\cfrac{\cfrac{f(u) = f(v) = 0}{uv : r \vdash u : p, uv : p}}
{u : p \Rightarrow r \vdash u : p}}
{1 : p \Rightarrow (p \Rightarrow r) \vdash} \qquad
\cfrac{
\cfrac{\vdots}{1 : p \Rightarrow (p \Rightarrow r), 1 : q \Rightarrow (q \Rightarrow r) \vdash p \Rightarrow (q \Rightarrow r)}}{}}
{\cfrac{1 : p \Rightarrow (p \Rightarrow r) \vdash (q \Rightarrow (q \Rightarrow r)) \Rightarrow (p \Rightarrow (q \Rightarrow r))}
{\vdash 1 : (p \Rightarrow (p \Rightarrow r)) \Rightarrow ((q \Rightarrow (q \Rightarrow r)) \Rightarrow (p \Rightarrow (q \Rightarrow r)))}}
$$

To prove completeness for AB_1 we introduce a new notion of validity for labelled sequents that coincides with the notion of validity defined in Definition 5 for sequents where all formulae have the label 1.

Definition 13 ($\models^*$). $\models^* \Gamma \vdash \Delta$ *iff for all valuations v in $\mathbb{Q}$ there exists a labelling function f such that* $\sum_{A \in f(\Gamma)} v(A) \geq \sum_{B \in f(\Delta)} v(B)$.

Note 6. $\models^* \Gamma^l \vdash \Delta^l$ iff $\models \Gamma \vdash \Delta$.

We now show that the rules of AB_1 pass $\models^*$ validity from conclusions to premises.

Definition 14 ($\models^*$-complete). *A rule with conclusion $\Gamma \vdash \Delta$ is said to be $\models^*$-complete iff for all premises of the rule, $\Gamma_i \vdash \Delta_i$, $\models^* \Gamma_i \vdash \Delta_i$ whenever $\models^* \Gamma \vdash \Delta$*

Lemma 1. *The rules of AB_1 are $\models^*$-complete.*

Proof. It is easy to see that the intensional rules are $\models^*$-complete; for any valuation the labelling function for the conclusion suffices for the premises. The $(\Rightarrow, l)$ and $(\Rightarrow, r)$ rules are only a little more complicated:

- $(\Rightarrow, l)$. If $\models^* \Gamma, x : A \Rightarrow B \vdash \Delta$ then given a valuation v we have a labelling function f such that:

$$\sum_{C \in f(\Gamma \cup \{x:A \Rightarrow B\})} v(C) \geq \sum_{D \in f(\Delta)} v(D)$$

  If $f(x) = 0$ then we extend f with $f(y) = 0$ for the required labelling function. Otherwise, if $v(A) \leq v(B)$ then we take $f(y) = 1$, if $v(A) > v(B)$ we take $f(y) = 0$. In both cases we get as required:

$$\sum_{C \in f(\Gamma \cup \{xy:B\})} v(C) \geq \sum_{D \in f(\Delta \cup \{xy:A\})} v(D)$$

- $(\Rightarrow, r)$. If $\models^* \Gamma \vdash \Delta, x : A \Rightarrow B$ then given a valuation v we have a labelling function f such that:

$$\sum_{C \in f(\Gamma)} v(C) \geq \sum_{D \in f(\Delta \cup \{x:A \Rightarrow B\})} v(D)$$

  Clearly:

$$\sum_{C \in f(\Gamma)} v(C) \geq \sum_{D \in f(\Delta)} v(D)$$

  Hence for the first premise f is the labelling function required. If $f(x) = 0$ then f is also the labelling function required for the second premise. If $f(x) = 1$ and $v(A) \leq v(B)$ then:

$$\sum_{C \in f(\Gamma)} v(C) \geq \sum_{D \in f(\Delta)} v(D) + v(B) - v(A)$$

  If $f(x) = 1$ and $v(A) \geq v(B)$ then:

$$\sum_{C \in f(\Gamma)} v(C) \geq \sum_{D \in f(\Delta)} v(D)$$

  Whence in both cases, as required:

$$\sum_{C \in f(\Gamma)} v(C) + v(A) \geq \sum_{D \in f(\Delta)} v(D) + v(B) \quad \square$$

Corollary 1. *If* $[\Gamma^l \vdash \Delta^l, \ldots, \Gamma_n \vdash \Delta_n]$ *is a branch of a proof in* AB_1 *then* $\models^* \Gamma_n \vdash \Delta_n$ *whenever* $\models \Gamma \vdash \Delta$.

Theorem 5 (Completeness of AB_1). *If* $\models \Gamma \vdash \Delta$ *then* $\Gamma^l \vdash \Delta^l$ *succeeds in* AB_1.

Proof. If $\Gamma^l \vdash \Delta^l$ fails in AB_1 then by applying the rules repeatedly we obtain at least one sequent $\Gamma_n \vdash \Delta_n$ that fails where Γ_n and Δ_n are multisets of labelled atoms. We consider the set of inequations:

$$S = \{\textstyle\sum_{p \in f(\Gamma_n)} p < \sum_{q \in f(\Delta_n)} q \mid f \text{ is a labelling function}\}$$

By Note 5 S must be *consistent* over $\mathbb{Q}$ (as otherwise we can apply $(succ)$). Hence there exists a valuation v satisfying all the inequations in S. But this means that there is no labelling function f for v such that $\sum_{A \in f(\Gamma_n)} v(A) \geq \sum_{B \in f(\Delta_n)} v(B)$. So $\not\models^* \Gamma_n \vdash \Delta_n$, whence by Corollary 1 $\not\models \Gamma \vdash \Delta$. $\square$

We take the opportunity to comment here that the labelled calculus AB_1 has a double significance in our work; it is both a first analytic, *terminating* calculus for **A** and also, as will be seen below, an extremely useful syntactic aid for proving the completeness of the unlabelled calculus, AB.

3.3 Adequacy of AB and AB_1

By Theorems 4 and 5 we have $AB \subseteq \mathbf{A} \subseteq AB_1$. To show $AB_1 \subseteq AB$ (and hence $AB = AB_1 = \mathbf{A}$) we add to sequents in AB_1 a store Π for formulae introduced by the $(\Rightarrow, l)$ rule in AB. Hence the rule for $(\Rightarrow, l)$ becomes:

$$\frac{\Gamma, xy : B|\Pi, B \Rightarrow A \vdash \Delta, xy : A \quad \text{y a new label}}{\Gamma, x : A \Rightarrow B|\Pi \vdash \Delta}$$

All the other rules for AB_1 stay the same except that for each conclusion and premise $\Gamma \vdash \Delta$ is replaced by $\Gamma|\Pi \vdash \Delta$. Notice that since the unlabelled formulae in the store are not processed by the rules of the calculus, this change does not affect the set of sequents provable in AB_1. What it *does* do is to allow us to prove inductively that the unlabelled sequents represented by the labelled sequent $\Gamma|\Pi \vdash \Delta$ can be reached in AB from the unlabelled sequent $\Gamma^{ul}, \Pi \vdash \Delta^{ul}$.

Definition 15 ($\Rightarrow -formula$, $atoms(\Gamma)$). *A $\Rightarrow$-formula is a formula with principal connective $\Rightarrow$, $atoms(\Gamma) = \{q \in \Gamma \mid q \text{ atomic }\}$.*

Lemma 2. *Given a branch of a proof in AB_1 $[\Gamma_1^l|\emptyset \vdash \Delta_1^l \ldots \Gamma|\Pi \vdash \Delta]$ where Δ is atomic and Γ contains only atoms and $\Rightarrow$-formulae, then for every labelling function f there exist multisets $\Gamma_f, \Gamma_e, \Gamma_r, \Delta_f$ and Δ_e such that:*

(1) $\Gamma^{ul} = \Gamma_f \cup \Gamma_e \cup \Gamma_r$ and $\Delta^{ul} = \Delta_f \cup \Delta_e$
(2) $\Gamma_f = atoms(f(\Gamma))$ and $\Delta_f = f(\Delta)$
(3) $\Gamma_e, \Pi \vdash \Delta_e$ succeeds in AB
(4) $\Gamma_e \subseteq \{A \mid x : A \in \Gamma, f(x) = 0\}$
(5) Γ_r contains only $\Rightarrow$-formulae

Proof. Omitted due to lack of space.

Theorem 6. $AB_1 \subseteq AB$

Proof. Given a proof of a sequent in AB_1 we apply the corresponding rules of AB up until the point on each branch when $(succ)$ is applied to a sequent $\Gamma|\Pi \vdash \Delta$ ie where there are labelling functions $f_1, \ldots, f_n$ such that $\cup_{i=1}^n f_i(\Gamma) = \cup_{j=1}^n f_j(\Delta)$. Now by Lemma 2, for $i = 1 \ldots n$ there exist multisets $\Gamma_f^i, \Gamma_e^i, \Gamma_r^i, \Delta_f^i, \Delta_e^i$ such that:

(1) $\Gamma^{ul} = \Gamma_f^i \cup \Gamma_e^i \cup \Gamma_r^i$ and $\Delta^{ul} = \Delta_f^i \cup \Delta_e^i$

(2) $\Gamma_f^i = atoms(f_i(\Gamma)) = f_i(\Gamma)$ and $\Delta_f^i = f_i(\Delta)$

(3) $\Gamma_e^i, \Pi \vdash \Delta_e^i$ succeeds in AB

(4) $\Gamma_e^i \subseteq \{A \mid x : A \in \Gamma, f_i(x) = 0\}$

(5) Γ_r^i contains only $\Rightarrow$-formulae

We have to show that $\Gamma^{ul}, \Pi \vdash \Delta^{ul}$ succeeds in AB. First we use (con) to step to:

$$\underbrace{\Gamma^{ul}, \ldots, \Gamma^{ul}}_{n}, \underbrace{\Pi, \ldots, \Pi}_{n} \vdash \underbrace{\Delta^{ul}, \ldots, \Delta^{ul}}_{n}$$

We then apply (wk) repeatedly to formulae in Γ_r^i for $i = 1 \ldots n$ obtaining:

$$\Gamma_f^1 \cup \Gamma_e^1, \ldots, \Gamma_f^n \cup \Gamma_e^n, \underbrace{\Pi, \ldots, \Pi}_{n} \vdash \Delta_f^1 \cup \Delta_e^1, \ldots, \Delta_f^n \cup \Delta_e^n$$

Since $\cup_{i=1}^n f_i(\Delta) = \cup_{j=1}^n f_j(\Gamma)$ we have that $\Gamma_f^1, \ldots, \Gamma_f^n \vdash \Delta_f^1, \ldots, \Delta_f^n$ succeeds in AB using $(mingle)$ and (id). Also $\Gamma_e^i, \Pi \vdash \Delta_e^i$ succeeds in AB for $i = 1 \ldots n$. So applying $(mingle)$ repeatedly, we have that $\Gamma^{ul}, \Pi \vdash \Delta^{ul}$ succeeds as required. □

Note 7. We can also use this idea of a store to make the $(\Rightarrow, l)$ rule for AB reduce the complexity of a sequent. When $(\Rightarrow, l)$ is applied to a formula $A \Rightarrow B$ not in the store the "reverse formula" $B \Rightarrow A$ is put in the store as above; when $(\Rightarrow, l)$ is applied to a formula in the store however no reverse formula is added.

4   Łukasiewicz Logic

[9,15] are good references for the philosophical background and historical details of Łukasiewicz logics. We confine ourselves here to definitions and some of the main results.

Definition 16 (Łukasiewicz Infinite-Valued Logic, Ł). $\supset$ *and* f *are primitive.* **Ł** *has the rule* (mp) *and the following definitions and axioms:*

D¬ $\neg A = A \supset f$ D∨ $A \vee B = (A \supset B) \supset B$

D∧ $A \wedge B = \neg(\neg A \vee \neg B)$ D⊕ $A \oplus B = \neg A \supset B$

L1 $A \supset (B \supset A)$ L3 $((A \supset B) \supset B) \supset ((B \supset A) \supset A)$

L2 $(A \supset B) \supset ((B \supset C) \supset (A \supset C))$ L4 $((A \supset f) \supset (B \supset f)) \supset (B \supset A)$

Definition 17 (Positive Łukasiewicz Infinite-Valued Logic, $\mathbf{L^+}$). $\supseteq$, $\vee$, $\wedge$ and t are primitive. $\mathbf{L^+}$ has the rule (mp) and the following axioms:

$L^+1\ (D \supseteq B) \supseteq ((D \supseteq C) \supseteq (D \supseteq (B \wedge C)))$ $L^+6\ (B \supseteq C) \vee (C \supseteq B)$
$L^+2\ B \supseteq (C \supseteq B)$ $L^+7\ (B \wedge C) \supseteq B$
$L^+3\ (B \supseteq C) \supseteq ((C \supseteq D) \supseteq (B \supseteq D))$ $L^+8\ (B \wedge C) \supseteq C$
$L^+4\ ((B \supseteq C) \supseteq C) \supseteq (B \vee C)$ $L^+9\ t$
$L^+5\ (B \vee C) \supseteq (C \vee B)$

The appropriate models for $\mathbf{L}$ are *MV-algebras* (see [5] for details). Let $[0,1] = \{x \in \mathbb{R} \mid 0 \leq x \leq 1\}$, $a \oplus b = max(0, a+b-1)$, $\neg a = 1 - a$ and $f = 1$ then we have that $[0,1] = \langle [0,1], \oplus, \neg, f \rangle$ is an MV-algebra with $a \to b = \neg a \oplus b = max(0, b-a)$. In fact $[0,1]$ assumes the same role for MV-algebras as $\mathbb{Z}$ for abelian l-groups.

Theorem 7 (Characterisation Theorem for $\mathbf{L}$). *The following are equivalent: (1) ϕ is a theorem of $\mathbf{L}$. (2) ϕ is valid in all MV-algebras. (3) ϕ is valid in $[0,1]$.*

Proof. See [5]. □

It turns out that Łukasiewicz infinite-valued logic is contained in abelian logic in a very natural way. Consider the following definitions:

Definition 18 (Enthymematic Implication ($\supseteq$)). $B \supseteq C = (t \wedge B) \to C$

Definition 19 (Material Implication ($\supset$)). $B \supset C = (t \wedge B) \to (f \vee C)$

Meyer [11] shows that fragments obtained using these new implications frequently correspond to other well-known logics; for example the material and enthymematic fragments of $\mathbf{R}$ are classical logic and positive intuitionistic logic respectively. We now investigate the corresponding fragments for $\mathbf{A}$.

Definition 20 (Enthymematic Fragment of $\mathbf{A}$, $\mathbf{A_E}$). $\mathbf{A_E}$ *is built up from propositional variables, t, $\wedge$, $\vee$ and $\supseteq$.*

Definition 21 (Material Fragment of $\mathbf{A}$, $\mathbf{A_M}$). $\mathbf{A_M}$ *is built up from propositional variables, f and $\supset$.*

Theorem 8. $\mathbf{L^+} = \mathbf{A_E}$

Proof. See [10]. □

Proposition 5. *(mp) is admissible for $\mathbf{A_M}$.*

Proof. Consider $\mathbf{A_M}$ formulae, A and B where $\models A \supset B$ and $\models A$. Since $\models A$ we have $A \leq t$, whence $A \supset B = (A \wedge t) \to (B \vee f) = B \vee f \leq t$. If B is a propositional variable then by taking a valuation $v(B) = v(f) = 1$ in $\mathbb{Z}$ we have $v(A \supset B) > t$, a contradiction. So either $B = t$ or $B = C \supset D$. If the former then clearly $\models B$, if the latter then we have $B \leq f$ whence $B \vee f = B \leq t$ and $\models B$ as required. □

Proposition 6. *L1-L4 are theorems of $\mathbf{A}$.*

Proof. We show the validity of L1–L4 in **A** using the sequent calculus AB. To aid the presentation of the proof we adopt the abbreviations $A^t = A \wedge t$ and $B_f = B \vee f$ (recalling that $A \supset B = A^t \to B_f$), and combine proof steps where convenient.

L1: $A \supset (B \supset A)$

$$\frac{\dfrac{A \vdash A}{A^t, B^t \vdash A_f}}{\vdash A \supset (B \supset A)}$$

L2: $(A \supset B) \supset ((B \supset C) \supset (A \supset C))$

$$\cfrac{\cfrac{B \vdash B \quad \cfrac{\cfrac{\cfrac{B \vdash B}{B, A^t \vdash B_f}}{B \vdash A \supset B} \quad B, (A \supset B) \Rightarrow t \vdash t}{B, (A \supset B) \Rightarrow t \vdash B^t}}{B, (A \supset B) \Rightarrow t, C_f \vdash C_f, B^t}}{\cfrac{f \vdash f \quad B, (A \supset B) \Rightarrow t, (B \supset C)^t \vdash C_f}{\cfrac{B_f, (A \supset B) \Rightarrow t, (B \supset C)^t \vdash C_f}{\cfrac{B_f, (A \supset B) \Rightarrow t, (B \supset C)^t, A^t \vdash C_f, A^t}{\cfrac{A \supset B, (A \supset B) \Rightarrow t, (B \supset C)^t, A^t \vdash C_f}{\cfrac{(A \supset B)^t, (B \supset C)^t, A^t \vdash C_f}{\vdash (A \supset B) \supset ((B \supset C) \supset (A \supset C))}}}}}}$$

L3: $((A \supset B) \supset B) \supset ((B \supset A) \supset A)$

$$\cfrac{\cfrac{B \vdash B \quad \cfrac{f \vdash f \quad B \vdash B}{f, B^t \vdash B, A_f} \quad \cfrac{\cfrac{\cfrac{A \vdash A \quad B \vdash B}{A^t, B^t \vdash B, A_f}}{A^t \vdash B, B \supset A}}{(B \supset A) \Rightarrow t, A^t \vdash B} \quad B_f, (B \supset A) \Rightarrow t, A^t \vdash B, B_f}{\cfrac{B_f, (B \supset A) \Rightarrow t \vdash B \quad B_f, (B \supset A) \Rightarrow t \vdash B, A \supset B}{\cfrac{B_f, (B \supset A) \Rightarrow t \vdash B, (A \supset B)^t}{\cfrac{((A \supset B) \supset B)^t, (B \supset A) \Rightarrow t \vdash B^t}{\cfrac{((A \supset B) \supset B)^t, (B \supset A) \Rightarrow t, A_f \vdash A_f, B^t}{\cfrac{((A \supset B) \supset B)^t, (B \supset A)^t \vdash A_f}{\vdash ((A \supset B) \supset B) \supset ((B \supset A) \supset A)}}}}}}$$

L4: $((A \supset f) \supset (B \supset f)) \supset (B \supset A)$

$$
\cfrac{
  \cfrac{
    f \vdash f \quad
    \cfrac{
      f \vdash f \quad
      \cfrac{
        f \vdash f \quad B^t \vdash B^t
      }{f, B^t \vdash f, B^t}
    }{f, B^t \vdash f}
    \quad
    \cfrac{
      \cfrac{
        f \vdash f \quad
        \cfrac{
          \cfrac{
            f \vdash f \quad B^t \vdash B^t
          }{f, B^t \vdash f, B^t}
        }{B \supset f, B^t \vdash f}
      }{(B \supset f)_f, B^t \vdash f}
      \cfrac{}{(B \supset f)_f, B^t, A^t \vdash A, f}
    }{(B \supset f)_f, B^t \vdash A, (A \supset f)}
  }{(B \supset f)_f, B^t \vdash A_f, (A \supset f)^t}
}{
  \cfrac{
    ((A \supset f) \supset (B \supset f))^t, B^t \vdash A_f
  }{\vdash ((A \supset f) \supset (B \supset f)) \supset (B \supset A)}
}
$$

Theorem 9. $\mathbf{L} = \mathbf{A_M}$

Proof. $\mathbf{L} \subseteq \mathbf{A_M}$ follows from Propositions 5 and 6 . To prove $\mathbf{A_M} \subseteq \mathbf{L}$ we show that if $\not\models_{\mathbf{L}} \phi$ then $\not\models_{\mathbf{A}} \phi$. Given a valuation v for $[0, 1]$ such that $v(\phi) > 0$, define a valuation v' in the abelian l-group $\mathbb{Q}$ as follows: $v'(f) = 1$, $v'(p) = v(p)$ for all propositional variables p. We claim that for all formulae ψ: (1) if $v(\psi) > 0$ then $v'(\psi) = v(\psi)$, (2) if $v(\psi) = 0$ then $v'(\psi) \leq 0$. We would then have $v'(\phi) = v(\phi) > 0$ as required. We prove the claim by induction on the complexity of ψ. The base case holds by stipulation. If $\psi = \psi_1 \supset \psi_2 = (t \wedge \psi_1) \rightarrow (f \vee \psi_2)$, then if $v(\psi_1) < v(\psi_2)$, $v(\psi) = v(\psi_2) - v(\psi_1)$. $v(\psi_2) > 0$ so we have $v'(f \vee \psi_2) = v(\psi_2)$. Also $v'(t \wedge \psi_1) = v(\psi_1)$, whence $v'(\psi) = v(\psi_2) - v(\psi_1)$. If $v(\psi_1) \geq v(\psi_2)$ then if $v(\psi_2) = 0$ we have $v'(f \vee \psi_2) \leq 0$ by the induction hypothesis and $v'(t \wedge \psi_1) \geq 0$ by definition, whence we have $v'(\psi) \leq 0$; if $v(\psi_2) > 0$ then $v(\psi_1) > 0$ and we have $v'(\psi_1) = v(\psi_1)$ and $v'(\psi_2) = v(\psi_2)$ whence $v'(\psi) = v(\psi_2) - v(\psi_1) \leq 0$. $\square$

5   Conclusions

In this paper we have presented the first labelled and unlabelled analytic sequent calculi for abelian logic, the former providing a decision procedure. For the latter a careful analysis of algorithms for solving linear programming problems (eg Gaussian elimination) promises to give a bound for the contraction rule. In combination with the introduction of a store to restrict the $(\Rightarrow, l)$ rule this will give us a terminating unlabelled calculus.

Our proof that Łukasiewicz logic coincides with the material fragment of abelian logic allows us to also give $\mathbf{L}$ both a new terminating labelled calculus and a first single sequent calculus that is analytic and internal. Here there are clear connections with other approaches in the literature. In [1] a proof calculus is given exploiting the fact that any formula valid in $\mathbf{L}$ is also valid in $\mathbf{L_n}$ where n is a function of the number of occurrences of variables in the formula. This calculus uses multiple sequents that seem to perform the same role as the (con) rule albeit with a different semantic interpretation. In [7] a labelled tableaux reduction of $\mathbf{L}$ to mixed integer programming is presented. Although similar in output (ie mathematical programming problems) the method is significantly different to ours in that constraints (ie equations) are generated dynamically as a proof progresses rather than one single labelled equation being maintained per branch. It is important to note also that the reduction in [7] is to a single mixed integer programming problem of *polynomial* size (hence proving the satisfiability problem of **Ł** is in NP). In contrast, the (*succ*) rule of AB_l is applied to a number of linear programming problems of *exponential* size ie one for each branch. We are convinced however that deciding the (*succ*) rule as applied to the atomic labelled sequents *generated by* AB_l can be performed in polynomial time; the reason being that the set of inequations to be tested for inconsistency can be reduced to a polynomially sized set by adding further constraints on the labels. Since linear programming can be decided in polynomial time, this would prove the satisfiability problem of abelian logic to be in NP. The details of this argument will be given in future work.

Acknowledgements. We are grateful to the referees for their careful reading and for their helpful suggestions and remarks.

References

1. S. Aguzzoli and A. Ciabattoni. Finiteness in infinite-valued Łukasiewicz logic. Journal of Logic, Language and Information, 9(1), 2000.
2. A. R. Anderson and N. D. Belnap Jr. Entailment: The Logic of Relevance and Necessity, Volume 1. Princeton, University Press, 1975.
3. E. Casari. Comparative Logics and Abelian l-Groups. In Logic Colloquium '88, Ferro et al. Ed, Elsevier, 1989.
4. A. Ciabattoni and D. Luchi. Two connections between linear logic and Łukasiewicz logics. In Proceedings of Computational Logic and Proof Theory, G. Gottlöb, A. Leitsch and D. Mundici Eds, Lecture Notes in Computer Science, Vol. 1289, Berlin: Springer-Verlag, 1997.
5. R. Cignoli, I. M. L. D'Octaviano and D. Mundici. Algebraic foundations of many-valued reasoning. Kluwer, 2000.
6. R. Giles. Lukasiewicz logic and fuzzy set theory. In Fuzzy Reasoning and its Applications, E. H. Mamdani and B. R. Gaines Eds, London:Academic Press, 1981.
7. Reiner Hähnle. Automated Deduction in Many-Valued Logics. Oxford University Press, 1994.
8. P. Hájek. Metamathematics of Fuzzy Logic. Kluwer, 1998.
9. G. Malinowski. Many-Valued Logics. Oxford, 1993.
10. R. K. Meyer and K. Slaney. Abelian Logic (from A to Z). In Paraconsistent Logic Essays on the Inconsistent, G. Priest et al. Ed, Philosophia Verlag, 1989.
11. R. K. Meyer. Intuitionism, entailment, negation. In Truth, Syntax, Modality, H. Leblanc Ed, Amsterdam, 1973.
12. D. Mundici and N. Olivetti. Resolution and model building in the infinite-valued calculus of Łukasiewicz. Theoretical Computer Science, 200(1-2), 1998.
13. N. Olivetti. Tableaux for infinite-valued Łukasiewicz logic. To appear in Studia Logica, 2002.
14. A. Prijatelj. Bounded Contraction and Gentzen style formulation of Łukasiewicz Logics. Studia Logica, 57, 437-456, 1996.
15. A. Urquhart. Many-valued logic. In Handbook of Philosophical Logic Volume 3, Dov Gabbay and F. Guenthner Eds, Kluwer, 1986.

Analytic Tableau Systems for Propositional Bimodal Logics of Knowledge and Belief

Linh Anh Nguyen

Institute of Informatics, Warsaw University
ul. Banacha 2, 02-097 Warsaw, Poland
nguyen@mimuw.edu.pl

Abstract. We give sound and complete analytic tableau systems for the propositional bimodal logics $\mathbb{KB}$, $\mathbb{KB}_C$, $\mathbb{KB}_5$, and $\mathbb{KB}_{5C}$. These logics have two universal modal operators $\mathbb{K}$ and $\mathbb{B}$, where $\mathbb{K}$ stands for knowing and $\mathbb{B}$ stands for believing. The logic $\mathbb{KB}$ is a combination of the modal logic $S5$ (for $\mathbb{K}$) and $KD45$ (for $\mathbb{B}$) with the interaction axioms $I : \mathbb{K}\phi \to \mathbb{B}\phi$ and $C : \mathbb{B}\phi \to \mathbb{K}\mathbb{B}\phi$. The logics $\mathbb{KB}_C$, $\mathbb{KB}_5$, $\mathbb{KB}_{5C}$ are obtained from $\mathbb{KB}$ respectively by deleting the axiom C (for $\mathbb{KB}_C$), the axioms 5 (for $\mathbb{KB}_5$), and both of the axioms C and 5 (for $\mathbb{KB}_{5C}$). As analytic sequent-like tableau systems, our calculi give simple decision procedures for reasoning about both knowledge and belief in the mentioned logics.

1 Introduction

Modal logics can be used to reason about knowledge and belief. Between basic modal logics, the logic $S5$ (resp. $KD45$) is the most suitable for reasoning about knowledge (resp. belief). Both of these logics have the axioms $4 : \Box\phi \to \Box\Box\phi$ and $5 : \neg\Box\phi \to \Box\neg\Box\phi$, which mean that knowledge and belief satisfy positive and negative introspection. Furthermore, the logic $S5$ has the axiom $T : \Box\phi \to \phi$, which means that knowledge is veridical, while $KD45$ has the axiom $D : \Box\phi \to \neg\Box\neg\phi$, which means that belief is consistent. These logics can be combined to reason about both knowledge and belief. To distinguish the modalities, we use $\mathbb{K}$ and $\mathbb{B}$ as the modal operators standing respectively for knowing and believing. As interaction axioms between $\mathbb{K}$ and $\mathbb{B}$, one can adopt $I : \mathbb{K}\phi \to \mathbb{B}\phi$ and $C : \mathbb{B}\phi \to \mathbb{K}\mathbb{B}\phi$. The axiom[1] I means that knowledge is understood to be stronger than belief, and the axiom C means that one is conscious about one's beliefs. This combined logic, denoted by $\mathbb{KB}$, is discussed in [18] by Hoek and Meyer.

Analytic tableau systems have been developed for all 15 basic modal logics, i.e. the ones obtained from the logic K by adding any combination of the axioms D, T, B, 4, 5 (see the works by Fitting [6], Goré [10], Massacci [14], and ours [15]). As some recent works devoted to developing tableau systems for modal logics about knowledge or belief, there are the works by Fitting et al [7], Rosati

---

[1] The axioms I and C are named by us.

U. Egly and C.G. Fermüller (Eds.): TABLEAUX 2002, LNAI 2381, pp. 206–220, 2002.
© Springer-Verlag Berlin Heidelberg 2002

[17], Baldoni et al [2], and Wooldridge et al [20]. Besides, tableau algorithms have been also developed for description logics, which are a family of knowledge representation formalisms (see the overview by Baader and Sattler [1]). The mentioned works [7,17,2,20], however, do not suit to reasoning about both knowledge and belief: the multimodal logics studied in [7,20] have modalities of the same type, the grammar logics considered in [2] have modalities of different types but do not contain the axioms D and 5.

In this paper, basing on known tableau systems for the monomodal logics $S5$, $KD45$, $S4$, and $KD4$, we develop analytic sequent-like tableau systems for the logic $\mathbb{KB}$ and three other bimodal logics $\mathbb{KB}_5$, $\mathbb{KB}_C$, and $\mathbb{KB}_{5C}$. These latter logics are obtained from $\mathbb{KB}$ by deleting the axioms 5 – for $\mathbb{KB}_5$, the axiom C – for $\mathbb{KB}_C$, and both of the axioms 5 and C – for $\mathbb{KB}_{5C}$. We choose these logics because $\mathbb{KB}$ is a popular modal logic for reasoning about both knowledge and belief, $\mathbb{KB}_5$ eliminates some undesirable properties of $\mathbb{KB}$ (e.g. $\mathbb{B}\mathbb{K}\phi \rightarrow \phi$), and $\mathbb{KB}_C$, $\mathbb{KB}_{5C}$ are interesting from the theoretical point of view as combinations of the component logics with the only interaction axiom I. Our tableau systems are sound and complete. As analytic sequent-like tableau systems, they give simple set-based backtracking decision procedures for the considered logics. Using the systems, we show that the satisfiability problem in $\mathbb{KB}_5$ and $\mathbb{KB}_{5C}$ is PSPACE-complete, in $\mathbb{KB}$ and $\mathbb{KB}_C$ is NP-complete.

In [3], Beckert and Gabbay developed a method for fibring tableaux. They described how to uniformly construct a sound and complete tableau calculus for the combined logic from "well-behaved" calculi for the component logics. In this paper, we do not apply the method as there are interaction axioms between $\mathbb{K}$ and $\mathbb{B}$, and the calculi considered in [3] are labeled tableau systems. The combination of modal logics has gained a lot of attention in the past years (see e.g. [12,19,5,8,13,9,4]). The logics considered in this paper are fusions of the component logics (with some interaction axioms). In the way of [4], the logic $\mathbb{KB}_C$ is denoted by $S5 \oplus_{\subseteq} KD45$, and $\mathbb{KB}_{5C}$ by $S4 \oplus_{\subseteq} KD4$.

The formulation of our systems is based on the work by Goré [10]. We use a similar technique to prove completeness of the systems. To show completeness of a calculus $\mathcal{C}L$ we give an algorithm that, given a finite $\mathcal{C}L$-consistent formula set X, constructs an L-model graph that satisfies every one of its formulae at the corresponding world.

2 Preliminaries

2.1 Definitions for Bimodal Logics

A modal formula, hereafter simply called a *formula*, is defined by the following rules: any primitive proposition p is a formula, $\perp$ is a formula (which stands for falsity), and if ϕ and ψ are formulae then so are $\neg\phi$, $\phi \wedge \psi$, $\mathbb{K}\phi$, and $\mathbb{B}\phi$. The modal operator $\mathbb{K}$ stands for knowing and $\mathbb{B}$ for believing. We write $\phi \vee \psi$ and $\phi \rightarrow \psi$ to denote the shortened forms of $\neg(\neg\phi \wedge \neg\psi)$ and $\neg(\phi \wedge \neg\psi)$, respectively.

We use small letters p and q to denote primitive propositions, Greek letters like ϕ and ψ to denote formulae, and block letters like X, Y, Z to denote formula sets. A *classical literal* is either a primitive proposition or negation of a primitive proposition (i.e. $\neg p$ for some p).

A (bimodal) Kripke *frame* is a tuple $\langle W, \tau, R, S \rangle$, where W is a nonempty set of possible worlds, $\tau \in W$ is the actual world, R and S are binary relations on W called accessibility relations. If $R(w, u)$ (resp. $S(w, u)$) holds, then we say that the world u is accessible (or reachable) from u via R (resp. S).

A (bimodal) Kripke *model* is a tuple $\langle W, \tau, R, S, h \rangle$, where $\langle W, \tau, R, S \rangle$ is a Kripke frame and h is a function that maps each world of W to a set of primitive propositions.

Given some Kripke model $M = \langle W, \tau, R, S, h \rangle$ and some $w \in W$, the satisfaction relation $M, w \vDash \phi$ is defined recursively as follows.

$$M, w \nvDash \bot$$
$$M, w \vDash p \quad \text{iff} \quad p \in h(w);$$
$$M, w \vDash \neg \phi \quad \text{iff} \quad M, w \nvDash \phi;$$
$$M, w \vDash \phi \wedge \psi \quad \text{iff} \quad M, w \vDash \phi \text{ and } M, w \vDash \psi;$$
$$M, w \vDash \mathbb{K}\phi \quad \text{iff} \quad \text{for all } u \in W \text{ such that } R(w, u), \; M, u \vDash \phi;$$
$$M, w \vDash \mathbb{B}\phi \quad \text{iff} \quad \text{for all } u \in W \text{ such that } S(w, u), \; M, u \vDash \phi.$$

We say that M *satisfies* ϕ *at* w, and ϕ is *satisfied at* w *in* M iff $M, w \vDash \phi$. If $M, \tau \vDash \phi$ then we say that M *satisfies* ϕ and ϕ is *satisfied in* M. If M satisfies ϕ then we also call M a *model of* ϕ.

The axiom schemata mentioned in the introduction are mirrored by certain properties of the accessibility relations. The axioms T, D, 4 and 5 correspond respectively to reflexivity (of R), seriality (of S), transitivity and euclideanness[2] (of R and S). The axiom $I : \mathbb{K}\phi \to \mathbb{B}\phi$ corresponds to the property $S \subseteq R$, while $C : \mathbb{B}\phi \to \mathbb{K}\mathbb{B}\phi$ corresponds to the condition $\forall x, y, z \; R(x, y) \wedge S(y, z) \to S(x, z)$. The classes of admissible interpretations for the logics $\mathbb{KB}_{5C}$, $\mathbb{KB}_5$, $\mathbb{KB}_C$, and $\mathbb{KB}$ are specified by the frame restrictions given in Table 1. For L being one of these logics, we refer to the restrictions as *L-frame restrictions*.

We call a model M an *L-model* if the accessibility relations of M satisfy all *L-frame restrictions*. We say that ϕ is *L-satisfiable* if there exists an *L-model* of ϕ. A formula ϕ is *L-valid* if it is satisfied in every *L-model*.

The logics $\mathbb{KB}_{5C}$, $\mathbb{KB}_5$, $\mathbb{KB}_C$, and $\mathbb{KB}$ are axiomatized by the standard axioms for the classical propositional logic, the *modus ponens* inference rule, plus the axioms mentioned in the Introduction, the K-axioms: $\Box(\phi \to \psi) \to (\Box\phi \to \Box\psi)$, and the necessitation rules: $\vdash \phi \Longrightarrow \vdash \Box\phi$, where $\Box$ can be either $\mathbb{K}$ or $\mathbb{B}$. It can be shown that for L being one of the considered logics, a formula is provable by the axiomatization system of L iff it is *L-valid* (see [18] for $\mathbb{KB}$). In this paper we use only the fact that all axioms of L are *L-valid*.

2.2 Definitions for Tableau Systems

Our tableau formulation is adopted from the work by Goré [10], which in turn is related to the ones by Hintikka [11] and Rautenberg [16]. A number of terms and notations used in this work are borrowed from Goré [10].

---

[2] i.e. $\forall x, y, z \; R(x, y) \wedge R(x, z) \to R(y, z)$, and similarly for S

Table 1. Frame restrictions for the logics $\mathbb{KB}_{5C}$, $\mathbb{KB}_5$, $\mathbb{KB}_C$, and $\mathbb{KB}$.

Logic	Frame Restrictions
$\mathbb{KB}_{5C}$	R is reflexive and transitive, S is serial and transitive, $S \subseteq R$
$\mathbb{KB}_5$	the conditions as for $\mathbb{KB}_{5C}$ plus $\forall x, y, z \ R(x,y) \wedge S(y,z) \rightarrow S(x,z)$
$\mathbb{KB}_C$	R is reflexive, transitive, and euclidean, S is serial, transitive, and euclidean, $S \subseteq R$
$\mathbb{KB}$	the conditions as for $\mathbb{KB}_C$ plus $\forall x, y, z \ R(x,y) \wedge S(y,z) \rightarrow S(x,z)$

A *tableau rule* δ consists of a numerator N above the line and a (finite) list of denominators D_1, D_2, ..., D_k (below the line) separated by vertical bars.

$$\frac{N}{D_1 \mid D_2 \mid \ldots \mid D_k}$$

The numerator is a finite formula set and so is each denominator. As we shall see later, each rule is read downwards as "if the numerator is L-satisfiable, then so is one of the denominators". The numerator of each tableau rule contains one or more distinguished formulae called the *principal formulae*.

A *tableau system* (or *calculus*) CL is a finite set of tableau rules.

A CL-tableau for X is a tree with root X whose nodes carry finite formula sets. A tableau rule with numerator N is applicable to a node carrying a set Y if Y is an instance of N. The steps for extending a tableau are:

- choose a leaf node n carrying Y where n is not an end node (defined below), and choose a rule δ which is applicable to n;
- if δ has k denominators then create k successors nodes for n, with successor i carrying an appropriate instance of denominator D_i;
- all with the proviso that if a successor s carries a set Z and Z has already appeared on the branch from the root to s then s is an *end node*.

Let Δ be a set of tableau rules. We say that Y is *obtainable from X by applications of rules from Δ* if there exists a tableau for X which uses only rules from Δ and has a node that carries Y.

A branch in a tableau is *closed* if it ends with $\bot$. A tableau is *closed* if every its branch is closed. A tableau is *open* if it is not closed. A finite formula set X is said to be CL-*consistent* if every CL-tableau for X is open. If there is a closed CL-tableau for X then we say that X is CL-*inconsistent*.

A tableau system CL is said to be *sound* if for any finite formula set X, if X is L-satisfiable then X is CL-consistent. A tableau system CL is said to be *complete* if for any finite formula set X, if X is CL-consistent then X is L-satisfiable.

Table 2. Tableau systems for the logics $\mathbb{KB}_{5C}$, $\mathbb{KB}_5$, $\mathbb{KB}_C$, and $\mathbb{KB}$.

$$(\bot) \ \frac{X;\phi;\neg\phi}{\bot} \qquad (\neg) \ \frac{X;\neg\neg\phi}{X;\phi} \qquad (\wedge) \ \frac{X;\phi\wedge\psi}{X;\phi;\psi} \qquad (\vee) \ \frac{X;\neg(\phi\wedge\psi)}{X;\neg\phi \mid X;\neg\psi}$$

$$(T_K) \ \frac{X;\mathbb{K}\,\phi}{X;\mathbb{K}\,\phi;\phi} \qquad\qquad (D_B) \ \frac{X}{X;\neg\mathbb{B}\bot}$$

$$(T'_K) \ \frac{X;Y}{X;Y;\neg\mathbb{K}\,\neg(Y)} \qquad\qquad (T''_K) \ \frac{X;Y;\mathbb{B}\,U;\neg\mathbb{B}\,V}{X;Y;\mathbb{B}\,U;\neg\mathbb{B}\,V;\neg\mathbb{K}\,\neg(Y;\mathbb{B}\,U;\neg\mathbb{B}\,V)}$$

where in the rules (T'_K) and (T''_K), Y is a set of classical literals

$$(4I_B) \ \frac{X;\mathbb{K}\,Y;\mathbb{B}\,Z;\neg\mathbb{B}\,\phi}{\mathbb{K}\,Y;Y;\mathbb{B}\,Z;Z;\neg\phi} \qquad\qquad (45I_B) \ \frac{X;\mathbb{K}\,Y;\mathbb{B}\,Z;\neg\mathbb{K}\,U;\neg\mathbb{B}\,V;\neg\mathbb{B}\,\phi}{\mathbb{K}\,Y;Y;\mathbb{B}\,Z;Z;\neg\mathbb{K}\,U;\neg\mathbb{B}\,V;\neg\mathbb{B}\,\phi;\neg\phi}$$

$$(4_K) \ \frac{X;\mathbb{K}\,Y;\neg\mathbb{K}\,\phi}{\mathbb{K}\,Y;Y;\neg\phi} \qquad\qquad (45_K) \ \frac{X;\mathbb{K}\,Y;\neg\mathbb{K}\,U;\neg\mathbb{K}\,\phi}{\mathbb{K}\,Y;Y;\neg\mathbb{K}\,U;\neg\mathbb{K}\,\phi;\neg\phi}$$

$$(4C_K) \ \frac{X;\mathbb{K}\,Y;\mathbb{B}\,Z;\neg\mathbb{K}\,\phi}{\mathbb{K}\,Y;Y;\mathbb{B}\,Z;\neg\phi} \qquad\qquad (45C_K) \ \frac{X;\mathbb{K}\,Y;\mathbb{B}\,Z;\neg\mathbb{K}\,U;\neg\mathbb{B}\,V;\neg\mathbb{K}\,\phi}{\mathbb{K}\,Y;Y;\mathbb{B}\,Z;\neg\mathbb{K}\,U;\neg\mathbb{B}\,V;\neg\mathbb{K}\,\phi;\neg\phi}$$

Calculus	Static Rules	Transitional Rules
$\mathcal{C}\mathbb{KB}_{5C}$	$(\bot),(\neg),(\wedge),(\vee),(T_K),(D_B)$	$(4I_B),(4_K)$
$\mathcal{C}\mathbb{KB}_5$	$(\bot),(\neg),(\wedge),(\vee),(T_K),(D_B)$	$(4I_B),(4C_K)$
$\mathcal{C}\mathbb{KB}_C$	$(\bot),(\neg),(\wedge),(\vee),(T_K),(T'_K),(D_B)$	$(45I_B),(45_K)$
$\mathcal{C}\mathbb{KB}$	$(\bot),(\neg),(\wedge),(\vee),(T_K),(T'_K),(D_B)$	$(45I_B),(45C_K)$

Let δ be one of the rules of $\mathcal{C}L$. We say that δ is sound wrt. L if for any instance δ' of δ, if the numerator of δ' is L-satisfiable then so is one of the denominators of δ'. It is clear that if $\mathcal{C}L$ contains only rules sound wrt. L then $\mathcal{C}L$ is sound.

3 Tableau Systems for the Logics $\mathbb{KB}_{5C}$, $\mathbb{KB}_5$, $\mathbb{KB}_C$, $\mathbb{KB}$

By a sequence $\phi_1;\phi_2;\ldots;\phi_n$ we denote the set $\{\phi_1,\phi_2,\ldots,\phi_n\}$. If X and Y are formula sets and ϕ is a formula, then by $X;Y$ (resp. $X;\phi$) we denote the set $X\cup Y$ (resp. $X\cup\{\phi\}$). We use $\mathbb{K}\,X$ to denote the set $\{\mathbb{K}\,\phi \mid \phi \in X\}$. The sets $\mathbb{B}\,X$ and $\neg X$ are defined similarly. If X is a formula set, then by (X) we denote the formula being the conjunction of formulae of X. Note that $\neg\mathbb{K}\,\neg(X)$ is different to $\neg\mathbb{K}\,\neg X$. In Table 2, we give tableau rules and calculi for the logics $\mathbb{KB}_{5C}$, $\mathbb{KB}_5$, $\mathbb{KB}_C$, and $\mathbb{KB}$.

Following Goré [10], we categorize each rule either as a *static rule* or as a *transitional rule*. The intuition behind this sorting is that in the static rules, the numerator and the denominators represent the same world (in the same model), whereas in the transitional rules, the numerator and the denominator represent different worlds (in the same model). In our systems thinning is built into the transitional rules, whereas in [10] Goré uses an explicit thinning rule.

The meaning of the static rules $(\bot)$, $(\neg)$, $(\wedge)$, $(\vee)$, (T_K), and (D_B) is quite clear. For intuition and soundness of the transitional rules, see the proof of Lemma 1. The transitional rule (4_K) is often used in tableau systems for the monomodal logics $K4$, $KD4$, and $S4$, while the transitional rule (45_K) is often used in tableau systems for the monomodal logics $K45$, $KD45$, and $S5$ (see [10]).

The rule $(4I_B)$ is just a simple modification of the rule (4_K) for dealing with the modal operator $\mathbb{B}$. It uses the axiom $I : \mathbb{K}\phi \rightarrow \mathbb{B}\phi$. The rule $(4C_K)$ differs from $(4I_B)$ in the point that Z does not occur in the denominator. The reason is that the modal operator $\mathbb{B}$ is weaker than $\mathbb{K}$. In the transitional rule $(4C_K)$, the presence of $\mathbb{B}Z$ in the denominator is due to the axiom $C : \mathbb{B}\psi \rightarrow \mathbb{K}\mathbb{B}\psi$. Similar things can be said about the transitional rules $(45I_B)$ and $(45C_K)$ in comparison with the rule (45_K).

The static rule (T'_K) plays a similar role as the rule (π) in Fitting's tableau system $\mathcal{C}S5\pi$ for the logic $S5$ (see [6,10]). As we will see, we may apply this rule only once, before applying transitional rules. The rule (T''_K) is similar to (T'_K), but it cannot be replaced by (T'_K) for $\mathcal{C}\mathbb{K}\mathbb{B}_C$ because that in the rule (45_K) formulae of the form $\mathbb{B}\psi$ or $\neg\mathbb{B}\psi$ are not transferred from the numerator to the denominator as in the rule $(45C_K)$ of $\mathcal{C}\mathbb{K}\mathbb{B}$. The presence of $\neg\mathbb{K}\neg(Y; \mathbb{B}U; \neg\mathbb{B}V)$ in the denominator of (T''_K) guarantees that we can reconsider the content of the current world in the future when having more information.

Example 1. Suppose that we want to prove $(\mathbb{K}p \wedge (\mathbb{B}p \rightarrow \mathbb{K}q)) \rightarrow q$ in $\mathbb{K}\mathbb{B}$, where $\rightarrow$ has the usual meaning. Denote the formula by ϕ. By Lemma 1 given below, $\mathcal{C}\mathbb{K}\mathbb{B}$ is sound, hence it suffices to show that there exists a closed $\mathcal{C}\mathbb{K}\mathbb{B}$-tableau for $\neg\phi = (\neg q; \mathbb{K}p; \neg(\mathbb{B}p \wedge \neg\mathbb{K}q))$. Here is such a tableau:

$$
(\vee) \frac{\neg q; \mathbb{K}p; \neg(\mathbb{B}p \wedge \neg\mathbb{K}q)}{(45I_B)\frac{\neg q; \mathbb{K}p; \neg\mathbb{B}p}{(\bot)\frac{\neg q; \mathbb{K}p; p; \neg\mathbb{B}p; \neg p}{\bot}} \quad \mid \quad (\neg)\frac{\neg q; \mathbb{K}p; \neg\neg\mathbb{K}q}{(T_K)\frac{\neg q; \mathbb{K}p; \mathbb{K}q}{(\bot)\frac{\neg q; \mathbb{K}p; \mathbb{K}q; q}{\bot}}}}
$$

We write $Sf(\phi)$ to denote the set of all subformulae of ϕ, and by $Sf(X)$ we denote the set $\bigcup_{\phi \in X} Sf(\phi)$. By $\widetilde{X}$ we denote the set $Sf(X) \cup \neg Sf(X) \cup \{\bot\}$. By $Ss(X)$ we denote the set of formulae of the form (Y) with $Y \subseteq X$.

A tableau system $\mathcal{C}L$ has the *analytic superformula* property iff to every finite set X we can assign a finite set $X^*_{\mathcal{C}L}$ such that $X^*_{\mathcal{C}L}$ contains all formulae that may appear in any tableau for X. Our systems have the analytic superformula property, with $X^*_{\mathcal{C}L} = \widetilde{X}$ for $L \in \{\mathbb{K}\mathbb{B}_{5C}, \mathbb{K}\mathbb{B}_5\}$, and $X^*_{\mathcal{C}L} = \widetilde{X} \cup \neg\mathbb{K}\neg Ss(\widetilde{X}) \cup \neg\neg Ss(\widetilde{X})$ for $L \in \{\mathbb{K}\mathbb{B}_C, \mathbb{K}\mathbb{B}\}$.

Lemma 1. *The calculi* $\mathbb{K}\mathbb{B}_{5C}$, $\mathbb{K}\mathbb{B}_5$, $\mathbb{K}\mathbb{B}_C$, *and* $\mathbb{K}\mathbb{B}$ *are sound.*

Proof. We show that $\mathcal{C}L$ contains only rules sound wrt. L, where L is $\mathbb{K}\mathbb{B}_{5C}$, $\mathbb{K}\mathbb{B}_5$, $\mathbb{K}\mathbb{B}_C$, or $\mathbb{K}\mathbb{B}$. Suppose that the numerator of the considered rule is satisfied at a world w in a model $M = \langle W, \tau, R, S, h \rangle$. It can be shown that if the considered rule is static, then one of the denominators is satisfied at w, else the only denominator is satisfied at some world reachable from w (via R or S). Nontrivial cases are when the considered rule is one of the transitional rules.

Consider the rule (4_K) of $\mathcal{CKB}_{5C}$. We have $M, w \vDash X; \mathbb{K}Y; \neg\mathbb{K}\phi$. Since $M, w \vDash \neg\mathbb{K}\phi$, there exists u such that $R(w, u)$ and $M, u \vDash \neg\phi$. Since R is transitive and $M, w \vDash \mathbb{K}Y$, we have $M, u \vDash \mathbb{K}Y; Y$. Hence the denominator of the rule is satisfied at u.

Consider the rule $(4I_B)$ of $\mathcal{CKB}_{5C}$ and $\mathcal{CKB}_5$. We have $M, w \vDash X; \mathbb{K}Y; \mathbb{B}Z; \neg\mathbb{B}\phi$. Since $M, w \vDash \neg\mathbb{B}\phi$, there exists u such that $S(w, u)$ and $M, u \vDash \neg\phi$. We have $M, u \vDash Y; Z$. Since $M, w \vDash \mathbb{K}Y; \mathbb{B}Z$, by the axioms 4, we have $M, w \vDash \mathbb{K}\mathbb{K}Y; \mathbb{B}\mathbb{B}Z$, and by the axiom I, $M, w \vDash \mathbb{B}\mathbb{K}Y; \mathbb{B}\mathbb{B}Z$. Hence $M, u \vDash \mathbb{K}Y; \mathbb{B}Z$, and the denominator of the rule is satisfied at u.

Consider the rule $(4C_K)$ of $\mathcal{CKB}_5$. We have $M, w \vDash X; \mathbb{K}Y; \mathbb{B}Z; \neg\mathbb{K}\phi$. Since $M, w \vDash \neg\mathbb{K}\phi$, there exists u such that $R(w, u)$ and $M, u \vDash \neg\phi$. Since R is transitive and $M, w \vDash \mathbb{K}Y$, it follows that $M, u \vDash \mathbb{K}Y; Y$. For any world v such that $S(u, v)$, by the property $\forall x, y, z\ R(x, y) \wedge S(y, z) \rightarrow S(x, z)$, we have $S(w, v)$ (since $R(w, u)$), hence $M, v \vDash Z$ (since $M, w \vDash \mathbb{B}Z$). Therefore $M, u \vDash \mathbb{B}Z$, and the denominator of the rule is satisfied at u.

Consider the rule (45_K) of $\mathcal{CKB}_C$. We have $M, w \vDash X; \mathbb{K}Y; \neg\mathbb{K}U; \neg\mathbb{K}\phi$. Since $M, w \vDash \neg\mathbb{K}\phi$, there exists u such that $R(w, u)$ and $M, u \vDash \neg\phi$. Similarly as for the rule (4_K), we have $M, u \vDash \mathbb{K}Y; Y$. Since $M, w \vDash \neg\mathbb{K}U; \neg\mathbb{K}\phi$, by the axiom 5, we have $M, w \vDash \mathbb{K}\neg\mathbb{K}U; \mathbb{K}\neg\mathbb{K}\phi$. Hence $M, u \vDash \neg\mathbb{K}U; \neg\mathbb{K}\phi$. Therefore the denominator of the rule is satisfied at u.

Consider the rule $(45I_B)$ of $\mathcal{CKB}_C$ and $\mathcal{CKB}$. We have $M, w \vDash X; \mathbb{K}Y; \mathbb{B}Z; \neg\mathbb{K}U; \neg\mathbb{B}V; \neg\mathbb{B}\phi$. Since $M, w \vDash \neg\mathbb{B}\phi$, there exists u such that $S(w, u)$ and $M, u \vDash \neg\phi$. Analogously as for the rule $(4I_B)$, we derive $M, u \vDash \mathbb{K}Y; Y; \mathbb{B}Z; Z$. Since $M, w \vDash \neg\mathbb{K}U; \neg\mathbb{B}V; \neg\mathbb{B}\phi$, by the axioms 5, we have $M, w \vDash \mathbb{K}\neg\mathbb{K}U; \mathbb{B}\neg\mathbb{B}V; \mathbb{B}\neg\mathbb{B}\phi$. By the axiom I, it follows that $M, w \vDash \mathbb{B}\neg\mathbb{K}U$. Hence $M, u \vDash \neg\mathbb{K}U; \neg\mathbb{B}V; \neg\mathbb{B}\phi$, and the denominator of the rule is satisfied at u.

Finally, consider the rule $(45C_K)$ of $\mathcal{CKB}$. We have $M, w \vDash X; \mathbb{K}Y; \mathbb{B}Z; \neg\mathbb{K}U; \neg\mathbb{B}V; \neg\mathbb{K}\phi$. Since $M, w \vDash \neg\mathbb{K}\phi$, there exists u such that $R(w, u)$ and $M, u \vDash \neg\phi$. Analogously as for the rule $(45I_B)$, we derive $M, u \vDash \mathbb{K}Y; Y; \neg\mathbb{K}U; \neg\mathbb{K}\phi$. Since $M, w \vDash \mathbb{B}Z$, similarly as for the rule $(4C_K)$, we have $M, u \vDash \mathbb{B}Z$. Since $M, w \vDash \neg\mathbb{B}V$, by the axiom T, $M, w \vDash \neg\mathbb{K}\mathbb{B}V$. Hence, by the axiom 5, $M, w \vDash \mathbb{K}\neg\mathbb{K}\mathbb{B}V$, and by the axiom I, $M, w \vDash \mathbb{B}\neg\mathbb{K}\mathbb{B}V$. Hence $M, u \vDash \neg\mathbb{K}\mathbb{B}V$, and by the axiom C, $M, u \vDash \neg\mathbb{B}V$. Therefore the denominator of the rule is satisfied at u.

4   Completeness of the Calculi

We prove completeness of our calculi via model graphs in a similar way as Rautenberg [16] and Goré [10] do for their systems. Let L denote one of the logics $\mathbb{KB}_{5C}$, $\mathbb{KB}_5$, $\mathbb{KB}_C$, $\mathbb{KB}$; and $\mathcal{C}L$ denote the corresponding calculus. To show

completeness of CL we give an algorithm that, given a finite CL-consistent formula set X, constructs an L-model graph (defined in Section 4.2) for X that
satisfies every one of its formulae at the corresponding world.

4.1 Saturation

In the rules $(\neg)$, $(\wedge)$, $(\vee)$, the principal formula does not occur in the denominators. For δ being one of these rules, let δ' denote the rule obtained from δ
by adding the principal formula to each of the denominators. Let $\mathcal{SCL}$ denote
the set of static rules of CL with $(\neg)$, $(\wedge)$, $(\vee)$ replaced by $(\neg')$, $(\wedge')$, $(\vee')$. Note
that for any rule of $\mathcal{SCL}$ except $(\bot)$, the numerator is included in each of the
denominators.

For X being a finite CL-consistent formula set, a formula set Y is called a
CL-saturation of X if Y is a maximal CL-consistent set obtainable from X by
applications of the rules of $\mathcal{SCL}$.

A set X is *closed wrt. a tableau rule* if, whenever the rule is applicable to X,
one of the corresponding instances of the denominators is equal to X.

As stated by the following lemma, CL-saturations have the same nature as
"downward saturated sets" defined in the works by Hintikka [11] and Goré [10].

Lemma 2. *Let X be a finite CL-consistent formula set and Y a CL-saturation
of X. Then $X \subseteq Y \subseteq X^*_{CL}$ and Y is closed wrt. the rules of $\mathcal{SCL}$. Furthermore,
there is an effective procedure that, given a finite CL-consistent formula set X,
constructs some CL-saturation of X.*

Proof. It is clear that $X \subseteq Y \subseteq X^*_{CL}$. Observe that if a rule of $\mathcal{SCL}$ is applicable to Y, then one of the corresponding instances of the denominators is
CL-consistent. In fact, in a sequence of applications of the rules of $\mathcal{SCL}$, the
second application of a rule with the same principal formula does not change
the formula set; and when applying a transitional rule, formulae that may be
principal formulae of static rules are ignored. Since Y is a CL-saturation (of X),
Y is closed wrt. the rules of $\mathcal{SCL}$.

We construct a CL-saturation of X as follows: let $Y = X$; while there is some
rule δ of $\mathcal{SCL}$ applicable to Y with the property that one of the corresponding instances of the denominators, denoted by Z, is CL-consistent and strictly
contains Y, set $Y = Z$.

At each iteration, $Y \subset Z \subseteq X^*_{CL}$. Hence the above process always terminates.
It is clear that the resulting set Y is a CL-saturation of X.

4.2 Proving Completeness via Model Graphs

A *model graph* is a tuple $\langle W, \tau, R, S, H \rangle$, where $\langle W, \tau, R, S \rangle$ is a Kripke frame,
and H is a function that maps each world to a formula set. We sometimes treat
model graphs as models with $h(w)$ being $H(w)$ restricted to the set of primitive
propositions. A model graph is called an *L-model graph* if its frame satisfies all
L-frame restrictions. A model graph $\langle W, \tau, R, S, H \rangle$ is said to be *saturated* if it
satisfies the following conditions for every $w \in W$:

- if $\neg\neg\phi \in H(w)$, then $\phi \in H(w)$;
- if $\phi \wedge \psi \in H(w)$, then $\{\phi, \psi\} \subseteq H(w)$;
- if $\neg(\phi \wedge \psi) \in H(w)$, then $\neg\phi \in H(w)$ or $\neg\psi \in H(w)$;
- if $\mathbb{K}\phi \in H(w)$, then for every u such that $R(w, u)$, $\phi \in H(u)$;
- if $\neg\mathbb{K}\phi \in H(w)$, then there exists $u \in W$ such that $R(w, u)$ and $\neg\phi \in H(u)$;
- if $\mathbb{B}\phi \in H(w)$, then for every u such that $S(w, u)$, $\phi \in H(u)$;
- if $\neg\mathbb{B}\phi \in H(w)$, then there exists $u \in W$ such that $S(w, u)$ and $\neg\phi \in H(u)$.

A saturated model graph is said to be *consistent* if every one of its worlds does not contain $\bot$ nor a pair of formulae ϕ and $\neg\phi$. We use the term "model graph" merely to denote a data structure, while in the definition by Rautenberg's model graphs are required to be saturated and consistent.

Lemma 3. *If* $M = \langle W, \tau, R, S, H \rangle$ *is a consistent saturated model graph, then* M *is a model of* $H(\tau)$.

This lemma can be proved by induction on the construction of ϕ that if $\phi \in H(w)$ then $M, w \models \phi$.

Given a finite $\mathcal{C}L$-consistent set X, as an L-model for X we construct a consistent saturated L-model graph $M = \langle W, \tau, R, S, H \rangle$ such that $H(\tau) \to X$ is L-valid. If for every $w \in W$, $H(w)$ is a $\mathcal{C}L$-saturation of some set, then the first three conditions of being a *saturated* model graph are satisfied. The constructions given in the next subsections differ by frame properties of the constructed model graphs: for both $\mathbb{KB}_C$ and $\mathbb{KB}$, $R = W \times W$; and additionally for $\mathbb{KB}$, $S = W \times W_B$ for some $W_B \subset W$, $\tau \notin W_B$.

4.3   Completeness of $\mathcal{C}\mathbb{KB}_{5C}$ and $\mathcal{C}\mathbb{KB}_5$

In this subsection, let L denote either $\mathbb{KB}_{5C}$ or $\mathbb{KB}_5$. In the following algorithm, the worlds of the constructed model graph are marked either as *unresolved* or as *resolved*.

Algorithm 1
Input: a finite $\mathcal{C}L$-consistent set X of formulae.
Output: an L-model graph $M = \langle W, \tau, R, S, H \rangle$ satisfying X.

1. Let $W = \{\tau\}$, $R_0 = S_0 = \emptyset$, and $H(\tau)$ be a $\mathcal{C}L$-saturation of X. Mark τ as unresolved.
2. While there are unresolved worlds, take one, denoted by w, and do the following:
   a) For every formula $\neg\mathbb{B}\phi$ in $H(w)$:
      i. Let Y be the result of the application of the rule $(4I_B)$ to $H(w)$, i.e.
      $$Y = \{\neg\phi\} \cup \{\psi \mid \mathbb{K}\psi \in H(w) \text{ or } \mathbb{B}\psi \in H(w)$$
      $$\text{or } \psi \text{ is of the form } \mathbb{K}\zeta \text{ or } \mathbb{B}\zeta\}.$$
      and let Z be a $\mathcal{C}L$-saturation of Y.
      ii. If there exists a world $u \in W$ such that $H(u) = Z$, then add the pair (w, u) to S_0. Otherwise, add a new world w_ϕ with content Z to W, mark it as unresolved, and add the pair (w, w_ϕ) to S_0.

b) For every formula $\neg \mathbb{K} \phi$ in $H(w)$:

   i. Let δ be the rule (4_K) if $L = \mathbb{KB}_{5C}$, or $(4C_K)$ if $L = \mathbb{KB}_5$. Let Y be the result of the application of δ to $H(w)$, i.e.

$$Y = \{\neg\phi\} \cup \{\psi \mid \mathbb{K}\psi \in H(w) \text{ or } \psi \text{ is of the form } \mathbb{K}\zeta\}$$
$$\cup \{\mathbb{B}\zeta \mid \mathbb{B}\zeta \in H(w) \text{ and } L = \mathbb{KB}_5\}$$

and let Z be a $\mathcal{C}L$-saturation of Y.

   ii. If there exists a world $u \in W$ such that $H(u) = Z$, then add the pair (w, u) to R_0. Otherwise, add a new world w_ϕ with content Z to W, mark it as unresolved, and add the pair (w, w_ϕ) to R_0.

c) Mark w as resolved.

3. Let R and S be respectively the least extensions of R_0 and S_0 such that $\langle W, \tau, R, S\rangle$ is an L-frame.

This algorithm always terminates because H is one-to-one, and for any world w, $H(w) \subseteq X_{\mathcal{C}L}^*$.

Lemma 4. *Let X be a finite $\mathcal{C}L$-consistent formula set and $M = \langle W, \tau, R, S, H\rangle$ be the model graph constructed by the above algorithm for X. Then M is a consistent saturated L-model graph satisfying X.*

Proof. It is clear that M is an L-model graph and for any $w \in W$, $H(w)$ is $\mathcal{C}L$-consistent. We now show that M is a saturated model graph. For this aim it is sufficient to show that for every $w \in W$,

- if $\mathbb{K}\phi \in H(w)$, then for every u such that $R(w, u)$, $\phi \in H(u)$;
- if $\mathbb{B}\phi \in H(w)$, then for every u such that $S(w, u)$, $\phi \in H(u)$.

The first assertion follows from the observation that for any $x \in W$, if $\mathbb{K}\phi \in H(x)$ then $\phi \in H(x)$ (by the rule (T_K)) and for any $y \in W$ such that $R_0(x, y)$ or $S_0(x, y)$, $\{\mathbb{K}\phi, \phi\} \subseteq H(y)$.

Consider the second assertion. Note that for any $x, y \in W$, if $\mathbb{B}\phi \in H(x)$ and $S_0(x, y)$ then $\{\mathbb{B}\phi, \phi\} \subseteq H(y)$. This implies the second assertion for the case $L = \mathbb{KB}_{5C}$. The assertion also holds for the case $L = \mathbb{KB}_5$ because that for any $x, y \in W$ with $\mathbb{B}\phi \in H(x)$, if $S_0(x, y)$ then $\{\mathbb{B}\phi, \phi\} \subseteq H(y)$, if $R_0(x, y)$ then $\mathbb{B}\phi \in H(y)$.

Since $X \subseteq H(\tau)$, by Lemma 3, M satisfies X.

The following theorem follows from Lemmas 1 and 4.

Theorem 1. *The calculi $\mathcal{C}\mathbb{KB}_{5C}$ and $\mathcal{C}\mathbb{KB}_5$ are sound and complete.*

Let L still denote $\mathbb{KB}_{5C}$ or $\mathbb{KB}_5$. By the above theorem, a formula set X is L-satisfiable iff every $\mathcal{C}L$-tableau for X has an unclosed branch. Thus checking L-satisfiability can be reduced to searching an and-or tree. It can be shown that the depths of $\mathcal{C}L$-tableaux for X as well as the sizes of formula sets carried by nodes of the search tree are bounded by a polynomial in the size of X. Hence the satisfiability problem in $\mathbb{KB}_{5C}$ and $\mathbb{KB}_5$ is decidable in PSPACE, and then is PSPACE-complete (since the satisfiability problem in $S4$ is PSPACE-complete).

4.4   Completeness of $C\mathbb{KB}$

Let $X_\#$ denote the set $\{\phi \in X \mid \phi$ is of the form $\mathbb{K}\psi, \mathbb{B}\psi, \neg\mathbb{K}\psi,$ or $\neg\mathbb{B}\psi\}$. Note that if Y is obtainable from X by applications of the rules of $C\mathbb{KB}$, then $X_\# \subseteq Y_\#$. Given a finite $C\mathbb{KB}$-consistent set X of formulae, in order to construct a $\mathbb{KB}$-model graph for X, we first repeatedly apply the rules of $C\mathbb{KB}$ to X until obtaining a set Y such that for any set Y' obtainable from Y by applications of the rules of $C\mathbb{KB}$, $Y'_\# = Y_\#$.

For δ being one of the transitional rules of $C\mathbb{KB}$, X being a formula set, and $\phi \in X$ being an instance of the principal formula of δ, let $apply(\delta, X, \phi)$ denote the result of the application of δ to X with ϕ being the principal formula, i.e.

$$apply((45I_B), X, \neg\mathbb{B}\,\phi) = \{\neg\phi\} \cup X_\# \cup \{\psi \mid \mathbb{K}\,\psi \in X \text{ or } \mathbb{B}\,\psi \in X\}$$
$$apply((45C_K), X, \neg\mathbb{K}\,\phi) = \{\neg\phi\} \cup X_\# \cup \{\psi \mid \mathbb{K}\,\psi \in X\}$$

Algorithm 2

Input: a finite $C\mathbb{KB}$-consistent set X of formulae.
Output: a $\mathbb{KB}$-model graph $M = \langle W, \tau, R, S, H \rangle$ satisfying X.

1. Let X_1 be a $C\mathbb{KB}$-saturation of X, and let $Y = X_1$.
2. While there exist $\neg\mathbb{B}\,\phi$ (resp. $\neg\mathbb{K}\,\phi$) from Y and a $C\mathbb{KB}$-saturation Y' of the set $apply((45I_B), Y, \neg\mathbb{B}\,\phi)$ (resp. $apply((45C_K), Y, \neg\mathbb{K}\,\phi)$) with the property that $Y_\# \subset Y'_\#$, let $Y = Y'$.
3. Let $X_2 = Y$ and $W_K = W_B = \emptyset$.
4. Let Z be the set of all classical literals from X_1. We have $\neg\mathbb{K}\neg(Z) \in X_1$, and hence $\neg\mathbb{K}\neg(Z) \in X_2$. Let $H(\tau)$ be a $C\mathbb{KB}$-saturation of the set $apply((45C_K), X_2, \neg\mathbb{K}\neg(Z))$.
5. For every $\neg\mathbb{B}\,\phi \in X_2$, add a new world w to W_B with $H(w)$ being a $C\mathbb{KB}$-saturation of the set $apply((45I_B), X_2, \neg\mathbb{B}\,\phi)$.
6. For every $\neg\mathbb{K}\,\phi \in X_2$, add a new world w to W_K with $H(w)$ being a $C\mathbb{KB}$-saturation of the set $apply((45C_K), X_2, \neg\mathbb{K}\,\phi)$.
7. Let $W = \{\tau\} \cup W_K \cup W_B$, $R = W \times W$ and $S = W \times W_B$.

It is clear that this algorithm always terminates.

Lemma 5. *Let X be a finite $C\mathbb{KB}$-consistent formula set and $M = \langle W, \tau, R, S, H \rangle$ be the model graph constructed by the above algorithm for X. Then M is a consistent saturated $\mathbb{KB}$-model graph satisfying X.*

Proof. Clearly, M is a $\mathbb{KB}$-model graph and for every $w \in W$, $H(w)$ is $C\mathbb{KB}$-consistent. We show that M is a saturated model graph. Since for $w \in W$, $H(w)$ is a $C\mathbb{KB}$-saturation of some set, it suffices to show that

- if $\mathbb{K}\phi \in H(w)$, then for every $u \in W$, $\phi \in H(u)$;
- if $\neg\mathbb{K}\phi \in H(w)$, then there exists $u \in W$ such that $\neg\phi \in H(u)$;
- if $\mathbb{B}\phi \in H(w)$, then for every $u \in W_B$, $\phi \in H(u)$;
- if $\neg\mathbb{B}\phi \in H(w)$, then there exists $u \in W_B$ such that $\neg\phi \in H(u)$.

These assertions hold because for any $w \in W$, $H(w)_{\#} = X_{2\#}$.

We now show that $H(\tau) \to X$ is $\mathbb{KB}$-valid. We have $Z \cup X_{1\#} \subseteq H(\tau)$. Hence $X_1 - H(\tau)$ is a subset of $X_1 - (Z \cup X_{1\#})$, which contains only formulae of the form $\neg\neg\phi$, $\phi \wedge \psi$, or $\neg(\phi \wedge \psi)$. Since X_1 is a $\mathcal{CKB}$-saturation (of X), it follows that $H(\tau) \to X_1$ is $\mathbb{KB}$-valid. By Lemma 3, M satisfies $H(\tau)$, hence it also satisfies X_1 and X.

The following theorem follows from Lemmas 1 and 5.

Theorem 2. *The calculus $\mathcal{CKB}$ is sound and complete.*

If the language does not contain the modal operator $\mathbb{B}$, then we have the monomodal logic $S5$. As a corollary of Theorem 2, the rules $(\bot)$, $(\neg)$, $(\wedge)$, $(\vee)$, (T_K), (T'_K), and (45_K) form a sound and complete *cut-free* tableau system for the logic $S5$. The system has the analytic superformula property and can give a decision procedure for $S5$.

When constructing a $\mathbb{KB}$-model graph for a $\mathcal{CKB}$-consistent formula set, we may use the rule (T'_K) only once, for the actual world after saturating its content. In fact, suppose that we modify the definition of $\mathcal{CKB}$-saturation by excluding the rule (T'_K) from the set $\mathcal{SCKB}$ and replacing step 1 of Algorithm 2 by: "Let X' be a $\mathcal{CKB}$-saturation of X, and let $Y = X_1 = X' \cup \neg\mathbb{K}\neg(Z)$, where $Z = \{\phi \in X' \mid \phi$ is a classical literal$\}$". Then the proof of Lemma 5 can still be used for the modified algorithm.

With the above mentioned modifications, computing a $\mathcal{CKB}$-saturation of a $\mathcal{CKB}$-consistent set U is done in nondeterministic polynomial time in the size of U. In the modified algorithm, the formula sets X_1, Y, X_2 have size bounded by a polynomial in the size of X. Hence the modified algorithm terminates in nondeterministic polynomial time in the size of X. A nondeterministic execution of the modified algorithm gives a correct solution if the resulting model graph is consistent. Therefore the satisfiability problem in $\mathbb{KB}$ is NP-complete (the lower bound is taken as the complexity of the satisfiability problem in $S5$).

4.5   Completeness of $\mathcal{CKB}_C$

Let $X_{\#K}$ denote the set $\{\phi \in X \mid \phi$ is of the form $\mathbb{K}\psi$ or $\neg\mathbb{K}\psi\}$. Note that if Y is obtainable from X by applications of the rules of $\mathcal{CKB}_C$, then $X_{\#K} \subseteq Y_{\#K}$. Despite that $X_{\#K}$ does not contain formulae of the form $\mathbb{B}\phi$ or $\neg\mathbb{B}\phi$, it contains information about such formulae because of the rule (T''_K). Similarly as for the case of $\mathcal{CKB}$, to construct a $\mathbb{KB}_C$-model graph for a $\mathcal{CKB}_C$-consistent set X of formulae we first repeatedly apply the rules of $\mathcal{CKB}_C$ to X until obtaining a set Y such that for any Y' obtainable from Y by applications of the rules of $\mathcal{CKB}_C$, $Y'_{\#K} = Y_{\#K}$.

We also use $X_{\#B}$ to denote the set $\{\phi \in X \mid \phi$ is of the form $\mathbb{B}\psi$ or $\neg\mathbb{B}\psi\}$.

For $\neg\mathbb{B}\phi \in X$, let $apply((45I_B), X, \neg\mathbb{B}\phi)$ be defined as in the previous subsection. For $\neg\mathbb{K}\phi \in X$, let $apply((45_K), X, \neg\mathbb{K}\phi)$ be the result of the application of the rule (45_K) to X with $\neg\mathbb{K}\phi$ being the principal formula, i.e. $apply((45_K), X, \neg\mathbb{K}\phi) = \{\neg\phi\} \cup X_{\#K} \cup \{\psi \mid \mathbb{K}\psi \in X\}$.

Algorithm 3
Input: a finite $\mathcal{CKB}_C$-consistent set X of formulae.
Output: a $\mathbb{KB}_C$-model graph $M = \langle W, \tau, R, S, H \rangle$ satisfying X.

1. Let X_1 be a $\mathcal{CKB}_C$-saturation of X, and let $Y = X_1$.
2. Repeat the following until $Y_{\#K} = Y_{0\#K}$ (after executing step 2d).
   a) Let $Y_0 = Y$.
   b) If there exist $\neg\mathbb{B}\phi \in Y$ and a set Z being a $\mathcal{CKB}_C$-saturation of the set $apply((45I_B), Y, \neg\mathbb{B}\phi)$ such that $Y_{\#K} \subset Z_{\#K}$, then let $Y = Z$.
   c) If there exist $\neg\mathbb{K}\phi \in Y$ and a set Z being a $\mathcal{CKB}_C$-saturation of the set $apply((45_K), Y, \neg\mathbb{K}\phi)$ such that $Y_{\#K} \subset Z_{\#K}$, then let $Y = Z$.
   d) If there exist formula sets Z_1, Z_2, and formulae $\neg\mathbb{K}\neg(U) \in Y$, $\neg\mathbb{B}\phi \in Z_1$ such that:
      - Z_1 is a $\mathcal{CKB}_C$-saturation of $apply((45_K), Y, \neg\mathbb{K}\neg(U))$,
      - Z_2 is a $\mathcal{CKB}_C$-saturation of $apply((45I_B), Z_1, \neg\mathbb{B}\phi)$, and
      - $Y_{\#K} \subset Z_{2\#K}$,
      then let $Y = Z_2$.
3. Let X_2 be the set obtained from Y by deleting every formula $\neg\mathbb{K}\neg(U)$ such that there exists $\neg\mathbb{K}\neg(U') \in Y$ with $U' \supset U$.
4. For each formula $\neg\mathbb{K}\neg(U) \in X_2$, create a new world w with $H(w)$ being a $\mathcal{CKB}_C$-saturation of $apply((45_K), X_2, \neg\mathbb{K}\neg(U))$. Let W_K be the set of such worlds.
5. Let $W = W_K$ and $S_0 = \emptyset$.
6. For each $w \in W_K$ do the following:
   a) Let $U = H(w)_{\#B}$.
   b) Let $\neg\mathbb{K}\neg(U_w)$ be a formula of X_2 such that $U_w \supseteq U$ and there is no $\neg\mathbb{K}\neg(U') \in X_2$ with $U'_{\#B} \supset U_{w\#B}$.
   c) Let Z_w be a $\mathcal{CKB}_C$-saturation of $apply((45_K), X_2, \neg\mathbb{K}\neg(U_w))$.
   d) For each formula $\neg\mathbb{B}\phi \in Z_w$, create a new world u with $H(u)$ being a $\mathcal{CKB}_C$-saturation of $apply((45I_B), Z_w, \neg\mathbb{B}\phi)$, add u to W and the pair (w, u) to S_0.
7. Let τ be a world of W_K such that $H(\tau)$ contains all classical literals and formulae of the form $\mathbb{B}\psi$ or $\neg\mathbb{B}\psi$ that belong to X_1.
8. Let $R = W \times W$ and S be the euclidean closure of S_0.

Due to the rule (T''_K), the existences of $\neg\mathbb{K}\neg(U_w)$ at step 6b and τ at step 7 are guaranteed. It is clear that this algorithm always terminates.

Lemma 6. *Let X be a finite $\mathcal{CKB}_C$-consistent formula set and $M = \langle W, \tau, R, S, H \rangle$ be the model graph constructed by the above algorithm for X. Then M is a consistent saturated $\mathbb{KB}_C$-model graph satisfying X.*

Proof. It is easily seen that S is serial (because of the rule (D_B)), transitive and euclidean. Hence M is a $\mathbb{KB}_C$-model graph. M is consistent because $H(w)$ is $\mathcal{CKB}_C$-consistent for every $w \in W$.

We now show that M is a saturated model graph. Since for every $w \in W$, $H(w)$ is $\mathcal{CKB}_C$-saturation of some set, it is sufficient to show that, for every $w \in W$,

- if $\mathbb{K}\phi \in H(w)$, then for every $u \in W$, $\phi \in H(u)$;
- if $\neg\mathbb{K}\phi \in H(w)$, then there exists $u \in W$ such that $\neg\phi \in H(u)$;
- if $\mathbb{B}\phi \in H(w)$, then for every u such that $S(w,u)$, $\phi \in H(u)$;
- if $\neg\mathbb{B}\phi \in H(w)$, then there exists $u \in W$ such that $S(w,u)$ and $\neg\phi \in H(u)$.

The first two of the above assertions hold because that if ψ is of the form $\mathbb{K}\phi$ or $\neg\mathbb{K}\phi$, and $\psi \in H(w)$ for some w, then $\psi \in X_{2\#K}$ (because of the step 2).

For the third assertion, suppose that $S(w,u)$ holds and $\mathbb{B}\phi \in H(w)$. If $w \in W_K$ and $S_0(w,u)$, then $\phi \in H(u)$ follows from $\mathbb{B}\phi \in H(w)$. If $w \notin W_K$ then there exists $v \in W_K$ such that $S_0(v,w)$ and $S_0(v,u)$. By the step 6b and the rules $(45I_B)$, (T''_K), we have $U_{v\#B} = H(w)_{\#B}$. This implies that $\mathbb{B}\phi \in U_v$, and hence $\mathbb{B}\phi \in Z_v$ and $\phi \in u$. Therefore the third assertion holds.

For the fourth assertion, suppose that $\neg\mathbb{B}\phi \in H(w)$. If $w \in W_K$, then there exists u such that $S_0(w,u)$ and $\neg\phi \in H(u)$. Suppose that $w \notin W_K$. There exists $v \in W_K$ such that $S_0(v,w)$. Since $\neg\mathbb{B}\phi \in H(w)$, similarly as for the case of the third assertion, we derive that $\neg\mathbb{B}\phi \in U_v$. It follows that $\neg\mathbb{B}\phi \in Z_v$ and there exists u such that $S_0(v,u)$ and $\neg\phi \in H(u)$. It is clear that $S(w,u)$ holds.

We now show that M satisfies X. Since M is a saturated model graph, by Lemma 3, $M \vDash H(\tau)$. Let V be the set of formulae of X_1 that are of the form $\neg\neg\phi$, $\phi \wedge \psi$, or $\neg(\phi \wedge \psi)$. We have $(X_1 - V) \subseteq H(\tau)$. Hence $M \vDash (X_1 - V)$. Since X_1 is a $\mathcal{CKB}_C$-saturation of some set, it follows that $M \vDash X_1$. Therefore $M \vDash X$. This completes the proof.

Theorem 3. *The calculus $\mathcal{CKB}_C$ is sound and complete.*

This theorem follows from Lemmas 1 and 6. Now consider the complexity of the satisfiability problem in $\mathbb{KB}_C$. We first adopt some restrictions on the use of the rule (T''_K). Assume that when applying the rule (T''_K), a formula of the form $\neg\mathbb{K}\neg(U)$ is created in the denominator only for U being the largest set satisfying the condition of the rule. Also assume that when computing a $\mathcal{CKB}_C$-saturation of some set, the rule (T''_K) is applied only once as the last rule, and if in the resulting set there are $\neg\mathbb{K}\neg(U)$ and $\neg\mathbb{K}\neg(U')$ with $U \subset U'$ then the formula $\neg\mathbb{K}\neg(U)$ is deleted from the set. Consider Algorithm 3 under such restrictions: computing a $\mathcal{CKB}_C$-saturation of a set U is done in nondeterministic polynomial time in the size of U, and the sets X_1, Y, X_2 have size bounded by a polynomial in the size of X. Hence the new algorithm terminates in nondeterministic polynomial time in the size of X. Analogously as for $\mathbb{KB}$, we conclude that the satisfiability problem in $\mathbb{KB}_C$ is NP-complete.

5   Conclusions

We have given analytic sequent-like tableau systems for the propositional bimodal logics $\mathbb{KB}$, $\mathbb{KB}_C$, $\mathbb{KB}_5$, and $\mathbb{KB}_{5C}$. They are sound and complete and can be used to reason about both knowledge and belief. Using the systems and their completeness proofs, we have shown that the satisfiability problem in $\mathbb{KB}_5$ and $\mathbb{KB}_{5C}$ is PSPACE-complete, in $\mathbb{KB}$ and $\mathbb{KB}_C$ is NP-complete. Our tableau systems can be used to prove the Craig interpolation lemma for the considered logics, as done in our work [15] for other logics.

Acknowledgements. The author would like to thank the anonymous reviewers for useful comments.

References

1. F. Baader and U. Sattler. An overview of tableau algorithms for description logics. *Studia Logica*, 69:5–40, 2001.
2. M. Baldoni, L. Giordano, and A. Martelli. A tableau calculus for multimodal logics and some (un)decidability results. In *H. de Swart, editor, Proceeding of TABLEAUX'98, LNCS 1397*, pages 44–59. Springer-Verlag, 1998.
3. B. Beckert and D. Gabbay. Fibring semantic tableaux. In *H. de Swart, editor, Proceeding of TABLEAUX'98, LNCS 1397*, pages 77–92. Springer-Verlag, 1998.
4. S. Demri. Complexity of simple dependent bimodal logics. In *Roy Dyckhoff (Ed.): TABLEAUX 2000, LNAI 1847*, pages 190–204. Springer, 2000.
5. K. Fine and G. Schurz. Transfer theorems for stratified multimodal logics. In *J. Copeland, editor, Logic and Reality, Essays in Pure and Applied Logic. In Memory of Arthur Prior*, pages 169–213. Oxford University Press, 1996.
6. M. Fitting. *Proof Methods for Modal and Intuitionistic Logics*. Volume 169 of Synthese Library. D. Reidel, Dordrecht, Holland, 1983.
7. M. Fitting, L. Thalmann, and A. Voronkov. Term-modal logics. *Studia Logica*, 69:133–169, 2001.
8. D. Gabbay. Fibred semantics and the weaving of logics part 1: Modal and intuitionistic logics. *The Journal of Symbolic Logic*, 61(4):1057–1120, 1996.
9. D. Gabbay and V. Shehtman. Products of modal logics, part 1. *Logic Journal of the IGPL*, 6(1):73–146, 1998.
10. R. Goré. Tableau methods for modal and temporal logics. In D'Agostino Gabbay Hähnle Posegga, editor, *Handbook of Tableau Methods*, pages 297–396. Kluwer Academic Publishers, 1999.
11. K.J.J. Hintikka. Form and content in quantification theory. *Acta Philosophica Fennica*, 8:3–55, 1955.
12. M. Kracht and F. Wolter. Properties of independently axiomatisable bimodal logic. *Journal of Symbolic Logic*, 56:1469–1485, 1991.
13. M. Kracht and F. Wolter. Simulation and transfer results in modal logic - a survey. *Studia Logica*, 59:149–177, 1997.
14. F. Massacci. Single step tableaux for modal logics. *Journal of Automated Reasoning*, 24(3):319–364, 2000.
15. L.A. Nguyen. Analytic tableau systems and interpolation for the modal logics KB, KDB, K5, KD5. *Studia Logica*, 69(1):41–57, 2001.
16. W. Rautenberg. Modal tableau calculi and interpolation. *Journal of Philosophical Logic*, 12:403–423, 1983.
17. R. Rosati. A sound and complete tableau calculus for reasoning about only knowing and knowing at most. *Studia Logica*, 69:171–191, 2001.
18. W. van der Hoek and J.-J. Meyer. Modalities for reasoning about knowledge and uncertainties. In Patrick Doherty, editor, *Partiality, Modality, and Nonmonotonicity*. CSLI Publications, 1996.
19. A. Visser. A course on bimodal provability logic. *Annals of Pure and Applied Logic*, 73:109–142, 1995.
20. M. Wooldridge, C. Dixon, and M. Fisher. A tableau-based proof method for temporal logics of knowledge and belief. *Journal of Applied Non-Classical Logics*, 8(3):225–258, 1998.

A Confluent Theory Connection Calculus

Uwe Petermann

Leipzig University of Applied Sciences
Dept. of Computer Science
D-04251 Leipzig, P.O.B. 300066, Germany
uwe@imn.htwk-leipzig.de,
http://www.imn.htwk-leipzig.de/~uwe

Abstract. In the present paper we combine two different enhancements of connection method based theorem proving calculi: a confluent version of a connection calculus [5] and a general approach for building-in theories [17] in connection calculi.

1 Introduction

This work is concerned with the combination of two different improvements of proof procedures based on the connection method [1,6]. In [5] the lack of proof confluence in proof procedures which are based on the connection method has been identified as a cause for sever inefficiencies during the proof search. A proof confluent version of the first-order connection method has been presented in the mentioned paper. In the present paper we generalize the approach of [5] to the case of reasoning with a built-in theory.

For this purpose we use our approach developed in [17]. This approach has been applied to various classes of theories. For an overview see [4] and for further results concerning hybrid theories see [19].

This paper is organized as follows. Necessary general notions will be introduced in section 2. An introductory example illustrating the presented calculus will be given in section 3. Section 4 is devoted to the presentation of a generic approach to building in theories into theorem provers. The application of the general approach to reasoning in a confluent calculus will be presented in Section 5. In particular we have to formulate certain restrictions concerning the theory to be built in. However, the restrictions are sufficiently weak in order to admit a large class of theories.

In the present paper we consider only the case of total theory reasoning, i.e. the case where in every inference step a whole theory connection is detected. Nevertheless it should be possible to generalize the approach in order to treat partial theory reasoning as well.

Related work. A general approach to building in theories into theorem provers via theory connections has been suggested in [7] by the treatment of equality by so-called eq-connections. A systematic approach to theory reasoning in the context of resolution based theorem proving can be found in [20]. In [13] so

U. Egly and C.G. Fermüller (Eds.): TABLEAUX 2002, LNAI 2381, pp. 221–234, 2002.

called theory links, obtained by a certain completion method, are used in the context of a matrix method.

Among the applications of theory reasoning are several methods translating non-standard logics into first-order logics with built-in theories [10,9,16]. Other approaches [8] consider theories given by classes of models or even theories combined from different sub-theories [19]. For an overview on relevant results in unification theory see [2].

2 Preliminaries

In order to keep the paper self-contained we recall basic notions concerning logic in general and theory reasoning in particular. We assume that the reader is familiar with the basic notions of first-order logic in clause form (cf. [11]). A clause with at most (exactly) one positive literal will be called a *Horn (definite) clause*. A definite clause consisting only of equational literals will be called a *conditional equation*. A *clause* is represented as a multi-set of literals. A *matrix* is a multi-set of clauses. Multi-Sets will be denoted as sequences of their elements. A set of pairwise variable disjoint copies of clauses of a matrix M will be called an *amplification* of M (see [12] for a more general definition of this notion). Clauses will be abbreviated also by Γ, C, D etc. Γ_1, Γ_2 denotes the union $\Gamma_1 \cup \Gamma_2$, whereas Γ, L denotes $\Gamma \cup \{L\}$ etc. A clause $L_1, \ldots, L_n$ means the disjunction $(L_1 \vee \ldots \vee L_n)$ of its elements. The meaning of a matrix $C_1, \ldots, C_n$ is the conjunction $C_1 \wedge \ldots \wedge C_n$.

This paper will focus on a family of proof procedures that generate goal driven a set of instances of clauses such that its unsatisfiability in a given theory may be proved by checking a simple sufficient criterion. In order to formulate this criterion we first of all need the notions of a path and of a spanning theory mating. A *(partial) path (in) through* a matrix M is a multi-set containing (at most) exactly one literal from each clause of M. Paths will be abbreviated also by p or q. A set of partial paths in a matrix M is called a *mating*[1] in M. A partial path u in a matrix M is *spanning* a path p through M if $u \subseteq p$. A mating U in a matrix M is *spanning* if for every path p through M exists an element $u \in U$ which is spanning p. If M' and M'' are disjoint subsets of a matrix M and then for sets of paths P through M' and P' through M'' the set $P \circ P'$ denotes the set of all paths which are the concatenation of a path from P and a path from P'.

If L is a positive literal then $\bar{L}$ denotes the literal $\neg L$. If L has the form $\neg K$ then $\bar{L}$ denotes the literal K. If p is the path $L_1, \ldots, L_n$ then $\bar{p}$ denotes the clause $\bar{L}_1, \ldots, \bar{L}_n$. And, vice versa, if Γ is the clause $L_1, \ldots, L_n$ then $\bar{p}$ denotes the path $\bar{L}_1, \ldots, \bar{L}_n$. The set of variables occurring in a term t, literal L, clause Γ or path p will be denoted by $Var(t)$, $Var(L)$, $Var(\Gamma)$ or $Var(p)$ respectively.

---

[1] In the case of theory theory reasoning we have to consider connections of very different form. Therefore we decided to distinguish the notion of a mating, consisting of any partial paths, from that of a theory mating which consists only of partial paths which satisfy a certain semantic condition.

A *substitution* is a mapping from the set of variables into the set of terms which is almost everywhere equal to the identity. The *domain* of a substitution σ is the set $D(\sigma) = \{X \mid \sigma(X) \neq X\}$. The set of *variables introduced by* σ is the set $I(\sigma) = \bigcup_{x \in D(\sigma)} Var(\sigma(X))$. If the variables $X_1, \ldots, X_n$ are the elements of the domain of a substitution σ and the terms $t_1, \ldots, t_n$ are the corresponding values then σ will be denoted by $\{X_1 \mapsto t_1, \ldots, X_n \mapsto t_n\}$. A substitution σ may be extended canonically to a mapping from the set of terms into the set of terms. This extension will be denoted by σ too. For a set of variables V and substitutions σ and ρ we write $\sigma =_V \rho$ if for every element $X \in V$ holds $\sigma(X) = \rho(X)$. In the previous equation the lower index V may be omitted if V is the set of all variables. The *composition* $\sigma\theta$ of substitutions σ and θ is the substitution which assigns to every variable X the term $\theta(\sigma(X))$. A substitution σ is called *idempotent* if $\sigma = \sigma\sigma$. A substitution σ is idempotent iff $D(\sigma) \cap I(\sigma) = \emptyset$. If M is the multi-set of clauses $C_1, \ldots, C_n$ then $M' = C'_1, \ldots, C'_k$ is a *sub-matrix* of M iff there is a sequence of pairwise disjoint indices $i_1, \ldots, i_k$ s.t. C'_l is a sub-multi-set of C_{i_l} for each l with $1 \leq l \leq k$. A set of matrices which is closed w.r.t. the application of substitutions, forming amplifications and sub-matrices will be called a *query language*. For a path $p = L_1, \ldots, L_n$ and a query language $\mathcal{Q}$ we will write $p \in \mathcal{Q}$ in order to abbreviate $\{\{L_1\}, \ldots, \{L_n\}\} \in \mathcal{Q}$.

Let $\mathcal{T}$ be an open, i.e. quantifier-free, theory. A $\mathcal{T}$-model is an interpretation satisfying $\mathcal{T}$. A query (a clause, a path, a literal) S is $\mathcal{T}$-*satisfiable* if there is a $\mathcal{T}$-model satisfying S. It is $\mathcal{T}$-*unsatisfiable* otherwise.

3   An Introductory Example

In this paper we introduce a generalization of the confluent connection calculus [5] towards theory reasoning. In order to illustrate the calculus we consider the following, very simple, theory $\mathcal{T}$.

$$\neg\, l(X, Y) \vee g(Y) \tag{1}$$
$$\neg\, p(X) \vee \neg\, l(X, Y) \vee c(Y) \tag{2}$$
$$p(a) \tag{3}$$

We try to construct a derivation for the following matrix.

$$\forall\, X\ (l(X, s) \vee \neg\, p(X))$$
$$\wedge$$
$$\forall\, Y\ (\neg\, c(Y) \vee \neg\, g(Y)) \tag{4}$$
$$\wedge$$
$$\forall\, Z\ p(Z)$$

Figure 1 shows a four-step derivation under the built-in theory $\mathcal{T}$ given by the axioms (1), ..., (3). Because of space restrictions the last two derivation steps had to be drawn as one "double" step.

Every $\mathcal{T}$-connection is indicated by a (multiple) arc. In each deduction step will be detected one $\mathcal{T}$-connection. Its first occurrence is in the destination of that step. The paths spanned by this new $\mathcal{T}$-connection are all those which are continuations of one of the partial paths consisting of the boxed literals in the source of the step. Moreover, one of the most general $\mathcal{T}$-unifiers of the $\mathcal{T}$-connection has been applied to those clauses the matrix which contain literals of the considered $\mathcal{T}$-connection. If the application of a $\mathcal{T}$-unifier changes a clause, then the original version of this clause will not be overwritten, rather its modified version will be adjoined to the matrix.

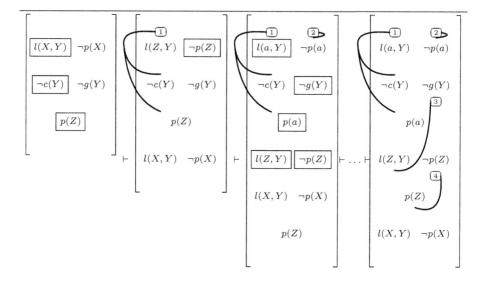

Fig. 1. A Sample Deduction in Matrix Notation

Four new instances of certain clauses of the original matrix have been generated, and four $\mathcal{T}$-connections have been found. The first $\mathcal{T}$-connection consists of three literals, the second of one, whereas the remaining two connections consist of two literals. The $\mathcal{T}$-connections are indicated by arcs connecting their elements. The final proof state is reached in the rightmost matrix in Figure 1. The mating U formed by those $\mathcal{T}$-connections is spanning the set of clauses in the final state of the derivation.

We have to point out some specific properties of the confluent (theory) connection calculus. First of all variables are considered free. Therefore each occurrence of a variable name in different clauses means the same variable. Or in other words, variables are not bound (by implicit quantifiers) to a certain clause.

New variables are introduced by so called *variant steps*. In the discussed derivation only one variant step occurs, that one constructing the initial matrix. The remaining steps are connection steps. Those steps construct new clauses by instantiation. The substitutions used for instantiations are $\mathcal{T}$-unifiers of

$\mathcal{T}$-connections. The reader should observe that clauses are never removed from the matrix. For example from clause $l(X, Y), \neg p(X)$, which is element of the first matrix, clause $l(Z, Y), \neg p(Z)$ in the second matrix has been constructed. Besides this new clause also the original clause $l(X, Y), \neg p(X)$ occurs in the second matrix.

4   A Generic Approach to Theory Reasoning

In the present section we introduce a formal framework for constructing complete confluent total theory reasoning calculi for open, i.e. quantifier free, theories. A complete theory reasoning calculus for an open theory needs the following key capabilities: (1) finding theory connections, (2) computing unifiers for theory connections, (3) managing amplifications and representations of sets of paths which are not spanned by a currently found theory mating, and (4) a fair rule for choosing clauses for further connection steps. The ingredients for constructing a complete confluent theory reasoning calculus — a complete set of theory connections (Definition 3) with a solvable unification problem (Definition 4) and a calculus managing amplifications of matrices and keeping track of unsolved goals — will be introduced in the subsections 4.1, 4.2 and 5.2 respectively. In the present section we formalize what it means to have for a given theory "enough" theory connections in order to prove all theory unsatisfiable matrices which belong to a given query language. We formulate a Herbrand theorem (cf. 1) by use of this notion. The notion of a complete set of unifiers for a theory connection generalizes the notion of complete set of theory unifiers of a pair of terms.

4.1   Complete Sets of Theory Connections

In order to formulate sufficient conditions for the completeness of a theory reasoning calculus we introduce the notion of a set of theory connections which is complete with respect to a given query language.

Definition 1. *(* $\mathcal{T}$*-complementary,* $\mathcal{T}$*-unifier) A path u is called $\mathcal{T}$-complementary if and only if the conjunction of the elements of u, $\bigwedge_{L \in u} L$, is $\mathcal{T}$-unsatisfiable. A substitution σ is a $\mathcal{T}$-unifier of u if and only if $\sigma(u)$ is $\mathcal{T}$-complementary.*

Remark 1. The $\mathcal{T}$-complementarity of a path u has been defined via the $\mathcal{T}$-unsatisfiability of the conjunction of the elements of u according to the negative representation which has been chosen in the present paper. In the positive representation $\mathcal{T}$-complementarity of a path u we would have been defined via the $\mathcal{T}$-validity of the disjunction of the elements of u. The remaining notions and results may be defined independently on the chosen representation.

Definition 2. *(Connection,* $\mathcal{T}$*-Connection) Let $\mathcal{T}$ be a theory, M a matrix, $\mathcal{U}$ a set of multi-sets of literals and $\mathcal{Q}$ a query language. Any partial path u in M will be called a $\mathcal{T}$-connection in M if there exists a $\mathcal{T}$-unifier for u. If $\mathcal{T}$ is the empty theory then the prefix $\mathcal{T}$ may be omitted.*

Definition 3. *(Complete set of theory connections)* *Let* $\mathcal{T}$ *be a theory, M a matrix, $\mathcal{U}$ a set of $\mathcal{T}$-connections and $\mathcal{Q}$ a query language.*

(1) *Any set of $\mathcal{T}$-connections in a matrix M, which are elements of $\mathcal{U}$, is called a $\mathcal{U}$-mating in M.*
(2) *A decidable set $\mathcal{U}$ of $\mathcal{T}$-connections which is closed w.r.t. application of substitutions will be called $\mathcal{T}$-complete w.r.t. $\mathcal{Q}$ if*
    a) *for each $\mathcal{T}$-complementary ground path $p \in \mathcal{Q}$ exists $u \in \mathcal{U}$ such that $u \subseteq p$ and*
    b) *for each $\mathcal{T}$-complementary ground path of the form $\sigma(u) \in \mathcal{U}$ such that $u \in \mathcal{Q}$ holds $u \in \mathcal{U}$.*

Example 1. If theory $\mathcal{T}$ consists of conditional equations and the equality symbol does not occur in the query language then the set $\mathcal{U}_{\mathcal{T}}$ of connections of the form $p(t_1, \ldots, t_n), \neg p(s_1, \ldots, s_n)$ for simultaneously pairwise $\mathcal{T}$-unifiable terms t_i and s_i is complete w.r.t. to the query language $\mathcal{Q}_{\mathcal{T}}$.

The less literals a connection consists of the more paths it may span. Therefore, we are interested to find theory connections which are minimal with respect to set-theoretical inclusion. Every extra literal may cause that additional subgoals have to be solved. The following proposition makes sure that a complete set of theory connections contains also all minimal connections. Having a complete set of theory connections a Herbrand theorem may be proved.

Proposition 1. *Properties of complete sets of theory connections Let the set of $\mathcal{T}$-connections $\mathcal{U}$ be $\mathcal{T}$-complete with respect to the query language $\mathcal{Q}$. Let u be a path such that $u \in \mathcal{Q}$. If u is minimally $\mathcal{T}$-complementary then $u \in \mathcal{U}$.*

Theorem 1. *(Herbrand's theorem) Let $\mathcal{T}$ be an open theory, $\mathcal{Q}$ a query language, $\mathcal{U}$ a set of $\mathcal{T}$-connections which is complete w.r.t. to $\mathcal{Q}$. Then for every $\mathcal{T}$-unsatisfiable matrix $M \in \mathcal{Q}$ there exists an amplification M' of M, a $\mathcal{U}$-mating U which is spanning in M' and a substitution σ such that $\sigma(u)$ is minimally $\mathcal{T}$-complementary for each $u \in U$.*

4.2   The Unification Problem for Sets of Theory Connections

In order to obtain a proof calculus for a given complete set of $\mathcal{T}$-connections $\mathcal{U}$ we also need to be able to compute or to represent for every $u \in \mathcal{U}$ all substitutions σ such that $\sigma(u)$ is $\mathcal{T}$-complementary. This will be formulated in the following definition.

Definition 4. *(more general $\mathcal{T}$-unifier, $\mathcal{T}$-unification problem in $\mathcal{U}$)*
    Let $\mathcal{U}$ be a set of multi-sets of literals.
(1) *Let ϱ and σ be $\mathcal{T}$-unifiers of some $u \in \mathcal{U}$ such that $D(\varrho), D(\sigma) \subseteq Var(u)$. Then ϱ is called more general than σ if there exists η such that $\varrho\eta =_{Var(u)} \sigma$. This will be denoted by $\varrho \leq \sigma$.*
(2) *A set S of $\mathcal{T}$-unifiers of a multi-set $u \in \mathcal{U}$ will be called complete if for each $\mathcal{T}$-unifier σ of u exists a substitution $\varrho \in S$ such that $\varrho \leq \sigma$.*
(3) *We say that the $\mathcal{T}$-unification problem in $\mathcal{U}$ is solvable if*

    a) for every $u \in \mathcal{U}$ there exists an enumerable complete set S_u of $\mathcal{T}$-unifiers for u and

    b) for a given $u \in \mathcal{U}$ it is decidable whether $S_u \neq \emptyset$.

(4) A substitution σ is called a simultaneous $\mathcal{T}$-unifier of a set U of multi-sets of literals if and only if $\sigma(u)$ is $\mathcal{T}$-complementary for every $u \in U$.

Remark 2. The syntactic structure of the considered query language is important for the complexity of the related $\mathcal{T}$-unification problem. If the restrictions concerning query language in example 1 would be relaxed admitting the equality symbol in queries then for an reasonable treatment transformations of the query language according to [3] would be necessary. If on the other hand the considered equational theory is associative with unit then the following restriction of the query language would be helpful. Let $\mathcal{U}_{\mathcal{T}}^{upp}$ be the subset of $\mathcal{T}$-connections defined in Example 1 obeying the following, so called, unique prefix property (cf. [9]). A formula or a term has the unique prefix property if each variable α occurs always in the same left context. Formulas obtained by the algebraic translation of modal formulas have this property. For those restricted $\mathcal{T}$-unification problems exists an efficient unification algorithm [9].

While for syntactical unification most general unifiers for unifiable terms never introduce variables not occurring in the unification problem this is not true in the theory case. The following example illustrates the problem.

Example 2. Let $\mathcal{T}$ consist of an associative binary function symbol $*$. Then the $\mathcal{T}$-connection 5 in Figure 2 has the most general $\mathcal{T}$-unifier (6).

$$\left\{ \begin{array}{c} p(X * Y) \\ \neg p(a * Z) \end{array} \right\} \qquad (5) \qquad\qquad \{X \mapsto a * W,\ Z \mapsto W * Y\} \quad (6)$$

Fig. 2. A theory unifier introducing a new variable

This unifier introduces a "new" variable W. If the unification problem occurs as a sub-problem in a proof task then those "new" variables must not occur in the matrix under consideration. Otherwise binding them might prevent the solution of further unification problems.

Moreover one can observe, that the "new" variable W occurs only as a proper sub-term. Therefore the application of this $\mathcal{T}$-unifier increases the term depth.

Definition 5. *We say that a solution to the $\mathcal{T}$-unification problem has the shielding property iff for every $\mathcal{T}$-unifier σ of a $\mathcal{T}$-connection u and every variable $X \in dom(\sigma)$ the term $\sigma(X)$ is not a variable not occurring in u.*

In a connection calculus we have to find a *simultaneous* $\mathcal{T}$-unifier of a spanning mating of $\mathcal{T}$-connections incrementally. The solvability of the unification problem in a set of theory connections $\mathcal{U}$ implies the solvability of the simultaneous unification problem in $\mathcal{U}$.

Proposition 2.   *Let the $\mathcal{T}$-unification problem be solvable for the set of $\mathcal{T}$ -connections $\mathcal{U}$ and S_u denote the complete set of $\mathcal{T}$-unifiers for each $u \in \mathcal{U}$. Then every simultaneous $\mathcal{T}$-unifier θ of a set of $\mathcal{T}$-connections $U \subseteq \mathcal{U}$ can be approximated incrementally. Indeed, for each enumeration $u_1, \ldots, u_n$ of the elements of U may be constructed sequences $\{\sigma_i\}_{i=1}^n$, $\{\eta_i\}_{i=0}^n$, $\{\varrho_i\}_{i=0}^n$ such that*

(1) $\eta_0 = \theta$ and $\varrho_0 = \{\ \}$,
(2) for every $i, 1 \leq i \leq n$:
      (a) $\sigma_i \in S_{\varrho_{i-1}(u_i)}$, (b) $\sigma_i \eta_i = \eta_{i-1}$, (c) $\varrho_i = \varrho_{i-1} \sigma_i$ and
(3) $\varrho_n \eta_n = \theta$.

5   A Confluent Connection Calculus with Built-in Theory

5.1   The Calculus Definition

Now we are going to define a Confluent Theory Connection Calculus (CTCC). The constituents are the *inference rules*, the notion of a *derivation*, and following [5], a *fairness condition* for derivations. We assume the following properties of the considered query language $\mathcal{Q}$, theory $\mathcal{T}$, the set $\mathcal{U}$ of $\mathcal{T}$-connections complete w.r.t. $\mathcal{Q}$ and the solution to the $\mathcal{T}$-unification problem in $\mathcal{U}$:

(1) For each $u \in \mathcal{U}$ exist at most finitely many $\mathcal{T}$-unifiers.
(2) For each $u \in \mathcal{U}$ and for each finite set of variables X not occurring in u any $\mathcal{T}$-unifier σ for u which introduces new variables may be chosen so that none of those new variables belongs to X.
(3) The solution to the $\mathcal{T}$-unification problem in $\mathcal{U}$ has the shielding property.

The mentioned conditions are satisfied by a large class of theories, however not by all theories. They are trivially satisfied by the empty theory.

A *state of a derivation* maintains information about the clause instances which have been constructed and the open paths in that state. Open paths are those which are not yet spanned by one of the theory connections which have been found up to the current derivation state.

Definition 6. *A state (for the confluent theory connection calculus) is a triplet (P, M, N)*

(1) A set P of paths through matrix M,
(2) N a set of variants of clauses of the original matrix, and
(3) M a set of instances of clauses of the original clause set (i.e. including N).

Definition 7. *(Theory Connection Rule Application) The connection rule may be applied to state (P, M, N) if*

(1) there is an $\mathcal{U}$-connection u
(2) spanning all paths out of some non-empty subset P' of P, which are not yet spanned, and
(3) having a $\mathcal{T}$-unifier σ.

The resulting state is $((\sigma(P) \setminus P'') \circ (M \setminus \sigma(M)), \sigma(M) \cup M, N)$ *for some non-empty subset* P'' *of* $\sigma(P')$.

$\sigma(M) \setminus M$ *is called the set of new clauses (of this inference step).*

Definition 8. *(Variant Generation) The* variant rule *adjoins a set* K *of new copies of the clauses of the matrix to the state* (P, M, N). *The obtained state is the triplet* $(P \circ K, M \cup K, N \cup K)$.

Definition 9. *(Progressive Rule Application) An inference rule application is called* progressive *iff it introduces new clauses. For any natural number* T *a progressive deduction step is called* T-progressive *if one of the newly constructed clauses has a term nesting depth not greater than* T.

Definition 10. *(Derivation) An* initial state *in a derivation is a triplet* (P, M, M) *where* M *is a copy of the original clause set and* P *is the set of all paths through* M. *Now a* derivation *may be defined as a sequence of rule applications which starts from an initial state. A derivation is called* ground *if the unifier in every* $\mathcal{T}$-connection step is empty. A finite derivation is successful if the component P in its last element is empty.*

The calculus is sound, because in every state of a derivation the set P contains all those paths, which are not spanned by the theory connections which have been found so far in that derivation.

Proposition 3. *(Soundness) The confluent theory connection calculus is sound.*

5.2 Fairness

Following [5] we define a notion of fairness as an intermediate concept. It will be shown that fair derivations for $\mathcal{T}$-unsatisfiable matrices are successful. Moreover a procedure which ensures fairness will be given. Fairness means that each deduction step which might contribute to the success of a derivation at a certain state of that derivation will be applicable further on unless its effect has been achieved by other steps.

Definition 11. *Let* n *be a natural number or the least infinite ordinal number. Let* $\{M_i\}_{i<n}$ *be the sequence of matrices of a derivation. The derivation is called* fair *iff it is successful or if the following two conditions are satisfied:*

(1) *For every* i *there is a* j, *such that* $i < j$ *and* $j + 1 < n$ *and* M_{j+1} *results from* M_j *by a variant step.*

(2) *For every* i *and every connection* u *with* $\mathcal{T}$-unifier σ *which is a candidate for a progressive connection step in* M_i *there is a* j *such that* $i < j < n$ *and one of the following conditions is satisfied:*

   a) $\sigma(M_i) \subseteq M_j$.

   b) *Every path* p *through* M_j *which is spanned by* u *is closed.*

Condition (1) requires that there will be no latest variant step. This implies that infinitely many new variables will occur in subsequent variant steps. Condition (2) formalizes that any progressive connection step either remains applicable (2a) or its effect will be achieved by other connection steps (2b).

The mentioned fairness condition is a global property of a derivation. Thus, we need to formulate a condition which may be checked with reasonable effort at any state of a derivation and which implies fairness of a derivation.

Definition 12. *(The CTCC Procedure) Let T be a natural number.*

(1) Initialize (P, M, N) with M and N being the original matrix, P being the set of all paths through M. Moreover, let T the maximum term nesting depth of the clauses in S.

(2) While P is not empty repeat:

    a) Modify M by applying one variant step and increment T.

    b) Repeat

            to modify M by applying a T-progressive connection step until no such step is applicable any more.

Theorem 2. *(Fairness theorem) Suppose that the complete set $\mathcal{U}$ of $\mathcal{T}$-connections has a solution of the unification problem such that for each $u \in \mathcal{U}$ each unifier $\sigma \in S_u$ has the shielding property.*

Any derivation (starting from any finite input clause set) constructed by the procedure defined in (12) is fair.

Proof. First of all let us observe that the inner loop (2b) of the considered procedure always terminates. We consider the following cases a, b and c:

a: Only finitely many of the applied $\mathcal{T}$-unifiers in the inner loop are not renamings. Therefore only a finite number of T-progressive connection steps is possible.

b: Infinitely many of the applied $\mathcal{T}$-unifiers are not renamings. But only finitely many steps introduce new variables. This would contradict the T-progressiveness of those $\mathcal{T}$-connection steps because the term depth of the generated clauses would exceed all bounds.

c: Infinitely many of the applied $\mathcal{T}$-unifiers are not renamings and infinitely many new variables are introduced. Since the $\mathcal{T}$-unification method is assumed to have the shielding property also this assumption contradicts the T-progressiveness of those $\mathcal{T}$-connection steps.

Thus, the inner loop (2b) terminates.

Since successful derivations are fair by definition, it remains to consider an infinite derivation. Each of the steps (2a), (2b) of the outer loop terminates, therefore step (2a) is performed infinitely often, i.e. condition (1) of the fairness definition (11) is satisfied.

In order to prove condition (2) of definition (11) consider any index i where a progressive $\mathcal{T}$-connection step is applicable to some $\mathcal{T}$-connection u in M_i

with some $\mathcal{T}$-unifier $\sigma \in S_u$. Let T_0 be the minimal natural number, so that the mentioned step is T_0-progressive. Further let j be the number of the last step in the inner loop of the execution of the outer loop with threshold T_0. Suppose that neither condition (2a) nor condition (2b) of the fairness definition is satisfied. I.e. $\sigma(M_i) \not\subseteq M_j$ and some path p through M_j which is spanned by u is not closed. Then the current step will be either the execution of just the $\mathcal{T}$-connection step with u and σ or any other step which causes one of the conditions (2a) or (2b) being satisfied. Otherwise the inner loop would be finished by this step contrary to the assumption about j.

5.3 Strong Herbrand Theorem

Having a complete set $\mathcal{U}$ of theory connections with a solvable $\mathcal{T}$-unification problem a strong Herbrand theorem may be proved for fair derivations. The following version of Herbrand's theorem applies to the discussed example 1.

Theorem 3. *(Strong Herbrand theorem) Let $\mathcal{T}$ be an open theory, $\mathcal{Q}$ a query language, $\mathcal{U}$ a set of $\mathcal{T}$-connections which is complete w.r.t. to $\mathcal{Q}$. Then for every $\mathcal{T}$-unsatisfiable matrix $M \in \mathcal{Q}$ any fair derivation is successful.*

Proof. Let n_0 be the least number such that there exist an amplification M' of matrix M consisting of n_0 copies of M, a minimal $\mathcal{U}$-mating U which is spanning in M' and a substitution σ such that $\sigma(u)$ is minimally $\mathcal{T}$-complementary for each $u \in U$.

Now, let D be a fair derivation $\{M_i\}_{i \in \mathcal{N}}$ starting from M. We assume, contrary to the hypothesis, that D is not successful. Since D is fair, the variant rule must be applied infinitely often. Therefore exists a minimal index, say l, such that for each clause of M exist n_0 copies in M_l. There exists a minimal $\mathcal{U}$-mating U spanning the amplification of M which is subset of M_l and having a simultaneous $\mathcal{T}$-unifier σ.

Let $u_1, \ldots, u_i, \ldots, u_m$ be any enumeration of the elements of U. We construct sequences $\{\tau_j\}_{j=0}^{m}$ of substitutions, $\{N_j\}_{j=0}^{m}$ of matrices, $\{U_j\}_{j=0}^{m}$ of matings and $\{i_j\}_{j=0}^{m}$ of indeces such that $\bigcup_{j=0}^{m} N_j \subseteq M_{i_j}$ and for each index j, $j \le m$, U_j is a mating in N_j and τ_j is a simultaneous $\mathcal{T}$-unifier of U_j.

Initialization: $U_0 = U$, $N_0 = M_l$, $\tau_0 = \sigma$ and $i_0 = l$
For $j = 0$ To $m - 1$ Repeat:

   Invariant:

      $\bigcup_{j'=0}^{j} N_{j'} \subseteq M_{i_j}$
      τ_j is simultaneous $\mathcal{T}$-unifier of U_j.
      Every path through $\bigcup_{i \in \mathcal{N}} M_i$ which is spanned by some of the elements of $U \setminus U_j$ is also spanned by some $\mathcal{T}$-unsatisfiable $\mathcal{T}$-connection in $\bigcup_{i \in \mathcal{N}} M_i$.

   If $U_j = \emptyset$ then let $\tau_{j+1} = \tau_j$, $U_{j+1} = U_j$, $N_{j+1} = N_j$ and $i_{j+1} = i_j$.
   Otherwise choose some $u \in U_j$.
   Case distinction:

(1) u is $\mathcal{T}$-unsatisfiable in N_j: Let $\tau_{j+1} = \tau_j$, $U_{j+1} = U_j \setminus \{u\}$, $N_{j+1} = N_j$ and $i_{j+1} = i_j$.

(2) u is not $\mathcal{T}$-unsatisfiable in N_j and for some $\mathcal{T}$-unifier $\tau_j' \in S_u$ the $\mathcal{T}$-connection u is not progressive with τ_j':

Choose (according to item (1) of definition 4) some non-progressive $\mathcal{T}$-unifier τ_j' of u and let τ_j'' be the substitution such that $\tau_j(u) = \tau_j''(\tau_j'(u))$. Then $\tau_j'(N_j) \subseteq N_j$.

Let $\tau_{j+1} = \tau_j''$, $U_{j+1} = \tau_j'(U_j \setminus \{u\})$, $N_{j+1} = N_j$ and $i_{j+1} = i_j$.

(3) u is not $\mathcal{T}$-unsatisfiable in N_j and for every $\mathcal{T}$-unifier $\tau_j' \in S_u$ the $\mathcal{T}$-connection u is progressive with τ_j'.

Then one of the following sub-cases holds according to the fairness definition 11:

a) Suppose that for none of the $\mathcal{T}$-unifiers $\tau_j' \in S_u$ condition (2b) of the fairness definition 11 is satisfied.

Let $\tau_{j+1} = \tau_j''$, $U_{j+1} = \tau_j'(U_j \setminus \{u\})$, $N_{j+1} = N_j \cup \tau_j'(N_j)$ and i_{j+1} is the minimal index j' such that $N_{j+1} \subseteq M_{j'}$.

b) Contrary to the previous sub-case suppose that for some $\mathcal{T}$-unifier $\tau_j' \in S_u$ condition (2b) of the fairness definition 11 is satisfied.

Let $\tau_{j+1} = \tau_j''$, $U_{j+1} = \tau_j'(U_j \setminus \{u\})$, $N_{j+1} = N_j$ and $i_{j+1} = i_j$.

According to the referred assumptions the previous construction will be successful. In its final state the following is true:

Every path through $\bigcup_{i \in \mathcal{N}} M_i$ which is spanned by some of the elements of U is also spanned by some $\mathcal{T}$-unsatisfiable $\mathcal{T}$-connection in $\bigcup_{i \in \mathcal{N}} M_i$.

On the other hand side we can show that for every infinite fair derivation exists a path through $\bigcup_{i \in \mathcal{N}} M_i$ which is not spanned by any $\mathcal{T}$-unsatisfiable $\mathcal{T}$-connection. This contradiction to the previous claim would close the proof.

Indeed, we can construct an infinite tree with finite degree as follows. The nodes of the tree are paths through M_i for some $i \in \mathcal{N}$ which are not spanned by any $\mathcal{T}$-connection. For each $i \in \mathcal{N}$ any path through M_{i+1} is successor of its proper sub-path being a path through M_i. The tree is infinite since the considered derivation is infinite. By König's lemma there exists an infinite path in the constructed tree. The union of its elements is an infinite path through $\bigcup_{i \in \mathcal{N}} M_i$ which is not spanned by any $\mathcal{T}$-unsatisfiable $\mathcal{T}$-connection.

6   Refinements

In the present section we discuss certain refinements of the result derived above. Details of the proofs for the outlined results remain to be worked out.

Pool calculus. The confluent theory connection calculus has been presented in a very abstract form. In particular the question how to represent open paths has not been answered. It seems that the pool calculus (see [15] for the basic form and [18] for its theory version) might be suitable for this purpose. Having this conjecture in mind we did not require to remove all paths which are spanned by a found theory connection from the set of open paths in definition 7. Probably it will be easier to represent a superset of the set of open paths and to ensure that every connection step closes some of the represented paths.

Non-normal forms. There are (at least) two ways for considering non-normal form formulas. One way is to apply structure preserving normal form transformations. Since this causes the introduction of new predicate symbols hybrid theories [19] have to be considered.

The other way is to generalize the theory pool calculus towards reasoning with non-normal form matrices. We conjecture that the fairness condition from definition 11 implies a fairness definition formulated in section 4 in [17]. This would allow us to use the completeness theorem 6.1 proved in [17] in order to prove the completeness of a confluent non-normal form theory connection calculus.

Partial theory reasoning. For certain theories $\mathcal{T}$ it is unpossible to estimate the number of elements of a theory connection. In those cases it is more suitable to approximate theory connections by several so called partial theory reasoning inferences [20] than to guess a whole theory connection at once. Each of those partial theory inferences finds some further literals of a connection and some approximation of the $\mathcal{T}$-unifier and return a remainder, the so called residue [20]. This reasoning scheme has been described for the pool calculus in [14]. Along this line a confluent partial theory connection calculus might be developed.

7   Conclusion

We introduced a confluent theory connection calculus. We formulated sufficient restrictions concerning the character of the theory unification problem of theory connections. The restrictions seem to be rather mild so that a large class of theories is covered by the formulated result. The proof technique used in the completeness proof exhibits the relevant properties of the theory: the form of theory connections and the character of the theory unification problem.

Acknowledgments. First of all many thanks to Harry de Swart for inviting the author to the Symposium on Automated Deduction in Eindhoven in December 2001, where a first idea of this work has been presented. Moreover, the author wishes to thank the referees for their constructive remarks.

References

1. Andrews, P.: Theorem Proving via General Matings. J.ACM **28** (1981) 193–214
2. Baader, F., Schulz, K.U.: Unification theory. In Bibel, W., Schmitt, P.H., eds.: Automated Deduction. A Basis for Applications. Volume I. Kluwer Academic Publishers Group, Dordrecht, The Netherlands (1998) 225–263
3. Bachmair, L., Ganzinger, H., Voronkov, A.: Elimination of equality via transformations with ordering constraints. In Kirchner, C., Kirchner, H., eds.: Proceedings, 15th International Conference on Automated Deduction (CADE), Lindau, Germany. Volume 1421 of Lecture Notes in Computer Science., Springer (1998) 175–190

4. Baumgartner, P., Petermann, U.: Theory Reasoning. In Bibel, W., Schmitt, P.H., eds.: Automated Deduction. A Basis for Applications. Volume I. Kluwer Academic Publishers Group, Dordrecht, The Netherlands (1998) 191–224

5. Baumgartner, P., Eisinger, N., Furbach, U.: A confluent connection calculus. In Hölldobler, S., ed.: Intellectics and Computational Logic – Papers in Honor of Wolfgang Bibel. Kluwer (1999)

6. Bibel, W.: Matings in matrices. In Siekmann, J., ed.: German Workshop on Artificial Intelligence, Berlin, Springer (1981) 171–187

7. Bibel, W.: Automated Theorem Proving. Vieweg Verlag, Braunschweig (1982)

8. Bürckert, H.J.: A resolution principle for constrained logics. Artificial Intelligence **66** (1994) 235–271

9. Debart, F., Enjalbert, P.: A case of termination for associative unification. In H.Abdulrab, J.P., ed.: Words Equations and related Topics: Second International Workshop IWWERT '91, Berlin, Springer-Verlag (1992)

10. Frisch, A.M., Scherl, R.B.: A general framework for modal deduction. In Allen, J., Fikes, R., Sandewall, E., eds.: Proceedings of the 2nd International Conference on Principles of Knowledge Representation and Reasoning, San Mateo, Morgan Kaufmann (1991) 196–207

11. Loveland, D.W.: Automated Theorem Proving: a Logical Basis. 1 edn. North-Holland, Amsterdam (1978)

12. Miller, D.A.: Proofs in Higher-Order Logic. PhD thesis, Carnegie Mellon University, Pittsburg Pa. (1983)

13. Murray, N., Rosenthal, E.: Theory Links: Applications to Automated Theorem Proving. J. of Symbolic Computation (1987) 173–190

14. Neugebauer, G., Petermann, U.: Specifications of inference rules and their automatic translation. In: Workshop on Theorem Proving with Analytic Tableaux and Related Methods. Lecture Notes in Computer Science (1995)

15. Neugebauer, G., Schaub, T.: A pool-based connection calculus. In Bozşahin, C., Halıcı, U., Oflazar, K., Yalabık, N., eds.: Proceedings of Third Turkish Symposium on Artificial Intelligence and Neural Networks, Middle East Technical University Press (1994) 297–306

16. Ohlbach, H.J., Schmidt, R.A.: Functional translation and second-order frame properties of modal logics. Journal of Logic and Computation **7** (1997) 581–603

17. Petermann, U.: How to Build-in an Open Theory into Connection Calculi. Journal on Computer and Artificial Intelligence **11** (1992) 105–142

18. Petermann, U.: Completeness of the pool calculus with an open built in theory. In Gottlob, G., Leitsch, A., Mundici, D., eds.: 3rd Kurt Gödel Colloquium '93. Volume 713 of Lecture Notes in Computer Science., Berlin, Springer-Verlag (1993)

19. Petermann, U.: Combining Semantical and Syntactical Theory Reasoning. In Gabbay, D.M., de Rijke, M., eds.: Frontiers of Combining Systems 2, FroCoS'98, Research Studies Press Limited (1999)

20. Stickel, M.E.: Automated deduction by theory resolution. Journal of Automated Reasoning **4** (1985) 333–356

On Uniform Word Problems Involving Bridging Operators on Distributive Lattices

Viorica Sofronie-Stokkermans

Max-Planck-Institut für Informatik, Stuhlsatzenhausweg 85, Saarbrücken, Germany
sofronie@mpi-sb.mpg.de

Abstract. In this paper we analyze some fragments of the universal theory of distributive lattices with many sorted bridging operators. Our interest in such algebras is motivated by the fact that, in description logics, numerical features are often expressed by using maps that associate numerical values to sets (more generally, to lattice elements). We first establish a link between satisfiability of universal sentences with respect to algebraic models and satisfiability with respect to certain classes of relational structures. We use these results for giving a method for translation to clause form of universal sentences, and provide some decidability results based on the use of resolution or hyperresolution. Links between hyperresolution and tableau methods are also discussed, and a tableau procedure for checking satisfiability of formulae of type $t_1 \leq t_2$ is obtained by using a hyperresolution calculus.

1   Introduction

In description logics, numerical information is often associated to concepts. This is achieved, for instance, by using so-called "bridging functions" (terminology introduced in [Ohl01] in the context of set-description languages). An example of a bridging function on a lattice $(L, \cup, \cap, \emptyset, L)$ of sets, where $L \subseteq \mathcal{P}(X)$, is maxcost : $L \rightarrow [0, n]$ defined, for every $A \in L$, by maxcost$(A) = \max\{\mathsf{cost}(a) \mid a \in A\}$, where cost : $X \rightarrow [0, n]$ is a given map. Then, maxcost$(\emptyset) = 0$ and, for all $A, B \in L$ maxcost$(A \cup B) = \max(\mathsf{maxcost}(A), \mathsf{maxcost}(B))$, i.e. maxcost preserves all finite joins (i.e. it is a *join hemimorphism*). Note that maxcost does not preserve all meets: in general maxcost$(A \cap B) \neq \min(\mathsf{maxcost}(A), \mathsf{maxcost}(B))$.

Bridging functions such as maxcost are special instances of the more general concept of many sorted join hemimorphisms, which can be analyzed in a general algebraic framework. This kind of operators encompass very general types of bridging functions, not necessarily with numerical values.

The main contributions of this paper are the following:

- We formally define a class of many sorted bridging functions between bounded distributive lattices, which we call *many sorted join hemimorphisms*.
- We show that the Priestley representation theorem can be extended in a natural way to encompass such operators.

U. Egly and C.G. Fermüller (Eds.): TABLEAUX 2002, LNAI 2381, pp. 235–250, 2002.

- We show that the results in [SS01] can be adapted also to this more general type of operators:
  - we define a structure-preserving translation to clause form for uniform word problems for such classes of lattices with operators, and
  - obtain resolution-based decision procedures for several classes of algebras of this type.
- We also analyze refinements of resolution such as hyperresolution and its relationship with the definition of tableau calculi (cf. also [HS00]).

In what follows we briefly explain the links between the results presented here and previous work. In [SS99] we gave a method for automated theorem proving in the universal theory of varieties of distributive lattices with operators that were either hemimorphisms or antimorphisms in every argument (hence, generalizations of the modal operators ◇ and □). In [SS01], the arguments were extended to operators that are hemimorphisms in some arguments and antimorphisms in other arguments. This allowed us to deal in a simple and uniform way with various classes of operators, including both generalizations of modal operators □ and ◇, but also those obtained by considering e.g. weakened implications, which satisfy identities such as:

$$0 \to z = 1 \ (x \vee y) \to z = (x \to z) \wedge (y \to z), \tag{1}$$
$$x \to 1 = 1, \ x \to (y \wedge z) = (x \to y) \wedge (x \to z). \tag{2}$$

This allowed us to obtain resolution-based decision procedures for classes of distributive lattices with operators that satisfy *generalized residuation conditions*. The main idea was to think of an operator that is a hemimorphism in some arguments and antimorphism in other arguments as a map of type $\varepsilon_1 \ldots \varepsilon_n \to \varepsilon$, where $\varepsilon_1, \ldots, \varepsilon_n, \varepsilon \in \{-1, +1\}$, such that $f : L^{\varepsilon_1} \times \cdots \times L^{\varepsilon_n} \to L^{\varepsilon}$ is a join hemimorphism, where $L^1 = L$ and $L^{-1} = L^d$, the order-dual of L.

In the present paper we show that the results in [SS99,SS01] can be generalized in a very natural way to many sorted algebras $(\{L_s\}_{s \in S}, \{\sigma_L\}_{\sigma \in \Sigma})$ where, for each sort $s \in S$ L_s is a bounded distributive lattice, endowed with operators which are many sorted join hemimorphisms $f : L_{s_1} \times \cdots \times L_{s_n} \to L_s$. Some "bridging functions" ([Ohl01]), such as maxcost : $L \to [0, n]$, are many sorted join hemimorphisms; others, such as e.g. mincost are join hemimorphisms from L into the order-dual, $[0, n]^d$, of $[0, n]$.

1.1   Idea

We illustrate the idea of the algorithm we propose on a simple example. Consider the formula ϕ below:

$$(\forall a, b : \mathsf{lat})(\forall c, d : \mathsf{num}) \ (\mathsf{maxcost}(a) = c \wedge \mathsf{maxcost}(b) = d \to \mathsf{maxcost}(a \wedge b) \leq c \wedge d)$$

where the variables a and b are of sort lat (range over elements in lattices), the variables c and d are of sort num (range over elements in a numeric domain), and maxcost is a unary function symbol of type lat → num.

Let $D_{01}O^n$, where n is an arbitrary but fixed natural number, be the class of all algebras with two sorts $S = \{\mathsf{lat}, \mathsf{num}\}$, of the form $(\mathbf{L}, \mathbf{C_n}, \mathsf{maxcost})$, with the property that $\mathbf{L} = (L, \wedge, \vee, 0, 1)$ is a bounded distributive lattice, $\mathbf{C_n}$ is the n-element chain with elements $\{1, \ldots, n\}$, and $\mathsf{maxcost} : \mathbf{L} \to \mathbf{C_n}$ is a join hemimorphism.

One possibility for proving that ϕ holds in $D_{01}O^n$ is to show that ϕ is a consequence of the bounded distributive lattice axioms to which a description of the lattice $\{1, \ldots, n\}$ is added. However, complications may already arise for one-sorted formulae: as shown in [SS99,SS01], there exist formulae for which even powerful theorem provers such as SPASS or WALDMEISTER could not find reasonably short proofs by using equational resoning in distributive lattices.

Instead, we use the fact that every bounded distributive lattice L is isomorphic to a sublattice of the lattice of all upwards-closed subsets of a preordered set X_L (suprema are unions and infima intersections). In particular, the linearly ordered finite lattice $\{0, \ldots, n\}$ is isomorphic to the lattice of all order-filters of $D(n) = (\{\uparrow i \mid 1 \leq i \leq n\}, \subseteq)$, where $\uparrow i = \{j \mid i \leq j \leq n\}$.

As a consequence, $\mathsf{D_{01}O}^n \models \phi$ iff for every preordered set $(X, \leq)$, ϕ holds for every assignment that replaces its variables of sort lat with upwards-closed subsets of $(X, \leq)$ and those of sort num with upwards-closed subsets of $(D(n), \subseteq)$, if $\vee$ is interpreted as union and $\wedge$ as intersection, and an increasing relation $R_{\mathsf{maxcost}} \subseteq X \times D(n)$ is associated with the map $\mathsf{maxcost}$. We will show that ϕ is true in all algebras in $D_{01}O^n$ if and only if the following family of set constraints is unsatisfiable:

$$
\left\{
\begin{array}{lll}
(\mathsf{Dom_s}) & (X, \leq) \text{ preordered set} & \\
 & (D(n), \leq) \text{ is a preordered set with } n \text{ elements, } \uparrow n \leq \cdots \leq \uparrow 1 & \\
 & (\forall x : \mathsf{lat})(\forall x_i, x_j : \mathsf{num})(x_i \leq x_j \wedge R_{\mathsf{maxcost}}(x, x_i) \to R_{\mathsf{maxcost}}(x, x_j)) & \\
 & & \\
(\mathsf{Her_s}) & x_1 \in I_e, x_1 \leq x_2 \to x_2 \in I_e & \text{for all } e \in ST(\phi) \\
 & & \text{of sort } \mathsf{lat} \text{ or } \mathsf{num} \\
(\mathsf{Ren_s}) & (\wedge) I_{a \wedge b} = I_a \cap I_b \qquad I_{c \wedge d} = I_c \cap I_d & \\
 & (\mathsf{m}) I_{\mathsf{maxcost}(e)} = \{\uparrow i \mid \exists x_1 \in I_e : R_{\mathsf{maxcost}}(x_1, \uparrow i)\} & \text{for } e \in \{a, b, a \wedge b\} \\
 & & \\
(\mathsf{P_s}) & I_{\mathsf{maxcost}(a)} = I_c & \\
 & I_{\mathsf{maxcost}(b)} = I_d & \\
(\mathsf{N_s}) & I_{\mathsf{maxcost}(a \wedge b)} \not\subseteq I_{c \wedge d} & \\
\end{array}
\right.
$$

where $ST(\phi)$ is the set of all subterms occurring in ϕ. We encode every set I_e, $e \in ST(\phi)$, by a unary predicate P_e. We obtain again a many-sorted structure with sorts lat and num, where for every $e \in ST(\phi)$, the predicate P_e accepts arguments of the same sort as the expression e.

With this encoding we can reduce the problem of testing the satisfiability of the family of set constraints above to the problem of testing the satisfiability of the following conjunction in first-order logic:

$$
\left\{
\begin{array}{lll}
\text{(Dom)} & & \\
\quad \forall x : \mathsf{s} & x \leq x & \mathsf{s} \in \{\mathsf{lat}, \mathsf{num}\} \\
\quad \forall x, y, z : \mathsf{s} & x \leq y, y \leq z \rightarrow x \leq z & \\
& \uparrow n \leq \cdots \leq \uparrow 1 & \\
\quad \forall x : \mathsf{num}, \forall x_i, x_j : \mathsf{num} & x_i \leq x_j, R_{\mathsf{maxcost}}(x, x_i) \rightarrow R_{\mathsf{maxcost}}(x, x_j) & \\
\text{(Her)} & & \\
\quad \forall x, y : \mathsf{s} & x \leq y, P_e(x) \rightarrow P_e(y) & e \in ST(\phi) \text{ of sort } \mathsf{s} \\
\text{(Ren)} & & \\
\quad (\wedge)\forall x : \mathsf{s} & P_{e_1 \wedge e_2}(x) \leftrightarrow P_{e_1}(x) \wedge P_{e_2}(x) & e_1 \wedge e_2 \in ST(\phi) \text{ of sort } \mathsf{s} \\
\quad (\vee)\forall x : \mathsf{s} & P_{e_1 \vee e_2}(x) \leftrightarrow P_{e_1}(x) \vee P_{e_2}(x) & e_1 \vee e_2 \in ST(\phi) \text{ of sort } \mathsf{s} \\
\quad (\mathsf{m})\forall x_i : \mathsf{num} & P_{\mathsf{maxcost}(e)}(x_i) \leftrightarrow (\exists x : \mathsf{lat})(P_e(x) \wedge R_{\mathsf{maxcost}}(x, x_i)) & \\
& & \mathsf{maxcost}(e) \in ST(\phi) \\
\text{(P)} & & \\
\quad \forall x : \mathsf{num} & P_{\mathsf{maxcost}(a)}(x) \leftrightarrow P_c(x) & \\
\quad \forall x : \mathsf{num} & P_{\mathsf{maxcost}(b)}(x) \leftrightarrow P_d(x) & \\
\text{(N)} & & \\
\quad \exists y : \mathsf{num} & P_{\mathsf{maxcost}(a \wedge b)}(y) \wedge \neg P_{c \wedge d}(y). & \\
\end{array}
\right.
$$

We obtain a structure-preserving translation to first-order logic, and, ultimately, to clause form. The satisfiability of the set of clauses obtained this way can be checked for instance by ordered resolution with selection.

In this paper we show that similar ideas can be used for many classes of many sorted bounded distributive lattices with so-called bridging functions. Moreover, we show that refinements of resolution can successfully be used to obtain decision procedures for the universal Horn theories of many such classes, and show how hyperresolution can be used to define a set of sound and complete tableau rules for deciding validity of problems of the type $s \leq t$.

2   Representation of Distributive Lattices with Operators

This section discusses an extension of representation theorems for distributive lattices with bridging operators.

2.1   Distributive Lattices with Bridging Operators

A structure $(L, \vee, \wedge)$, consisting of a non-empty set L together with two binary operations $\vee$ (join) and $\wedge$ (meet) on L, is called *lattice* if $\vee$ and $\wedge$ are associative, commutative and idempotent and satisfy the absorption laws. A *distributive lattice* is a lattice that satisfies either of the distributive laws $(D_\wedge)$ or $(D_\vee)$, which are equivalent in a lattice.

$$(D_\wedge) \quad x \wedge (y \vee z) = (x \wedge y) \vee (x \wedge z) \qquad (D_\vee) \quad x \vee (y \wedge z) = (x \vee y) \wedge (x \vee z).$$

A lattice $(L, \vee, \wedge)$ has a *first element* if there is an element $0 \in L$ such that $0 \wedge x = 0$ for every $x \in L$; it has a *last element* if there is an element $1 \in L$ such that $1 \wedge x = x$ for every $x \in L$. A lattice having both a first and a last element is called *bounded*. If $\mathbf{L} = (L, \vee, \wedge, 0, 1)$ is a bounded lattice we denote by $\mathbf{L}^d$ the order-dual of $\mathbf{L}$, i.e. the lattice $(L, \vee^d, \wedge^d, 0^d, 1^d)$, where for every $x, y \in L$, $x \vee^d y = x \wedge y$, $x \wedge^d y = x \vee y$; $0^d = 1$; and $1^d = 0$. A filter in a lattice $(L, \vee, \wedge)$

is a non-empty order-filter closed under meets. A filter F is said to be *prime* if $F \neq L$ and for every $x, y \in L$, if $x \vee y \in F$ then $x \in F$ or $y \in F$. In what follows the set of prime filters will be denoted by $\mathcal{F}_p(L)$.

Definition 1. *Let $\{\mathbf{L}_s\}_{s \in S}$ be a family of bounded lattices $\mathbf{L}_s = (L_s, \vee, \wedge, 0, 1)$ and let $s_1, \ldots, s_n, s \in S$. A join hemimorphism of type $s_1 \ldots s_n \to s$ is a function $f : L_{s_1} \times \cdots \times L_{s_n} \to L_s$ such that for every $i, 1 \leq i \leq n$,*

(1) $f(a_1, \ldots, a_{i-1}, 0, a_{i+1}, \ldots, a_n) = 0$,
(2) $f(a_1, \ldots, a_{i-1}, b_1 \vee b_2, a_{i+1}, \ldots, a_n) =$
$\quad = f(a_1, \ldots, a_{i-1}, b_1, a_{i+1}, \ldots, a_n) \vee f(a_1, \ldots, a_{i-1}, b_2, a_{i+1}, \ldots, a_n).$

Example 1.

1. The modal operator $\diamond$ on a Boolean algebra $\mathbf{B}$ is a join hemimorphism. The modal operator $\square$ on $\mathbf{B}$ is a meet hemimorphism, i.e. a join hemimorphism on the dual $\mathbf{B}^d$ of $\mathbf{B}$. If we consider 2-sorted algebras $(\mathbf{B}, \mathbf{B}^d)$ with sorts $S = \{\text{bool}, \text{bool}_d\}$, $\diamond$ is a join hemimorphism of type $\text{bool} \to \text{bool}$ and $\square$ is of type $\text{bool}_d \to \text{bool}_d$.
2. Let $\mathbf{L}$ be a lattice, and $(\mathbf{L}, \mathbf{L}^d)$ the 2-sorted algebra with sorts $S = \{\text{lat}, \text{lat}_d\}$. The operation $\to$ satisfying the conditions (1) and (2) on page 236 is a join hemimorphism of type $\text{lat}, \text{lat}_d \to \text{lat}_d$.
3. Let $(\mathbf{L}, \mathbf{C}_{n+1})$ be the 2-sorted algebra with sorts $S = \{\text{lat}, \text{num}\}$, where L is a bounded lattice, and $C_{n+1} = (\{0, 1, \ldots, n\}, \vee, \wedge, 0, n)$ is the $n+1$-element chain. A function $f : \mathbf{L} \to \mathbf{C}_{n+1}$ that associates with every element of L an element of $\{0, 1, \ldots, n\}$ such that $f(x \vee y) = f(x) \vee f(y)$ and $f(0) = 0$ is a join hemimorphism of type $\text{lat} \to \text{num}$.

2.2   Representation Theorems

We now present a simplified version of Priestley's representation theorem stating that every bounded distributive lattice is isomorphic to a lattice of sets.

Theorem 1 ([Pri70]). *Let $\mathbf{L}$ be a distributive lattice, let $D(\mathbf{L}) = (\mathcal{F}_p(\mathbf{L}), \subseteq)$ be the partially-ordered set having as points the prime filters of $\mathbf{L}$, ordered by inclusion, and let $\mathcal{H}(D(\mathbf{L}))$ be the lattice of all upwards-closed subsets of $D(\mathbf{L})$. Then the map $\eta_L : L \to \mathcal{H}(D(\mathbf{L}))$, defined for every $x \in L$ by $\eta_L(x) = \{F \in \mathcal{F}_p(\mathbf{L}) \mid x \in F\}$ is an injective lattice homomorphism.*

In what follows we will refer to the space $D(\mathbf{L})$ as the dual of $\mathbf{L}$.

It was shown that operators on a bounded distributive lattice induce in a canonical way maps resp. relations on $D(\mathbf{L})$ [JT52,Gol89,SS00,SS01]. We now show that these canonical definitions can be formulated in a very general way, which enables us to extend them to many sorted join hemimorphisms. If $f : \mathbf{L}_{s_1} \times \cdots \times \mathbf{L}_{s_n} \to \mathbf{L}_s$ is a join hemimorphism, then a relation $R_f \subseteq D(\mathbf{L}_{s_1}) \times \cdots \times D(\mathbf{L}_{s_n}) \times D(\mathbf{L}_s)$ can be defined by:

$$R_f(F_1, \ldots, F_n, F) \text{ iff } f(F_1, \ldots, F_n) \subseteq F.$$

Proposition 1. *Let* $\{\mathbf{L}_s\}_{s \in S}$ *be a family of bounded distributive lattices. Let* $f : \mathbf{L}_{s_1} \times \cdots \times \mathbf{L}_{s_n} \to \mathbf{L}_s$ *be a join hemimorphism of type* $s_1 \ldots s_n \to s$. *Then* R_f *is an increasing relation*[1].

Proposition 1 justifies the definition of S-sorted RT Σ-relational structures.

Definition 2. *An S-sorted RT Σ-relational structure $(\{(X_s, \leq)\}_{s \in S}, \{R_X\}_{R \in \Sigma})$ is an S-sorted family of sets, each endowed with a reflexive and transitive relation $\leq$ and with additional maps and relations indexed by Σ, where, if $R \in \Sigma$ is of type $s_1 \ldots s_n \to s$, $R_X \subseteq X_{s_1} \times \cdots \times X_{s_n} \times X_s$ is increasing.*

For every S-sorted RT Σ-relational structure $\mathbf{X} = (\{(X_s, \leq)\}_{s \in S}, \{R_X\}_{R \in \Sigma})$, we denote by $\mathcal{H}(\mathbf{X})$ the many sorted algebra $(\{(\mathcal{H}(X_s), \cup, \cap, \emptyset, X_s)\}_{s \in S}, \{f_R\}_{R \in \Sigma})$, where, for every $s \in S$, $(\mathcal{H}(X_s), \cup, \cap, \emptyset, X_s)$ is the bounded distributive lattice of all hereditary (i.e. upwards-closed with respect to $\leq$) subsets of X_s, and the operators $\{f_R\}_{R \in \Sigma}$ are defined as follows.

If $R \subseteq X_{s_1} \times \cdots \times X_{s_n} \times X_s$ is an increasing relation then $f_R : \mathcal{H}(X_{s_1}) \times \cdots \times \mathcal{H}(X_{s_n}) \to \mathcal{H}(X_s)$ is defined, for every $(U_1, \ldots U_n) \in \mathcal{H}(X_{s_1}) \times \cdots \times \mathcal{H}(X_{s_n})$ by

$$f_R(U_1, \ldots, U_n) = R^{-1}(U_1, \ldots, U_n),$$

where $R^{-1}(U_1, \ldots, U_n) = \{x \mid \exists x_1 \ldots x_n (x_1 \in U_1, \ldots, x_n \in U_n, R(x_1, \ldots, x_n, x))\}$.

Proposition 2. *Let X be an S-sorted RT Σ-relational structure. If $R \in \Sigma$ is of type $s_1 \ldots s_n \to s$ then $f_R : \prod_{i=1}^{n} \mathcal{H}(X_{s_i}) \to \mathcal{H}(X_s)$ is a join hemimorphism.*

We will denote the class of all S-sorted distributive lattices with operators in Σ by DLO_Σ^S. The class of S-sorted RT Σ-relational structures will be denoted by RT_Σ^S. In the one-sorted case the index S will usually be omitted. The following result extends the representation theorems in [Gol89,SS00,SS02] to the more general classes of operators we consider here.

Theorem 2. *For every $\mathbf{A} = (\{\mathbf{L}_s\}_{s \in S}, \{f_A\}_{f \in \Sigma}) \in \mathsf{DLO}_\Sigma^S$, $D(\mathbf{A}) \in RT_\Sigma^S$, and $\eta_A : A \to \mathcal{H}(D(A))$ defined for every $s \in S$ and every $x \in L_s$ by $\eta_A^s(x) = \{F \in \mathcal{F}_p(\mathbf{L}_s) \mid x \in F\}$ is an injective homomorphism between algebras in DLO_Σ^S.*

Proof: Similar to the proof of Theorem 14 in [SS02]. ☐

3   The Universal Theory of DLO_Σ^S and Subclasses Thereof

In this section we show that the representation theorems discussed before allow, under certain conditions, to avoid the explicit use of the full algebraic structure of distributive lattices with S-sorted bridging operators and use, instead, lattices of sets over structures in RT_Σ^S. This justifies a structure-preserving translation to clause form. The proofs, which we do not provide here, are easy generalizations of those in [SS01,SS02].

---

[1] A relation $R \subseteq X_1 \times \cdots \times X_n \times X$ is increasing if for every $\overline{x} \in X_1 \times \cdots \times X_n$, and every $y, y' \in X$ (if $R(\overline{x}, y)$ and $y \leq y'$ then $R(\overline{x}, y')$).

3.1   Generalities

Let $\mathcal{V}$ be a class of (many sorted) algebras. The *universal theory* of $\mathcal{V}$ is the collection of those closed formulae valid in $\mathcal{V}$ which are of the form

$$\forall x_1 \ldots \forall x_k \left(\bigwedge_{i=1}^{m} ((\neg)t_{i1} = s_{i1} \vee \cdots \vee (\neg)t_{in_i} = s_{in_i}) \right). \tag{3}$$

Since a conjunction is valid iff all its conjuncts are valid, we can restrict, without loss of generality, to formulae of the type $(\bigwedge_{i=1}^{n} s_{i1} = s_{i2} \rightarrow \bigvee_{j=1}^{m} t_{j1} = t_{j2})$.

The *universal Horn theory* of $\mathcal{V}$ is the collection of those closed formulae valid in $\mathcal{V}$ which are of the form $\forall x_1 \ldots \forall x_n (\bigwedge_{i=1}^{n} s_{i1} = s_{i2} \rightarrow t_{j1} = t_{j2})$.

If $\mathcal{V}$ is a class of algebras which is closed under direct products then, by a result of McKinsey, the decidability of the universal Horn theory of $\mathcal{V}$ implies the decidability of the universal theory of $\mathcal{V}$.

3.2   A Link between Algebraic and Relational Models

We establish a link between truth of universal sentences in classes of distributive lattices with operators and truth in classes of S-sorted RT Σ-relational structures. We consider subclasses $\mathcal{V}$ of DLO_Σ^S that satisfy the following condition:

(K)   There exists a $\mathcal{K} \subseteq RT_\Sigma^S$ such that (i) for every $\mathbf{A} \in \mathcal{V}$, $D(\mathbf{A}) \in \mathcal{K}$;
       (ii) for every $\mathbf{X} \in \mathcal{K}$, $\mathcal{H}(\mathbf{X}) \in \mathcal{V}$.

Proposition 3 ([SS01]). *Assume that $\mathcal{V}$ satisfies condition (K). Then for every* $\phi = \forall x_1, \ldots, x_k (\bigwedge_{i=1}^{n} s_{i1} = s_{i2} \rightarrow \bigvee_{j=1}^{m} t_{j1} = t_{j2})$,

$$\mathcal{V} \models \phi \text{ if and only if for every } \mathbf{X} \in \mathcal{K}, \mathcal{H}(\mathbf{X}) \models \phi.$$

For automated theorem proving it is important to find subclasses of RT_Σ^S with good theoretical and logic properties, for instance subclasses which are *first-order definable*. Although this is not always possible, such classes can often be obtained by abstracting properties of the Priestley duals of algebras in $\mathcal{V}$.

Lemma 1. *Condition (K) holds in the following cases:*

1. $\mathcal{V} = \mathsf{DLO}_\Sigma^S = \{((\{\mathbf{L}_s\}_{s \in S}, \{f\}_{f \in \Sigma}) \mid \mathbf{L}_s \in \mathsf{D}_{01} \text{ for all } s \in S; f : \prod_{i=1}^{n} \mathbf{L}_{s_i} \rightarrow \mathbf{L}_s \text{ join hemimorphism, for every } f \in \Sigma_{s_1 \ldots s_n \rightarrow s}\}$ and $\mathcal{K} = RT_\Sigma^S$.

2. $\mathcal{V} = \mathsf{BAO}_\Sigma^S = \{(\{\mathbf{B}_s\}_{s \in S}, \{f\}_{f \in \Sigma}) \mid \mathbf{B}_s \in \mathsf{Bool} \text{ for all } s \in S; f : \prod_{i=1}^{n} \mathbf{B}_{s_i} \rightarrow \mathbf{B}_s \text{ join hemimorphism, for every } f \in \Sigma_{s_1 \ldots s_n \rightarrow s}\}$ and $\mathcal{K} = R_\Sigma^S$ *the subclass of RT_Σ^S consisting only of those S-sorted spaces in which all supports are discretely ordered.*

3. *If $\mathbf{A} \in \mathsf{D}_{01}$ is an arbitrary but fixed finite lattice and $S = \{\mathsf{lat}, \mathsf{num}\}$:* $\mathcal{V} = \mathsf{DLO}_\Sigma^A = \{(\mathbf{L}, \mathbf{A}, \{f_L\}_{f \in \Sigma_L}, \{f_b\}_{f \in \Sigma_b}) \mid \mathbf{L} \in \mathsf{D}_{01}; f_L : \mathbf{L}^k \rightarrow \mathbf{L} \text{ join hemimorphism, for every } f \in \Sigma_L, \text{ of type } \mathsf{lat}^k \rightarrow \mathsf{lat}; f_b : \mathbf{L}^m \rightarrow \mathbf{A} \text{ join hemimorphism for every } f \in \Sigma_b, \text{ of type } \mathsf{lat}^m \rightarrow \mathsf{num}\}$, and $\mathcal{K} = \{(X, D(\mathbf{A}), \{R_f\}_{f \in \Sigma_L}, \{R_g\}_{g \in \Sigma_b}) \mid (X, \{R_f\}_{f \in \Sigma_L}) \in RT_{\Sigma_L} \text{ and } R_g \subseteq X^m \times D(\mathbf{A}) \text{ increasing for all } g \in \Sigma_b \text{ of type } \mathsf{lat}^m \rightarrow \mathsf{num}\}$.

3.3   Structure-Preserving Translation to Clause Form

We show that, if a subclass $\mathcal{V}$ of DLO_Σ^S satisfies condition (K) for some first-order definable subclass $\mathcal{K}$ of RT_Σ^S, then the problem of checking whether a formula $\phi = \forall x_1, \ldots, x_k (\bigwedge_{i=1}^n s_{i1} = s_{i2} \rightarrow \bigvee_{j=1}^m t_{j1} = t_{j2})$ holds in $\mathcal{V}$ can be reduced to the problem of checking the satisfiability of a set of clauses.

Let $ST(\phi)$ be the set of all subterms of s_{il} and t_{jp}, $1 \leq i \leq n, 1 \leq j \leq m, l, p \in \{1, 2\}$ (including the variables and s_{il}, t_{jp} themselves).

Proposition 4. *Let $\mathcal{K} \subseteq RT_\Sigma^S$. The following are equivalent:*

(1) *For every $\mathbf{X} \in \mathcal{K}$, $\mathcal{H}(\mathbf{X}) \models \phi$.*
(2) *For every $\mathbf{X} = (\{(X_s, \leq)\}_{s \in S}, \{R\}_{R \in \Sigma}) \in RT_\Sigma^S$ and every family of subsets of X indexed by all subterms of ϕ, $\{I_e \subseteq X_s \mid e \in ST(\phi) \text{ of sort } s \in S\}$, if:*

$$
\left\{
\begin{array}{lll}
(\mathsf{Dom}_s) & \mathbf{X} \in \mathcal{K}, & \\
(\mathsf{Her}_s) & I_e \in \mathcal{H}(X_s) & \forall e \in ST(\phi) \text{ of sort } s, \\
(\mathsf{Ren}_s) & (1, 0) \quad I_{1_s} = X_s, \quad I_{0_s} = \emptyset, & \\
(\wedge) & I_{e_1 \wedge e_2} = I_{e_1} \cap I_{e_2}, & \\
(\vee) & I_{e_1 \vee e_2} = I_{e_1} \cup I_{e_2}, & \\
(\Sigma_{s_1 \ldots s_n \rightarrow s}) & I_{f(e_1, \ldots, e_n)} = R_f^{-1}(I_{e_1}, \ldots, I_{e_n}), & \\
(\mathsf{P}_s) & I_{s_{i1}} = I_{s_{i2}} & \text{for all } i = 1, \ldots, n, \\
\end{array}
\right.
$$

then

$\quad (\mathsf{C}_s) \quad$ *for some $j \in \{1, \ldots, m\}$ $I_{t_{j1}} = I_{t_{j2}}$,*

where the rules in (Σ) range over all terms in $ST(\phi)$ starting with an operator in $\Sigma_{s_1 \ldots s_n \rightarrow s}$. (We used the abbreviation $R^{-1}(U_1, \ldots, U_n) := \{x \mid \exists x_1 \in U_1 \ldots \exists x_n \in U_n : R(x_1, \ldots, x_n, x)\}$.)

If the class $\mathcal{K}$ is first-order definable, Proposition 4 justifies a structure-preserving translation of universal formulae to sets of clauses.

Proposition 5. *Let $\mathcal{K}$ be a subclass of RT_Σ^S which is definable by a finite set C of first-order sentences. Then the following are equivalent:*

(1) For every $\mathbf{X} \in \mathcal{K}$, $\mathcal{H}(\mathbf{X}) \models \phi$.
(2) The conjunction of $(\mathsf{Dom}) \cup (\mathsf{Her}) \cup (\mathsf{Ren}) \cup (\mathsf{P}) \cup (\mathsf{N}_1) \cup \cdots \cup (\mathsf{N}_m)$ is unsatisfiable, where:

(Dom) $\qquad\qquad C,$

$\qquad \leq \subseteq X_s \times X_s$ is *reflexive and transitive for every sort $s \in S$,*

$\qquad R_f \subseteq \prod_{i=1}^{n+1} X_{s_i}$ is *increasing* $\qquad$ *for every $f \in \Sigma_{s_1 \ldots s_n \rightarrow s_{n+1}}$,*

(Her) $\forall x, y \quad (x \leq y \wedge P_e(x) \rightarrow P_e(y))$

(Ren)

$\quad (1) \quad \forall x \qquad\qquad P_{1_s}(x) \qquad\qquad\qquad$ *for every sort $s \in S$,*

$\quad (0) \quad \forall x \qquad\qquad \neg P_{0_s}(x) \qquad\qquad\qquad$ *for every sort $s \in S$,*

$\quad (\wedge) \quad \forall x \qquad (P_{e_1 \wedge e_2}(x) \leftrightarrow P_{e_1}(x) \wedge P_{e_2}(x))$

$\quad (\vee) \quad \forall x \qquad (P_{e_1 \vee e_2}(x) \leftrightarrow P_{e_1}(x) \vee P_{e_2}(x))$

$\quad (\Sigma) \quad \forall x \qquad (P_{f(e_1, \ldots, e_n)}(x) \leftrightarrow \exists x_1 \ldots x_n (\bigwedge_{i=1}^n P_{e_i}(x_i) \wedge R_f(x_1, \ldots, x_n, x)))$

$(\mathsf{P}) \quad \forall x \qquad (\bigwedge_{i=1}^n P_{s_{i1}}(x) \leftrightarrow P_{s_{i2}}(x))$

$(\mathsf{N}_1) \quad \exists x_1 \qquad (P_{t_{11}}(x_1) \not\leftrightarrow P_{t_{12}}(x_1))$

$\qquad\qquad \cdots \qquad\qquad\qquad \cdots$

$(\mathsf{N}_m) \quad \exists x_m \qquad (P_{t_{m1}}(x_m) \not\leftrightarrow P_{t_{m2}}(x_m))$

where the unary predicates P_e are indexed by elements in $ST(\phi)$, and the formulae in Σ range over all operators $f \in \Sigma_{s_1 \ldots s_n \to s}$.

In addition, polarity of subformulae can be used for using only one direction of the implications in (Ren). Similar ideas can be used for obtaining translations to clause form for formulae of the form $\bigwedge_{i=1}^{n} s_{i1} \leq s_{i2} \to \bigwedge_{j=1}^{m} t_{j1} \leq t_{j2}$. Then only the direct implications are necessary in (P) and (N).

Theorem 3. *Assume that $\mathcal{V}$ and $\mathcal{K}$ satisfy condition (K), where $\mathcal{K}$ is a class of RT Σ-structures definable by a finite set C of first-order sentences. The following are equivalent:*

(1) $\mathcal{V} \models \phi$.

(2) *The conjunction of* (Dom) $\cup$ (Her) $\cup$ (Ren) $\cup$ (P) $\cup$ (N$_1$) $\cup \cdots \cup$ (N$_m$) *(as defined above) is unsatisfiable.*

Proof: Direct consequence of Propositions 3, 4 and 5. □

4   Some Decidability Results

In the following sections we present some examples in which decidability results can be obtained easily. We show that

- orderer resolution with selection decides in exponential time the universal Horn theory of DLO_Σ^S and of DLO_Σ^A, where $A \in \mathsf{D}_{01}$ is finite;
- hyperresolution is a decision procedure for deciding whether $t_1 \leq t_2$ holds in the class DLO_Σ^S and in the class DLO_Σ^A, where $A \in \mathsf{D}_{01}$ is finite;
- hyperresolution can be used to synthesize tableau calculi.

4.1   Ordered Resolution with Selection

Let $\succ$ be a total well-founded ordering on ground atoms, and let S be an arbitrary selection function that assigns with every clause a multiset of negative selected literals. Let $R_S^\succ$ be the following inference system for ground clauses, consisting of ordered resolution with selection S and ordered factoring:

Ordered resolution:
$$\frac{C \vee A \quad D \vee \neg A}{C \vee D}$$

where (i) A is strictly maximal[2] in $C \vee A$, and C contains no selected atoms; (ii) $\neg A$ is either selected by S in $D \vee \neg A$ or else $D \vee \neg A$ contains no selected literals and $\neg A$ is maximal in $D \vee \neg A$.

Ordered (positive) factoring:
$$\frac{C \vee A \vee A}{C \vee A}$$

where A is a positive atom which is maximal in C, and no atom in C is selected.

---

[2] We say that a literal L is maximal in a clause C if $L' \succ L$ for no literal L' in C; and that L is strictly maximal in C if $L' \succeq L$ for no literal $L' \neq L$ in C.

Ordered resolution with selection can be lifted to non-ground clauses by viewing non-ground expressions to represent the set of their ground instances and by employing unification to avoid the explicit enumeration of ground instances (for details cf. e.g. [BG01]).

The results of [SS01] can be easily adapted to prove the following theorem.

Theorem 4. *Ordered resolution with selection decides in time* exponential in the size of the input *if the arity of operators in Σ has an upper bound, and* exponential in the square of the size of the input *in general the universal Horn theory of (1)* DLO_Σ^S, *and (2)* DLO_Σ^A, *where A is a finite distributive lattice.*

Idea of the Proof: (1) The results of [SS01], Section 5.1 can be easily adapted to prove (1). As pointed out in [SS01], the selection strategy we adopt for this purpose shows, as a by-product, that in this case inferences with the clauses containing the $\leq$ symbol are not needed for refutational completeness.
(2) In a similar way we can show that inferences with the clauses containing the $\leq$ symbol applied to arguments of sort lat are not needed in the case of DLO_Σ^A. Since $D(A)$ is finite, the monotonicity and heredity rules for sort num, can be replaced with their instances with elements in $D(A)$. For instance the monotonicity and heredity rule can alternatively be expressed by:

$$R_f(x_1, \ldots, x_n, a) \rightarrow R_f(x_1, \ldots, x_n, b) \qquad \text{for all } a, b \in D(A), a \leq b \quad (4)$$
$$P_e(a) \rightarrow P_e(b) \qquad \text{for all } a, b \in D(A), a \leq b \quad (5)$$

We can now introduce $D(A)$ copies for every predicate symbol with last argument of sort num, e.g. by replacing, for every $a \in D(A)$, $R_f(x_1, \ldots, x_n, a)$ with $R_f^a(x_1, \ldots, x_n)$ and $P_e(a)$ with P_e^a. Arguments in [SS01], Section 5.2 can now be applied and also in this case yield the desired complexity results. $\qquad \square$

Similar arguments can be also used for (many sorted) Boolean algebras with operators, by considering, in addition, the renaming rules for Boolean negation.

4.2   Hyperresolution

Hyperresolution can be simulated by resolution with maximal selection. This means that the selection function selects all the negative literals in any non-positive clause. Let H be the calculus consisting of negative hyperresolution, (positive) factoring, splitting and tautology deletion.

Negative hyperresolution:

$$\frac{C_1 \vee A_1 \quad \ldots \quad C_n \vee A_n \qquad \neg A_1 \vee \cdots \vee \neg A_n \vee D}{C_1 \vee \cdots \vee C_n \vee D}$$

where D and $C_i \vee A_i$, $1 \leq i \leq n$ are positive clauses; and no A_i occurs in C_i.

Hyperresolution can be combined with ordering restrictions, and can be lifted to non-ground clauses by viewing non-ground expressions to represent the set of their ground instances and by employing unification to avoid the explicit enumeration of ground instances (cf. e.g. [BG01]). Ordered resolution and hyperresolution can be combined with splitting: Suppose that a set N of clauses contains a clause $C = C_1 \vee C_2$, where C_1 and C_2 are non-trivial and have no variables in common. In order to show that N is unsatisfiable, one proves that $(N \setminus \{C\}) \cup \{C_i\}$, $i = 1, 2$ are both unsatisfiable. The components in the variable partition of a clause are called split components. Two split components do not share variables. A clause that cannot be split is called *a maximally split clause*.

We now show that hyperresolution with splitting can be used for the simpler problem of checking whether $\mathsf{DLO}_\Sigma^S \models t_1 \leq t_2$ or $\mathsf{DLO}_\Sigma^A \models t_1 \leq t_2$. Though much more special than uniform word problems, problems of this type often occur in non-classical logics. For instance, in some relevant logics [AB75] or in variants of the (full) Lambek calculus [Ono93], it can be proved that a formula ϕ is a theorem iff $\mathcal{V} \models \phi \geq e$, where $\mathcal{V}$ is the class of all algebraic models of the respective logic and e is a special constant.

Theorem 5. *For all terms t_1, t_2, H decides whether $\mathsf{DLO}_\Sigma^S \models t_1 \leq t_2$.*

Proof: By Theorem 3 and Lemma 1 as well as the fact that, by the proof of Theorem 4, in this case all clauses containing the symbol $\leq$ can be ignored, $\mathsf{DLO}_\Sigma^S \models t_1 \leq t_2$ iff the clause form of (Ren) $\cup$ (N) is unsatisfiable. Since the premise of the formula ϕ is empty, there are no clauses in (P). (N) consists of the unit clauses $P_{t_1}(c)$ and $\neg P_{t_2}(c)$ for some constant c.

We show that any H-derivation terminates on the set of clauses (Ren) $\cup$ (N) associated with $\phi = (t_1 \leq t_2)$, in which all predicates P_e are fully labeled, in the sense that for every non-variable subterm $e \in ST(\phi)$, the precise occurrence π of e in t_1 or t_2 is indicated (e.g. in the form $P_e^{t_i^\pi}$).

All non-unit clauses of (Ren) contain a negative (hence selected) literal. Therefore they can only be used as negative premises of resolution steps. (Ren)(1) can only be used in inferences with the clause $\neg P_{t_2}(c)$ if $t_2 = 1$, and (Ren)(0) only in inferences with $P_{t_1}(c)$, if $t_1 = 0$; in both cases the empty clause is obtained.

Except for (Ren)(1), at the beginning there is only one candidate for a positive premise, namely the positive (ground) conjunct of (N), $P_{t_1}(c)$. It can be checked that hyperresolution inferences with such unit ground clauses will, in a first step, generate maximally split clauses of the form $P_e(s)$ or $R_f(c_1(s), \ldots, c_n(s), s)$ for some term s which contains only the constant c, and such that (i) the terms e are subterms of t_1, (ii) the Skolem functions introduced by (Ren)(Σ) that occur in s are all labeled with subterms of t_1, (iii) for every literal $P_e(s)$ obtained this way, the sum between the height of e and the height of s does not exceed the height $h(t_1)$ of t_1, and (iv) for every literal $R_f(c_1^{f(e_1, \cdots e_n)}(s), \ldots, c_n^{f(e_1, \cdots e_n)}(s), s)$ obtained this way, such that $c_1^{f(e_1, \cdots e_n)}, \ldots, c_n^{f(e_1, \cdots e_n)}$ are Skolem functions introduced by (Ren)(Σ), the sum between the height of e and the height of s is does not exceed $h(t_1) - 1$. Since the depth of the arguments can be bounded, this part of the procedure obviously terminates. Moreover, it can be seen that for each argument s generated this way, all labels of the Skolem functions occurring in s correspond to subterms occurring along one branch in the tree representation of the term t_1. This shows that the number of arguments of literals generated this way is bounded by the number of subterms of t_1. Hence, the number of positive ground atoms generated in this part of the procedure is polynomial in the size of t_1. Note that in this phase only inferences with clause forms of direct implications in Ren are possible.

After generating all unit clauses of the form $P_p(s)$, where p is a propositional variable (by the remarks above, in all such cases the height of s does not exceed $h(t_1)$), inferences with rules in (Ren) involving subformulae of t_2 are possible. Only inferences with clause forms of inverse implications in Ren lead to non-redundant clauses. A similar argument as before shows that also in this case the depth of the arguments can grow with at most $h(t_2)$. This shows that H terminates on the set of clauses associated with $\phi = t_1 \leq t_2$. □

The termination proof above shows that the number of different literals in any derivation tree is polynomial in the size of the input. The arguments in Theorem 5 can be also adapted to many sorted Boolean algebras with operators for which every term has a negation normal form (in particular, for modal algebras).

Theorem 6. *Let A be an arbitrary, but fixed, finite bounded distributive lattice. Then for all terms t_1, t_2, H decides whether $\mathsf{DLO}_\Sigma^A \models t_1 \leq t_2$.*

Idea of the proof: Without loss of generality we assume that t_1 and t_2 are formulae of sort A (otherwise, as all bridging functions are of type lat...lat → num no subterms of sort num occur in $ST(t_1 \leq t_2)$, and so Theorem 5 can be applied.). The proof proceeds along the same lines as that of Theorem 5, with the following differences. Instead of using a Skolem constant c for the negation of the premise, we test unsatisfiability of (Dom) ∪ (Her) ∪ (Ren) ∪ (N_a) for all variants of (N), (N_a) : $P_{t_1}(a) \wedge \neg P_{t_2}(a)$, where $a \in D(A)$. Heredity clauses for A and monotonicity conditions of the form (5) resp. (4) for bridging functions and predicates of sort num have to be also taken into account. The inferences of $P_{t_1}(a)$ with the heredity clauses for P_{t_1} yield all unit ground literals of the form $P_{t_1}(b)$, $a \leq b \in D(A)$. The proof continues along the same lines as that of Theorem 5. □

4.3 Tableau Calculi

Selection refinements of resolution, and in particular hyperresolution, are closely related to standard (modal) tableau calculi [HS99,HS00].

A tableau is a finitely branching tree whose nodes are sets of labeled formulae. Tableaux are used for testing satisfiability of formulae. If ϕ is a formula to be tested for satisfiability, the root node is the set $\{a : \phi\}$. Successor nodes are constructed according to a set (Exp) of expansion rules of the form

$$\frac{X}{X_1 \mid \cdots \mid X_n}$$

The expansion rule above can be applied for a formula F if F is an instance of X. n successor nodes are created which contain the formulae of the current node and the appropriate instances of X_i. A branch in a semantic tableau is *closed* if it contains $\perp$ or labeled formulae of the form $a : F$ and $a : \neg F$. Otherwise the branch is called *open*. A tableau is *closed* if each of its branches is closed. A formula ϕ is satisfiable (w.r.t. (Exp)) if a tableau can be constructed (with the set (Exp) of expansion rules) which contains an open maximal branch.

In many papers in which tableau methods are given for modal or description logics, the formula ϕ whose satisfiability is tested is supposed to be in negation normal form. This ensures that all subformulae of ϕ that are not propositional variables have positive polarity, hence only the direct implications of the renaming rules need to be used in a hyperresolution procedure.

When checking satisfiability of formulae of type $t_1 \not\leq t_2, t_1$ (or, in clause form, P_{t_1}) has positive polarity and t_2 (in clause form, P_{t_2}) has negative polarity. In what follows we show that tableau rules as used in modal and description logics can be formulated when t_2 is a constant k. In this case, the root node is the set $\{a : t_1, a : \neg k\}$. Successor nodes are constructed according to the set T_Σ^S of expansion rules below. We will also indicate how a (non-standard) variant of tableaux with polarities can be used for checking satisfiability of formulae of type $t_1 \not\leq t_2$. In that case the root node is the set $\{a : t_1^p, a : \neg t_2^n\}$, and successor nodes are constructed according to a set $T_\Sigma^S(ext)$ of rules.

Let T_Σ^S be the following set of tableau rules:

$$(\perp) \quad \frac{s : 0}{\perp} \qquad \frac{s : \neg 1}{\perp} \qquad \frac{s : e, s : \neg e}{\perp} \qquad (\wedge) \quad \frac{s : e_1 \wedge e_2}{s : e_1, s : e_2} \qquad (\vee) \quad \frac{s : e_1 \vee e_2}{s : e_1 \mid s : e_2}$$

$$(f) \quad \frac{s : f(e_1, \ldots, e_n)}{(s_1, \ldots, s_n, s) : R_f, s_1 : e_1, \ldots, s_n : e_n} \qquad \text{with } s_1, \cdots s_n \quad \text{new to the branch.}$$

Theorem 7. *The formula $t_1 \not\leq k$, where k is a constant, is unsatisfiable in* DLO_Σ^S *iff a tableau in which every branch is closed can be constructed from* $\{c{:}t_1, c{:}\neg k\}$ *using the set T_Σ^S of tableau rules (and, in addition, $\frac{s:\neg k}{s:\neg R_k}$ or $\frac{s:R_k}{s:k}$).*

Proof: The proof uses ideas on the link between resolution and tableaux in [HS99, HS00]. By the soundness, completeness and termination of the hyperresolution calculus H, $t_1 \not\leq k$ is unsatisfiable in DLO_Σ^S iff on all split branches the empty clause is derived from (Ren) and (N) in H.

Assume that $t_1 \not\leq k$ is unsatisfiable in DLO_Σ^S. Then the empty clause is derived from (Ren) and (N) in H on all branches caused by splitting. By polarity considerations, only the direct implications of the definitions of subterms of t_1 in (Ren) are used. If $k = 1$, $\neg P_k(c)$ produces the empty clause with $P_1(x)$. If $k = 0$, $\neg P_k(c)$ is subsumed by Ren(0). If $k \notin \{0, 1\}$ the inference of $\neg P_k(c)$ with (Ren)(k) produces $\neg R_k(c)$. Since tableau rules are macro-inference steps of H on the clause form of the direct implications of the definitions in (Ren), based on the hyperresolution proof of the empty clause, a tableau can be constructed from $\{c : t_1, c : \neg k\}$ in which every branch is closed.

Conversely, assume that a tableau can be constructed from $\{c : t_1, c : \neg k\}$ in which every branch is closed. Let h be the map that associates literals to labeled formulae defined by $h(s : e) = h_1(e)(h_2(s))$, where $h_1(e) = P_e$ for every subformula e of $t_1 \leq t_2$, $h_1(R_f) = R_f$; $h_2(s_i) = c_i^{f(e_1,\ldots,e_m)}(h(s))$ if s_i was introduced by (f), where $c_i^{f(e_1,\ldots,e_m)}$ is the Skolem function associated with e_i and $f(e_1, \cdots e_n)$; and $h_2(s) = s$ otherwise. Then derivations in H correspond to the tableau rules above. For instance, the following derivation corresponds to rule (f). From $P_{f(e_1,\ldots,e_n)}(s)$ derive $P_{e_i}(c_i^{f(e_1,\ldots,e_n)})(s)$, $i = 1, \ldots, n$ and $R_f(c_1^{f(e_1,\ldots,e_n)}(s), \ldots, c_n^{f(e_1,\ldots,e_n)}(s), s)$ using (Ren)(Σ) in $n+1$ steps. $\square$

A set of tableau rules for checking satisfiability in DLO_Σ^A of formulae of the form $t_1 \leq k$ can be obtained from T_Σ^S by adding the rules:

$$(\mathsf{Her_A}) \frac{a : e}{\bigwedge_{b \in D(A), b \geq a} b : e} \qquad (\mathsf{Mon_g}) \frac{(s_1, \ldots, s_n, a) : R_g}{\bigwedge_{b \in D(A), b \geq a}(s_1, \ldots, s_n, b) : R_g}$$

for all elements $a \in D(A)$, where the labels $s_1, \ldots s_n$ are of type lat, e is a formula of type A and g a bridging function with values of type A.

Validity of formulae of the form $t_1 \leq t_2$, where t_2 is a term can be tested by using a fairly unusual extension of the notion of tableaux to what we call *tableaux with polarities*, in which the direction in which a rule is applied is determined by the polarity of the formula. Both polarities are associated with propositional variables. Let $T_\Sigma^S(ext)$ be the set of rules containing $(\bot)$ and:

$$(\wedge^p) \frac{s : (e_1 \wedge e_2)^p}{s : e_1^p, s : e_2^p} \quad (\vee^p) \frac{s : (e_1 \vee e_2)^p}{s : e_1^p \mid s : e_2^p} \quad (\wedge^n) \frac{s : e_1^n, s : e_2^n}{s : (e_1 \wedge e_2)^n} \quad (\vee^n) \frac{s : e_i^n}{s : (e_1 \vee e_2)^n}$$

$$(f^p) \frac{s : f(e_1, \ldots, e_n)^p}{(s_1, \ldots, s_n, s) : R_f, s_1 : e_1^p, \ldots, s_n : e_n^p} \quad (f^n) \frac{(s_1, \ldots, s_n, s) : R_f, s_1 : e_1^n, \ldots, s_n : e_n^n}{s : f(e_1, \ldots, e_n)^n}$$
$$(\text{with } s_1, \cdots s_n \text{ new to the branch})$$

These rules encode macro-inference steps of H with the clause form of direct implications in (Ren) for subterms of t_1 $((\wedge^p), (\vee^p), (f^p))$ resp. the inverse implications in (Ren) for subterms of t_2 $((\wedge^n), (\vee^n), (f^n))$. Similar arguments as those used in Theorem 7 can be used to show that the formula $t_1 \not\leq t_2$ is unsatisfiable in DLO_Σ^S iff a tableau in which every branch is closed can be constructed starting from the root $\{c : t_1^p, c : \neg t_2^n\}$ and using the rules in $T_\Sigma^S(ext)$, with the restriction that $(\wedge^n), (\vee^n)$ and (f^n) can only be applied if the result is a subexpression of t_2.

5   Conclusions

We formally defined a class of many sorted bridging functions between bounded distributive lattices, showed that the Priestley representation theorem can be extended in a natural way to encompass such operators, and then analyzed some fragments of the universal theory of distributive lattices with many sorted bridging operators. In particular, we showed that a structure-preserving translation to clause form for uniform word problems for such classes of lattices with operators can be defined also in this case using the same pattern used in [SS99] for join hemimorphisms. Using this translation, the results in [SS99] can be extended in a straightforward way to prove that ordered resolution with selection is a decision procedure for the universal theory of many-sorted distributive lattices with bridging operators. We then proved that hyperresolution can be used for simpler problems such as the problem of checking validity of formulae of type $t_1 \leq t_2$ in $\mathsf{DLO}_{\Sigma}^{S}$ and $\mathsf{DLO}_{\Sigma}^{A}$. Based on this we sketched a way of designing tableau calculi.

Bridging functions such as "cardinality" are, in general, not join hemimorphisms, but satisfy the subadditivity condition $f(a \vee b) \geq f(a) \vee f(b)$ or conditional additivity axioms such as $x \wedge y = 0 \Rightarrow f(x \vee y) = f(x) + f(y)$. We would like to extend the results presented here to such more general operators.

Acknowledgements. I thank Harald Ganzinger for inspiring discussions, and for bringing the results on bridging functions in [Ohl01] to my attention, and the referees for their helpful comments.

References

[AB75]   A.R. Anderson and N.D. Belnap. *Entailment – The Logic of Relevance and Necessity*. Princeton University Press, 1975.

[BG01]   L. Bachmair and H. Ganzinger. Resolution theorem proving. In A. Robinson and A. Voronkov, editors, *Handbook of Automated Reasoning*. Elsevier, 2001.

[Gol89] R. Goldblatt. Varieties of complex algebras. *Annals of Pure and Applied Logic*, 44(3):153–301, 1989.

[HS99]   U. Hustadt and R. A. Schmidt. On the relation of resolution and tableaux proof systems for description logics. In T. Dean, editor, *Proceedings of IJ-CAI'99*, volume 1, pages 110–115. Morgan Kaufmann, 1999.

[HS00]   U. Hustadt and R. A. Schmidt. Using resolution for testing modal satisfiability and building models. In I. P. Gent, H. van Maaren, and T. Walsh, editors, *Proceedings of SAT 2000*, volume 63 of *Frontiers in Artificial Intelligence and Applications*. IOS Press, Amsterdam, 2000.

[JT52]   B. Jónsson and A. Tarski. Boolean algebras with operators, Part I&II. *American Journal of Mathematics*, 73&74:891–939&127–162, 1951&1952.

[Ohl01] H.J. Ohlbach. Set description languages and reasoning about numerical features of sets. Technical Report PMS-FB-2001-1, Institut f. Informatik, LMU, München, April 2001.

[Ono93] H. Ono. Semantics for substructural logics. In P. Schroeder-Heister and K. Došen, editors, *Substructural Logics*, pages 259–291. Oxford University Press, 1993.

[Pri70] H.A. Priestley. Representation of distributive lattices by means of ordered Stone spaces. *Bull. London Math. Soc.*, 2:186–190, 1970.

[SS99]   V. Sofronie-Stokkermans. On the universal theory of varieties of distributive lattices with operators: Some decidability and complexity results. In *Proceedings of CADE-16*, LNAI 1632, pages 157–171, Trento, Italy, 1999. Springer.

[SS00]   V. Sofronie-Stokkermans. Duality and canonical extensions of bounded distributive lattices with operators, and applications to the semantics of non-classical logics I. *Studia Logica*, 64(1):93–132, 2000.

[SS01]   V. Sofronie-Stokkermans. Resolution-based decision procedures for the universal theory of some classes of distributive lattices with operators. Research Report MPI-I-2001-2-005, Max-Planck-Institut für Informatik, Saarbrücken, Germany, September 2001.

[SS02]   V. Sofronie-Stokkermans. Representation theorems and the semantics of non-classical logics and applications to automated theorem proving. In M. Fitting and E. Orlowska, editors, *Theory and Applications of Multiple-Valued Logic* Springer-Verlag series Studies in Fuzziness and Soft Computing, to appear, 2002.

Question Answering: From Partitions to Prolog[*]

Balder ten Cate[1] and Chung-chieh Shan[2]

[1] Institute for Logic, Language and Computation, Universiteit van Amsterdam
Nieuwe Doelenstraat 15, 1012 CP, Amsterdam, The Netherlands
`b.ten.cate@hum.uva.nl`
[2] Division of Applied and Engineering Sciences, Harvard University
33 Oxford Street, Cambridge MA 02138, USA
`ccshan@post.harvard.edu`

Abstract. We implement Groenendijk and Stokhof's partition semantics of questions in a simple question answering algorithm. The algorithm is sound, complete, and based on tableau theorem proving. The algorithm relies on a syntactic characterization of answerhood: Any answer to a question is equivalent to some formula built up only from instances of the question. We prove this characterization by translating the logic of interrogation to classical predicate logic and applying Craig's interpolation theorem.

1 The Partition Theory of Questions

An elegant account of the semantics of natural language questions from a logical and mathematical perspective is the one provided by Groenendijk and Stokhof [8]. According to them, a question denotes a partition of a logical space of possibilities. In this section, we give a brief summary of this influential theory, using a notation slightly different from Groenendijk's presentation [7].

A question is essentially a first order formula, possibly with free variables. We will denote a question by $?\phi$, where ϕ is a first order formula. (We will also denote a set of questions by $?\Phi$, where Φ is a set of first order formulas.) An answer is also a first order formula, but one that stands in a certain *answerhood* relation with respect to the question, to be spelled out in Sect. 2. For example, the statement "Everyone is going to the party" $(\forall x Px)$ will turn out to be an answer to the question "Who is going to the party?" $(?Px)$.

We assume that equality is in the language, so one can ask questions such as "Who is John?" $(?x \approx j)$. We also assume that, for every function symbol— including constants—it is indicated whether it is interpreted rigidly or not. Intuitively, for a function symbol to be rigid means that its denotation is known.

[*] We would like to thank Patrick Blackburn, Paul Dekker, Jeroen Groenendijk, Maarten Marx, Stuart Shieber, and the anonymous referees for their useful comments and discussions. The 13th European Summer School in Logic, Language and Information, the 13th Amsterdam Colloquium, and Stanford University's Center for the Study of Language and Information provided stimulating environments that led to this collaboration. The second author is supported by the United States National Science Foundation under Grant IRI-9712068.

U. Egly and C.G. Fermüller (Eds.): TABLEAUX 2002, LNAI 2381, pp. 251–265, 2002.
© Springer-Verlag Berlin Heidelberg 2002

For example, under the notion of answerhood that we will introduce in Sect. 2, it is only appropriate to answer "Who is going to the party?" ($?Px$) with "John is going to the party" (Pj) if it is known who "John" is—in other words, if j is rigid. Also, for "Who is John?" ($?x \approx j$) to be a non-trivial question, "John" must have a non-rigid interpretation.

Questions are interpreted relative to first order modal structures with constant domain. That is, a model is of the form (W, D, I), where W is a set of worlds, D is a domain of entities, and I is an interpretation function assigning extensions to the predicates and function symbols, relative to each world. Furthermore, we only consider models that give rigid function symbols the same extension in every world. Relative to such a model $M = (W, D, I)$, a question $?\phi$ expresses a partition of W, in other words an equivalence relation over W:

$$[?\phi]_M = \{ (w, v) \in W^2 \mid \forall g \colon M, w, g \models \phi \Leftrightarrow M, v, g \models \phi \} \ . \tag{1}$$

Roughly speaking, two worlds are equivalent if one cannot tell them apart by asking the question $?\phi$. In general, any set of questions $?\Phi$ also expresses a partition of W, namely the intersection of the partitions expressed by its elements:

$$[?\Phi]_M = \bigcap_{\phi \in \Phi} [?\phi]_M$$
$$= \{ (w, v) \in W^2 \mid \forall \phi \in \Phi \colon \forall g \colon M, w, g \models \phi \Leftrightarrow M, v, g \models \phi \} \ . \tag{2}$$

Entailment between questions is defined as a *refinement* relation among partitions (i.e., equivalence relations): An equivalence relation A is a subset of another equivalence relation B if every equivalence class of A is contained in a class of B.

$$?\Phi \models ?\psi \quad \text{iff} \quad \forall M \colon [?\Phi]_M \subseteq [?\psi]_M \ . \tag{3}$$

A more fine-grained notion of entailment is as follows [7]. Let χ be a first order formula with no free variables, and let $M \models \chi$ mean that $M, w \models \chi$ for all w.

$$?\Phi \models_\chi ?\psi \quad \text{iff} \quad \forall M \colon M \models \chi \Rightarrow [?\Phi]_M \subseteq [?\psi]_M \ . \tag{4}$$

Pronunciation: The questions $?\Phi$ entail the question $?\psi$ *in the context of* χ (or, *given* χ). The context χ is intended to capture assertions in the common ground: If it is commonly known that everyone who got invited to the party is going, and vice versa ($\forall x(Ix \leftrightarrow Px)$), then the questions "Who got invited?" ($?Ix$) and "Who is going?" ($?Px$) entail each other.

1.1   Translation to First Order Logic

Groenendijk and Stokhof [8] do not provide an inference system for the above entailment relation, but we can use the following entailment-preserving translation procedure to ordinary first order logic.

The intuition behind the translation is simple: One question entails another iff the former distinguishes between more worlds than the latter does. In other words, one question entails another iff every pair of worlds considered equivalent by the first question is also considered equivalent by the second. For instance, the question "Who is going to the party?" ($?Px$) entails the question "Is John going to the party?" ($?Pj$). After all, if exactly the same people are going to two parties $(\forall x(Px \leftrightarrow P'x))$, then either John is going to both parties, or he is going to neither of them $(Pj \leftrightarrow P'j)$.

For any first order formula ϕ, let ϕ^* be the result of priming all occurrences of non-rigid non-logical symbols. Formally, define

$$
\begin{aligned}
(Pt_1 \ldots t_n)^* &= P't_1^* \ldots t_n^* & f(t_1, \ldots, t_n)^* &= \begin{cases} f(t_1^*, \ldots, t_n^*) & \text{if } f \text{ is rigid} \\ f'(t_1^*, \ldots, t_n^*) & \text{otherwise} \end{cases} \\
(s \approx t)^* &= (s^* \approx t^*) & & \\
(\phi \wedge \psi)^* &= \phi^* \wedge \psi^* & x^* &= x & (5) \\
(\neg \phi)^* &= \neg(\phi^*) & \top^* &= \top \\
(\exists x \phi)^* &= \exists x(\phi^*) & \bot^* &= \bot \ .
\end{aligned}
$$

Furthermore, for any question $?\phi$, let $?\phi^{\#}$ be the first order formula $\forall \vec{x}(\phi \leftrightarrow \phi^*)$, where $\vec{x}$ are the free variables of ϕ. For any set of questions $?\Phi$, let $?\Phi^{\#}$ be the set of first order formulas $\{ ?\phi^{\#} \mid \phi \in \Phi \}$. Now, we can reduce entailment between questions to ordinary first order entailment, as follows.

Theorem 1. *The following entailments are equivalent.*

1. $?\Phi \models_{\chi} ?\psi$
2. $?\Phi^{\#}, \chi, \chi^* \models ?\psi^{\#}$

Proof. [$\Rightarrow$] By contraposition. Suppose $?\Phi^{\#}, \chi, \chi^* \not\models ?\psi^{\#}$. Then there is a first order model $M = (D, I)$ that verifies the formulas $?\Phi^{\#}, \chi, \chi^*$ but not $?\psi^{\#}$.

Now consider the first order modal structure $N = (\{w, v\}, D, I')$, where for all non-logical symbols α, we let $I'_w(\alpha) = I(\alpha)$ and $I'_v(\alpha) = I(\alpha')$. By construction, $(w, v) \in [?\Phi]_N$ and $(w, v) \notin [?\psi]_N$. Furthermore, $N \models \chi$. Therefore, $?\Phi \not\models_{\chi} ?\psi$.

[$\Leftarrow$] Again by contraposition. Suppose $?\Phi \not\models_{\chi} ?\psi$. Then there is a first order modal structure $M = (W, D, I)$ with $w, v \in W$ such that $(w, v) \in [?\Phi]_M$ yet $(w, v) \notin [?\psi]_M$. Furthermore, $M, w \models \chi$ and $M, v \models \chi$.

Now consider the first order model $N = (D, I')$, where for all non-logical symbols α, we let $I'(\alpha) = I_w(\alpha)$ and $I'(\alpha') = I_v(\alpha)$. By construction, N verifies the formulas $?\Phi^{\#}, \chi, \chi^*$ but not $?\psi^{\#}$. Therefore, $?\Phi^{\#}, \chi, \chi^* \not\models ?\psi^{\#}$. □

By this theorem, we can determine whether an entailment between questions holds, by translating the formulas involved to ordinary predicate logic. For example, suppose that a is a rigid constant, and consider the supposed entailment

$$?Px \models ?Pa \ . \tag{6}$$

In order to determine whether the entailment is valid, we need only translate the two formulas to ordinary first order logic, giving

$$\forall x(Px \leftrightarrow P'x) \models Pa \leftrightarrow P'a \ . \tag{7}$$

As can be easily seen, this is indeed valid. On the other hand, if a were non-rigid then the entailment would not be valid. As a second example, consider

$$?Px \models_{\forall x(Px \leftrightarrow Qx)} ?Qa \ . \tag{8}$$

Given that a is rigid, this is again valid, as we can see from the translation

$$\forall x(Px \leftrightarrow P'x), \forall x(Px \leftrightarrow Qx), \forall x(P'x \leftrightarrow Q'x) \models Qa \leftrightarrow Q'a \ . \tag{9}$$

1.2 Varying Domains

The partition theory as formulated in the previous section makes some natural predictions regarding question entailment. For example, the question "Who is going to the party?" ($?Px$) entails the question "Is everyone going to the party?" ($?\forall x Px$). Intuitively, whenever one knows (completely) who is going to the party, one also knows whether everyone is going to the party. As a matter of fact, much of the motivation for the partition theory of questions comes from its natural account of entailment relations between sentences embedding such questions.[1]

Unfortunately, the theory also makes some counterintuitive predictions. For example, the question $?j \approx b$ ("Is John the same person as Bill?", where j and b are interpreted rigidly) is entailed by every question, including the trivial question $?\top$. Likewise, $?\exists x \exists y \neg (x \approx y)$ ("Does there exist more than one entity?") is entailed by every question.[2] For this reason, an alternative semantics has been discussed, in which the questions are interpreted with respect to first order modal structures with *varying* domains [9]. That is, each world w is associated with its own domain of entities D_w. This semantics is more general, since it allows more models: Every constant domain model is also a varying domain model, so fewer entailments between questions are valid for varying domains. In particular, $?\exists x \exists y \neg (x \approx y)$ is no longer entailed by every question. Also, $?Px$ no longer entails $?\neg Px$, though the entailment $?Px, ?x \approx x \models ?\neg Px$ remains valid.

It is not entirely trivial to generalize the partition semantics of questions to varying domains, since it is unclear in (1) which assignments g should be quantified over. One generalization, which Groenendijk and Stokhof [9] seem to suggest but do not state, is to define

$$[?\phi]_M = \{ (w,v) \in W^2 \mid \forall g:$$
$$(g \in D_w^\phi \ \& \ M,w,g \models \phi) \Leftrightarrow (g \in D_v^\phi \ \& \ M,v,g \models \phi) \} , \tag{10}$$

where D_w^ϕ denotes the set of assignment functions that map all free variables in ϕ to entities in D_w. Question entailment, as defined in (4), remains the same.

Various generalizations of the partition theory to varying domains, including that in (10), can be straightforwardly reduced to the constant domain version by introducing an *existence predicate* E. In the case of (10), one would *relativize* all quantifiers—that is, replace $\exists x \phi$ by $\exists x (Ex \wedge \phi)$ and $\forall x \phi$ by $\forall x (Ex \rightarrow \phi)$—and consider questions of the form $?(Ex_1 \wedge \ldots \wedge Ex_n \wedge \phi)$, where $x_1, \ldots, x_n$ are the free variables of ϕ. Theorem 1 can then be applied after the reduction.

In the rest of this paper, we will restrict ourselves to constant domain models.

2   A Syntactic Characterization of Answerhood

Groenendijk and Stokhof's entailment relation between questions, as discussed in the previous section, allows us to define a notion of answerhood.

---

[1] Cf. Nelken and Francez [13] for one of the few competing theories in this respect.

[2] In Sect. 2, we will see exactly which such counterintuitive predictions are made by the theory. For now, the reader can use Theorem 1 to check that the theory indeed makes these predictions.

Definition 1 (Answerhood). *Let ?ϕ be a question and ψ a first order formula without free variables. We say that ψ is an* answer *to ?ϕ if ?$\phi \models$?ψ.*

According to this notion (also termed *licensing* by Groenendijk [7]), "Everyone is going to the party" ($\forall x Px$) is an answer to "Who is going to the party?" (?Px), because ?$Px \models$?$\forall x Px$. (We will generalize to sets of questions in Sect. 2.2.)

Note that, under this definition, any contradiction or tautology counts as an answer to any question. Groenendijk and Stokhof [7, 8] define a stricter notion of *pertinence*, which excludes these two trivial cases by formalizing Grice's Maxims of Quality and Quantity, respectively. In this paper, however, we will stick to the simpler criterion of answerhood as defined above, which corresponds to Grice's Maxim of Relation.

We now have a semantic notion of answerhood, telling us what counts as an answer to a question. However, for practical purposes, it is useful to have also a *syntactic* characterization of this notion. Can one give a simple syntactic property that is a necessary and sufficient condition for answerhood? As we will see in a minute, one can.

First, let us look at a partial result discussed by Groenendijk and Stokhof [8] and Kager [11]. Define rigidity of terms and formula instances as follows.

Definition 2 (Rigidity). *A* term *is* rigid *if it is composed of variables and rigid function symbols. A formula ϕ is a* rigid instance *of another formula ψ if ϕ can be obtained from ψ by uniformly substituting rigid terms for variables. An identity statement $s \approx t$ is* rigid *if the terms s and t are rigid.*

For example, if c is a rigid constant and f is a rigid function symbol, then rigid instances of Px include Pc, Px, $Pf(c)$, and $Pf(x)$. The identity statement $c \approx x$ is also rigid. Notice that rigid instances are not necessarily rigid: If c is rigid, then Rcd is a rigid instance of Rxd even if the constant d is not rigid.

Groenendijk and Stokhof [8] and Kager [11] observed that rigid instances of a question constitute answers to that question. By a simple inductive argument, one can generalize this a bit.

Definition 3 (Development). *A formula ψ is a* development *of another formula ϕ (written "$\phi \leq \psi$") if ψ is built up from rigid instances of ϕ and rigid identity statements using boolean connectives and quantifiers, or if ψ is $\top$ or $\bot$.*

For example, if c and d are rigid constants, then $Pc \wedge Pd$ and $\exists x(Px \wedge \neg(x \approx c))$ are both developments of Px.

Theorem 2. *If $\phi \leq \psi$ then ?$\phi \models$?ψ.*

Proof. By induction on the size of ϕ. □

Using the translation procedure in Sect. 1, together with Craig's interpolation theorem for first order logic, we can prove the converse as well.

Theorem 3. *Let $\vec{y}$ be the free variables of some formula ψ. If ?$\phi \models_\chi$?ψ, then there exists some formula ϑ with no free variables beside $\vec{y}$ such that $\phi \leq \vartheta$ and $\chi \models \forall \vec{y}(\psi \leftrightarrow \vartheta)$.*

Proof. First, we will prove the special case where ϕ is an atomic formula, say $P\vec{x}$. Suppose that $?P\vec{x} \models_\chi ?\psi(\vec{y})$. Then, by Theorem 1,

$$\forall \vec{x}(P\vec{x} \leftrightarrow P'\vec{x}), \chi, \chi^* \models \forall \vec{y}(\psi(\vec{y}) \leftrightarrow \psi^*(\vec{y})) \ . \tag{11}$$

As a fact of first order logic, we can replace the universally quantified variables in the consequent by some freshly chosen constants $\vec{c}$. This results in

$$\forall \vec{x}(P\vec{x} \leftrightarrow P'\vec{x}), \chi, \chi^* \models \psi(\vec{c}) \leftrightarrow \psi^*(\vec{c}) \ , \tag{12}$$

and, from this,

$$\forall \vec{x}(P\vec{x} \leftrightarrow P'\vec{x}), \chi^*, \psi^*(\vec{c}) \models \chi \rightarrow \psi(\vec{c}) \ . \tag{13}$$

By Craig's interpolation theorem for first order logic, we can construct an interpolant $\vartheta(\vec{c})$ such that

$$\forall \vec{x}(P\vec{x} \leftrightarrow P'\vec{x}), \chi^*, \psi^*(\vec{c}) \models \vartheta(\vec{c}) \ , \tag{14}$$
$$\vartheta(\vec{c}) \models \chi \rightarrow \psi(\vec{c}) \ , \tag{15}$$

and the only non-logical symbols in $\vartheta(\vec{c})$ are those occurring on both sides of (13). From the way the translation procedure $(\cdot)^*$ is set up, it follows that the only non-logical symbols that χ^* and ψ^* on the one hand, and χ and ψ on the other hand, have in common, are rigid function symbols. Thus, $\vartheta(\vec{c})$ contains no non-logical symbols beside P, $\vec{c}$, and rigid function symbols.

Removing primes uniformly from all predicate and function symbols in (14), we get $\chi \models \psi(\vec{c}) \rightarrow \vartheta(\vec{c})$. From (15), we get the converse: $\chi \models \vartheta(\vec{c}) \rightarrow \psi(\vec{c})$. Together, this gives us

$$\chi \models \psi(\vec{c}) \leftrightarrow \vartheta(\vec{c}) \ . \tag{16}$$

Since the constants $\vec{c}$ do not occur in χ, we can replace them by universally quantified variables. This results in

$$\chi \models \forall \vec{y}(\psi(\vec{y}) \leftrightarrow \vartheta(\vec{y})) \ . \tag{17}$$

Furthermore, $\vartheta(\vec{y})$ contains no non-logical symbols beside P and rigid function symbols. From this, it follows that $\vartheta(\vec{y})$ is a development of $P\vec{x}$.

As for the general case, suppose $?\phi(\vec{x}) \models_\chi ?\psi$. Choose a fresh predicate symbol P with the same arity as the number of free variables of ϕ. Then it follows that $?P\vec{x} \models_{\chi \wedge \forall \vec{x}(P\vec{x} \leftrightarrow \phi(\vec{x}))} ?\psi$. Apply the above strategy to obtain a development ϑ of $?P\vec{x}$ such that $\chi \wedge \forall \vec{x}(P\vec{x} \leftrightarrow \phi(\vec{x})) \models \forall \vec{y}(\vartheta \leftrightarrow \psi)$. Let ϑ' be the result of replacing all subformulas in ϑ of the form $P\vec{z}$ by $\phi(\vec{z})$. Then ϑ' is a development of ϕ, and $\chi \models \forall \vec{y}(\psi \leftrightarrow \vartheta')$. □

Thus, the syntactic notion of development corresponds precisely to the semantic notion of entailment between questions.

Recall that the formula χ in Theorem 3 represents an assertion in the common ground. If no assumptions on the common ground are made (i.e., $\chi = \top$), then Theorem 3 reduces to the following syntactic characterization of answerhood.

Corollary 1. *ψ is an answer to $?\phi$ iff ψ is equivalent to a development of ϕ.*

This syntactic characterization is useful for several purposes. First of all, it makes possible a thorough investigation of the predictions made by Groenendijk and Stokhof's theory of answerhood: It shows what their semantic theory really amounts to, syntactically speaking.

Second, this result opens the way to practical question answering algorithms. Now that we have a syntactic characterization of answerhood, we can address the question answering problem purely in terms of symbolic manipulation without having to refer to the semantics. This will be the topic of Sect. 3.

Another advantage is that it becomes possible to compare different theories of questions and answers. For instance, while at first sight Prolog and the partition theory of questions seem incomparable, we will see in Sect. 3.2 that they are in fact closely related.

2.1   Languages without Equality

What if we do not have equality in the language? This is an interesting question for at least two reasons. First, as we saw in Sect. 1.2, a number of counterintuitive predictions of the partition semantics involve equality. For example, sentences such as $\neg(j \approx b)$ ("John is not Bill", where j and b are interpreted rigidly) and $\exists x \exists y \neg(x \approx y)$ ("There exist at least two entities") are answers to every question. Removing equality would prevent these predictions, though then answers like "Only John is going to the party" would no longer be expressible.

The second reason why eliminating equality from the language is interesting is more practical. In question answering algorithms, it is convenient not to have to deal with equality, since equality reasoning is very expensive. From the theorem proving literature, one can conclude that dealing with equality is not feasible for many practical applications.

As it turns out, the syntactic characterization result is even simpler for first order languages without equality. The corresponding notion of *development of ϕ* is simply *a formula built from rigid instances of ϕ using boolean connectives and quantifiers, or $\top$ or $\bot$*. The same proof of Theorem 3 goes through, since Craig's interpolation theorem holds regardless of whether equality is present.

2.2   Multiple Questions

The notion of answerhood that we introduced earlier (Definition 1) generalizes trivially to multiple questions: If ψ is a first order formula without free variables, we say that ψ is an answer to $?\Phi$ if $?\Phi \models ?\psi$. The notion of development (Definition 3) also generalizes: A formula ψ is a development of Φ if ψ is built up from rigid instances of elements of Φ and rigid identity statements using boolean connectives and quantifiers, or if ψ is $\top$ or $\bot$. The proof of Theorem 3 then generalizes directly to multiple questions, as does Corollary 1: ψ is an answer to $?\Phi$ iff ψ is equivalent to a development of Φ.

Multiple questions arise naturally in two settings. First, a query like "Who got invited to the party, and who is going to the party?" corresponds to a set of questions like $?\Phi = \{?Ix, ?Px\}$. According to the above generalization of answerhood, one answer to this query is $\forall x(Ix \leftrightarrow Px)$: "Everyone invited is going, and vice versa."

Second, suppose that, as part of their common ground, the questioner and the answerer both know the complete true answers to a certain set of questions $?\Theta$. For example, if it is commonly known who got invited, then $?\Theta$ contains $?Ix$. Extend the notion of entailment in (4) to handle questions as contexts in the following way: If χ is a first order formula with no free variables, then

$$?\Phi \models_{\chi,?\Theta} ?\psi \quad \text{iff} \quad \forall M = (W,D,I): \qquad (18)$$
$$M \models \chi, \; [?\Theta]_M = W^2 \Rightarrow [?\Phi]_M \subseteq [?\psi]_M \; .$$

Intuitively, given the common ground $?\Theta$, a formula ψ is an answer to a question $?\phi$ just in case the entailment $?\phi \models_{?\Theta} ?\psi$ holds. Indeed, the entailment

$$?Px \models_{?Ix} ?\forall x(Ix \leftrightarrow Px) \qquad (19)$$

is valid: If it is commonly known who got invited, then in response to "Who is going to the party?" one can answer "Everyone invited is going, and vice versa." In fact, we have

$$?\Phi \models_{\chi,?\Theta} ?\psi \quad \text{iff} \quad ?\Theta, ?\Phi \models_\chi ?\psi \; . \qquad (20)$$

In particular,

$$?\phi \models_{?\Theta} ?\psi \quad \text{iff} \quad ?\Theta, ?\phi \models ?\psi \; . \qquad (21)$$

This result means that asking a question $?\phi$ under some common ground $?\Theta$ is exactly like asking the set of questions $?\Theta \cup \{?\phi\}\cup$ under no common ground, in terms of what counts as an answer. So multiple questions arise again [7].

We are about to present a question-answering algorithm. For simplicity, we will assume that there is only a single question to answer, and that the context is empty. The algorithm we will present generalizes trivially to handle multiple questions at once, and hence to handle questions in the context.[3]

3   Finding the Answer to a Question

The general task of question answering is the following.

> Given a finite first order theory Σ and a question $?\phi$, find an answer to $?\phi$ that is entailed by Σ and that is as informative as possible.

In other words, we wish to find an informative formula ψ, such that $\Sigma \models \psi$ and $?\phi \models ?\psi$. Here the theory Σ is intended to capture the answerer's private knowledge, and we measure how *informative* an answer is by its logical strength: One answer is more informative than another if the former entails the latter. For example, an answerer who knows that John is going to the party and that it rains ($\Sigma = \{Pj, R\}$) might reply to "Who is going to the party?" ($?\phi = ?Px$) with the statement "Someone is going to the party" ($\psi = \exists x Px$). If the constant

---

[3] In passing, we mention that the semantics of multiple questions can be reduced to that of single questions, provided that the domain contains at least two elements. More specifically, any two questions $?\phi_1$ and $?\phi_2$ are equivalent to the single question $?\big((x{\approx}y{\wedge}\phi_1)\vee(\neg(x{\approx}y){\wedge}\phi_2)\big)$. This reduction is of practical importance to the reader who encounters a fairy that promises to answer a single eternal burning question.

symbol j is rigid, then the statement "John is going to the party" (Pj) would be an answer and preferred because it is more informative.

The first question that comes to mind when considering the task of question answering is: *Is there always an optimal answer?* In other words, given a finite theory Σ and a question $?\phi$, is there always (modulo logical equivalence) a unique most informative answer to $?\phi$ entailed by Σ? The answer is *no*.

Theorem 4. *There is a finite theory Σ and a question $?\phi$ such that, for every answer to $?\phi$ entailed by Σ, there is a strictly more informative answer to $?\phi$ entailed by Σ.*

Proof. Let Σ be the theory

$$\{\forall xyz(x < y \wedge y < z \rightarrow x < z),\ \forall x \neg(x < x),\ \forall x \exists y(x < y)\} \qquad (22)$$

("$<$ is an unbounded strict order"), and ψ_n $(n \in \mathbb{N})$ be the formula

$$\exists x_1 \ldots \exists x_n \bigwedge_{i,j \leq n;\ i \neq y} \neg(x_i \approx x_j) \qquad (23)$$

("there are at least n different objects"). Every ψ_n is entailed by Σ. Furthermore, every ψ_n is an answer to the question $?\top$. (This follows either via Theorem 2, or directly from how question entailment was defined in (4).) The optimal answer would have to entail each ψ_n and, furthermore, contain no non-logical symbols. It follows from the compactness theorem that there is no such formula.   □

Equality is not essential to this counterexample. Indeed, the same argument goes through if we replace the equality sign $\approx$ by a non-logical binary relation I, use $?Ixy$ as the question, and extend the theory Σ with *replacement axioms* [5]:

$$\Sigma^+ = \Sigma \cup \{\ \forall x Ixx,\ \forall xyzu(Ixz \wedge Iyu \wedge x < y \rightarrow z < u), \\ \forall xyzu(Ixz \wedge Iyu \wedge Ixy \rightarrow Izu)\ \}\ . \qquad (24)$$

Moreover, in the absence of equality there is a second problem, concerning undecidability. It is undecidable whether the given formula is the most specific answer to a question entailed by a theory. This follows from a simple reduction argument: Suppose we do not have equality in the language, and suppose the theory Σ does not contain any rigid function symbols. Then Σ is satisfiable iff $\top$ is the most specific answer to $?\top$ entailed by Σ. But as we all know, first order satisfiability is undecidable.

Notwithstanding these negative results, it is possible to construct a sound and complete question answering algorithm. The output of the algorithm is a sequence of answers that is *cofinal* in the set of all answers entailed by the theory Σ. Cofinality means that, for any answer that is entailed by Σ, there is a more informative answer in the sequence generated by the algorithm. Formally:

Definition 4 (Cofinality). *A set of formulas Φ is cofinal in another set of formulas Ψ if each formula in Ψ is entailed by some formula in Φ.*

We call a question answering algorithm *sound* if it generates only formulas that are answers to the question and that are entailed by the theory. We call the

$$\left.\begin{array}{l} \text{Theory } \Sigma \\ \text{Question } ?\phi \end{array}\right\} \xrightarrow{\text{INPUT}} \boxed{\text{QA Algorithm}} \xrightarrow{\text{OUTPUT}} \text{Sequence of answers } \psi_1, \psi_2, \dots$$

$$\begin{array}{ll} \textit{Soundness:} & \forall i : \Sigma \models \psi_i \ \& \ ?\phi \models ?\psi_i \\ \textit{Completeness:} & \forall \psi : \Sigma \models \psi \ \& \ ?\phi \models ?\psi \implies \exists i : \psi_i \models \psi \end{array}$$

Fig. 1. A question answering algorithm

algorithm *complete* if the sequence it generates is always cofinal in the set of all answers to the question entailed by the theory. A question answering algorithm with these properties is depicted in Fig. 1.

To show that there are indeed algorithms satisfying these constraints, we will now discuss a rather trivial algorithm. Recall that, to answer a question $?\phi$ given a theory Σ, it suffices to find developments of ϕ that are entailed by Σ. The search for answers can be conducted using any theorem proving technique, including tableaux. A first stab at a question answering algorithm, then, is to syntactically enumerate and check all potential answers ψ.

Algorithm 1. To answer the question $?\phi$ given the theory Σ, repeat in dovetail fashion for every development ψ of ϕ:

1. Initialize a tableau with a single branch, consisting of Σ and $\neg\psi$.
2. Keep applying tableau expansion and closure rules.
3. If the tableau becomes closed, report ψ as an answer. □

This algorithm is sound and complete, because tableau-based first order theorem proving is. However, it is also horribly inefficient, since it considers every development of ϕ as a potential answer, without taking the theory Σ into account.

The challenge, then, is to construct an question answering algorithm that is sound and complete (like Algorithm 1) yet as efficient as possible. In the next section, we will make a start by providing a more intelligent algorithm.

3.1 Tableau-Based Question Answering

We will now introduce a sound and complete question answering algorithm based on free variable tableaux [5]. Without loss of generality, we assume that the question $?\phi$ consists of a single atomic formula $P\vec{x}$, called the *answer literal* [6]. (If that is not so, simply add the formula $\forall\vec{x}(P\vec{x} \leftrightarrow \phi)$ to the theory, where P is a new predicate symbol and $\vec{x}$ are the free variables of ϕ.) We also assume that the theory Σ is Skolemized; that is, any existential quantifier in Σ has been eliminated with the help of additional, non-rigid function symbols. Finally, we will disregard equality for the moment, but the algorithm can be extended to deal with equality as well (we will return to this issue at the end of this section).

Table 1 summarizes the tableau calculus for first order logic without equality given by Fitting [5]. (We omit the existential rule since the theory is Skolemized.)

Table 1. Tableau expansion and closure rules for theorem proving

Conjunction	$\dfrac{\phi \wedge \psi}{\phi, \psi}$	$\dfrac{\neg(\phi \wedge \psi)}{\neg\phi \mid \neg\psi}$
Quantification	$\dfrac{\neg\exists x \phi}{\neg\phi[x/y]}$	where y is fresh
Negation	$\dfrac{\neg\neg\phi}{\phi}$	

Closure   A branch is closed if it contain a formula and its negation.
A tableau is closed if all its branches are closed.
A substitution σ is *closing* if the tableau is closed after applying σ.

In the algorithm that we will introduce shortly, besides the usual tableau expansion rules, one other operation is allowed. At any stage of tableau construction, one is allowed to create a copy of the question—renaming its free variables to new variables—and either add the copy to all branches or add its negation to all branches. We term this operation the *Add Instance* rule, shown in Table 2.

Table 2. The Add Instance rule for question answering

Add Instance	$\overline{P\vec{y}}$	$\overline{\neg P\vec{y}}$

where $?P\vec{x}$ is the question, and $\vec{y}$ are fresh variables

Note that, whereas the rules in Table 1 are only applied to a single branch at a time, the Add Instance rule is always applied to the entire tableau. This difference is not essential—completeness is not lost if we restrict the application of the Add Instance rule to single branches—but it increases efficiency and it renders the generated answers more concise.

Example 1. A partially developed tableau is given in Fig. 2, where we are given the theory $\Sigma = \{(Pa \wedge Pc) \vee (Pb \wedge Pc)\}$ and wish to answer the question $?Px$. Note the use of the Add Instance rule, indicated by "!". Also note that $y := c$ is a closing substitution: After applying it, the tableau is closed.

Every closing substitution generates an answer, in the following way. Suppose we face a partially developed tableau T, and it can be closed by a substitution σ. Let Φ be the (finite) set of all instances of the question that have been added so far using the Add Instance rule. Then $\neg \bigwedge \Phi^\sigma$ is an appropriate answer. In fact, we can even do a little better and give a slightly more informative answer, by only considering those added instances that participate in closure.

Definition 5 (Closure). *Let T be a tableau, σ be a substitution over T, and κ be a set of formula occurrences in T. The pair (σ, κ) is a closure if κ^σ contains, on each branch, some formula and its negation.*

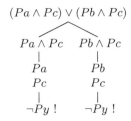

$$(Pa \wedge Pc) \vee (Pb \wedge Pc)$$

$Pa \wedge Pc$	$Pb \wedge Pc$
Pa	Pb
Pc	Pc
$\neg Py$!	$\neg Py$!

Fig. 2. A partially developed tableau

For every closing substitution σ, there is at least one closure (σ, κ). Let Φ_κ consist of exactly those formulas in Φ that appear in κ. With ANS(σ, κ) we will denote the result of universally quantifying all free variables in $\neg \bigwedge (\Phi_\kappa)^\sigma$.

Example 2. Consider again the tableau in Fig. 2. Let σ be the substitution $y := c$, and let κ contain the occurrences of Pc and $\neg Py$ on both branches. Then the pair (σ, κ) is a closure. It generates the answer ANS$(\sigma, \kappa) = \neg\neg Pc$.

When generating answers from closures, we will only be interested in the *most general* closures. One closure (σ_1, κ_1) is more general than another (σ_2, κ_2) if σ_1 is more general than σ_2 and κ_1 is a subset of κ_2. Closures that are more general do as little as possible besides closing the tableau, and so generate answers that are more informative. When there is more than one most general closure, we compute all the corresponding answers and take their conjunction.

One remaining difficulty concerns rigid function symbols. According to our syntactic characterization of answerhood, non-rigid constants and function symbols are not allowed to occur in generated answers. For instance, suppose the theory is $\{Pc\}$, where c is a non-rigid constant. To the question $?Px$, we must answer $\exists x Px$ rather than Pc. Moreover, Skolem functions created during tableau expansion are also considered non-rigid and disallowed in answers. For instance, given the theory $\{\exists x Px\}$ and the question $?Px$, we must answer $\exists x Px$, rather than "Ps, where s is the Skolem constant such that Ps". Our algorithm achieves this by applying Chadha's *unskolemization* procedure [4].

The complete question answering algorithm is as follows.

Algorithm 2. To answer the question $?P\vec{x}$ given the theory Σ, start by initializing a tableau for Σ. Next, do one of the following, repeatedly, *ad infinitum*.

1. Apply a tableaux expansion rule (Table 1).
2. Apply the Add Instance rule (Table 2).
3. Take the conjunction $\psi_0 = \bigwedge$ ANS(σ, κ) over all most general closures (σ, κ). Unskolemize ψ_0 to remove any non-rigid or Skolem function symbols, and report the result as the next answer.   □

Theorem 5. *Algorithm 2 is sound and complete, provided the non-deterministic choices are made in a* fair *manner.*

Proof sketch. Call a formula ψ a *pre-answer* if ψ is built up from instances of the answer literal $P\vec{x}$—allowing non-rigid and Skolem function symbols—using boolean connectives and quantifiers, or if ψ is $\top$ or $\bot$. We first prove that the algorithm, minus unskolemization, generates pre-answers in a sound and complete manner. Soundness means that the algorithm only generates (yet-to-be-unskolemized) conjunctions ψ_0 that are pre-answers and that are entailed by the theory. Completeness means that the sequence of conjunctions generated is cofinal in the set of all pre-answers entailed by the theory.

Soundness: Because $\mathrm{ANS}(\sigma, \kappa)$ is always a pre-answer, so is any generated conjunction ψ_0. Moreover, any closure (σ, κ) for our question-answering tableau gives rise to to a closed theorem-proving tableau for $\Sigma \cup (\Phi_\kappa)^\sigma$. Since tableau theorem proving is sound, the theory Σ must entail $\mathrm{ANS}(\sigma, \kappa)$. Hence Σ entails ψ_0.

Completeness: Suppose that ψ is a pre-answer entailed by Σ. By completeness of tableau theorem proving, we can find a closed theorem-proving tableau for $\Sigma \cup \{\neg\psi\}$, and systematically transform it into a question-answering tableau for $(\Sigma, ?P\vec{x})$ that generates a pre-answer ψ_0 entailing ψ. Given this, it can be shown that in fact any fair question-answering tableau expansion procedure will eventually generate a pre-answer entailing ψ.

We now need to relate pre-answers to answers. The unskolemization procedure is sound; that is, unskolemizing ψ_0 always gives a formula entailed by ψ_0. Besides, unskolemizing any pre-answer gives an answer, so Algorithm 2 is sound. The unskolemization procedure is also complete; that is, whenever a pre-answer ψ_0 entails some answer ψ, the result of unskolemizing ψ_0 also entails ψ. Besides, every answer is a pre-answer, so Algorithm 2 is complete.   □

One way to guarantee fairness in Algorithm 2 is to implement it with *depth first iterative deepening*, just as Beckert and Posegga [2] did in their leanT^AP prover. In fact, we have modified leanT^AP to become a lean question answerer.

The difference between Algorithms 1 and 2 is that the latter waits until closing the tableau before deciding which answer to prove to follow from the theory. In other words, Algorithm 2 does not commit to the rigid instances that constitute the development until they are determined by the closure. This ability to postpone commitment is exactly the strength of free variable tableau calculi as compared to ground tableaux [5].

This algorithm can be extended to deal with equality in two steps. First, add the tableau rules necessary for theorem proving with equality [1, 5]. Second, generalize the Add Instance rule, so that not only instances of the question but also (in)equalities can be added to the tableau.

3.2   Prolog as a Special Case

A precise connection can be established between Prolog and our algorithm. Prolog performs question answering in a sense more restrictive than considered here, because it makes extra assumptions about the theory Σ and the question $?\phi$:

1. The theory Σ is required to be in Skolemized Horn form and the question must consist of a single atom, in order to make computation feasible.

2. There is no equality predicate in the basic language of Prolog.
3. Prolog assumes that all function symbols and constants are rigid, making Pc a potential answer to $?Px$ even if the symbol c resulted from Skolemization.
4. Due to its depth-first search strategy, Prolog is complete only for some theories, for example theories without cycles among predicate symbols.

Subject to all these restrictions, Prolog is an optimal question answering algorithm: Given a theory and a question, it produces answers optimal in the sense of the partition theory of questions.[4]

As we can see, Prolog is a question answering algorithm that makes many extra assumptions. The present work makes it possible to distinguish and identify these assumptions, and eliminate them. A broad spectrum of generalizations of Prolog can then be considered.

4   Conclusion

This paper makes two contributions. First, we presented a syntactic characterization of answerhood for the partition semantics of questions. The applications of this result are mainly internal to the partition semantics: It explains the meaning of a question in terms of the form of its answers.

Second, our tableau-based question answering algorithm connects two important research traditions: question answering systems such as Prolog, and the formal semantics of natural language questions. We feel that the link between these two fields of research has been neglected in the past, and hope to bring them together.

We want to mention three directions of further research (we stress the third).

Logical. Some theoretical issues are still to be addressed: How can answerhood be characterized syntactically when the semantics allows varying domains? Also, is it decidable whether a given answer is the optimal answer to a question entailed by a theory? Without equality, this problem is undecidable, as we proved in Sect. 3. We have yet to find a similar reduction argument for the case with equality.

Linguistic. We want to bring our theoretical results to bear on the semantics of questions in natural language. In particular, our syntactic characterization result clarifies the linguistic predictions made by the partition semantics [14].

Computational. We want to use this work as a unifying framework to compare different approaches to question answering. In particular, we want to investigate a variety of Prolog generalizations and determine which assumptions made by Prolog are feasible to drop.

Like us, Green [6] and Luckham and Nilsson [12] have applied theorem proving to question answering, but their criteria for answerhood are tied

---

[4] One apparent difference between Prolog and our algorithm is that Prolog is based on resolution, whereas we used tableaux. However, the two methods are closely related, and Prolog can be interpreted as a variant of so-called *connection tableaux* [10].

to the syntax of formulas in prenex normal form. This difference explains why their algorithms omit unskolemization, a step necessary for soundness under the notion of answerhood we adopt here. Also, Bos and Gabsdil [3] have devised a simplified version of the partition semantics for computational purposes. These efforts seem to fit nicely in our picture.

References

[1] Beckert, Bernhard. 1994. Adding equality to semantic tableaux. In *Proceedings of the 3rd workshop on theorem proving with analytic tableaux and related methods*, ed. Krysia Broda, Marcello D'Agostino, Rajeev Goré, Rob Johnson, and Steve Reeves, 29–41. Tech. Rep. TR-94/5, Department of Computing, Imperial College, London.

[2] Beckert, Bernhard, and Joachim Posegga. 1995. leanT^AP: Lean, tableau-based deduction. *Journal of Automated Reasoning* 15(3):339–358.

[3] Bos, Johan, and Malte Gabsdil. 2000. First-order inference and the interpretation of questions and answers. In *Proceedings of Götalog 2000*, ed. Massimo Poesio and David Traum, 43–50. Gothenburg Papers in Computational Linguistics 00-5.

[4] Chadha, Ritu. 1991. Applications of unskolemization. Ph.D. thesis, Department of Computer Science, University of North Carolina.

[5] Fitting, Melvin C. 1996. *First order logic and automated theorem proving*. 2nd ed. Berlin: Springer-Verlag.

[6] Green, Claude Cordell. 1969. The application of theorem proving to question-answering systems. Ph.D. thesis, Department of Electrical Engineering, Stanford University. Reprinted by New York: Garland, 1980.

[7] Groenendijk, Jeroen. 1999. The logic of interrogation: Classical version. In *SALT IX: Semantics and linguistic theory*, ed. Tanya Matthews and Devon Strolovitch, 109–126. Ithaca: Cornell University Press.

[8] Groenendijk, Jeroen, and Martin Stokhof. 1984. Studies on the semantics of questions and the pragmatics of answers. Ph.D. thesis, Universiteit van Amsterdam.

[9] ———. 1996. Questions. In *Handbook of logic and language*, ed. Johan van Benthem and Alice ter Meulen, 1055–1124. Amsterdam: Elsevier Science.

[10] Hähnle, Reiner. 2001. Tableaux and related methods. In *The handbook of automated reasoning*, ed. Alan Robinson and Andrei Voronkov, vol. 1, chap. 3, 100–178. Amsterdam: Elsevier Science.

[11] Kager, Wouter. 2001. Questions and answers in query logic. Master's thesis, Universiteit van Amsterdam.

[12] Luckham, David, and Nils J. Nilsson. 1971. Extracting information from resolution proof trees. *Artificial Intelligence* 2:27–54.

[13] Nelken, Rani, and Nissim Francez. 2000. A calculus of interrogatives based on their algebraic semantics. In *Proceedings of TWLT16/AMILP2000*, ed. Dirk Heylen, Anton Nijholt, and Giuseppe Scollo, 143–160.

[14] Shan, Chung-chieh, and Balder ten Cate. 2002. The partition semantics of questions, syntactically. In *Proceedings of the ESSLLI-2002 student session*, ed. Malvina Nissim.

A General Theorem Prover for Quantified Modal Logics

V. Thion[1], S. Cerrito[1], and Marta Cialdea Mayer[2]

[1] Université de Paris-Sud, L.R.I.
[2] Università di Roma Tre, Dipartimento di Informatica e Automazione

Abstract. The main contribution of this work is twofold. It presents a modular tableau calculus, in the free-variable style, treating the main domain variants of quantified modal logic and dealing with languages where rigid and non-rigid designation can coexist. The calculus uses, to this end, light and simple semantical annotations. Such a general proof-system results from the fusion into a unified framework of two calculi previously defined by the second and third authors. Moreover, the work presents a theorem prover, called **GQML-Prover**, based on such a calculus, which is accessible in the Internet. The fair deterministic proof-search strategy used by the prover is described and illustrated via a meaningful example.

1 Introduction

This work presents a theorem prover, called **GQML-Prover** for quantified analytic modal logics, having the following features:

1. it deals with formulae possibly containing both rigid and non-rigid terms;
2. it is parametric with respect to three domain variants: constant, increasing and freely varying domains;
3. it is parametric with respect to five propositional bases of the logic: **D**, **K**, **K4**, **T**, **S4**.

The prover is implemented in Objective Caml and is based on a global modular tableau calculus in the free variable style, that results from the fusion into a same framework of two calculi presented, respectively, in [3,4] and [2], i.e.:[1]

- free-variable tableaux parametric w.r.t. rigid and non-rigid designation of terms, increasing or varying domains and propositional analytical bases, and
- a free variable calculus for constant domain quantified modal logics, with both rigid and non-rigid symbols.

The general proof-system is not simply the justapposition of two different calculi. To start with, it deals with both rigid and non-rigid designation coexisting in the same language, for all domains. Such a feature is absent in [3,4], where varying and increasing domains are treated, while present in [2], where constant domains

---

[1] For the sake of simplicity, in this work we do not consider non-local terms, that are taken into account in [3,4].

U. Egly and C.G. Fermüller (Eds.): TABLEAUX 2002, LNAI 2381, pp. 266–280, 2002.

are dealt with. Having both kinds of designation in the language is interesting for many applications, for instance in database modeling, where both rigid and non-rigid attributes need to be dealt with (e.g. *birth-date*, and, respectively, *salary*).

As a second point, the present system uses a unique labeling technique for all domain variants, while the node labelling mechanism was slightly different in the cited previous works.

The final, and more important, point concerns the treatment of the expansion rule for existential formulae. In fact, the calculi in [3,4] use the "traditional" δ-rule to expand existential quantified formulae, where the arguments of Skolem functions are *all* the free variables (of appropriate level) in the set of formulae $\exists x A(x), S$ to be expanded. On the contrary, [2] shows that the "liberalized" δ^+-rule, where the only arguments of Skolem functions are the free variables actually occurring in A, and that is proved sound for classical logic in [10], characterizes constant domains, in the absence of any semantical annotation. So, the fusion of the two approaches requires proving soundness of the "liberalized" δ^+-rule for non-constant domain logics, in the annotated calculi we consider. This is not a trivial task: the proof requires some subtleties (see the end of Section 3).

Section 2 introduces the syntax and semantics of Quantified Modal Logics (QML). The general tableau system is presented in Section 3, together with the soundness proof of the liberalized δ^+-rule used by the **GQML-Prover** for all domain variants. The main feature of the system, in comparison with other approaches such as prefixed tableaux [6], matrix methods [15] and others, such as those cited in [2,4], is the effort to minimize expression labelling.

A further important issue that must be faced in order to turn a tableau calculus into an automated theorem prover is the definition of a complete proof-search strategy. The issue is not trivial, because of the interplay of applications of the γ-rule, possible sources of an infinite number of instantiations of a universal formula, and the choice of closing substitutions with the "dynamical" modal rules, which cause one to forget the past. Section 4 presents the **GQML-Prover** and the underlying search strategy. In order to ensure termination of proof search, the strategy uses two upper bounds on the size of candidate proofs, whose values are entered by the user. It is complete in the sense that if a formula is valid, then a proof is found, provided that the input bounds are big enough. Note that, although some theorem provers for non-classical logics exist (for instance, Mod-LeanTap [1] deals with propositional modal logics, while IleanTap [12] deals with quantification, but only in a intuitionistic logic setting), up to our knowledge, not much has been done on QML.

Section 5 concludes this work with a discussion on equality.

2   Quantified Modal Logics

In Kripke semantics for quantified modal logic an interpretation is, roughly, a set of first-order classical interpretations (the "possible worlds") connected by an accessibility relation. The worlds can either all have the same object domain (constant domains) or the domains can be allowed to be different (varying domains), possibly monotonically increasing with the accessibility relation (cumulative domains). Terms can designate the same object in each world (rigid terms) or can be allowed to designate differently in different worlds (non-rigid terms). Rigid and non-rigid functional symbols may coexist in the same language: the set L_F of functional symbols of a language is partitioned into a set L_{F_R} of rigid functional symbols, and a disjoint set $L_{F_{NR}}$ of non-rigid functional symbols.

From now on, we consider modal formulae in negation normal form, i.e. built out of literals (atoms and negated atoms) by use of $\wedge$, $\vee$, $\square$, $\lozenge$ and the quantifiers $\forall$ and $\exists$. Negation over non-atomic formulae and implication are considered as defined symbols.

Below, we recall standard definitions on quantified modal logics [6]. A first-order modal interpretation $\mathcal{M}$ of a language L is a tuple $\langle W, w_0, R, D, \delta, \phi, \pi \rangle$ such that:
- W is a non empty set (the set of "possible worlds");
- w_0 is a distinguished element of W (the "initial world");
- R is a binary relation on W (the *accessibility relation*); wRw' abbreviates $\langle w, w' \rangle \in R$;
- D is a non empty set (the "global" object domain);
- δ is a function assigning to each $w \in W$ a non empty subset of D, the domain of w: $\delta(w) \subseteq D$;
- ϕ represents the interpretation of constants and functional symbols in the language: for every world $w \in W$ and k-ary functional symbol $f \in L_F$ (with $k \geq 0$),
$$\phi(w, f) \in D^k \to D$$
Moreover, if $f \in L_{F_R}$, then for all $w, w' \in W$, $\phi(w, f) = \phi(w', f)$. We consider here only *local* terms, i.e. for all $w \in W$ and $f \in L_F$, if $d_1, ..., d_n \in \delta(w)$, then $\phi(w, f)(d_1, ..., d_n) \in \delta(w)$.
- π is the interpretation of predicate symbols: if p is a k-ary predicate symbol and $w \in W$, then $\pi(w, p) \subseteq D^k$ is a set of k-ples of elements in D.

The accessibility relation R of a modal structure can be required to satisfy additional properties, characterizing different logics: seriality (**D**), reflexivity (**T**), transitivity (**K4**), both reflexivity and transitivity (**S4**). When no additional assumption on R is made, the logic is **K**.

On the first-order side, the main "domain variants" of QML are characterized as follows:
Constant domains: for all $w \in W$, $\delta(w) = D$.
Cumulative domains: for all $w, w' \in W$, if wRw' then $\delta(w) \subseteq \delta(w')$.
Varying domains: no restrictions on $\delta(w)$.

If $\mathcal{M}$ is an interpretation with object domain D, a variable assignment on $\mathcal{M}$ is a function $s : X \to D$, where X is the set of variables of the language. If s is a variable assignment, x is a variable and $d \in D$, then s_x^d is the variable assignment such that $s_x^d(x) = d$ and $s_x^d(y) = s(y)$ for all $y \neq x$.

Given a world $w \in W$ and a variable assignment s, the interpretation of a term t in w according to s, $s(w, t)$, is inductively defined as follows:

1. If x is a variable, then $s(w, x) = s(x)$.
2. If c is a constant, then $s(w, c) = \phi(w, c)$.
3. If f is a k-ary functional symbol and $t_1, ..., t_k$ are terms, then $s(w, f(t_1, ..., t_k)) = \phi(w, f)(s(w, t_1), ..., s(w, t_k))$.

If t is a ground term, its designation is independent from the variable assignment and is denoted by $\mathcal{M}(w, t)$.

The relation $\models$ between an interpretation $\mathcal{M} = \langle W, w_0, R, D, \delta, \phi, \pi \rangle$, a variable assignment s on $\mathcal{M}$, a world $w \in W$ and a formula is defined inductively as follows:[2]

1. $\mathcal{M}, s, w \models p(t_1, ..., t_n)$ iff $\langle s(w, t_1), ..., s(w, t_n) \rangle \in \pi(w, p)$.
2. $\mathcal{M}, s, w \models \neg A$ iff $\mathcal{M}, s, w \not\models A$.
3. $\mathcal{M}, s, w \models A \wedge B$ iff $\mathcal{M}, s, w \models A$ and $\mathcal{M}, s, w \models B$.
4. $\mathcal{M}, s, w \models A \vee B$ iff $\mathcal{M}, s, w \models A$ or $\mathcal{M}, s, w \models B$.
5. $\mathcal{M}, s, w \models \forall x A$ iff for all $d \in \delta(w)$, $\mathcal{M}, s_x^d, w \models A$
6. $\mathcal{M}, s, w \models \exists x A$ iff there exists $d \in \delta(w)$ such that $\mathcal{M}, s_x^d, w \models A$
7. $\mathcal{M}, s, w \models \Box A$ iff for all $w' \in W$ such that wRw', $\mathcal{M}, s, w' \models A$
8. $\mathcal{M}, s, w \models \Diamond A$ iff there is a $w' \in W$ such that wRw' and $\mathcal{M}, s, w' \models A$

A formula A is true in $\mathcal{M}$ iff for all variable assignments s on $\mathcal{M}$: $\mathcal{M}, s, w_0 \models A$, and it is valid iff it is true in all interpretations. Note that, if t is a ground term and $w \in W$, then for all variable assignment s, $s(w, t) \in \delta(w)$. However, if domains are allowed to vary without restrictions, if $\mathcal{M}, s, w \models \exists x \Diamond p(f(x))$, and d is the element of $\delta(w)$ such that $\mathcal{M}, s_x^d, w \models \Diamond p(f(x))$, then (by definition) there exists a world w' accessible from w and such that $\mathcal{M}, s_x^d, w' \models p(f(x))$; but $s_x^d(w', f(x))$ is not necessarily in the domain of the world w', unless $d \in \delta(w')$.

3   The Tableaux Systems

In this section we introduce the calculi which are the basis of the **GQML-Prover**. They result from the fusion into a same framework of the free-variable tableaux systems described in [3,4] and [2], but for the fact that a liberalized δ-rule is used in all calculi, and not only for the constant domain case. The soundness proof for the varying and cumulative domain logics can be found at the end of the section.

In the calculi we are going to describe, tableau nodes are labelled by $n : S$ where n is a positive integer (the "name" of a possible world) and S a set of annotated formulae. The integer n is called the *depth* of the node. In an annotated formula, functional symbols can be annotated by a superscript natural number: the "name" of the world where they are meant to designate. If f is a rigid symbol of the original language, it always occurs as f^0 in the tableau. If f is non-rigid, it occurs either with no annotation or as $f^1, f^2, ...$ The language of a tableau includes also annotated *free variables*, $v_0^k, v_1^k, v_2^k, ...$, and annotated

---

[2] The reader will recognize that this approach to the interpretation of non-rigid functional symbols corresponds to the "narrow-scope" approach discussed in [8].

Skolem functional symbols. Skolem functions and annotated functional symbols are considered as rigid symbols.

The initial tableau for a set S of formulae is $1 : S^*$, where S^* is obtained from S by annotating rigid symbols with 0 and *non-modal occurrences* of non-rigid symbols with 1 – where a symbol occurrence is non-modal if it is in the scope of no modal operators.

The formulation of the expansion rules require the definition of *depth* of a term, that – intuitively – establishes a relation between annotated terms and positive integers. So, "t is at depth n" means its intended designation belongs to the domain of the world named by n.

A term t is at **depth** n iff every functional symbol in t is annotated and such symbols are only annotated with:
> **varying domains:** n and 0;
> **cumulative domains:** $k \leq n$;
> **constant domains:** any k.

Similarly, we define the world domains over which a variable may range:

A free variable v^n **ranges** over depth k iff:
> **varying and cumulative domains:** $k = n$;
> **constant domains:** $k \in \mathbb{N}$ (i.e. always)

Non-rigid symbols occurring in the scope of some modal operator are initially non-annotated. They get their annotation when, by application of a modal expansion rule, they come to the surface. The annotation they are given is the label of the tableau node in which they occur. The definition of the expansion rules requires then the following last definition: if A is a modal formula and $n \in \mathbb{N}$, then A^n is obtained from A by annotating each non-modal occurrence of a non-rigid functional symbol with n. If S is a set of modal formulae, then $S^n = \{A^n \mid A \in S\}$.

As a leading example we consider the case of QMLs based on **S4**. The other analytic propositional bases treated by the **GQML-Prover**, i.e. **K, D, T** and **K4**, are obtained simply by modification of the modal rules. The tableau expansion rules for **S4** are shown in Figure 1, where S, S' are sets of annotated modal formulae, $\Box S$ stands for $\{\Box A \mid A \in S\}$, S' is a set of non-boxed modal formulae, comma is set union. Rules generating a new node label are called *dynamic* (only π_4 in the case of **S4**), the others are *static*.

Note that, in the case of varying or cumulative domains, in the δ^+-rule, $k_1 = k_2 = ... = k_m = n$. In the case of constant domains, instead, the annotation of free-variables and Skolem functional symbols can actually be ignored. In this variant, in fact, the only relevant annotations are those on non-rigid symbols, which are taken into account by unification (symbols annotated differently are considered as different symbols).

Besides the expansion rules, the calculi provide a substitution rule. The notion of substitution however takes into account the depth of terms:

A modal substitution σ is a set of pairs $\{t_1/v_1^{k_1}, ..., t_m/v_m^{k_m}\}$, where each t_i is at depth k_i.

Note again that, in the case of constant domains, the annotation of symbols is not relevant, since any term is at any depth.

The substitution rule of the calculus is the *MGU atomic closure rule*: if $\mathcal{T}$ is a tableau for a set S of sentences and some leaf of $\mathcal{T}$ contains P and $\neg Q$, where P and Q are atomic, then $\mathcal{T}\sigma$ is also a tableau for S, where σ is a most general unifier of P and Q.

A tableau is closed iff each of its leaves contains a pair of complementary literals, i.e. literals P and $\neg P$. A closed tableau for a formula $\neg A$ is a tableau proof of A, and a closed tableau for a set of formulae S is a refutation of S.

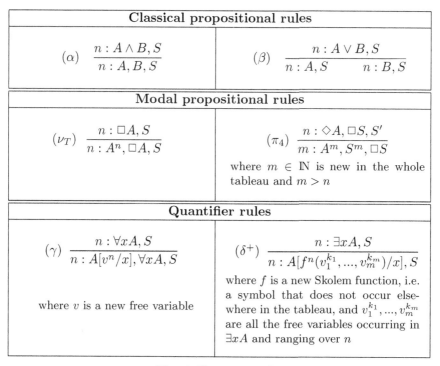

Fig. 1. Expansion rules

Note that the δ^+-rule only requires free-variables actually occurring in $\exists x A$ to be taken as parameters of the Skolem function. In free-variable calculi with no annotation, the δ^+-rule characterizes constant domains [2]. An intuitive justification of the soundness of the δ^+-rule in the cumulative or varying domain cases can be given as follows: in a non-annotated calculus we need the full δ-rule because the substitution of a free variable v, introduced at a given depth n, with a Skolem term t introduced at a greater depth must be forbidden, because v ranges over a domain that may not contain the designation of t. But such a constraint is automatically satisfied when depths of terms are taken into consideration by the notion of substitution itself.

The main difficulty in adapting the soundness proof of the δ^+-rule for classical logic to the modal non-constant domain cases is due to the interplay between the

δ^+-rule and substitution, in presence of the fact that tableau nodes can contain variables ranging over different world domains and terms denoting in different worlds. The proof sketched below makes use of an unrestricted grounding substitution rule, that must always be applied before dynamic rules, so that one doesn't have to keep track of the domains of previously considered worlds.

Let us consider the tableau calculi obtained by replacing the MGU atomic closure rule with unrestricted substitution: if $\mathcal{T}$ is a tableau for S and σ is a modal substitution then $\mathcal{T}\sigma$ is a tableau for S. Clearly, if there is a closed tableau for S using the MGU atomic closure rule, then there is a closed tableau for S using the unrestricted substitution rule.

Now, let $\mathcal{T}\sigma$ be a closed tableau for a set S of sentences, where σ is the composition of all the modal substitutions used to close $\mathcal{T}$. We may assume, without loss of generality, that σ is a grounding substitution, i.e. that $\mathcal{T}\sigma$ is a ground tableau. In fact, if $\mathcal{T}\theta$ is closed and it contains the free variables $v_1^{k_1}, ..., v_n^{k_n}$, and $a_1^1, a_2^2, ...$ are a new constants (the "dummy" constants, one for each annotation), then clearly

$$\mathcal{T}(\theta \circ \{a_{k_1}^{k_1}/v_1^{k_1}, ..., a_{k_n}^{k_n}/v_n^{k_n}\})$$

is a ground and closed tableau for S.

If $max(\mathcal{T})$ is the maximal label of a node in $\mathcal{T}$, we may assume, without loss of generality, that whenever a tableau $\mathcal{T}$ is expanded by means of a dynamic rule, the new integer m used to label the expansion is equal to $1 + max(\mathcal{T})$. For all $i = 1, ..., n = max(\mathcal{T})$, let $\mathcal{T}_i$ be the maximal subtree of $\mathcal{T}\sigma$ where the label of every node is less than or equal to i. We can assume that $\mathcal{T}\sigma$ is built as the sequence $\mathcal{T}_1, ..., \mathcal{T}_n = \mathcal{T}\sigma$. In other words, at first all the static rules are applied to the initial node, then σ is applied (so that the ground tableau $\mathcal{T}_1$ is obtained), then a dynamic rule is applied, followed by a sequence of static rules; then σ is applied again (obtaining $\mathcal{T}_2$) before the next dynamic rule application, and so on.

Note that, for all k, while building $\mathcal{T}_k$ starting from $\mathcal{T}_{k-1}$, tableau nodes only contain free-variables annotated with k. In fact, $\mathcal{T}_{k-1}$ is a ground tableau, and the new expansion rules applied to obtain $\mathcal{T}_k$ from $\mathcal{T}_{k-1}$ only affect nodes labelled with k, so if any new free variable is introduced by means of the γ-rule, it is annotated with k. Moreover, in the construction of the sequence $\mathcal{T}_1, ..., \mathcal{T}_n$, only "grounding substitutions" are applied, i.e. when σ is applied, the result is a ground tableau.

In order to prove soundness, it is sufficient to show that if S is satisfiable then there is no sequence $\mathcal{T}_1, ..., \mathcal{T}_n$ of tableaux, built as illustrated above, and such that $\mathcal{T}_n$ is closed. This, in turn, amounts to proving soundness of the calculus Tab^*, allowing the general substitution rule but with the additional constraints that:

– when a substitution is applied, the result is a ground tableau, and
– when a dynamic rule is applied, the tableau contains no free variables.

This can be done along standard lines, by showing that if S is satisfiable then any Tab^*-tableau for S is satisfiable. However, the notion of satisfiability of a tableau requires some machinery. We first define when a "static" tableau is satisfiable, i.e. a tableau that has never been expanded by application of a dynamic rule.

In general, the interpretation of a language with annotations is a modal interpretation where:

- symbols annotated differently are considered as different symbols;
- annotated functional symbols are rigid.

Definition 1. *If $\mathcal{T}$ is a static Tab^*-tableau, whose nodes are all labelled by n, $\mathcal{M}$ is an interpretation of the language of $\mathcal{T}$ and w a world in $\mathcal{M}$, then $\mathcal{M}, w \models \mathcal{T}$ ($\mathcal{M}$ satisfies $\mathcal{T}$ at w) iff for all variable assignment s, if $s(v^n) \in \delta(w)$ for all free-variable v^n annotated by n, then there exists a leaf $n : S$ of $\mathcal{T}$ such that $\mathcal{M}, s, w \models S$.*

A static tableau is satisfiable iff there exists an interpretation $\mathcal{M}$ and a world w in $\mathcal{M}$ such that $\mathcal{M}, w \models \mathcal{T}$.

Satisfiability of a generic tableau amounts to satisfiability of one of its maximal static terminal sub-tableaux:

Definition 2. *If $\mathcal{T}$ is a tableau, then its terminal sub-tableaux are all the static sub-trees $\mathcal{T}'$ of $\mathcal{T}$ such that:*

- *the root of $\mathcal{T}'$ is either the root of $\mathcal{T}$ itself, or a node obtained by application of a dynamic rule;*
- *all the leaves of $\mathcal{T}'$ are leaves of $\mathcal{T}$.*

A tableau $\mathcal{T}$ is satisfiable iff it has a satisfiable terminal sub-tableau.

Soundness of Tab^* follows from the following

Lemma 1. *If S is satisfiable, then any Tab^*-tableau $\mathcal{T}$ for S is satisfiable.*

The proof is by induction on $\mathcal{T}$, showing how to build an interpretation $\mathcal{M}$ of the annotated language of $\mathcal{T}$ and a world w in $\mathcal{M}$ such that for some terminal sub-tableau $\mathcal{T}'$ of $\mathcal{T}$, $\mathcal{M}, w \models \mathcal{T}'$. The same induction shows that, if the nodes in $\mathcal{T}'$ are labelled by n, then for every ground term t at depth n in the language of the tableau (i.e. symbols occurring in the tableau and dummy constants), $\mathcal{M}(w, t) \in \delta(w)$. This fact is needed when the substitution rule is applied.

The base case is immediate: the interpretation $\mathcal{M}$ is obtained from the model of the initial set of formulae given by the hypothesis, extending it in the obvious way to symbols annotated with 1 (the constant a_1^1 is mapped to any element of the domain of the initial world).

For the induction step, let $\mathcal{T}'$ be a satisfiable terminal sub-tableau of $\mathcal{T}$ (with nodes labelled by n), $\mathcal{M}$ a modal interpretation and w a world in $\mathcal{M}$ such that $\mathcal{M}, w \models \mathcal{T}'$. If $\mathcal{T}$ is expanded by application of an expansion rule to a leaf that is not in $\mathcal{T}'$, then:

- if the applied rule is not the δ^+-rule, then obviously $\mathcal{M}, w \models \mathcal{T}$ is still true.
- If the δ^+-rule is applied, introducing a new Skolem function f, then the interpretation $\mathcal{M}$ is extended to $\mathcal{M}'$ by establishing that $\mathcal{M}'(f) = \lambda(d_1, ..., d_k).d$, where d is any element in the domain of w. Since f does not occur in $\mathcal{T}'$, $\mathcal{M}', w \models \mathcal{T}'$. And it is still true that the interpretation of every ground term at depth n is in the domain of w.

The interesting cases are when $\mathcal{T}'$ is expanded to $\mathcal{T}''$. We consider the following two different cases, according to the applied rule.

1. The applied rule is not the substitution rule and the expanded node is $n : S$. If $\mathcal{T}'$ is expanded by means of a classical rule, the proof is the same as in the classical case, since $\mathcal{T}''$ is still a classical tableau. The only point to be taken care of is to ensure that, when the δ^+-rule is applied, introducing the Skolem function f^n, the interpretation of every ground term $f^n(t_1, ..., t_k)$ at depth n is in the domain of w. But this follows immediately from the induction hypothesis and the fact that $t_1, ..., t_k$ are at depth n too.

   Also the case of static modal rules are straightforward. If $\mathcal{T}'$ is expanded by application of a dynamic rule to $n : S$, $n : S$ contains no free-variables. So the proof of this case is the same as in the soundness proof of the ground tableau calculi presented in [3,4].

2. The applied rule is the substitution rule. There, a Modal Substitution Theorem is applied, that, in QML, holds in the following form:

   Let $\mathcal{M}$ be a modal interpretation, w a world in $\mathcal{M}$, s a variable assignment, and t a rigid term (i.e. a term containing no non-rigid symbol). If $s(w, t) = d$, then $\mathcal{M}, s_x^d, w \models A$ if and only if $\mathcal{M}, s, w \models A[t/x]$.

   Now, let us assume that $\mathcal{T}''$ is obtained from $\mathcal{T}'$ by application of the grounding substitution rule, with substitution σ. Then, if $v_1^n, ..., v_k^n$ is a sequence of all the free variables (all annotated with n) occurring in $\mathcal{T}'$, σ has the form $\{t_1/v_1, ..., t_k/v_k\}$, where $t_1, ..., t_k$ are ground terms at depth n.

   Let $\mathcal{M} = \langle W, w, R, D, \delta, \phi, \pi \rangle$ be a model of $\mathcal{T}'$. By definition, for all variable assignment s', if $s'(v^n) \in \delta(w)$ for all free-variable v^n annotated by n, then there exists a leaf $n : S$ of $\mathcal{T}'$ such that $\mathcal{M}, s', w \models S$. Moreover, by the induction hypothesis, for every ground term t at depth n, $\mathcal{M}(w, t) \in \delta(w)$.

   Let s be any variable assignment such that $s(v^n) \in \delta(w)$ for all free-variable v^n annotated by n. If t_j/v_j^n is any element of σ, since t_j is a ground term at depth n, $\mathcal{M}(w, t_j) \in \delta(w)$. Now, let $d_j = \mathcal{M}(w, t_j)$, for any $j = 1, ..., k$, and consider the assignment $s' = s_{v_1, ..., v_k}^{d_1, ..., d_k}$. Clearly, for all free variable v^n, $s'(v^n) \in \delta(w)$. As a consequence, by hypothesis there is a leaf $n : S$ in $\mathcal{T}'$ such that $\mathcal{M}, s', w \models S$. Since $s(w, t_i) = d_i = s'(v_i)$ and t_i is a rigid term, by the Modal Substitution Theorem $\mathcal{M}, s, w \models S\sigma$.

4   The GQML-Prover

The aim of the **GQML-Prover** is to detect whether a given sentence is a theorem of a given QML. Obviously, termination must be forced with the loss of completeness. The **GQML-Prover** exploits, to this end, two numerical bounds limiting the proof depth and entered by the user. The role of such bounds is explained below. Besides them, the user enters the sentence to prove, the propositional base of the considered logic, the domain variant, and the non-rigid functional symbols.

The **GQML-Prover** is implemented in Objective Caml. It is accessible on line at http://www.lri.fr/~thion/Proto. One just needs a standard web browser to use it. The Objective Caml program is compiled on the LRI[3] server. The user formulates a query by filling the form in the web page. A *php* function calls the execution of the program on the LRI server and the answer is given in a frame under the form. In order to help the user, a pre-defined set of sentences to test and help topics supplement the form. The tool will be part of a more important application allowing to test preservation of integrity constraints in data bases.

Like any tableau calculus, the system presented in Section 3 is intrinsically non-deterministic, since a node might be expanded by means of several rules. Hence, the crucial passage from a proof system to an algorithm consists in defining a fair and complete strategy guiding rule application.

Tableau building strategies have been proposed for different logics in [11,5, 13,9]. The strategy used in our implementation is partially inspired by these papers but is specifically designed to deal with our calculus.

A first classical choice in the strategy underlying the **GQML-Prover** consists in applying deterministic rules (in our case static rules) before a non-deterministic (a dynamic) one.

QML tableaux and tableaux systems for classical logic share the difficulty that, in principle, a γ-rule might need to be applied an unlimited number of times to the same formula (in each given world), in order to achieve completeness. A classical way to deal with this problem is to set an upper bound to the number of γ-rule applications to the same formula in a given world [7]. This is the role of the first bound entered by the user of the **GQML-Prover**: the γ-rule will never be applied more than K_γ times to the same formula at the same depth.

However, when K_γ is large, applying always K_γ times a γ-rule to the same formula in each world leads immediately to an explosion of the search space. In order to overcome this problem, at the first attempt to close a branch, the γ-rule is applied only once to the same formula in each world. If the branch cannot be closed, then the γ-rule is applied again to each formula, i.e. the number of γ-rule applications is increased as an effect of backtracking. The advantage of such a choice is that if a proof exists where the γ-rule is applied a number of times strictly inferior to K_γ, such a proof is found.

The second bound, which we here call K_π, limits the number of dynamic rule applications allowed in a single branch, which will never exceed $K_\pi - 1$.

In order to describe the proof search strategy, we introduce the following classification of the expansion rules of the system:

- *Dynamic rules*, which introduce a new node label and are non-reversible rules; the dynamic rules are the π-rules of all the considered logics, and the ν-rule of system **D**.
- *Looping rules*, that may need to be triggered more than once on the same formula in the same world (i.e. at the same depth). The only looping rule is the γ-rule.

---

[3] Laboratoire de Recherche Informatique, *Université Paris-Sud*, France

- *Branching rules*, that generates two branches. The only branching rule is the β-rule.
- *Simple rules:* all the others, i.e. static, non-looping and non-branching rules. These are all the rules α, δ^+ and ν_T.

Proof search in the **GQML-Prover** proceeds depth-first, and the construction of a single branch proceeds by stages, as follows:

Step 1: Initialize p with 0.

Step 2: Simple rules are applied as far as possible.

Step 3: For each γ-formula A resulting from the previous step, the γ-rule is applied once, if A has been expanded less than K_γ times at the same depth.

Step 4: Branching rules are applied as far as possible, and a branch is chosen to be expanded next (this is not a choice point: every branch must be expanded, sooner or later).

Step 5 (Choice point): either choose, if any, a substitution that closes the branch and apply it to the whole tableau, or go on to step 6.

Step 6 (Choice point): either go on to step 7, or go back to step 2 (if some formula can still be expanded either by simple rules or by the γ-rule).

Step 7: Increase p by one (one "world" has been explored).

Step 8 (Choice point): If $p \leq K_\pi$, choose a formula (if any) that can be expanded by means of a dynamic rule, expand it and go back to step 2.

Each iteration between steps 2 and 4 constitutes the construction of a *block*. The construction of a branch ends in any case when it contains (at most) K_γ applications for every universal formula at each depth, and (at most) $K_\pi - 1$ applications of dynamic rules (i.e. K_π different node labels). The attempt to close a branch fails when the branch cannot be expanded any more and no substitution can close it. A more detailed description of the algorithm is given in Figure 2.

The strategy described above is sound and complete, provided that, by iterative deepening, the bounds K_γ and K_π are incremented as far as needed (this corresponds to using an "unbounded" version of the strategy). The soundness and completeness proofs can be found in [14].

In order to illustrate the proof-search strategy, consider the formula $F \equiv \neg(\forall x \exists y (\neg p(x) \wedge p(y)) \wedge \Diamond r(a)) \wedge \Diamond(q(a) \rightarrow \Box q(a))$, where the constant a is rigid. F is a theorem of **S4**-QML with varying domains. Below, we show the construction, according to the strategy illustrated above, of a closed tableau rooted at $\neg F \equiv (\forall x \exists y (\neg p(x) \wedge p(y)) \wedge \Diamond r(a)) \vee \Box(q(a) \wedge \Diamond \neg q(a))$, when the bounds $K_\gamma = 2$ and $K_\pi = 2$.

PROVABLE (A) /* returns a boolean */
return IS-CLOSED $(\{\text{INITIAL-TABLEAU}\ (\neg A)\}, 0)$
                /* INITIAL-TABLEAU returns the node representing
                the initial tableau for a formula */

IS-CLOSED $(nodes, p)$
/* $nodes$ is the set of open leaves to expand, all having the same depth;
    p is the number of "worlds" already explored in the branch $(p \leq K_\pi)$ */
if $nodes = \emptyset$ **then return** true
else let $N =$ an element of $nodes$
    and $rest = nodes - \{N\}$
    and $expansions =$ EXPAND-A-BLOCK (N)
    and $N1 =$ an element of $expansions$
    and $siblings = expansions - \{N1\}$
    return
      there exists a substitution σ that closes $N1$
        such that IS-CLOSED $((siblings \cup rest)\ \sigma, p)$
      or $p < K_\pi$
        and there exists an expansion $N2$ of $N1$ by a dynamic rule
              such that IS-CLOSED $(\{N2\}, p+1)$
        and IS-CLOSED $((siblings \cup rest)\ \sigma, p)$
            where σ is the substitution used to close $N2$
      or $expansions \neq \{N\}$ /* if $expansions = \{N\}$ nothing happened
                          when expanding a block in N */
        and IS-CLOSED $(expansions \cup rest, p)$

EXPAND-A-BLOCK (N)
    /* expands node N and returns all the nodes that can be obtained
        by application of simple rules, a single application of the γ-rule
        to each formula that has not yet reached the limit, and the β-rule */
let $N1 =$ the node resulting from N by applying simple rules
        as far as possible
and $N2 =$ the node resulting from $N1$ by expanding once more each γ-formula
        that has already been expanded less than K_γ times at this depth
return the leaves of the tableau obtained from $N2$ by
        applying the β-rule as far as possible

Fig. 2. The algorithm of the GQML-Prover, where K_π and K_γ are global variables,
assumed to have a positive value.

The initial node is:

$$1 : (\forall x \exists y(\neg p(x) \wedge p(y)) \wedge \Diamond r(a^0)) \vee \Box(q(a^0) \wedge \Diamond \neg q(a^0))$$

Such a node can be expanded neither by simple rules nor by the γ-rule, while
the β-rule can be applied:

$$\frac{1 : \forall x \exists y (\neg p(x) \wedge p(y)) \wedge \Diamond r(a^0) \vee \Box (q(a^0) \wedge \Diamond \neg q(a^0))}{1 : \forall x \exists y (\neg p(x) \wedge p(y)) \wedge \Diamond r(a^0) \qquad \qquad 1 : \Box (q(a^0) \wedge \Diamond \neg q(a^0))} \ (\beta)$$

At first, one tries to close the first branch. When the first branch is closed, the second one will be treated (by depth-first search).

Dealing with the first branch. The node $1 : \forall x \exists y (\neg p(x) \wedge p(y)) \wedge \Diamond r(a^0)$ is expanded, and the tableau shown below is built. Note that the γ-rule is applied only once, and is not followed by an application of the α-rule, even if it would be possible, because, in a single block, the α-rule is always applied only before the γ-rule.

$$\frac{\dfrac{1 : \forall x \exists y (\neg p(x) \wedge p(y)) \wedge \Diamond r(a^0)}{1 : \forall x \exists y (\neg p(x) \wedge p(y)), \ \Diamond r(a^0)} \ (\alpha)}{1 : \forall x \exists y (\neg p(x) \wedge p(y)), \ \Diamond r(a^0), \ \exists y (\neg p(v_1^1) \wedge p(y))} \ (\gamma)$$

Since there are no closing substitutions for the leaf of this branch, the construction goes on with an application of the π_4-rule:

$$\vdots$$

$$\frac{1 : \forall x \exists y (\neg p(x) \wedge p(y)), \ \Diamond r(a^0), \ \exists y (\neg p(v_1^1) \wedge p(y))}{1 : r(a^0)} \ (\pi_4)$$

This branch cannot be expanded any further, and it cannot be closed. Thus, the algorithm backtracks before the application of the π_4-rule, the simple rules are applied again as far as possible and the γ-rule once again to each formula (no application of the β-rule is possible):

$$\vdots$$

$$\frac{\dfrac{\dfrac{1 : \forall x \exists y (\neg p(x) \wedge p(y)), \ \Diamond r(a^0), \ \exists y (\neg p(v_1^1) \wedge p(y))}{1 : \forall x \exists y (\neg p(x) \wedge p(y)), \ \Diamond r(a^0), \ \neg p(v_1^1) \wedge p(f^1(v_1^1))} \ (\delta^+)}{1 : \forall x \exists y (\neg p(x) \wedge p(y)), \ \Diamond r(a^0), \ \neg p(v_1^1), \ p(f^1(v_1^1))} \ (\alpha)}{1 : \forall x \exists y (\neg p(x) \wedge p(y)), \ \Diamond r(a^0), \neg p(v_1^1), \ p(f^1(v_1^1)), \ \exists y (\neg p(v_2^1) \wedge p(y))} \ (\gamma)$$

At the end of this second block, since again there are no closing substitutions, the π_4-rule is applied again, leading to a tableau that can be neither closed nor expanded further:

$$\vdots$$

$$\frac{1 : \forall x \exists y (\neg p(x) \wedge p(y)), \ \Diamond r(a^0), \neg p(v_1^1), \ p(f^1(v_1^1)), \ \exists y (\neg p(v_2^1) \wedge p(y))}{1 : r(a^0)} \ (\pi_4)$$

So the algorithm backtracks once more before the application of the π_4-rule and builds the third block. At this point, the γ-rule has already been applied twice to the formula $\forall x \exists y (\neg p(x) \wedge p(y))$ at the current depth (during the two previous blocks), so the K_γ bound has been reached and the γ-rule cannot be applied anymore to that formula (at this depth).

$$\vdots$$

$$\frac{\displaystyle 1 : \forall x \exists y (\neg p(x) \wedge p(y)),\ \Diamond r(a^0),\ \neg p(v_1^1),\ p(f^1(v_1^1)),\ \exists y(\neg p(v_2^1) \wedge p(y))}{\displaystyle \frac{1 : \forall x \exists y (\neg p(x) \wedge p(y)),\ \Diamond r(a^0), \neg p(v_1^1),\ p(f^1(v_1^1)),\ \neg p(v_2^1) \wedge p(g^1(v_2^1))}{1 : \forall x \exists y (\neg p(x) \wedge p(y)),\ \Diamond r(a^0),\ \neg p(v_1^1),\ p(f^1(v_1^1)),\ \neg p(v_2^1),\ p(g^1(v_2^1))}\ (\alpha)}\ (\delta^+)$$

Finally, this branch is closed by the substitution $\sigma = \{g^1(v_2^1)/v_1^1\}$.

Dealing with the second branch. The application of σ to the rightmost branch leaves it unchanged, since there are no occurrences of v_1^1. The first block of the rightmost branch is:

$$\frac{\displaystyle 1 : \Box(q(a^0) \wedge \Diamond \neg q(a^0))}{\displaystyle \frac{1 : q(a^0) \wedge \Diamond \neg q(a^0),\ \Box(q(a^0) \wedge \Diamond \neg q(a^0))}{1 : q(a^0),\ \Diamond \neg q(a^0),\ \Box(q(a^0) \wedge \Diamond \neg q(a^0))}\ (\alpha)}\ (\nu_T)$$

Since the leaf cannot be closed, the π_4-rule is applied and the branch is expanded by application of simple rules (now $p = 1$, so this is the last application of the π_4-rule in the branch):

$$\vdots$$

$$\frac{\displaystyle 1 : q(a^0),\ \Diamond \neg q(a^0),\ \Box(q(a^0) \wedge \Diamond \neg q(a^0))}{\displaystyle \frac{2 : \neg q(a^0),\ \Box(q(a^0) \wedge \Diamond \neg q(a^0))}{\displaystyle \frac{2 : \neg q(a^0),\ q(a^0) \wedge \Diamond \neg q(a^0),\ \Box(q(a^0) \wedge \Diamond \neg q(a^0))}{2 : \neg q(a^0),\ q(a^0),\ \Diamond \neg q(a^0),\ \Box(q(a^0) \wedge \Diamond \neg q(a^0))}\ (\alpha)}\ (\nu_T)}\ (\pi_4)$$

Finally, also the second branch closes.

Note that if either $K_\pi < 2$ or $K_\gamma < 2$, no proof would be found.

5   Concluding Remarks

The addition of suitable rules handling equality to the general calculus presented in Section 3 presents a major difficulty, due to the nature of dynamic rules, which lead to a loss of information, in contrast with the fact that equality is to be interpreted as a rigid predicate symbol. To make this point clear, consider the following simple example. Let A be the formula $\exists x\, \exists y\, ((\Diamond x = y) \wedge (\Diamond x \neq y))$. Since equality is identity everywhere ($\mathcal{M}, s, w \models t_1 = t_2$ iff $s(t_1) = s(t_2)$), the formula A is unsatisfiable. In fact, if $s(x) = s(y)$ in a given world w, then it cannot be $s(x) \neq s(y)$ in w'. However, no matter which set of "reasonable" rules for $=$ (including, for instance, reflexivity and replacement) we add to our calculus, no tableau rooted at $1 : A$ closes, since, after two applications of the δ^+-rule and an application of the α-rule, one gets

$$1 : \Diamond\, a^1 = b^1,\ \Diamond\, a^1 \neq b^1$$

When this latter node is expanded by means of a π-rule, the information about one $\diamond$-successor of the world named 1 is necessarily lost: two different expansions can be produced, but in two distinct tableaux, namely $2 : a^1 = b^1$ and $2 : a^1 \neq b^1$. Clearly, neither the first nor the second tableau closes.

This failure to capture equality (at least in a simple way) is intrinsic in the nature of "standard" (i.e. unprefixed) tableaux, because of the presence of non-reversible rules (the dynamic ones).

A natural way of overcoming such a difficulty is resorting to prefixed tableaux, in the style of [6], that represent a way of keeping track of several different tableaux in the same prefixed one. In other terms, node labels are replaced by prefixes on formulae. Prefixes, in turn, are structured objects, encoding the accessibility relation between possible worlds, and symbol annotations have the same structure. Of course, this would constitute an important depart from the framework of the proof systems proposed in this work.

References

1. B. Beckert and R. Goré. Free variable tableaux for propositional modal logics. In *Proc. of TABLEAUX'97*, pages 91–106. Springer, 1997.
2. S. Cerrito and M. Cialdea Mayer. Free-variable tableaux for constant-domain quantified modal logic with rigid and non-rigid designation. In *First Int. Joint Conf. on Automated Reasoning (IJCAR 2001)*, pages 137–151. Springer, 2001.
3. M. Cialdea Mayer and S. Cerrito. Variants of first-order modal logics. In *Proc. of TABLEAUX 2000*, pages 175–189. Springer, 2000.
4. M. Cialdea Mayer and S. Cerrito. Ground and free-variable tableaux for variants of quantified modal logics. *Studia Logica*, 69:97–131, 2001.
5. F. M. Donini and F. Massacci. EXPTIME tableaux for ALC. *Artificial Intelligence*, 124:87–138, 2000.
6. M. Fitting. *Proof Methods for Modal and Intuitionistic Logics*. Reidel, 1983.
7. M. Fitting. *First-Order Logic and Automated Theorem Proving*. Springer, 1996.
8. M. Fitting and R Mendelsohn. *First-Order Modal Logic*. Kluwer, 1998.
9. R. Goré. Automated reasoning project. Technical report, TR-ARP-15-95, 1997.
10. R. Hähnle and P. H. Schmitt. The liberalized δ-rule in free variable semantic tableaux. *Journal of Automated Reasoning*, 13:211–222, 1994.
11. U. Hustadt and R. A. Schmidt. Simplification and backjumping in modal tableau. In *Proc. of TABLEAUX'98*, pages 187–201. Springer, 1998.
12. Jens Otten. ileanTAP: An intuitionistic theorem prover. In *Proc. of TABLEAUX'97*, pages 307–312. Springer, 1997.
13. J. Posegga and P. Schmitt. Implementing semantic tableaux. In M. D'Agostino, G. Gabbay, R. Hähnle, and J. Posegga, editors, *Handbook of tableau method*, pages 581–629. Kluwer, 1999.
14. V. Thion. A strategy for free variable tableaux for variant of quantified modal logics. Technical report, L.R.I., 2002. http://www.lri.fr/~thion.
15. L. A. Wallen. *Automated Deduction in Nonclassical Logics: Efficient Matrix Proof Methods for Modal and Intuitionistic Logics*. MIT Press, 1990.

Some New Exceptions for the Semantic Tableaux Version of the Second Incompleteness Theorem

Dan E. Willard⋆

State University of New York at Albany

Abstract. This article continues our study of axiom systems that can verify their own consistency and prove all Peano Arithmetic's Π_1 theorems. We will develop some new types of exceptions for the Semantic Tableaux Version of the Second Incompleteness Theorem.

1 Introduction

Gödel's Second Incompleteness Theorem states that sufficiently strong axiom systems are unable to formally verify their own consistency. Let us define an axiom system α to be **Self-Justifying** iff

i) one of α's theorems will assert α's consistency (using some reasonable definition of consistency),
ii) and the axiom system α is in fact consistent.

It is well known [5,6,14] that Kleene's Fixed Point Theorem implies every r.e. axiom system α can be easily extended into a broader system α^* which satisfies condition (i). Kleene's proposal [6] was essentially for the system α^* to contain all α's axioms plus the one added axiom sentence below.

+   There exists no proof of 0=1 from the union of α with *"this sentence"*.

Kleene noted that it was easy to apply the Fixed Point Theorem to formally encode a self-referencing statement, similar to the sentence above. The catch is that α^* can be inconsistent even while its added axiom formally asserts α^*'s consistency. For this reason, Kleene, Rogers and Jeroslow [5,6,14] each emphatically warned their readers that most axiom systems similar to α^* were useless on account of their inconsistency, *although they were technically well-defined*. This problem arises in both Gödel's paradigm (where α extends Peano Arithmetic), as well in many more general settings [1,2,4,12,16,19,25], where a Gödel-like diagnoalization argument can be constructed to show that the *very presence* of the axiom + causes the system α^* to become inconsistent.

We have recently published four articles [20,23,24,25] about generalizations of the Second Incompleteness Theorem and exceptions to it that exist for Semantic Tableaux deductive calculi. Let $A(x, y, z)$ and $M(x, y, z)$ denote $x + y = z$ and $x * y = z$, and let us say an axiom system α *recognizes* Addition and

---

⋆ Supported by NSF Grant CCR 99-02726. Email = dew@cs.albany.edu.

U. Egly and C.G. Fermüller (Eds.): TABLEAUX 2002, LNAI 2381, pp. 281–297, 2002.

Multiplication as **Total Functions** iff it can prove $\forall x \forall y \exists z \ A(x,y,z)$ and $\forall x \forall y \exists z \ M(x,y,z)$. We showed in [23,25] that all axiom systems recognizing Addition and Multiplication as total functions and containing one additional Π_1 axiom, called "V", are unable to recognize their self–consistency, under the paradigm of the Semantic Tableaux Deductive Calculi. On the other hand, our papers [20,24] did show that systems can verify some forms of their Tableaux self-consistency while retaining an ability to prove at least analogs of Peano Arithmetic's Π_1 theorems, if they treat Addition as a total function and Multiplication as a "non–total" 3–way relation $M(x,y,z)$.

Our objective in this paper will be to establish crisper and stronger versions of the preceding results. This topic is mathematically complex because there are several plausible definitions D_1 , D_2 , D_3 , ... indicating that an axiom system α can verify its "Semantic Tableaux Consistency". These definitions are equivalent to each other under strong logics, but a weak axiom system α is typically unable to prove these definitions of consistency are equivalent to each other. Thus, the question naturally arises as to which definition of self–justification is one choosing to study ?

In general, it is desirable to use the weakest possible definition among the alternatives D_1 , D_2 , D_3 , ... when one is seeking to generalize the Second Incompleteness Theorem. On the other hand, the opposite is true when one seeks to develop "boundary–case exceptions" to the Second Incompleteness Theorem that introduce some new type of "Self–Justifying formalism". They become more wide–reaching when they use the strongest feasible D_i available.

A system α 's weakest possible definition of Tableaux–Self–Justification is that α can prove the non–existence of a Smullyan–like Semantic Tableaux proof p of the theorem $0 = 1$, in a context where p's proper axioms are drawn from the system α (itself). This was the formal definition of Self-Justification we used in our Tableaux–2000 conference paper [23], as well as in [25]. The preceding paragraph explained why weaker definitions of Self–Justification *are better,* when developing generalizations of the Second Incompleteness Theorem. Thus, we need not further improve the results from our prior generalizations [23, 25] of the Second Incompleteness Theorem because there is little room available for further improvement, at least in the context of axioms systems that extend Q+V and recognize the consistency of their Semantic Tableaux deductive calculi.

On the other hand, there are substantial open questions remaining about whether and how far our exceptions to the Second Incompleteness Theorem, involving for example the "IS(A)" formalism of [20,24], can indeed be further improved. The reason the latter topic is much more open than the former is that *weaker is certainly not better than stronger* for it. This is because one would ideally like the boundary–case exceptions to the Second Incompleteness Theorem to use the the strongest possible definition of Self–Justification, among the available alternatives D_1 , D_2 , D_3 , ...

For example, our IS(A) system of [20,24] could recognize the non–existence of any Smullyan–like Tableaux proof p of the theorem $0 = 1$, all of whose proper axioms are drawn from IS(A). However *for fully arbitrary sentence* Ψ ,

IS(A) was not able to prove the unavailability of two Smullyan–like Tableaux contradictory proofs for Ψ and $\neg\,\Psi$ from IS(A).

Essentially, this paper will seek to investigate how close we can come to establishing the above effect for extensions of IS(A). The next section will define the notion of a " Π_1^- " sentence that will help clarify this issue. Section 1.2 will then define a new axiom system, called IS-1(A), that recognizes that no pair of contradictory Semantic Tableaux proofs of the two sentences Ψ and $\neg\,\Psi$ from IS-1(A) can exist, whenever Ψ is a " Π_1^- " sentence. The Remark 5 (at the end of Section 1.2) will give a short 1-paragraph summary of a recent discovery by us, showing that the preceding boundary–case exceptions to the Second Incompleteness Theorem do not generalize from Π_1^- to Π_2^- sentences.

1.1. Notation and Statement of Main Theorem

Some added notation is needed before we can state our main theorems. Say a function $F(a_1, a_2, ...a_j)$ satisfies the **Non-Growth** property iff F satisfies $F(a_1, a_2, ...a_j) \leq Maximum(a_1, a_2, ...a_j)$ for all values of $a_1, a_2, ...a_j$. Seven examples of non-growth functions are *Integer Subtraction* (where $x - y$ is defined to equal zero when $x \leq y$), *Integer Division* (where $x \div y$ is defined to equal x when $y = 0$, and we round down to the nearest integer), $Maximum(x, y)$, $Logarithm(x)$, $Predecessor(x) = \text{Max}(x - 1, 0)$, $Root(x, y) = \lceil x^{1/y} \rceil$ and $Count(x, j)$ designating the number of "1" bits among x's rightmost j bits. These functions are called the **Grounding Functions**.

We will use a slight variant of Logic's conventional notation when discussing grounding functions. A *term* will be defined to be a constant, variable or function symbol (whose input arguments are recursively defined terms). If t is a term then the quantifiers in the wffs $\forall\, v \leq t\;\; \Psi(v)$ and $\exists\, v \leq t\;\; \Psi(v)$ are called *bounded quantifiers*. If Φ is a formula that uses the Grounding primitives as its function symbols and the two relation symbols of " $=$ " and " $\leq$ ", then this formula will be called both " Π_0^-" and " Σ_0^-" whenever all its quantifiers are bounded. For $n \geq 1$, a formula Υ shall be called " Π_n^- " iff it is written in the form $\forall v_1 \forall v_2 \, ... \, \forall v_k \quad \Phi$, where Φ is " Σ_{n-1}^- ". Likewise, Υ is called " Σ_n^- " iff it is written in the form $\exists v_1 \exists v_2 \, ... \, \exists v_k \quad \Phi$, where Φ is " Π_{n-1}^- ".

Our definitions of Σ_n^- and Π_n^- formulae are the same as the conventional definitions of Σ_n and Π_n formulae, except that the Addition and Multiplication function symbols are replaced with Grounding primitives. Since Subtraction and Division can represent Addition and Multiplication as relations, every conventional Π_1 formula can be translated into an Π_1^- formula that is equivalent to it under sufficiently strong models of Arithmetic.

Using the preceding notation, we can provide a more succinct summary of our main result. Let us say an axiom system α has a **Level-N** understanding of its own Semantic Tableaux consistency iff it can recognize that there exists no Smullyan-like Semantic Tableaux proofs, using α's proper axioms, of both the theorems Ψ and $\neg\,\Psi$, for all Π_N^- sentences Ψ. Let us say α has a **primitive** understanding of its own Semantic Tableaux consistency iff it can recognize that there exists no Smullyan-like Semantic Tableaux proof, using α's proper axioms, of the theorem $0 = 1$. Our prior IS(A) system of [20,24] technically had only a primitive understanding of its own Semantic Tableaux consistency. However, we could have easily improved this result to the Level-Zero. In this paper, we will show how a stronger version of IS(A), called IS-1(A), can have a Level-1 understanding of its own Semantic Tableaux consistency. This is a non–trivial improvement over our prior result because there exists no decision procedure for enumerating all true Π_1^- sentences.

1.2 Definition of IS-1(A)

Let A denote an axiom system that proves theorems about the Grounding Functions. Our new axiom system, called IS-1(A), will be a 4-part self-justifying axiom system. Its Group-Zero, 1 and 2 axiom schemes will be defined analogously to their counterparts in the IS(A) formalism of [20,24] (except for some unimportant notational changes). However IS-1(A)'s Group-3 scheme will have a quite different definition than IS(A)'s counterpart. It will essentially assert that the IS-1(A) formalism is Level-1 consistent. The formal 4-part defintion of IS-1(A) is given below:

Group-Zero: Two of the Group-zero axioms will define two initial constants that correspond to the integers 0 and 1. The third Group-zero axiom will indicate that Addition is a total function. (It will thus provide a means to define integers larger than 1.) Since our Grounding Function formalism does not technically use an Addition function symbol, the axiom (1) below will view Addition as an operation that is the inverse of Subtraction:

$$\forall x \, \forall y \, \exists z \quad x = z - y \tag{1}$$

Group-1: This axiom group will consist of a finite set of Π_1^- sentences, denoted as F , which assures that the seven Grounding functions have their conventional properties with regards to the "=" and "<" predicates when they are given constants as inputs. By this we mean that for each grounding function G , k-tuple $(n_1, n_2, ...n_k)$ and added constant m , the union of axiom system F with (1)'s added axiom will be sufficient to prove whichever one of the three conditions of $G(n_1, n_2, ...n_k) = m$, $G(n_1, n_2, ...n_k) < m$ or $G(n_1, n_2, ...n_k) > m$ is true. (Any finite set of Π_1^- sentences F with this property may be used to define Group-1. Our prior published papers expressed no strong preference about which F was employed.)

Group-2: Let $\mathrm{Prf}_A^\Phi(x, y)$ denote a Σ_0^- formula indicating that y is a proof of the theorem Φ from the axiom system A . For each Π_1^- sentence Φ, the Group-2 schema will contain an axiom of the form (2). Thus, the Group-2 scheme shall trivially endow IS-1(A) with a capacity to verify all A's Π_1^- theorems.

$$\forall y \, \{ \mathrm{Prf}_A^\Phi (y) \supset \Phi \} \tag{2}$$

Group-3: This group will consist of one Π_1^- sentence stating essentially:

* There exists no two Semantic Tableaux proofs from the **Union** of the Group-1 and 2 axioms with **this sentence looking at itself** of both some Π_1^- sentence and its negation.

In order to formally encode * as a Π_1^- sentence, let $\text{Pair}(x, y)$ denote a Σ_0^- formula indicating x is the Gödel number of a Π_1^- sentence and y is x's negation. Also, let $\text{Prf}_{\text{IS-1}(A)}(a, b)$ denote a Σ_0^- formula that indicates that b is the Gödel number of a semantic tableaux proof of the theorem a from the axiom system IS-1(A). In this context, the formal Gödel encoding of the axiom sentence * can be approximated as:

$$\forall\, x \,\forall\, y \,\forall\, p \,\forall\, q \quad \neg\, [\ \text{Pair}(x, y) \ \wedge\ \text{Prf}_{\text{IS-1}(A)}(x, p) \ \wedge\ \text{Prf}_{\text{IS-1}(A)}(y, q)\ ] \quad (3)$$

Remark 1. The full formal description of IS-1(A)'s Group-3 axiom is somewhat more complicated than the abbreviated descriptions of this axiom's structure, given either by the Sentence * or by the analogous Equation (3). The main added complication arises because the Group-3 axiom declares the consistency of a formal set of axioms that includes "itself" (in the words of Sentence *.) The general notion of an axiom including formally "itself" when it refers to the consistency of an axiom schema goes back to Kleene's 1938 paper [6] (as the first paragraph of this article had already indicated). Kleene's abbreviated description is insufficient to establish that Equation (3) can be encoded precisely as a Π_1^- sentence. To do this, one needs techniques similar to Appendixes B through D from our article [24]. We will not repeat such a construction here.

Remark 2. One can easily become initially confused by IS-1(A)'s Group-3 axiom because IS-1(A) is *not automatically consistent* by virtue of the simple fact that its Group-3 axiom declares: *"I am consistent"*. Using the nomenclature from the opening paragraph of our article, the difficulty is that it is plausible that IS-1(A) could satisfy Part–i but not the *equally important* Part-ii of the definition of Self–Justification (as had happened with the example of α^* , in the first paragraph of this article). The next chapter will prove that this difficulty does not occur with IS-1(A).

Remark 3. We wish to reinforce the point made by the preceding paragraph, and graphically illustrate how some seemingly minor modifications in IS-1(A)'s formalism will result in the construction of an inconsistent system. Pudlák has proven that no consistent extension α of Robinson's axiom system Q can prove that all Hilbert-styled proofs employing α's axioms are assured to be free of inconsistencies. Solovay subsequently observed [16] it was possible to use methods of Nelson and Wilkie-Paris [9,19] to incrementally refine this particular theorem of Pudlák's so that it will generalize for essentially all axiom systems that simultaneously recognize Successor as a total function and that retain a capacity to prove all Peano Arithmetic's Π_1^- theorems. Hence, IS-1(A) will automatically *become inconsistent* if its Group-3 axiom *is simply revised* so that "Prf" specifies a Hilbert rather than Semantic Tableaux variant of proof.

Remark 4. Similarly, our "Q+V" version of the Second Incompleteness Theorem from [23,25] demonstrates that it is infeasible to modify the IS-1(A) axiom system so that it can simultaneously recognize Multiplication as a total function and retain a *logically valid* analog of Equation (3)'s Group-3 axiom. There is insufficient space to explain here why Multiplication's totality is central for effectuating the Semantic Tableaux version of the Second Incompleteness Theorem. However, the reader can find some very good and detailed intuitive explanations for this phenomena in either the passage spanning pages 328–331 in our article [20] or in Remark 4.5 of [24].

Remark 5. During the last three months while this article was being refereed, we developed a new version of the Second Incompleteness Theorem which states that there exists a Π_1^- sentence W , provable from the $I\Sigma_0$ fragment of Peano Arithmetic, such that no consistent axiom system α can prove W , prove Addition is a total function and simultaneously recognize its own Level-2 Semantic Tableaux consistency. There is no space to insert the proof of this added theorem here, and we will display it elsewhere. It implies that when A has the strength of Peano Arithmetic, it is impossible to devise a modification of IS-1(A) that is consistent and whose Group-3 axiom precludes the possibility of there existing simultaneous Semantic Tableaux proofs of both an arbitrary Π_2^- sentence and its negation. This inability to generalize our results from Level-1 to Level-2 consistency makes the main theorem-proofs, presented in the next chapter, even the more interesting.

Remark 6. Let us say that a formula $\Upsilon(v)$ is an **Initialization Segment** *relative to* an axiom system α if α can formally prove:

$$\Upsilon(0) \quad \text{and} \quad \forall v \ \{ \ \Upsilon(v) \ \supset \ \Upsilon(v+1) \ \} \tag{4}$$

Kriesel-Takeuti, Nelson, Pudlák, Visser and Wilkie-Paris [4,8,9,12,18,19] have illustrated several examples of Initialization-Formulae $\Upsilon(v)$, where an axiom system α can prove its *Semantic Tableaux* consistency local to such Initialization Segments. Thus if " BadTableaux $_\alpha$ (y) " denotes that y is a semantic tableaux proof of the theorem 0=1 from α, then there are several known axiom systems α that can prove localized consistency statements similar to:

$$\forall y \ \{ \ \Upsilon(y) \ \supset \ \neg \, \text{BadTableaux} \, _\alpha \, (\, y \,) \ \} \tag{5}$$

The earliest version of (5) was discovered by Kriesel-Takeuti [8] in the rather specialized context of a Second Order Logic generalization of the Cut-Free Sequent Calculus. Nelson [9] showed that Robinson's Arithmetic Q can prove a version of Equation (5) about itself. Pudlák [4,12] proved a much more general theorem showing a similar effect was applicable to any finitely axiomatized sequential theory (and also allowing for Wilkie-Paris's notion [19] of a Herbrand-restricted-consistency). This literature is not exactly relevant to Self-Justifying axiom systems, because our axiom systems do not have their consistency statements localized by an analog of Equation (5)'s formula $\Upsilon(y)$. However, this literature is probably the closest analog to our results that has been explored by other researchers. We especially encourage the readers to examine Pudlák's work [4,12] because it proves Equation (5)'s effect generalizes *for all* finitely axiomatized sequential theories, which is a quite *noteworthy phenomena !*

2   Proof of Main Theorem

Let $I(\bullet)$ denote a function that maps an initial axiom system A onto a second axiom system, denoted as $I(A)$. Let us call the mapping–formalism $I(\bullet)$ **Consistency-Preserving** iff $I(A)$ is consistent whenever the union of the axiom system A with Section 1.2's Group-Zero and Group-1 axiom schemes is consistent. Our objective will be to prove that IS-1($\bullet$) is "Consistency-Preserving". In our discussion, a sentence Ψ will be called PRENEX* iff it is written in the form $Q_1 x_1 Q_2 x_2... Q_n x_n \ \theta(x_1, x_2...x_n)$ where $\theta(x_1, x_2...x_n)$ is a Σ_0^- formula and Q_i denotes either the symbol $\forall$ or $\exists$.

Our definition of a semantic tableaux proof will be very similar to the definitions used in say Fitting's or Smullyan's textbooks [3,15]. Define a Φ**-Based Candidate Tree** for the axiom system α to be a tree structure whose root corresponds to the sentence $\neg \Phi$ *rewritten in PRENEX* normal form* and whose all other nodes are either axioms of α or deductions from higher nodes of the tree. Let the notation "$\mathcal{A} \implies \mathcal{B}$" indicate that $\mathcal{B}$ is a valid deduction when $\mathcal{A}$ is an ancestor of $\mathcal{B}$ in the candidate tree T. In this notation, the deduction rules allowed in a candidate tree are:

1. $\Upsilon \wedge \Gamma \implies \Upsilon$ and $\Upsilon \wedge \Gamma \implies \Gamma$.
2. $\neg\neg\Upsilon \implies \Upsilon$. Other valid Tableaux rules for the "$\neg$" symbol include:
   $\neg(\Upsilon \vee \Gamma) \implies \neg\Upsilon \wedge \neg\Gamma$, $\neg(\Upsilon \supset \Gamma) \implies \Upsilon \wedge \neg\Gamma$, $\neg(\Upsilon \wedge \Gamma) \implies \neg\Upsilon \vee \neg\Gamma$,
   $\neg \exists v \, \Upsilon(v) \implies \forall v \neg \, \Upsilon(v)$ and $\neg \forall v \, \Upsilon(v) \implies \exists v \, \neg\Upsilon(v)$
3. A pair of sibling nodes Υ and Γ is allowed in a candidate tree when their ancestor is $\Upsilon \vee \Gamma$.
4. A pair of sibling nodes $\neg\Upsilon$ and Γ is allowed in a candidate tree when their ancestor is $\Upsilon \supset \Gamma$.
5. $\exists v \, \Upsilon(v) \implies \Upsilon(u)$ where u denotes a newly introduced "Parameter Symbol".
6. $\forall v \, \Upsilon(v) \implies \Upsilon(t)$ where t denotes a parameter term. The "Parameter Terms" here are built out of the Grounding Functions, whose inputs are any set of constant symbols $c_1, c_2, .., c_m$ and parameter symbols $u_1, u_2, .., u_n$, where each symbol u_i **was previously** introduced by an ancestor of the node storing the new deduction "$\Upsilon(t)$".

Define a particular leaf-to-root branch in a candidate tree T to be **Closed** iff it contains both some sentence Υ and its negation $\neg\Upsilon$. A **Semantic Tableaux** proof of Φ is defined to be a candidate tree whose root stores the sentence $\neg\Phi$ (written in PRENEX* normal form) and all of whose root-to-leaf branches are closed. The only distinction between our definition of a semantic tableaux proof and some other conventional definitions in [3,15,19] is that we require Φ's proof tree to have its root store $\neg \Phi$ *rewritten in PRENEX* normal form,* whereas some other conventional definitions do not have the PRENEX* requirement. All our theorems will also hold if we drop the PRENEX* requirement, but the notation in our main proofs will be greatly simplified if we begin with the assumption that the root has been normalized into PRENEX* form.

Let T denote a Φ-Based Candidate Tree, β denote a branch of T, L and M denote two fixed constants, and VAL($\bullet$) denote a function that maps each term s (from β) onto an integer VAL(s), subject to the following constraints:

A. Suppose u represents a new parameter symbol that is introduced at a depth level d along the branch β. Then its value will satisfy the constraint:

$$\text{Val}(u) \leq \text{Min}(M , L \cdot 2^d) \tag{6}$$

B. VAL($\overline{c_K}$) $= K$ when $\overline{c_K}$ corresponds to one of the two particular constants, c_0 or c_1, defined by IS-1(A)'s Group-zero axiom and representing the two numbers of zero and one.

C. VAL(s)'s definition will generalize in the natural manner for terms s that contain function symbols F, i.e. VAL($F(s_1, s_2)$) $= F(\text{VAL}(s_1), \text{VAL}(s_2))$.

Our next definition will require the added notation convention listed below.

Let Ψ^M denote a sentence identical to Ψ except that all the *previously-unrestricted* universal quantifiers will have their ranges *redefined* in Ψ^M to correspond to the subset of non-negative integers $\leq M$. (Bounded universal quantifiers and both bounded and unbounded existential quantifiers in Ψ will not have their ranges changed under Ψ^M.)

Our next definition will use the fact that a Φ-Based Candidate Tree **IS NOT** a Semantic Tableaux proof of Φ when at least one of the branches of this tree fails to be closed. Let us say a branch β of such a Φ-Based Candidate Tree is **Conservative** iff there exists an ordered triple (L, M, VAL) where β satisfies the preceding conditions A–C, plus the following additional fourth constraint below. (We will also call such a branch **(L,M)–Conservative** in the special case where the particular values for (L, M) are fixed and known in advance.)

D. All sentences Ψ appearing on the branch β will be sentences where Ψ^M is valid in the Standard Model of the Natural Numbers.

Before proceeding further, it would be useful to explain the significance of Conservative Branches. Lemma 1 will state that no "candidate tree" can be a "semantic tableaux proof" when it draws its proper axioms from IS-1(A) and *simultaneously contains* a Conservative Branch. This fact will enable us to develop a formal proof–by–contradiction that the IS-1($\bullet$) axiom mapping must be Consistency-Preserving, because otherwise the algorithm PROBE (which shall defined be in Section 2.2) will construct the particular type of Conservative Branch, whose existence will be *strictly forbidden* by Lemma 1.

Lemma 1. . *Let α denote an axiom system whose every axiom sentence is written in PRENEX* normal form (similar to IS-1(A)). Then none of candidate trees drawing their proper axioms from α can simultaneously contain a Conservative Branch and constitute a "semantic tableaux proof".*

Proof. Very trivial because all α's axioms, as well as any sentence stored in a proof-tree's root, are written in PRENEX* form. In such a context, it is simply impossible for a branch β in a proof tree p to be closed without β containing both some Σ_0 sentence Υ and its negation $\neg \Upsilon$. The latter cannot possibly occur in a Conservative branch, because Part-D of our definition of conservativeness would then require that Υ and its negation $\neg \Upsilon$ both be simultaneously valid sentences in the Standard Model of the Natural Numbers. $\square$

We will now explain roughly how we will use Lemma 1 to devise a proof–by–contradiction that verifies that the IS-1($\bullet$) axiom mapping is Consistency–Preserving. Let $\omega(x, y, p, q)$ be the Σ_0^- formula that corresponds to the square bracket expression on the right-side of Equation (3). This means that IS-1(A)'s Group-3 axiom (defined by Equation (3)) can be simply rewritten as:

$$\forall x \ \forall y \ \forall p \ \forall q \quad \neg \ \omega(x, y, p, q) \tag{7}$$

For any second formula $\theta(x, y, p, q)$, let us examine the properties of the following second sentence:

$$\forall x \ \forall y \ \forall p \ \forall q \quad \{ \ \omega(x, y, p, q) \supset \theta(x, y, p, q) \ \} \tag{8}$$

Let us call Equation (8) a **Vacuous Truth** iff it satisfies the following conditions:

a. Equation (8) is a logically valid statement.
b. Although it is a valid sentence, Equation (8) will actually not indicate what it may first appear to imply. This is because no tuple (x, y, p, q) will actually satisfy either $\omega(x, y, p, q)$ or $\theta(x, y, p, q)$.

It is well known that "vacuous truths" are often useful intermediate steps appearing in proofs-by-contradiction. For example, a proof-by-contradiction can verify Equation (7)'s assertion by employing Equation (8)'s "vacuous truth" and showing that no tuple (x, y, p, q) can satisfy $\theta(x, y, p, q)$.

Our formal proof of IS-1($\bullet$)'s Consistency–Preserving property will rest on a proof–by–contradiction of this type. Its invoked formal constraint sentence " $\forall x \forall y \forall p \forall q \ \neg \ \theta(x, y, p, q)$ " will turn out to be a fairly simple consequence of Lemma 1. Our objective will be to use this θ–statement and (8) to establish (7). The only moderately difficult part of our proof will be because the full meaning of vacuous truths are always awkward to directly visualize, because of the inherently non–constructive nature of their statements. However, it will be ultimately easy to follow our proof, provided one remembers the inherently non–constructive nature of vacuous truths.

2.1 Structure of Main Proof

We begin by listing some notation that our proof will require:

1. $\mathrm{Max}(p, q)$ will denote the maximum of the two numbers p and q.
2. $\mathrm{Top}(P, Q)$ will be an abbreviation for the following formula:

$$\forall p \ \forall q \ \forall x \ \forall y \ \{ \ \mathrm{Max}(p, q) < \mathrm{Max}(P, Q) \ \supset \ \neg \ \omega(x, y, p, q) \ \} \tag{9}$$

3. $\mathrm{Check}(X, Y, P, Q)$ will denote a Boolean formula. In particular, let us recall that the condition $\omega(X, Y, P, Q)$ indicates P is a proof from the axiom system IS-1(A) of a Π_1^- sentence, called X , and Q is the proof of the negation of this sentence, called Y . In order to simplify our notation, let us assume that X denotes the sentence " $\forall a \ \phi(a)$ " and Y denotes " $\exists a \ \neg \ \phi(a)$ ". Then the symbol $\mathrm{Check}(X, Y, P, Q)$ will yield a Boolean

value of TRUE if and only if the following statement is valid in the Standard Model of the Natural Numbers:

$$\forall a \quad [\, a \le \frac{1}{2} \cdot \text{Max}(P,Q)\,] \quad \supset \quad \phi(a) \tag{10}$$

4. Constraint(t,β) is a formula indicating that t denotes the Gödel number of a Semantic Tableaux "Candidate Tree" and β is a conservative branch in t. (Note that Lemma 1 indicates that when Constraint(t,β) is satisfied, t **CANNOT** possibly represent a semantic tableaux proof. This fact will be used by our proofs–by–contradiction to justify Theorems 1 and 2.)

We will now use the preceding notation to outline the structure of the proof of our main theorem, asserting the consistency of the IS-1(A) formalism. Our proof can be viewed as having two parts. One part (appearing in Section 2.2) will establish the validity of the two statements (11) and (12), listed at the bottom of this paragraph. Both these statements are vacuous truths, characterized by the usual property that there exists no tuple (X,Y,P,Q) satisfying the square-bracket condition on the left side of their horn clause. As a result of their vacuous nature, some readers may have difficulty fully visualizing the meaning of (11) and (12), until Section 2.2's proof for them is examined. We suggest that the readers not feel particularly concerned to decipher their exact meaning at this current juncture. Rather, one should just treat (11) and (12) as simply purely formal mathematical objects. Our present goal will be to show how our main theorem, asserting the consistency of the IS-1(A) formalism, follows easily from these statements, when one uses a method of proof–by–contradiction. In conjunction with our formal proofs of (11) and (12), given later in Section 2.2, this analysis will establish that the IS-1(A) axiom system is, indeed, consistent.

$$\forall X\ \forall Y\ \forall P\ \forall Q \quad \{\ [\ \text{Check}(X,Y,P,Q)\ \wedge\ \omega(X,Y,P,Q)\ \wedge\ \text{Top}(P,Q)\ ]$$
$$\supset\ \exists \beta\ \text{Constraint}(Q,\beta)\ \} \tag{11}$$

$$\forall X\ \forall Y\ \forall P\ \forall Q \quad \{\ [\ \neg\text{Check}(X,Y,P,Q)\ \wedge\ \omega(X,Y,P,Q)\ \wedge\ \text{Top}(P,Q)\ ]$$
$$\supset\ \exists \beta\ \text{Constraint}(P,\beta)\ \} \tag{12}$$

We need one preliminary proposition before we can prove our main result.

Theorem 1. *The combination of Equations (11) and (12) immediately imply the validity of the following statement:*

$$\forall X\ \forall Y\ \forall P\ \forall Q \quad \{\ \text{Top}(P,Q)\ \supset\ \neg\,\omega(X,Y,P,Q)\ \} \tag{13}$$

Proof. Our proof rests on separately examining the two cases where the tuple (X,Y,P,Q) does and does not satisfy the condition Check(X,Y,P,Q).

In the first case, we can infer from Equation (11) that the formal predicate condition " $\omega(X,Y,P,Q)\ \wedge\ \text{Top}(P,Q)$ " does imply the validity of

$$\exists \beta\ \text{Constraint}(Q,\beta)\ . \tag{14}$$

However, Lemma 1's formal statement, translated into our new notation, amounts to the assertion that it is impossible for Equation (14) and $\omega(X, Y, P, Q)$ to be simultaneously valid (see the footnote [1] for the formal details substantiating this point). Hence, our forced conclusion is that if the condition Check(X, Y, P, Q) is valid, then the identity " Top$(P, Q) \supset \neg \omega(X, Y, P, Q)$ " must automatically hold in this case.

We can use almost the identical technique to prove the validity of the identity " Top$(P, Q) \supset \neg \omega(X, Y, P, Q)$ " in the alternate case where the condition Check(X, Y, P, Q) is false. The only difference is that the second case will use Equation (12) rather than (11) to arrive at a similar proof–by–contradiction. (In particular, its proof will be the same as the preceding case, except that our counterpart of Equation (14)'s intermediate step will now be the observation that β satisfies Constraint(P, β) .) $\square$

Theorem 2. *Suppose the union of the axiom system* A *with Section 1.2's "Group-1" axiom schema is a consistent system. Then IS-1(A) is also a consistent axiom system. (In our formal nomenclature, this amounts to stating that the axiom–mapping formalism IS-1$(\bullet)$ is "consistency–preserving".)*

Proof. It is easy to derive Theorem 2 from Theorem 1 by using the method of proof–by–contradiction. In particular, suppose that the theorem was false and IS-1(A) was inconsistent. Using our notation convention, there would then exist a tuple (x, y, p, q) satisfying $\omega(x, y, p, q)$. From such a tuple (x, y, p, q) , we can certainly find a second such tuple (X, Y, P, Q) , that also satisfies this ω−condition, but additionally possesses the minimal possible value for MAX(P, Q) among all tuples satisfying $\omega(x, y, p, q)$. In our notation, this means that (X, Y, P, Q) will satisfy the following dual condition:

$$\omega(X, Y, P, Q) \ \wedge \ \text{Top}(P, Q) \tag{15}$$

However, the point is that Theorem 1 precludes the possibility that any tuple could satisfy Equation (15) (because the latter blatantly contradicts the invariant (13), established by Theorem 1). Hence, our proof–by–contradiction forces us to conclude that the Theorem 2 must be valid, because otherwise the formal statement of Theorem 1 would be contradicted. $\square$

The remainder of this chapter will justify the vacuous truths, from Equations (11) and (12), so that our proofs for Theorem 1 and 2 shall be formally completed.

2.2 Proofs of Equations (11) and (12)

To prove Equations (11) and (12), we need to first introduce some notation. Let T denote a candidate tree, and (L, M) denote the parameters used to define

---

[1]   The basic reason for this inherent incompatibility is that the formula $\omega(X, Y, P, Q)$, by definition, implies Q is a semantic tableaux proof of the theorem Y . In this context, the formula Constraint(Q, β) flatly contradicts the preceding statement, since Lemma 1 indicates that the presence of Q's "conservative branch" β demonstrates that it is impossible for the "candidate" tree Q to be a formal tableaux-style proof.

an (L, M)−Conservative Branch. The symbol PROBE will denote an algorithm which given these inputs, seeks to construct a valuation VAL($\bullet$) and a (L, M)−Conservative Branch for T, called Beta(T, L, M). The four algorithmic rules for constructing Beta(T, L, M) and VAL($\bullet$) are listed below:

1. The top node along the path Beta(T, L, M) will always be T's root.
2. Suppose the first i nodes along the path Beta(T, L, M) are $N_1, N_2, N_3,$ ... N_i, and the node has N_i has two children denoted as N_a and N_b. In this case, the candidate tree T has used either the $\vee$−Elimination or $\supset$−Elimination to justify this binary split, and we will let Ψ_a and Ψ_b denote the two sentences stored in these two nodes. In this case, our algorithm PROBE(T, L, M) will make the "left child" N_a constitute the next element along Beta(T, L, M)'s path when the sentence Ψ_a^M is valid (in the Standard Model of the Natural Numbers). Otherwise, it will make N_b be Beta(T, L, M)'s next node.
3. If the first i nodes along the Beta(T, L, M)'s path are $N_1, N_2, N_3,$ ... N_i and N_i has only one child, denoted as N_{i+1}, then the algorithm PROBE(T, L, M) will "attempt" to make N_{i+1} the next node along Beta(T, L, M)'s path. This "attempt" may not be successful. The difficulty arises when N_{i+1}'s sentence is constructed via the $\exists$−Elimination Rule (and it thus introduces a new parameter–symbol, called say u_j). In this case, the procedure PROBE(T, L, M) will attempt to assign VAL(u_j) the smallest possible value (consistent with the assignments it previously gave to $u_1, u_2,$ ... u_{j-1}). If the resulting quantity VAL(u_j) is sufficiently small to satisfy Equation (6)'s inequality, then PROBE(T, L, M)'s attempt will be considered successful. Otherwise, the procedure PROBE(T, L, M) will simply "quit" and cease attempting to build T's (L, M)−conservative branch, called Beta(T, L, M).
4. The procedure PROBE(T, L, M) will iteratively repeat Steps 2 and 3 to make the path Beta(T, L, M) become longer and longer, until either it reaches the candidate tree's desired leaf–level or a failure occurs in Step 3.

Our next two lemmas will show how we may apply the procedure PROBE(T, L, M) to corroborate the validity of Equations (11) and (12).

Lemma 2. . *Suppose the union of the axiom system A with IS-1(A)'s Group-zero and Group-1 axioms is a consistent axiom system and that the 4-tuple (X, Y, P, Q) satisfies the square-bracket expression on the left side of Equation (11). (This expression is rewritten below.)*

$$Check(X, Y, P, Q) \wedge \omega(X, Y, P, Q) \wedge Top(P, Q) \tag{16}$$

Let us set $L = 1$, $M = \frac{1}{2} \cdot Max(P, Q) - 1$ and $T = Q$. Then for these input values for (T, L, M), the procedure PROBE will successfully find an (L, M)−Conservative Branch lying in the candidate tree Q.

Lemma 3. . *Let us again suppose that the union of the axiom system A with IS-1(A)'s Group-zero and Group-1 axioms is a consistent axiom system. Also,* *suppose that the* (X, Y, P, Q) *satisfies the square-bracket expression on the left side of Equation (12). (This expression is rewritten below.)*

$$(\neg \ Check(X, Y, P, Q) \ ) \ \wedge \ \omega(X, Y, P, Q) \ \wedge \ Top(P, Q) \tag{17}$$

Let us set $L = \frac{1}{2} \cdot Max(P, Q)$, $M = Max(P, Q) - 1$ *and* $T = P$. *Then for these input values for* (T, L, M), *the procedure PROBE will successfully find an* $(L, M) - Conservative$ *Branch lying in the candidate tree* P .

PROOF OF LEMMA 2. We will use the Principle of Induction to prove Lemma 2. Our inductive proof shall assume that the i highest nodes $N_1, N_2...N_i$ along the path Beta(T,L,M) satisfy the $(L, M) - Conservative$ condition, and it will use this fact to deduce that the node N_{i+1} will also be $(L, M) - Conservative$. Our inductive proof will be divided into eight sub–cases because we must separately consider the possibilities that N_{i+1} constitutes T's root, stores an axiom of IS-1(A), or is deduced from a higher node of the candidate tree T via one of the six Elimination rules for the $\exists, \forall, \wedge, \vee, \supset$ or $\neg$ symbols.

1. The Case where N_{i+1} **designates** T's **root:** We will employ the notation from Equation (10)'s definition of Check(X, Y, P, Q). It indicated that if for some Σ_0^- formula $\phi(a)$, X denotes the sentence " $\forall a \ \phi(a)$ " and Y denotes " $\exists a \ \neg \ \phi(a)$ ", then Check(X, Y, P, Q) denotes the statement:

$$\forall a \ [\ a \leq \frac{1}{2} \cdot Max(P, Q) \ ] \ \supset \ \phi(a) \tag{18}$$

In a context where Lemma 2 sets $M = \frac{1}{2} \cdot Max(P, Q) - 1$ and $[\neg Y]$ denotes $\neg Y$ rewritten in Prenex* Normal form, Equation (18) implies that the sentence $[\neg Y]^M$ is valid. Moreover since Q represents a proof of the sentence Y , the root of Q's proof tree is the sentence " $\neg Y$ ". Hence the last two sentences show that the root satisfies Part-D of the definition of $(L, M) - Conservativeness$. (We do not need to verify it also satisfies the other three parts of this definition because the root contains no parameter symbols u , and thus these conditions hold trivially, by default.) □

2. The Case where N_{i+1} **stores one of IS-1(A)'s formal axioms.** Let Ψ denote the axiom sentence stored in N_{i+1} . Similar to the preceding case, the only non–trivial aspect of this case is the demonstration that Ψ satisfies Part-D of the definition of $(L, M) - Conservativeness$ (i.e. that Ψ^M is valid under the Standard Model). The proof of this fact is divided into three sub–cases:

1. *Sub-case where* Ψ *is one of IS-1(A)'s Group-zero or Group-1 axioms:* In this case Ψ is automatically valid under the Standard Model of the Natural Numbers, and hence so is Ψ^M .

2. *Sub-case where* Ψ *is one of IS-1(A)'s Group-2 axioms:* Lemma 2's hypothesis indicates that the union of A with IS-1(A)'s Group-zero and Group-1 schemes is a consistent system. This fact implies that every Group-2 axiom is valid under the Standard Model. Moreover, Equation (2)'s definition of a Group-2 axiom indicates that these axioms are encoded as Π_1^- sentences. Such Π_1^- sentences Ψ have the property that Ψ's validity automatically implies the validity of Ψ^M .

3. *Sub-case where* Ψ *is IS-1(A)'s Group-3 axioms (formally defined by Equation (3)):* Unlike the other sub-cases, we shall not assume the validity of the sentence Ψ at the start of the proof of this sub-case (see footnote [2]). However, Lemma 2's hypothesis does indicate validity of $Top(P,Q)$ (i.e. see Equation (16)). The latter, combined with M's definition, immediately implies that Ψ^M is valid when Ψ denotes IS-1(A)'s Group-3 axiom.   □

3. The Case where N_{i+1} is generated by the ∃-Elimination Rule: This Elimination rule, defined in Section 2's second paragraph, allows N_{i+1} to represent a sentence $\phi(u^*)$, containing a new parameter symbol u^*, when an ancestor of N_{i+1} represents the sentence $\exists v \ \phi(v)$. A key aspect of IS-1(A) is that Equation (1) is its only axiom using unbounded existential quantifiers. Let MaxVal(i) denote the maximum of 1 and of the largest quantity, Val(u), stored in the nodes $N_1, N_2, N_3, ... N_i$. It is clear that the elimination of an existential quantifier, originating from Equation (1), will cause Val(u^*) $\leq 2 \cdot$ MaxVal(i).

Moreover since neither any of IS-1(A)'s other proper axioms nor its root contains unbounded existential quantifiers, the preceding inequality clearly implies MaxVal($i+1$) $\leq 2 \cdot$ MaxVal(i). This latter inequality, combined with the facts that MaxVal(1)= 1 and the height of Q's proof tree is certainly less than $\frac{1}{3}$ Log$_2(M)$ immediately shows that the Val(u^*) will satisfy Equation (6)'s constraint. The proof that the node N_{i+1} will satisfy the other parts of the definition of (L, M)-Conservativeness is trivial.   □

4. The Case where N_{i+1} is generated by the ∀-Elimination Rule: This Elimination rule, allows N_{i+1} to represent a sentence $\phi(u^*)$, when an ancestor of N_{i+1} stores the sentence $\forall v \ \phi(v)$ and u^* represents a parameter symbol used in one of N_{i+1}'s ancestors, one of the constants of 0 or 1, or a term generated from these primitive objects. In each of these cases, a routine inductive argument shows that $\phi(u^*)$ must satisfy the (L, M)-Conservative Condition because the parameter symbols appearing inside u^* satisfied Equation (6) and because the higher node storing "$\forall v \ \phi(v)$" should be inductively presumed to be (L, M)-Conservative.   □

5. The Case where N_{i+1} is generated by the ∧-Elimination Rule: Trivial because a sentence Υ will automatically satisfy the (L, M)-Conservative Condition when some ancestor of it storing the sentence $\Upsilon \wedge \Theta$ does.   □

6. The Case where N_{i+1} is generated by a ¬ Elimination Rule: It is, once again, trivial that a sentence Υ will automatically satisfy the (L, M)-Conservative Condition when some ancestor of it storing the sentence $\neg \neg \Upsilon$ does. Also, a similar trivial argument applies to the other variants of ¬ Elimination (formally defined in Section 2's second paragraph). □

7. The Case where N_{i+1} is generated by the ∨-Elimination Rule: This rule introduces a pair of sibling nodes Υ and Θ when they have a common ancestor $\Upsilon \vee \Theta$. Since the inductive hypothesis implies $\Upsilon \vee \Theta$ satisfies the

---

[2] It turns out that IS-1(A)'s Group-3 axiom is a valid statement. However, we cannot assume its validity during the course of Lemma 2's proof because Lemma 2's purpose is to help prove Theorem 2, and the validity of IS-1(A)'s Group-3 axiom is not evident until Theorem 2 is formally proven.

(L, M)-Conservative Condition, one of Υ or Θ must also satisfy this condition. Our algorithm PROBE will automatically select this satisfying node. □

8. The Case where N_{i+1} is generated by the $\supset$-Elimination Rule: Essentially the same as the preceding Case 7. □

PROOF OF LEMMA 3.   The general structure of Lemma 3's proof will be analogous to Lemma 2's proof, in that it will again demonstrate the node N_{i+1} satisfies the $(L, M)-$Conservative condition with an inductive argument that presumes that the i higher nodes $N_1, N_2...N_i$ along the path Beta(T,L,M) already satisfy the $(L, M)-$Conservative condition. Our inductive proof will be divided into eight cases, six of which are the same as their analogs in Lemma 2's proof (i.e. Cases 2 and 4–8). The remaining two cases appear below:

A) The Case where N_{i+1} designates T's root: This case differs from the Case 1 of Lemma 2's proof because a proof of P of X stores $\neg X$ (which corresponds to Y rewritten in Prenex* Normal form) in its root, rather than $\neg Y$ (which corresponds to X in Prenex* Normal form). Another distinction is that Lemma 3's hypothesis assumes the validity of the condition $\neg$ Check(X, Y, P, Q), whereas Lemma 2's hypothesis presumed Check(X, Y, P, Q). The salient point is that this shift in Check(X, Y, P, Q)'s Boolean value allows us to conclude that the new sentence stored in T's root, under Lemma 3, is also valid in the Standard Model of the Natural Numbers. Hence if Ψ denotes the root's sentence, we can again conclude the Ψ^M is valid, showing that the root satisfies Part-D of the definition of $(L, M)-$Conservativeness. (Once again, it is trivial that the root satisfies the other three parts of the definition of $(L, M)-$Conservativeness.) □

B) The Case where N_{i+1}'s Stored Sentence is generated by the $\exists$-Elimination Rule: The reason this case is different from the Case 3 of Lemma 2's proof is that the root of T's candidate tree will, for some Π_0^- formula $\phi(v)$, correspond to a sentence of the form " $\exists \, v \, \phi(v)$ " in the current case. Moreover from the fact that Lemma 3's hypothesis indicates that the condition $\neg$ Check(X, Y, P, Q) is valid, we can presume our valuation will assure that Val$(u) \le L$, whenever N_{i+1}'s stored sentence " $\phi(u)$ " is deduced by eliminating the existential quantifier from " $\exists \, v \, \phi(v)$ " .

The remainder of our proof for the current case is analogous to Case 3 from Lemma 2's proof. It uses again the fact that the only proper axiom of IS-1(A) containing an unbounded existential quantifier is Equation (1)'s axiom. In particular, let MaxVal(i) again denote the maximum of 1 and of the largest quantity, Val(u), stored in the nodes $N_1, N_2, N_3, ...N_i$. We already noted in Lemma 2's proof that MaxVal$(i+1) \le 2 \cdot$ MaxVal(i), whenever the node N_{i+1} introduces a new parameter u, generated by eliminating an existential quantifier stemming from Equation (1). Hence, this observation, combined with the inequality from the preceding paragraph, implies MaxVal$(i+1) \le$ Max $[\, L \, , 2 \cdot$ MaxVal$(i)\,]$.

This recurrence relation, together with the facts that $L = \frac{1}{2} \cdot$ Max(P, Q) , $M =$ Max$(P, Q) - 1$ and that P's proof tree has height less than $\frac{1}{3}$ Log$_2(M)$, demonstrates that the parameter u, generated by the $\exists$-Elimination Rule meets Equation (6)'s requirements. It is, again, trivial to justify it satisfies the other parts of the definition of (L, M)-Conservativeness. □

The preceding proofs of Lemmas 2 and 3 also complete our justification for Theorems 1 and 2. This is because Section 2.1's proof of these two theorems had pre-supposed the correctness of Equations (11) and (12), an assumption which Lemmas 2 and 3 do now corroborate.

Generalizations of Theorem 2 and Added Perspectives. Let H denote a list of ordered pairs (t_1, p_1), $(t_2, p_2)...(t_n, p_n)$, where p_k is a Semantic Tableaux proof of the theorem t_k. Define H to be a **R(i,j) Tableaux-Hierarchy Proof** of the theorem T from the axiom system α iff $T = t_n$ and H also satisfies the following two conditions:

1. The formal axioms used in p_m's proof are either one of $t_1, t_2, ...t_{m-1}$ or come from α.
2. Each of the sentences $t_1, t_2, ...t_{n-1}$ are required to have a Π_i^* or Σ_j^* format.

Consider a revised form of the IS-1(A) that uses $R(1,1)$ deduction rather than conventional semantic tableaux as its underlying formalism. Thus, this version of IS-1(A), which perhaps should be called IS-1*(A), will have an identical definition as IS-1(A) except that its Group-3 axiom will employ a variant of Eq (3) where "Prf" now denotes a $R(1,1)$ proof rather than a conventional tableaux proof. Thus IS-1*(A)'s Group-3 axiom will be identical to IS-1(A)'s counterpart except that it will have this type of Prf $_{\text{IS-1*}(A)}$ predicate replace Prf $_{\text{IS-1}(A)}$.

A longer version of this paper generalizes Theorem 2 to establish that the IS-1*($\bullet$) axiom–mapping formalism is "consistency–preserving". Moreover, all our formalisms can also be further strengthened so that they support the additional properties of our article [24]'s Tangibility Reflection Principle.

It also turns out that Theorem 2 and its generalizations collapse when $R(2,1)$ deduction replaces $R(1,1)$. In this case, a generalization of the Second Incompleteness Theorem can establish there exists a Π_1^- sentence W, provable from the $I\Sigma_0$ fragment of Peano Arithmetic, such that no consistent axiom system α can prove W, prove Addition is a total function and simultaneously recognize the assured non-existence of a $R(2,1)$ proof of 0=1 using α's axioms.

References

1. Z. Adamowicz, "Herbrand Consistency and Bounded Arithmetic", *Fundamenta Mathematica* 171 (2002) pp. 279-292.
2. S. Buss, *Bounded Arithmetic,* Proof Theory Lecture Notes #3, Bibliopolic 1986.
3. M. Fitting, *First Order Logic & Automated Theorem Proving,* SpringerVerlag 1990.
4. P. Hájek and P. Pudlák, *Metamathematics of First Order Arithmetic,* Springer Verlag 1991.
5. R. Jeroslow, "Consistency Statements in Formal Mathematics", *Fundamenta Mathematica* 72 (1971) pp. 17-40.
6. S. Kleene, "On the Notation of Ordinal Numbers", *Journal of Symbolic Logic* 3 (1938), pp. 150-156.
7. J. Krajícek, *Bounded Propositional Logic and Complexity Theory,* Cambridge University Press, 1995.
8. G. Kreisel and G. Takeuti, "Formally Self-Referential Propositions for Cut-Free Classical Analysis", Dissertationes Mathematicae 118 (1974) pp. 1–55

9. E. Nelson, *Predicative Arithmetic,* Math Notes, Princeton Press, 1986.

10. R. Parikh, "Existence and Feasibility in Arithmetic", *Journal of Symbolic Logic* 36 (1971), pp.494-508.

11. J. Paris and C. Dimitracopoulos, "A Note on the Undefinability of Cuts", *Journal of Symbolic Logic* 48 (1983) pp. 564-569.

12. P. Pudlák, "Cuts, Consistency Statements and Interpretations", *Journal of Symbolic Logic* 50 (1985) pp.423-442.

13. P. Pudlák, "On the Lengths of Proofs of Consistency", in *Collegium Logicum: Annals of the Kurt Gödel Society Volume 2,* published (1996) by Springer-Wien-NewYork, pp 65-86.

14. H. Rogers, *Recursive Functions and Effective Compatibility,* McGrawHill 1967.

15. R. Smullyan, *First Order Logic,* Springer Verlag, 1968.

16. R. Solovay, Private Communications (1994) about his generalization of one of Pudlák's theorems from [12]. Solovay never published any of his observations about "Definable Cuts" that several logicians [4,7,9,11,12,13,19] have attributed to his private communications. We provide our short 4-page interpretation of Solovay's revised form of Pudlák's Incompleteness Theorem in Appendix A of [24].

17. G. Takeuti, *Proof Theory,* Studies in Logic Volume 81, North Holland, 1987.

18. A. Visser, "An Inside View of Exp", *Journal of Symbolic Logic* 57 (1992) 131–165

19. A. Wilkie and J. Paris, "On the Scheme of Induction for Bounded Arithmetic", *Annals of Pure and Applied Logic* (35) 1987, 261-302

20. D. Willard, "Self-Verifying Axiom Systems", *Third Kurt Gödel Colloquium* (1993), Springer-Verlag LNCS#713, pp. 325-336.

21. D. Willard, "The Tangibility Reflection Principle", *Fifth Kurt Gödel Colloquium* (1997), Springer-Verlag LNCS#1289, pp. 319–334.

22. D. Willard, "Self-Reflection Principles and NP-Hardness", *Dimacs Series #* 39 (1998), pp. 297–320 (AMS Press).

23. D. Willard, "The Semantic Tableaux Version of the Second Incompleteness Theorem Extends Almost to Robinson's Arithmetic Q", in *Semantic Tableaux 2000 Conference Proceedings,* SpringerVerlag LNAI#1847, pp. 415-430.

24. D. Willard, "Self-Verifying Systems, the Incompleteness Theorem and the Tangibility Reflection Principle", in *Journal of Symbolic Logic* 66 (2001) pp. 536-596.

25. D. Willard, "How to Extend The Semantic Tableaux And Cut-Free Versions of the Second Incompleteness Theorem Almost to Robinson's Arithmetic Q", *Journal of Symbolic Logic* 67 (2002) pp. 465-496.

A New Indefinite Semantics for Hilbert's Epsilon

Claus-Peter Wirth

FR Informatik, Saarland Univ., D–66041 Saarbrücken, Germany
cp@ags.uni-sb.de

Abstract. After reviewing the literature on semantics of Hilbert's epsilon symbol, we present a new one that is similar to the referential interpretation of indefinite articles in natural languages.

1 Motivation

In [10] we have studied the combination of mathematical induction in the style of Fermat's *descente infinie* with state-of-the-art logical deduction into a formal system in which a working mathematician can straightforwardly develop his proofs. This system's soundness proof required a notion of reduction like the one of Def. 5.19 below that *"preserves solutions"*. By this we mean the following: All solutions that transform a proof attempt (to which a proposition has been reduced) into a closed proof (i.e. the "closing substitutions" for the free variables) are also solutions of the original proposition, just as a proof in Prolog computes answers of a query proposition. The *liberalized* δ-rules as found in [4] do not satisfy this notion. The addition of our choice-conditions—which can be understood as a new semantics for Hilbert's ε-symbol that mirrors the referential interpretation of indefinite articles in natural languages—finally turned out to be the only way to repair this defect of the liberalized δ-rules. As Hilbert's ε is of universal interest and applicability, we suppose that our new semantics will turn out to be useful in many other areas where logic is applied as a tool for description and reasoning. The paper organizes as follows: Sect. 2 introduces the ε. In Sect. 3 we show the problems with indefinite and committed choice and review the literature on the ε's semantics w.r.t. adequacy and Hilbert's intentions. Sect. 4 introduces our new approach to the ε's semantics informally. A formal discussion follows in Sect. 5, where proofs are omitted but can be found in [10].

2 What Is Hilbert's ε?

Just like Bertrand Russell's ι-symbol (cf. e.g. [7, Vol. I]), Hilbert's ε-symbol is a binder that takes a variable x and a formula A and produces the term $\varepsilon x. A$.

Example 2.1 (ι) *(Buggy!)*
Let III and IV denote Henry III and Henry IV, resp., and consider Father to be a predicate for which Father(III, IV) holds, i.e. "Henry III is father of Henry IV". Now, *"the* father of Henry IV" can be denoted by $\iota x.$ Father(x, IV), and because this is nobody but Henry III, i.e. III $= \iota x.$ Father(x, IV), we know that

U. Egly and C.G. Fermüller (Eds.): TABLEAUX 2002, LNAI 2381, pp. 298–314, 2002.

$\mathsf{Father}(\iota x.\ \mathsf{Father}(x, \mathsf{IV}), \mathsf{IV})$ holds. Similarly,
$$\mathsf{Father}(\iota x.\ \mathsf{Father}(x, \mathsf{Adam}), \mathsf{Adam}), \qquad\qquad (\text{Ex. 2.1.1})$$
and thus $\exists y.\ \mathsf{Father}(y, \mathsf{Adam})$, but, oops! Adam and Eve do not have any fathers. If you think differently on this, consider the following problem that occurs when somebody has two fathers:
$$\mathsf{Father}(\mathsf{HolyGhost}, \mathsf{Jesus}) \ \wedge\ \mathsf{Father}(\mathsf{Joseph}, \mathsf{Jesus}). \qquad (\text{Ex. 2.1.2})$$
Then the Holy Ghost is *the* father of Jesus and Joseph is *the* father of Jesus, i.e.
$$\mathsf{HolyGhost} = \iota x.\ \mathsf{Father}(x, \mathsf{Jesus}) \ \wedge\ \mathsf{Joseph} = \iota x.\ \mathsf{Father}(x, \mathsf{Jesus}) \quad (\text{Ex. 2.1.3})$$
which implies something the Pope may not accept, namely that $\mathsf{HolyGhost} = \mathsf{Joseph}$, and he anathematized Henry IV in the year 1076.

Thus, in order to be able to write down $\iota x.\ A$ without further consideration, following the (well justified) standard in classical non-modal logics that any term uniquely denotes something that exists, we have to treat $\iota x.\ A$ as an uninterpreted term about which we only know
$$\exists! x.\ A \ \Rightarrow\ A\{x \mapsto \iota x.\ A\}$$
or in different notation $(\exists! x.\ (A(x))) \ \Rightarrow\ A(\iota x.\ (A(x)))$. Now the problems of Ex. 2.1 disappear because (Ex. 2.1.1) and (Ex. 2.1.3) are not valid. The price we have to pay for this is that—roughly speaking— $\iota x.\ A$ is of no use unless the unique existence $\exists! x.\ A$ can be derived.

Compared to this, the ε is more useful than the ι because it comes with the stronger axiom
$$\exists x.\ A \ \Rightarrow\ A\{x \mapsto \varepsilon x.\ A\} \qquad\qquad\qquad (\varepsilon_0)$$
As the basic methodology of David Hilbert's formal program is to treat all symbols as meaningless, he does not give us any semantics but only the axiom (ε_0). Although no meaning is required, it furthers the understanding, and therefore Paul Bernays writes [7, Vol. II, p. 12] in the fundamental book on the work of David Hilbert and his group on the foundations of mathematics that

> $\varepsilon x.\ A$ ... "is an object of the universe for which—according to the semantical translation of the formula (ε_0)—*the predicate A holds, provided that A holds for any object of the universe.*" (our translation)

Example 2.2 (ε **instead of** ι) *(continuing Ex. 2.1)*
We still have $\mathsf{III} = \varepsilon x.\ \mathsf{Father}(x, \mathsf{IV})$ and $\mathsf{Father}(\varepsilon x.\ \mathsf{Father}(x, \mathsf{IV}), \mathsf{IV})$. But, from the contrapositive of (ε_0) and $\neg\mathsf{Father}(\varepsilon x.\ \mathsf{Father}(x, \mathsf{Adam}), \mathsf{Adam})$, we now can conclude that $\neg\exists y.\ \mathsf{Father}(y, \mathsf{Adam})$.

David Hilbert did not need any semantics or precise intention for the ε-symbol because it was introduced merely as a formal syntactic device to facilitate proof-theoretic investigations, motivated by the possibility to get rid of the existential and universal quantifiers via
$$\exists x.\ A \ \Leftrightarrow\ A\{x \mapsto \varepsilon x.\ A\} \qquad\qquad\qquad (\varepsilon_1)$$
and
$$\forall x.\ A \ \Leftrightarrow\ A\{x \mapsto \varepsilon x.\ \neg A\} \qquad\qquad\qquad (\varepsilon_2)$$
Cf. [9] for an excellent modern treatment of the subject.

Wilhelm Ackermann, Paul Bernays, and David Hilbert finally succeeded [7, Vol. II] in giving a proof of the fact that the ε (just as the ι [7, Vol. I]) is a conservative extension in the sense that any formal proof of an ε-free formula can be transformed into a formal proof that does not use the ε at all ("ε-*elimination theorems*"). Generally, this is not the case anymore if we go beyond first-order logic, e.g. by considering finite structures only, cf. [3] for references.

While the historical and technical research on ε-elimination is still going on, this is not the subject of this paper. Moreover, it is my opinion that in our days we should be less interested in Hilbert's formal program and the consistency of mathematics than in the powerful use of logic in creative processes. And, instead of the tedious syntactical proof transformations that easily lose their usefulness and elegance within their technical complexity and that—more importantly— can only refer to an already existing logic, we need *semantical* means for finding new logics and new applications. And the question that then arises here—esp. for classical logic—is: What would be the proper semantics for Hilbert's ε?

3   Is Indefinite Choice the Proper Semantics?

Just as the ι-symbol is generally taken to be the referential interpretation of the *definite* article in natural languages, it is our opinion that the ε-symbol should be that of the *indefinite* one.

Example 3.1 (ε instead of ι)   *(continuing Ex. 2.1)*
It may well be the case that
    HolyGhost $= \varepsilon x.$ Father(x, Jesus) $\wedge$ Joseph $= \varepsilon x.$ Father(x, Jesus)
i.e. that "The Holy Ghost is $\underline{a}$ father of Jesus and Joseph is $\underline{a}$ father of Jesus." But this does not bring the Pope into trouble because we do not know whether any father of Jesus is equal to any father of Jesus. This will become clearer when reconsidering this example in Ex. 4.4.

3.1   Committed Choice

Closely connected to indefinite choice (also called "indeterminism" or "don't care nondeterminism") is the notion of "*committed choice*". E.g., when you have a new telephone, you *don't care* which number you get, but once the provider has chosen a number for your telephone, you want the provider to *commit to its choice*, i.e. not to change your phone number between two incoming calls.

Example 3.2 (Committed Choice)   *(Buggy!)*
Suppose we want to prove $\exists x.\ (x \neq x).$
According to (ε_1) this reduces to $\varepsilon x.\ (x \neq x)\ \neq\ \varepsilon x.\ (x \neq x).$
Since there is no solution to $x \neq x$ we can replace $\varepsilon x.\ (x \neq x)$ with anything.
Thus, the above reduces to $0\ \neq\ \varepsilon x.\ (x \neq x),$
and then, by exactly the same argumentation, to $0\ \neq\ 1,$
which is valid.

Thus we have proved our original formula $\exists x.\ (x \neq x)$, which, however, happens to be invalid. What went wrong? Of course, we have to commit to our choice for the ε-term introduced for the elimination of the existential quantifier.

The following lengthy example shows that the elimination of $\forall$- and $\exists$-quantifiers with the help of ε-terms may be more difficult than one might think. The problem is that some ε-terms may become "subordinate" to others. An ε-term $\varepsilon v.\ B$ (or more generally a binder on v) is *superordinate* to an (occurrence of an) ε-term $\varepsilon x.\ A$ if $\varepsilon x.\ A$ is a subterm of B and an occurrence of the variable v in $\varepsilon x.\ A$ is free in B. An (occurrence of an) ε-term a is *subordinate* to an ε-term b if b is superordinate to a. These subordinate ε-terms [7, Vol. II, p. 24] are responsible for the difficulty to prove the theorems on ε-elimination constructively.

Example 3.3 (Subordinate ε-terms)

Consider the formula $\forall x.\ \exists y.\ \forall z.\ \mathsf{P}(x, y, z)$. Let us apply (ε_1) and (ε_2) in order to completely remove the three quantifiers. The resulting term does not depend on the order in which we do this, but it is quite deep; in general n nested quantifiers result in an ε-nesting depth of $2^n - 1$. Moreover, huge ε-terms occur up to n-times with commitment to their choice. Therefore, we should carefully identify the terms that have multiple occurrence. The result is $\mathsf{P}(x_1, y_2, z_4)$, where

$z_4 = \varepsilon z.\ \neg\mathsf{P}(x_1, y_2, z)$
$y_2 = \varepsilon y.\ \mathsf{P}(x_1, y, z_3(y))$ with $z_3(y) = \varepsilon z.\ \neg\mathsf{P}(x_1, y, z)$
$x_1 = \varepsilon x.\ \neg\mathsf{P}(x, y_1(x), z_2(x))$ with $z_2(\underline{x}) = \varepsilon z.\ \neg\mathsf{P}(\underline{x}, y_1(\underline{x}), z)$
         and $y_1(\underline{x}) = \varepsilon y.\ \mathsf{P}(\underline{x}, y, z_1(\underline{x}, y))$ with $z_1(\underline{x}, y) = \varepsilon z.\ \neg\mathsf{P}(\underline{x}, y, z)$.

Firstly note that the equations for z_3, z_2, y_1, z_1 are a little problematic because the underlined variables $\underline{x}$ and $\underline{y}$ occurring on the right-hand sides are only seemingly free but actually bound by the next ε to the left, to which the closest ε-term thus becomes subordinate. E.g., the ε-term $z_3(y)$ is subordinate to the ε-term y_2. Secondly, the top ε-binders on the right-hand sides are exactly those that require a commitment to their choice. This means that each of $z_1, z_2, z_3,$ z_4 and of y_1, y_2 may be chosen differently without affecting soundness of the equivalence transformation. Note that the variables are strictly nested into each other. Thus we must choose in the order of $z_1, y_1, z_2, x_1, z_3, y_2, z_4$. Moreover, for z_3, z_2, y_1, z_1 we actually have to choose a function instead of a simple value. In Hilbert's view, however, there are no objects at all, but only terms, where x_1 reads

    $\varepsilon x.\ \mathsf{P}(x, \varepsilon y.\ \mathsf{P}(x, y, \varepsilon z_1.\ \mathsf{P}(x, y, z_1)), \varepsilon z_2.\ \mathsf{P}(x, \varepsilon y.\ \mathsf{P}(x, y, \varepsilon z_1.\ \mathsf{P}(x, y, z_1)), z_2))$
and y_2 and z_4 take several lines to write them down.

For $\forall x.\ \forall y.\ \forall z.\ \mathsf{P}(x, y, z)$ instead of $\forall x.\ \exists y.\ \forall z.\ \mathsf{P}(x, y, z)$,   we get the same exponential explosion as in Ex. 3.3 when we eliminate the ε-terms completely using (ε_2). The only difference is that we get two more occurrences of '$\neg$'. But when we have quantifiers of the same kind like '$\exists$' or '$\forall$', we had better choose them in parallel, e.g., for $\forall x.\ \forall y.\ \forall z.\ \mathsf{P}(x, y, z)$ we take $v_1 := \varepsilon v.$ $\neg\mathsf{P}(1\mathrm{st}(v), 2\mathrm{nd}(v), 3\mathrm{rd}(v))$, and then $x_1 = 1\mathrm{st}(v_1)$, $y_2 = 2\mathrm{nd}(v_1)$, $z_4 = 3\mathrm{rd}(v_1)$.

3.2   Free Existential and Weak Free Universal Variables

Suppose we want to prove the existential property $\exists x.\ A$. While in old-fashioned inference systems the γ-rules (according to Smullyan's classification) require us to choose a witnessing term t immediately when removing the quantifier, more modern inference systems like the ones in [4] enable us to delay the choice of the term t (which is crucial for the success of the later proof) until the state of the proof attempt provides information that is sufficient to make a success-ful decision. This delay is achieved with a special kind of variable, sometimes called "dummy", "free variable", or "meta variable". We will call these variables *free existential variables* and write them like $x^{\exists}$. Now, $\exists x.\ A$ is first reduced to $A\{x \mapsto x^{\exists}\}$ and later in the proof we can globally substitute $x^{\exists}$ with an appropriate term.

In theorem proving, cf. [10] e.g., the explosion of Ex. 3.3 is reduced by not removing the quantifiers below ε-binders and by replacing existentially quanti-fied variables with free existential variables. For the case of Ex. 3.3, this yields $z_4 = \varepsilon z.\ \neg\mathsf{P}(x_1, y_1^{\exists}, z)$ and $x_1 = \varepsilon x.\ \neg \exists y.\ \forall z.\ \mathsf{P}(x, y, z)$. Thus, in general, the binder nesting does not become deeper than $\frac{1}{4}(n+1)^2$. Moreover, if we are only interested in reduction and not in equivalence transformation of a formula, we can even abstract Skolem terms from the ε-terms and just consider $z_4 = z^{\forall,\mathsf{w}}(y_1^{\exists})$ and $x_1 = x^{\forall,\mathsf{w}}$. Here $x^{\forall,\mathsf{w}}$ and $z^{\forall,\mathsf{w}}$ are *weak free universal variables*. These vari-ables play the role of parameters and stand for an arbitrary object of which nothing is known. The small 'w' stands for "weak".

Note that with Skolemization we have no explosion at all and the same will be the case for our approach to ε-terms.

After a glimpse into the literature on a semantics for Hilbert's ε in the next two sections, we will further introduce into indefinite choice in Sect. 4.

3.3   Functional Semantics

Nearly all the semantics for Hilbert's ε in the literature is functional. Cf. [9] and the references there for an overview. There, a functional behavior is required for the ε, which contrasts the above suggested indefiniteness.

The omnipresence of the functionality requirement may have its historical justification in the fact that the dots "..." in the quotation preceding Ex. 2.2 actually contain the word "function", which could be understood in its mathe-matical sense to denote a (right-) unique relation. And, what kind of function could it be but a choice function, choosing an element from the set of objects that satisfy A? In [6], Hilbert even writes

> "Above that, the ε has the role of the choice function, i.e. in the case where $A(a)$ may hold for several things, $\varepsilon x.(A(x))$ is *an arbitrary one* of the things a for which A holds." (our translation)

Regarding the question of an intended unique behavior, these statements are ambiguous in the German original. Hilbert most probably wanted to have what today we call "*committed choice*", but, as this technical term did not exist at his time and he was not interested in semantics anyway, simply used the word "function". The strongest argument against Hilbert's intention of a functional behavior is that the implied formula

$$\forall x.\,(A{\Leftrightarrow}B) \quad \Rightarrow \quad \varepsilon x.\,A = \varepsilon x.\,B \qquad\qquad (E2)$$

cannot be derived form Hilbert's axiomatization.

To be precise, the notion of a "choice function" must be generalized here because—in order to have a total function on the power set of the universe—a value must be supplied even on the empty set: f is defined to be a *generalized choice function* if $f : \mathrm{dom}(f) \to \bigcup(\mathrm{dom}(f))$ and $\forall x \in \mathrm{dom}(f).$ $(x = \emptyset \;\lor\; f(x) \in x)$. Different possible choices for the value on the empty set are described in [9], but as the consequences of any special choice are quite queer, the only solution that is found to be sufficiently adequate in [9] is to consider validity in *any* model given by *each* generalized choice function on the power set of the universe. Note, however, that, in each single model, the behavior of the ε is still a *function* from the set of objects that satisfy A. This can be expressed by (E2) which, roughly speaking, together with (ε_1) and (ε_2) is shown in [9] to be complete for first-order ε predicate calculus w.r.t. this semantics.

In [5] the above treatment of [9] is called the *extensional* one because the value of $\varepsilon x.\,A$ in each semantical structure $\mathcal{A}$ is functionally dependent on the extension of the formula A, i.e. on $\{\, o \mid \mathrm{eval}(\mathcal{A}{\uplus}\{x{\mapsto}o\})(A) \,\}$, where 'eval' is the standard evaluation function that maps a structure (or interpretation) (possibly including a valuation of the free variables) to a function from terms (and formulas) to values. In order to get more freeness for the definition of a semantics of ε, in [5] the value of $\varepsilon x.\,A$ may depend on the syntax besides the semantics. It is given as a function depending on a structure and on the *term* $\varepsilon x.\,A$. In [5, p. 177] we read: "This definition contains no restriction whatsoever on the valuation of ε-terms." This is, however, not true because it imposes the restriction of a functional behavior, which denies the possibility of an indefinite behavior as we will see below.

3.4   Indefinite Semantics in the Literature

The only occurrences of an indefinite semantics for Hilbert's ε in the literature seem to be [3] and the references there. Consider $\varepsilon x.\,(x{=}x) = \varepsilon x.\,(x{=}x)$ from [3] or the even simpler

$$\varepsilon x.\;\mathsf{true} \;=\; \varepsilon x.\;\mathsf{true} \qquad\qquad (R)$$

which may be valid or not, depending on the question whether the same object is taken on both sides of the equation or not. In natural language this like "Something is equal to something" whose truth is indefinite. If you do not think so, take $\varepsilon x.\;\mathsf{true} \neq \varepsilon x.\;\mathsf{true}$ instead, i.e. "Something is unequal to something". In [3], Kleene's strong three valued logic is taken as a mathematically elegant means to solve the problems with indefiniteness. From a practical point of view, however, we do not think this to be an adequate solution because it severely restricts the applicability of the logic: Logical arguments outside the academical world are never made explicit because the presence of logic is either not realized at all or taken to be trivial. In applications, a logic is not the object of investigation but a meta-logical tool. Thus, regarding applications in the western world we have to stick to our common meta-logic which is a subset of classical (modal) logic. A western court can accept that Lee Harvey Oswald killed John F. Kennedy as well as that he did not; but cannot accept a third possibility, a tertium, as required for Kleene's strong three valued logic, and esp. not the interpretation given in [3] that he *both* did and did not kill him.

4   Introduction to a New Indefinite Semantics for the ε

From the discussion above one could get the impression that an indefinite logical treatment of the ε is not easy to find. Indeed, there is the problem that the substitutivity $s = t \Rightarrow f(s) = f(t)$ (cf. (E2)) and the reflexivity axiom $t = t$ (cf. (R)) cannot be taken for granted. This means that it is not definitely okay to replace a subterm by an equal term and that even syntactically equal terms may not be definitely equal.

Therefore, it may be interesting to see that in programs we are quite used to an indefinite behavior of choosing including committed choice and that the violation of substitutivity and even reflexivity is no problem there: Consider the following ML function, returning the first element of a list that implements a set:

```
fun choose s = case s of Set (i :: _) => i | _ => raise Empty;
```

The behavior of the function `choose` is indefinite for a given set, but any time it is called for an implemented set, it chooses a special element and *commits to this choice*, i.e. when called again, it returns the same value. In this case we have `choose s = choose s`, but $s = t$ does not imply `choose s = choose t`. In an implementation where some parallel reordering of lists may take place, even `choose s = choose s` may be wrong. The question of `choose s = choose s` is indefinite until the choice steps have actually been performed. *This is exactly what we will do with the ε.* The steps that are performed in logic are proof steps. Thus, on the one hand, when we want to prove $\varepsilon x.\ \mathrm{true} = \varepsilon x.\ \mathrm{true}$ we can choose 0 for both occurrences of $\varepsilon x.\ \mathrm{true}$, get $0 = 0$, and the proof is successful. On the other hand, when we want to prove $\varepsilon x.\ \mathrm{true} \neq \varepsilon x.\ \mathrm{true}$ we can choose 0 for one occurrence and 1 for the other, get $0 \neq 1$, and the proof is successful, too. This procedure may seem wondrous again, but is very similar to something quite common with free existential variables, cf. Sect. 3.2: On the one hand, when we want to prove $x^\exists = y^\exists$ we can choose 0 to substitute for both $x^\exists$ and $y^\exists$, get $0 = 0$, and the proof is successful. On the other hand, when we want to prove $x^\exists \neq y^\exists$ we can choose 0 to substitute for $x^\exists$ and 1 to substitute for $y^\exists$, get $0 \neq 1$, and the proof is successful, too.

4.1   Replacing ε-Terms with Strong Free Universal Variables

An important difference between the inequations $\varepsilon x.\ \mathrm{true} \neq \varepsilon x.\ \mathrm{true}$ and $x^\exists \neq y^\exists$ is that the latter does not violate the reflexivity axiom. And we are going to cure the violation of the former immediately by introducing a new kind of free variables, namely the *strong free universal variables*, which we write like $x^{\forall,\mathrm{s}}$.

Now, instead of $\varepsilon x.\ \mathsf{true} \neq \varepsilon x.\ \mathsf{true}$ we write $x^{\vee,s} \neq y^{\vee,s}$ and remember what these strong free universal variables stand for by storing this into a function C, called a *choice-condition*: $C(x^{\vee,s}) := C(y^{\vee,s}) := \mathsf{true}$.

At first, suppose that our ε-terms are not subordinate to any outside binder that binds variables inside the ε-term. In this case, we replace each ε-term $\varepsilon z.\ A$ with a new strong free universal variable $z^{\vee,s}$ and extend the partial function C by $C(z^{\vee,s}) := A\{z \mapsto z^{\vee,s}\}$.

By this procedure we eliminate all ε-terms without loosing any syntactical information, the substitutivity and reflexivity axioms are immediately regained, and the problems discussed above disappear.

Another reason for replacing the ε-terms with strong free universal variables is that the latter can solve the question whether a committed choice is required: We can express—on the one hand—a committed choice by using a single strong free universal variable and—on the other hand—a choice without commitment by using several variables with the same choice-condition. Indeed, this solves our problems with committed choice of Ex. 3.2: Now, again using (ε_1), $\exists x.\ (x \neq x)$ reduces to $x^{\vee,s} \neq x^{\vee,s}$ with $C(x^{\vee,s}) := (x^{\vee,s} \neq x^{\vee,s})$ and the proof attempt immediately fails due to the now regained reflexivity axiom.

We still have to explain what to do with subordinate ε-terms. If the ε-term $\varepsilon z.\ A$ contains occurrences of variables $v_0,\ \dots,\ v_{l-1}$ that are not bound by quantifiers or other binders inside but outside the ε-term, then we have to replace it with $z^{\vee,s}(v_0)\cdots(v_{l-1})$ for a new strong free universal variable $z^{\vee,s}$ and to extend the choice-condition C by $C(z^{\vee,s}) := \lambda v_0.\ \dots \lambda v_{l-1}.\ (A\{z \mapsto z^{\vee,s}(v_0)\cdots(v_{l-1})\})$.

Example 4.1 (Higher-Order Choice-Condition) *(continuing Ex. 3.3)*
In our framework the elimination of the $\forall$- and $\exists$-quantifiers turns $\forall x.\ \exists y.\ \forall z.\ \mathsf{P}(x,y,z)$ into $\mathsf{P}(x_1^{\vee,s}, y_2^{\vee,s}, z_4^{\vee,s})$, and the subordinate ε-terms are replaced with the following higher-order choice-condition:

$$C(z_4^{\vee,s}) = \neg\mathsf{P}(x_1^{\vee,s}, y_2^{\vee,s}, z_4^{\vee,s}) \qquad C(y_2^{\vee,s}) = \mathsf{P}(x_1^{\vee,s}, y_2^{\vee,s}, z_3^{\vee,s}(y_2^{\vee,s}))$$
$$C(z_3^{\vee,s}) = \lambda y.\ \neg\mathsf{P}(x_1^{\vee,s}, y, z_3^{\vee,s}(y)) \qquad C(x_1^{\vee,s}) = \neg\mathsf{P}(x_1^{\vee,s}, y_1^{\vee,s}(x_1^{\vee,s}), z_2^{\vee,s}(x_1^{\vee,s}))$$
$$C(z_2^{\vee,s}) = \lambda x.\ \neg\mathsf{P}(x, y_1^{\vee,s}(x), z_2^{\vee,s}(x)) \qquad C(y_1^{\vee,s}) = \lambda x.\ \mathsf{P}(x, y_1^{\vee,s}(x), z_1^{\vee,s}(x)(y_1^{\vee,s}(x)))$$
$$C(z_1^{\vee,s}) = \lambda x.\ \lambda y.\ \neg\mathsf{P}(x, y, z_1^{\vee,s}(x)(y))$$

4.2   Variable-Conditions

In some inference systems Skolemization is unsound, e.g. for higher-order systems like the one in [8] or the system in [10] for *descente infinie*. In these systems a δ-step (according to Smullyan's classification) substitutes a previously universally quantified variable (say z in $\forall z.\ \neg A$) not with a new Skolem term say $f(x_0^{\exists}, \dots, x_{l-1}^{\exists})$ but with a new free universal variable $y^{\vee}$ (resulting in $\neg A\{z \mapsto y^{\vee}\}$) and the dependencies $\{\ (x_i^{\exists}, y^{\vee}) \mid i \prec l\ \}$ are stored in a so-called *variable-condition*, which disallows the instantiation of the $x_i^{\exists}$ with $y^{\vee}$ and takes over the part of the occur-check of unification in the Skolemizing inference systems.

While the benefit of the introduction of free existential variables in γ-rules is to delay the choice of a witnessing term, it is sometimes unsound to instantiate a free existential variable $x^\exists$ with a term containing a free universal variable $y^\forall$ that was introduced later than $x^\exists$:

Example 4.2 $\qquad\qquad\qquad\qquad\qquad\qquad\qquad\qquad \exists x.\ \forall y.\ (x = y)$
is not deductively valid. We can start a proof attempt via:

γ-step: $\qquad\qquad\qquad\qquad\qquad\qquad\qquad\qquad\qquad \forall y.\ (x^\exists = y)$
δ-step: $\qquad\qquad\qquad\qquad\qquad\qquad\qquad\qquad\qquad\quad (x^\exists = y^\forall)$
Now, if we were allowed to substitute the free existential variable $x^\exists$ with the free universal variable $y^\forall$, we would get the tautology $(y^\forall = y^\forall)$, i.e. we would have proved an invalid formula. In order to prevent this, the δ-step has to record $(x^\exists, y^\forall)$ in the variable-condition, which disallows the instantiation step.

In order to restrict the possible instantiations as little as possible, we should keep our variable-conditions as small as possible. While in [1] Wolfgang Bibel is quite generous in that he lets his variable-conditions become quite big, the variable-conditions of Michaël Kohlhase in [8] are too small for soundness, cf. [10]. Our variable-conditions of Sect. 5.1 do not have these problems.

Note that variable-conditions do not add unnecessary complexity to applications where Skolemization is no problem and variable-conditions are not needed: Firstly, if they are superfluous we can work with an empty variable-condition as if there would be no variable-condition at all. Secondly—and more importantly—we need the variable-conditions anyway to guarantee that our choice-conditions do not end up in meaningless (vicious) cycles, cf. Ex. 5.11 below.

The above δ-step on $\forall z.\ \neg A$ may be *liberalized* or not. If it is not liberalized, the introduced free universal variable is a weak one. If the δ-step is liberalized, however, it introduces a new strong free universal variable say $y^{\forall,s}$ with choice-condition $C(y^{\forall,s}) := A\{z \mapsto y^{\forall,s}\}$. The advantage of the liberalized version is a smaller variable-condition which enables additional proofs on the same level of multiplicity, cf. [10].

4.3   Instantiating Strong Free Universal Variables

We now have to explain how to replace strong free universal variables with terms that satisfy their choice-condition. Just like the free existential variables, the strong free universal variables must be substituted globally! While a free existential variable $x^\exists$ can be replaced with nearly everything, the replacement of a strong free universal variable $y^{\forall,s}$ requires some proof work, and a weak free universal variable $z^{\forall,w}$ cannot be instantiated at all (unless for lemma or induction hypothesis application, when the formula becomes a tool instead of a task). More precisely, a free existential variable $x^\exists$ may be instantiated with any term that does not violate the current variable-condition. The instantiation of a strong free universal variable $y^{\forall,s}$ additionally requires some proof work. In general, if a substitution σ substitutes—possibly among other free existential and strong free universal variables—the strong free universal variable $y^{\forall,s}$ for which the choice-condition $C(y^{\forall,s}) = \lambda v_0.\ \ldots \lambda v_{l-1}.\ B$ is given, then we must prove

$$\forall v_0. \ \ldots \forall v_{l-1}. \ \left(\ \exists y. \ (B\{y^{\forall,\mathsf{s}} \mapsto y\}) \ \right) \ \Rightarrow \ B \ )\sigma$$

in order to know that the global instantiation with σ is a sound proof step.

Example 4.3   Suppose that our domain is natural numbers and that $y^{\forall,\mathsf{s}}$ has the choice-condition $C(y^{\forall,\mathsf{s}}) = (z^{\forall,\mathsf{w}} = y^{\forall,\mathsf{s}}+1)$. Then, before we may replace $y^{\forall,\mathsf{s}}$ with $\mathsf{p}(z^{\forall,\mathsf{w}})$, we have to prove $\exists y. \ (z^{\forall,\mathsf{w}} = y+1) \Rightarrow (z^{\forall,\mathsf{w}} = \mathsf{p}(z^{\forall,\mathsf{w}})+1)$, which is true for the predecessor function p.

Example 4.4 (Canossa 1077)   *(continuing Ex. 3.1)*   The situation of Ex. 3.1 now reads $\mathsf{HolyGhost} \ = \ z_0^{\forall,\mathsf{s}} \ \wedge \ \mathsf{Joseph} \ = \ z_1^{\forall,\mathsf{s}}$ (Ex. 4.4.1)
with $C(z_0^{\forall,\mathsf{s}}) = \mathsf{Father}(z_0^{\forall,\mathsf{s}}, \mathsf{Jesus})$ and $C(z_1^{\forall,\mathsf{s}}) = \mathsf{Father}(z_1^{\forall,\mathsf{s}}, \mathsf{Jesus})$.
On the one hand, this does not bring the Pope into trouble because we do not know whether $z_0^{\forall,\mathsf{s}} = z_1^{\forall,\mathsf{s}}$. On the other hand, from knowing (Ex. 2.1.2) we can prove (Ex. 4.4.1) by substituting $z_0^{\forall,\mathsf{s}}$ with $\mathsf{HolyGhost}$ because this solves $C(z_0^{\forall,\mathsf{s}})$, and $z_1^{\forall,\mathsf{s}}$ with Joseph because this solves $C(z_1^{\forall,\mathsf{s}})$.

5   Formal Discussion of the ε's New Indefinite Semantics

We use '$\uplus$' for the union of disjoint classes and 'id' for the identity function. For classes R, A, and B we define $_A{\restriction}R := \{ (a,b) \in R \mid a \in A \}$; $R{\restriction}_B := \{ (a,b) \in R \mid b \in B \}$; $\langle A \rangle R := \{ b \mid \exists a \in A. \ (a,b) \in R \}$; $R\langle B \rangle := \{ a \mid \exists b \in B. \ (a,b) \in R \}$. A relation R [on A] is *wellfounded* if any non-empty class B [$\subseteq A$] has an R-minimal element, i.e. $\exists a \in B. \ \neg \exists a' \in B. \ a' R a$.

We define a *sequent* to be a (disjunctive) list of formulas. We assume the following four sets of symbols to be disjoint: $V_\exists$, *free existential variables*, i.e. the free variables of [4]; $V_\forall$, *free universal variables*, i.e. nullary parameters, our substitute for Skolem functions; V_{bound}, *bound variables*, i.e. variables for bound use only; Σ, *constants*, i.e. the function and predicate symbols from the signature. We split the free universal variables $V_\forall$ into *weak free universal variables* $V_{\forall,w}$ and *strong free universal variables* $V_{\forall,s}$: $V_\forall = V_{\forall,w} \uplus V_{\forall,s}$. We define the *free variables* by $V_{free} := V_\exists \uplus V_\forall$ and the *variables* by $V := V_{bound} \uplus V_{free}$. For k being any of these kinds of variables and Γ being a term, formula, sequent, &c., we use '$V_k(\Gamma)$' to denote the set of variables from V_k occurring in Γ. For a substitution σ we denote with '$\Gamma\sigma$' the result of replacing in Γ each occurrence of a variable $x \in \text{dom}(\sigma)$ with $\sigma(x)$. In default situations, we tacitly assume that all occurrences of variables from V_{bound} in terms and formulas on top level and in the ranges of substitutions are *bound occurrences* (i.e. that a variable $x \in V_{bound}$ occurs only in the scope of a binder on x) and that each substitution σ satisfies $\text{dom}(\sigma) \subseteq V_{free}$, so that no bound occurrences of variables can be replaced and no additional variable occurrences can become bound (i.e. captured) when applying σ.

Validity is expected to be given with respect to some Σ-structure $\mathcal{A}$, assigning a non-empty universe (or "carrier" or "object domain"). For $X \subseteq V$ we denote the set of total $\mathcal{A}$-valuations of X (i.e. functions mapping variables to objects of the universe of $\mathcal{A}$) with $X \to \mathcal{A}$ and the set of (possibly) partial $\mathcal{A}$-valuations of X with $X \rightsquigarrow \mathcal{A}$. For $\tau \in X \to \mathcal{A}$ we denote with '$\mathcal{A}\uplus\tau$'

the extension of $\mathcal{A}$ to the variables of X. More precisely, we assume the existence of some evaluation function 'eval' such that $\text{eval}(\mathcal{A}\uplus\tau)$ maps any term whose free occurring symbols are from $\Sigma\uplus X$ into the universe of $\mathcal{A}$ (respecting types) such that for all $x \in X$: $\text{eval}(\mathcal{A}\uplus\tau)(x) = \tau(x)$. Moreover, $\text{eval}(\mathcal{A}\uplus\tau)$ maps any formula B whose free occurring symbols are from $\Sigma\uplus X$ to TRUE or FALSE, such that B is valid in $\mathcal{A}\uplus\tau$ iff $\text{eval}(\mathcal{A}\uplus\tau)(B) = \text{TRUE}$. We assume that the *Substitution-Lemma* (cf. e.g. [4, p. 120]) holds in the sense that, for any substitution σ, Σ-structure $\mathcal{A}$, valuation $\tau \in V \rightsquigarrow \mathcal{A}$, and term or formula B, if the variables that occur free in $B\sigma$ belong to $\text{dom}(\tau)$: $\text{eval}(\mathcal{A}\uplus\tau)(B\sigma) = \text{eval}\big(\mathcal{A} \;\uplus\; (\sigma \;\uplus\; _{V\setminus\text{dom}(\sigma)}\!\restriction\!\text{id}) \circ \text{eval}(\mathcal{A}\uplus\tau)\big)(B)$. Note that we assume the operator '$\circ$' to have higher priority than the operators '$\cup$' and '$\uplus$'. Finally, we assume that the value of the evaluation function on a term or formula B does not depend on the variables that do not occur free in B: For X being the set of the variables that occur free in B, we require: $\text{eval}(\mathcal{A}\uplus\tau)(B) = \text{eval}(\mathcal{A} \;\uplus\; _X\!\restriction\!\tau)(B)$. Further properties of validity or evaluation are definitely not needed. Note that we have left open what our formulas and what our Σ-structures are. All we need are the above basic requirements. We can assume any classical logic here, esp. forms of higher-order logic. Moreover, we can even include those modal logics where the Substitution-Lemma only holds for the substitution of rigid and rigidified (grounded, annotated) terms, although we do not take care of the then necessary restrictions in this paper.

5.1   Existential Substitutions and Valuations

Several binary relations on free variables will be introduced. The overall idea is that when (x, y) occurs in such a relation this means something like "x is older than y" or "the value of y depends on or is described in terms of x".

Definition 5.1 (Variable-Condition)
A *variable-condition* is a subset of $V_{\text{free}} \times V_{\text{free}}$.

Definition 5.2 (E_σ, U_σ)
For a substitution σ we define the *existential relation* to be
$$E_\sigma := \{\, (z^\exists, x) \mid z^\exists \in \mathcal{V}_\exists(\sigma(x)) \wedge x \in \text{dom}(\sigma) \,\},$$
and the *universal relation* to be
$$U_\sigma := \{\, (y^\forall, x) \mid y^\forall \in \mathcal{V}_\forall(\sigma(x)) \wedge x \in \text{dom}(\sigma) \,\}.$$

Definition 5.3 ([[Quasi-]Existential] R-Substitution)
Let R be a variable-condition, cf. Def. 5.1.
σ is an *R-substitution* if σ is a substitution and $R \cup E_\sigma \cup U_\sigma$ is wellfounded.
σ is *existential* if $\text{dom}(\sigma) \subseteq V_\exists$. σ is *quasi-existential* if $\text{dom}(\sigma) \subseteq V_\exists \uplus V_{\text{v,s}}$.

Note that, regarding syntax, $(x, y^\forall) \in R$ is intended to mean that an R-substitution σ may not replace x with a term in which $y^\forall$ occurs, i.e. $(y^\forall, x) \in U_\sigma$ must be disallowed, i.e. $R \cup U_\sigma$ must be wellfounded. Note that in practice w.l.o.g. R, E_σ, and U_σ can always be chosen to be finite, so that $R \cup E_\sigma \cup U_\sigma$ is wellfounded iff it is acyclic.

After application of an R-substitution σ, in case of $(x, y^{\scriptscriptstyle\forall}) \in R$, we have to update our variable-condition R in order to ensure that x is not replaced with $y^{\scriptscriptstyle\forall}$ via a future application of another R-substitution that replaces a free variable say $u^{\scriptscriptstyle\exists}$ occurring in $\sigma(x)$ with $y^{\scriptscriptstyle\forall}$. In this case, the transitive closure of the updated variable-condition has to contain $(u^{\scriptscriptstyle\exists}, y^{\scriptscriptstyle\forall})$. But we have $u^{\scriptscriptstyle\exists} \; E_\sigma \; x \; R \; y^{\scriptscriptstyle\forall}$. This means that $R \cup E_\sigma$ must be a subset of the updated variable-condition. Besides this, we have to add steps with U_σ again.

Definition 5.4 (σ-Update)
Let R be a variable-condition and σ be a substitution.
The σ-*update of* R is $R \cup E_\sigma \cup U_\sigma$.

Let $\mathcal{A}$ be some Σ-structure. We now define a semantical counterpart of our existential R-substitutions, which we will call "existential $(\mathcal{A}, R)$-valuation". Suppose that e maps each free existential variable not directly to an object of $\mathcal{A}$, but can additionally read the values of some free universal variables under an $\mathcal{A}$-valuation $\tau \in V_{\scriptscriptstyle\forall} \to \mathcal{A}$, i.e. e gets some $\tau' \in V_{\scriptscriptstyle\forall} \rightsquigarrow \mathcal{A}$ with $\tau' {\subseteq} \tau$ as a second argument; short: $e : V_{\scriptscriptstyle\exists} \to (V_{\scriptscriptstyle\forall} \rightsquigarrow \mathcal{A}) \rightsquigarrow \mathcal{A}$. Moreover, for each free existential variable $x^{\scriptscriptstyle\exists}$, we require the set of read free universal variables (i.e. $\mathrm{dom}(\tau')$) to be identical for all τ; i.e. there has to be some "semantical relation" $S_e \subseteq V_{\scriptscriptstyle\forall}{\times}V_{\scriptscriptstyle\exists}$ such that for all $x^{\scriptscriptstyle\exists} \in V_{\scriptscriptstyle\exists}$: $e(x^{\scriptscriptstyle\exists}) : (S_e\langle\!\langle\{x^{\scriptscriptstyle\exists}\}\rangle\!\rangle \to \mathcal{A}) \to \mathcal{A}$. Note that, for each $e : V_{\scriptscriptstyle\exists} \to (V_{\scriptscriptstyle\forall} \rightsquigarrow \mathcal{A}) \rightsquigarrow \mathcal{A}$, at most one semantical relation exists, namely $S_e := \{\, (y^{\scriptscriptstyle\forall}, x^{\scriptscriptstyle\exists}) \mid y^{\scriptscriptstyle\forall} \in \mathrm{dom}(\bigcup(\mathrm{dom}(e(x^{\scriptscriptstyle\exists})))) \wedge x^{\scriptscriptstyle\exists} \in V_{\scriptscriptstyle\exists} \,\}$.

Definition 5.5 (Semantical Relation (S_e))
Let $e : X \to (Y \rightsquigarrow \mathcal{A}) \rightsquigarrow \mathcal{A}$. The *semantical relation of* e is
$$S_e := \{\, (y, x) \mid y \in \mathrm{dom}(\bigcup(\mathrm{dom}(e(x)))) \wedge x \in X \,\}.$$
e is *semantical* if $e(x) : (S_e\langle\!\langle\{x\}\rangle\!\rangle \to \mathcal{A}) \to \mathcal{A}$ for all $x \in X$.

Definition 5.6 (Existential $(\mathcal{A}, R)$-Valuation)   Let R be a variable-condition and $\mathcal{A}$ a Σ-structure. e is an *existential $(\mathcal{A}, R)$-valuation* if $e : V_{\scriptscriptstyle\exists} \to (V_{\scriptscriptstyle\forall} \rightsquigarrow \mathcal{A}) \rightsquigarrow \mathcal{A}$, e is semantical, and $R \cup S_e$ is wellfounded.

Definition 5.7 (ϵ)   We define the function
$$\epsilon : \quad (X \to (Y \rightsquigarrow \mathcal{A}) \rightsquigarrow \mathcal{A}) \quad \rightsquigarrow \quad (Y \to \mathcal{A}) \to X \to \mathcal{A}$$
by ($e : X \to (Y \rightsquigarrow \mathcal{A}) \rightsquigarrow \mathcal{A}$ being semantical, $\tau \in Y \to \mathcal{A}$, $x \in X$)
$$\epsilon(e)(\tau)(x) := e(x)(_{S_e\langle\!\langle\{x\}\rangle\!\rangle}\!\restriction\!\tau).$$

We are now going to define R-validity of a set of sequents with free variables, in terms of validity of a formula.

Definition 5.8 (Validity)   Let R be a variable-condition, $\mathcal{A}$ a Σ-structure, and G a set of sequents. G is R-*valid in* $\mathcal{A}$ if there is an existential $(\mathcal{A}, R)$-valuation e such that G is $(e, \mathcal{A})$-valid. G is $(e, \mathcal{A})$-*valid* if G is $(\tau, e, \mathcal{A})$-valid for all $\tau \in V_{\scriptscriptstyle\forall} \to \mathcal{A}$. G is $(\tau, e, \mathcal{A})$-*valid* if G is valid in $\mathcal{A} \uplus \epsilon(e)(\tau) \uplus \tau$. G is *valid in* $\mathcal{A}$ if Γ is valid in $\mathcal{A}$ for all $\Gamma \in G$. A sequent Γ is *valid in* $\mathcal{A}$ if there is some formula listed in Γ that is valid in $\mathcal{A}$.

Example 5.9 (Validity)

For $x^∃ ∈ V_∃$, $y^∀ ∈ V_∀$, the sequent $x^∃=y^∀$ is $∅$-valid in any $\mathcal{A}$ because we can choose $S_e := V_∀×V_∃$ and $e(x^∃)(τ) := τ(y^∀)$ for $τ ∈ V_∀ → \mathcal{A}$, resulting in $ε(e)(τ)(x^∃) = e(x^∃)(S_e ⟨\!⟨x^∃⟩\!⟩ \uparrow τ) = e(x^∃)(V_∀ \uparrow τ) = τ(y^∀)$. This means that $∅$-validity of $x^∃=y^∀$ is the same as validity of $∀y. ∃x. x=y$. Moreover, note that $ε(e)(τ)$ has access to the $τ$-value of $y^∀$ just as a raising function f for x in the raised (i.e. dually Skolemized) version $f(y^∀)=y^∀$ of $∀y. ∃x. x=y$.

Contrary to this, for $R := V_∃×V_∀$, the same formula $x^∃=y^∀$ is not R-valid in general because then the required irreflexivity of $S_e∘R$ implies $S_e = ∅$, and $e(x^∃)(S_e ⟨\!⟨x^∃⟩\!⟩ \uparrow τ) = e(x^∃)(∅ \uparrow τ) = e(x^∃)(∅)$ cannot depend on $τ(y^∀)$ anymore. This means that $(V_∃×V_∀)$-validity of $x^∃=y^∀$ is the same as validity of $∃x. ∀y. x=y$. Moreover, note that $ε(e)(τ)$ has no access to the $τ$-value of $y^∀$ just as a raising function c for x in the raised version $c=y^∀$ of $∃x. ∀y. x=y$.

For a more general example let $G = \{ A_{i,0} … A_{i,n_i-1} \mid i∈I \}$, where for $i∈I$ and $j≺n_i$ the $A_{i,j}$ are formulas with free existential variables from $\boldsymbol{x}$ and free universal variables from $\boldsymbol{y}$. Then $(V_∃×V_∀)$-validity of G means validity of
$$∃\boldsymbol{x}. ∀\boldsymbol{y}. ∀i∈I. ∃j≺n_i. A_{i,j}$$
whereas $∅$-validity of G means validity of
$$∀\boldsymbol{y}. ∃\boldsymbol{x}. ∀i∈I. ∃j≺n_i. A_{i,j}$$

5.2   Choice-Conditions

Definition 5.10 (Choice-Condition, Extension)

C is an R-*choice-condition* if R is a wellfounded variable-condition, C is a partial function from $V_{∀,s}$ into the set of formulas, and $z \, R^+ \, y^{∀,s}$ for all $y^{∀,s} ∈ dom(C)$ and $z ∈ \mathcal{V}_{free}(C(y^{∀,s}))\backslash\{y^{∀,s}\}$.

More generally, the values of C can be formula-valued $λ$-terms where, for $y^{∀,s} ∈ dom(C)$ and $C(y^{∀,s}) = λv_0. … λv_{l-1}. B$, B is a formula whose free occurring variables from V_{bound} are among $\{v_0, …, v_{l-1}\} ⊆ V_{bound}$ and where, for $v_0 : α_0, …, v_{l-1} : α_{l-1}$, we have $y^{∀,s} : α_0 → … → α_{l-1} → α_l$ for some type $α_l$, and any occurrence of $y^{∀,s}$ in B must be of the form $y^{∀,s}(v_0)···(v_{l-1})$.

(C', R') is an *extension* of (C, R) if C is an R-choice-condition, C' is an R'-choice-condition, $C⊆C'$, and $R⊆R'$.

Example 5.11 (Choice-Condition)   *(continuing Ex. 4.1)*

On the one hand, if R is a wellfounded variable-condition that satisfies
$$z_1^{∀,s} \, R \, y_1^{∀,s} \, R \, z_2^{∀,s} \, R \, x_1^{∀,s} \, R \, z_3^{∀,s} \, R \, y_2^{∀,s} \, R \, z_4^{∀,s},$$
then the C of Ex. 4.1 is an R-choice-condition, indeed.

On the other hand, if some clever person would like to do the complete quantifier-elimination of Ex. 4.1 by the simpler $C'(z_4^{∀,s}) = ¬P(x_1^{∀,s}, y_2^{∀,s}, z_4^{∀,s})$, $C'(y_2^{∀,s}) = P(x_1^{∀,s}, y_2^{∀,s}, z_4^{∀,s})$, $C'(x_1^{∀,s}) = ¬P(x_1^{∀,s}, y_2^{∀,s}, z_4^{∀,s})$, then he would—among other things—need $z_4^{∀,s} \, R \, y_2^{∀,s} \, R \, z_4^{∀,s}$, which renders R non-wellfounded. Thus, this C' cannot be an R-choice-condition for any R.

Definition 5.12 (Compatibility)

Let C be an R-choice-condition, $\mathcal{A}$ a Σ-structure, and e an existential $(\mathcal{A}, R)$-valuation. π is $(e, \mathcal{A})$-*compatible with* (C, R) if

1. $\pi : V_{\forall,s} \rightarrow (V_{\forall,w} \rightsquigarrow \mathcal{A}) \rightsquigarrow \mathcal{A}$ is semantical (cf. Def. 5.5) and $R \cup S_e \cup S_\pi$ is wellfounded.
2. For all $y^{\forall,s} \in \mathrm{dom}(C)$ with $C(y^{\forall,s}) = \lambda v_0. \ldots \lambda v_{l-1}. B$ and $\tau \in V_{\forall,w} \rightarrow \mathcal{A}$ and $\chi \in \{v_0, \ldots, v_{l-1}\} \rightarrow \mathcal{A}$:

    If, for some $\eta \in \{y^{\forall,s}\} \rightarrow \mathcal{A}$,
    B is $\left(V_{\forall,s}\setminus\{y^{\forall,s}\} 1 (\epsilon(\pi)(\tau)) \uplus \eta \uplus \tau \uplus \chi, \ e, \ \mathcal{A}\right)$-valid,
    then B is $(\epsilon(\pi)(\tau) \uplus \tau \uplus \chi, e, \mathcal{A})$-valid.

Item 1 of this definition is quite technical and needed for lemma application. Roughly speaking, it says that the flow of information between variables expressed in R, e, and π is acyclic.

Item 2 of $(e, \mathcal{A})$-compatibility of π with say $(\{(y^{\forall,s}, \lambda v_0. \ldots \lambda v_{l-1}. B)\}, R)$ means that a different choice for the $\epsilon(\pi)(\tau)$-value of $y^{\forall,s}$ cannot give rise to a previously not given validity of the formula B in $\mathcal{A} \uplus \epsilon(e)(\epsilon(\pi)(\tau) \uplus \tau) \uplus \epsilon(\pi)(\tau) \uplus \tau \uplus \chi$, or that $\epsilon(\pi)(\tau)(y^{\forall,s})$ is chosen such that B becomes valid if such a choice is possible. This is closely related to Hilbert's ε-operator in the sense that $y^{\forall,s}$ is given the value of $\lambda v_0. \ldots \lambda v_{l-1}. \varepsilon y. (B\{y^{\forall,s}\mapsto y\})$ for $y \in V_{\mathrm{bound}} \setminus \mathcal{V}(B)$.

Since the choice for $y^{\forall,s}$ depends on the other free variables of $\lambda v_0. \ldots \lambda v_{l-1}. B$ (i.e. the free variables of $\lambda v_0. \ldots \lambda v_{l-1}. \varepsilon y. (B\{y^{\forall,s}\mapsto y\})$), we required the inclusion of this dependency into the transitive closure of R in Def. 5.10.

Note that the empty function $\emptyset$ is an R-choice-condition for any wellfounded (which in the following will always be the case) variable-condition R. Moreover, any $\pi : V_{\forall,s} \rightarrow \{\emptyset\} \rightarrow \mathcal{A}$ is $(e, \mathcal{A})$-compatible with $(\emptyset, R)$ due to $S_\pi = \emptyset$. Indeed, a compatible π always exists:

Lemma 5.13 *Let C be an R-choice-condition, $\mathcal{A}$ a Σ-structure, e an existential $(\mathcal{A}, R)$-valuation. Now, there is some π that is $(e, \mathcal{A})$-compatible with (C, R).*

Finally, we need means for expressing the requirement on a quasi-existential substitution that it replaces the strong free universal variables in a way that goes together well with the compatibility of Def. 5.12(2):

Definition 5.14 ($Q_{C,\sigma}$)

For a substitution σ and an R-choice-condition C, we require $Q_{C,\sigma}$ to be a function from $\mathrm{dom}(C) \cap \mathrm{dom}(\sigma)$ into the set of formulas such that for each $y^{\forall,s} \in \mathrm{dom}(C) \cap \mathrm{dom}(\sigma)$ with $C(y^{\forall,s}) = \lambda v_0. \ldots \lambda v_{l-1}. B$, we have $Q_{C,\sigma}(y^{\forall,s}) = \forall v_0. \ldots \forall v_{l-1}. (\exists y. (B\{y^{\forall,s}\mapsto y\}) \Rightarrow B)\sigma$ for some $y \in V_{\mathrm{bound}} \setminus \mathcal{V}(C(y^{\forall,s}))$.

Definition 5.15 (Extended σ-Update)
Let C be an R-choice-condition and σ a substitution. The *extended σ-update* (C', R') of (C, R) is given by:
$C' := \{ (x, B\sigma) \mid (x, B) \in C \wedge x \notin \mathrm{dom}(\sigma) \}$, R' is the σ-update of R.

Lemma 5.16 (Extended σ-Update)
Let C be an R-choice-condition, σ an R-substitution, and (C', R') the extended σ-update of (C, R). Now: C' is an R'-choice-condition.

5.3   Strong Validity

Definition 5.17 (Strong Validity)
Let C be an R-choice-condition, $\mathcal{A}$ a Σ-structure, and G a set of sequents.
G is (C, R)-*strongly valid in* $\mathcal{A}$ if there is an existential $(\mathcal{A}, R)$-valuation e such that G is (C, R)-strongly $(e, \mathcal{A})$-valid. G is (C, R)-*strongly* $(e, \mathcal{A})$-*valid* if G is strongly $(\pi, e, \mathcal{A})$-valid for some π that is $(e, \mathcal{A})$-compatible with (C, R). G is *strongly* $(\pi, e, \mathcal{A})$-*valid* if G is $(\epsilon(\pi)(\tau) \uplus \tau, e, \mathcal{A})$-valid for each $\tau \in V_{\mathsf{v,w}} \to \mathcal{A}$. The rest is given by Def. 5.8.

Note that strong validity is called "strong" because it treats the strong free universal variables properly, whereas (weak) validity of Def. 5.8 does not. It is generally not the case, however, that strong validity is logically stronger than weak validity.

It should be pointed out that the "some π" in the above definition is something we can play around with, e.g. even "each π" is possible here.

Example 5.18   In our framework the formula (E2) of Sect. 3.3 looks like
$\forall x.\ (A \Leftrightarrow B) \quad \Rightarrow \quad x_0^{\mathsf{v,s}} = x_1^{\mathsf{v,s}}$ for some new strong free universal variables $x_0^{\mathsf{v,s}}$ and $x_1^{\mathsf{v,s}}$ with $R = V_{\mathrm{free}}(A) \times \{x_0^{\mathsf{v,s}}\} \cup V_{\mathrm{free}}(B) \times \{x_1^{\mathsf{v,s}}\}$ and R-choice-condition $C = \{(x_0^{\mathsf{v,s}}, A\{x \mapsto x_0^{\mathsf{v,s}}\}), (x_1^{\mathsf{v,s}}, B\{x \mapsto x_1^{\mathsf{v,s}}\})\}$. On the one hand, for the definition via "some π", this formula becomes (C, R)-strongly valid because after choosing a value for $x_0^{\mathsf{v,s}}$ we can take the same value for $x_1^{\mathsf{v,s}}$ simply because $x_1^{\mathsf{v,s}}$ is new and can read all weak free universal variables. On the other hand, for the definition via "each π", this formula only becomes valid when there is a unique solution for the choice-condition on $x_0^{\mathsf{v,s}}$.

The reason why we prefer "some π" to "each π" here and in [10] is that the latter results in more valid formulas (e.g. (E2)) and makes theorem proving easier. Contrary to "each π" and to all semantics in the literature, the "some π" frees us from considering all possible choices: We just have to pick a single one and fix it in a proof step. As the major notion here and in [10] is not strong validity but reduction (cf. Def. 5.19), where the quantification of π must be universal no matter how we quantify in the notion of strong validity, changing the quantification of π in Def. 5.17 would only have very local consequences. Roughly speaking, only Theor. 5.20(a) for the case of $O \neq \emptyset$ becomes false for a different choice on the quantification of π in Def. 5.17.

5.4   Reduction

Definition 5.19 (Reduction)
Let C be an R-choice-condition, $\mathcal{A}$ a Σ-structure, and G_0, G_1 sets of sequents.
G_0 (C, R)-*reduces to* G_1 *in* $\mathcal{A}$ if for each existential $(\mathcal{A}, R)$-valuation e and each π that is $(e, \mathcal{A})$-compatible with (C, R):
    if G_1 is strongly $(\pi, e, \mathcal{A})$-valid, then G_0 is strongly $(\pi, e, \mathcal{A})$-valid.

Theorem 5.20 (Reduction) *Let C be an R-choice-condition; $\mathcal{A}$ a Σ-structure; G_0 and G_1 sets of sequents. For a quasi-existential R-substitution σ and the extended σ-update (C', R') of (C, R), and for O, N with $O \subseteq \mathrm{dom}(C) \cap \mathrm{dom}(\sigma) \subseteq O \uplus N$, $N \subseteq \mathrm{dom}(C) \setminus O$, $\mathrm{dom}(C) \cap \langle N \rangle R^+ \subseteq N$, $N \cap \mathcal{V}(G_0, G_1) = \emptyset$, and $\mathcal{V}_{\forall,s}(\mathrm{ran}(\sigma)) \cap (\mathrm{dom}(\sigma) \cup N) = \emptyset$:*

(a) If $G_0 \sigma \cup \langle O \rangle Q_{C,\sigma}$ is (C', R')-strongly valid in $\mathcal{A}$,
    then G_0 is (C, R)-strongly valid in $\mathcal{A}$.

(b) If G_0 (C, R)-reduces to G_1 in $\mathcal{A}$,
    then $G_0 \sigma$ (C', R')-reduces to $G_1 \sigma \cup \langle O \rangle Q_{C,\sigma}$ in $\mathcal{A}$.

Suppose that G_0 is a proposition we want to prove and G_1 represents the current state of our proof attempt with variable-condition R and R-choice-condition C. Then G_0 (C, R)-reduces to G_1. E.g., in [10, Sect. 14] G_0 is $z_0^{\exists}(x_0^{\forall,\mathsf{w}})(y_0^{\forall,\mathsf{w}}) \prec \mathsf{ack}(x_0^{\forall,\mathsf{w}}, y_0^{\forall,\mathsf{w}})$, which says that Ackermann's function has a lower bound that is to be determined during the proof, and the current state G_1 of the proof attempt reduces to a known lemma when we apply the substitution $\sigma := \{z_0^{\exists} \mapsto \lambda x.\, \lambda y.\, y\}$. Now, setting $O := N := \emptyset$, Theor. 5.20(b) says that the instantiated (and $\lambda\beta$-reduced) theorem $y_0^{\forall,\mathsf{w}} \prec \mathsf{ack}(x_0^{\forall,\mathsf{w}}, y_0^{\forall,\mathsf{w}})$ (C', R')-reduces to the instantiated proof state and thus is (C', R')-strongly valid.

Let us have a careful look at the assumptions of Theor. 5.20, which is by far the deepest result in this paper. When strong free universal variables are replaced besides free existential variables, we cannot set O and N to the empty set as above. We use the set O to form the set of formulas $\langle O \rangle Q_{C,\sigma}$ (cf. Def. 5.14) that—as explained around Ex. 4.3—captures the soundness of the substitution σ. The possibility that the set O is a proper subset of the set $\mathrm{dom}(C) \cap \mathrm{dom}(\sigma)$ (of strong free universal variables that are conditioned by C and replaced by σ) is not a sophistication but of practical importance as will be explained later. The set N that contains the other variables from $\mathrm{dom}(C) \cap \mathrm{dom}(\sigma)$ should be thought of as the set of variables that are not relevant for our local context. Thus, these variables must not occur in G_0 and G_1. Moreover, N must be closed according to $\mathrm{dom}(C) \cap \langle N \rangle R^+ \subseteq N$, which says that the C-conditioned variables that depend on the variables of N are in N again, i.e. also not relevant for our local context. Finally, the assumption of $\mathcal{V}_{\forall,s}(\mathrm{ran}(\sigma)) \cap (\mathrm{dom}(\sigma) \cup N) = \emptyset$ simply says that the strong free universal variables that are globally replaced by σ are not at the same time introduced again by σ. Now we still have to explain why we need the set N.

Example 5.21 *(continuing Ex. 4.3)*
Suppose that $\exists y.\, (z^{\forall,\mathsf{w}} = y{+}1) \Rightarrow (z^{\forall,\mathsf{w}} = \mathsf{p}(z^{\forall,\mathsf{w}}){+}1)$ is one of our lemmas and that we want to use this lemma as justification for replacing $y^{\forall,\mathsf{s}}$ under R-choice-condition $C(y^{\forall,\mathsf{s}}) = (z^{\forall,\mathsf{w}} = y^{\forall,\mathsf{s}}{+}1)$ globally with $\mathsf{p}(z^{\forall,\mathsf{w}})$, which is possible because it is equal to $Q_{C,\sigma}(y^{\forall,\mathsf{s}})$ for $\sigma := \{y^{\forall,\mathsf{s}} \mapsto \mathsf{p}(z^{\forall,\mathsf{w}})\}$.

The problem we get here is that the lemma is applied globally. Esp. problematic is the possibility that $y^{\forall,\mathsf{s}}$ occurs in the proof of the lemma itself. Unless we are very careful, the lemma becomes a lemma of itself, which results in a cyclic lemma application relation of a globally applied lemma. Then our whole proof work is in vain because no validities can be inferred. Therefore, we either have to reintroduce the lemma as an open lemma and prove it again or had better take a closer look on which of our (possibly open) lemmas L really depend on the justifying lemma $Q_{C,\sigma}(y^{\forall,s})$ after global application of σ.

Let us sketch how to do the latter now. Let M be the set of all strong free universal variables that occur in the lemma L, in its open goals (i.e. its state of proof attempt), or in the lemmas that have been applied in its proof attempt. Set $O := \mathrm{dom}(C) \cap \mathrm{dom}(\sigma) \cap R^*\langle M \rangle$ and $N := \mathrm{dom}(C) \cap \langle (\mathrm{dom}(C) \cap \mathrm{dom}(\sigma)) \setminus O \rangle R^*$. Now, setting $G_0 := \{L\}$ and G_1 to the open goals and applied lemmas of the proof attempt of L, as a consequence of Theor. 5.20(b)—provided that $\mathcal{V}_{\forall,s}(\mathrm{ran}(\sigma)) \cap (\mathrm{dom}(\sigma) \cup N) = \emptyset$; the other conditions on O and N being automatically satisfied—we know that $L\sigma$ (which now depends on $G_1\sigma$ w.r.t. reduction) depends on the lemma $Q_{C,\sigma}(y^{\forall,s})$ *only if* $y^{\forall,s} \in O$. With these refined dependencies we get a smaller lemma application relation that breaks the cycles discussed in Ex. 5.21 for reasonable substitutions σ. Detailed and further information on this can be found in Theor. 10.6 of [10] and its proof.

6   Conclusion

We have proposed a semantics for Hilbert's ε which ...

- is similar to the referential use of the indefinite article in natural languages.
- makes obvious the requirements on a commitment of the choice, cf. Sect. 4.1.
- is based on an abstract formal approach that extends a semantics for closed formulas (satisfying only weak requirements, cf. Sect. 5) to a semantics with several kinds of free variables (universal, existential, ε-constrained), which is esp. designed for developing proofs in the style of a working mathematician.
- makes proof work most simple because we do not have to consider all proper choices (as in all other approaches) but only a single arbitrary one, which is fixed in a proof step just as choices are settled in program steps, cf. Sect. 4.

[1] Wolfgang Bibel (1987). *Automated Theorem Proving.* 2nd rev. ed., Vieweg, Braunschweig.

[2] Wolfgang Bibel, Peter H. Schmitt (eds.) (1998). *Automated Deduction — A Basis for Applications.* Kluwer Acad. Publ..

[3] Andreas Blass, Yuri Gurevich (2000). *The Logic of Choice.* J. Symbolic Logic **65**, pp. 1264-1310.

[4] Melvin C. Fitting (1996). *First-Order Logic and Automated Theorem Proving.* 2nd extd. ed., Springer.

[5] Martin Giese, Wolfgang Ahrendt (1999). *Hilbert's ε-Terms in Automated Theorem Proving.* 8th TABLEAU 1999, LNAI 1617, pp. 171-185, Springer.

[6] David Hilbert (1928). *Die Grundlagen der Mathematik.* Abhandlungen aus dem mathematischen Seminar der Univ. Hamburg **6**, pp. 65-85.

[7] David Hilbert, Paul Bernays (1968/70). *Grundlagen der Mathematik.* 2nd ed., Springer.

[8] Michaël Kohlhase (1998). *Higher-Order Automated Theorem Proving.* In: [2], Vol. 1, pp. 431-462.

[9] A. C. Leisenring (1969). *Mathematical Logic and Hilbert's ε-Symbol.* Gordon and Breach, New York.

[10] Claus-Peter Wirth (2000). *Descente Infinie + Deduction.* Report 737/2000, FB Informatik, Univ. Dortmund. Extd. version, Feb. 1, 2002. `http://ags.uni-sb.de/~cp/p/tab99/new.html` (Feb. 01, 2002).

A Tableau Calculus for Combining Non-disjoint Theories

Calogero G. Zarba

Stanford University and University of Catania

Abstract. The Nelson-Oppen combination method combines ground satisfiability checkers for first-order theories satisfying certain conditions into a single ground satisfiability checker for the union theory. The most significant restriction that the combined theories must satisfy, for the Nelson-Oppen combination method to be applicable, is that they must have disjoint signatures. Unfortunately, this is a very serious restriction since many combination problems concern theories over non-disjoint signatures.

In this paper we present a tableau calculus for combining first-order theories over non-disjoint signatures. The calculus generalizes the Nelson-Oppen combination method to formulae with quantifiers and to the union of *arbitrary* theories over non necessarily disjoint signatures.

1 Introduction

In many areas of computer science such as program verification and problem solving one often has to reason about mixed constraints over several different constraint domains. Thus, it is important to build frameworks for combining into a single general-purpose reasoner the specialized and efficient constraint reasoners for the several constraint domains.

One of the first and most important results in the field of combination was obtained in 1979 when Nelson and Oppen presented a method for combining decision procedures for first-order theories satisfying certain conditions into a single decision procedure for the union theory [9,15].

Although the Nelson-Oppen combination method is still considered to be state of the art, it has three major restrictions:

1. it does not support quantifiers;
2. the theories to combine must be stably infinite;
3. the signatures of the theories must be disjoint.

Of the three restrictions, the disjointness one is the most serious, since many combination problems involve theories over non-disjoint signatures. The disjointness restriction has also revealed very hard to lift, as witnessed by the fact that, more than 20 years after Nelson and Oppen's original work was published, non-disjoint combination research is still in its infancy.

Indeed, some limited results on non-disjoint combination exist in term rewriting for rewriting systems sharing constructors [6,10], in unification for equational

U. Egly and C.G. Fermüller (Eds.): TABLEAUX 2002, LNAI 2381, pp. 315–329, 2002.

theories sharing either constant symbols [11] or constructors [2,4], and in constraint satisfiability for theories sharing constructors [12]. A recent and extensive theoretical study on non-disjoint combination can be found in [16].

This paper introduces *N-O-tableaux*, an extension of Smullyan semantic tableaux [5,13] which generalize the Nelson-Oppen combination method to formulae with quantifiers and to the union of *arbitrary* universal theories, not necessarily stably infinite and not necessarily over disjoint signatures.

Using as black boxes a ground decision procedure P_1 for an universal Σ_1-theory $\mathcal{T}_1$ and ground decision procedure P_2 for an universal Σ_2-theory $\mathcal{T}_2$, N-O-tableaux provide a sound and complete method that allows to check the $(\mathcal{T}_1 \cup \mathcal{T}_2)$-validity of any $(\Sigma_1 \cup \Sigma_2)$-sentence φ. No syntactical or semantic restriction is made over $\mathcal{T}_1$ and $\mathcal{T}_2$ (except universality), and absolutely no hypothesis is made over the intersection of the signatures Σ_1 and Σ_2.

The great generality of N-O-tableaux comes however at the price of a very large and potentially infinite search space. Therefore, in this paper we address the problem of reducing the search space by recognizing some conditions under which restrictions can be imposed to the applications of the tableau rules without losing completeness. At the quantifier-free level, there are cases where we can even make the search space finite, thus obtaining decidability results.

We also address the problem of making the tableau construction more efficient with the introduction of a residue rule. This rule is inspired by a recent work of Tinelli [14] in which, using a restricted version of the Craig Interpolation Lemma, he presented a multi-theory reasoning tableau calculus where the background reasoners cooperate by exchanging residues over a common signature. It should be noted, however, that while in Tinelli's calculus residues are disjunctions of literals, in our N-O-tableaux completeness is not lost even if residues are restricted to disjunctions of *positive* literals.

1.1   Other Related Work

Several generalizations of the Nelson-Oppen combination method are present in literature. Tiwari [17] generalizes the Nelson-Oppen and Shostak combination methods into one single framework. Armando, Ranise and Rusinowitch [1] recast the Nelson-Oppen combination method in a rewriting framework based on a superposition calculus. Both [17] and [1] deal only with quantifier-free formulae, and limit themselves to the combination of stably infinite theories over disjoint signatures.

Kaufl and Zabel [7] generalize the Nelson-Oppen combination method to formulae with quantifiers by embedding it into a ground tableau calculus. They consider only stably infinite theories over disjoint signatures.

A preliminary version of N-O-tableaux first appeared in [18] for the quantifier-free case only. This paper greatly generalizes our earlier results in [18].

1.2 Organization of the Paper

The paper is organized as follows. In Section 2 we give some preliminary notions that will be needed in what follows. In Section 3 we formally define N-O-tableaux, and we prove that N-O-tableaux are sound and complete. In Section 4 we address the problem of reducing the search space. In Section 5 we describe how it is possible to make the tableau construction more efficient by employing a residue propagation mechanism similar to the one of [14]. Finally, in Section 6 we conclude the paper by pointing at directions for future research.

2   Preliminaries

2.1   Syntax

A *signature* Σ is composed by a set Σ^{C} of constants, a set Σ^{F} of function symbols, and a set Σ^{P} of predicate symbols.

Given a set V of variables, we denote with $T(\Sigma, V)$ the set of terms built from the variables in V and the symbols in Σ. An element of $T(\Sigma, V)$ is a Σ-*term*. $T(\Sigma)$ stands for $T(\Sigma, \emptyset)$.

A Σ-*atom* is either an expression of the form $P(t_1, \dots, t_n)$, where $P \in \Sigma^{\mathrm{P}}$ and $t_1, \dots, t_n$ are Σ-terms, or an expression of the form $s \approx t$, where $\approx$ is the equality logical symbol and s, t are Σ-terms. Σ-*formulae* are constructed by applying in the standard way the connectives $\neg, \wedge, \vee, \rightarrow$ and the quantifiers $\forall, \exists$ to Σ-atoms. A Σ-formula is *universal* if it is in prefix normal form, and its (possibly empty) quantifier prefix contains only universal quantifiers. Σ-*Literals* are Σ-atoms or their negations. Σ-*Sentences* are Σ-formulae with no free variables. A Σ-formula is *ground* if it has no variables.

When Σ is irrelevant or clear from the context, we will simply write atom, formula, literal, and sentence in place of Σ-atom, Σ-formula, Σ-literal, and Σ-sentence.

2.2   Semantics

Definition 1. *Let Σ be a signature. A Σ-STRUCTURE $\mathcal{A}$ with domain A is a map which interprets each constant $c \in \Sigma^{\mathrm{C}}$ as an element $c^{\mathcal{A}} \in A$, each function symbol $f \in \Sigma^{\mathrm{F}}$ of arity n as a function $f^{\mathcal{A}} : A^n \rightarrow A$, and each predicate symbol $P \in \Sigma^{\mathrm{P}}$ of arity n as a subset $P^{\mathcal{A}}$ of A^n.*

Let $\mathcal{A}$ be a Σ-structure with domain A,[1] and let V be a set of variables. For a term $t \in T(\Sigma, V)$ and an assignment $\alpha : V \rightarrow A$, we denote with $t_\alpha^{\mathcal{A}}$ the evaluation of the term t under the interpretation $(\mathcal{A}, \alpha)$. Similarly, we denote with $\varphi_\alpha^{\mathcal{A}}$ the truth-value of the formula φ under the interpretation $(\mathcal{A}, \alpha)$. Note

---

[1] In this paper we are using the convention that the calligraphic letters $\mathcal{A}$, $\mathcal{B}$, and $\mathcal{M}$ denote structures, and that the corresponding Roman letters denote the domains of the structures.

that if t is ground then $t_\alpha^{\mathcal{A}} = t_\beta^{\mathcal{A}}$, for all substitutions α, β. Thus, we will simply write $t^{\mathcal{A}}$ in place of $t_\alpha^{\mathcal{A}}$ when t is ground. We will also write $\varphi^{\mathcal{A}}$ in place of $\varphi_\alpha^{\mathcal{A}}$ when φ is a sentence. If T is a set of ground terms and $\mathcal{A}$ is a structure, $T^{\mathcal{A}}$ denotes the set $\{t^{\mathcal{A}} : t \in T\}$.

Let Ω be a signature and let $\mathcal{A}$ be an Ω-structure. For a subset Σ of Ω, we denote with $\mathcal{A}^{\Sigma}$ the Σ-structure obtained by restricting $\mathcal{A}$ to interpret only the symbols in Σ.

Definition 2. *Let Σ be a signature, and let $\mathcal{A}$ and $\mathcal{B}$ be Σ-structures. A map $h : A \to B$ is an* HOMOMORPHISM *of $\mathcal{A}$ into $\mathcal{B}$ if the following conditions hold:*

- $h(c^{\mathcal{A}}) = c^{\mathcal{B}}$, *for each constant $c \in \Sigma^{\mathrm{C}}$;*
- $h(f^{\mathcal{A}}(a_1, \dots, a_n)) = f^{\mathcal{B}}(h(a_1), \dots, h(a_n))$, *for each n-ary function symbol $f \in \Sigma^{\mathrm{F}}$ and $a_1, \dots, a_n \in A$;*
- $(a_1, \dots, a_n) \in P^{\mathcal{A}}$ *if and only if $(h(a_1), \dots, h(a_n)) \in P^{\mathcal{B}}$, for each n-ary predicate symbol $P \in \Sigma^{\mathrm{P}}$ and $a_1, \dots, a_n \in A$.*

An ISOMORPHISM *of $\mathcal{A}$ into $\mathcal{B}$ is a bijective homomorphism of $\mathcal{A}$ into $\mathcal{B}$.*

We write $\mathcal{A} \cong \mathcal{B}$ to indicate that there exists an isomorphism of $\mathcal{A}$ into $\mathcal{B}$.

2.3   Uniform Notation

In the rest of the paper we will make use of Smullyan's uniform notation [13]. Accordingly, we divide non-literals into five categories: $\neg\neg$, α, β, γ, and δ. More specifically:

- a formula φ is a $\neg\neg$-formula if it is of the form $\neg\neg Z$, for some Z.
- α- and β-formulae, and their components α_1, α_2 and β_1, β_2 are defined in the following way:

α	α_1	α_2
$X \wedge Y$	X	Y
$\neg(X \vee Y)$	$\neg X$	$\neg Y$
$\neg(X \to Y)$	X	$\neg Y$

β	β_1	β_2
$X \vee Y$	X	Y
$\neg(X \wedge Y)$	$\neg X$	$\neg Y$
$X \to Y$	$\neg X$	Y

- γ- and δ-formulae, and their instances $\gamma_0(x)$ and $\delta_0(x)$, are defined in the following way:

γ	$\gamma_0(x)$
$(\forall x)\varphi$	φ
$\neg(\exists x)\varphi$	$\neg\varphi$

δ	$\delta_0(x)$
$(\exists x)\varphi$	φ
$\neg(\forall x)\varphi$	$\neg\varphi$

The following equivalences hold:

$$\alpha \equiv \alpha_1 \wedge \alpha_2 \qquad \beta \equiv \beta_1 \vee \beta_2 \qquad \gamma \equiv (\forall x)\gamma_0(x) \qquad \delta \equiv (\exists x)\delta_0(x).$$

2.4   First-Order Theories

Definition 3. *Let Σ be a signature. A Σ-THEORY is any set of Σ-sentences. Given a theory $\mathcal{T}$, a structure $\mathcal{A}$ is a $\mathcal{T}$-MODEL if $\varphi^{\mathcal{A}}$ evaluates to true, for each sentence φ in $\mathcal{T}$.*

Definition 4. *A Σ-theory $\mathcal{T}$ is STABLY INFINITE if every $\mathcal{T}$-satisfiable quantifier-free Σ-formula φ is satisfiable in an infinite $\mathcal{T}$-model.*

Definition 5. *A Σ-theory $\mathcal{T}$ is CONVEX if for every conjunction φ of Σ-literals and for every disjunction $\psi_1 \vee \cdots \vee \psi_k$ of Σ-atoms, if $\mathcal{T} \cup \varphi \models \psi_1 \vee \cdots \vee \psi_n$ then $\mathcal{T} \cup \varphi \models \psi_i$, for some $i \in \{1, \dots, n\}$.*

Given a Σ-theory $\mathcal{T}$, a Σ-sentence φ is

- $\mathcal{T}$-*valid*, if it evaluates to true under all $\mathcal{T}$-models;
- $\mathcal{T}$-*satisfiable*, if it evaluates to true under some $\mathcal{T}$-model;
- $\mathcal{T}$-*unsatisfiable*, if it evaluates to false under all $\mathcal{T}$-models;

The notion of $\mathcal{T}$-validity, $\mathcal{T}$-satisfiability and $\mathcal{T}$-unsatisfiability naturally extend to sets of sentences.

In this paper we will consider only *universal* theories, that is theories whose sentences are universal. The restriction to universal theories is necessary for completeness reasons because only for such theories the following Theorem 1 holds, a theorem that can be seen as a positive version of the famous Herbrand Theorem. Note, however, that the restriction is not essential, since existential quantifiers can be removed by skolemization.

Theorem 1 (Herbrand). *Let $\mathcal{T}$ be an universal Σ-theory, and let $\Sigma^{\mathrm{C}} \neq \emptyset$. Then $\mathcal{T}$ is satisfiable if and only if there exists a $\mathcal{T}$-model $\mathcal{A}$ with domain $A = [T(\Sigma)]^{\mathcal{A}}$.*

The following theorem was first proved in [12] and [15].

Theorem 2. *Let Σ_1 and Σ_2 be two not necessarily disjoint signatures, and let $\mathcal{T}_i$ be a Σ_i-theory, for $i = 1, 2$. Then $\mathcal{T}_1 \cup \mathcal{T}_2$ is satisfiable if and only if there exists a $\mathcal{T}_1$-model $\mathcal{A}$ and a $\mathcal{T}_2$-model $\mathcal{B}$ such that $\mathcal{A}^{(\Sigma_1 \cap \Sigma_2)} \cong \mathcal{B}^{(\Sigma_1 \cap \Sigma_2)}$.*

3   N-O-Tableaux

For the rest of this section we fix two not necessarily disjoint signatures Σ_1 and Σ_2, along with an universal Σ_1-theory $\mathcal{T}_1$ and an universal Σ_2-theory $\mathcal{T}_2$.

We now define a tableau calculus that is sound and complete for the $(\mathcal{T}_1 \cup \mathcal{T}_2)$-validity of any given $(\Sigma_1 \cup \Sigma_2)$-sentence φ.

Definition 6. *Let φ be a $(\Sigma_1 \cup \Sigma_2)$-sentence. An INITIAL N-O-TABLEAU for φ is a tree consisting of one branch whose only node is labeled with φ. A N-O-TABLEAU for φ is either an initial N-O-tableau for φ or is obtained by applying the rules in Figure 1 to an initial N-O-tableau for φ.*

Propositional rules

$$\frac{\neg\neg Z}{Z} \qquad \frac{\alpha}{\begin{array}{c}\alpha_1\\\alpha_2\end{array}} \qquad \frac{\beta}{\beta_1 \mid \beta_2}$$

Quantifier rules

$$\frac{\gamma}{\gamma_0(t)} \qquad\qquad \frac{\delta}{\delta_0(p)}$$

Where t is any ground term in $T(\Sigma_1 \cup \Sigma_2 \cup \mathbf{par})$ and $p \in \mathbf{par}$ is new.

Abstraction rule

$$\frac{}{t \approx p}$$

Where t is any ground term in $T(\Sigma_1 \cup \Sigma_2 \cup \mathbf{par})$ and $p \in \mathbf{par}$ is new.

Purification rule

$$\frac{\begin{array}{c}\varphi[t]\\t \approx p\end{array}}{\varphi[p]}$$

Where φ is a literal and $p \in \mathbf{par}$.

Decomposition rules

$$\frac{}{p \approx q \mid p \not\approx q} \qquad\qquad \frac{}{P(p_1,\dots,p_n) \mid \neg P(p_1,\dots,p_n)}$$

Where $p, q, p_1, \dots, p_n \in \mathbf{par}$ and $P \in \Sigma_1^{\mathrm{P}} \cap \Sigma_2^{\mathrm{P}}$.

Fig. 1: N-O-tableau rules.

Note that while the formulae to prove are given in the signature $\Sigma_1 \cup \Sigma_2$, N-O-tableaux are made of formulae in an extended signature $\Sigma_1 \cup \Sigma_2 \cup \mathbf{par}$, where **par** is an enumerable collection of *parameters* disjoint from $\Sigma_1 \cup \Sigma_2$.

We still need to define when a N-O-tableau is closed.

Definition 7. *Let* B *be a (not necessarily finite) branch of a N-O-tableau* T. *We say that* B *is* $\langle \mathcal{T}_1, \mathcal{T}_2 \rangle$-CLOSED *if there exists a finite set* θ_i *of* Σ_i-*literals such that* $\theta_i \subseteq$ B *and* θ_i *is* $\mathcal{T}_i$-*unsatisfiable. A branch which is not* $\langle \mathcal{T}_1, \mathcal{T}_2 \rangle$-*closed is* $\langle \mathcal{T}_1, \mathcal{T}_2 \rangle$-OPEN.

A N-O-tableau is $\langle \mathcal{T}_1, \mathcal{T}_2 \rangle$-CLOSED *is so are all its branches; otherwise it is* $\langle \mathcal{T}_1, \mathcal{T}_2 \rangle$-OPEN.

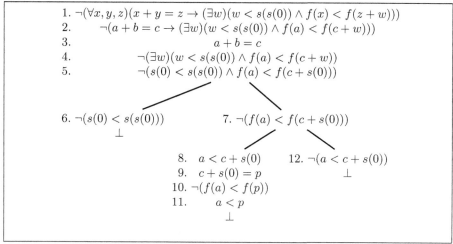

1. $\neg(\forall x, y, z)(x + y = z \rightarrow (\exists w)(w < s(s(0)) \land f(x) < f(z + w)))$
2. $\neg(a + b = c \rightarrow (\exists w)(w < s(s(0)) \land f(a) < f(c + w)))$
3. $\qquad a + b = c$
4. $\neg(\exists w)(w < s(s(0)) \land f(a) < f(c + w))$
5. $\neg(s(0) < s(s(0)) \land f(a) < f(c + s(0)))$

6. $\neg(s(0) < s(s(0)))$ 7. $\neg(f(a) < f(c + s(0)))$
$\bot$

8. $\quad a < c + s(0)$ 12. $\neg(a < c + s(0))$
9. $\quad c + s(0) = p$ $\bot$
10. $\neg(f(a) < f(p))$
11. $\qquad a < p$
$\bot$

Fig. 2: A N-O-tableau.

Note that checking the closure of a branch can be effectively done if we have available, for each $i = 1, 2$, a decision procedure P_i that can decide the $\mathcal{T}_i$-satisfiability of every conjunction of ground $(\Sigma_i \cup \mathbf{par})$-literals.

Definition 8. *A branch* B *of a N-O-tableau* T *is* SATURATED *if no application of any rule in Figure 1 can add new formulae to* B.

Definition 9. *Let* $\mathcal{T}$ *be a* Σ-theory, for some signature Σ. A branch B of a N-O-tableau T is $\mathcal{T}$-SATISFIABLE if the collection of its formulae is $\mathcal{T}$-satisfiable. A N-O-tableau is $\mathcal{T}$-SATISFIABLE if at least one of its branches is $\mathcal{T}$-satisfiable.*

3.1 An Example

Let $\mathcal{P}$ be the theory of Presburger arithmetic over the signature $\Sigma = \{0, s, +, <\}$. Formally, $\mathcal{P}$ is defined as the collection of universal Σ-sentences that are true in the standard model of arithmetic $\langle \mathbb{N}, 0, s, +, < \rangle$.

Also, let $\mathcal{T}$ be the Ω-theory

$$\mathcal{T} = \{(\forall x, y)(x < y \rightarrow f(x) < f(y)\},$$

where $\Omega = \{<, f\}$. Note that $\Sigma \cap \Omega \neq \emptyset$.

Figure 2 shows a $\langle \mathcal{P}, \mathcal{T} \rangle$-closed N-O-tableau that proves the $(\mathcal{P} \cup \mathcal{T})$-validity of

$$(\forall x, y, z)(x + y = z \rightarrow (\exists w)(w < s(s(0)) \land f(x) < f(z + w))). \qquad (1)$$

Denoting with φ_i the formula labeling node i, the construction of the N-O-tableau in Figure 2 can be justified as follows:

- φ_2 is obtained from φ_1 by means of three applications of the γ-rule.
- φ_3 and φ_4 are obtained from φ_2 by means of an application of the α-rule.
- φ_5 is obtained from φ_4 by means of an application of the δ-rule.
- φ_6 and φ_7 are obtained from φ_5 by means of an application of the β-rule. Note that the left branch is $\langle \mathcal{P}, \mathcal{T} \rangle$-closed because φ_6 is $\mathcal{P}$-unsatisfiable.
- φ_8 and φ_{12} are obtained by means of an application of the second decomposition rule. Note that the right branch is $\langle \mathcal{P}, \mathcal{T} \rangle$-closed because $\{\varphi_3, \varphi_{12}\}$ is $\mathcal{P}$-unsatisfiable.
- φ_9 is obtained by means of an application of the abstraction rule.
- φ_{10} is obtained from φ_7 and φ_9 by means of an application of the purification rule.
- φ_{11} is obtained from φ_8 and φ_9 by means of an application of the purification rule. Note the branch is $\langle \mathcal{P}, \mathcal{T} \rangle$-closed because $\{\varphi_{10}, \varphi_{11}\}$ is $\mathcal{T}$-unsatisfiable.

3.2   Soundness

N-O-tableaux are clearly sound, as the following theorem states.

Theorem 3 (soundness). *Let φ be a $(\Sigma_1 \cup \Sigma_2)$-sentence. If there exists a $\langle \mathcal{T}_1, \mathcal{T}_2 \rangle$-closed N-O-tableau for φ, then φ is $(\mathcal{T}_1 \cup \mathcal{T}_2)$-unsatisfiable.*

Proof. Let T be a $\langle \mathcal{T}_1, \mathcal{T}_2 \rangle$-closed N-O-tableau for φ, and suppose, for a contradiction, that φ is $(\mathcal{T}_1 \cup \mathcal{T}_2)$-satisfiable. Since the rules in Figure 1 preserve tableau $(\mathcal{T}_1 \cup \mathcal{T}_2)$-satisfiability, it follows that there exists some branch B of T which is $(\mathcal{T}_1 \cup \mathcal{T}_2)$-satisfiable. But since T is $\langle \mathcal{T}_1, \mathcal{T}_2 \rangle$-closed, B must also be $\langle \mathcal{T}_1, \mathcal{T}_2 \rangle$-closed, which is a contradiction because a $\langle \mathcal{T}_1, \mathcal{T}_2 \rangle$-closed branch cannot be $(\mathcal{T}_1 \cup \mathcal{T}_2)$-satisfiable.   □

3.3   Completeness

We now prove that N-O-tableaux are complete.

Lemma 1. *Let B be a (not necessarily finite) $\langle \mathcal{T}_1, \mathcal{T}_2 \rangle$-open branch of a N-O-tableau T, and let θ_i be the collection of $(\Sigma_i \cup \mathbf{par})$-literals occurring in B, for $i = 1, 2$. Then θ_i is $\mathcal{T}_i$-satisfiable, for $i = 1, 2$.*

Proof. Since B is $\langle \mathcal{T}_1, \mathcal{T}_2 \rangle$-open, every finite subset of θ_1 is $\mathcal{T}_1$-satisfiable. Hence, every finite subset of $\mathcal{T}_1 \cup \theta_1$ is satisfiable. By compactness, $\mathcal{T}_1 \cup \theta_1$ is satisfiable, implying that θ_1 is $\mathcal{T}_1$-satisfiable. Similarly one can show that θ_2 is $\mathcal{T}_2$-satisfiable.   □

For the rest of this section, let us fix a $\langle \mathcal{T}_1, \mathcal{T}_2 \rangle$-open and saturated branch B, and let θ_i be the collection of $(\Sigma_i \cup \mathbf{par})$-literals occurring in B, for $i = 1, 2$.

By Lemma 1, there exist a $\mathcal{T}_1$-model $\mathcal{A}$ satisfying θ_1 and a $\mathcal{T}_2$-model $\mathcal{B}$ satisfying θ_2. In addition, since $\mathcal{T}_1$ and $\mathcal{T}_2$ are universal, by Theorem 1 and saturation with respect to the abstraction rule, we can assume without loss of generality that $A = \mathbf{par}^{\mathcal{A}}$ and $B = \mathbf{par}^{\mathcal{B}}$. Thus, we can fix a function $name_{\mathcal{A}} : A \to \mathbf{par}$ such that

$$[name_{\mathcal{A}}(a)]^{\mathcal{A}} = a , \qquad\qquad \text{for each } a \in A .$$

The next step of the completeness proof is to merge the structures $\mathcal{A}$ and $\mathcal{B}$ into a single structure $\mathcal{M}$ satisfying $\mathcal{T}_1 \cup \mathcal{T}_2 \cup \theta_1 \cup \theta_2$. Clearly, this goal can be accomplished by an application of Theorem 2 if we can show that $\mathcal{A}^{(\Sigma_1 \cap \Sigma_2) \cup \mathbf{par}}$ and $\mathcal{B}^{(\Sigma_1 \cap \Sigma_2) \cup \mathbf{par}}$ are isomorphic. Accordingly, we define a function $h : A \to B$ by letting

$$h(a) = [name_{\mathcal{A}}(a)]^{\mathcal{B}}, \qquad\qquad \text{for each } a \in A.$$

The following five lemmas show that h is an isomorphism of $\mathcal{A}^{(\Sigma_1 \cap \Sigma_2) \cup \mathbf{par}}$ into $\mathcal{B}^{(\Sigma_1 \cap \Sigma_2) \cup \mathbf{par}}$.

Lemma 2. $p^{\mathcal{A}} = q^{\mathcal{A}}$ *if and only if* $p^{\mathcal{B}} = q^{\mathcal{B}}$, *for every* $p, q \in \mathbf{par}$.

Proof. By saturation with respect to the first decomposition rule. □

Lemma 3. $h(p^{\mathcal{A}}) = p^{\mathcal{B}}$, *for every* $p \in \mathbf{par}$.

Proof. Let $p^{\mathcal{A}} = a$ and let $name_{\mathcal{A}}(a) = q$. Then $p^{\mathcal{A}} = q^{\mathcal{A}}$, which implies $p^{\mathcal{B}} = q^{\mathcal{B}}$ by Lemma 2. Thus $h(p^{\mathcal{A}}) = h(a) = [name_{\mathcal{A}}(a)]^{\mathcal{B}} = q^{\mathcal{B}} = p^{\mathcal{B}}$. □

Lemma 4. h *is injective.*

Proof. Let $h(a_1) = h(a_2)$. Then, by putting $name_{\mathcal{A}}(a_i) = p_i$, for $i = 1, 2$, it follows that $p_1^{\mathcal{B}} = p_2^{\mathcal{B}}$. By Lemma 2, $p_1^{\mathcal{A}} = p_2^{\mathcal{A}}$, which in turn implies $a_1 = a_2$. □

Lemma 5. h *is surjective.*

Proof. Let $b \in B$. Then there exists a parameter $p \in \mathbf{par}$ such that $p^{\mathcal{B}} = b$. By Lemma 3, $h(p^{\mathcal{A}}) = p^{\mathcal{B}} = b$, and therefore h is surjective. □

Lemma 6. h *is an homomorphism of* $\mathcal{A}^{(\Sigma_1 \cap \Sigma_2) \cup \mathbf{par}}$ *into* $\mathcal{B}^{(\Sigma_1 \cap \Sigma_2) \cup \mathbf{par}}$.

Proof. Lemma 3 implies that $h(p^{\mathcal{A}}) = p^{\mathcal{B}}$, for each $p \in \mathbf{par}$. On the other hand, if $c \in \Sigma_1^C \cap \Sigma_2^C$, then by saturation with respect to the abstraction rule a literal of the form $c \approx p$ must occur in B, and therefore $h(c^{\mathcal{A}}) = h(p^{\mathcal{A}}) = p^{\mathcal{B}} = c^{\mathcal{B}}$.

Next, let $f \in \Sigma_1^F \cap \Sigma_2^F$, and let $a = f^{\mathcal{A}}(a_1, \ldots, a_n)$, where $a_1, \ldots, a_n \in A$. Then there exist parameters $p_1, \ldots, p_n \in \mathbf{par}$ such that $a_i = p_i^{\mathcal{A}}$, for each $i = 1, \ldots, n$. By Lemma 3 we have that $h(a_i) = p_i^{\mathcal{B}}$, for each $i = 1, \ldots, n$. Note also that $[f(p_1, \ldots, p_n)]^{\mathcal{A}} = [name_{\mathcal{A}}(a)]^{\mathcal{A}}$, which by Lemma 2 yields $[f(p_1, \ldots, p_n)]^{\mathcal{B}} = [name_{\mathcal{A}}(a)]^{\mathcal{B}}$. Thus, we obtain $h(f^{\mathcal{A}}(a_1, \ldots, a_n)) = h(a) = [name_{\mathcal{A}}(a)]^{\mathcal{B}} = [f(p_1, \ldots, p_n)]^{\mathcal{B}} = f^{\mathcal{B}}(p_1^{\mathcal{B}}, \ldots, p_n^{\mathcal{B}}) = f^{\mathcal{B}}(h(a_1), \ldots, h(a_n))$.

Next, assume that $(a_1, \ldots, a_n) \in P^{\mathcal{A}}$, where $P \in \Sigma_1^P \cap \Sigma_2^P$ and $a_i \in A$, for $i = 1, \ldots, n$. Then there exist parameters $p_1, \ldots, p_n \in \mathbf{par}$ such that $a_i = p_i^{\mathcal{A}}$, for each $i = 1, \ldots, n$. By Lemma 3 we have $h(a_i) = p_i^{\mathcal{B}}$, for each $i = 1, \ldots, n$. By saturation with respect to the second decomposition rule, $P(p_1, \ldots, p_n)$ is in B, so that $(p_1^{\mathcal{B}}, \ldots, p_n^{\mathcal{B}}) \in P^{\mathcal{B}}$. But this implies $(h(a_1), \ldots, h(a_n)) \in P^{\mathcal{B}}$.

Analogously one can prove that if $(h(a_1), \ldots, h(a_n)) \in P^{\mathcal{B}}$ then $(a_1, \ldots, a_n) \in P^{\mathcal{A}}$. □

We are now able to apply Theorem 2 and obtain the existence of a $(\mathcal{T}_1 \cup \mathcal{T}_2)$-model $\mathcal{M}$ satisfying $\theta_1 \cup \theta_2$. Indeed, by also appealing to the fact that B is a saturated branch, we can prove the following stronger result.

Lemma 7. *Let* B *be a* $\langle \mathcal{T}_1, \mathcal{T}_2 \rangle$-*open and saturated branch of a N-O-tableau* T. *Then* B *is* $(\mathcal{T}_1 \cup \mathcal{T}_2)$-*satisfiable.*

Proof. Let θ_i be the collection of $(\Sigma_i \cup \mathbf{par})$-literals in B, for $i = 1, 2$. By Lemma 1 there exists a $\mathcal{T}_1$-model $\mathcal{A}$ satisfying θ_1 and a $\mathcal{T}_2$-model $\mathcal{B}$ satisfying θ_2. After letting $h(a) = [name_{\mathcal{A}}(a)]^{\mathcal{B}}$, for every $a \in \mathcal{A}$, Lemmas 4, 5, and 6 imply that h is an isomorphism of $\mathcal{A}^{(\Sigma_1 \cap \Sigma_2) \cup \mathbf{par}}$ into $\mathcal{B}^{(\Sigma_1 \cap \Sigma_2) \cup \mathbf{par}}$. Thus, we can apply Theorems 1 and 2, obtaining the existence of a $(\mathcal{T}_1 \cup \mathcal{T}_2)$-model $\mathcal{M}$ satisfying $\theta_1 \cup \theta_2$ such that $M = [T(\Sigma_1 \cup \Sigma_2 \cup \mathbf{par})]^{\mathcal{M}}$.

By saturation with respect to the purification rule it follows that all literals in B are true in $\mathcal{M}$, and by saturation with respect to the propositional and quantifiers rules and the fact that $M = [T(\Sigma_1 \cup \Sigma_2 \cup \mathbf{par})]^{\mathcal{M}}$ it follows that all sentences in B are true in $\mathcal{M}$.   □

We now have everything we need to finish the proof of completeness of N-O-tableaux.

Theorem 4 (completeness). *Let* φ *be a* $(\Sigma_1 \cup \Sigma_2)$-*sentence. If* φ *is* $(\mathcal{T}_1 \cup \mathcal{T}_2)$-*unsatisfiable, then* φ *has a* $\langle \mathcal{T}_1, \mathcal{T}_2 \rangle$-*closed N-O-tableau.*

Proof. Assume, for a contradiction, that φ has no $\langle \mathcal{T}_1, \mathcal{T}_2 \rangle$-closed N-O-tableau, and let T be the initial N-O-tableau for φ. Using a fair strategy, apply to T the rules in Figure 1 in all possible ways, obtaining a tableau limit T^∞. Note that, since φ has no $\langle \mathcal{T}_1, \mathcal{T}_2 \rangle$-closed N-O-tableau, T^∞ must contain a $\langle \mathcal{T}_1, \mathcal{T}_2 \rangle$-open and saturated branch B. By Lemma 7, B is $(\mathcal{T}_1 \cup \mathcal{T}_2)$-satisfiable, which implies that also φ is $(\mathcal{T}_1 \cup \mathcal{T}_2)$-satisfiable, a contradiction.   □

4   Restricting the Search Space

The calculus presented in Section 3 has a very large search space: in order to implement the γ and abstraction rules, a fair enumeration of all ground terms in $T(\Sigma_1 \cup \Sigma_2 \cup \mathbf{par})$ is needed, which, by traditional methods, is often so blind that the right instances may appear relatively late.

In literature, the problematic γ-rule is handled by either introducing free-variable tableaux, or by developing sophisticated strategies for ground term selection [3,8], but this is beyond the scope of this paper.

Thus, in this section we turn our attention to the abstraction rule. More specifically, we identify several conditions under which we can impose restrictions to the applications of the abstraction rule that lead to a smaller search space and, in some favorable cases, to decidability results.

4.1 Stably Infinite Theories over Disjoint Signatures

Let Σ_1 and Σ_2 be disjoint signatures, and let $\mathcal{T}_i$ be a stably infinite Σ_i-theory, for $i = 1, 2$. In this case completeness is not lost if the abstraction rule is subject to the following restriction.

> **Restriction 1.** A literal $t \approx p$ can be added to a branch B by means of an application of the abstraction rule only if t is a subterm of an impure[2] literal $\varphi[t]$ already occurring in B.

Without entering too much into details, the basic idea of the completeness argument is as follows. Let B be a $\langle \mathcal{T}_1, \mathcal{T}_2 \rangle$-open branch such that no application of any rule in Figure 1 complying with Restriction 1 can add new formulae to B. Also, let θ_i be the collection of $(\Sigma_i \cup \mathbf{par})$-literals occurring in B, for $i = 1, 2$. Since $\Sigma_1 \cap \Sigma_2 = \emptyset$, in order to apply Theorem 2 to a $\mathcal{T}_1$-model $\mathcal{A}$ satisfying θ_1 and a $\mathcal{T}_2$-model $\mathcal{B}$ satisfying θ_2, one has to show that $\mathcal{A}^{\mathbf{par}} \cong \mathcal{B}^{\mathbf{par}}$. Indeed, the stable infiniteness of $\mathcal{T}_1$ and $\mathcal{T}_2$ ensures that $|A| = |B|$, so that saturation with respect to the first decomposition rule enforces $\mathcal{A}^{\mathbf{par}} \cong \mathcal{B}^{\mathbf{par}}$.

Finally, note that we re-obtain Nelson and Oppen's original decidability result when the root-formula of the tableau is of the form $\neg(\forall x_1, \dots, \forall x_n)\varphi$, with φ quantifier-free, since in this case the tableau construction must eventually terminate.

4.2 Stably Infinite Theories Sharing Constants

The case in which the theories to combine share constants is not much different from the disjoint case, since the shared constants can be treated as parameters.

More specifically, assume that $\Sigma_1 \cap \Sigma_2$ is a set of constants, and let $\mathcal{T}_i$ be a stably infinite Σ_i-theory, for $i = 1, 2$. Then it is easy to see that completeness is not lost if the abstraction rule is subject to the following restriction.

> **Restriction 2.** A literal $t \approx p$ can be added to a branch B by means of an application of the abstraction rule only if t is either a subterm of an impure literal $\varphi[t]$ already occurring in B, or a constant in $\Sigma_1^{\mathrm{C}} \cap \Sigma_2^{\mathrm{C}}$.

Note also that completeness is not lost even if one retains Restriction 1, but extends the first decomposition rule to terms p, q in $\mathbf{par} \cup (\Sigma_1^{\mathrm{C}} \cap \Sigma_2^{\mathrm{C}})$.

Finally, note that we obtain a decidability result if $\Sigma_1^{\mathrm{C}} \cap \Sigma_2^{\mathrm{C}}$ is finite and the root-formula of the tableau is of the form $\neg(\forall x_1, \dots, \forall x_n)\varphi$, with φ quantifier-free, since in this case the tableau construction must eventually terminate.

4.3 Σ-Generated Theories

We now consider the case of Σ-*generated* theories.

Definition 10. *Let $\mathcal{T}$ be an Ω-theory, and let $\Sigma \subseteq \Omega$. We say that $\mathcal{T}$ is Σ-*GENERATED *if every $\mathcal{T}$-satisfiable collection θ of ground $(\Omega \cup \mathbf{par})$-literals is satisfiable in a $\mathcal{T}$-model $\mathcal{A}$ with domain $A = [T(\Sigma \cup \mathbf{par})]^{\mathcal{A}}$.*

---

[2] We say that a literal φ is impure if it is neither a Σ_1-literal nor a Σ_2-literal.

Note that, by Theorem 1, any universal Σ-theory is Σ-generated.

Let $\mathcal{T}_i$ be a Σ_i-generated Ω_i-theory, for $i = 1, 2$. Then completeness is not lost if the abstraction rule is subject to the following restriction.

Restriction 3. A literal $t \approx p$ can be added to a branch B by means of an application of the abstraction rule only if t is either a subterm of an impure literal $\varphi[t]$ already occurring in B, or a term in $T(\Sigma_1 \cup \Sigma_2 \cup \mathbf{par})$.

The basic idea of the completeness argument is as follows. Let B be a $\langle \mathcal{T}_1, \mathcal{T}_2 \rangle$-open branch such that no application of any rule in Figure 1 complying with Restriction 3 can add new formulae to B. Also, let θ_i be the collection of $(\Omega_i \cup \mathbf{par})$-literals occurring in B, for $i = 1, 2$. Then, given a $\mathcal{T}_1$-model $\mathcal{A}$ satisfying θ_1 and a $\mathcal{T}_2$-model satisfying θ_2, saturation with respect to the abstraction rule, even if subject to Restriction 3, ensures that $A = \mathbf{par}^{\mathcal{A}}$ and $B = \mathbf{par}^{\mathcal{B}}$. From here, the completeness proof continues exactly as in Section 3.3.

5   Residue Propagation in N-O-Tableaux

N-O-tableaux are essentially a *total multi-theory reasoning* calculus where the *foreground reasoner* decides what tableau rules to apply, and the two *background reasoners*—the ground decision procedures for $\mathcal{T}_1$ and $\mathcal{T}_2$—are in charge of detecting branch closure. The cooperation of the two background reasoners is done with the decomposition rules. The decomposition rules are, however, inherently nondeterministic, and a blind search performed by the foreground reasoner is unlikely to find the applications of the decomposition rules that lead to the shorter proofs.

The problem is that the foreground reasoner has no knowledge of the features of the theories to combine. The background reasoners, with their better domain-specific knowledge, are more qualified to direct the search toward the "best" applications of the decomposition rules. Our goal is therefore to devise a mechanism to make the background reasoners help the foreground reasoner make the tableau construction more efficient and less nondeterministic.

Following an idea of Tinelli [14], this can be done in a *partial multi-theory reasoning* setting, by allowing the background reasoners to return *residues*. More precisely, we define a residue version of N-O-tableaux by replacing the decomposition rules with the residue rule shown in Figure 3.

It should be noted, however, that in Tinelli's calculus residues are disjunctions of literals, whereas in our calculus residues are restricted to disjunctions of atoms.

The residue rule in Figure 3 helps making the exploration of the search space more efficient. In addition, the rule effectively reduces the search space in the presence of convex theories. In fact, while in general residues are disjunctions of atoms, when $\mathcal{T}_i$ is convex the residues returned by the background reasoner for $\mathcal{T}_i$ are restricted to atoms.

5.1   An Example

Let $\mathcal{P}$ and $\mathcal{T}$ be the theories defined in Section 3.1. Figure 4 shows an N-O-tableau with residues that proves the $(\mathcal{P} \cup \mathcal{T})$-validity of (1).

Residue rule

$$\varphi_1$$
$$\vdots$$
$$\varphi_h$$

$$\overline{\psi_1 \mid \ \ldots \ \mid \psi_k}$$

Provided there is an index $i \in \{1, 2\}$ such that:
- if $\mathcal{T}_i$ is convex, then $k = 1$;
- $\varphi_1, \ldots, \varphi_h$ are Σ_i-literals;
- for each $j = 1, \ldots, k$, ψ_j is either of the form $p \approx q$ or of the form $P(p_1, \ldots, p_n)$, with $p, q, p_1, \ldots, p_n \in \mathbf{par}$ and $P \in \Sigma_1^{\mathrm{P}} \cap \Sigma_2^{\mathrm{P}}$;
- $\mathcal{T}_i \cup \{\varphi_1, \ldots, \varphi_h\} \models \psi_1 \vee \cdots \vee \psi_k$.

Fig. 3: The residue rule.

1. $\neg(\forall x, y, z)(x + y = z \rightarrow (\exists w)(w < s(s(0)) \wedge f(x) < f(z + w)))$
2. $\quad \neg(a + b = c \rightarrow (\exists w)(w < s(s(0)) \wedge f(a) < f(c + w)))$
3. $\qquad\qquad\qquad\qquad a + b = c$
4. $\qquad\qquad \neg(\exists w)(w < s(s(0)) \wedge f(a) < f(c + w))$
5. $\qquad\qquad \neg(s(0) < s(s(0)) \wedge f(a) < f(c + s(0)))$

6. $\neg(s(0) < s(s(0)))$ 7. $\neg(f(a) < f(c + s(0)))$
$\qquad\quad \bot$ 8. $\qquad a < c + s(0)$
                             9. $\qquad c + s(0) = p$
                          10. $\qquad \neg(f(a) < f(p))$
                          11. $\qquad\qquad a < p$
                                $\bot$

Fig. 4: A N-O-tableau.

Note that while in Figure 2 the literal $a < c + s(0)$ was added by means of an application of the second decomposition rule, in Figure 4 the same literal is added by means of an application of the residue rule.[3]

5.2   Soundness and Completeness

Soundness of the residue version of N-O-tableaux immediately follows by inspection of the residue rule, whereas completeness is a consequence of the following theorem.

Theorem 5. *Let* B *be a* $\langle \mathcal{T}_1, \mathcal{T}_2 \rangle$-*open branch, and assume that no application of any propositional, quantifier, abstraction, purification, and residue rule can add new formulae to* B. *Then* B *is* $(\mathcal{T}_1 \cup \mathcal{T}_2)$-*satisfiable.*

---

[3] Exploiting the fact that $\mathcal{P} \cup \{a + b = c\} \models a < c + s(0)$.

Proof. Consider the set $\mathsf{B}' = \mathsf{B} \cup \{\neg\psi : \psi \text{ is an atom and } \psi \notin \mathsf{B}\}$. Clearly, B' is saturated (with respect to Definition 8). Therefore, if we show that B' is $\langle \mathcal{T}_1, \mathcal{T}_2 \rangle$-open, by Lemma 7 we obtain that B is $(\mathcal{T}_1 \cup \mathcal{T}_2)$-satisfiable.

Thus, assume, for a contradiction, that B' is $\langle \mathcal{T}_1, \mathcal{T}_2 \rangle$-closed. Then there exists an index $i \in \{1, 2\}$ and a finite set θ_i of Σ_i-literals such that $\theta_i \subseteq \mathsf{B}'$ and θ_i is $\mathcal{T}_i$-unsatisfiable. Without loss of generality, let $\theta_i = \{\varphi_1, \ldots, \varphi_h, \neg\psi_1, \ldots, \neg\psi_k\}$, where $\varphi_1, \ldots, \varphi_h$ occur in B and $\psi_1, \ldots, \psi_k$ are atoms not occurring in B. Note that, since B is $\langle \mathcal{T}_1, \mathcal{T}_2 \rangle$-open, we must have $k > 0$. Moreover, $\mathcal{T}_i \cup \{\varphi_1, \ldots, \varphi_h\} \models \psi_1 \vee \cdots \vee \psi_k$. In addition, if $\mathcal{T}_i$ is convex, then $\mathcal{T}_i \cup \{\varphi_1, \ldots, \varphi_h\} \models \psi_j$, for some $j \in \{1, \ldots, k\}$. But then, by saturation with respect to the residue rule, it follows that $\{\psi_1, \ldots, \psi_k\} \cap \mathsf{B} \neq \emptyset$, a contradiction.   □

6   Conclusion

We presented a tableau calculus for combining decision procedures for *arbitrary* universal theories over non necessarily disjoint signatures. Since our tableau calculus can be seen as a generalization of the Nelson-Oppen combination method to the case of non-disjoint signatures, we gave the name of N-O-tableaux to the tableaux constructed with our calculus.

We then recognized several cases in which restrictions can be imposed to the applications of the tableau rules in such a way to reduce the search space. We also provided a residue propagation mechanism that can make the exploration of the search space more efficient.

We plan to continue our research on N-O-tableaux by lifting the results of this paper to the free-variable level, and by recognizing more cases where efficiency can be achieved by restricting the tableau rules.

Acknowledgments. We thank Cesare Tinelli and the anonymous reviewers for useful comments.

This research was supported in part by NSF(ITR) grant CCR-01-21403, by NSF grant CCR-99-00984-001, by ARO grant DAAD19-01-1-0723, and by ARPA/AF contracts F33615-00-C-1693 and F33615-99-C-3014.

References

1. Alessandro Armando, Silvio Ranise, and Michaël Rusinowitch. Uniform derivation of decision procedures by superposition. In Laurent Fribourg, editor, *Computer Science Logic*, volume 2142 of *Lecture Notes in Computer Science*, pages 513–527. Springer, 2001.
2. Franz Baader and Cesare Tinelli. Combining decision procedures for positive theories sharing constructors. In Sophie Tison, editor, *Rewriting Techniques and Applications*, Lecture Notes in Computer Science. Springer, 2002.
3. Jean-Paul Billon. The disconnection method. A confluent integration of unification in the analytic framework. In Pierangelo Miglioli, Ugo Moscato, Daniele Mundici, and Mario Ornaghi, editors, *Theorem Proving with Analytic Tableaux and Related Methods*, volume 1071 of *Lecture Notes in Artificial Intelligence*, pages 110–126. Springer, 1996.

4. Eric Domenjoud, Francis Klay, and Christophe Ringeissen. Combination techniques for non-disjoint equational theories. In Alan Bundy, editor, *Automated Deduction – CADE-12*, volume 814 of *Lecture Notes in Artificial Intelligence*, pages 267–281. Springer, 1994.

5. Melvin C. Fitting. *First-Order Logic and Automated Theorem Proving.* Graduate Texts in Computer Science. Springer, 2nd edition, 1996.

6. Bernhard Gramlich. On termination and confluence properties of disjoint and constructor-sharing conditional rewrite systems. *Theoretical Computer Science*, 165(1):97–131, 1996.

7. Thomas Kaufl and Nicolas Zabel. Cooperation of decision procedures in a tableau-based theorem prover. *Reveu d'Intelligence Artificielle*, 4(3):99–126, 1990.

8. Shie-Jue Lee and David A. Plaisted. Eliminating duplication with the hyper-linking strategy. *Journal of Automated Reasoning*, 9(1):25–42, 1992.

9. Greg Nelson and Derek C. Oppen. Simplification by cooperating decision procedures. *ACM Transactions on Programming Languages and Systems*, 1(2):245–257, 1979.

10. Enno Ohlebusch. Modular properties of composable term rewriting systems. *Journal of Symbolic Computation*, 20(1):1–41, 1995.

11. Christophe Ringeissen. Unification in a combination of equational theories with shared constants and its application to primal algebras. In Andrei Vonronkov, editor, *Logic Programming and Automated Reasoning*, volume 624 of *Lecture Notes in Artificial Intelligence*, pages 261–272. Springer, 1992.

12. Christophe Ringeissen. Cooperation of decision procedures for the satisfiability problem. In Franz Baader and Klaus U. Schulz, editors, *Frontiers of Combining Systems*, volume 3 of *Applied Logic Series*, pages 121–140. Kluwer Academic Publishers, 1996.

13. Raymond M. Smullyan. *First-Order Logic.* Springer, 1968.

14. Cesare Tinelli. Cooperation of background reasoners in theory reasoning by residue sharing. Technical Report 02-03, Department of Computer Science, University of Iowa, 2002.

15. Cesare Tinelli and Mehdi T. Harandi. A new correctness proof of the Nelson-Oppen combination procedure. In Franz Baader and Klaus U. Schulz, editors, *Frontiers of Combining Systems*, volume 3 of *Applied Logic Series*, pages 103–120. Kluwer Academic Publishers, 1996.

16. Cesare Tinelli and Christophe Ringeissen. Unions of non-disjoint theories and combinations of satisfiability procedures. Technical Report 01-02, Department of Computer Science, University of Iowa, 2001.

17. Ashish Tiwari. *Decision Procedures in Automated Deduction.* PhD thesis, State University of New York at Stony Brook, 2000.

18. Calogero G. Zarba. Combining non-disjoint theories. In Rajeev Goré, Alexander Leitsch, and Tobias Nipkow, editors, *International Joint Conference on Automated Reasoning (Short Papers)*, Technical Report DII 11/01, pages 180–189. University of Siena, Italy, 2001.

LINK: A Proof Environment Based on Proof Nets

L. Habert[*], J.-M. Notin, and D. Galmiche

LORIA–Université Henri Poincaré
Campus Scientifique, BP 239
Vandœuvre-lès-Nancy, France

1 Introduction

LINK is a proof environment including proof nets-based provers for multiplicative linear logics: mixed linear logic, or recently called non-commutative logic (MNL) [1], commutative linear logic (MLL) and non-commutative (or cyclic) linear logic (MCyLL). Its main characteristic is the provability analysis through automatic proof nets construction. A proof net is a particular graph-theoretic representation of proofs that appears appropriate for proof-search in MLL and MCyLL [4,5]. It is a powerful alternative to deal with proof search and its problems about non-permutability and resource management [3]. In the context of system verification, such a semantical and graphical representation of proof can be useful from a software engineering point of view. It allows to analyse provability (through proof nets) or non-provability (through proof structures that can be seen as counter-models).

The LINK proof engine is based on one specific algorithm dedicated to MLL [8] that has been adapted to deal with non-commutative connectives (MCyLL) and also with both commutative and non-commutative connectives (MNL). This first version of LINK includes provers that can be also seen as implementations of new connection methods for these linear logic fragments [4]. Further work, in addition to standard improvements, will concern the development of this proof technology for other substructural logics and of tools dedicated to the analysis of related semantic structures. LINK illustrates that proof nets-based theorem proving is an appropriate and promising proof-theoretical but also proof-engineering approach of proof search in linear logic fragments.

2 Basic Principles of LINK

LINK is a proof environment that includes provers for three multiplicative linear logics, but each of them is based on the same initial principles presented for MLL in [8] and refined in [5]. Let us summarize its underlying concepts and principles. A proof structure for a sequent Γ is composed of its decomposition tree and axiom-links between leaves, labelled with dual atomic formulae X and $X^\perp$.

---

[*] École Normale Supérieure Ulm, Paris, France, in a training period at LORIA.

U. Egly and C.G. Fermüller (Eds.): TABLEAUX 2002, LNAI 2381, pp. 330–334, 2002.

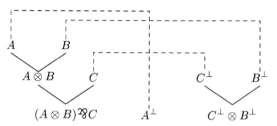

Fig. 1. A MLL proof structure

Figure 1 shows a proof structure of a MLL sequent $\vdash (A \otimes B)\mathbin{\bindnasrepma}C, A^{\perp}, C^{\perp} \otimes B^{\perp}$. Among proof structures, there are some corresponding to a proof in the sequent calculus. Such a proof structure is called a proof net and there are criteria characterizing a proof structure that is a proof net. Our approach is based on an inductive definition of proof nets leading to an automatic construction of proof nets from the decomposition tree and thus to an automatic search of appropriate axiom-links. For instance, the inductive definition of MLL proof nets is the following: 1) an axiom $(X, X^{\perp})$, where X is a atom, is a proof net; 2) let Π_1 and Π_2 be disjoint proof nets, with conclusions Γ, A and B, Δ respectively, then the extension of Π_1 and Π_2, from A and B, with a conjunctive link ($\otimes$) between A and B is a proof net Π, with conclusions $\Gamma, A \otimes B, \Delta$; 3) let Π_1 be a proof net with conclusions Γ, A, B, then the extension of Π, from A and B, with a disjunctive link ($\mathbin{\bindnasrepma}$) is a proof net Π, with conclusions $\Gamma, A\mathbin{\bindnasrepma}B$. Let us summarize the principles of construction for MLL. The algorithm starts with the decomposition tree of the sequent, that is a frame guiding the proof net search. The main idea is to build, step by step but automatically, axiom-links that are elementary proof nets and to link and extend them in order to have new sub-proof nets (further called subnets) and finally a proof net that "covers" the decomposition tree. Coming back to our example, from figure 1, we can first build the axiom-links $(A, A^{\perp})$ and $(B, B^{\perp})$ that are two elementary proof nets and connect and extend them with a conjunctive link ($\otimes$). Then, this new proof net and the axiom-link $(C, C^{\perp})$ can be connected and extended with a conjunctive link ($\otimes$), providing a new proof net. Finally, as $A \otimes B$ and C are conclusions of the same proof net, we can extend it with a disjunctive link ($\mathbin{\bindnasrepma}$) and we have a proof net with $(A\otimes B)\mathbin{\bindnasrepma}C$, $A^{\perp}$ and $C^{\perp}\otimes B^{\perp}$ as conclusions, that covers the initial decomposition tree. A main and necessary principle is to deal with conjunctive links before additive links. More details about the algorithm can be found in [4,8].

A major problem arising in such proof nets construction is the choice of appropriate axiom-links. If we replace, in our example, B and C by A, $B^{\perp}$ and $C^{\perp}$ by $A^{\perp}$, we need to detect the right axiom-links among all the possible $(A, A^{\perp})$. Some automatic choices are wrong choices, w.r.t. provability, and thus backtracking is necessary at some points. Our algorithm includes strategies to detect most of the failure cases: for instance, when two premises of a conjunctive link (resp. disjunctive link) are (resp. cannot be) in the same subnet. The impact of the strategies is significant and the backtracking is then strongly reduced. Let us mention that this approach, compared to bottom-up proof search in a sequent calculus, is often very efficient to detect and analyse the non-provability of a sequent.

3 The LINK Prover

The LINK prover is written in the OCaml[1] language. The program and its sources are available at http://www.loria.fr/~notin/LINK with information about how to install and use LINK. Thanks to the module system of OCaml, most part of the code is shared between the different provers (for MLL, MCyLL and MNL). Therefore, LINK proposes a single command line interface allowing the user to choose the logic, and to enter the formula to prove. Figure 2 shows a typical session of LINK. If the display mode is available, the proof net in construction is drawn in a graphic window. The user can also choose to have a step by step proof net construction in this window; this mode is very useful to understand the basic principles of the provers, as it shows the main stages like creation of axiom-links or extension of subnets by conjunctive and disjunctive links.

```
$mnld                        We choose to work in MNL, using dependencies.
((a*b)<c)|a^|(c^@b^)          We enter a first formula.
F = (((((a*b)<c)|a^)|(c^@b^)))
Disproved in 0.00 seconds    The formula is not provable.
((a@b)<c)|a^|(c^@b^)          We enter a second formula.
F = (((((a@b)<c)|a^)|(c^@b^)))
Proved in 0.00 seconds       This one is provable.
(* represents ⊗, @ represents ⊙, | represents ⅋ and < represents ⊲)
```

Fig. 2. A session example

LINK is composed of four main modules: *Select* (for the choice of literals), *CC* (Connected Components - to handle subnets already built) and *PW* (Par Waiting - to handle disjunctive links, the premises of which do not belong to the same subnet). The fourth module, *Build*, is common to all provers and contains the procedures that implement the basic proof nets construction algorithm.

The algorithm for MLL is implemented from the basic principles we previously mentioned. Following [5], MCyLL proof nets can be seen as particular MLL proof nets such that there is no crossing between axiom-links. Then, to build a prover for MCyLL, we only have to modify the *Select* module in order to have a choice of literals in accordance with this restriction. The design of a prover for MNL is more complicated because this logic combines both commutative $(\otimes, \⅋)$ and non-commutative $(\odot, \⊲)$ connectives [1]. The underlying idea is to apply the previous principles with $\otimes$ and $\odot$ as conjunctive links and $\⅋$ and $\⊲$ as disjunctive links and to capture the actual interactions between connectives during proof search with an appropriate semantic structure (based on labels or dependencies) that is built in parallel with the partial proof nets. Following [7],

---

[1] OCaml is available at http://caml.inria.fr/ocaml

in which we provide a new definition of MNL proof nets based on dependency relations, a first prover builds, step by step, partial proof nets like in MLL, but also in parallel dependency graphs on which one has to verify some conditions when a non-commutative disjunction ($\lhd$) link must be extended. Therefore, the CC and PW modules have to be adapted to deal with such dependency graphs associated to subnets. In particular, the procedures performing the extension of subnets by disjunctive and conjunctive links (included in the CC module) include the computation of the dependency set associated to the new subnet.

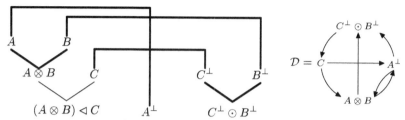

Fig. 3. A step of MNL proof net construction

Figure 3 shows, for the MNL sequent $\vdash (A \otimes B) \lhd C, A^\perp, C^\perp \odot B^\perp$, a partial MNL proof net (in bold) and the associated dependency set $\mathcal{D}$. The algorithm has extended axiom-links by $A \otimes B$ and then by $C^\perp \odot B^\perp$. Then, it has to check a condition on the dependency graph, related to the $\lhd$ connective. When, like here, the condition is not verified then the extension of the $\lhd$ link is impossible. As there is no other choice for axiom-links, the algorithm cannot perform any backtracking and the construction fails. In such a case of non-provability, the partial proof net (in bold) and the dependency graph in LINK are displayed. Then, such a graph is an essential semantic tool to analyse the provability in MNL. If $A \otimes B$ is replaced by $A \odot B$ then the condition is verified and a final proof net is built. The MLL strategies are extended to MNL and are very efficient to reduce backtracking when many choices are possible for axiom-links construction. LINK also includes two other MNL provers that are based on other semantic structures. One, following [6], with labels that are propagated in partial proof structures (decomposition tree plus axiom-links already built) during the proof net search. Another, following [11], with implementations of a contractibility criterion with a particular graph (a seaweed) and contraction rules applied on the associated structure.

Further work will be devoted to refinements on the first MNL prover, focusing on the analysis and manipulation of dependency graphs. The performances of LINK provers have been tested on various examples, of provable and non-provable formulae and the results are good. They illustrate the efficiency of the based-on proof net theorem proving, mainly in case of non-provability. With our algorithms, we can directly build, in parallel, a sequent proof for Γ, each link extension corresponding to a sequent rule application. Depending on the strategy, we can obtain a sequent proof in various canonical forms (for instance with focusing [2]). Moreover, these provers are implementations of new connection methods for linear logics [4,10], with automatic generation of connections and parallel construction of sequent proofs.

4   Conclusion and Perspectives

LINK is a proof environment based on an original and alternative concept, w.r.t. proof-search, namely proof net. It illustrates the actual interest of this concept, completed with semantic structures, to provide proof search and proof analysis in some linear logic fragments. The main prover of LINK deals with MNL, that appears appropriate to specify particular programming concepts or system properties [9] and for which no automatic prover has been designed before. The LINK provers are efficient, especially for non-provability, and also provide semantic structures that can be analysed in this case. Further developments of this version will include refinements of strategies, parallel construction of the sequent proof and graphical representations of semantic structures like dependency graphs. Tools for the manipulation and the analysis of these structures will be studied, with a software engineering and users point of view. We aim to use the LINK environment and their further extensions (with additives, quantifiers) for the verification and analysis of system properties [9], focusing on the failure analysis from the graph-theoretical proof representation.

References

1. M. Abrusci and P. Ruet. Non-commutative logic I : the multiplicative fragment. *Annals of Pure and Applied Logic*, 101:29–64, 2000.
2. J.M. Andreoli and R. Maieli. Focusing and proof-nets in linear and non-commutative logic. In *Int. Conf. on Logic for Programming and Automated Reasoning, LPAR'99, LNCS 1705*, pages 320–333, Tbilisi, Georgia, September 1999.
3. I. Cervesato, J. Hodas, and F. Pfenning. Efficient resource management for linear logic proof search. *Theoretical Computer Science*, 232(1-2):133–163, 2000.
4. D. Galmiche. Connection Methods in Linear Logic and Proof nets Construction. *Theoretical Computer Science*, 232(1-2):231–272, 2000.
5. D. Galmiche and B. Martin. Proof nets construction and automated deduction in non-commutative linear logic - extended abstract. *Electronic Notes in Theoretical Computer Science*, 17, 1998.
6. D. Galmiche and J.M. Notin. Proof-search and proof nets in mixed linear logic. *Electronic Notes in Theoretical Computer Science*, 37, 2000.
7. D. Galmiche and J.M. Notin. Calculi with dependency relations for mixed linear logic. In *International Workshop on Logic and Complexity in Computer Science, LCCS'2001*, pages 81–102, Créteil, France, 2001.
8. D. Galmiche and G. Perrier. A procedure for automatic proof nets construction. In *LPAR'92, International Conference on Logic Programming and Automated Reasoning, LNAI 624*, pages 42–53, St. Petersburg, Russia, July 1992.
9. D. Gray, G. Hamilton, J. Power, and D. Sinclair. Specifying and verifying TCP/IP using Mixed Intuitionistic Linear Logic. Technical report, Dublin City Univ., 2001.
10. C. Kreitz, H. Mantel, J. Otten, and S. Schmitt. Connection-based proof construction in linear logic. In *14th Int. Conference on Automated Deduction*, pages 207–221, Townsville, North Queensland, Australia, 1997.
11. V. Mogbil. Quadratic correctness criterion for non commutative logic. In *15th Int. Workshop on Computer Science Logic, CSL 2001, LNCS 2142*, pages 69–83, Paris, France, 2001.

DCTP 1.2 – System Abstract

Gernot Stenz

Institut für Informatik
Technische Universität München
D-80290 Munich, Germany
stenzg@in.tum.de

Abstract. We describe version 1.2 of the theorem prover DCTP, which
is an implementation of the disconnection calculus. The disconnection
calculus is a confluent tableau method using non-rigid variables. This
current version of DCTP has been extended and enhanced significantly
since its participation in the IJCAR system competition in 2001. We
briefly sketch the underlying calculus and the proof procedure and describe some of its refinements and new features. We also present the
results of some experiments regarding these new features.

1 Introduction

In this paper we present the latest version of the theorem prover DCTP, which is
based on the disconnection tableau calculus [3]. The calculus provides a natural
decision procedure for the Bernays-Schönfinkel class unlike most resolution and
rigid-variable tableau calculi and it is proof confluent, so that it can be used
for model generation. The extraction of a model from a saturated branch is one
of the main motivations and advantages of the traditional semantic tableau approach. It is important to emphasise that this advantage is lost in contemporary
free-variable tableau calculi like connection tableaux or model elimination [5] or
certain confluent variants of tableaux [1] or hyper tableaux [2], in which free variables are treated in a rigid manner. DCTP 1.2 is an extension of the prototypical
prover first presented in [6] and has been enhanced significantly since its original
inception. After briefly describing the underlying calculus, we give an overview
of the new features that were included in DCTP 1.2. We also describe some key
issues of the implementation. We conclude with the results of an experimental
evaluation that show both the progress achieved over the previous version and
a comparison with other first-order provers.

2 The Disconnection Tableau Calculus

Essentially, the disconnection tableau calculus can be viewed as an integration
of Plaisted's clause linking method [4] into a tableau control structure. For a
description of the proof method see [6,7]. The disconnection tableau calculus
consists of a single complex inference rule, the so-called *linking rule* that extends

U. Egly and C.G. Fermüller (Eds.): TABLEAUX 2002, LNAI 2381, pp. 335–339, 2002.

the tableau by renamed instances of the input clauses. The link selection is restricted to links occurring on the *current active path* (i.e. tableau branch). Branches are closed by ∀-*complementary* pairs of literals, i.e. literals that become complementary when all their variables are identified ($P(x, y)$ and $\neg P(v, v)$ are ∀-complementary). No variables are instantiated by closing branches and no hidden form of Smullyan's γ rule is used in the calculus.

3   Design and Proof Search

The disconnection calculus employed by DCTP is proof confluent. This means that only a single tableau is constructed. This single tree is processed in a backtracking-driven manner, since even though all inferences performed on a closed branch remain fixed, we still need to solve all remaining open subgoals in the tableau. In order to save space, closed tableau branches are discarded. A confluent calculus invariably places many redundant clauses on the tableau. To avoid the repeated solution of redundant subgoals we use the techniques of tableau pruning similar to [8].

The actual tableau proof search is preceded by a formula preprocessing as described in the next section. Then an initial active path is selected from the input clauses. Starting with the links occurring on the initial active path, a tableau is constructed below the last subgoal of the initial path to solve that subgoal. First, a linking step is executed, extending the tableau by new subgoals. These new subgoals then are themselves solved in a depth-first manner by adding their new links and by applying linking steps. The evaluation of this main loop is continued until either no open subgoals are left or the available links on a branch are exhausted. The main loop of the tableau construction comprises two forms of non-determinism, the selection of the next open branch and the selection of a link on the branch for tableau expansion. The former represents a don't-care non-determinism, while the latter has to respect some form of fairness condition, i.e. it must be guaranteed that every link on an open branch must eventually be selected. Both of these selections are heuristically guided, some of the heuristics used are described in Section 5. An important part of the proof search is the integration of a unit theory: unit clauses (or *lemmas*) are dynamically generated and used for subsuming new clauses or simplifying open subgoals.

4   New Refinements

For the version 1.2 of DCTP, a number of new refinements were added to the calculus to enhance the prover performance, which we will briefly describe now. *Equality handling.* The most significant improvement of the system over its previous version concerns the handling of the equality predicate. Equality is now treated by means of an integrated theory. Several methods of equality handling were incorporated in DCTP. The most successful of these is *ordered eq-linking*, an adaption of ordered paramodulation to a tableau framework. Unfortunately, eq-linking is incompatible with the powerful regularity restriction. In addition

DCTP uses destructive term rewriting based on a Knuth-Bendix ordering to normalise subgoals. Term rewriting is currently used in a restricted form only, where each new selected subgoal is normalised w.r.t. the unit equations on the path before it is solved.

Input preprocessing. DCTP also permits to perform a large number of satisfiability preserving transformations on the input clause set before actually starting the tableau proof. Among these are the elimination of isolated connections, the deletion of clauses with pure literals and tautological clauses, a certain form of demodulation and static clause splitting. Additionally, existing techniques like unit subsumption and unit simplification are used.

Variant subsumption. Full subsumption between non-unit clauses is not allowed in the disconnection calculus. However, we employ a stronger version of the clause variant pruning described in [6] that we call variant subsumption. A clause c is variant subsumed if a subclause of c is a variant of a clause on the current path.

Clause splitting. In addition to the static splitting performed during preprocessing, DCTP can also apply dynamic splitting to new clause instances that can be divided into several subclauses with disjoint variable sets. A minimum size for the new subclauses can be defined. These subclauses are connected via new propositional splitting literals.

t-closedness. In contrast to the use of $\forall$-closure, where all variables on the path are mapped to a new constant symbol, an arbitrary but fixed term can also be selected for the mapping of the path variables. The term t is automatically selected from the set of constants in the input clauses.

Factoring. Clause factoring is a standard resolution technique for obtaining shorter clauses. For the disconnection calculus, dynamic clause factoring during the proof search turned out to be unfeasible. However, good results could be obtained by integrating factoring together with full subsumption into the formula preprocessing. For example, the problem called *Andrew's challenge* that could not be solved previously due to the enormous branching factor of the tableau could be easily solved after the factorisation of the input set.

5   Implementation Issues

The subgoals of the initial active path are selected in the same way as the next open subgoal to be solved during the proof search, preferring subgoals that are maximal in their clause with respect to either their degree of instantiation or their term complexity. The generation of new links is performed by checking the new open subgoal against the list of potentially linked path literals. For each link a link weight is computed according to a mixed weighing scheme that is based upon the number of new non-simplifiable subgoals created by an application of each link and the maximum weighted term complexity of the new subgoals. Additional factors take the involvement of units or relevance information into account. Basically, linking steps introducing short and simple clauses are preferred. All links are bucket sorted into link lists according to their link weight. For each linking step, the newest link of the lowest link weight available is chosen. The inclusion of the maximum complexity of new terms into the link weight computation guarantees the fairness of the proof procedure. DCTP alternates its link selection in a user controllable way. Two types of alternation occur. The first one is between non-equality links and equality links, because it is hard to define a uniform link weight measure suitable for both types of links. By default, standard links and eq-links are chosen in relation to the number of non-equality and equality literals in the input. The second type of alternation is for each of the former types between the links of lowest weight and the oldest links, a successful heuristic also used in a variety of other provers. Unit subsumption and simplification are performed by matching each new subgoal against discrimination tree indexes of the unit lemmas available. Additional indexes for storing path literals and clause instances are used when checking for $\forall$-closedness or clause variants, resp. The theorem prover DCTP is implemented in the Scheme dialect *bigloo*. The system can be obtained from the author.

6   Future Extensions

Model extraction. As mentioned above, the disconnection calculus allows the extraction of models from failed proof attempts. The theory of model extraction for the non-equality case has been discussed in [7]. However an implementation of this has yet to be done.

Rewriting. After the successful implementation of equality handling a number of improvements still remain. These are mostly concerned with rewriting. In order to improve the performance for equality problems the use of a rewrite index is vital. Furthermore, currently each tableau subgoal is normalised only once just before it is solved. An incremental normalisation also of path subgoals by new unit equations is needed. Also, to obtain better guidance for the proof search it would be necessary to normalise all potential new clauses before computing the weights of their respective links. Unfortunately, this is hard to integrate into the inference mechanism of DCTP, but may be important for improving the performance of DCTP in the domain of unit equality problems.

Universal variables. Universal variables, i.e. variables that are implicitly universally quantified w.r.t a single literal instead of a clause can be used to extend some of the techniques for unit lemmas to non-unit clauses. Branch-local variables, an easily detectable subset of universal variables shall be used for non-unit subsumption and simplification.

7   Evaluation

In order to demonstrate the performance gain that the improvements described in this paper have caused, we present a comparison of the evaluations of DCTP 0.1 and DCTP 1.2 (denoted as DCTP in the table below) over the problems contained in the TPTP library version 2.4.1.[1] The first set of columns shows

---

[1] The largest and most comprehensive problem library available.

the results for all 4419 clause problems, the second one shows the results for the 2894 equality problems among those. The time limit for all tests was 300 seconds per problem on Sun Ultra 60 machines with 300 MHz processors and 384 MB of main memory. Currently, DCTP can solve about 20 problems that could not be solved by other provers before.

	TPTP		TPTP-Eq		CASC-JC MIX			CASC-JC SAT		
System	DCTP	DCTP 0.1	DCTP	DCTP 0.1	DCTP	e-SETHEO	Otter	DCTP	Gandalf	MACE
Proofs	1714	1138	953	468	42	93	31	-	-	-
Models	356	278	128	45	-	-	-	50	48	25

For the problems of the CASC-JC system competition, DCTP 1.2 gives decent to very good results. All new experiments were conducted under competition conditions. The third set of columns in the table above shows the results for the MIX class of the competition with 120 problems, which was won by e-SETHEO and VampireJC.[2] While still being far behind the really successful systems in this category, DCTP with eq-linking performs better than some other well known systems. The fourth set of columns gives the results for SAT category of CASC-JC with 90 problems. In this category, the new DCTP 1.2 is very successful and even outperforms the winner GandalfSat.

References

1. P. Baumgartner, N. Eisinger, and U. Furbach. A confluent connection calculus. In Harald Ganzinger, editor, *Proc. CADE-16, Trento, Italy*, LNAI 1632, pages 329–343. Springer, 1999.
2. P. Baumgartner, U. Furbach, and I. Niemelä. Hyper tableaux. In José Júlio Alferes et al., editors, *Proc. JELIA-96: Logics in Artificial Intelligence, LNAI* 1126, pp. 1–17, Berlin, 1996. Springer.
3. Jean-Paul Billon. The disconnection method: a confluent integration of unification in the analytic framework. In P. Migliolo et al., editors, *Proc. 5th Tableaux Workshop, LNAI* 1071, pp. 110–126, Berlin, 1996. Springer.
4. S.-J. Lee and D. Plaisted. Eliminating duplication with the hyper-linking strategy. *Journal of Automated Reasoning*, pp. 25–42, 1992.
5. Reinhold Letz, Johann Schumann, Stephan Bayerl, and Wolfgang Bibel. SETHEO: A high-performance theorem prover. *Journal of Automated Reasoning*, 8(2):183–212, 1992.
6. Reinhold Letz and Gernot Stenz. DCTP: A Disconnection Calculus Theorem Prover. In Rajeev Goré, Alexander Leitsch, and Tobias Nipkow, editors, *Proc. IJCAR-2001, Siena, Italy, LNAI* 2083, pp. 381–385. Springer, Berlin, 2001.
7. Reinhold Letz and Gernot Stenz. Proof and Model Generation with Disconnection Tableaux. In Andrei Voronkov, editor, *Proc. LPAR 2001, Havanna, Cuba*, pp. 142–156. Springer, Berlin, 2001.
8. F. Oppacher and E. Suen. HARP: A tableau-based theorem prover. *Journal of Automated Reasoning*, 4:69–100, 1988.

---

[2] Both systems are meta-provers combining different search methods.

Author Index

Lecture Notes in Artificial Intelligence (LNAI)

Lecture Notes in Computer Science